ARTILLERY

Other Titles in ABC-CLIO's
WEAPONS AND WARFARE SERIES

ARTILLERY

AN ILLUSTRATED HISTORY
OF ITS IMPACT

Jeff Kinard

A B C ⬤ C L I O

Santa Barbara, California • Denver, Colorado • Oxford, England

Library of Congress Cataloging-in-Publication Data
Kinard, Jeff, 1954-
Artillery : an illustrated history of its impact / Jeff Kinard.
p. cm. — (Weapons and warfare series)
Includes bibliographical references and index.
ISBN-13: 978-1-85109-556-8 (hardcover : alk. paper)
ISBN-13: 978-1-85109-561-2 (ebook)
1. Artillery—History. I. Title.

UF15.K55 2007
623.4'109—dc22

2006103178

11 10 09 08 07 / 10 9 8 7 6 5 4 3 2 1

This book is also available on the World Wide Web as an eBook.
Visit abc-clio.com for details.

ABC-CLIO, Inc.
130 Cremona Drive, P.O. Box 1911
Santa Barbara, California 93116-1911

This book is printed on acid-free paper. ∞
Manufactured in the United States of America

Senior Production Editor, Cami Cacciatore
Editorial Assistant, Sara Springer
Production Manager, Don Schmidt
Media Manager, Caroline Price
Media Editor, J. R. Withers
File Management Coordinator, Paula Gerard

CONTENTS

CHAPTER SEVEN

The Interwar Years and World War II, 1921–1945   269

CHAPTER EIGHT

Post–World War II and
Late-Twentieth-Century Developments   299

REFERENCE SECTION

INTRODUCTION TO

WEAPONS AND WARFARE SERIES

WEAPONS BOTH FASCINATE AND REPEL. They are used to kill and maim individuals and to destroy states and societies, and occasionally whole civilizations, and with these the greatest of man's cultural and artistic accomplishments. Throughout history tools of war have been the instruments of conquest, invasion, and enslavement, but they have also been used to check evil and to maintain peace.

Weapons have evolved over time to become both more lethal and more complex. For the greater part of human existence, combat was fought at the length of an arm or at such short range as to represent no real difference; battle was fought within line of sight and seldom lasted more than the hours of daylight of a single day. Thus individual weapons that began with the rock and the club proceeded through the sling and boomerang, bow and arrow, sword and axe, to gunpowder weapons of the rifle and machine gun of the late nineteenth century. Study of the evolution of these weapons tells us much about human ingenuity, the technology of the time, and the societies that produced them. The greater part of technological development of weaponry has taken part in the last two centuries, especially the twentieth century. In this process, plowshares have been beaten into swords; the tank, for example, evolved from the agricultural caterpillar tractor. Occasionally, the process is reversed and military technology has impacted society in a positive way. Thus modern civilian medicine has greatly benefited from advances to save soldiers' lives, and weapons technology has impacted such areas as civilian transportation or atomic power.

Weapons can have a profound impact on society. Gunpowder weapons, for example, were an important factor in ending the era of the armed knight and the Feudal Age. They installed a kind of rough democracy on the battlefield, making "all men alike tall." We can only wonder what effect weapons of mass destruction (WMD) might have on our own time and civilization.

This series will trace the evolution of a variety of key weapons systems, describe the major changes that occurred in each, and illustrate and identify the key types. Each volume begins with a description of the particular weapons system and traces its evolution, while discussing its historical, social, and political contexts. This is followed by a heavily illustrated section that is arranged more or less along chronological lines that provides more precise information on at least eighty key variants of that particular weapons system. Each volume contains a glossary of terms, a bibliography of leading books on that particular subject, and an index.

Individual volumes in the series, each written by a specialist in that particular area of expertise, are as follows:

Aircraft Carriers
Ancient Weapons
Artillery
Ballistic Missiles
Battleships
Cruisers and Battle Cruisers
Destroyers
Helicopters
Machine Guns
Medieval Weapons
Military Aircraft, Origins to 1918
Military Aircraft, 1919–1945
Military Aircraft in the Jet Age
Pistols
Rifles
Submarines
Tanks

We hope that this series will be of wide interest to specialists, researchers, and even general readers.

Spencer C. Tucker
Series Editor

PREFACE

THIS VOLUME TRACES THE HISTORY of artillery and its place in society from the ancient world to the present. The term "artillery" is derived from the Latin *ars,* or *artis,* terms for "craft" that later evolved through the Old French *atillier,* meaning "to deck, adorn with care or arrange"; *atil,* meaning "decoration, armor or equipment"; and *attillement,* or "apparatus." In 1268, Etienne Boileau defined an *artillier* as "a manufacturer of war engines, especially bows and offensive weapons." Throughout the Middle Ages "artillery" remained a general term for all types of military equipment. According to Gillaume Guiart in the early fourteenth century, "Artillery is the waggon-train which by duke, count or king or by any earthly lord is loaded with quarrels for war, crossbows, darts, lances and shields of similar kind" (Contamine, 193).

By about 1500, the term "artillery" had reached its current meaning, describing the actual cannons themselves, as well as their ammunition, support equipment, and operating personnel. Deriving from the Greek word *kanun* and Latin *canna,* or "tube," the word *canones* is found first in a document written in Italy in 1326. Antoine de Lalaing describes cannons in "the arsenal of Maximilian von Habsburg at Innsbruck" as *pieces d'artillerie* (ibid., 139). The word "cannon" was first used in France in 1339 and in England in 1378. Geoffrey Chaucer mentions cannons in his poems written between 1375 and 1400; "cannon" was more often used in France, with the term "gun" seeing more usage in England. The first English use of the word "gun" to describe a firearm was in 1339. Earlier forms were *gunne, gone,* and *gunna,* with possible etymological sources from Old Norse (Hall, 44).

"Artillery" can also describe weapons capable of launching heavier, more destructive projectiles at longer ranges than those of the ordinary infantry or cavalry arms. Early nongunpowder siege weapons of the Greeks and Romans and the Middle Ages fall into that category and are treated in Chapter 1. Chapter 2 covers the invention and uses of gunpowder in China and its application by medieval European inventors. These early gunpowder artillery pieces include the bronze *pots de fer* and wrought-iron cannons, such as both the muzzle-loaded and breech-loaded heavy bombards. This volume also assesses the effectiveness of early artillery in such medieval battles as Crecy and its affect on siege operations. In addition, the medieval period witnessed advancements in and uses of more mobile field artillery, including the fifteenth-century contributions of the Bureau brothers and Charles VIII.

Chapter 3 covers the major developments of the sixteenth and seventeenth centuries, addressing the contributions of Henry VIII of England and Sweden's Gustavus Adolphus. Discussions concerning the evolving nature of both naval and land gunnery, as well as the use of trains of artillery, track the continuing development of artillery and its impact on warfare. Chapters 4 and 5 cover the great strides in artillery technology during the eighteenth and nineteenth centuries. Such towering innovators as Gribeauval, Congreve, Maritz, Cavalli, Krupp, Armstrong, Whitworth, and Dahlgren emerged to revolutionize artillery designs and manufacturing techniques. Their efforts led to improvements in smoothbore weapons, long-range rifled guns, breechloading cannons, as well as rocket artillery and rapid-fire weapons. Case studies of the wars of Louis IV, the Napoleonic Wars, the American Civil War, and the Franco-Prussian War will help illustrate the impact of these developments.

Chapters 6, 7, and 8 address the continuing evolution of modern artillery from the late ninetheenth century through World Wars I and II, the Korean War, Vietnam, and the wars of the late twentieth century. Discussions include the mechanization of artillery and its application to antiaircraft roles, as well as recoilless weapons and rocket advancements. The volume concludes with a discussion concerning the future of artillery.

ACKNOWLEDGMENTS

I AM VERY GRATEFUL for the guidance of series editor Dr. Spencer Tucker and book editor Dr. Alex Mikaberidze and senior production editor Cami Cacciatore of ABC-Clio for their valuable insights. Ms. Renee Burrows and the staff of the GTCC Learning Resource Center were also extremely helpful in providing their interlibrary loan expertise. I especially thank my wife and son, Kelly and Luka, for their patience and support.

CHAPTER ONE

Ancient and Medieval Artillery

ANCIENT ARTILLERY

Pregunpowder artillery relied on nonexplosive principles to propel missiles, and it is thus generally referred to as mechanical artillery. Archeological evidence suggests that some forms of mechanical artillery may have been developed in early Mesopotamia, but written sources are much more complete for the Mediterranean region. Achieving a high degree of sophistication with the Greeks and used by the Romans and during the Middle Ages, these weapons played key roles in siege warfare and, to a lesser extent, field actions. Although no ancient siege weapons have survived, excavated metal components, written sources (primarily Biton, Diodorus, Heron, Philon, and Vitruvius), and contemporary artworks provide a rich source for modern students of the subject. Scholars' efforts—often including the construction and testing of working models based on the ancient sources—provide insights into early warfare and engineering capabilities.

Still, the nomenclature for early artillery is somewhat problematic, as ancient writers tended to use terms for weapons interchangeably, thus engendering some confusion. As a general rule, however, the term "ballista," used in a generic sense, usually refers to long-range antipersonnel weapons in the form of smaller, bow-powered engines projecting a large arrow or bolt in a relatively flat trajectory. In contrast, the term "catapult" describes a larger weapon that usually launched stone shot in a high arc and was used primarily against stone fortifications. Another self-descriptive term, "lithobolos," or "stone-thrower," appeared in about 335 BC. This term refers to weapons evolving from the oxybeles (a large, tension-powered weapon), including ballistae of various sizes capable of accurately hurling 10- to 180-pound projectiles over ranges of to up 500 yards—a performance that compares favorably to that of many late-eighteenth-century field pieces.

Ancient sources suggest that the first Greek artillery pieces appeared in Sicily in 399 BC. In that year, Dionysius I, tyrant of the colony of Syracuse, initiated a remarkably comprehensive program to develop new types of warships, siege engines, and other weapons in anticipation of hostilities with nearby Carthaginian strongholds. Infamous for his ruthlessness, Dionysius also proved imminently pragmatic: he assembled teams of highly paid engineers and craftsmen to establish, in effect, the first true ordnance research and development facility. Two years later, in 397 BC, their efforts enabled Syracuse to field a number of specialized siege engines when it attacked the nearby Carthaginian island outpost of Motya. These weapons included massive rolling siege towers and the earliest recorded artillery pieces in the form of mechanical, tension-powered catapults.

THE GASTRAPHETES

Tensional catapults are weapons based on the crossbow principle, thus relying on a horizontally mounted bow to provide the power to propel a stone or large arrow. The catapults used during the siege of Motya were probably the gastraphetes, or "belly bow," a large, one-man crossbow that required the user to push down with his stomach against the concave butt of the weapon to cock the highly tensioned bowstring. The Assyrians had possibly used the crossbow principle earlier, in a more primitive form, but the gastraphetes proved a truly practical weapon. It provided the starting point for the development of larger artillery forms.

The heart of the gastraphetes was its compound bow, consisting of a wooden core sandwiched between a rear layer of horn and a layer of flexible animal sinew. Its other components included the wood stock, a wood slider, the bowstring, and a simple trigger mechanism. To prepare the gastraphetes for use, one first pressed with his stomach against the U-shaped butt to force the slider to the rear. The slider, riding on grooves cut into the stock, thus tensioned the bow and bowstring. Metal-reinforced ratchets in the stock engaged with the triggering device in the rear of the slider to hold it in place for loading. A large arrow, also known as a dart or bolt, was then placed in a corresponding groove cut into the top of the slider. Firing the gastraphetes was accomplished by releasing the trigger.

Deployed as a siege weapon—as were nearly all forms of early mechanical artillery—the gastraphetes proved a key factor in deciding Dionysius's victory over Motya. At some 250 meters, its range exceeded that of the Carthaginians' conventional bow weapons by some 50 meters, allowing the Syracusans to clear the city's walls of defenders. That enabled the Greek sappers to maneuver their new six-story siege towers into position against the city's fortifications. As a new and thus unknown weapon, the gastraphetes also provided the attackers with a distinct psychological advantage over the defenders, as well as the crews of a Carthaginian fleet that unsuccessfully attempted to come to Motya's aid.

The success of Dionysius's artillery at Motya sparked an arms race throughout the Mediterranean as the competing powers rushed to arm themselves with the new engines of war. Kings, tyrants, and polis councils competed with one another to lure artillery designers into their service with promises of wealth and privilege. Previously scorned as mere artisans, the engineers who designed the catapults found a new and exalted status as appreciation of their talents spread. Paradoxically, there seems to have been little effort to maintain secrecy among the various powers; the engineers, for the most part, moved freely from patron to patron in search of the most profitable arrangements. Within a few years, Athens, Byzantium, Halicarnassus, and Tyre all had acquired large numbers of catapults with which to defend their city walls.

THE OXYBELES

A much larger tension-powered gastraphetes appeared soon after the early gastraphetes, in about 375 BC. Although sometimes called the oxybeles, or "bolt-shooter," variants of these weapons were also capable of firing stone shot. The oxybeles incorporated a sturdy wooden tripod to support its weight, as well as a winch and lever arrangement to draw its powerful bow. Despite requiring a crew to operate it

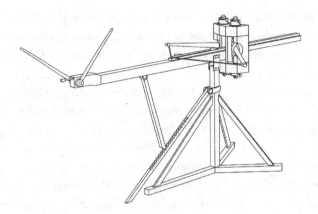

Oxybeles (Courtesy Art-Tech)

efficiently, its increased size and power combined with the stability of its platform enabled the oxybeles to fire significantly larger projectiles much farther and more accurately than its predecessor. The addition of a universal joint between the base and the firing mechanism of later models was a considerable improvement on earlier machines. The incorporation of the universal joint eliminated the need for multiple crewmen to position the heavy base for each shot and made it possible for a single man to aim the weapon.

The Greeks called the most powerful of these machines—firing bolts capable of penetrating the shield and armor of an opponent at ranges of up to 400 yards—the katapeltes, or "shield-piercer." One type of oxybeles, probably developed by the inventor Zopyrus of Tarentum in about 330 BC, was fitted with an approximately 9-foot bow and boasted even greater lethality, in that it was capable of simultaneously shooting two heavy 6-foot bolts from its double-slotted slider. The largest weapons, fitted with bows approaching 15 feet, were capable of hurling a 40-pound stone shot about 300 yards. Some fragmentary evidence even hints that an advanced form of tension artillery incorporating a steel bow, known as the "thunderbolt," appeared in the late Roman Empire.

The evolution of the oxybeles made possible new siege warfare techniques, and the special skills required for its operation helped to promote artillery as a specialized branch of ancient armies. The oxybeles, like the one-man gastraphetes, was essentially a direct-fire weapon, in that it fired its relatively light projectiles at a relatively flat trajectory. This limitation was more than offset, however, by the ability of its various forms to fire both stone projectiles and bolts. The bolt-shooting weapons, most commonly firing 27-inch arrows, proved effective in clearing defenders from battlements, whereas the stone-shooting engines were best suited for battering the upper masonry and wood fortifications on a city's upper walls.

TORSION ARTILLERY

As the size of siege engines increased, ancient artillery designers soon realized the limitations of bow-powered weapons. A later form of the oxybeles, appearing sometime before 340 BC, introduced the torsion principle for launching missiles. Torsion engines replaced the bow with powerful, vertically mounted twin springs on either side of the slider bed. These were composed of tightly wound skeins of sinew or hair wrapped around a wooden axis. The base of a wooden arm, approximately 2 to 3 feet in length, was mounted into each spring with the exposed end providing the attaching point for the bowstring. The introduction of the torsion principle quickly rendered the earlier tension-powered engines obsolete and opened new possibilities for huge weapons capable of projecting much more destructive projectiles at significantly greater distances.

THE EUTHYTONE AND PALINTONE

The two early types of such torsion weapons, the euthytone and the palintone, derived their names from comparisons to hand bows in the angles described by their cocked spring and arm assemblies. In Greek, *euthytone* means "straight-spring" (as in straight bow); *palintone* means "V-spring" (or curved composite bow). The palintone evolved from the euthytone, and its arms could be drawn farther back than those of its predecessor, thus generating more energy. As the more powerful weapon, the larger and more sturdily built palintone was most often used to hurl heavy stone shot, while the euthytone was primarily an antipersonnel bolt-shooting weapon. Both weapons saw continual improvements by the Greeks and later Romans, with some later models of the palintone weighing several tons.

The inherent complexity of torsion artillery, in comparison to earlier types, necessitated an unprecedented need for more sophisticated personnel for its maintenance and operation. Larger weapons required disassembly into their various components for transport, whereas the very largest were constructed on site. Artillery officers would thus have found it necessary to master not only military but also engineering skills to operate effectively. In addition, the two torsion springs demanded careful initial winding to ensure maximum strength and balance for the highest efficiency—an operation that required constant attention and adjustments—because the springs were prone to stretching (and thus weakening) as a result of repeated use or wet conditions.

The need to maintain consistent accuracy further complicated the ancient artilleryman's job: a bolt was useless unless it hit its living target, and heavy stone shot required multiple hits in a concentrated area to bring down a wall. To achieve optimum accuracy engineers developed standardized bolts and stone shot, according to weight and size, to fit their corresponding weapons. Stone shot, in addition, required careful shaping by masons to ensure an acceptably smooth and round contour, to minimize damage to the catapult's bearing surfaces and to enhance their flight characteristics.

Once in position, with a properly constructed and tuned catapult and its correct ammunition, an ancient artillerist still faced challenges that his infantry or cavalry colleagues would have been ill prepared to meet. Rather than face his enemy face to face in direct combat, the artillerist would have applied mathematical principles to calculate the angles of elevation of his piece in relation to the weight of the projectile and the tension of the torsion springs. These new demands were instrumental in the early definition of artillery as a specialized service requiring elite troops and officers with technical skills beyond those of the typical rank-and-file soldier.

The advent of such a relatively impersonal, mechanical mode of war especially appalled those classical warriors who put such great value in personal valor. In 368 or 367 BC, the Spartan king Archidamus, after witnessing the new weapons, probably sent by Dionysius I to the Peloponnese, declared, "Heracles, man's martial valor is of no avail any more" (Marsden, *Historical Development,* 65). Despite such reservations, Dionysius's gifts seem not to have offended Archidamus's sensibilities to the point that he refused to use them successfully against the Arcadians and the Argives.

Apparently the Spartans were not the only beneficiaries of Dionysius's largesse, as Athenian inventories from around 370 BC list large numbers of catapult bolts in storage. That Athens awarded an honorary crown to Dionysius in 368 BC and the next year entered into an alliance with Syracuse strongly suggests that these projectiles and presumably the weapons to fire them were gifts from the Syracusan tyrant. The Athenians quickly grasped the implications of artillery as a defensive weapon and began their own building program, producing both torsion and nontorsion bolt-shooters. During the ensuing years the Athenians manufactured large numbers of catapults, including dual-purpose machines capable of firing both bolts and shot by merely changing sliders.

Athens also realized the need to maintain a trained core of skilled specialists to design and fabricate the machines, as well as to crew them. To that end, in about 335 BC, the polis instituted formal artillery training for its ephebes—young men eighteen to twenty years of age performing their military service—under the tutelage of an expert instructor. In the same vein, other Greek cities incorporated catapult marksmanship competitions in their gymnasia programs, using both stone and bolt-firing machines.

MACEDONIAN ARTILLERY

Although Dionysius I of Syracuse introduced artillery, it was Philip II (r. 359–336 BC) of Macedon who fully integrated the new technology into his military. Upon taking the throne, Philip (father of Alexander the Great) set about remaking the Macedonian army by replacing its traditional infantry phalanx of citizen-soldier hoplites with a professional fighting force. Philip's innovations included new weapons and more flexible infantry formations and tactics, as well as elite cavalry units—components previously unseen in Greek warfare. A defeat in 353 BC at the hands of the Phocian general Onomarchus and his stone-throwing artillery during the Third Sacred War (356–345 BC) probably also prompted Philip to develop artillery for his own army. The Phocians were allies of both Sparta and Athens at the time, and most probably they had received their catapult knowledge from at least one of the two city-states.

In a brilliant maneuver, Onomarchus lured Philip's troops into a crescent-shaped killing ground bordered by hills where he had concealed infantry and stone-throwing artillery. Once Philip's phalanx came into range, the Phocian artillery unleashed a devastating barrage of approximately 5-pound stones that opened wide gaps in the Macedonian formation. Although Philip later downplayed his defeat, the Phocian infantry exploited the damage and confusion inflicted by their artillery to rout the Macedonians from the field. The significance of the battle was twofold. First, it marks the first well-documented use of field artillery as a tactical component in support of infantry, as opposed to a strictly siege application as at Motya. Second, the weapon's effectiveness was not lost on the shrewd Philip. Soon after his defeat, the Macedonian became obsessed with equipping his army with the most advanced artillery available. To that end he employed the Thracian engineer Polyidus and his apprentices Chaerias and Diades to design movable siege towers and artillery pieces.

Yet despite Philip's efforts, his most ambitious deployment of artillery—during the siege of Perinthus in 340 BC—ultimately proved a failure. Philip attacked the city with a large force including 120-foot siege towers and considerable numbers of bolt-shooting catapults, possibly including torsion models. At first, the catapults proved highly effective in providing cover fire by clearing the walls of the city of defenders. That allowed the Macedonian sappers to undermine the walls and weaken them with battering rams and ultimately breach the city's outer defenses. The desperate Perinthians also recognized the catapults' potential, however, and soon obtained nontorsion bolt-shooters from the neighboring city of Byzantium. The siege of Perinthus thus saw both the offensive and defensive use of siege artillery, with the defenders eventually gaining the upper hand and forcing Philip to withdraw.

Alexander (356–323 BC), Philip's son and successor, later drew upon his father's experience at Perinthus; he also held the advantage of possessing new and more powerful stone-throwing torsion artillery. Tactically, his siege of Halicarnassus in 334 BC differed little from his father's at Perinthus. Alexander too employed massive siege towers, with artillery providing antipersonnel covering fire for his sappers. Although the Persian defenders fought back desperately with bolt-firing catapults, the city eventually fell, leaving Alexander free to push south along the eastern coast of the Mediterranean.

Halicarnassus was, in effect, the prelude to Alexander's greatest siege operation, the seven-month siege of Tyre (332 BC). Having defeated the Persian king Darius III at Issus (November, 333 BC), Alexander next moved south along the Mediterranean coast toward Egypt. In his path, off the coast of modern-day Lebanon, lay the Phoenician fortress-city of Tyre. As a Persian ally, Tyre posed a threat to Alexander's supply lines, leading him to see its capture as a critical factor in the success of his operations in the region.

Tyre posed a daunting obstacle. It had repelled numerous earlier sieges and was generally considered impregnable. The city presented massive 150-foot walls mounting large numbers of bolt-firing artillery manned by a well-trained and well-supplied garrison with a ready supply of fresh water. In addition, two fortified ports allowed the Phoenician galleys free access to the sea. To further complicate an attacker's operations, the city occupied an island one-half mile off the coast—a particularly thorny problem for Alexander, as he had no fleet.

True to character, however, in January 332 BC the Macedonian forged ahead, ordering his engineers to begin construction of a 200-foot-wide earthen bridge—or a mole—to span the 18-foot-deep waters between the coast and the city. As the mole came within range of the city, Alexander positioned two siege towers and his artillery on it, to bring the walls under fire. A new form of siege warfare was then born as Alexander's bolt-firing catapults began sweeping Tyre's walls of its defenders, while his heavier stone-throwers battered the walls themselves—a function previously performed by undermining and battering rams.

The tenacious Tyrians responded with their own catapults, raining bolts on the Macedonian construction crews and artillery in what would, in later centuries, be termed counter-battery fire. As the mole grew closer and the Macedonian barrage became more intense and accurate, the Tyrians answered with ingenious antiartillery measures, erecting giant spinning wooden wheels on the facing wall to deflect incoming bolts, while simultaneously positioning padding on the wall face to soften the impact of stone shot. Despite such measures, however, the mole's progress continued, leading the Phoenicians to attack it with their galleys and fire ships, a move that resulted in damage to the mole and the destruction of the siege towers and numerous artillery pieces.

The raid, however, bought only a brief respite for the defenders, as the Macedonians quickly repaired the damage and constructed new towers. More ominously for the Tyrians, their success apparently compelled Alexander to acquire his own fleet in order to neutralize Tyre's naval advantage and threaten the city's entire perimeter, rather than simply the narrow, heavily reinforced wall facing the mole. To that end Alexander coerced a number of nearby cities to contribute warships and support vessels to his cause, ultimately building a fleet including some 250 triremes.

As his triremes blockaded the city, cutting off food and supplies, Alexander mounted siege towers and catapults on the more stable transport vessels. These ships ranged around the city, suppressing defending fire from the walls with bolt-shooters in their towers, while shot-firing pieces on the decks tested the walls for weaknesses. Although the Phoenicians fought back furiously, dropping huge boulders from their walls and firing incendiary bolts coated in pitch, naphtha, and other flammable materials at the artillery platforms, their situation eventually became desperate. Finally, in August 332 BC, its defenders weakened by starvation and its walls crumbling, Tyre fell to the Macedonians at the cost of some 8,000 defenders killed in the fighting, with the remaining 30,000 citizens being sold into slavery.

At Tyre, by combining the systematic research and development begun by his father with his own talent for field expediency, Alexander achieved the culmination of Macedonian ingenuity in the use of artillery in siege warfare. This legacy included the use of mobile siege towers combined with bolt-firing catapults in an antipersonnel covering role in conjunction with heavy stone-throwers, used to concentrate fire on stone fortifications. Equally far-reaching, Alexander's pioneering use of ship-mounted artillery was to revolutionize naval warfare. The lessons learned at Tyre stood Alexander well in his later campaigns, such as the subsequent siege of the Persian stronghold of Gaza (September–November 332 BC).

Although a relatively easy victory in comparison with Tyre, Gaza did mount a spirited defense that nearly claimed the Macedonian king's life. While countering a sally by the Persians, Alexander was struck in the shoulder by a bolt from the Gazans' artillery that penetrated both his shield and his armor. The wound evidently so enraged the volatile Alexander that, in imitation of his hero Achilles' treatment of the body of Hector, he dragged the body of the city's commander, Batis, around the city walls behind his chariot. For good measure, upon the city's fall, he then ordered the execution of the male citizens and sold the women and children into slavery.

Alexander also recognized both the advantages and limitations of the use of artillery in nonsiege applications, as what would later be termed field artillery. The artillery used by Onomarchus in 353 BC against Alexander's father, Philip, had wreaked havoc among the Macedonians, but was of relatively short range, and thus vulnerable to fast-moving infantry and archers. Onomarchus had thus positioned his artillery on high ground and protected it with infantry in preparation of Philip's advance, a lesson that Alexander later took to heart.

On more than one occasion Alexander protected his artillery by deploying it behind rivers to provide both defensive and offensive covering fire for his troops as they crossed. This tactic proved effective in 335 BC during a retreat across the Eordaicus River. Alexander later claimed that covering fire by his archers and long-range artillery against the pursuing forces of Glaucus and Cleitus of Pelium made possible controlled withdrawal without casualties. In 329 he positioned his artillery behind the Jaxartes River in preparation for crossing the river against the Scythians. As renowned horsemen, the Scythians managed to avoid many of the incoming salvoes. But they were nevertheless unfamiliar with artillery and were amazed at the long range and devastating effects of those missiles that did hit their targets. In the face of the new terror weapon the Scythians withdrew, allowing the Macedonians to cross the river into their territory.

HELLENISTIC ARTILLERY

Upon the death of Alexander in 323 BC the Wars of the Diadochi ("Successors") (322–315 BC) erupted as his generals and satraps—including such men as Antipater, Antigonus, Ptolemy, and Seleucus—vied for individual supremacy. Antigonus, also known as Monophthalmos ("One-eyed"), died battling the armies of Lysimachus and Seleucus at the Battle of Ipsus in 301 BC and was succeeded by his son, Demetrius I Poliorcetes ("Besieger") (336–283 BC). Demetrius's title was indeed appropriate, as he had gained a formidable reputation in siege craft and the use of artillery while fighting alongside his father.

In 307 BC Demetrius launched a campaign to force Cassander (358–297 BC), son of Antipater and ruling king of Macedonia, out of Athens and surrounding Attica. Cassander was an intelligent but ruthless man who had executed such real and perceived political threats as Alexander the Great's surviving family, including his mother, Olympias; his wife, Roxanne; and his son, Alexander IV. Utilizing both stone- and bolt-shooting catapults, Demetrius rather easily defeated Cassander's local governor, Demetrius of Phalerum, by battering down the defensive walls of the city's port, Piraeus, and the nearby fortress of Munychia. Following the liberation of Athens, Demetrius moved on to prosecute what would become known as two of the most spectacular feats of siege craft in the ancient world.

Demetrius first targeted Salamis, a strategic Cyprian city controlling the trade routes in the eastern Mediterranean. Claimed by Alexander's former general and the current king of Egypt, Ptolemy I (r. 323–285 BC) and commanded by his brother Menelaus, the city was strongly fortified and manned and was well equipped with artillery. In 306 BC Demetrius attacked the city with the most sophisticated siege equipment of the period, including a huge siege tower designed by the Athenian engineer Epimachus. Christened the helepolis ("destroyer of cities"), the tower was, in effect, an ingenious mobile and armored artillery platform that rose above the city's defenses.

As described by such ancient authors as Diodorus Siculus and Vitruvius, the nine-story tower rose over 100 feet in height and rolled on four huge wooden wheels. It was manned by approximately 200 artillerists and required thousands of men to roll into position. The various artillery pieces were positioned in the tower according to weight, with the heaviest stone throwers, firing projectiles weighing some 150 pounds (80 kg), on the lowest levels; heavy bolt-shooters were on the middle levels, and light stone and arrow shooters occupied the highest floors. The helepolis was apparently not deployed to destroy the walls themselves—a duty reserved for Demetrius's giant battering rams and masonry drills—but to demolish their upper defensive fighting levels.

Despite demolishing the city's upper battlements, Demetrius faced fierce opposition from the Ptolemaic defenders in the form of incendiary counter-battery fire and the arrival of a large fleet under the command of Ptolemy himself. During the ensuing sea battle—the largest up to that time—Demetrius also proved himself a formidable admiral, routing the Egyptian king and leaving Menelaus no alternative but to capitulate.

One year later, in 305 BC, Demetrius launched his unsuccessful yet most famous operation, the siege of Rhodes, a yearlong investment well documented by Diodorus from on-scene reports by Hieronymus of Cardia. The siege itself was very much a fight between well-matched engineers and artillerymen. Rhodes was a wealthy city with a large complement of the latest artillery, sophisticated harbor defenses, and a powerful fleet. The key to their defense lay in the defense of their harbor, the lifeline by which their fleet could supply the city and maintain a naval threat to an attacker's rear. Alerted to Demetrius's impending attack, the Rhodians prepared by reinforcing and heightening the existing walls in the harbor and improvising new defensive positions. These included powerful batteries of stone- and bolt-firing artillery on raised platforms on the harbor's mole and on cargo ships moored behind it.

The Rhodians' efforts were well rewarded. Despite repeated attacks against the harbor defenses, Demetrius failed to gain a stable foothold on the city's seaward side and at last altered his strategy by targeting the city's landward defenses. To that end Epimachus designed another nine-level—but even larger and more sophisticated—

helepolis, rising a reported 150 feet in height from a 72-foot square base and weighing an estimated 150 tons. Its tapered, iron-plated sides were designed to deflect stone shot and incendiary bolts, and padded covers over the mechanically raised firing ports protected the artillery crews while reloading. This behemoth was equipped with eight 15-foot-diameter wooden casters rather than simply wheels, thus allowing it to be rolled in any direction by a crew of some 3,400 men pushing from behind as well as operating a sophisticated capstan device within the structure.

As at Salamis, the helepolis provided covering fire for other siege weapons, as well as the sappers and infantry. From their positions well above the city's outer wall, the tower's crews inflicted severe damage to the walls' upper fighting platforms and inner defensive works.

Still, despite finally breaking through the outer wall, Demetrius found his match at Rhodes. Anticipating the breach, the city's defenders constructed secondary walls as well as defensive ditches that blocked the advance of the heavy siege engines. Also, the defending artillerists proved their own skill by concentrating the fire of their heavy stone throwers to dislodge a number of the iron plates protecting the face of the helepolis. The crews of the lighter bolt-shooting catapults then targeted the vulnerable, exposed wooden substructure with incendiary projectiles, forcing Demetrius to order the tower to be pulled back to safety. The arrival of relief forces dispatched by his old enemy Ptolemy at last convinced Demetrius of the futility of the enterprise. After a year-long siege, having failed to close the city's harbor and facing artillery equal to his own, he at last withdrew by sea, leaving much of his wrecked siege equipment scattered around the battered walls of Rhodes. For their part, the citizens of Rhodes later commemorated their victory by selling the equipment left behind by the frustrated Demetrius to fund the construction of the legendary Colossus of Rhodes, one of the Seven Wonders of the World.

The basic principles of tension- and torsion-powered artillery were well established by the end of the Hellenistic period. Experiments in testing alternative methods of powering torsion machines—such as those of Ctesibius of Alexandria, who attempted to replace the sinew and hair torsion springs with bronze or pistons—ultimately proved failures. Other ingenious designs, such as a hopper-fed, chain and cam operated repeating catapult by a fellow Alexandrian, Dionysius, also proved impractical. With the rise of Rome, the next stage of artillery development would essentially be one of adapting and perfecting existing forms.

ROMAN ARTILLERY

The Romans are well known for their talent in appropriating and modifying other cultures' inventions for their own needs. The adoption of existing Greek artillery forms including tension-powered and torsion weapons by the Romans was thus much in keeping with Roman practice, as was their subsequent modifications to fit their particular tactical requirements. Apart from their Latin designations, the artillery of the Republic and early empire was virtually identical to the earlier Greek weapons. The Greek bolt-shooting euthytone thus became the catapulta, and the stone-throwing palintone, the ballista. Rome was, however, rather late in its appreciation of artillery—a lesson hard learned at the hands of the birthplace of artillery, its Greek neighbor Syracuse, during the Second Punic War.

Following the city's declaration of alliance with Carthage, a Roman armada of sixty quinqueremes (ships with five tiers of oars) under the command of Marcus Claudius Marcellus (268–208 BC), with a large land force under Appius Claudius Pulcher (Consul 212 BC), besieged the city in 213 BC. Despite their numbers—25,000 men— the Romans had little artillery and were probably equipped only with conventional short-range missile weapons, including javelins, bows, and slings. For their part, the Syracusans enjoyed sophisticated defense works, nearly two centuries of constant artillery development from the days of Dionysius I, and a living resident genius who had contributed much to his city's defense.

That genius—none other than the famous Archimedes (287–212 BC)—had carefully prepared the city defenses by placing large numbers of stone- and bolt-shooting artillery that, according to their size, range, and projectile, would inflict the most damage to an attacking force. By precalculating the ranges from the city walls, Archimedes had set up a sophisticated system by which the Syracusan artillerists could open fire on an attacker at long range with their largest engines, and then "walk" their fire ever closer to the city's walls with lighter weapons as the enemy advanced. Frustrated by the effectiveness of the Syracusans' defense, the Roman commanders at last resorted to a blockade of the city; after some eight months, the starving inhabitants at last fell to a Roman assault. According to Polybius by way of Livy and Plutarch, Archimedes met his end at the hands of an enraged Roman soldier who cut him down during the ensuing sack of the city.

The Roman army gradually integrated artillery into its arsenal as it gained large stocks of captured weapons from the Carthaginians and

Greeks. These were used by Scipio Aemilianus (185/4–129 BC) in the siege of Carthage itself during the Third Punic War in 147–146 BC. (Some accounts relate that in a desperate attempt to delay disaster, the Carthaginian women donated their own hair to repair the springs of the city's catapults.) The process, however, was not consistent; during his siege of the Piraeus beginning in 87 BC, Sulla (138–78 BC) began operations without the benefit of artillery. Daunted by the use of the defenders' weapons, however, he soon after obtained artillery pieces from nearby cities and organized work crews to construct new engines, some of which hurled heavy lead shot to great effect.

As with the Greeks, the historical sources of Roman artillery development are fragmentary, based on a limited number of authors—primarily the first-century B.C. engineer Vitruvius (ca. 90–20 BC) and Flavius Vegitius Renatus, writing at the time of Valentinian I (364–375 AD). These accounts are further supplemented by intriguing archeological evidence and a limited number of artistic depictions. In use and design, Roman artillery, or *tormenta*, differed little in principle from the earlier Greek forms.

THE BALLISTA

As described by Vitruvius during the time of Julius Caesar in about 50 BC, the Roman ballista was a two-armed torsion machine used as an antipersonnel weapon in sieges and operated by a two-man firing crew. Caesar equipped each of his legions with thirty ballistae, providing his forces with a highly mobile and effective covering fire capability.

Although some ballistae were much larger, many were relatively small, for portability in rough terrain—a practical asset for campaigns in wild, barbarian territories such as Britain and Gaul. Arm lengths varied from 2 to 4 feet, with larger stone-throwing weapons hurling shot weighing from 7 to a more typical 60 pounds; ranges were up to 550 yards. Bolt-firing ballistae were recorded firing 26-inch to 3-foot projectiles up to 300 yards. Traveling at a velocity of about 115 mph, the ballista's projectiles were capable of devastating results on the human body. The Jewish historian Flavius Josephus (AD 37–ca. 100) recorded that during the siege of Jotapata in AD 67, the future emperor Vespasian (AD 9–79) surrounded the city with 160 siege engines, most probably including ballistae.

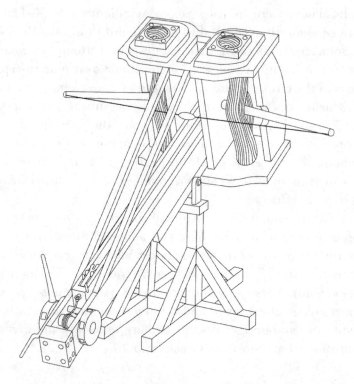

Ballista (Courtesy Art-Tech)

Josephus's rare first-hand account of the effect of these weapons graphically illustrates their ability to inflict terror and destruction:

[T]he engines could not be seen at a great distance, and so what was thrown at them was hard to be avoided; for the force with which these weapons threw stones and darts made them hurt several at a time, and the violent noise of the stones that were cast by the engines was so great, that they carried away the pinnacles of the wall, and broke off the corners of the towers; for no body of men could be so strong as not to be overthrown to the last rank by the largeness of the stones; and any one may learn the force of the engines by what happened this very night; for as one of those that stood round about Josephus was near the wall, his head was carried away by such a stone, and his skull was flung as far as three furlongs [a furlong equals 220 yards]. In the daytime also, a woman with child had her belly so violently struck, as she was just come out of her house, that the infant was carried to the distance of half a furlong; so great was the force of that engine. The noise of the instruments themselves was very terrible, the sound of the darts and stones that were thrown by them was so also; of the same sort was that noise the dead bodies made, when they were dashed against the wall; and indeed dreadful was the clamor which these things raised in the women within the city, which was echoed back at the same time by the cries of such as were slain; while the whole space of ground whereon they fought ran with blood. . . . (Josephus, 650)

THE ONAGER

The onager, meaning "wild ass," derived its name from its powerful recoil, or kick, upon discharge; it was built in a number of sizes. Although possibly originating as early as the third century BC, it was most commonly used in the fourth century AD. Resembling the modern conception of a catapult, it mounted a throwing arm attached to the center of a single horizontal torsion spring, with a leather sling attached to the opposite end of the arm to accept projectiles. A winch allowed the crew to lower the arm to its cocked position, where a metal rod would secure it for loading either stone shot—the equivalent of shrapnel, consisting of smaller stones—or ceramic balls filled with incendiary pitch. Striking the retaining pin with a mallet released the throwing arm to fly forward and release its projectile upon striking a large pad on an upper wooden cross-beam; this violent action earned the onager its name. Although five to six men could effectively man the onager, Vegitius recommended an eleven-man crew for optimum efficiency. That number included four men to operate the winch, a gunner and commander to aim the piece, and ammunition handlers.

The onager held the advantages of being the simplest and least expensive of the Roman siege weapons, and it was capable, in its largest models, of hurling stone shot weighing up to 180 pounds. But it also had its limitations. As the largest siege engine, it weighed from 2 to 6 tons and was difficult to transport, even when disassembled; its use was thus limited mainly to the Continent as a garrison weapon. Its weight further complicated its crew's duties, as it was very difficult to shift from side to side to adjust angle of fire. It was also less accurate than two-armed artillery, as it hurled its stones in a high, arcing trajectory much like a modern mortar or howitzer. In addition, although Josephus described an onager in action hurling a 100-pound stone over 400 yards, most onagri achieved a shorter range than the ballista, thus exposing their crews to enemy archers.

Still, onagri were used extensively, being effective against fortifications and for defending camps in the field. They were particularly
terrifying to barbarians. As recorded by Tacitus, a large onager also
figured prominently in a famous incident during the civil wars of AD
69. During the Second Battle of Bedriacum (near Cremona), troops
of the Fifteenth Legion under Vitellius moved the weapon forward to
deliver a punishing fire on Danubian troops under Antonius Primus,
a commander loyal to Vespasian. Their exposed position, however,
enabled two of Antonius's legionnaires, concealing their allegiance
with captured Vitellian shields, to overpower its crew and cut its
sinew springs. Graphically illustrating the vulnerability of artillery
insufficiently supported by infantry, the action of the two soldiers
disabled the weapon for the duration of the battle—a battle that ultimately resulted in the ascension of Vespasian to the throne.

THE SCORPION

As described by Vitruvius, the scorpion (or scorpio) was a relatively
lightweight and mobile weapon that appeared in the mid-first century B.C. It was a torsion-powered weapon with the improvement of
curved, tapered arms similar to an archer's recurved bow to increase
their strength. The evolution of the scorpion's construction illustrates the Romans' use of much more metal than the Greeks to reinforce stress points: bronze for frames and iron for surfaces subject to
wear. The Romans manufactured both stone- and bolt-firing scorpi-
ons, with the stone-throwers capable of hurling a 7- to 10-pound
shot 300 yards. Bolt-firing weapons typically fired a 27-inch arrow
fitted with a pyramidal iron head and three wooden fletches.

THE CHEIROBALLISTRA

The cheiroballistra probably appeared in the late first century AD and
was the most sophisticated Roman two-armed siege and field
weapon. Its torsion springs were supported by all-metal frames and
often were protected from the weather by bronze casings. The
frames themselves were secured by metal components, with some
possibly constructed with all-iron frames and two front-mounted
wheels for rapid deployment.

Ranged by adjusting a ratchet controlling the firing cord tension, the cheiroballistra was highly accurate, being aimed with a simple rear sight aligned with the bolt tip. Capable of three to four shots a minute, it was particularly suited as a rapid-fire field piece, the majority of its up to ten-man crew serving as ammunition handlers.

Archeologists have excavated a relatively large number of metal cheiroballistra components and bolts; the finds have also been supported by a number of surviving artistic representations. Three scenes from Trajan's Column (A.D. 106–113) show what appear to be larger types of cheiroballistrae used as defensive weapons in fortifications. Two scenes show smaller cheiroballistrae transported by wagon—a mode of transportation supported by Vegitius (fl. ca. AD 390), who reported that they were pulled by mule teams. The so-called Cupid Gem, a late Hellenistic or possibly early Augustine ornament, features a cheiroballistra in a rather humorous light, as it portrays Cupid aiming the weapon, in favor of his traditional bow, presumably at a particularly difficult and desirable object of affection.

PRODUCTION AND DEPLOYMENT
OF ROMAN ARTILLERY

In light of their profound military and engineering talents, the Romans were apparently strangely belated in appreciating systematic artillery acquisition and production. Whereas the great Hellenistic kingdoms had large and well-organized artillery manufacturing facilities in such cities as Alexandria, Pergamum, and Rhodes, the Romans seem to have used their arsenals, the *armamentaria publica,* mainly for armor and small arms fabrication. During the Republican period, commanders in the field were often forced to resort to requisitioning artillery from local Greek cities and hiring local experts to operate it. As late as 63 BC, Pompey the Great (106–47 BC) found it necessary to obtain artillery from Tyre for his siege of Jerusalem.

Julius Caesar (100–44 BC), however, exhibited a great appreciation of artillery and did maintain at least a minimal complement on a permanent basis; it was used to great effect against the Belgae and other tribes on the Continent. Caesar himself recorded the outstanding accuracy of his catapult crews during the twenty-seven-day siege of Avaricum (Bourges) in 52 BC. Over the course of an entire night, Roman artillery crews picked off Gaulish troops one by one as they attempted to fling burning pitch onto the attackers' siege works. Caesar also recognized artillery's inherent vulnerability during field operations. As had Sulla before him, he protected his catapults during field operations by placing them in small forts or by positioning them on high ground with infantry and archer support.

Early records are extremely fragmentary, but a certain standardization for distribution of artillery appears to have begun under Augustus (31 BC–14 AD). This included one ballista fielded by each cohort and one scorpion per century, with an actual total of possibly fifty engines per legion. By the time of Constantine the Great (r. AD 307–337), Roman artillery was apparently organized in specialized legions attached to field armies and fielding approximately fifty pieces. Troops especially trained and experienced as artillerists, known as *ballistarii*, were highly valued and were afforded elite status with special privileges. During the first centuries of the empire, possibly two *ballistari* were attached to each century, with approximately ten *libritors*, or crewmen, attached to each piece.

One of the best accounts of the deployment of Roman field artillery in battle comes from the *Order of Battle Against the Alans* by Lucius Flavius Arrianus, also known as Arrian (ca. AD 85–after 146). Although a Greek and well known as a historian, Arrian was a close friend of the emperor Hadrian (r. AD 117–138), a consul, and served as the Roman governor of Cappadocia. In that capacity, in AD 134 he also exhibited his considerable military skills as he successfully led two legions—the Legio XV Apollinaris and the Legio XII Fulminata—against the Alans, a nomadic tribe from the northern steppes sometimes referred to by the Romans as the Scythians.

Arrian formed his two legions into a crescent-shaped battle line with its flanks arcing toward the expected assault. With his light infantry and archers protecting his mobile artillery (most likely cheiroballistrae) occupying his extended flanks, Arrian thus safely maximized the range of his long-range weapons ahead of his main battle line. He anchored the center of his line with his heavy infantry, which, in turn, shielded his largest, least mobile ballistae— bolt- and stone-throwers that were positioned to fire over the main battle line at the approaching enemy.

Arrian's account does not describe the battle itself, but his preliminary orders to his officers apparently reflect the standard Roman tactics of the time for countering an attacking mounted force. Troops were to maintain strict and utter silence until the enemy came into artillery and bow range. At that point, they were to erupt into their battles cries and simultaneously release an overwhelming missile barrage in an assault calculated to devastate the less disciplined barbarians both psychologically and physically.

The Romans also used ballistae in civil roles. Prompted by a devastating fire in Rome in AD 6, the emperor Augustus ordered the establishment of a permanent paramilitary police and fire-fighting organization known as the Vigiles. Organized into seven cohorts of 1,000 men and commanded by centurions of the Praetorian guard, the Vigiles were exclusively former slaves who, by their service, were eventually granted full Roman citizenship. Modern scholars theorize that the Vigiles, as did the regular legionaries, fielded one ballista per century. Although there is some debate concerning the use of these weapons, bolt-firing ballistae may have been used for riot control purposes, while stone-throwers were possibly used to knock down burning buildings to create firebreaks. Some evidence indicates that ballistae were also used to launch grappling hooks attached to climbing ropes to allow access to roofs and the upper stories of buildings. As the Romans were well aware of the fire-suppressant qualities of wine vinegar, another theory asserts that the Vigiles launched vinegar-filled jugs or other containers into fires with their ballistae.

ROMAN AND BYZANTINE NAVAL ARTILLERY

As with the Greeks before them, the early Roman use of maritime artillery was essentially an adaptation of standard forms to meet immediate needs. During the civil war, Caesar met such an improvised threat during his siege of Massilia in 49 BC when its defenders hurriedly mounted catapults not only on warships but on fishing boats as well. That same year he, himself, probably used raft-mounted catapult towers at Brundesium. Earlier, during his invasion of Britain in 55 BC, Caesar had effectively covered his landings on the Kentish coast with ship-mounted artillery, and both bolt- and stone-firing artillery were certainly aboard his ships when he entered the harbor of Alexandria in 48 BC.

Naval artillery continued to develop during the civil wars that resumed after Caesar's assassination. Marcus Agrippa (ca. 63–12 BC), an experienced general and the later adoptive son of Octavian, the future emperor, Augustus (r. 27 BC–AD 14), made use of ship-borne artillery and apparently invented a catapult-launched grappling hook first used at the battle of Naulochus in 36 BC. At a time when naval tactics were still based on first ramming and then boarding enemy vessels, Agrippa's innovations also made possible long-range ship-to-ship artillery fire that probably contributed to his victory over the fleet of Marc Antony (83–30 BC) and Cleopatra (69–30 BC) at the decisive battle of Actium in 31 BC. The increasing use of ship-borne artillery, however, did lead to new designs in ship architecture, as the catapults in use, weighing some two tons, required more stable platforms. As a result, Roman ships eventually increased in size and incorporated artillery towers to accommodate the heavy weapons.

GREEK FIRE

In the seventh century AD, the Byzantines introduced a new form of incendiary weapon known variously as marine fire, liquid fire, or more commonly, Greek fire. Although its exact formula has been lost, Greek fire probably consisted of varying amounts of liquid petroleum, naphtha, pitch or tar, sulfur, and quicklime. Although more typically projected through a pressurized bronze tube, various catapults could also launch it in ceramic jars. Owing to its composition it stuck to nearly any surface and burned fiercely even on water, much like modern napalm, making it particularly effective against enemy ships and wooden siege towers. The only known methods of extinguishing Greek fire were dousing it with wine vinegar or smothering it with sand.

The Byzantines, who claimed that the formula had been passed directly to Constantine the Great (r. AD 307–337) by an angel from God, jealously guarded the formula for Greek fire as a state secret. Although warning that those who imparted its secrets were liable to be struck from above by lightning, they did supply allies with quantities of the prepared substance. Despite such measures and dire warnings, by the time that the Crusaders reached the Holy Land and Egypt, the use of Greek fire had spread to the Muslims, who, in turn, used it against the European invaders.

During the siege of Mansura (Mansourah) in Egypt in 1249, the Muslims used ballistae against the French Crusaders to launch tubs of Greek fire with spectacular and terrifying effect. The Sieur de Joinville (1224–1319), companion and biographer of King Louis IX (1214–1270), described one of the flaming missiles fired at night by what he identifies as a pierrière: "It was like a big tun [wine cask] and had a tail of the length of a large spear: the noise which it made resembled thunder, and it appeared like a great fiery dragon flying through the air, giving such a light that we could see in our camp as clearly as in broad day" (Partington, 25–26). Still, despite such impressive pyrotechnics and the destruction of some siege towers, Joinville records few if any actual casualties resulting from Greek fire.

MEDIEVAL ARTILLERY

Other than its terminology, little distinguished early medieval siege engines from their late Roman predecessors. Artillery development appears to have lapsed in Western Europe following the collapse of the Roman Empire, but it was eventually reintroduced by way of contact with the Byzantines and the Muslim-Arabs of the Near East and through the Moors in Spain. The onager and ballista survived for a limited time, although in the West, through a shift in terminology, the term "ballista" gradually came to describe what the Romans had called the onager. Attesting to its continuing survival in the Muslim world, the same weapon was known to the Arabs as the *ziyar*.

Other weapons also survived and probably made their way back to the West by way of the Islamic world. In that way the ancient gastraphetes reappeared as the "great crossbow," and the larger form of the gastraphetes, the oxybeles, as the espringale (also seen as "espringal"). The espringale was essentially a medieval translation of the oxybeles that fired a 4-foot iron bolt, or, with modification, stone shot. It launched its projectile at a relatively flat trajectory and achieved an effective range of about 150 yards. The powerful arms were spanned with either winches or screw devices, and the entire engine mounted on various forms of wooden stands.

The espringale and great crossbow were efficient long-range antipersonnel weapons, as well as being useful in providing counterbattery fire against enemy artillery crews. They were lighter than other types of early artillery and were often used to defend gates and as naval weapons. The great crossbow and espringale also fascinated the great Renaissance figure Leonardo da Vinci (1452–1519), who, between 1485 and 1487, recorded a number of detailed plans and improvements of the devices in one of his manuscripts, the *Codex Atlanticus*. It was, however, the later development of the large pivoting-beam, counterpoise engines exemplified by the trebuchet that dominated the medieval siege.

THE MANGONEL

As with many early designations, the term "mangonel" seems to have been used by early writers to indicate a number of different types of siege engine, including torsion machines like the onager. It may also describe an early pivoting-beam engine powered by human traction or a fixed (rather than the later free-swinging) counterweight. Chinese records indicate human traction-powered pivoting-beam engines nearly identical to medieval European engines described as mangonels being used in that country before the third century BC. A poem, "De Bellis Parisiacae Urbis" ("The Wars of the City of Paris") by the French monk Abbon de Saint-Germain-des Prés (850–923), appears to refer to such a weapon used by the Vikings in their siege of Paris in 885–886. That the supposedly primitive Northmen could build such sophisticated weapons initially startled the Franks defending the city. The Vikings, however—who apparently also used some form of Greek fire during the siege—may well have come in contact with both weapons through their travels in Muslim- and Byzantine-controlled territories. Paris was eventually saved in that, although adaptable, the Vikings did not fully grasp the true capabilities of siege machinery and thus did not exploit it to its fullest extent. Having failed to breach the walls but succeeding in intimidating the city's population, the Vikings contented themselves with extorting an acceptable amount of tribute and subsequently left for other opportunities.

Still, a new invention, probably originating in China, arrived in Europe by way of the Muslim world in the seventh century and gradually led to the obsolescence of the older Greco-Roman tension and torsion engines. It consisted of two large wooden A-frames mounted on a base and connected at the top by a freely rotating wooden axle. A throwing beam or arm passed through the center of the axle with one-quarter of its length facing the target and the remaining three-quarter length extending rearward. A heavy leather sling attached by rope to the long portion of the throwing arm couched the weapon's projectile, while the short end mounted a counterweight (or counterpoise) to provide the machine's energy. These engines eventually evolved into the trebuchet, the primary heavy siege weapon that remained in use well after the advent of gunpowder artillery. Gilles Colonne (d. 1316), writing in about 1280, identified several distinct models of the machine, suggesting a continual process of experimentation and modification of the pivoting arm and crossbeam principle. Egidio Colonna also wrote of the same device.

THE PIERRIÈRE AND THE BRICOLE

Probably the earliest of these machines (also confusingly referred to as mangonels in some records), the pierrière (also called petraria), was also the smallest and the most simple in construction and operation. The smallest pierrière could be operated by one person. That the Arabs introduced it to the West is suggested by their use of an identical type of weapon, called the *lu'ab*. To operate the pierrière, the crew simply placed a stone in a sling attached to the longer end of the firing arm and, by applying human traction power, vigorously pulled a rope attached to the other end. To achieve a slightly greater range, one or two other soldiers could be added as rope-pullers. During the Third Crusade, the French contingent under King Philip Augustus carried three such engines identified as "patrariae" to the Holy Land.

The bricole (sometimes called a biffa) was essentially a somewhat larger pierrière that supplemented or replaced the rope with a movable counterweight as its energy source. Owing to their relatively small size, the bricole and pierrière were often used as defensive weapons mounted on top of fortifications and sometimes reported to be served by women. Such was the case in 1115, when forces of King Louis VI "the Fat" (b. 1081; r. 1108–1137) of France besieged rebellious citizens of Amiens in a fortified tower known as le Castillon. To counter the king's two movable siege towers, the citizens constructed an equal number of engines of the human traction–powered mangonel or pierrière type. A contemporary chronicler recorded that the designer and commander of the two stone-throwers "set almost four-score women to throwing the stones he had piled up. . . .And while the men defended their ramparts with the spirit of Achilles, the women with equal courage hurled stones from the catapults and shattered both of the towers" (Nicolle, 45–46). In another incident, during the siege of Toulouse in 1218–1219, the commander of the attacking forces, Simon de Montfort (1168–1218), was struck and killed by a stone launched by a pierrière crewed by townswomen.

Both the pierrière and the bricole offered a number of advantages to early medieval armies. They were inexpensive to manufacture, and both their construction and operation required relatively unskilled personnel. They were also easily portable and could sustain a high rate of short- to medium-range fire; with a suitable pile of rocks at hand, the crew could fire at a rate comparable to that of a simple slinger. One example of the astounding rate of fire that could be delivered by such engines occurred in 1147, when two English weapons manned in shifts rained 5,000 projectiles on the defenders of Lisbon in ten hours.

THE TREBUCHET

The trebuchet was the most effective type of heavy artillery in the pregunpowder age. Nevertheless, throughout its career, the size and the complexity of the trebuchet limited its deployment during major sieges to a maximum of about twenty engines, often firing in batteries. Such engines often reached gigantic proportions, mounting throwing arms of up to 50 feet in length. In its refined forms it was capable, at 300 yards, of concentrating repeated hits on a specific area with stone shot weighing 300 pounds or more, to crumble sections of even the stoutest fortifications and achieve breaches. Typically hinged to the short end of the throwing arm, free-swinging counterweights provided the energy to throw these huge stones. These counterweights were large wooden hoppers up to 9 feet across and 12 feet deep, holding as much as 10 tons of stone, lead, earth, or sand. Because of their size, trebuchets were usually constructed on site using local materials such as timber, with manufactured components including metal fittings and rope being hauled in by wagons and oxen.

Accounts of the siege of Scottish-held Stirling Castle by King Edward I (Longshanks; b. 1239; r. 1272–1307) in 1304 attest to the scale of such a project, as well as to the affection of soldiers for particular artillery pieces. The strategic stronghold was manned by only thirty defenders—the last holdouts of the Scottish revolt—but was well situated and protected by massive walls. Edward, who had defeated the famed William Wallace at Falkirk six years earlier, was determined to put an end to the threat to his authority; he besieged the castle with his army and twelve siege engines, their counterweight hoppers filled with the lead roofing plates stripped from nearby churches. Edward, however, ordered an additional engine to be built, a particularly large trebuchet that apparently became his obsession.

It took famed engineer Master James of St. George and a team of master carpenters supervising forty-nine workmen to erect the monster, affectionately christened "War Wolf" by its creators. Edward, who nearly lost his life twice during the siege—once when struck by

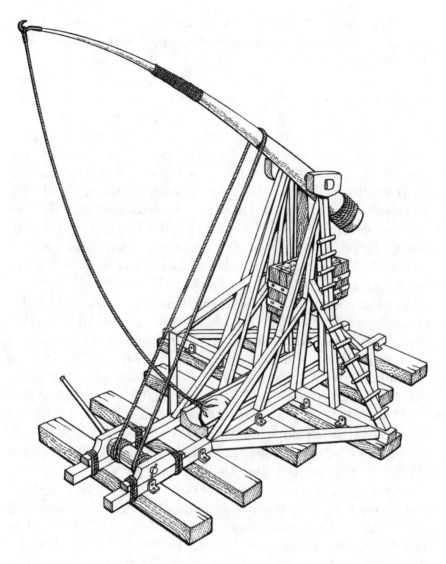

Trebuchet (Courtesy Art-Tech)

a crossbow bolt and again when his horse was killed by a stone from a defending engine—actually delayed accepting the surrender of the castle until War Wolf's completion. Finally, after three months of continuous construction, and viewed by a number of ladies especially invited by the king, War Wolf hurled one stone against the battlements. It could only have been a great relief for the starving defenders that, his point made, Edward at last accepted the castle's surrender. Ammunition preparation also proved labor intensive; as recorded at the siege of Berwick in 1296, forty-three stonemasons and quarrymen labored at cutting and shaping stone shot.

The operation of the larger weapons also required significant manpower, with crews for single trebuchets often numbering more than fifty men. To prepare the trebuchet for firing, some twenty men were necessary to operate two winches or capstans to lower the firing arm into its ready position, where it would be secured by a metal pin. Other crewmen would then place the projectile in the leather sling attached to the throwing arm, and the officer of the piece would sight the weapon. Careful adjustment of the length of the ropes attaching the sling and the weight of the counterpoise enabled the trebuchet to achieve remarkable accuracy. To fire the trebuchet, the operator pulled a lanyard to release the retaining pin. This freed the counterweight to swing down, lifting the arm and sling and allowing the projectile to slide up a smooth wooden ramp until the arm reached the vertical, at which point one end of the sling fell free and released the projectile at the apogee of its arc.

Although it certainly appeared some years earlier, the first reliable documentary evidence of a trebuchet was recorded in Italy in 1199, describing its use during the siege of Castelnuovo. The trebuchet went on to dominate medieval siegecraft from the twelfth through the early fourteenth centuries, and it saw considerable use during the Crusades and the early battles of the Hundred Years' War (1337–1453). As with later artillery pieces, these individual engines often earned an affection similar to that of Edward for War Wolf. Their crews bestowed upon them such names as "Parson" and "Vicar" (Contamine, 104–106, 194; Nicolle, 19.)

Such large and complicated machines also earned special status and sometimes extraordinary recognition for those who possessed the special skills required to supervise their design and construction. In 1249, during the Seventh Crusade, Jocelin de Cornaut held the title *mestre engingneur* (master engineer) and oversaw the erection of eighteen engines in Egypt. Jean de Mézos of Gascony even rose from *mestre engingeur* to a knighthood in 1254 as a reward for his talents. That royal governments understood the importance of maintaining arsenals of such heavy ordnance is indicated by documentary evidence of round stone shot being manufactured under the auspices of the English Crown by 1244.

The trebuchet was capable of launching various types of projectiles, ranging from the field expedient to the carefully shaped and weighed shot of the French and English royal arsenals. Its accuracy was graphically illustrated by a 1340 account of a counterbattery exchange during the siege of Mortagne, when the defenders constructed a smaller trebuchet to neutralize a larger engine employed by their besiegers from the city of Valenciennes: "With its first shot the stone fell a dozen feet short of the Valenciennes one, the second fell right alongside, and the third 'was so well aimed that it struck the main beam of the engine and broke it in two'."(Contimine, 194) In 1211, during the siege of Castelnaudry, the attacking Occitanian artillerists used relatively brittle rocks found nearby as antipersonnel ammunition that, upon impact, "disintegrated but not before causing great injury to those who were inside the town" (Contamine, 104.

Medieval besiegers also found the trebuchet suitable for incendiary, biological, and psychological warfare. Incendiary projectiles consisting of pots or barrels filled with Greek fire or other flammable materials proved effective when launched into cities or against exposed troops. Incendiary shot also served as tracers during night operations, as it aided crews in tracking hits on their targets. Night bombardments also provided the added advantages of concealing the trebuchet operators from enemy archers and making possible a continuous hail of projectiles to wear down a city's defenders. Medieval besiegers also grasped at least a rudimentary notion of biological warfare, as they at times launched the carcasses of dead animals and the corpses of plague victims over cities' walls with the intention of spreading disease among the defenders. To this grisly ammunition they sometimes added the severed heads of captured enemies or even living prisoners, in the hope of shaking the defenders' will to resist.

THE TRIPANTUM AND COUILLARD

Gilles Colonne identified another type of trebuchet, the tripantum, as being a more accurate and even longer-ranged weapon than the standard model. This was apparently owing to its combination of two counterweights—one fixed to the throwing arm and the other movable for fine-tuning the range adjustments. The couillard, or couillart (Old French for testicles), was a sophisticated machine that could be erected more rapidly than the standard trebuchet and could thus be put into action much more quickly. It was distinguished by its two, rather than one, free-swinging counterweights.

Although gunpowder artillery (cannons) appeared in the fourteenth century and became more prevalent in the fifteenth century, it did not immediately replace mechanical artillery. The armies of the time instead slowly integrated these primitive gunpowder weapons into their arsenals, alongside their sophisticated trebuchets and mangonels. That was a tactically sound move, as the later trebuchets were much more powerful, accurate, and versatile than the essentially experimental and often unreliable early cannons.

CHAPTER TWO

Early Gunpowder Artillery

BLACK POWDER

No reliable account of the origin of black powder (or gunpowder)—a mixture of carbon (charcoal), sulfur, and saltpeter (potassium nitrate)—has survived. The earliest medieval European accounts credit its discovery to various diabolical characters practicing magic or alchemical experiments. Although various explosive compounds had been known for centuries, a Chinese official named Tseng Kung-Liang recorded the first accurate formula for black powder in 1044, in a reference work entitled *Wujung Zongyao*. By 1300, the mixture was in wide use by the Chinese and Mongols for rockets, fire arrows, and bombs. Beginning in the mid-thirteenth century, Muslim artillerists were using it to create explosive trebuchet projectiles. It later passed to the Near East and, by way of the Muslims, on to Europe, where its critical ingredient, saltpeter, belied its discoverers under such names as Chinese snow and Chinese salt. The English scholar and alchemist Roger Bacon (ca. 1214–1292) recorded the first reliable Western account of the formula in 1267.

Bacon's writings indicate that gunpowder was known in Europe in the thirteenth century and widely used for amusement in firecrackers. He also clearly understood the destructive potential of the compound: "There is a child's toy of sound and fire made in various parts of the world with powder of saltpeter, sulphur and charcoal of hazelwood. This powder is enclosed in an instrument of parchment the size of a finger, and since this can make such a noise that it seriously distresses the ears of men, especially if one is taken unawares, and the terrible flash is also very alarming, if an instrument of large size were used, no one could stand the terror of the noise and flash. If the instrument were made of solid material the violence of the explosion would be much greater" (Partington, 78).

Saltpeter, deriving from "saltpetre," from the medieval Latin *sal petrae,* or "stone salt," is also known as potassium nitrate. It is essential as the oxidizing agent when combined with sulfur and carbon to create the explosive force in black powder. Saltpeter occurs naturally in some caves and other areas rich in decaying organic material such as bat or bird guano, but it requires processing to be effective as a component in black powder. Bacon's experiments revealed through trial and error that he could purify naturally occurring saltpeter by dissolving it in water, filtering it, and then allowing it to dry in glass containers. This process resulted in white, rod-shaped crystals more suitable for his alchemical experiments. His final black powder formula, written in code to frustrate the unworthy, instructs one to "take 7 parts saltpeter, 5 parts young hazelwood [charcoal] and 5 sulphur" (ibid., 74). As Europe had few natural sources of saltpeter, Western gunpowder manufacturers found it necessary to import it from the East, a situation that greatly increased the cost and limited the production. It was not until the 1380s that Europeans developed the means to produce the material for themselves.

Although quite sufficient for firecrackers and other pyrotechnics, Bacon's mixture lacked the combustive qualities to make it a truly viable propellant for use in firearms. Other advances, however, improved the distillation of saltpeter, and experiments by the German monk and alchemist St. Albertus Magnus (1206?–1280) resulted in a more explosive mixture. With time, further research eventually arrived at the ideal mixture of 74.64 percent saltpeter, 11.85 percent sulfur, and 13.51 percent charcoal.

EARLY CANNONS

Cheap, plentiful, and easy to work, wood appealed to some early makers as an ideal material from which to make cannons. It may possibly have been used in China soon after their discovery of black powder, and in 1344, the Italian poet and humanist Petrarch (1304–1374) mentions small wooden cannons being used in Europe. Experiments soon proved, however, that although economical, wood is incapable of withstanding the pressures of the large powder charges required to throw any significant projectile. Still, Henry VIII used wooden guns in the siege of Boulogne as late as 1544—weapons depicted as being 8 feet long with 2-foot bores. Some modern scholars believe, however, that they may have been dummies disguising a smaller metal tube inside, to convince the Boulognese that they were facing much more destructive weapons.

The first European metal cannons appeared soon after the invention of true black powder, but their origins are also obscured by time and legend. A now generally discredited though persistent tradition credits the German monk Berthold Schwartz with first igniting black powder in a metal tube to fire a projectile. Black Berthold, however, was most probably a fiction invented by the Germans to support nationalistic pride. The surviving documentary evidence, for its part, is riddled with obvious forgeries and is so contradictory—placing him in both the thirteenth and fourteenth centuries, and possibly being a Dane or Greek—that it is now generally accepted that he never existed.

Dating from the early fourteenth century, the earliest cannons were rather small affairs and probably the handiwork of bell casters, the only medieval craftsmen who would have had the necessary casting and metal-working skills necessary for their production. Contemporary manuscript illuminations and a few rare surviving examples suggest that these were vase-shaped, giving them their respective French and Italian names, *pots de fer* and *vassi*. Although the graphic evidence portrays weapons possibly 2 to 4 feet long, a pot de fer in the Statens Historika Museum in Sweden is only 18 inches long with a 36mm bore. Illustrations show such pieces resting on wooden tables and set off with a glowing hot iron or slow match of saltpeter-impregnated cord. They are firing iron, antipersonnel, crossbow-type bolts or quarrels with possibly brass, leather, or tin flights. Although without a doubt more spectacular to the observer, such a weapon would probably have been slower to load and would have had no greater effective range than a contemporary crossbow; also, they were capable of considerably less accuracy.

Still, such weapons represented progress, and they were added to European arsenals as attested by ordnance lists from Ghent dated 1313, reports of cannons firing iron balls at the siege of Metz in 1324, and an order by the city of Florence dated 11 February 1326 for brass cannons (*canones de metallo*) and iron balls. An early account of naval artillery is also found in a 1338 document recounting a French fleet's mission against England carrying a 25-pound pot de fer, 3 pounds of powder, and 48 projectiles. Within two decades the new technology appears to have spread throughout Western Europe, creating a demand for new and more effective cannons and sparking a new medieval arms race. From the early fourteenth century onward, battlefields would increasingly be shrouded in white, acrid gun smoke, and soldiers deafened by the roar of artillery.

As these early cannons were essentially an extension of the bell founders' craft, the early cannon founders began casting their guns of their customary copper, or of brass or bronze, alloys made up of a mixture of copper and zinc. The accepted mixture for bells in the Middle Ages was as much as five parts copper to one part tin, with experience and experiments eventually arriving at a mixture of nine parts copper to one of tin for what was termed "gun-metal." The casting process consisted of pouring molten metal into a mold formed of a clay core built around an iron support rod and incased in an outer clay shell reinforced by iron bands. Upon cooling, the mold and core would be removed, and the bore and outer surfaces filed and ground smooth. For early guns, copper, brass, and bronze held the advantages of melting at a relatively low heat and being easily worked. Their major disadvantage—especially with copper—lay in their brittleness, which necessitated a heavy tube to withstand the shock of ignition without splitting or otherwise self-destructing. Soon after the introduction of brass cannons, gun founders began experimenting with wrought iron, a stronger and more resilient metal but one with its own inherent deficiencies.

The process of forging wrought iron cannon barrels required an extremely high temperature, bellows-aided furnace capable of heating iron rods until red hot and then positioning them around a wooden mandrel. These rods would then be secured by a number of white-hot iron hoops, which would shrink upon cooling. The assembly would then be reheated to soften the metal, so that a blacksmith could hammer and fuse the iron together and in the process sufficiently char or incinerate the wooden mandrel so that it could be removed from the bore. Early gun tubes used from two to six iron-securing hoops, whereas hoops strengthened the entire outer surface of later guns. The founders then filled any gaps between the iron components with molten lead. The whole process very much resembled that of cooping, and thus it may have been one source of the term "barrel" to describe a cannon tube.

The introduction of wrought iron guns made possible the manufacture of much larger weapons than were possible with brass. But, owing to the inexact metallurgy of the time, as with cast bronze guns, the manufacturing process was incapable of producing bores with precise tolerances, which reduced the cannons' accuracy. Of greater concern, the tubes were still regularly capable of exploding upon discharge. The very nature of the hoop-and-stave construction of wrought iron guns made the elimination of all internal faults impossible, and cast pieces often concealed internal air bubbles within the tubes' walls. Although guns with such faults could often withstand a number of firings with no visible damage, repeated use or a heavy gunpowder charge eventually resulted in a burst barrel. By at least 1375 makers began testing barrels for structural integrity by repeatedly firing them with excessive charges before releasing them for use. These pieces were then stamped with a proof mark to indicate their structural integrity.

Still, the self-destructive nature of cannons persisted throughout the Middle Ages, and many gun founders and gunners in the field were maimed or killed by their own exploding ordnance, the most famous possibly being Scotland's King James II (b. 1430; r. 1437–1460), who was killed by fragments of one of his exploding guns in 1460 during the siege of Roxburgh Castle. Gunners eventually arrived at the safest position for firing a cannon—ten paces back and to the left of the breech—a distance that would have required a correspondingly long pole to hold the slow match or hot iron. Despite all precautions, bombards and other early cannons had a tendency to burst if overheated.

During the first half of the fourteenth century, gun foundries produced both breech- and, to a lesser extent, muzzleloading brass and wrought iron guns. Inasmuch as the early cannon founders found it difficult to plug the breech of the gun tubes satisfactorily, they most typically incorporated an open space at the rear of the tube to accept removable, wrought or cast iron cylindrical or bottle-shaped powder chambers. Secured in the rear with a wedge, these chambers, often called "thunder boxes," were often fitted with handles and could quickly be removed and replaced. Although it was necessary to load the projectiles at the muzzle of these early breechloaders, the removable powder chambers did provide a rapid rate of fire and efficient unloading. Such removable powder chambers were most effective in smaller guns; in larger pieces they were less efficient owing to their bulk and excessive weight. Consequently, many found muzzleloading cannon more efficient in chambering larger caliber ammunition. Still, foundries did produce large breechloaders with screw-on powder chambers.

Early fourteenth-century cannons were not mounted on carriages but transported by horse- or ox-drawn wagons to the field and then secured to wooden frameworks erected on site. This lack of mobility was not considered an overwhelming disadvantage at the time; however, as artillery was essentially limited to siege craft. For firing, smaller weapons were strapped to heavy wooden beams, whereas larger pieces were tied into large wooden frameworks called *teleria*, with their breeches against heavy wooden backstops secured to the ground with stakes. Heavier tubes were later fabricated with two metal loops attached to their center of gravity, to allow placement with block-and-tackle and cranes.

EARLY AMMUNITION

In addition to the quarrels used in pots de fer, artillery ammunition consisted of round lead, iron, or stone shot. Iron shot was preferable against stone fortifications; also, because it was cast, it generally provided a more consistently precise fit in a cannon's bore. Cast iron balls, however, were expensive to manufacture and were often prohibitively heavy to transport in larger calibers. Stone shot was thus often preferable for use in larger caliber artillery pieces and, being lighter, also offered the advantage of requiring less powder to achieve the same range. Furthermore, by using less powder it produced less pressure, thereby lessening the chances of exploding the tube. Stone shot, however, required careful shaping by skilled stonemasons using wooden or parchment sizing gauges. In addition, owing to their comparative fragility, stone balls were prone to disintegrate upon firing or against stone fortifications. Still, that disadvantage proved an advantage when used against defenders within a city; shattering upon impact, it showered enemy troops with deadly fragments.

Whether using stone, iron, or lead shot, loading and firing an early cannon was a complicated and hazardous proposition. Owing to the tendency of its ingredients to separate as the heavier sulfur settled during storage and transportation, gunpowder was typically mixed on site. The gunners then measured the powder and, in larger guns, loaded it in the powder chamber with chargers—long-handled wooden scoops. The next step, packing the powder with a rammer, also required particular attention, as powder compressed too tightly or too loosely failed to ignite efficiently.

The efficiency of any gunpowder weapon is also dependent on a secure gas seal of the firing chamber. That allows the powder to burn sufficiently to create enough pressure to fire the projectile at a high velocity. The technical expertise of the early ordnance industry, however, was incapable of manufacturing balls sufficiently sized to the cannons' bores. Thus there was blow-by of the explosive gasses past the projectile, with a resultant significant loss of energy. This gap between the projectile and the sides of the bore, known as windage, was a persistent and inherent problem with early cast and wrought iron guns. One method of reducing the loss of pressure consisted of pounding a tapered alder or willow plug into the mouth of the chamber before inserting the ball—a tricky process, as if the plug was driven in too tightly, the gun was in danger of exploding.

Firing the cannon was accomplished by applying a smoldering slow match of saltpeter-impregnated cord or a red-hot iron to a vent hole drilled into the top of the powder chamber and filled with fine priming powder. The process was often as dangerous to the gunners as to their intended targets: any spark could easily ignite the highly volatile gunpowder prematurely, and the cannons themselves were prone to explode without warning. The inherent dangers and skills involved in the artillerist's craft were such that few soldiers actually manned cannons during the Middle Ages. The duty instead fell to civilian professional artillerists, often known as bombardiers, cannoniers, or artists, who contracted their services to commanders as needed.

These specialists, who included some women, ensured their unique position by adopting Saint Barbara, the saint of thunder and lightning, as their patron and often organized in the same manner as contemporary craft guilds. Master gunners were also unique among battlefield personnel, as, owing to the technical nature of their profession, many were literate, so as to exchange the latest technological advances in their field. Aided by the invention of the printing press, artillery treatises such as the *Feurwerkbuch* of before 1420 circulated widely throughout Europe and were read by such famous figures as Leonardo da Vinci, who held a keen interest in artillery.

Still, artillerists were typically seen as a breed apart from regular medieval soldiers. More lightly armored than other personnel, owing to the heavy manual nature of their work, artillerists were often shunned by common soldiers within their own ranks for their association with the new "infernal machines" and the implication that they were somehow in league with the devil. In one instance, after the fighting at Metz in 1437, a master bombard gunner who had achieved the astounding rate of fire of three rounds in one day found it necessary to make a pilgrimage to Rome to allay the fears of his fellow soldiers that he had received satanic aid. What's more, as mercenary experts, artillerists also faced a somewhat uncertain fate if captured. Enraged enemies who saw their long-range killing as unchivalrous often killed gunners outright; more pragmatic captors at times struck a deal on the spot to turn their expertise against their former patrons.

Despite its primitive nature, artillery proliferated rapidly during the mid-fourteenth century, prompting both awe and concern among thoughtful observers. In 1344, Petrarch (1304–1374) wrote in a letter of a small wooden cannon firing explosive bronze projectiles, and his apprehension of the new weapon: "I am surprised that you have not also those bronze acorns which are thrown with a jet of flame and a horrible noise of thunder. It is not enough to have the anger of an immortal God thundering in the vault of heaven but, oh the cruel mixture of pride, man, sorry creature, must also have his thunder. Those thunders which Vergil thought to be inimitable, man, in his rage for destruction, has come to imitate. He throws them from an infernal machine of wood as they are thrown from the clouds" (Partington, 103–104).

EARLY BOMBARDS

Although far from standardized, specific types of cannons began to emerge as the various kingdoms and cities established formal ordnance production. Until about 1420 bombards held the field as the dominant artillery type used by the major European powers. Although later used as a general term to designate larger, wrought iron cannons, during the early fourteenth century "bombard" described diminutive weapons, some no larger than a pot de fer. Deriving their name from the Greek *bombos*, describing the loud buzz of a bee, or the Italian *bombo et ardor* ("thunder and lightning"), early bombards were made of a number of materials and fired a variety of projectiles. A typical bombard presented a markedly stepped profile, as the powder chamber was usually of a smaller diameter than the actual barrel. German records of 1360 list three sizes of such weapons, including 130-pound guns firing stone shot, 36-pound guns firing arrows, and 24-pound guns firing lead shot. The term later variously applied to squat, mortar-like guns and much larger weapons including both breech- and muzzle loading bombards, the largest breechloaders fitted with massive screw-on powder chambers.

Bombard (Courtesy Art-Tech)

The Hundred Years' War

Spanning the years 1337 through 1453, the intermittent conflict between England and France known as the Hundred Years' War saw the steady development of gunpowder artillery throughout Europe. At first Burgundy and France tended to lead other powers in the use of gunpowder weapons, but they were soon matched by England, and later by Germany, Spain, and Italy. By the middle of the fifteenth century guns were well on the way to replacing traditional medieval weapons such as the trebuchet, crossbow, and even the English longbow. During the period the new artillery forced military architects to redesign fortifications to accommodate defensive guns and to withstand the destructive power of besieging cannons. Even more far reaching, the long-range weapons also foretold the end of mounted chivalry, one of the key foundations of the old European feudal structure.

Early French and Burgundian Artillery

Spurred by the Hundred Years' War, French cannon and munitions production spread rapidly during the fourteenth century. Records from 1340 through 1382 list facilities in Lille, St. Omer, Toulouse, Cahors, Tournay, Montauban, Bioule, Agen, Laon, Chartres, Caen, and Chalon. The accounts suggest that these cities manufactured not only cannons but also their gunpowder and projectiles. The variety of cannons include small, cast bronze arrow-firing guns, as well as large pieces including an iron gun weighing 2,300 pounds forged in forty-two days in Caen in 1375. Although making a number of large copper guns, French gunmakers found that metal too brittle and manufactured guns of bronze and, preferably, iron. The ammunition manufactured at the French facilities included quarrels (arrows), medium and large stone and iron balls, and small iron and lead balls for antipersonnel use. A September 1346 entry from Tournay offers the rather odd image of an experimental cannon built by a pewterer named Peter of Bruges firing a 2-pound lead cube that penetrated a wall and a house before killing a man. Although the records do not specify whether they were bronze or iron guns, in 1345 the foundry at Cahors cast twenty-four cannon, with Caen casting iron guns by 1374 and Lille by 1414.

In 1376, Philip the Bold, Duke of Burgundy (b. 1342; r. 1363–1404), ordered that a large facility be set up at Chalon capable of producing a variety of cannon including large cast iron guns. Under the supervision of two famed cannon smiths, Jacques and Roland of Majorca, Chalon manufactured heavy guns in various calibers capable of firing stone shot weighing from 20 to 130 pounds. An example of such guns was a cast 384-pound, 11-inch-diameter piece that used 1.5 pounds of powder to fire a 60-pound stone ball. This gun was dwarfed in 1377, when Jacques and Roland were joined by another well-known craftsman, Jacques of Paris, to finish in eighty-eight days a goliath gun of at least 21-inch bore and capable of firing 450-pound stone balls.

The observant Christine of Pisa (1363–1431), daughter of the Venetian councilor to Charles V (b.1338 r. 1364–1380), noted even larger guns, as well as the French tendency to bestow feminine names on their largest guns. Garite (Margaret) was such a gun: it could throw stone balls weighing from 400 to 500 pounds. John the Fearless (1404–1419), son of Philip the Bold, continued in his father's footsteps by deploying ever larger artillery pieces. Between 1409 and 1410, at the siege of Velloxon near Calais, he fielded guns capable of firing 320- to 600-pound balls. These guns required up to 25 pounds of powder per firing and were capable of firing only about 8 shots per day.

Still, during his 1411 siege of the castle of Ham, John demonstrated that the destructive power of such guns could often intimidate an enemy into capitulation with only a minimum expenditure of ammunition. At Ham he fielded his own huge Griette bombard made at St. Omer, and although its first shot passed over the castle and splashed into the Somme River, the second and third balls—despite falling short—rebounded against the fortifications, collapsing a tower and the surrounding sections of the walls. Before another shot could be fired, the castle surrendered.

A contemporary account of another Griette firing at Bourges in June 1412 graphically describes the effect of a large, well-handled bombard in action: "It shot stones of enormous weight at the cost of large quantities of gunpowder and much hard and dangerous work on the part of its expert crew. Nearly twenty men were required to handle it, and when it went off the thunderous noise could be heard 4 miles away, terrorizing the locals as if it were the noise made by the furies of hell. On the first day, it partly destroyed the foundations of one of the towers. On the second day it shot twelve times; two of its stones penetrated the tower, exposing many rooms and their inhabitants to injury" (Hall, 62).

Early English Artillery

The arms race engendered by the Hundred Years' War also caused the English to develop their own artillery train. Artillery development in England found an early patron in King Edward III (b. 1312; r. 1327–1377). Expense ledger entries of Robert de Mildenhale, the Keeper of the King's Wardrobe at the Tower of London, provide reliable lists of English ordnance procurements from 1344 to 1353. These include numerous orders for large amounts of saltpeter, sulfur, and charcoal, as well as mixed gunpowder and lead balls. Various types of cannons are also listed, including a number of examples of a light, cart-transported, multibarreled arrangement known as a ribauldequin. Mildenhale's accounts record shipments of ribauldequins to Edward's troops in France in February 1347 for use in the siege of Calaise.

The Tower continued to act as a clearinghouse for ordnance, commissioning guns and gunpowder ingredients from various sources and distributing them among England's field armies and castles. Records from 1345 through 1360 report orders for four copper mortars, and in 1365 the Tower transported two "great guns" and nine smaller cannons to Queensborough Castle in Sheppey. In 1371 it provided six guns and saltpeter to Dover Castle, as well as to troops in Ireland and France. After 1380 this trickle of activity intensified, and by the end of the decade gunpowder and cannon production, centered around London, had become a major industry.

Following the Hundred Years' War, England fell somewhat behind the Continent in the development of improved cannons and artillery tactics. During the War of the Roses, from 1455 through 1485, both belligerents employed artillery, operated chiefly by foreign mercenary gunners, but guns rarely played a decisive role in the engagements. The war, a conflict between the houses of York and Lancaster over the succession to the throne, eventually culminated in a Lancastrian victory at the Battle of Bosworth on 22 August. The battle resulted in the crowning of the first Tudor king of England, Henry VII (b. 1457; r. 1485–1509). Henry, however, made little real progress in furthering English artillery development. It would be his son, Henry VIII (b. 1491; r. 1509–1547) who would lead England into the sixteenth century as a major artillery power.

Early Italian Artillery

The earliest known Italian references to cannons are from Florence in 1326, and into the middle of the century, records indicate that their use had spread to Friuli (1331), Terni (1340), Lucca (1341), Frassineto (1346), Turin (1347), Saluerolo, Modena (1350), Perugia (1351), and Ravenna (1358). The materials for the guns were bronze and, as described by Leonardo da Vinci, of welded or wrought iron. Other documents list cast iron bombards reinforced by wrought iron bands being manufactured in Parma at the end of the fourteenth century, and small cast iron cannons were recorded as being produced in Como in 1429. Italian ammunition was in keeping with that of other European countries, consisting of arrows or lances and stone, lead, and iron balls.

Early German Artillery

Although firearms probably appeared in Germany between 1325 and 1331, existing records of early German firearms development are rare, the earliest reliable records surviving from Frankfurt and dating to 1348. As described, the Frankfurt gun was of bronze, weighed only about 34 pounds and firing arrows. Frankfurt eventually assumed a leading role in Germany in the production of ordnance, manufacturing gunpowder, projectiles, and the guns themselves. Later records list a wrought iron cannon manufactured in 1377 and a large copper gun firing 100-pound stone balls the next year. Bronze guns are noted in 1381, and the records claim that iron guns were first cast in 1391.

By 1394, Frankfurt cannon makers were producing much larger guns, including a bronze muzzleloaded gun capable of firing 350-pound stone balls and requiring a team of sixteen horses for transport. It was also fitted with a shield to protect its crew from enemy fire. This gun was reportedly used at the 15 July 1410 Battle of Tannenberg (also called the Battle of Grunwald), in which united Polish and Lithuanian forces crushed the Teutonic Knights. Contemporary accounts of the battle state that both armies fielded artillery, with the Lithuanians' sixteen cannons being vastly outnumbered by the Teutonic Knights' approximately one hundred guns. The German artillery's numerical superiority, however, was minimized by both natural and tactical factors.

The Teutonic guns, positioned in the front lines with some infantry, opened the battle but reportedly managed to fire only twice before being overrun by Polish and Lithuanian light cavalry and infantry. Heavy rains of the previous day may have dampened the Germans' powder, rendering it unreliable and prone to misfires. Another critical factor was the decision by the Polish and Lithuanian commanders to hold back their heavily armed knights and lead their attack with irregularly spaced light cavalry and infantry. That deployment minimized the effect of individual artillery projectiles and enabled the fast-moving Union troops to overrun the vulnerable guns with minimal casualties. The Battle of Tannenberg ultimately illustrated that field artillery tactics in the early fifteenth century still remained at an experimental stage. As with so many early artillery deployments, the big guns played only a small role, with the majority of the battle following a typical medieval pattern of armored knights and archers deciding the outcome.

Artillery development continued, however, and at this time Frankfurt makers also produced smaller types of guns called *fustbusse*, a name possibly derived from its fist-size, 10-pound shot. Probably weighing from 1,600 to 2,000 pounds, these breechloaded guns were made either of bronze or wrought iron and were transported on carriages or carts pulled by four horses. In 1413, Frankfurt makers also produced a number of small breechloading guns of cast copper and wrought iron.

Inventories also list artillery either being made or stored in a number of other German cities, including Marienburg, Naumburg, Cologne, Augsburg, Erfurt, Nürnberg, Dortmund, Wesel, Linz, Göttingen, and Brunswick. These include a Marienburg record of a large cannon cast by Johannn von Christburg in 1408 for the Prussian Order. As did a number of German founders,

Von Christburg added a small amount of lead to his bronze alloy, and the cannon itself was of a two-piece construction with a screw-on breech section.

Early Spanish and Portuguese Artillery

Spain was affected by both European and Moorish influences and applied artillery to both land and naval uses. The earliest surviving Spanish cannons include both breech- and muzzleloading examples, being of wrought iron and relatively small. Although Spain was somewhat slower than other European powers at fully integrating artillery into its military, a 1359 Spanish account notes the use of a ship-mounted bombard, and by 1371 guns were a regular part of ships' armaments. Portugal began using cannons somewhat later than Spain, in 1370, and used them in the defense of Lisbon in 1384.

The 14 August 1385 Battle of Aljubarotta saw the first tactical use of field artillery on the Iberian peninsula and ensured Portugal's independence. It pitted the Portuguese pretender, John, Master of Avis, and his English allies against King John of Castile, who was aided by a large contingent French troops. Despite being outnumbered by the Castilians and French, the Portuguese and English were better organized and assumed strong defensive positions. Moreover, although the Castilians fielded some sixteen small cannons at Aljubarotta, those weapons did not decide the battle. Despite the confusion wreaked by the guns, the highly effective English longbowmen proved a much more decisive factor—a demonstration of the still experimental nature of the new gunpowder weapons.

Artillery was a much more decisive factor in the Portuguese acquisition of the strategic North African city of Ceuta on the Straits of Gibraltar on 14 August 1415. The Portuguese forces, including the twenty-one-year-old Prince Henry the Navigator (1394–1460), attacked the Muslim port on 14 August with 200 ships, artillery, and some 45,000 troops. The battle, in which Henry was wounded, gained Portugal a foothold in formerly Muslim territory and a key position on the Straits, and also opened new possibilities for the young prince in exploration and Portuguese expansion.

The marriage in 1469 of Queen Isabella I (1451–1504) of Castile and King Ferdinand II (1452–1516) of Aragon led, with the final conquest of Moorish Grenada in 1492, to a unified Spain. That victory was in no small part owing to Isabella's efforts, beginning in about 1482, to expand Spain's artillery resources. To that end,

Castile and Leon began producing and stockpiling large stores of guns and ammunition in Huesca in 1483. Spanish ammunition during this period included large stone balls, as well as incendiary projectiles composed of gunpowder and other flammable materials. In 1487, Spain again escalated its artillery program by obtaining both gunpowder and skilled workmen from abroad.

The guns produced in Spain during this period, although numerous, were of somewhat inferior quality, as suggested by one surviving 12-foot-long example showing rather shoddy workmanship in its wrought iron construction. These guns were also awkward in the field, as they were rigidly mounted on their carriages and thus could not be readily repositioned for sighting. Still, they were capable of firing formidable projectiles, including iron balls and stone shot ranging from 14-inch, 175-pound marble shot up to balls weighing 550 pounds.

LARGE BOMBARDS

By the late fourteenth century the term "bombard" had come to describe extremely large guns capable of launching massive balls with crushing effect. From about 1380 the bombards' range (sometimes over a mile), destructive power, and psychological impact were instrumental in the phasing out of mechanical engines such as the trebuchet in favor of gunpowder siege weapons. They were used throughout Europe during the late fourteenth and early fifteenth centuries, and the dukes of Burgundy—Philip the Bold (b. 1342; r. 1363–1404) and his son, John the Fearless (b. 1371; r. 1404–1419)—were particularly fond of the large guns; a number of famous bombards were made under their auspices. Philip the Good (b. 1396; r. 1419–1467) went so far as to establish his artillery as a separate branch of the Burgundian military structure by instituting the office of *matre d'artillerie* ("master of artillery").

Despite their ability to deliver highly destructive missiles, the very size of the bombards restricted their use to a static offensive siege role; their heavy recoil—capable of damaging stone battlements—denied their mounting on walls for defensive use. Transportation over the crude roads of the period was especially difficult and expensive. Conveying a single bombard weighing several tons required a large wooden wagon pulled by dozens of horses or oxen at a rate of only about 3 miles a day. In addition, the gun's train included spare draft animals, as well as wagons carrying equipment for mounting the gun on site, gunpowder ingredients, and the gun's projectiles. The personnel required to manage the livestock, maintain the wagon, mount, and serve the gun once in position, often numbered well over 100 men.

Preparing and firing a bombard on site were also massive and backbreaking undertakings, limiting the bombards to a maximum of some seven firings a day. Work gangs, with the aid of cranes, blocks, and tackle, first erected a stout wooden support for the gun and secured it into position by pounding stakes into the ground attached to its base. Other crews mixed the gunpowder ingredients and prepared the stone balls for firing. Owing to the gun's recoil jarring it out of alignment with each discharge, the crew also laboriously had to readjust the entire arrangement after each firing and wait for the barrel to cool for another loading. The great guns were also vulnerable to counterfire; despite their own superior range, to deliver maximum damage they were often positioned within the defenders' artillery and crossbow range. As a countermeasure, therefore, workmen were also required to erect large wooden shields that could be swung into position to protect the gun crews during the loading process.

Still, the large guns apparently engendered a certain affection among their makers, owners, and crews, who often assigned personalities and appropriate names to individual bombards. One example of such sentiment is engraved in verse on one great gun:

> I am Dragon the venomous serpent who desires with furious blows to drive off our enemies.
> John the Black, master gunner, Conrad, Coin and Cradinteur all together master founders made me on time in 1476. (Contamine, 142–143)

Variations on the name "Margaret" seem to have been popular among the Burgundians. The great Flemish bombard Dulle Griete ("Mad Meg") of Ghent bears the name of a legendary Flemish housewife who went insane and led an army of women into the depths of hell to wreak havoc on Satan and his minions. The great Flemish master Pieter Brueghel the Elder (ca. 1525/1530–1569) later immortalized her story in his painting Dulle Griete of 1562. For its part, the Flemish bombard was also capable of inflicting its own form of hellish havoc and destruction.

Although Dulle Griete bears the arms of Philip the Good, Duke of Burgundy (b. 1396; r. 1419–1467), it was possibly made around 1382 during the reign of his father, Philip the Bold. Now displayed in Ghent, Belgium, it is constructed of wrought iron and weighs approximately 13 tons. Capable of launching a 700-pound granite ball, and nearly 16.5 feet long, with a 25-inch bore, Dulle Griete was made with a tapered powder chamber 10 inches across the front and 6 inches at the rear. There are few records of Dulle Griete's actual use in battle, but it is probable that it was used by Ghent in its siege of Oudenarde in 1454.

In 1457, Philip the Good presented a pair of large bombards, acquired from the famed cannon dealer Jean Cambier and made in the town of Mons, to his nephew by marriage and fellow artillery aficionado King James II of Scotland. Philip probably felt little loss from his transfer of the guns to James, as Burgundy, like most Continental powers, by midcentury had essentially abandoned bombards as obsolete owing to their size and lack of mobility. For their part, James and his fellow Scots were impressed with what—in Scotland—was considered the latest in siege weaponry.

The one surviving gun, Mons Meg ("Mons Margaret"), is now exhibited in Edinburgh Castle. Another wrought iron, muzzleloaded gun, Mons Meg weighs some 6 tons, is bored to about 20 inches, and fired a 330-pound ball. Some estimates give approximately 100 pounds as the necessary amount of gunpowder to launch such a projectile. Unfortunately, James, having enthusiastically overloaded another gun during the siege of Roxburgh Castle, was killed when it exploded, leaving Mons Meg to see most of its use in the service of his successors. James IV (b. 1473; r. 1488–1513) later used the bombard in his successful siege of Norham Castle in 1513 and in his second siege of Dumbarton Castle.

Relegated to Edinburgh Castle for ceremonial use in the sixteenth century, Mons Meg was fired in 1558 to celebrate the marriage of Mary Queen of Scots (1542–1587) to the French dauphin, Francis. The ball was later reportedly found some 2 miles from the castle. Mons Meg fired its last shot in 1681 in honor of the future King James VII (of Scotland) and II (of England) (b. 1633; r. 1685–1688). On that occasion the barrel split, and the gun was discarded outside the castle's gate, where it lay until being carried to the Tower of London in 1754. Mons Meg at last returned to Scotland with great pomp and circumstance in 1829, following a campaign for its return by Sir Walter Scott and the Society of Antiquaries of Scotland.

Turkish Bombards:
The Fall of Constantinople

It is not without some irony that bombards, all but abandoned as obsolete by most European powers by 1453, played a critical role that year in the fall of Constantinople, the last Christian stronghold in the East. For centuries the Byzantine capital's great walls and defenders had repulsed invaders, including an earlier 1422 attempt by Sultan Murad II (r. 1421–1451). Although Murad had employed bombards against the city, they were rather ineffective, and he subsequently withdrew. His successor, however, Mohammad II, sometimes known as Mehmed II (b. 1432; r. 1444–1446, 1451–1481), and also known as Muhammad the Conqueror, possessed an innate appreciation for artillery and its use in siege craft.

Muhammad, lacking technical experts among his own subjects, subsequently obtained the services of Christian gun founders to design and build cannons especially suited for the siege. Among these was reportedly a famed Hungarian cannon maker known as Urban. Urban (or Orban) had previously been hired by the Byzantines but had deserted their cause after they failed to meet his fees. Muhammad, unlike the Byzantines, appreciated Urban's considerable, although mercenary, talents and "welcomed him with open arms, treated him honorably and provided him with food and clothing; and then he gave him an allowance so generous, that a quarter of the sum would have sufficed to keep him in Constantinople" (De Vries, X 356).

Urban quickly established a gun foundry at Adrianople where he oversaw the casting of both a number of large iron and bronze guns. These included at least one huge bombard of cast iron reinforced with iron hoops and with a removable, screw-on breech. Typical of such large breechloading cannons, the gun was fitted with slots around the breech's circumference to accept stout wooden beams. For loading and unloading, these beams were inserted in the slots to act as a capstan and provide the leverage to unscrew the heavy powder chamber. Weighing more than 19 tons, the gun was capable of firing stone balls weighing from approximately 800 to 875 pounds. The sheer size of the bombard, known as Basilica, required forty-two days and a team of sixty oxen and a thousand men to traverse the 120 miles to its firing site at Constantinople.

Muhammad began preparations for the siege in February and ordered the positioning of fourteen artillery batteries around the city.

As a further preparation, he ordered his navy, also equipped with artillery, to cut Constantinople off from the sea. For his part, the Byzantine emperor, Constantine XI (b. 1409; r. 1449–1453), did possess some artillery, but it was for the most part obsolete and numerically insufficient to reply to Muhammad's forces. The Byzantines had long lost the technological superiority they had held in previous centuries, and they soon found themselves reckoning with their shortsightedness in snubbing Urban the Hungarian.

Muhammad began the bombardment of the city on 6 April 1453. With a keen eye for the city's weaknesses, he concentrated his guns against its most vulnerable points, including the Gate of St. Romanus, where they effected a breach on 11 April. His success was short lived, however, as the defenders counterattacked and repaired the damage. Muhammad also faced other setbacks when Urban was killed when a cannon he was supervising exploded, and when his giant bombard cracked after a few days of firing, necessitating repairs. The sultan, however, proved his own resourcefulness in the use of artillery and made much better use of his smaller guns—weapons that were capable of a much higher rate of fire than Basilica's three rounds a day and were also more maneuverable. These included eleven bombards capable of firing 500-pound shot and fifty guns firing 200-pound balls.

The Ottoman barrage continued day and night, wearing down both the city's walls and its defenders. A witness described its effect:

> And the stone, borne with tremendous force and velocity, hit the wall, which it immediately shook and knocked down, and was itself broken into many fragments and scattered, hurling the pieces everywhere and killing those who happened to be near by. Sometimes it demolished a whole section, and sometimes a half-section, and sometimes a larger or smaller section of tower or turret or battlement. And there was no part of the wall strong enough or resistant enough or thick enough to be able to withstand it, or to wholly resist such force and such a blow of the stone cannon-ball. (ibid., X 357–358)

Finally, on 29 May 1453, the walls on either side of the St. Romanus Gate collapsed, and the Turks stormed the city. The Emperor Constantine fought valiantly in the defense of his city, but he was killed as overwhelming numbers of Turkish troops rampaged through the city for three days, killing, looting, and raping. With the fall of its capital, the Byzantine Empire collapsed, and with it the last vestiges of the Roman Empire.

The Czar Cannon

Also known as the Great Mortar of Moscow, the Czar Cannon was cast of bronze in 1586 and was the last and the largest of the bombards. Cast by master metalworker Andrei Chokov for Czar Fyodor I (b. 1557; r. 1584–1598), son of Ivan the Terrible (b. 1530; r. 1547–1584), the great gun has never been fired and is now exhibited in Moscow. Already an anachronism when cast, it is, however, a masterpiece of the bronze-caster's art and is awe-inspiring in its scale (although it would probably burst if actually fired).

The Moscow cannon is 18 feet long, weighs more than 40 tons, and is 36 inches at the muzzle. Essentially a straight tube, it is decorated with equestrian portraits of Czar Fyodor and has four handles molded into each side to aid in transporting its bulk. Although originally designed to fire grape shot, the Czar Cannon is now exhibited with four large balls weighing approximately 2,000 pounds each and rests on a huge, decorative gun carriage.

IMPROVEMENTS IN MEDIEVAL ARTILLERY

As gunpowder and cannon technology progressed, a certain degree of standardization of types of guns developed according to their size and use. Whereas the term "bombard" had evolved from a generic descriptive of several types of cannons to refer more specifically to large siege guns, other terms emerged for the numbers of smaller weapons that were used during the medieval period. A key factor in this process was the introduction of cast iron as well as cast bronze guns, a process that, after the initial casting, made possible a more precisely drilled and polished bore that, in turn, yielded more precise calibers and a certain interchangeability of ammunition between weapons of similar type. A tendency to lengthen the barrels in relation to bore size also became common beginning in the middle of the fifteenth century. The trend culminated in the late sixteenth century, with barrels reaching as much as thirty times or more their bore diameters.

The mid-fifteenth century onward also saw great improvements in the transportation of artillery. Earlier guns were essentially large, heavy metal tubes that were carried to the field or siege site in four-wheel wagons or sledges and then laboriously secured to wooden frameworks for firing. A French innovation of the 1490s at last made field artillery possible. Their introduction of trunnions, from the

French *trognon,* meaning "stump" (metal projections on either side of the gun tube slightly forward of its balancing point) provided a way of mounting the gun on a more mobile two-wheeled carriage. In addition, by providing a pivoting point, the trunnions allowed for much easier elevation and depression of the tube, making aiming the piece more efficient.

The process of "corning," or graining, gunpowder, introduced in about 1429, and improved methods of refining saltpeter greatly increased its efficiency and reliability. Prior to that date powder mills, powered either by water or horses, had ground the ingredients on marble slabs into a powder that was then sifted through cloth, producing a very fine consistency. Powder produced by this method, known as "serpentine," tended to separate—the heavier saltpeter settling to the bottom and the lighter charcoal shifting to the top—during storage or transportation. This shifting of ingredients produced a propellant with uneven burning qualities and subsequent poor performance when ignited in a gun. Adding to that problem, the fine nature of the powder did not allow for the adequate circulation of oxygen through the mixture, again reducing its explosive potential.

Corning powder involved wetting the powdered ingredients with vinegar, spirits, wine, or "the urine of a wine-drinking man." The resulting paste was then allowed to dry in the sun or in a dry room and was then crushed into uniform granules. The larger granules allowed more oxygen to circulate among the mixture, resulting in much more consistent burning. The powder factories then graded the powders from coarse to fine according to their intended use, with the coarsest mixtures most suited for the largest guns. Taking advantage of the new powder, during the 1430s artillerists also began prepackaging their powder into cartridges in premeasured linen or vellum bags.

Projectiles also improved steadily over the period. The earliest artillery ammunition was simply an adaptation of existing projectiles such as the crossbow bolt or the mechanical artillery's stone shot. Although not effective against stone battlements, lead, because of its low melting point and density, also lent itself well for casting into shot. In addition, early experiments showed that coating stone shot with a layer of lead produced significant advantages. Its malleability allowed it to fill in any imperfections in the hard stone core, thus producing a more precise spherical shape and, as a side benefit, reducing the possibility of damage to the bore. Lead-coated shot was also potentially more accurate, in that it reduced the gap between the ball and the walls of the bore and thus reduced the loss of propulsive gasses upon firing.

Iron shot was also used at an early date, but, because of the primitive metallurgy of the time, it proved impractical for all but the smaller guns, with stone shot being preferred for larger pieces. As cannon technology and casting techniques improved, artillerists returned to iron as a useful material for projectiles. By 1431, Philip the Good, the Duke of Burgundy, was including cast iron balls in his ordnance lists, and in Naumburg, Germany, shops were producing wrought iron shot in 1446 and cast iron balls in 1449. By the mid-sixteenth century large cast-iron balls were common in England, as is demonstrated by the recovery of 65-pound balls from the wreck of Henry VIII's flagship, the *Mary Rose*, lost in 1545.

Experiments in the fifteenth century also produced a number of other specialized types of ammunition. Whereas solid stone or iron shot was ideal for use against fortifications, they were relatively ineffective against advancing troops at close range. To that end, gunners at times found it expedient in the field to load their guns with a very primitive form of what was later called case shot, known as langridge. Langridge consisted of whatever lay at hand, including nails, scrap metal, or even gravel. By 1410 this amalgam was being contained or cased in a bag or some other container to ease handling. Various European arsenals also developed other, more formalized, types of antipersonnel ammunition. This included canister rounds made up of cans of lead or iron balls that would scatter upon leaving the muzzle. This shotgun effect greatly increased the killing potential of small guns and could be devastating upon infantry and cavalry at close range. A similar loading, grape shot, also appeared, and was made up of a cloth bag filled with iron or stone balls.

As bombardments during sieges were typically carried out day and night, artillerists invented an incendiary projectile to aid in aiming during night operations. Ignited by the detonation of the gun, these early "tracers" consisted of a stone or iron ball smeared with a sticky mixture of resin and tallow and then covered in gunpowder. To add to such pyrotechnic displays, gunners also found that by mixing small amounts of different ingredients into their gunpowder they could produce a variety of colors, including red, yellow, and orange.

TYPES OF MEDIEVAL ARTILLERY

Medieval writers were by no means consistent in their terminology in describing various types of artillery pieces. Still, a very general nomenclature for late-fourteenth- and fifteenth-century cannons can be pieced together. These included the bombards that were generally of wrought iron, 15 to 20 feet in length and fired projectiles of 300 pounds or more. A smaller version, the medium or common bombard, was about 10 feet in length and fired a stone shot of about 50 pounds. Another large gun, the basilisk, possibly derived its name from a legendary snake that could kill victims at a distance by merely looking at them. It was 22 to 25 feet long and fired a 20- to 48-pound bronze or iron ball. First mentioned about 1410, the veuglaire (or "fowler"), an often breechloaded siege weapon, was somewhat more than 8 feet in length and was bored from 9.75 to 19.5 inches. It was typically mounted on a wooden two-wheeled carriage fitted with a bed extending along the entire length of the barrel. Other heavier guns included the 48-pound cannon royal, also known as a carthoun, and the half-carthoun, firing a 24-pound ball. The courtaud was about 12 feet long and fired a 60- to 100-pound stone ball, while the passe-volant was 18 feet long and fired an 18-pound lead or iron shot. Mortars were first mentioned around 1460 and were squat, 5- or 6-foot weapons that fired a 200- to 300-pound stone in a high, arcing trajectory.

The culverin (or coulverine) possibly derived its name from *colubra,* a Latin word for serpent, or a legendary fire-breathing snake. It was first mentioned in 1410 and proved to be one of the most versatile and long-lived of cannons, seeing both field and naval use well into the seventeenth century. The typical culverin exhibited a rather graceful appearance, with a rather long and slender barrel, often embellished with the owner's coat of arms. It was a long-range gun capable of firing at a flat trajectory with reasonable accuracy. The two basic sizes were the demiculverin, firing an 8-pound ball, and the full-sized or whole culverin, firing an 18-pound projectile. The larger culverins were capable of firing a 17- to 18-pound ball accurately to about 350 yards and achieved an extreme range of 2,500 yards. Its trunnions made possible mounting on a variety of carriages, and a typical culverin field gun was mounted on a two-wheeled wooden carriage with an elevation screw behind the breech to facilitate raising and lowering of the barrel. Some writers also used the term "serpentine" interchangeably with "culverin" in describing a wide range of guns, from heavy weapons to small 1.5-inch-bore 4-pounders.

The saker, named for a European falcon, was not as large as the demiculverin and was applied to both land and naval use. It fired a 5- to 8-pound shot up to 350 yards with reasonable accuracy and was capable of extreme ranges of 17,000 yards. Sakers presented a

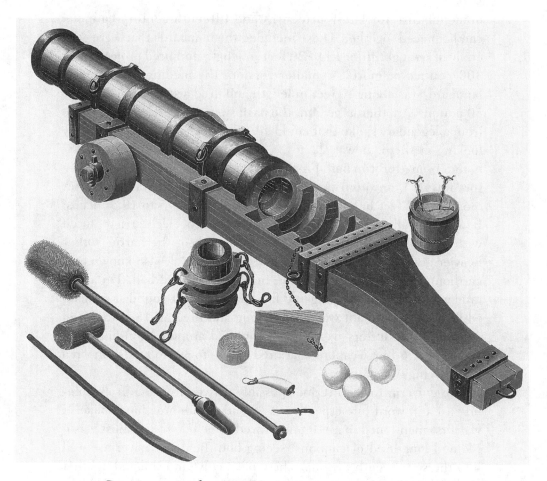

Generic cannon showing various components and implements
(Courtesy Art-Tech)

rather graceful appearance, with long, slender barrels. The cerbottana was 8 to 10 feet long and fired a 2- to 3-pound lead shot; the 8-foot-long espingarde fired a 10- to 15-pound stone ball.

Other smaller guns included the crapaudeaux (or "toad") and crapaudines, first recorded in 1430; the courtauds in 1460; and the faucons and fauconneaux in 1480. The falcon—another name for faucon—was typically swivel-mounted on a pintle as secondary armament for naval use and fired a stone or iron shot. Many falcons were fitted with a metal or wooden tailpiece at the breech to provide a handle for aiming. The falconet was another related light gun suitable for mounting on a two-wheeled field carriage or for shipboard use as a swivel gun. It was typically of a 2-inch bore and fired balls weighed from 1 to 3 pounds. Minions were diminutive guns used as late as the seventeenth century, of a 3.25-inch bore and firing a

Falconet with breech removed (Courtesy Art-Tech)

4- to 4.5-pound ball. Drakes were of cast brass, saw both land and naval use, and fired a 6-pound shot, as did the dragon. The term "bastard" described a gun of any size that did not fall within a specific type.

The slow firing rate of medieval cannons eventually spurred artillery makers to experiment with producing multiple-fire guns. The ribauldequin, or ribaude, was an early form of field artillery, probably named for the lowest class of royal servant. It consisted of a four- or two-wheeled cart transporting and supporting two or more small barrels that could be fired singly or in volley. A similar design, known as an orgelgeschutze, also appeared in Germany in the mid-fifteenth century. Owing to its maneuverability and multibarrel design, the ribauldequin was an effective weapon for field use against both infantry and cavalry, and as a support weapon to protect heavier

Burgundian Falcon (Courtesy Art-Tech)

bombards. The largest ribauldequins ever made were probably three examples built in Italy incorporating approximately 20-foot-tall horse-drawn wagons supporting three squared logs with groups of as many as twelve small bombards attached on each side. This allowed the gunners, in theory, to fire 12 guns at one time, swivel the cart and beams to fire the other banks in turn, and thus provide a form of volley fire from a total of 144 guns. Unfortunately, when deployed by the Veronese against the Paduan army at the Battle of Castagno in 1389, the three Ribauldequins became mired in the mud and did not play a role in the battle.

FIELD ARTILLERY IN THE MEDIEVAL PERIOD

Highly vulnerable owing to their slow rate of fire, limited range, and lack of mobility, early cannons were best suited for siege use. Still, their potential as effective tactical field weapons was apparent to medieval commanders who gradually introduced guns into their forces in the field.

The Battle of Crécy

Although contemporary sources are contradictory, the first tactical field use of gunpowder artillery most likely occurred during the

Hundred Years' War at the 26 August 1346 Battle of Crécy. The timing of the battle, between the forces of England's Edward III and the French king Philip VI, no doubt influenced the ambiguous nature of the historical record. As a relatively new and experimental weapon, the cannon was still primitive, unreliable, and often more dangerous to its crew than to the enemy. It—as well as the crossbow—was thus overshadowed by another new yet much less technologically advanced weapon, the English longbow. There is also evidence that artillery was deemed unchivalrous by some early chroniclers, who expunged the mention of cannons at Crécy from their original manuscripts.

Still, surviving contemporary accounts suggest that the English fielded three and as many as six small cannons, quite possibly pots de fer (also called roundelades in some accounts, bombards in others) at Crécy. Although some accounts reported that they fired small iron balls, they may have also fired quarrels as well. The plausibility of Edward's use of artillery at Crécy is further reinforced by his earlier use of guns against Scotland in 1327 and later at Cambrai in 1338, Tournay in 1339, and Quesnoy in 1339–1340.

If Edward did indeed deploy artillery at Crécy, it played, at most, a very minor role and did not affect the outcome of the battle. The battle pitted the French army, numbering as many as 60,000 troops, against possibly 20,000 English troops, an advantage of approximately three to one. Edward, however, had chosen his position well, with one flank protected by a river and the other by woods and hastily dug ditches. His artillery was probably near his center, and his longbowmen were positioned to pour converging fire into attackers. Following a brief, soaking thunderstorm, Philip opened the battle by sending his Genoese mercenary crossbowmen forward. Most accounts agree that the English guns, their powder possibly dampened by the rain, probably managed no more than one volley during the opening stages of the battle.

Superior tactics and the English longbowmen, capable of loosing 10 to 12 arrows a minute, decided Crécy. Their first flight of thousands of arrows stunned the Genoese crossbowmen, who were capable, at the very best, of only 2 shots a minute. The Italians immediately broke ranks and scrambled for the rear, only to be trampled by excited French knights rushing forward to meet the English. The knights, in turn, fared no better than the crossbowmen, and the Battle of Crécy devolved into a series of futile charges by mounted French knights against peasant archers. The next day found a victorious English army occupying a field littered with the remains of the French nobility.

It is unknown whether any of the Genoese or French troops were actually injured or killed by the English cannons. The effect of the little guns was apparently more psychological in nature. The smoke and report—they "made a sound like thunder" (Norris, 16)—of the guns apparently surprised the Genoese and panicked the French knights' horses. Although Crécy marked the ascendance of the longbow over chivalry, it also foretold the coming of artillery as a battlefield weapon of the future.

The Battle of Bevershoutsveld

For nearly four decades after its appearance at Crécy, artillery continued to play only incidental roles in field actions. It was not until the Battle of Bevershoutsveld near Bruges in the spring of 1382 that cannons at last decided a battle's outcome. The origins of the battle lay in a local dispute over perceived injustices against the Flemish city of Ghent at the hands of the local count, Louis of Male (r. 1346–1384), the son-in-law of Philip the Bold of Burgundy. On 3 May, Philip van Artevelde (1340–1382), the leader of the Ghentish forces, led a small army of some 4,000 to 8,000 men against Philip's capital, the city of Bruges, and its garrison of some 20,000 to 40,000 troops.

Van Artevelde had apparently intended to besiege the city, as his train included a reported 200 carts full of artillery, some apparently carrying small antipersonnel ribauldequins. Although vastly outnumbered, van Artevelde held, in addition to his artillery, the advantage of commanding a highly motivated and well-organized force. His situation was also strengthened in that Bruges was not expecting an attack and was in the midst of celebrating a local holiday, the Procession of the Holy Blood. As one chronicler reported: "Many of the Brugeois were drinking, and drunk, and full of food" (DeVries, XIII, 297). Still, those who were not totally incapacitated attempted to sally from the city and make the roughly hour-long march to Bevershoutsveld to confront the forces of Ghent.

Van Artevelde met them with not only well-ordered battle lines but also the artillery that he had intended to use against the Bruges fortifications. As the Brugeois approached, the Ghentenaars, according to a contemporary writer, "fired more than three hundred cannons all at the same time." As the Brugeois reeled from the unexpected barrage, van Artevelde wheeled his infantry into them, causing them to discard their weapons and run "like cowards and villains" (DeVries, XIII, 299). Van Artevelde quickly pressed his advantage and, in yet another innovative demonstration of his adaptability, moved his artillery forward with his infantry. There followed the typical slaughter as the Ghentenaars pursued the fleeing Brugeois into their city. Louis, however, escaped in the confusion to meet van Artevelde again a few months later at the Battle of Rosebeke, where the Ghentish leader was killed in the fighting.

The Battle of Agincourt

In 1415, with the ultimate goal of claiming the French throne, England's young King Henry V (b. 1387; r. 1413–1422) initiated a new stage of the Hundred Years' War by invading Normandy. He immediately besieged the port city of Harfleur in Normandy on 13 August with the aid of as many as twelve large bombards under the direction of a master gunner named Giles. On 22 September, English incendiary projectiles ignited fires within the city, eventually leading to its surrender, but Henry's army was weakened by lack of food and disease. He thus attempted a withdrawal of his no more than 6,000 men to the sanctuary of the English-held city of Calais. Charles d'Albret, the Count of Dreux and Constable of France, commanded the French army in Henry's path on behalf of the incapacitated King Charles VI, also known as Charles the Mad (b. 1368; r. 1380–1422).

On 24 October, d'Albret arrayed his force near the small village of Agincourt, forcing Henry to fight the next day. The resultant Battle of Agincourt, glorified in Shakespeare's *King Henry V,* pitted the English king's tiny, half-starved force against a French army of as many as 30,000 troops. Although both the English and French reportedly fielded cannons at Agincourt, they—if present—remained in a secondary role and had little, if any, effect on the battle's outcome. Reports indicate that Henry had some seventy-five gunners in his army, yet, owing to the depleted state of his army and roads muddied by recent heavy rains, Henry must have left the majority of his guns in Harfleur. For their part the French were reported to have fielded a number of cannons and serpentines, yet their effectiveness was again compromised by recent thunderstorms. The heavy rains dampened their powder and muddied the field to such an extent that the guns were probably immobilized in the rear of the main battle lines. As at Crécy, the English longbow, not artillery, decided the battle.

Joan of Arc

Joan of Arc, the "Maid of Orléans" (1412–1431), proved adept at the use of siege artillery in the service of the dauphin, the future Charles VII (b. 1403; r. 1422–1461), during her brief career in the Hundred Years' War. Although possibly embellished in retrospect, the testimony of the Duc d'Alençon at Joan's retrial following her death extolled her military skills: "[S]he acted so wisely and clearly in waging war, as if she was a captain who had the experience of twenty or thirty years; and especially in the setting up of artillery, for in that she held herself magnificently" (DeVries , IX, 1).

Both the French and English had considerable numbers of cannons at the pivotal February 1429 siege of Orléans in which the English commander, Thomas Montagu, the Earl of Salisbury, was killed by a French cannon ball. After her victory, Joan increased her artillery train with pieces abandoned by the English at Orléans and the surrounding defensive fortresses, notably the heavily supplied Tourelles. She went on to a string of victories in the spring of 1429 in which she was particularly successful in bombarding her objectives with continuous day and night artillery fire. During the twenty-four-hour siege of Jargeau on 12 June, one of Joan's artillerists, known as Jean the Cannonier, received special mention for his deadly work with his culverin. On 18 June, Meung also fell, following an intense bombardment.

Observers noted that the French made particularly good use of the lighter bronze culverins, which, firing lead balls, were capable of penetrating plate armor. Enemy artillery, however, also played a critical role in a number of Joan's defeats. The English defenders of St. Denis at Paris and Senlis frustrated her attempts to take their cities with intense artillery fire. In April 1430, Joan faced an even greater opponent when Philip the Good of Burgundy, the most formidable artillery power of the day, entered the conflict as an English ally. Besieged at Compiègne, she faced a minimum of five siege bombards, two veuglaires, and a large number of culverins, in addition to two mechanical siege engines. Although the Burgundians eventually gave up their siege of the town, Joan was captured on 23 May, sold to the English, and eventually burned at the stake for heresy on 30 May 1431.

French Artillery under Charles VII

Although harshly criticized for allowing Joan's execution, the French king Charles VII later instituted a number of military reforms that eventually led to the expulsion of English troops from France. A key component in these reforms was the establishment of a formal artillery component in his military organization structure. In 1434 the highly talented treasurer of France and lawyer Jean Bureau (d. 1463) assumed duties as Charles's artillery and siege expert; his brother, Gaspard (d. 1469), became his master of artillery. The two brothers subsequently built the French artillery train into the most efficient in the world. The Bureau brothers played a pivotal role in suppressing the short-lived rebellion against Charles known as the Praguerie (15 February 1439 to 17 July 1440) led by certain nobles, as well as a number of critical battles including the 15 April 1450 Battle of Formigny and the 17 July 1453 Battle of Castillon.

The Battle of Formigny (15 April 1450)

The Truce of Tours, a five-year cessation of hostilities between France and England, ended in 1449, prompting Charles to launch a campaign to retake Normandy from the English invaders. The Bureau brothers led the French army's artillery train on the expedition and contributed their skills in the rapid victories at the sieges of Rouen in October 1449, Harfleur in December, and Honfleur in January 1450. The French next intercepted a newly landed English relief force at Formigny at the base of the Cherbourg Peninsula.

At Formigny, the English employed the longbow and the dismounted men at arms tactics that had served them so well at Crécy and Agincourt. The French, apparently having learned little from those battles and dozens of other similar engagements over the decades before Formigny, launched two mounted attacks against the English positions, with predictable results. Later in the afternoon, however, the Bureaus arrived on the field and deployed their artillery—probably two breechloading culverins on wheeled carriages—in a field role to counter the English longbowmen.

The ensuing stage of the battle revealed the growing ascendancy of gunpowder artillery over the vaunted longbow, as well as setting a precedent for innumerable future field artillery actions. The Bureaus' guns were apparently capable of a high rate of fire and—more important—at last outranged the English longbows and were thus capable of delivering a punishing barrage with impunity. Unfortunately for the French, however, the fire was so effective that the frustrated English archers responded by rushing and temporarily taking the insufficiently defended guns. The battle was eventually decided in favor of the French by the timely arrival of heavy cavalry reinforcements, ultimately leading to the withdrawal of the English from the region. For their part, the Bureaus' two culverins had proven a major advantage (effective long-range rapid fire) and a weakness (vulnerability if insufficiently supported by infantry) of artillery deployed in a field role.

The Battle of Castillon, 17 July 1453

The Bureau brothers continued to serve the king well, and in 1451 they were instrumental in the recapture of the Guyenne region, including its major city of Bordeaux. The local Gascon population, however, quickly proved that their loyalty lay more with English trade than to their king, and in 1452 they ejected Charles's troops from their towns. They then invited England's Henry VI (1421–1471; r. 1422–1461, 1470–1471) to send an army to ensure their independence. Henry, who intended also to ensure their loyalty to himself, responded by dispatching a force under the command of the elderly veteran John Talbot, the Earl of Shrewsbury. The decisive battle of the inevitable campaign to reclaim the region again proved the versatility of the Bureaus—now in a defensive role—in the use of artillery.

The French army, under the overall command of Jean de Blois, the Comte de Perigord and Vicomte de Limoges, began the campaign by besieging the town of Castillon, on the Dordgone River east of Bordeaux, Talbot's base of operations. Talbot responded with a forced march with his Gascon allies on the French siege positions, arriving on the morning of 17 July. That the Bureaus anticipated Talbot's advance is suggested by their positioning of their sizable artillery force not within range of Castillon's walls but in an ideal location to receive an attacking force from the south and west. Moreover, having learned from Formigny, the Bureaus screened their artillery with a protective force of archers in the woods forward of the gun emplacements.

Their foresight was rewarded on the morning of 17 July when Talbot's men surprised the archers, who, despite fleeing, alerted the main French army of the approaching English. Talbot, convinced that the retreating archers and the departure of other forces signaled an impending French rout, dismounted his cavalry and rushed forward without waiting for reinforcements. The violent meeting of the impetuous Talbot and the pragmatic Bureaus that followed resulted in a slaughter, as the waiting gunners fired their pieces almost point blank into the onrushing English and Gascons. According to a witness, as the French cannon enfiladed the attackers, "each shot knocked five or six men down, killing them all" (Hall, 117).

Fierce hand-to-hand fighting continued as the trailing components of Talbot's force reached the battlefield, but the superbly positioned and numerically superior French counterattacked and drove them back in panic. The seventy-five-year-old Talbot, his horse killed by a cannon shot, died in the final stages of the battle. In July, following their victory at Castillon, the French put Bordeaux, the last English stronghold and center of Gascon resistance, under siege with an artillery train of approximately 250 pieces. On 19 October 1453, after a ten-week bombardment under the direction of Jean Bureau, the city finally fell, effectively signaling the end of the Hundred Years' War.

Jean and Gaspard Bureau contributed greatly to France's ultimate success during the Hundred Years' War. They were instrumental in improving cannon designs, in organizing and leading the country's artillery train, and in establishing it as a permanent, professional component of the French army. Under their direction French cannons proved their value in both defensive and offensive roles, and as tactical field weapons. They also proved eminently resourceful. To ensure a continuous bombardment of English-held Cherbourg in 1450, they positioned bombards below the high-water mark on the town's seaward side. Leaving the guns to be submerged during high tide, the gunners returned when the sea had ebbed to resume fire, "to the great astonishment to the English, who had never seen anything like it" (Norris, 70–71).

The brothers' contributions were not lost on their contemporaries. In an age when military command was the almost exclusive domain of the nobility, the Bureaus were commoners. It is true that the new artillery was deemed less chivalrous than the mounted knighthood of the era (cavalry commanders would continue to be of the nobility for many years to come), yet the brothers' sheer competence elevated them to the highest echelons of their country's military establishment. The son of and successor to Charles VII, Louis XI (b. 1423; r. 1461–1483), held no love for his father and little respect for his inner court; upon assuming the throne, he promptly dismissed the majority of Charles's advisors. It is indicative of their character and value that Louis retained both of the Bureau brothers as his chief artillerists.

The Battle of Fornovo (1495)

The Bureau brothers' legacy served the French monarchy well when King Charles VIII (b. 1470; r. 1483–1498) ignited the Italian Wars by invading Italy with approximately 25,000 men in 1494. At that time, his invasion army boasted possibly the best artillery train in the world, with as many as 300 pieces of artillery including seventy siege guns. They quickly proved their effectiveness by reducing the Castle of Monte San Giovanni—a fortification that had previously withstood a seven-year siege—in just three hours. Charles's rapid series of victories in Italy, culminating in the capture of Naples in February 1495, however, alarmed other European powers. In response to the French king's apparent imperial ambitions, Milan, Venice, Spain, England, the Holy Roman Emperor Maximilian I, and Pope Alexander VI formed an alliance to force him out of the country.

Charles, hearing of League forces gathering to the north in the Piedmont, divided his army, leaving half to garrison Naples, and moved toward the Pass of Pontremoli to secure his communication and supply lines. On 6 July 1496, Charles met the alliance's forces commanded by the Mantuan condottiere general Giovanni Francesco Gonzaga at the small village of Fornovo near the Taro River. Although Gonzaga blocked Charles's retreat route with a formidable Venetian and Milanese mercenary force of 4,000 men at arms, 2,500 light cavalry, and 15,000 infantry, his artillery was inferior to that of the French. For his part Charles commanded a combined force in the modern sense, by integrating his infantry, cavalry, and artillery on the field. Having pushed his troops through the pass, he aggressively deployed his artillery in a supporting role to his infantry and cavalry, thus forcing the Italians to abandon their attempts to trap the French in northern Italy.

The Hussite Wars

The one-eyed Bohemian general and veteran of the Battle of Tannenberg, Jan Éiûka (sometimes spelled Ziska) (1370–1424), emerged as possibly the most innovative artillery tactician of the early gunpowder age. In 1419 the country erupted in a civil-religious war following the Catholic Church's condemnation for heresy and execution of the religious dissenter John Huss (1369–1418). Huss's followers, known as Hussites, reacted to his execution by launching a military campaign to secure radical religious, social, and nationalistic reforms. Lasting from 1419 to 1434, the Hussite Wars pitted the two main branches of the movement—the Ultraquists and the more radical Taborites—against the Catholic Church and Holy Roman Emperor Sigismund (b. 1368; r. 1433–1437), who claimed the Bohemian throne.

At his fortified base at Tabor, Éiûka trained his predominately peasant army into an efficient, well-disciplined force. He also developed a unique tactical system based on a two-stage defensive-offensive principle possibly derived from tactics used earlier by the Russians and Lithuanians against the Tartars, Poles, and Teutonic Knights. Éiûka based his campaigns on the Hussite war wagon, a heavy, four-wheeled, horse-drawn vehicle with high armored sides fitted with firing ports. On campaign, Éiûka led his war wagons in column into enemy territory until reaching an ideal defensive position. There he would laager them in a *wagenburg* (wagon fortress), a circular or squared temporary fortress faced by a defensive ditch. The wagons themselves were linked together with heavy chains and acted as firing platforms for his crossbowmen, handgunners, and his light bombards. Pikemen guarded the gaps between the wagons, where Éiûka positioned his heavier bombards.

In a typical battle, Éiûka began an engagement by goading his opponents into attacking the wagenburg by opening fire with his large bombards. The resulting cavalry charge by the armored knights invariably resulted in heavy casualties and retreat as they came into range of the Hussites' smaller cannons, handguns, and crossbows. Exploiting the ensuing confusion, Éiûka next ordered his cavalry and pikemen forward to cut down any survivors. Éiûka continued to wage a series of successful campaigns with his war wagon tactics until his death in 1424. Although his successor, Andrew Prokop, also known as Procopius the Great (1380–1434), continued to inflict numerous defeats on royalist forces, he was ultimately defeated and killed in the 30 May 1434 Battle of Lipany (also called Cesky Brod).

The Hussite movement collapsed after Lipany, and with it the use of war wagon tactics on any appreciable scale. Although frequently cited as such, the cannons employed in war wagon tactics were not deployed as true field artillery in the modern sense, as, once positioned in the *wagenburg*, they acted as fixed defensive pieces. Still, Éiûka's use of artillery was much more innovative than any of his contemporaries and was the deciding factor in countless battles during the Hussite Wars.

EARLY NAVAL ARTILLERY

In general, the proliferation of shipboard artillery during the late fourteenth and early fifteenth centuries mirrored that on land. The earliest ship-borne cannons were thus relatively small and, combined with the primitive gunnery of the time, incapable of inflicting significant hull damage to enemy ships. They nevertheless provided effective antipersonnel armament for repelling boarders and could damage an opponent's rigging. As cannons grew larger, some bombards were also used against fixed land targets such as fortifications or moored ships.

By the late fourteenth century cannons had become standard armament for most European and Muslim ships. As early as 1337, English records indicate that the ship *All Hallow's Cog* was fitted with "a certain iron instrument for firing quarrels and lead pellets, with powder, for the defense of the ship" (DeVries, XIV, 390). Naval artillery also played at least a minor role in a number of engagements during the fourteenth century. In the 1387 Anglo-Flemish Battle of Dunkirk, guns may have played a key factor in deciding a battle's outcome when the outnumbered Flemish fleet, led by the *Jan Buuc,* armed with three guns, forced the attacking English ships to withdraw.

By the early fifteenth century, ships were regularly being armed with rather formidable complements of artillery. A contemporary ordnance order for a fleet of forty ships at the port of La Rochelle documents the installation of four culverins and two veuglaires in each vessel. English ships, such as the *Ghost of the Tower,* were similarly armed, boasting an armament of six cannons in 1422. The use of shipboard artillery grew steadily over the century, as suggested by English records of 1497 listing the *Sovereign* with 141 cannons and 419 powder chambers and the *Regent* carrying 181 pieces with 453 chambers.

Adapting artillery to shipboard use required at first improvisation and eventually resulted in a basic redesign of both the guns and naval architecture. The guns carried by such ships as the *Ghost of the Tower* and *Sovereign* were rather small breechloaders—actually an advantage before the advent of wheeled gun carriages—and for the most part placed limited stress on the ships' structures and stability. An improvement over their land-use counterparts, these early naval guns often offered the advantages of employing interchangeable breech chambers and loading both the powder and the projectile at the breech. The heaviest guns were placed on the main deck amidships, balanced with other large guns in the stern castle. The remainder—the smaller pieces—were distributed over the rest of the ship. These guns were most probably mounted on swivels, a new invention at the time, to allow placement on the gunwales and easy

Shipboard cannon on truck carriage with implements (Courtesy Art-Tech)

loading and firing against boarders. As naval cannons grew larger, shipwrights accommodated them by strengthening ships' construction and inventing gun ports to allow the use of large guns on the lower decks.

The ability of naval artillery to breach an enemy's hull became a reality by the end of the fifteenth century, as the size of naval guns increased and gunnery improved. Venetian and Turkish ships inflicted heavy damage on each other with their cannons at the 1499 Battle of Zonchio. Reports indicate that one Venetian ship was possibly sunk by cannon fire, and three Turkish ships were lost when their magazines were ignited by enemy artillery strikes. Later, in 1501, during an exchange off Calicut, Vasco da Gama reportedly sank three Indian ships with salvoes aimed at the ships' hulls.

Late in the fourteenth century an anonymous author lamented the passing of chivalry in the face of gunpowder weapons: "Hardly a man and bravery in matters of war are of use any longer because guile, betrayal, treachery together with the gruesome artillery pieces have taken over so much that fencing, fighting, hitting and armour, weapons, physical strength or courage are not of much use any more. Because it happens often and frequently that a virile brave hero is killed by some forsaken knave with a gun" (Norris, 52).

CHAPTER THREE

The Sixteenth and Seventeenth Centuries

SIXTEENTH-CENTURY ARTILLERY

Artillery came into its own as a decisive combat arm during the sixteenth century. The period witnessed improvements in artillery organization, cannon production, ammunition, and the standardization of more basic types of weapons. Mobility was also improved somewhat with the introduction of more maneuverable types of gun carriages and more efficient artillery trains. Cannons also played a key role in this Age of Exploration, and new and more specialized types were mounted on the ships that sailed to the New World and fought for the supremacy of the seas. Politically, the rise of artillery contributed to the rise of the modern centralized national state, as only powerful rulers could afford the expense of maintaining large modern armies with their extensive artillery trains. In the process, the concepts of knighthood and chivalry gradually faded away and were replaced by a more pragmatic and technologically oriented professional military.

The publication of *Nova Scientia* in 1537 by the famous Italian mathematician Niccolo Tartaglia (1499–1557) significantly advanced the art of gunnery. In his treatise Tartaglia applied mathematical applications to artillery trajectories, addressed the principles of ballistics, and set down prototypes for firing tables. In about 1545, Tartaglia invented the gunner's quadrant, an aiming instrument to calculate trajectory resembling a carpenter's square and incorporating a plumb bob. Other treatises that continued to advance the science of the artillerist's craft followed Tartaglia's. Two of the more influential were the *Platica Manual de Artilleria* published by Luis Collado in 1592, and Diego Ufano's *Artillerie* of 1621. As if to emphasize their elevated status above common soldiers, early artillerists adopted a ritualized drill that incorporated not only military pomp but also religious overtones, with prayers to Saint Barbara, the patron saint of artillery.

As artillery sights were almost nonexistent, aiming was a time-consuming procedure. Contemporary theory held that the first shot should be purposely aimed well short of the intended target, so as to provide the crew with a visual reference point. The gunners would then "walk" their subsequent shots ever closer to the target, until they established the proper range. With heavier pieces, elevation was accomplished by placing increasingly larger blocks of wood under the breech. A slightly more sophisticated device, the quoin, was a simple wooden wedge, sometimes fitted with a handle, that was shoved under the breech as needed. Lighter guns were fitted with a somewhat more sophisticated arrangement consisting of a vertical wooden plank drilled with holes through which a peg mated with a hole in the rear of the barrel bed. Under such circumstances, the optimal rate of fire was considered to be 8 shots per hour.

Aiming was greatly improved with the invention of the elevating screw, a threaded rod passing through the carriage under the barrel's breech. Turning a handle at the top of the screw allowed gunners to elevate or depress the piece with greater ease and with more precision than the other method, and greatly increased the efficiency of both heavy and field artillery. The origins of the elevating screw are somewhat obscure, but two renowned Renaissance artists and inventors, Leonardo da Vinci (1452–1519) and his German counterpart, Albrecht Durer (1471–1528), included depictions of the device in their manuscripts and engravings.

As the manufacturing technology of the time matured, it made possible lighter, more reliable gun tubes suitable not only for siege use but also for practical mobile field and naval applications. New metallurgical techniques enabled gun founders to abandon the older haphazard method of forging barrels from iron rods and instead cast lighter, more reliable tubes of iron and bronze. This trend was further enhanced by the almost universal addition of trunnions—lateral projections located near the barrel's balancing point. Deriving from the French word *trognon*, meaning "stump," trunnions acted as an axle and facilitated easier mounting and elevation of the barrel. So successful was the trunnion that gun founders reworked many earlier guns by welding on metal rings fitted with the improvement. "Dolphins" were another innovation that greatly aided in the transportation and manipulation of gun barrels. Often cast in the shape of the aquatic mammals, these were handles fixed to the top of the tube that provided a hooking point for cranes to raise and lower it onto its carriage. As a finishing touch, many gun founders often further enhanced their creations with elaborate cast or chased decoration depicting fanciful figures or the crests of their clients.

CARRIAGES

New carriage designs also played a critical role in the ascendancy of viable field artillery. The sheer mass of such earlier guns as the bombards had made them impossible to use in fluid battle situations and had restricted their use to fortification defenses or siege work. Such behemoths required heavy, four-wheeled wagons drawn by as many as twenty horses or oxen for transport, as well as additional wagons for ammunition and the equipment to set them up for firing. Owing to the primitive road conditions, the optimal speed for their transportation was only some 2 miles an hour. The actual setting up of the gun for firing—a process requiring several hours—further complicated the situation and made the crew particularly vulnerable to enemy attack.

Although far from perfected, the early two-wheeled trail carriage and the limber solved many of these problems and were key innovations in the development of field artillery. The new carriage, probably originating in Venice during the fifteenth century, provided a much lighter and more maneuverable support for the gun tube. Known as the "stock trail carriage," it consisted of stout hardwood beams bound together with iron straps that made up the bed, or base, of the carriage, and the trail, an extension to the rear. Oak was the most favored wood for carriages, but elm and walnut also saw use; in America, some carriage builders also used hickory or even cedar. Most carriages were also painted in bright, often contrasting colors, with red, blue, and green being particularly popular. On some Spanish and French guns, two poles were hinged to each side of early trails for the attachment of the horse or oxen teams. The trail allowed the gunners to traverse the piece more easily, by simply shifting it to the left or right as the situation required. Elevation, however, was a bit more of a problem, as the barrel was rather rigidly fixed to the bed by its trunnions, thus requiring the raising or lowering of the trail.

For transport, the trail, in turn, could be fixed to the horse-drawn limber to create a four-wheeled cart for transport. The limber, introduced by the French before midcentury, was essentially a small cart in which to carry an ammunition chest; it was fitted with a pole for the attachment of the horse team, as well as a pintle to accept the cannon's trail. The limber thus enabled a gun crew to move and operate more efficiently on a battlefield than any previous arrangement.

By 1550, most powers had replaced the solid stock trail carriage with the lighter and more versatile "flask trail carriage." The flask trail carriage consisted of two wooden sidepieces—known as "flasks"—connected on the bottom by a number of wooden crosspieces known as transoms. The upper part of each flask, the "cheek," was, in turn, drilled with a hole to accept the trunnion. This arrangement was not only much lighter than the earlier solid stock carriage but, in addition, the space between the flasks permitted the vertical movement of the barrel. The introduction of the quoin, a wedge-shaped wooden block, also aided the aiming process, as it could be placed on the transom underneath the breech to adjust the elevation.

Lighter, smaller-bored field guns also helped to alleviate the problems of transporting ammunition. For the most part, fifteenth-century artillery trains had been grossly inefficient affairs conducted by notoriously unreliable civilian contractors. Porters often pushed or pulled ammunition in carts or wheelbarrows, or carried powder and lighter projectiles on their backs. Heavier bombard projectiles, weighing several hundred pounds, required a train of slow and heavy wagons. Not only were the new limbers faster to deploy on the battlefield but the lighter ammunition also allowed them to carry many more individual loadings than the earlier alternatives. Commanders soon recognized the advantages of relatively mobile guns capable of maintaining a respectable level of fire on a fluid, hard-fought battlefield.

AMMUNITION

Artillery ammunition also evolved during the period into a number of specialized types that would endure relatively unchanged into the coming centuries. As the century progressed, cast iron cannon balls began to supplant the earlier stone balls so common in the fourteenth and fifteenth centuries. Improved casting methods allowed ammunition founders consistently to produce balls that fit more precisely into guns' bores, thus increasing their efficiency. Iron balls proved much more effective than friable stone shot in penetrating masonry fortifications and smashing ships' timbers. Iron balls also proved more stable in flight and were more effective at long ranges and at flatter trajectories. They were particularly effective against massed formations of infantry, as the ball could pass through numerous ranks, inflicting heavy casualties, before losing its momentum. Gunners also found that by depressing their guns they could bounce shot through enemy ranks for even greater potential damage.

Canister, metal cans filled with metal or stone bullets or scrap, also made its appearance during the century. Functioning as a giant shotgun cartridge, canister proved particularly effective as a close-range antipersonnel loading. Somewhat similar in function to canister, grape shot consisted of typically larger balls bound together in bags; it was effective both against enemy personnel and in wrecking ships' rigging. Although often as dangerous to the gunners as to the enemy, bombs—hollow iron balls filled with gunpowder and ignited by simple fuses—were designed to explode among enemy troops and against fortifications; they were most often used in mortars. In 1573 a German by the name of Zimmerman developed a hybrid combination of the bomb and grape shot known as "hail shot," a shot-filled container also packed with an explosive charge and detonated by a simple fuse.

As their guns, ammunition, and equipment improved, so did the organization of artillery train personnel. The major European powers abandoned the use of civilian mercenary contractors as the century progressed in favor of incorporating their artillery as a regular arm of their military organizations. As a result professionalism increased, and, now subject to military discipline, artillerists became less prone to abandon their positions when directly threatened by enemy forces. Still, despite such improvements, field artillery remained vulnerable to fast-moving cavalry and infantry, as well as massed musket fire.

CLASSIFICATION OF
SIXTEENTH-CENTURY CANNONS

Although seemingly infinite variations existed, the evolving standardization of cannon types offered some rudimentary consistency in defining artillery according to its design, ammunition, use, and nationality. As a general rule the various European powers shared basic designs with inevitable regional differences, such as the Spanish tendency to field heavier guns of similar type to those of England. By about 1550, King Henry II of France had made the significant step of standardizing his guns' calibers, a move that greatly simplified ordnance manufacture and supply. Typical French artillery types of the period included the 5,200-pound, 10.5-foot-long Cannon, firing a 33-pound ball; the 11-foot-long, 4,000-pound culverin 15-pounder; and the 7-foot-long, 410-pound falconet, the smallest category, which fired a 12-ounce ball.

In 1544, Germany's King Charles V attempted to impose some standardization on his artillery by limiting standard gun types within his artillery train. These included cannons firing 40-pound balls, the 24-pounder cannon moyane, 12-pounder culverins of two varieties, two models of 6-pounder culverins, and a light 3-pounder falcon. In Holland, Prince Maurice of Nassau moved to increase the efficiency of his ordnance by ordering the standardization of his gun types to 6-pounders, 12-pounders, 24-pounders, and 48-pounders. The issue of one standard carriage type capable of accepting any of these gun tubes further simplified Dutch artillery logistics.

By the end of the century Germany had emerged as the leader in artillery design and production, and in 1592 the Spaniard Luis Collado attempted to classify guns according to the Germans' system. Collado thus identified long-range guns such as culverins and sakers as first-class guns, and fortification battering cannons as second-class pieces (technically, the only "true" cannons of the period); pedreros, mortars, and bombards used to fire heavy stone shot against ships and to defend fortifications were third-class. Collado further subdivided these primary classifications into numerous subgroupings based on size and caliber.

The amount of metal used in manufacturing cannons was a constant concern for cannon makers as they strove to maintain the lightest possible guns without sacrificing safety. A key factor was the amount of gun-metal used—bronze being more flexible than the relatively brittle cast iron and thus requiring less metal in comparatively sized pieces. The thickness or "fortification" of the bore's walls became another form of gun classification. English gun founders, for example, rated cannons on an ascending scale of fortification as "bastard," "legitimate," and "double-fortified." The fortification of a particular gun determined the amount of gunpowder used in individual charges and thus directly affected the effective range of each piece.

The second-class reinforced cannon proved one of the most effective guns of the period, with a range and destructive power to rival those of the culverin. The so-called 60-pounder was one of the most popular sizes, as it was imminently versatile, rugged, and, despite its classification, fired a potent 55-pound shot. As they often fired lighter stone balls and required less powder, third-class guns often mounted barrels of lighter weight.

Gun founders also reduced the weight of guns by incorporating a powder chamber of somewhat smaller diameter than the bore. The only significant flaw inherent to early chambered guns lay in the tendency of less experienced crewmen to mistake the outer rim of the chamber for the rear of the gun while ladling powder, thus emptying the gunpowder at the chamber's mouth. The Spanish attempted to alleviate this problem by introducing a chamber with a tapered or bell-shaped mouth known as the encampanado. The Spanish cañon encampanado was one of the finest guns of its day, as it was both light and capable of long-range, accurate fire. One of the smallest artillery pieces of the period, the robinet, was generally strapped atop a simple wooden stock and used as an antipersonnel weapon mounted on castle walls or on ships to repel boarders. A surviving example of Austrian origin is held in the collection of Fort Nelson in England and made around 1570. It is of approximately 1.5-inch bore and fired a 1-pound ball. An inscription on its barrel alludes to the small yet deadly nature of its shot: "I am forsooth an uncouth peasant—who tastes my eggs won't find them pleasant" (Norris, 122).

ENGLAND
Henry VIII

The modern term "ordnance" apparently derived from the time of the reign of England's Henry VIII (b. 1491; r. 1509–1547). Cannons in Henry's artillery train were typically referred to at the time originally as "pieces of ordinance" or "ordinance guns," to denote their casting according to regulations or official ordinance. In the course of repeated usage the term eventually evolved into the modern term "ordnance" to describe artillery.

Upon assuming the throne in 1509 at the age of eighteen, Henry inherited an artillery organization suffering from years of neglect by his father, Henry VII. Although at the time the Tower of London and other royal arsenals held respectable numbers of cannons in their inventories, many were unserviceable. The English artillery train, moreover, was also in complete disarray, and the office of Master Gunner, or chief of artillery, had lain vacant for some time. To make matters worse, Henry also discovered that only one English foundry possessed the capability to cast cannon barrels.

The ambitious young monarch lost little time in initiating an arms program to remedy the appalling situation. Henry first appointed Humphrey Walker, apparently the only competent gun founder left in England, to the office of Master Gunner. The capable Walker then assumed command of twelve subordinate master gunners to oversee cannon production and to train professional gun crews. Henry's other efforts included, in 1537, the founding of the Guild of St. George as a professional organization for his ordnance experts. Eager to pursue his Continental ambitions, Henry also supplemented his domestic production by acquiring forty-eight cannons abroad in The Netherlands from the Master Founder of Malines, Hans Poppenruyter. These included a group of approximately 45-pounder guns christened the "Twelve Apostles" and another sixteen guns of a class weighing between 3,000 and 4,000 pounds each. The latter guns required fourteen draft horses each: specially bred mares that Henry also obtained from The Netherlands.

Henry's investment justified itself in 1513, when his artillery train played a major role in the relief of the English garrison of Calais at the 16 August Battle of Guinegate. Later that month Henry's artillery, reinforced by that of his ally, Maximilian I, proved equally effective in the taking of the town of Therouanne and, in September, Tournai.

During the early sixteenth century English cannon makers were capable of making large weapons, or "great cannons," weighing from 150 pounds up to 737 pounds. Henry vigorously promoted cannon production at Buxted, south of London in Sussex. Owing to his patronage, Buxted attracted an international mix of skilled gunmakers, including Italians, a Frenchman named Baude, a German named van Cullen, as well as the Englishmen Robert and John Owen and Ralphe Hogge. Although such professional master founders commanded considerable respect as well as high salaries and even pensions, other foundry workers were not so well compensated. Women and children were also employed by the foundries and were typically paid in food and wine or cider.

The inventories of Henry's artillery holdings at the Tower of London and other locations indicate that his arsenal ultimately included numerous types of guns, including bombards weighing approximately 3 tons each and requiring twenty-four horses for transport, large culverins and sakers, and smaller falconets. A number of examples of Tudor cannons still survive, such as an 840-pound falconet cast by John Owen in 1551 and a saker cast by Henry's Italian-born founders at Salisbury Place in 1519. The falconet is 7-feet, 3-inches in length with a 2.8-inch bore and was held in storage in the local parish in Jersey. The saker is a 6-foot, 11-inch weapon.

Gun founders did not gain the necessary skill to produce cast iron cannon on a practical basis until well into the sixteenth century. Records indicate that two Frenchmen, Rafe Hoge and Peter Bawd, poured the first English cast iron guns at Buxted in 1543. Other reports list Peter Bawde (sometimes spelled Bawd) and Peter van Collen as making cast iron mortars with 11- to 19-inch bores, as well as explosive cast iron balls. Although these early cast iron guns were still much heavier than bronze guns of comparable size, they were significantly safer, more reliable, and more accurate than wrought iron pieces. The new iron-working method also lent itself to other applications, and the town of Buxted continued as one of England's largest cast iron—manufacturing centers for three centuries, its other products including such diverse items as fireplace inserts and grave markers.

A new technique, applicable to both bronze and iron guns, further advanced the founding of gun barrels. During the sixteenth century founders began pouring barrels as a solid casting, rather than using a mold with a central mandrel to create the bore. Although this technique required drilling out the bore with a hardened steel reamer, it created a more precise fit for ammunition. It also helped to prevent flaws in the casting that led to cracks or air pockets within the metal— defects that led to early metal fatigue and burst barrels. The development of small air pockets in the molten metal, creating a honeycomb effect in the finished barrels, remained a problem for gun founders and was more apt to occur in cast iron barrels. Although bronze was less susceptible to the problem, its cost was some ten times that of iron. For this reason cannon makers continued to make bronze guns well into the nineteenth century. Cast iron guns also continued to be made despite their inherent danger, for simple economic reasons.

Henry's Artillery Forts

The proliferation of gunpowder artillery inevitably forced military engineers throughout Europe to rethink castle construction. In siege after siege the fifteenth century had proved that the towering, flat-faced masonry walls of early fortifications were hopelessly vulnerable to heavy guns. These medieval structures, moreover, had been constructed without consideration for the installation of heavy defensive guns.

Architects thus began re-engineering existing fortifications by lowering and thickening their walls. Another measure—the addition of thick earthen facings to the walls' outer surfaces—also provided a cushioning layer to lessen the impact of projectile strikes. The mounting of heavy defensive cannons required the construction of reinforced embrasures both to accommodate the guns themselves and to withstand the stresses of their weight and recoil. On the Continent, sophisticated new "Italian Trace" forts built specifically for artillery appeared and incorporated low, thick walls and bastions to provide multiple angles of fire over carefully prepared approaches. In addition, multileveled artillery towers, such as at Castelnaud in France, also made their appearance at strategic locations throughout Europe. Such towers employed the most advanced engineering principles of their day and were all but impregnable to any but the most determined besieger.

The improvements in defensive works, in turn, ultimately forced tacticians to devise new siege craft methods. The most effective method to emerge incorporated the construction of angled approach trenches. These ditches provided protection from the besieged castles' guns and allowed the gradual advancement of siege guns to within their most effective range.

Henry's break with the Roman Catholic Church and subsequent excommunication by Pope Paul II in 1538 set England on a collision course with the powerful Catholic kingdoms of Europe. Almost overnight Henry found himself facing a papal-backed coalition of France and Germany, and he began preparations to fortify England's coast in anticipation of invasion.

He subsequently ordered the construction of a string of forts along England's coast from Cornwall to Dover. Unlike the Italian Trace forts common to the Continent, Henry's "blockhouse" or "bulwark" castles incorporated dry moats, interlocking defenses, low profiles, and rounded, sloped ramparts to deflect artillery projectiles. Possibly based on original designs by the famous German Renaissance figure Albrecht Durer, Henry's forts also featured numerous cannons in well-designed embrasures with specially designed vents to carry away choking, target-obscuring gun smoke. Although never tested in battle, such castles as Deal and Walmar remain as testaments to Henry's zeal in protecting his kingdom.

England's military fortunes declined somewhat during the reigns of Henry's immediate successors. Edward VI (r. 1547–1553), son of his third wife, Jane Seymour, simply died before reaching full maturity and left no real mark on the kingdom's ordnance development. For her part, Edward's successor, Mary I (r. 1553–1558), daughter of Henry's first queen, Catherine of Aragon, was more concerned with religious than military matters. Her reign saw the loss of Calais, England's last stronghold in France. It was Henry's daughter by his ill-fated second queen, Anne Boleyn, who at last put England back on the path to military prominence. The long reign of Elizabeth I (r. 1558–1603) witnessed a renewed energy in the modernization of the English military, with the abandonment of the venerable longbow and the universal adoption of gunpowder weapons. This renewed energy ultimately made possible England's defeat of the Spanish Armada, and the establishment of England as a major colonial and sea power. During Elizabeth's reign, England's artillery stabilized into a range of calibers—6-, 9-, 12-, 18-, 24-, 32-, and 42-ponders—that would serve its army and navy into the nineteenth century.

Although no direct connection has been established, a large bronze basilisk now held at Dover Castle apparently honors the Virgin Queen's military abilities. Known as "Queen Elizabeth's Pocket Pistol," it measures 24 feet in length, has a 5-inch bore, and reportedly could throw a 12-pound ball some 7 miles. The Pocket Pistol was cast by the Dutch founder Jan Tolhuys in 1544 and was presented to the queen's father by Emperor Charles V. Although of a large type more popular in Charles's Germanic states than in England, the cannon saw use by Charles I in the English Civil War. The barrel of the piece bears a Dutch inscription that translated announces:

"Breaker my name of rampart and wall,
Over hill and dale I throw my ball.
Load me well and keep me clean,
I'll carry my ball to Calais Green." (Norris, 122)

ENGLAND'S FINAL WARS WITH SCOTLAND
The Battle of Flodden, 9 September 1513

Artillery played a major role in England's final subjugation of Scotland. In 1513 the Scottish king, James IV (r. 1488–1513), attempted to exploit Henry VIII's invasion of France by, in turn, invading

England. Henry, however, had left the defense of his kingdom in the very capable hands of Thomas Howard, the Earl of Surrey, who promptly moved to thwart the invasion. On 9 September 1513, Howard confronted James, who had established a strong defensive position on a hill called Flodden Edge. At Flodden, the Scot master gunner, Robert Borthwick, commanded a well-supplied artillery train including some seventeen guns, two of which were probably heavy bombards transported from Threave Castle.

Exploiting his opponent's known lack of patience and aggressiveness, Howard initially declined to attack and instead coolly held his troops back as he opened a long-range artillery barrage on the hill. True to form, the Scots, enraged and frustrated by their mounting casualties and the ineffectiveness of their pikes against the distant guns, swarmed down the hill precisely as Howard desired. James and 10,000 of his countrymen died in the subsequent fighting.

The Battle of Pinkie, 10 September 1547

The last set battle between and English and Scottish forces was the culmination of the English invasion of Scotland with an army of some 16,000 troops under the command of Edward Seymour, the Duke of Somerset and the Lord Protector of England. On 10 September 1547 the English army met a superior 23,000-man force under the Scottish regent, Earl James Hamilton of Arran, at the River Esk on the Firth of Forth. Somerset exploited the location's proximity to the sea by coordinating his land forces with the firepower afforded by the nearby English fleet under the command of Admiral Lord Edward Clinton. Somerset, supported by Clinton's guns, thus overcame Hamilton's numerical superiority with firepower. Subjected to a punishing barrage from both land and sea, the Scots ultimately surrendered at the cost of heavy casualties, in contrast to relatively light English losses. The Battle of Pinkie was one of the earliest combined operations between land and naval artillery, and the Scots' subsequent surrender proved a decisive factor in the collapse of organized resistance to English dominance.

GERMAN ARTILLERY

King of Germany and Holy Roman Emperor Maximilian I (b. 1459; r. 1493–1519) matched the English monarchs in his zeal to establish political and military dominance. In addition to his many political maneuverings, Maximilian founded the Landsknechts, an elite, highly disciplined mercenary force and accelerated a program to build his artillery train. Maximilian's cannon production centered in Innsbruck, and he supplemented domestic production, as did Henry VIII, by buying cannons in The Netherlands from Remy de Hallut and the prolific Hans Poppenruyter.

Maximilian's artillery train included large bombards, known as hauptstucke by the Germans, as well as smaller guns such as falcons and falconets. Contemporary accounts record that on campaign Maximilian could field a train of 105 cannons of various sizes, including both iron and bronze guns.

SIXTEENTH-CENTURY WARS

One of the most momentous periods in Western history, the early years of the sixteenth century saw the Renaissance reach its highest achievements, as well as the religious upheavals sparked by the Protestant Reformation. It was also the dawn of the Age of Exploration and the modern European powers. The inevitable rivalries and disputes engendered by such change, however, also made it a century of almost continuous warfare. At the beginning of the century artillery had yet to prove itself decisively in the field—it was the feared and highly disciplined Swiss pikeman who ruled the battlefield. By the end of the century, however, as artillery improved and commanders began to appreciate its full potential, cannons became an indispensable factor in deciding victory or defeat.

The Italian Wars, 1494–1559

During the Middle Ages, Italy had devolved politically into an assortment of relatively weak, independent city-states. Its vulnerability thus made it attractive to the various imperial ambitions of its more powerful European neighbors. From 1494 to 1559 the unfortunate peninsula became a battleground as the French Valois Dynasty and the Spanish Habsburgs confronted each other in an intermittent series of conflicts known as the Italian Wars. Marked by ever-shifting alliances, the wars proved a testing ground for artillery technology and tactics.

King Charles VIII (b. 1470; r. 1483–1498) of France initiated the wars by invading the Italian peninsula in 1494 and, in 1495, easily seizing Naples. His victory, however, was short-lived, as it prompted Spain, the Holy Roman Emperor, Venice, Milan, and the pope to form an alliance against him. Despite an efficient artillery train, a legacy of the Bureau brothers, Charles was unable to counter the coalition; following the 6 July 1495 Battle of Fornova, he abandoned Italy and returned to France. In 1499, Charles's successor, Louis XII (b. 1462; r. 1498–1515), renewed French designs on Italy by reinvading the peninsula and taking Milan and Genoa. Resorting to diplomatic maneuvering with the Spanish king, Ferdinand (b. 1452; reigned as Ferdinand V of Castile and León 1474–1504, and King Ferdinand II of Aragón 1479–1516), and Pope Alexander VI (b. 1431; r. 1492–1503), he then, through the Treaty of Granada, regained partial sovereignty over Naples only to lose it again with his acceptance of the 1505 Treaty of Blois.

Three years later, however, the ambitions of Venice allowed Louis another opportunity to extend his influence into Italy. Alarmed by the Venetians' escalating expansionist actions, Pope Julius II (1443–1513) countered with the League of Cambrai, a grand alliance including not only the Holy Roman Empire and Spain but also, ironically, France. Louis's subsequent victory over the Venetians at the 14 May 1509 Battle of Agnadello set off yet another chain of events and alliances to again eject the unwanted albeit invited French out of Italy. To that end, in 1510, Pope Julius initiated the Holy League, eventually consisting of the Papal States, Venice, the Swiss cantons, Ferdinand of Spain, Henry VIII (b. 1491; r. 1502–1547) of England, and the Holy Roman Emperor Maximilian I (b. 1459; r. 1493–1519).

The unsettled circumstances of Renaissance Italy during the pontificate of Julius II led to both the creation and destruction of a major work by the great Michelangelo. According to the contemporary artist and art historian Giorgio Vasari, Julius ordered Michelangelo to interrupt his work on the Sistine Chapel to complete a sculpture of a more political nature. To that end the artist cast a monumental bronze statue of the pontiff to be placed as a testament of his authority in the rebellious city of Bologna, only recently subdued by Julius's army. Although admired for its artistry, Michelangelo's creation did not survive the recapture of Bologna by the pope's enemies. The statue was subsequently broken up and melted down, to be recast into a large cannon that the insurgents mockingly christened the "Julia."

The 11 April 1512 Battle of Ravenna pitted Louis's army, under the capable command of young Count Gaston of Foix, Duke of Nemours, against Holy League forces commanded by Pedro

Navarro. The battle, one of the earliest effectively involving not only traditional cavalry and infantry but also gunpowder small arms and field artillery, began as Navarro attempted to draw Gaston away from his siege of Ravenna. Intending to goad the French into an attack, Navarro skillfully prepared his ground by digging trenches and field fortifications south of the town for his artillery. Navarro further supported his guns with pikemen and arquebusiers, as well as heavy armored carts.

Although Navarro outnumbered Gaston in arquebusiers and crossbowmen, the French commander, having diverted some of his artillery from their siege positions, held a numerical edge in cannons, with some fifty-four guns against Navarro's approximately thirty. The battle was marked by the first recorded field artillery duel, which lasted for some two hours and resulted in heavy casualties on both sides. Navarro's selection of ground gave the Spanish troops an initial advantage, as he had chosen a protective slope that allowed his men to lie down under the French fire; his own artillery, however, could fire directly into the French center, slaughtering Gaston's infantry.

Despite Navarro's efforts, the French artillery, under the personal direction of Gaston, eventually proved a decisive factor in the battle's outcome. In a dazzling display of mobility, the French guns, maneuvered behind the Spanish positions as well as onto their flanks, poured a devastating fire into their cavalry, being held in reserve behind their main lines. The French artillery's accurate long-rang enfilade fire was so damaging that it spurred the Spanish horsemen into uncoordinated attacks by individual units against the main French line. Their rash charges were met by the main French cavalry, resulting in a vicious melee in the center of the battlefield, followed by heavy infantry fighting along the Spanish trenches. Although Gaston lost his life in the final fighting, the French heavy cavalry of armored knights at last decided the outcome of the battle in France's favor, and captured the Spanish commander.

Artillery did not decide the final outcome at Ravenna, yet its potential was obvious. Applying the lessons learned at the battle, the French continued to develop and deploy their guns in a field artillery role, recognizing that cannons could not be safely fielded without support. As a consequence, French commanders began the regular practice of fortifying their artillery positions with field works and protecting them with crossbowmen, pikemen, and cavalry. These emerging techniques proved effective, as in such battles as that at

Bicocco on 27 April 1522, when cannons proved their superiority over pikes. Although formidable at close range, the densely packed squares of Swiss pikemen proved easy targets and thus were highly vulnerable to long-range artillery fire. Although squares of pikemen remained a factor on the battlefield, the rise of artillery eventually led to their obsolescence by the end of the century.

For his part, Louis ultimately failed to maintain a presence in Italy. Another shift in alliances forced him back to France in the summer of 1512, and the following year a Swiss army routed Gaston's successor, Marshal Louis de la Trémoille, at the 6 June Battle of Novara.

The ascension of Francis I (b. 1494; r. 1515–1547) to the French throne ushered in a new phase in the wars with yet another invasion, when, in 1515, Francis allied himself with Venice. In that year his forces, including a sizable artillery train including 140 guns, clashed with a Swiss army at the 13–14 September Battle of Marignano. During the first day of the battle, however, the highly disciplined Swiss pikemen moved so quickly that they caught Francis off guard, so that he was unable to get his slow-moving artillery into action. Francis did, however, manage to prepare his artillery for the second day, and his guns inflicted numerous casualties on the exposed Swiss infantry. The Swiss, although lacking their own artillery, fought aggressively, and the issue was finally settled in Francis's favor with the arrival of the Venetian cavalry. The final outcome of Marignano found Francis in control of Lombardy and Milan and the Swiss, having suffered some 12,500 casualties, reluctant to venture on further foreign national ventures.

Many combinations of alliances and indecisive battles followed Marignano, to finally culminate in the Battle of Pavia in 1525. Although Francis fielded a considerable force of some 28,000 troops and held artillery superiority with a train of fifty-three guns to the Imperialists' seventeen, he lost his advantage because the action progressed faster than he could move his guns. In the end Francis suffered one of the most humiliating defeats in French history, with the loss of 13,000 casualties, the capture of the artillery train, and his own surrender and subsequent forced signing of the Treaty of Madrid, renouncing his Italian claims. Francis later repudiated the treaty and resumed his campaigns into Italy, campaigns that his successor, Henry II (1547–1559), continued until finally agreeing to the Treaty of Cateau-Cambrésis in 1559, ceding all Italian claims to Spain's Philip II.

Henry IV

From 1562 to 1598 political and religious conflicts plunged France into the Wars of Religion (also known as the Huguenot Wars), a series of civil wars fought between Catholic forces and those of the Protestant Huguenots. Disputes over the royal succession further inflamed the controversy, pitting the Protestant leader and heir to the throne, Henry of Navarre (b. 1553; r. 1589–1610), against the Catholic League under Charles, the Duke of Mayenne (1554–1611). A skilled politician, Navarre also proved his military prowess at the 21 September 1589 Battle of Arques, where he commanded only some 8,000 troops against Mayenne's Catholic League army of some 24,000 French Catholic and Spanish troops. Navarre won the battle by luring Mayenne into a trap composed of prepared trenches and superbly placed and handled artillery. Seeing his opportunity following the death of Henry III (b. 1551; r. 1574–1589)—the last of the Valois kings—and his victory at Arques, Navarre at last declared himself the first of the Bourbon Dynasty as King Henry IV in 1589.

At the 14 March 1590 Battle of Ivry Henry, Navarre, with 11,000 men, again faced Mayenne, who managed to field an army of some 16,000. Henry again demonstrated his skill for coordinating his cavalry, arquebusiers, and artillery, resulting in a slaughter of the Catholic horsemen and ultimate Catholic losses of some 4,000 men. As a further testament to his leadership, Henry's losses totaled only some 500. As an act of reconciliation Henry eventually returned to Catholicism, leading to a reunification of France. With the 13 April 1598 Edict of Nantes, permitting religious freedom for Protestants, Henry at last ended the Wars of Religion. A man of infinite ambition, Henry was in the process of preparing his army to confront his Spanish and Austrian Habsburg rivals when he was assassinated in 1589.

The Netherlands

Although maintaining its power in Italy, Spain had much less success in controlling its claims in The Netherlands. Led by the talented Maurice of Nassau (1567–1625), the Dutch showed considerable skill in the use of both land and naval artillery. Despite his reputation as a formidable leader and victor of Lepanto in 1571, Spain's Alexander Farnese, Duke of Parma (1545–1592), found Maurice a difficult opponent. During actions against Parma in

France during September and October 1591, Maurice moved rapidly and used his artillery to gain a series of dazzling victories, including the capture of Hulst on 14 September and Nijmegen on 21 October. Parma died in France in December 1592, and his less talented successor, Peter of Mansfeldt, proved even less a match for Maurice. Other Spanish commanders were also not up to the challenge, enabling Maurice to continue his string of victories. In addition, the Dutch gained victories at sea by building a small yet effective fleet, utilizing better weaponry and tactics against the much larger Spanish fleet. Between the years 1604 and 1607 the Dutch continued to hold the Spanish in check, and in 1607, Admiral Jacob van Heemskerk won the Battle of Gibraltar, leading to a truce between the two nations.

Still, the Continent continued to be wracked by war as kings vied for superiority, and, sparked by the Reformation, religious conflicts erupted into bitter internecine struggles. In the process field artillery evolved steadily, and engineers integrated cannons into castle designs and redesigned and strengthened fortifications to withstand bombardments. Naval architects too accommodated heavier and more types of guns to ships.

ARTILLERY OF THE AGE OF EXPLORATION

Inevitably, artillery played a key role in the exploration and conquest of the Americas. It was reportedly a bombard, fired from the *Pinta*, that alerted Columbus's flagship, the *Santa Maria*, of the sighting of land on 12 October 1492. Other Spanish explorers—such as Magellan, during his circumnavigation of the globe—included cannons in their ships' armament. Such guns were probably 5-pounder sakers: light enough to take ashore if needed yet powerful enough to inflict damage at reasonably long ranges. In addition to the lethal potential of artillery, early explorers also quickly recognized the psychological effect of their guns on aborigines who had never before seen gunpowder weapons.

As a consequence, the conquistadors regularly dragged light cannons inland in their search for gold and new territory. During his campaign in Mexico, Hernando Cortez (1485–1547) fielded at least eighteen cannons against the Aztec capital Tenochtitlan; Francisco Pizarro hauled two cannons into Peru against the Inca in 1531; and between 1540 and 1542, Francisco Vásquez de Coronado took along seven bronze guns on his expedition to find the legendary Seven Cities of Gold. On his 1597–1598 expedition into modern-day New Mexico, Don Juan de Oñate carried three heavy bronze culverins, two smaller bronze breechloaders, and a small iron breechloading esmeril.

Although the Spanish explorers seemed to consider artillery indispensable, they did encounter numerous difficulties in transporting their unwieldy pieces through the New World's trackless wildernesses and deserts. During his 1539 explorations along the Mississippi River, Hernando De Soto found his cannons useless in the wilderness and made the best of the situation by presenting a local Indian chief with his pieces. For his part, Coronado left four of his guns behind before venturing deeper into the interior, where he found his lighter guns ineffective against the Indians' cliff dwellings. His expedition was also marred by an accident that cost one of his gunners a hand when a gun detonated prematurely during loading.

Still, Spain took great pains to arm its New World outposts with cannons, and such fortifications as the Castillo de San Marcos at St. Augustine boasted formidable ordnance. Built between 1672 and 1695, the fort had its heaviest weapons mounted toward the sea, the direction of greatest threat from enemy ships. A 1683 inventory of the castillo's ordnance listed twenty-seven pieces, including one 40-pounder cannon, one 18-pounder, three 16-pounders, two 12-pounders, two 10-pounders, three 9-pounders, one 8-pounder, five 7-pounders, five 5-pounders, two 4-pounders, one 3-pounder, and one 2-pounder.

Spain also took the lead in establishing cannon manufacturing facilities in the New World. The Presidio of San Francisco, California, currently holds in its collection a number of well-made Spanish cannons produced in Lima, Peru, during the seventeenth century. Cast between 1628 and 1693 and ranging from 8- to 12-pounders, the pieces are all fitted with dolphins and bear the crests of the appropriate viceroy of Peru at the time of their casting.

Other powers' colonists also considered artillery a necessity for the defense of settlements and fortifications. The settlers of the ill-fated 1587 "Lost Colony" at Roanoke carried ashore a number of pieces including falcons and sakers, most probably attached to swivel mounts on the fort's walls. In 1607 the Jamestown colonists defended the walls of their fort with sakers, falcons, and demiculverins that, by 1609, numbered some twenty-four pieces. The Pilgrims of the Plymouth Colony removed cannons directly from the *Mayflower*'s armament and included sakers as well as minions in its artillery inventory. The nearby Massachusetts Bay Colony fairly bristled with artillery. Castle William in Boston Harbor eventually mounted eighteen 32- and 42-pounders. On 3 March 1628, Samuel Sharpe received a commission from the colony as its master gunner and was followed as the overseer of ordnance affairs by John Samford and later Major Edward Gibbon. In 1638 the colonists established the Ancient and Honorable Artillery Company of Boston to ensure the colony's defense.

Portugal also played a significant role in the global spread of gunpowder artillery. In addition to their New World expeditions, the Portuguese explored the African coastlines and made inroads throughout the Indian Ocean and as far as Japan. As gunpowder weapons were virtually unknown in sub-Saharan Africa, they proved effective as terror weapons to intimidate local inhabitants and to help establish the Portuguese as the dominant slave traders in the region.

In India, however, gunpowder technology may actually have been in use before it reached Europe from China. Artillery was the deciding factor in the 21 April 1526 Battle of Panipat between a Mughal army of 10,000 under the command of Babur and Sultan Ibrahim's army of 100,000 Delhi Mohammedans. Despite Ibrahim's vast numerical superiority and 1,000 war elephants, Babur possessed artillery—either obtained from the Europeans or influenced by Portuguese designs. These guns served to panic Ibrahim's elephants, leading to a general collapse of his force and with it the Afghan Dynasty. Babur's new Mughal Empire continued to increase cannon production in the following years, and Babur's grandson, Akbar, again used artillery to preserve Mughal sovereignty against a Hindu and Muslim force at the 5 November 1556 Second Battle of Panipat.

NAVAL ARTILLERY

The oared galley, the dominant warship of the Mediterranean since the time of the Greeks and Phoenicians, was rapidly reaching obsolescence by the beginning of the sixteenth century. Its design offered a number of advantages that had stood it well over the centuries: although equipped with sails, its banks of oars allowed it to operate without wind and provided sufficient speed to ram and sink enemy ships with a reinforced beak mounted to the prow. The advent of gunpowder artillery, however, demanded a dramatic shift in naval tactics and a totally new form of warship. Initially, galley designers attempted to accommodate the mounting of artillery but, owing to the banks of oars in the ships' sides, were limited to placing larger guns in fore and aft castles. This arrangement necessarily limited the galleys' firepower and forced naval commanders to adopt tactics that more or less mimicked those of land engagements. As a result, fifteenth-century galley engagements typically culminated in scenes that would have been familiar to the combatants of Actium or Salamis—with ships closing to within boarding distance to allow hand-to-hand fighting between shipboard infantry.

Still, contemporary sailing ship designs offered few advantages over the galley. Often known as "round ships" owing to their stubby appearance, with just over a two-to-one length to beam ratio, they lacked maneuverability and sufficient space to mount heavy ordnance. Moreover, the placement of large guns on the round ships' decks tended to make the vessels unstable and prone to capsizing, owing to their relatively high center of gravity.

An early-sixteenth-century innovation, originally intended to more easily facilitate the loading of cargo vessels, at last solved the problem of mounting heavy broadside batteries on warships. Often credited to an obscure Brest shipwright known only as Descharges, the "port" was a hinged door fitted to the sides of cargo ships to allow the direct loading of cargo from the docks into the ships' holds. The gun port was merely an adaptation of Descharges' original idea and permitted ship designers to place multiple heavy guns on ships' lower decks, closer to their center of gravity.

The appearance of the gun port coincided with a new program initiated by Henry VIII to expand and improve the English Navy, as well as Spain's development of the galleon, an innovative type of warship. Although retaining the prominent fore and aft castles of the galley, the new three-masted, square-rigged galleon presented a much sleeker profile than the round ship and was also faster and more maneuverable than its predecessors. In addition, the galleon's reliance on wind rather than muscle power for propulsion greatly increased its range. The combination of the gun port and the basic galleon design in its various forms was to revolutionize naval warfare. Henry, well known for his interest in firearms and ships, ordered the alternate placement of wrought iron and bronze guns on the gun decks of his naval vessels.

Conditions unique to naval applications also required specialized gun carriages more suited to the gun decks' confined spaces. Ideally, a naval carriage needed to be compact and sufficiently maneuverable to roll forward enough for efficient aiming, and also inboard sufficiently to absorb recoil and allow reloading and the closing of the gun port. Early shipboard gun carriages were apparently slightly modified field carriages complete with trails and large wheels. Spanish ships mounted such carriages as late as the Armada, a significant factor in the expedition's defeat.

Evidence indicates that the Armada's large guns were mounted on unwieldy two-wheeled trail carriages that, once run out, were secured so as to absorb recoil but would not allow the muzzles inboard far enough for reloading. To recharge their pieces, Spanish gun crews were thus faced with two difficult and time-consuming options. The safest method required unfastening the gun's tackle so as to haul it farther inboard, a procedure that, owing to the large size of the carriages, often led to confusion on the gun deck as multiple crews attempted to reload simultaneously. The second, and more dangerous, choice was to leave the cannon in place and send crewmembers outside the ship to service the piece. This procedure involved manipulating heavy cannon balls, powder, and loading implements while maintaining one's balance on the hot gun barrel and otherwise steadying oneself with whatever rigging was at hand—a particularly unpleasant task if under fire and in heavy seas. Either method would have greatly restricted the Spanish ships' rate of fire, and recent underwater archeology has revealed that although well supplied with ammunition, many of the Armada's guns managed only one or two shots during the entire engagement.

Fifty years before the Armada, however, English ships had already begun going to sea equipped with the truck carriage, a much more compact and efficient gun support that lent itself superbly to lower gun decks. Fitted with four small and solid wooden wheels and no trail, the truck carriage was more maneuverable than its Spanish counterpart, took up much less space, and permitted inboard reloading. It was the combination of the gun port and the truck carriage that provided the standard method of arming warships from Henry's time onward through the Age of Sail.

The ambitious young king's modernization program, however, was not without its setbacks. Henry loved both cannons and ships, and in keeping with his personality he desired the largest, most heavily armed ships possible. Unfortunately, trial and error soon proved that sheer size and weight of metal were not ideal criteria for effective (or safe) warships: 43 heavy and 141 lighter cannons accounted for more than 100 tons of the 1,000-ton displacement of Henry's pride, the *Grace à Dieu*. Considered exceptionally large for its day, the *Grace à Dieu* proved too ponderous and top-heavy for effective maneuvering. In addition, Henry's ship builders had not yet come to appreciate the most efficient placement of guns to provide maximum damage to enemy vessels.

Rather than mounted on a lower gun deck, where they would have both added to the ship's stability and been more manageable, the *Grace à Dieu's* heavy guns were distributed not only on the gun deck but in the fore and aft castles as well. Whereas such placement had proved effective with lighter guns as an antipersonnel measure in earlier designs, it robbed the *Grace à Dieu* of its ability to concentrate damage to an opponent's waterline. Another of Henry's ships, the *Mary Rose,* had better gun placement but tragically proved the necessity of maintaining closed lower gun ports in heavy seas.

Launched in 1511 and mounting seventy-eight guns, the 600-ton *Mary Rose* capsized and sank with the loss of all hands when water poured into its open gun ports in 1545. By the time of the Armada, Elizabeth's navy had greatly benefited from the experience gained by her father's ship builders and seamen. The smaller Elizabethan ships were faster, more seaworthy, and mounted their heaviest guns on truck carriages on lower gun decks equipped with gun ports.

The designs of Spanish and English galleons reflected the differences in their respective countries' naval theories. Still somewhat clinging to the earlier galley theories of viewing ships as floating fortresses, Spain continued to crew its ships with large complements of fighting men to act as boarding crews for close-in combat. To that end, Spanish ships also typically presented a low bow and ramming beak and balanced the heavy ship-to-ship ordnance of its gun deck with large numbers of lighter antipersonnel weapons mounted in the castles and on swivel mounts along the gunwales.

For their part, Henry's ship builders followed a different route, concentrating on producing more seaworthy warships built for tactics based on superior long-range gunnery. Thus they eventually eliminating the ramming beak altogether, reduced the quantity of lighter ordnance, and dramatically lowered the castles to turn out sleek and maneuverable "race-built" ship killers. In the years that followed, English sea captains honed their sailing skills in the new ships and in the process achieved a level of seamanship second to no other power. Possibly the most talented and innovative of these men, Sir Francis Drake (1540–1596), was instrumental in England's supremacy at sea in the following centuries. The defining event leading to the island nation's ascendancy occurred in the English Channel in the summer of 1588.

THE SPANISH ARMADA

The so-called Spanish Armada was the key element of the plan to invade England—then ruled by Henry's daughter, Elizabeth I (1533–1603)—by Philip II of Spain (1527–1598). Philip placed overall command of the Armada on the competent yet militarily inexperienced Duke of Medina and Sidonia, Alonzo Pérez de Guzmán (1550–1615). To somewhat offset the duke's military deficiencies, Admiral Diego de Valdéz assumed the office of second-in-command. The fleet itself consisted of twenty large galleons, forty-four armed merchant vessels, four galleasses, four galleys, and thirty-five smaller, more lightly armed support ships. In keeping with the Spanish practice of evenly balancing the numbers of heavy guns and lighter antipersonnel weapons, of the 2,431 cannons mounted by the fleet, 1,100 were larger caliber, long-range pieces.

Across the Channel, Elizabeth, following custom, chose the aristocratic Lord Howard of Effingham (1536–1624) as her commander, in lieu of the more capable Drake, who, by dint of his common birth, would have been ineligible for such lofty command. As second-in-command, however, Drake was nevertheless to play a decisive role in the channel actions. The combined English fleet consisted of some ninety-eight warships and approximately fifty auxiliary vessels. In contrast to the Armada, the English fleet had fewer secondary guns and instead mounted some 1,800 heavy cannons, primarily long-range culverins.

On 21 July 1588 the superior English gunnery promoted by Drake proved its value in the first engagement of the campaign off the coast of Plymouth. Firing at long range, English culverins inflicted heavy casualties among the Spanish crews and seriously damaged a number of ships, sinking one. A protracted action two days later off the Devon coast further crippled the Spanish fleet. Although no ships were lost on either side, the Spanish gunners expended all of their ammunition for their heavy cannons and, cut off from their supply bases, were unable to replenish their magazines. Lacking long-range firing capability, the Spaniards were thus forced to seek shelter at Calais across the Channel until forced out by English fire ships on 28 July.

Although escaping the port, the Spanish ships were later battered and scattered by a series of storms that plagued the survivors into September. The final fate of the Armada was decided more by the elements and a lack of food, water, and supplies than by English gunnery and seamanship. Of the original 130 Spanish ships, 63 never returned to Spain. The casualties included about 15 vessels that were captured or sunk by the English, 19 that were wrecked, and some 33 that were never accounted for. Ultimately, despite the decisive role of the weather, the end of the Armada marked the beginning of English ascendancy in naval power and gunnery.

The Battle of Lepanto, 1571

The 7 October 1571 Battle of Lepanto was the last great galley battle and temporarily ended Muslim dominance of the western Mediterranean. Taking place in the Gulf of Patras off the western coast of Greece, the battle pitted the Holy League—an alliance of Philip II of Spain (r. 1527–1600), Pope Pius V (r. 1566–1572), and the city of Venice—against the Ottoman Turkish Empire under Selim "the Sot" (r. 1566–1577), son of Suleiman "the Magnificent" (r. 1520–1566). Only twenty-four at the time of the battle, Philip's illegitimate half-brother, Don Juan (or Don John) of Austria (1547–1578), commanded the Christian fleet. The most effective Ottoman commander was Ali Pasha (ca. 1511–1587), an Italian who had been captured and enslaved by the Ottomans as a young man but, after converting to Islam, had received his freedom and risen to prominence in the sultan's service.

Although both fleets were relatively evenly matched numerically—the Holy League presented 206 galleys and six galleasses to the Ottomans' 208 galleys—the Christian fleet mounted a heavier weight in guns. As the galleys' oar banks precluded the use of heavy broadside batteries, the main armament of both fleets was placed in the forecastles, with additional guns on the poop decks and secondary pivot guns mounted on the gunwales. Their typical bow armament consisted of one large gun mounted on a sledge along the ship's centerline that was flanked by two smaller pieces—or, in the case of about one-half of the Holy League ships and a few larger Ottoman galleys, four flanking guns—for a total of five bow guns.

Both the Ottoman and Christian fleets mounted bronze guns of various sizes. The bow battery of Don Juan's flagship consisted of one large *cañon* (cannon), two *media-culebrinas* (demiculverins), and two *sacres* (sakers). A fighting platform above the main battery mounted more versos, small swivel-mounted antipersonnel guns that fired musket balls or scrap metal at close range. Spanish ships also employed another pintle-mounted swivel gun used to fire stone balls—the so-called falcon pedrero—as secondary armaments on their fighting platforms and around their poop decks. Both the falcon pedreros and versos were fitted with wooden or metal projections on their breech to provide a handgrip for aiming. Confident of his fleet's firepower, Don Juan ordered his captains to remove their ships' traditional rams, to give their bow gunners unobstructed fields of fire.

As the opposing fleets approached each other, both were arrayed in three wings, or battles. The Christian strategy, however, relied on six heavily armed Venetian galleasses positioned ahead of the main fleet to disrupt the Ottomans' approach. Built from converted merchant ships with 25 banks of oars on each side and averaging 152 feet long and 26 feet at the beam, the galleasses were painfully slow and lacked maneuverability. Still, they were veritable floating fortresses, mounting large forecastles with as many as nine large-bore cannons and more artillery along the gunwales and in the stern.

The two galleasses in the center of the Christian northern battle proved their worth by drawing first blood when, opening at long range, they sank a Turkish galley with their third shot, striking it in the bow below the waterline. The galleasses in center also scored long-range strikes that, although failing to sink any Turkish ships, did disrupt their attacking battle line. As the battle progressed, the Holy League gunners played a major role in what developed as a major Christian victory. Throughout the battle they continued to exhibit superior skills, holding their fire until the most advantageous moment, whereas the Turks tended to fire continually, scoring fewer and less damaging hits. Following the battle, galleys continued to see service in the Mediterranean but eventually only in an auxiliary role. Having dominated the seas for millennia, they at last gave way to the superiority of the broadside battery sailing ships.

MUSLIM ARTILLERY
Turkish Artillery

Warfare also racked Eastern Europe as the Ottoman Turkish forces of Suleiman the Magnificent (b. 1494; r. 1520–1566) renewed militant Muslim expansion. A talented general in his own right, Suleiman owed much of his success to the artillery legacy of his forebears, most notably his great-grandfather, Sultan Mehmet (or

Mehomet) II, also known as Muhammad and as Mehmet the Conqueror (b. 1432; r. 1444–1446, 1451–1481), who took Constantinople in 1453.

Suleiman continued the Ottoman practice of employing large bombards for siege operations to great effect, and he supplemented them
with smaller guns for field operations. In 1521, Suleiman captured
Belgrade, and later victories brought large areas of Eastern Europe,
Asia Minor, North Africa, and the Mediterranean under his control.
Key engagements included the siege of the Knights Hospitalers of St.
John garrison on the island of Rhodes in 1522. At Rhodes, Suleiman
subjected the defenders to a three-month bombardment resulting in
heavy casualties before allowing the surviving knights to sail for Malta,
where the order maintained itself until 1798.

Suleiman next turned his attention to Eastern Europe. In 1524,
having secured an agreement with Poland, Suleiman attacked Hungary with an army of 300,000 troops supported by 300 pieces of artillery of various sizes. At the 29 August 1524 Battle of Mohacs, the
Hungarians, whose army totaled only some 25,000 effectives and
twenty guns, made a heroic but doomed stand, losing some 15,000
casualties. After Mohacs, where he ordered the decapitation of his
Hungarian prisoners, Suleiman continued his campaign into Austria
and in 1529 laid siege to Vienna. At Vienna the sultan at last met his
match in Marshal William von Roggendorf, who directed his artillery
in highly effective counter-battery fire against the Turkish guns
eventually forcing Suleiman to raise the siege.

Following a campaign against Persia, Suleiman again turned his
attention to Hungary in 1544, to counter an army raised by Holy Roman Emperor Ferdinand (r. 1558–1564). To meet the threat the sultan again amassed an overwhelming force, including his impressive
artillery train of sixty heavy siege bombards and eighty lighter field
guns. Unable to resist the Turkish onslaught, Ferdinand found himself forced to concede most of Hungary, leaving Suleiman in firm
control of much of Eastern Europe.

Mughal Artillery

Modern artillery also played a key role in the establishment of the
Mughal Empire in northern India. Determined to establish a dynasty
in the region, Zahir-ud-din Babur (r. 1483–1530) invaded India from
Afghanistan in 1526. Although vastly outnumbered by the forces of

the local sultan, Ibrahim Lodi, Babur's army was armed with matchlock muskets as well as artillery, weapons relatively unknown to the defending forces. At the 21 April 1526 First Battle of Panipat, Babar deployed his artillery so as to fire into the massed ranks of the opposing infantry and cavalry, inflicting heavy casualties and confusion. The noise of the bombardment also aided the Mughals, as it panicked the defenders' war elephants, which, in turn, stampeded through the Indians' ranks. Babur followed his victory at Panipat the following year at the 17 March Battle of Khanwa, when he again used his artillery to break a superior force under Rana Sanga, finally breaking local resistance and ensuring his authority.

Persian Artillery

The shahs of the Safavid Dynasty initially proved ineffective in preventing the neighboring Ottomans from conquering extensive Persian territory. Having assumed the Persian throne at sixteen, Shah Abbas I (r. 1587–1629) determined to revitalize the Persian army in order to reassert his authority in the region. He subsequently enlisted two English self-styled military experts, the brothers Robert and Anthony Sherley, as his ordnance advisors. Accompanied by a number of European cannon founders, the Sherleys arrived in Persia in 1598 and soon began to reorganize the shah's army and cannon production along European lines. As a result of the Sherleys' efforts, the revitalized Persian army went on to achieve success against the Ottomans as well as the Uzbeks, Portuguese, and—ironically—the English.

THE SEVENTEENTH CENTURY

The conflicts that plagued the sixteenth century carried into the next as religious and politically motivated wars continued into the seventeenth century. Swedish artillery took the lead at the start of the century under the towering figure of King Gustavus II Adolphus (r. 1611–1632). Adolphus, often known as the father of modern field artillery, perfected the use of cannons during his many campaigns and imposed a professionalism that became the model throughout Europe. As the century progressed artillery dominance eventually passed to Germany, then France, and finally Austria.

SWEDEN
Gustavus Adolphus

Apparently no aspect of military theory, organization, or armament escaped the attention of the keen mind of Sweden's King Gustavus II Adolphus (r. 1611–1632). His revolutionary innovations transformed the Swedish army into a truly modern force and were copied throughout Europe. Earlier tactics had relied on the use of the dense "Spanish square" formation of infantry in line-abreast columns with artillery placed in fixed positions in front of the main battle lines. The cavalry, in turn, protected the vulnerable artillery and flanks.

Gustavus Adolphus abandoned the Spanish square in favor of thinner battle lines, with his artillery interspersed among the infantry at regular intervals. He also developed a much more mobile field artillery to enhance his new linear tactics that would survive well into the nineteenth century. In the process he standardized ranks and military organization by grouping his men according to company, battalion, and brigade. His most far-reaching innovation was the integration of his cavalry, infantry, and artillery, so that his combined arms could move rapidly together and provide mutual support.

Like few others, Gustavus Adolphus recognized the potential of highly mobile field artillery on the battlefield. He saw it as indispensable to protect his cavalry and infantry and to provide shock value in massed fire against a concentrated target in preparation for attack. In about 1631, his brilliant twenty-seven-year-old artillery commander Lennart Torstensson organized the Swedish artillery into six companies including four companies of gunners, one company of sappers, and one of demolition specialists.

The king and Torstensson also identified the need for standardized calibers and higher mobility as the prerequisites for effective field artillery. Gustavus Adolphus further earned his sobriquet as the "father of modern field artillery" by improving artillery carriages and ammunition, and by lightening gun tubes to improve his guns' mobility and handling. To simplify logistics he standardized the types of guns to 24-pounders, 12-pounders, and the versatile 3-pounder regimental gun. In addition to those conventional weapons Gustavus Adolphus pushed his rationale for lightweight cannons to its extreme limit with experiments culminating in the so-called leatheren, or leather cannons.

The term "leather cannon" is somewhat misleading, as its construction integrated a number of unconventional materials. The bore consisted of a wrought copper tube capped at the rear with a brass breech. The copper tube was then reinforced with four iron bands, and built up with successive layers of mastic, tightly wrapped cord, and plaster. The varnished leather from which the gun got its name acted merely as the outer protective surface of the piece.

The leather cannon unquestionably achieved Adolphus's goal of producing a lightweight and maneuverable gun—it required only a two-man crew to pull into position and operate. It was, however, too delicate for heavy charges and extended use and ultimately proved impractical. Still, as late as 1647 the government of the Massachusetts Bay Colony broached the subject of producing leather guns for the colony's defense.

Having limited Sweden's field guns to nothing greater than 12-pounders, Gustavus Adolphus and Torstensson initially assigned each regiment of infantry and cavalry one and later two 4-pounder regimental guns, thus greatly increasing their mobile firepower—yet another idea copied and made standard by other European armies. These were cast iron pieces served by small three-man crews—a 9-pounder demiculverin and a 4-pounder weighing just 500 pounds and requiring only two men or one horse for transport. The Swedes also increased their firing rates by adopting fixed ammunition in lieu of the previous loose powder and ladle method of loading. Fixed ammunition consisted of a cartridge made up of a premeasured bag of gunpowder already attached to the projectile; by eliminating the ladling procedure, it made loading more precise, safer for the crew, and much faster.

The changes initiated by Gustavus Adolphus and Lennart Torstensson served to make the Swedish army a formidable force during the 1618–1648 Thirty Years' War. The war began as a Catholic-Protestant conflict in Germany, but quickly expanded into a continental war as the Catholic Holy Roman Empire's Habsburg Dynasty, allied with the German Catholic princes, Austria, and Spain, attempted to expand its power throughout Europe. These efforts were opposed by the other European powers, including the Protestant German princes, the Catholic French Bourbons, and Protestant Denmark and Sweden.

The Battle of Breitenfeld, 17 September 1631

The Swedish king's preparations stood him in good stead at the 17 September 1631 Battle of Breitenfeld. There Gustavus Adolphus commanded a combined force of Swedes and Saxons against a

Catholic League force under Count Tilly and Count Gottfried H. zu Pappenheim. In anticipation of Adolphus's approach, Tilly and Pappenheim established defensive positions 4 miles north of Leipzig at Breitenfeld, with their infantry holding the center and flanked by cavalry. Although the Catholic League commanders first seized the initiative by attacking and forcing the Saxons to retreat, Adolphus counterattacked with his newly trained and equipped Swedes. At Breitenfeld, Adolphus deftly moved his rapidly firing artillery to provide concentrated fire into the League's tightly packed Spanish Squares with devastating effect. His artillery's superior maneuverability and tactics ultimately decided the battle as it worked closely with the infantry and cavalry to provide fire support. After recovering the guns abandoned by the Saxons, as well as the less maneuverable guns left by the Catholic League, he pushed on to take Leipzig.

Owing to the imperial commander Count Albrecht von Wallenstein's strong defensive positions incorporating scrub-covered broken ground to his front, Adolphus suffered one of his rare defeats at the 31 August–4 September 1632 Battle of Alte Veste. Despite Adolphus's talents, the gullies and undergrowth across Wallenstein's front effectively neutralized the Swedes' tactics, making it impossible for Adolphus to deploy his cavalry and artillery effectively and forcing him to withdraw. Weeks later, during the 16 November 1632 Battle of Lützen, Adolphus was killed in a cavalry melee.

THE NETHERLANDS
The Howitzer

During the 1600s, Dutch artillerists first recognized the advantages of a hybrid weapon capable of launching explosive bombs at a high trajectory like a mortar yet possessing a range and mobility making it useful on a fluid battlefield. Their response, the howitzer (from the Dutch *houwitser*, originating from an old German word for "pile of rocks"), proved one of the most successful types of all artillery pieces. As primarily a field weapon the howitzer was mounted on a two-wheeled carriage, like the standard field guns of its day. It was, however, somewhat modified and fitted with a shorter trail that allowed it a higher elevation than the typical field gun. The howitzer barrel, although larger bored, was not as long as those of other field guns but was considerably longer than that of the mortar. This resulted in a range slightly less than that of the typical field gun but much greater than that of the mortar.

Not only was the howitzer capable of throwing explosive projectiles behind an opponent's front lines or into fortifications but it was also capable of firing large-caliber standard field ammunition, including solid shot, grape, and canister. Such versatility soon gained it the admiration of artillerists throughout Europe, and within a short period most Continental powers included the howitzer in their artillery trains.

ENGLAND

Civil war distracted the British Isles from its colonial and Continental affairs for much of the century. The English Civil Wars of 1642–1648 pitted the royalist Cavaliers and Charles I (b. 1600; r. 1625–1649) against the Puritan-controlled Parliament led by Oliver Cromwell (1599–1658) and the Roundheads. In January 1645, Parliament moved to create a more efficient, professional military in the form of the New Model Army. Reforms included a 22,000-man regular army divided into twelve regiments of infantry numbering 14,000 men; 11 regiments of cavalry totaling 6,600 men; 1,000 dragoons; and a professional artillery organization integrated into the army. These changes, also including promotions based on merit and the introduction of the red coat as standard uniform for the infantry, created a truly national, professional army.

The wars, ultimately resulting in the beheading of Charles on 30 January 1649 and the establishment of the Commonwealth, saw the rise of Cromwell as a preeminent military leader. Cromwell's skillful use of siege artillery against a number of Royalist bastions scattered through England, Scotland, Ireland, and Wales proved the effectiveness of modern siege artillery against essentially medieval strategy and fortifications.

One such siege, that of the fortified town of Drogheda north of Dublin on 11 September 1649, illustrated not only the effectiveness of the Parliamentarian artillery but also the savagery engendered by religious warfare. Drogheda's commander, the one-legged Sir Arthur Aston, was convinced that his position, fortified with walls 20 feet in height and 6 feet thick at the base, was invincible. He further relied on the age-old defensive strategy of waiting a siege out until disease or lack of food and supplies forced the enemy to abandon their attack.

Cromwell's artillery proved Aston wrong on all counts. As the local population carted in food to sell to the Parliamentarians, Cromwell ordered the emplacement of eleven siege guns that within a day reduced sections of the walls to rubble. In the general slaughter that followed, Cromwell's troops rampaged through the town, giving no quarter. In the end the Royalists lost some 3,500 killed, including Sir Aston, who was beaten to death with his own wooden leg.

English Naval Developments

During this period the revolutionary ideas of Robert Blake (1599–1657) established him as the leading naval theorist of the era. Blake served as a member of Parliament and distinguished himself as a general during the English Civil War. Later, a commissioner of the navy, he was instrumental in the creation of the English Navy's *Articles of War* and the *Fighting Instruction*—the twin canons of the Royal Navy during the Age of Sail. Blake also put his theories to the test, and, following his appointment as general-at-sea by Parliament, he went on to serve as one of England's greatest combat admirals.

The key to England's lead in naval superiority lay in its commanders' understanding and exploitation of their broadside warships' potential. The introduction of the gun port and truck carriage had given England an advantage in the sixteenth century, but recoil remained a problem. Earlier methods, during the time of the Armada, had relied on cannons being tightly lashed to the gunwale or ships' side to prevent their recoiling back on deck and causing injury to men and the ship. That arrangement, however, made it extremely difficult to reload with the muzzle projecting far out of the gun port over the water. Early in the seventeenth century English designers solved the problem of recoil by attaching ropes and tackle that permitted the guns to recoil enough for reloading yet still stopped them from causing damage. By midcentury the English had also initiated the practice of the line-ahead formation (probably invented by Blake), allowing ships to advance in an orderly fashion to deliver repeated broadsides.

During the Civil War, Blake's leadership won the parliamentarians a string of victories against the Royalist Navy. In the three Anglo-Dutch Wars that followed, his skill and the English superiority in naval gunnery continued to bring success. A naval conflict over East Indies trading rights, the First Anglo-Dutch War of 1652–1654, was relatively inconclusive, yet it did see the introduction in March 1653 of Blake's *Fighting Instructions*. The *Instructions* made official policy of the use of the line-ahead formation, consisting of ships spaced at 100 yards to optimize the efficiency of broadside sailing ships. By following this protocol, English ships were able to pour a continuous fire from their heavy guns at targets, with ship-killing effect. Other than England's acquisition of New Amsterdam in the Second Anglo-Dutch War of 1665–1667, it and the Third Anglo-Dutch War of 1672–1674 were little more world changing than had been the First.

FRANCE

The assassination of his father brought the young Louis XIII (b. 1601; r. 1610–1643) to the French throne in 1610. Owing to Louis's youth and inexperience, his chief minister, Cardinal Richelieu (1585–1642), served as the virtual ruler of France and was instrumental in setting the country on the path to absolutism. Richelieu's protege and successor, Cardinal Jules Mazarin (1602–1661), continued Richelieu's role as the advisor to Louis's son Louis XIV (r. 1643–1715), who came to the throne at the age of five following his father's death.

Following the domineering Mazarin's death in 1661, the twenty-two-year-old Louis at last fully asserted his own will. As the "Sun King," he worked diligently to make France the dominant European land power and at last centralized the army's command under his own authority. Influenced to a considerable degree by Swedish artillery, in 1671, Louis brought France to the forefront of artillery development by establishing a regular artillery regiment as well as schools specifically dedicated to the artillerists' craft. During his reign the French artillery was also classified as to its projectile weight, to include 4-, 8-, 12-, 16-, 24-, 32-, and 48-pounders.

French field artillery made great advances under the influence of a Spaniard, Antonio Gonzales, who began work in France in 1679. It was his introduction of a lighter, more efficient system known as *La Nouvelle Invention* that eventually paved the way for the great advances in French artillery that culminated under Napoleon. *Nouvelle Invention* cannons differed from their predecessors in the placement of the vent above rather than to the rear of the breech and the use of a powder chamber of a greater diameter than the bore. Although lighter and requiring less powder than other cannons of the period, the new pieces were more difficult to clean and suffered from recoil so excessive that over time it wrecked their gun carriages. These problems eventually led to the system's obsolescence in 1720.

The French navy also improved, but not quite to the extent of the English. During the 1680s, Louis XIV challenged English naval superiority as his naval yards adapted and improved existing English ship designs to create faster and technologically superior French vessels. His intensive building program also led to French numerical superiority. Ironically, for all his effort, Louis failed to exploit his new advantage, leaving England to continue its dominance of the sea. In addition, his considerable military legacy was also somewhat diminished by the severe debt incurred by the expense of his wars.

CHAPTER FOUR

Eighteenth- and Early-Nineteenth-Century Artillery

EIGHTEENTH-CENTURY DEVELOPMENTS

Spurred by evolving technology, organization, and tactics, smooth-bore artillery achieved its maturity during the eighteenth century. Constantly improving metallurgy allowed for lighter and shorter gun tubes that did not sacrifice safety or accuracy. In addition, new gun carriages greatly aided the mobility of field artillery. The growing use of at least nominally interchangeable components also presented a valuable advantage in facilitating repairs, especially in the field. Except for slight national differences, typically in decoration, artillery designers went on to partially reach their elusive goal of standardization of basic gun types. The period of the late seventeenth and early eighteenth centuries at last saw the end of cannons being designated by such confusing and fanciful names as saker, minion, and basilisk. Instead, artillery, still cast in both bronze and iron, was classified more precisely according to a basic type, as to its use, bore diameter, or the weight of its projectile.

Artillery's growing complexity and sophistication attracted the attention of some of the most talented scientists, mathematicians, and engineers of the period. The English engineer and mathematician Benjamin Robins (1707–1751) published *New Principles of Gunnery* in 1742 and conducted experiments concerning the calculation of muzzle velocities. He published the findings of these tests—conducted with contemporary flintlock muskets—in London in 1747, and translations in German and French soon followed. In 1775, Robins's fellow countryman and mathematics professor at the Royal Military Academy, Charles Hutton (1737–1823), continued his explorations. In that year Hutton applied Robins's methods to experiments with a 6-pounder cannon at Woolwich. On the Continent, Bernard Forest de Belidor (1698–1761), a Spanish-born mathematician, engineer, and professor of artillery at the French military academy at La Fère, applied his talents to ballistics. His studies led to more efficient powder measurements to make possible the use of less powder while achieving the same results as earlier cartridges.

A number of influential artillerists emerged during the century to play major roles in pushing smoothbore artillery to the limits of its capabilities. Chief among these were Joseph Wenzel, Prince Lichtenstein of Austria, General John Armstrong of Britain, and General Jean Vallière of France. It was, however, Vallière's fellow countryman Jean Baptiste Gribeauval who initiated considerable changes to all aspects of artillery design, organization, and tactics. By the end of the century the combination of perfected designs, organization, and tactics had elevated artillery to a role equal to that of the already established and celebrated infantry and cavalry.

The Napoleonic wars further helped to establish artillery as an independent arm. Earlier theory, based on the regimental guns pioneered by Gustavus Adolphus, relied on relatively small numbers of light guns parceled out piecemeal to infantry units. The Napoleonic campaigns, however, proved the effectiveness of heavier massed artillery fire at decisive moments. To that end, England and France led in establishing a central artillery command capable of providing critical firepower when needed.

As ordnance and artillery theory matured, so did the appreciation that professional artillerists required specialized training, as did members of the other technical or "scientific" arm, the engineers. To that end, France and Austria led the other European powers in establishing the first artillery schools and in fully integrating their artillery arms into their overall military structures. French artillery held an advantage early in the period owing to a series of reforms under Louis XIV and the work of General Jean Vallière in the 1730s. England's artillery initially lagged somewhat behind that of the major Continental powers, as early in the century it was not fully integrated into the army structure and remained under the overall authority of the master general of ordnance. Britain did, however, achieve a major advantage in the field, as it was the only power during the period to adopt the solid block trail carriage.

It eventually became evident that the training and education of artillerists must keep pace with the growing sophistication of their weapons. Having tentatively approached the issue with an informal training program at Douai in 1679, France took the lead in artillery schooling in 1720. In that year it established Europe's first national artillery school that, in effect, also broke ground as the world's first modern professional school. The French artillery school attracted some of the most brilliant teachers of the day and stressed a rigorous program incorporating mathematics, the sciences, and practical field exercises. Other nations soon followed the French example, providing a level of professionalism among artillerists matched only by their fellow "scientific" arm, the engineers. As the century progressed, both Vallière and Gribeauval continued to stress the need for educated artillery officers and men. Vallière emphasized mathematics, technical drawing, and theory, while Gribeauval added programs requiring hands-on skills and set up schools for noncommissioned officers.

CARRIAGES

Different artillery applications required specialized carriages for efficient operation. In general, field carriages were the lightest in weight, as mobility was of primary concern. Heavier guns, as used for garrison and siege operations, required sturdy, less maneuverable mounts, and naval carriages were compact because of the confined spaces of gun decks. Most of the hardware used in their construction was of iron, with some components being of bronze. The favored materials for the main body of the carriage were hardwoods such as oak, elm, or walnut, but many other types of woods were used as circumstances indicated. Although some carriages were left unpainted, most were painted in either the colors dictated by the national establishment or by individual commanders. Whereas such powers as England adopted a sober lead gray, France, under the Gribeauval System, used blue, and Russia apple green with black iron work. Other carriages were gaudy affairs decorated with wheels, spokes, and the main carriage body painted in contrasting colors.

Gun carriage wheels were, by necessity, much more robust than their civilian counterparts and were "dished"—using curved spokes—to withstand sharp turns while bearing the weight of the cannon tube. During the eighteenth century the standard British field carriage wheel was 4 feet, 2 inches in diameter, a size that was raised to 5 feet for most pieces (the 5.5-inch howitzer retained the earlier wheel) in about 1800. Owing to its ability to resist splitting, elm was used for hubs, with oak being the favored material for the spokes. The "fellos," or outer rim sections, were of very dense ash. Unlike the typical single-piece iron tires that were heat-shrunk to fit the wheel, cannon tires were made in sections to permit field repairs. Known as "streak tyres," they consisted of six curved iron fittings that were bolted and nailed to the fellos.

Draft animals were, of course, critical to the movement of cannons and their supporting rolling stock. Although oxen were at times used during the eighteenth century, horses, owing to their greater speed, were favored for use by the field artillery. Early in the century the English long 6-pounder gun required a team of seven horses, whereas fifteen horses were necessary to transport a 12-pounder gun efficiently. Later, as gun carriages were improved and lightened, fewer horses were needed. By 1850 the 18-pounder gun required twelve horses, with eight horses allotted for the commonly used 9-pounder gun and the 24- and 32-pounder howitzers. The 6-pounder gun and 12-pounder howitzer required only six horses.

The Flask Trail Carriage

As its twin wood trails made up the most obvious structural component of its construction, the main field mounting of the period was known variously as the flask trail, split trail, or double bracket trail carriage. Although the various details improved steadily throughout the eighteenth century, this carriage remained relatively consistent in its main design features. The brackets themselves were connected by three wood transoms and were cut at the top with two half-round "trunnion holes" to accept the barrel's trunnions, which were, in turn, secured by iron "capsquares." The central transom, under the barrel's breech, supported the quoin. Iron strapping reinforced sections of the assembly prone to wear or damage.

The axletree, a square-section beam secured to the bottom of the flasks, provided the means to mount the wheels. Originally of all-wood construction, by about 1700 the axletree was usually reinforced by an iron bar or plate along its lower surface. The tapered iron axletree arms were fitted to each end of the axletree and slid into the greased bronze bearing surface within the wheel hub, known as the pipe boxes. An iron drag washer, incorporating a ring for the attachment of drag ropes, passed over the axletree arm and capped the outer hub. This assembly was, in turn, secured by a lynch pin. By midcentury ammunition boxes were often mounted above the axles between the wheels and the main carriage body to allow the crew to go into action immediately upon reaching its firing position. In British service at the time of Waterloo, these boxes contained matches and smaller equipment. Only 6-pounders carried extra ammunition in the axletree boxes—six rounds of case shot.

The Galloper Gun and Carriage

Also known as "grasshoppers" in English service, owing to their tendency to leap into the air upon recoil, galloper guns were light weapons evolved from the earlier regimental guns introduced by Gustavus Adolphus. As such, they were designed for the most rapid deployment and intended to provide close artillery support to infantry units. The most common calibers were 1.5- and occasionally 3-pounders. Rather than incorporating a conventional trail, the light galloper carriage was instead fitted with two shafts for the hitching of a single draft horse or to be pulled by two men.

The Block Trail Carriage

During the last decade of the eighteenth century, England began fielding the most advanced field carriage of the smoothbore era. Invented by Lieutenant General Sir William Congreve (1741–1814), father of the rocket designer of the same name, the solid block trail carriage revolutionized artillery transportation. Most significantly, it did away with the heavy twin flasks in favor of a single, more graceful solid wood trail. Two wood "cheeks" cut for the trunnions were then bolted to its front section to mount the cannon tube. It was thus better balanced and lighter than the split trail carriage—and so maneuverable that a single crewman, by way of a handspike inserted into two metal rings at its base, could traverse the piece easily. It also made possible a much better turning radius than earlier designs. The block trail carriage was first mated with the 6-pounder gun in the 1790s, and the 9-pounder upon its reintroduction in 1808. Still, it was not adopted by the British artillery for mounting howitzers until after the Napoleonic Wars. Eventually, however, it became the almost universally favored type of field carriage throughout the world and was in use in some areas into the twentieth century.

Congreve's original carriage mounted a number of well designed fittings to ensure its efficient service in the field. Early models were fitted with portfire cutters and axletree boxes. Nearly all had cheek attachments for handspikes and a sponge bucket hook on the axletree at the front of the carriage. Two 3-foot breast chains were also bolted to the front of the axletree, their free ends allowing for the attachment of drag ropes for manhandling over rough terrain. Another chain, the 6-foot skid, or locking chain, was secured under the center of the trail, its free end mounting a skid pan. The skid pan itself acted to brake the carriage when placed under the wheels during steep descents. Two lifting handles were also bolted at the rear of the trail for limbering and unlimbering, as well as two metal locking or rubbing plates halfway along either side of the trail. These served to protect the wood trail against damage from the limber tires during tight turns.

BASIC CANNON TYPES
The Gun

The gun's long barrel allowed its heavy powder charge to burn efficiently, giving its projectile the highest possible velocity before leaving the muzzle. This high muzzle velocity, combined with the gun's relatively light ball, also produced a relatively flat trajectory and long-range capability. For field use it was particularly effective when fired at low elevation across flat, hard ground, allowing the ball to bounce with deadly force through enemy targets. Gunners did, however, have to take particular care in their sighting, as, if the trajectory was too great and the ground soft, the ball could bury itself harmlessly in the earth.

The gun's carriage was also designed to permit limited elevation capability. If deployed on flat ground, guns could thus not fire over the heads of infantry; to provide support fire they required positioning on high ground or on the flanks. Another of the gun's drawbacks lay in the ballistic inefficiency of its round shot, which, when combined with the bore's windage, limited its effective accurate range to less than 1,300 yards. Still, that was usually sufficient for most battlefield applications, as direct fire at targets within sight was the common practice of the day.

Mortar (heavy) (Courtesy Art-Tech)

Mortars

The direct opposite of the gun, the mortar was a squat weapon cast with either one or two dolphins and the trunnions at the base rather than the sides of the barrel. Its main purpose was to throw large, usually explosive or incendiary projectiles at a high trajectory over walls, trees, hills, or friendly troops. Most early British mortars were of bronze and were fitted to wooden beds consisting of stoutly constructed wood cheeks connected by cross-pieces to absorb their heavy downward recoil. Owing to their weight and lack of wheels, mortars were transported by wagon and then placed in battery on a stable firing platform consisting of a floor of wooden planks. To compensate for the constant movement of shipboard artillery, naval mortars were mounted on revolving bases.

As the mortar's elevation was usually set at about 45 degrees, range was originally adjusted by varying the charge, which was commonly loaded with loose powder. John Müller, the master gunner of Wool-wich, however, argued for the addition of an adjustable barrel, lead-ing to England's adoption of the elevating bed incorporating a quoin by the 1740s. To avoid loss of priming powder from the vent at the mortar's steep elevation, a receptacle very much like a flintlock mus-ket's priming pan was usually incorporated at the breech below the vent. To take maximum advantage of their relatively light charges, mortars were drilled with powder chambers smaller than the bore. Early chambers were of a straight, cylindrical profile, whereas later models were fitted with so-called Gomer chambers having a tapered mouth. This innovation allowed the mortar to accept the projectile more snugly and reduce the blow-by and resultant loss of power of the ignited charge.

Much to Müller's dismay, English mortars were usually longer and heavier than those of other nations. The 13-inch piece weighed some 2,800 pounds—about twice that of its French counterpart. The largest mortars, of 13- and 10-inch caliber, were for siege and naval use and were followed in descending size by the 8-inch siege mortar, the 5.8-inch Royal Mortar, and the mobile 4.6-inch coehorn mortar. Invented by Baron Menno van Coehoorn of Holland, the coehorn was attached to a solid wooden base and was light enough to be moved about the field and served by a two-man crew. British troops also used two, apparently unofficial, diminutive mortars of 2.25- and 3.5-inch lengths to throw grenades.

Howitzers

Adopted by the British army around 1720, howitzers were a hybrid mix of the better qualities of the gun and mortar. They were thus designed to fire explosive shells at a higher trajectory than guns yet at a much greater range than mortars. Howitzers typically fired a larger ball than guns of similar size but required less powder, as they incorporated a powder chamber to concentrate the charge's explosion. Carriages were also specifically designed to allow for the higher elevation of the barrel than those of guns. Early howitzer barrels were shorter than those made after 1820 and generated a muzzle velocity of only about 500 fps, as compared with the 1150–1250 fps of the later weapons. At times the British army used various howitzers of possibly unique design. These included a very few iron 24-pounders used in the Peninsular Campaign and lightweight 12-pounder gun-howitzers carried by pack mules, apparently issued to the Mountain Batteries of the Bombay Artillery in the 1850s.

NAVAL ARTILLERY

Naval artillery among the major powers was remarkably similar in gun design, carriages, ammunition, drill, and tactics. Britain, France, Spain, and the new United States all used the truck carriage with only minor variations and, by the end of the century, had moved away from the use of bronze cannons in favor of iron weapons. Tactics for large fleet actions often involved rows of ships arrayed in a line of battle so that each ship could, in turn, fire broadsides into the opposing fleet. The most effective use of this maneuver, known as "crossing the T," required the line of battle to cross either the bows or sterns of an opponent's line and thus rake its ships lengthwise with its fire. The main goal of naval gunnery, however, was not to sink enemy ships but, if possible, to cripple them and make them vulnerable to boarding and capture. This required shooting away rigging and steering gear and inflicting heavy casualties among the enemy crews.

Shipboard gunnery also presented unique problems not encountered on land. During battle, gunners constantly had to adjust their actions to hit moving targets—all the while adjusting for their own constantly moving firing platform, which was often pitching and rolling in heavy seas. In the cramped confines of the lower gun decks, men also had to manhandle the typically 3-ton guns while loading and aiming amid the smoke, flying splinters, and confusion of battle.

Trained gunners were capable of long-range, accurate shooting, but most naval battles were fought at comparatively close ranges. A 24-pounder gun fired at a flat trajectory had a point-blank range of some 250 yards, meaning that the ball would strike the water's surface at that distance. Sometimes gunners would attempt ricochet fire by firing point blank and skipping the shot over the water's surface to hole the enemy's hull. As this tactic was rarely effective and the primary goal was not to sink but capture the enemy, it was not often used. Instead, captains usually tried to maneuver as close as possible with the enemy, where the firing rate was more important than accuracy. Owing to the restrictions of naval gunnery, one shot in three minutes was considered an acceptable firing cycle.

As with land artillery, various types of ammunition were used to achieve specific goals. The most commonly used, solid round shot, was capable of punching holes through a ship's hull at the waterline and possibly sinking it, although that was relatively rare: ships' carpenters were skilled at quickly patching such holes. Round shot was most effective in smashing the ships' wooden sides, creating storms of deadly splinters to cripple and kill enemy crews or to shoot away steering gear or masts. Other loadings, such as grape shot, canister, and bar shot, were used to destroy rigging and as antipersonnel rounds, whereas flammable "carcasses," or explosive rockets, could set a ship ablaze in short order.

British Naval Artillery

During the late eighteenth century the British navy began replacing its earlier Armstrong pattern guns with those of the Blomefield pattern. Designed by Inspector of the Artillery Thomas Blomefield, the new design was tested and approved at Woolwich in 1786 and, although never fully replacing earlier patterns, became the primary British naval gun during the Napoleonic wars. The Blomefield guns exhibited cleaner lines and were more heavily reinforced in the breech than the Armstrong models, and they had less of a muzzle swell and a thinner neck diameter. They were also easily identified by a breeching loop cast above the cascabel through which a restraining rope passed for shipboard use. Although the navy did continue to use older 42-pounder guns, the 32-pounder was the most popular heavy gun of the period.

Ships' guns were mounted on the Pattern of 1791 truck carriage, a minor refinement of the 1732 pattern, the only significant difference being the latter's cheek steps having beveled rather than straight edges. Elevation was effected with a quoin and the cheeks' steps allowed leverage points when using the handspike to raise the breech of the gun. Various eyebolts bolted to the carriage allowed the attachment of the heavy 3-inch-diameter ropes needed to secure the piece in heavy seas. The ropes, rigged with blocks and tackle, also served to control the guns' recoil, to return it to firing position, and to traverse it in action.

Such guns required crews of up to thirteen men and a powder boy to bring cartridges from the ship's magazine. As British seamen of the period were landsmen usually involuntarily pressed into service, constant drill was required to achieve efficiency. Although essentially the same as that for land artillery, naval drill was necessarily adapted to the close quarters of a gun deck and the constant threat of fire aboard a wooden ship. The flexible rammer was one such adaptation. Instead of a rigid wooden pole, the flexible rammer consisted of a wood rammer head and sponge connected by a thick length of rope. This allowed the crew to serve the gun with the bore partially protruding from the port—a dangerous and slow process if attempted with a conventional rammer.

Unlike land artillery, from about 1755 naval guns were also typically fitted with flintlock firing mechanisms similar to those used on small arms of the day. Triggered by way of a lanyard, the flintlocks helped reduce the risk of fire and speeded the firing rate. Still, as such devices were prone to malfunction, linstocks were usually kept at hand in tubs between the guns during action.

Ships' guns were numbered from bow to stern and by the side of the ship they were mounted, such as Starboard No. 1 or Port No. 12. Individual guns were commanded by a seaman petty officer designated the gun captain who supervised its loading, laying, and firing. Depending on the size of the ship, guns were grouped into divisions that were commanded by various junior officers or midshipmen. Overall command fell to the ship's gunner, who answered both to the ship's captain and to the Ordnance Board. The ship's gunner was thus responsible for all aspects of gun maintenance, magazine organization and safety, and crew training.

Although the British navy was much vaunted for its gunnery, the Admiralty did not establish official standards for gunnery practice. That responsibility thus fell to individual captains. Whereas some captains were rather lax in this aspect of their duties, others, most notably Captain Philip Vere Broke of the frigate HMS *Shannon*, gained fame for their attention to shipboard artillery. Broke's innovations included the addition of raised disport sights to his guns' muzzles. Used in conjunction with tangent rear sights, the disport sight proved more accurate than the traditional crude aiming marks chiseled into the muzzle and breech. Broke also ordered modifications to the *Shannon* to reduce the effect of the smoke that so often obscured the gunners' vision during battle. By having the ship's gun decks painted with predetermined firing angles, officers above could coordinate simultaneous broadsides by merely communicating the targets' coordinates below decks.

During the War of 1812, Broke's well-trained crew rewarded his efforts on 1 June 1813 with *Shannon*'s capture of the U.S. frigate *Chesapeake* off Boston Harbor. *Shannon*'s accurate broadsides proved decisive by inflicting heavy casualties among the Americans, damaging her batteries, and crippling the *Chesapeake*'s steering. The entire battle lasted a mere eleven minutes and resulted in 148 U.S. casualties, including the ship's commander, Captain James Lawrence, who was mortally wounded and died three days later.

Carronades

The theories concerning the emerging science of ballistics as outlined by the Englishman Benjamin Robins in his 1742 *New Principles of Gunnery* led to the invention of a new type of cannon known as the carronade. Combining compactness with a large bore, the carronade originated at the Carron Foundry in Falkirk, Scotland, between 1759 and 1762 and entered general British service in 1779. Its invention was variously credited to General Robert Melville (1728–1809) and Charles Gascoigne, the foundry manager. The weapon was thus sometimes alternately known as the "melvillade" or a "gasconade," although gunners found the name "smasher" more appropriate. Although sometimes used in fortifications, the carronade was primarily intended for naval use, and its relatively small powder charge delivered a large projectile with devastating results at close quarters.

The carronade's short, relatively thin-walled barrel was also flared to ease loading and to reduce muzzle flash. Earlier barrels were attached to the carriage by way of a single, heavy ring cast on the bottom, but as that provided a relatively unsteady aiming platform, a number of later carronades were cast with the more traditional trunnions. Many were also fitted with elevation screws rather than the more typical quoins or wedges that, in turn, were mounted to a sliding, two-wheeled carriage rather than a typical truck model. The most common sizes were 12-, 18-, 24-, and 32-pounders, with some large 68-pounders seeing service on larger ships-of-the-line. During the 21 October 1805 Battle of Trafalgar, Nelson's flagship, the HMS *Victory,* mounted two such pieces that, loaded with a combination of round shot and kegs of musket balls, cleared the gun deck of the French *Bucentaure.*

The carronade's one main limitation—it lacked range owing to its short barrel length and limited charge (about half that of the gun)—was more than compensated for by its advantages. It was light enough to be mounted on the upper deck without affecting a ship's stability, and when mounted on smaller vessels it could

Carronade (Courtesy Art-Tech)

provide a measure of firepower unobtainable with conventional guns. In addition, heavy projectiles traveling at the carronade's low muzzle velocity tended to shatter the woodwork of enemy ships, creating deadly splinters rather than punching the cleaner holes of higher velocity ammunition. During the Napoleonic Wars and afterward, many smaller ships' main armament was made up exclusively of carronades, with possibly two cannons as bowchasers for long-range work. The carronade fell out of use in the British service in about 1840.

Swivel Guns

Sometimes called pivot guns, swivel guns were small cannons mounted on a pivoting U-shaped support to allow their use on ships' fighting tops, gunwales, and the walls of land fortifications. A number were cast with a receptacle in place of a cascabel to accept a curved aiming stick known variously as a tiller or monkey tail. As short-range antipersonnel weapons they were usually loaded with multiple projectiles and, owing to their diminutive size, were easily crewed by two men. A uniquely French form of swivel gun, the espingole, was cast of brass, including its integral tiller; it was fired with a lanyard-activated flintlock mechanism. Typical sizes ranged from 14.5- and 19-inch examples of 1.125-inch bore to 31.5-inch pieces of .875-inch bore.

French Naval Artillery

French gun drill was very similar to that of other powers in the late eighteenth century. Standardized in 1767, French naval ordnance fell under the authority of the Inspecteur Général de l'artillerie Manson. Owing to differences in national weight standards, the French heavy gun of the period, the 36-pounder, was equivalent to the British 32-pounder and was mounted on the lower gun decks; 18-pounders were mounted on upper decks, with 8-pounders being placed on the forecastles and quarterdecks. Although bronze guns remained in service, by the end of the century most French naval artillery was of iron.

French naval truck carriages, with some exceptions, were also similar to British models. The trucks were of oak or elm with elm—thought to be less prone to splintering—being the preferred material for the cheeks. The carriages were also somewhat squatter than British types, and the breeching rope passed through holes in the cheeks rather than through a breeching loop cast into the gun tube's breech.

ROCKETS

Sir William Congreve's son, Congreve the Younger, inherited his father's technical talents and went on to gain even greater fame through his invention of the rockets that bore his name. Having arrived first from China centuries earlier, rockets had long been used in India before the British arrived. The younger Congreve became fascinated by examples held in the Royal Artillery Museum of captured war rockets used by the sultan of Mysore, Tippo Sahib, against British forces at Seringapatam in India during the 1790s. Impressed by the rockets' incendiary capabilities and lack of recoil upon firing,

Congreve began a series of experiments that resulted in two primary types, specifically designed for naval and land use.

Their main body was a tube constructed of multiple layers of tightly wrapped paper to which was attached a long stabilizing stick. Congreve's earliest rockets were thus, in appearance and function, nothing more than giant versions of the modern toy bottle rocket. Although acceptable incendiaries, these prototypes, however, did not have sufficient compression to provide damaging concussion, while their paper wrappings were decidedly lacking in lethality as shrapnel for military purposes. Soon after, however, Congreve replaced the rockets' paper tubes with ones of more durable and potentially deadly sheet iron.

Britain began production of Congreve's rockets in 1805, and soon after field use indicated the need for further improvements, the chief of which addressed the placement of the stabilizing stick. The average naval and land-use Congreve stick was 15 feet in length, naval sticks being of one solid piece with land-use sticks being assembled from smaller segments on site to assist in transportation. Both types were initially attached to the outside of the length of the rocket tube before launching by means of three iron ferules. This arrangement, however, made the rockets somewhat unstable in flight, and thus gained them an early reputation for inaccuracy. Congreve eventually replaced the earlier arrangement by placing a threaded stick mounting in the center of the rocket's base plate, with the exhaust vents arrayed around it to produce a much more stable and accurate weapon. Still, although Congreve's invention had an extreme maximum range of approximately 3 miles, accuracy was always unreliable, making it necessary to fire barrages of rockets for appreciable effect.

Congreve's *The Rocket System*, published in 1814, indicates that the classification of his rocket warheads (not including the stick weight) closely matched the standard conventional artillery ammunition of the day. These included 6-, 7-, and 8-inch carcasses, as well as 32- and 42-pound carcasses. In addition, there were also 9-, 12-, 18-, 24-, and 32-pounder shells and case shot rockets and a 6-pounder shell. The 32-pounder was the most widely used, being the smallest size for siege work and the largest for field deployment. Its 15-foot stick was mounted on a 3-foot cylindrical body, with carcasses being fitted with a sharply pointed conical nose and shells a more rounded nose. By 1813 two artillery troops were attached to the Royal Horse Artillery, with 6-, 9-, 12-, and 18-pounder rockets being the most common sizes for field use.

Still, the new technology was far from perfected. A firsthand account by a British artillery officer at Waterloo gives a quite candid picture of the horse artillery rocketeers in action:

> Meanwhile the rocketeers had placed a little iron triangle in the road with a rocket lying on it. The order to fire is given—port-fire applied—the fidgety missile begins to sputter out sparks and wriggle its tail for a second or so, and then darts forth straight up the chaussée. A gun stands right in its way, between the wheels of which the shell in the head of the rocket bursts, the gunners fall right and left, and, those of the other guns taking their heels, the battery is deserted in an instant. Strange; but so it was. I saw them run, and for some minutes afterwards I saw the guns standing mute and unmanned, whilst our rocketeers kept shooting off rockets, none of which ever followed the course of the first; most of them, on arriving about the middle of the ascent, took a vertical direction, whilst some actually turned back upon ourselves—and one of these, following me like a squib until its shell exploded, actually put me in more danger than all the fire of the enemy throughout the day. (Mercer, 153)

Naval Rockets

Rockets used by the Royal Navy were typically larger than those intended for field use and were launched by specially outfitted sloops of war or smaller ship's boats. Whereas these naval launchers were of wood construction and securely mounted to the vessel, land launchers, or firing frames, were of metal and designed to be disassembled for transport. The Congreve firing frame consisted of two iron or steel front legs that attached at their apex to twin metal channels enabling the frame to launch two rockets in quick succession. Earlier frames, for firing side-mounted stick rockets, utilized "half pipes" or troughs that provided less than reliable initial guidance to the rockets. After about 1815, with the introduction of the center-stick rockets, these half-pipes were replaced with full-pipes or complete tubes that acted much like a gun barrel in aiming. Elevation was accomplished by adjusting the distance between the front legs, and ignition by pulling a cord attached to a flintlock mechanism similar to that used on small arms of the period.

Congreve advocated barrages of large numbers of rapid or preferably instantaneously fired rockets to attain maximum destructive effect on targets—sound advice in that the rockets, despite improvements, remained notoriously unreliable. This doctrine was first tested in 1806, when eighteen boats launched 200 rockets in thirty minutes with limited success against Boulogne. This early trial was dwarfed the following year, when British forces launched a sustained barrage of some 40,000 incendiary rockets against Copenhagen, igniting hugely destructive fires throughout the city. British forces also used rockets against the Americans in the War of 1812, burning areas of Washington, DC. They were less successful in their 1814 bombardment of Fort McHenry in Baltimore Harbor, accomplishing little more than providing inspiration to Francis Scott Key's composition of the *Star-Spangled Banner*.

Congreve the Younger went on to become a member of Parliament from 1818 to 1828 and took over his father's previous post as comptroller of the Royal Laboratory. He also continued to formulate rocket theory and tactics and in 1827 published the richly illustrated *Treatise on the General Principles, Powers, and Facility of Application of the Congreve Rocket System*. Owing to their inherent inaccuracy, British rockets proved most successful as incendiary weapons against large targets, such as cities, although their pyrotechnic characteristics proved effective in panicking cavalry mounts and undisciplined troops. Their other main deficiency—a tendency to fail to explode—provided those on the receiving end of rocket barrages the opportunity to recover dud examples for study. As a result, soon after the introduction of their secret weapon, the British had spread the new technology throughout Europe.

European Rockets

Although Britain maintained the lead in rocket technology and use for some fifty years, other European powers developed their own programs. The devastating use of Congreves against Copenhagen prompted the Danes to develop their own rockets, an endeavor greatly aided by Second Lieutenant Andreas Schumacher, of the Danish Engineers, who recovered a nearly intact Congreve that had had failed to detonate. Schumacher, having disassembled the British weapon, went on to add improvements to its design, including designing a number of larger models. By 1811, Schumacher's efforts led to the building of a rocket manufacturing facility at Frederiksvaerk and eventually the establishment of the Danish Raketkompagniet (Rocket Company). The Danes went on to share their new technology with their French allies, and they used rockets against Hamburg during their 1813–1814 siege of that city.

Prompted by the success of the British and Danes, Austria and France began their own significant domestic rocket research and development programs. First headed by Chief Fireworks Master Anton Mager and later by the capable Major Vincent Augustin, the Austrian program began in 1808 and eventually developed into the largest on the Continent. Augustin's efforts soon led to the establishment of rocket manufacturing facilities at Wiener-Neustadt near the capital that by May 1815 were engaged in mass production. That year Austria established its own rocket corps, or Raketenbatterie, which saw action at the Siege of Huningue.

The French rocket program also began with the recovery of unexploded Congreves—in their case, examples gathered after the British attack on the Île d'Aix in 1809. The discovery soon came to the attention of Napoleon, who ordered further research to create a French rocket program. Production later began under the supervision of army captain Charles Moreton de Chabrillan and navy captain Pierre Bourrée at Vincennes. After further tests at Toulon from 1810 to 1812, production facilities were set up at Brest, Cherbourg, Lorient, and Rochefort. A combination of their high cost and the poor performance of the rockets against Calaise, however, led to the abandonment of the project in the favor of conventional artillery.

Other powers including Portugal, Russia, and Sweden also experimented with rockets but were even less successful. A Portuguese artillery noncommissioned officer, Sergeant-Major Jeronimo Nogueira de Andrade, drew up plans and proposed the adoption of an incendiary weapon in 1796, but little was done in the higher levels of the bureaucracy. Russian programs were somewhat better, in that Czar Alexander offered some encouragement, and a military study committee was established in 1810. Still, although Lieutenant Alexander Zasydko provided competent leadership in rocket development, the program languished in comparison to those of Britain and Austria.

Sweden's efforts showed initial promise yet encountered resistance from a somewhat unexpected source. While visiting Copenhagen in 1810, the Swedish chemist Jons Jakob Berzelius was struck by the damage still apparent following the British rocket attack on the city three years earlier. Seeing the potential of rockets as a weapon in his own country's arsenal, Berzelius entered into a collaboration with the Danish physicist Hans Christian Orsted. Although assisted in his efforts by Danish army officers, Berzelius's rockets were ultimately rejected by the Danish military. Master of Ordnance Colonel Paul Schroderstein briefly resuscitated the

Danish rocket program in 1813, and Captain D. W. Silferstrope tried again in 1829, but Denmark eventually joined the other Continental powers in ultimately rejecting the weapons until the twentieth century.

MOUNTAIN ARTILLERY

Also called pack artillery, mountain artillery consisted of light cannons that, along with their carriages, could be readily disassembled and carried either by men or pack animals over difficult terrain. The practice probably originated with British forces in 1772, to meet the special needs of operating in the mountains of northeastern India. This earliest use was the result of improvisation to meet an immediate need, and few details of the experiment survived. It does appear, however, that the various artillery components were carried by locally recruited peasants.

More than a quarter-century later, in 1813, a Lieutenant W. L. Robe organized the first official British Mountain Battery in the Pyrenees, during the Peninsular Campaign. Lieutenant Robe's battery fielded six brass 3-pounder guns. Three mules were required to carry each complete gun and carriage—one for the 252-pound gun tube and the others for the carriage and wheels. Although the battery was decommissioned after the campaign and Robe was later mortally wounded at Waterloo, other mountain batteries followed. In 1819 a Captain Frith of the Madras Artillery organized a Pack Battery with the local camel as his choice of draft animal. The camel Pack Battery also required three animals per complete weapon and used the 252-pound, 4.4-inch howitzer.

SMOOTHBORE AMMUNITION

By the eighteenth century the formulation of gunpowder had resulted in reasonably reliable mixtures, although varying somewhat by nationality: British powder was considered the best, French quite reliable, and, on the other end of the scale, Russian rather poor. Artillerists had a number of choices of specialized projectiles to suit the needs of various situations. Spherical projectiles were often fitted with a wood shoe, or sabot, usually of elm, at their base, to which a powder bag could be tied to create a "fixed cartridge." The sabot was especially necessary in firing fused projectiles, as it kept the fuse facing forward in the barrel.

In most circumstances, during the eighteenth century the use of premeasured powder bags or cartridges gradually replaced the use of the loose powder and ladle for the charging of artillery pieces. This transition both lessened the risk of spreading the highly flammable powder grains and speeded the loading process. The earliest powder bags were apparently of paper, but that was later replaced by flannel and then serge, materials that burned very cleanly, leaving little residue in the bore. The invention of the powder cartridge has been variously credited to the Austrians, British, and a French Lieutenant General Brocard, with the fixed cartridge consisting of a powder bag fixed to the shot possibly an invention of Gribeauval. For some reason the Royal Navy continued to use paper cartridges soaked in alum and sizing long after the British army had transitioned to flannel.

Although in rare cases of stone or lead, the most commonly used projectile, solid or round shot, was a simple cast iron sphere. Making up to 80 percent of their ammunition chests' contents, it was most useful in guns, where its optimal destructive power was best achieved at a flat trajectory. Round shot was highly effective in battering masonry fortifications and as a long-range antipersonnel loading. Numerous battle accounts record single round shots killing more than a dozen men in densely packed formations, and the destructiveness of shots skipped over hard ground into their targets. Unlike other projectiles, solid shot could be reused numerous times, and a number of battles saw troops on either side scrambling to retrieve spent balls from the field—often for such rewards as extra rum rations. Unfortunately, few infantrymen of the time understood the latent kinetic energy of the slowly rolling projectiles. A number of eager men were recorded to have lost hands or feet in their haste to stop such balls before they came to a full rest.

In 1579, Poland's King Stephen Bathory invented an incendiary projectile by having round shot heated in furnaces until red hot. Such "hot shot" required tongs for loading and a wet wad between it and the powder charge, but it was extremely effective against wooden targets. It was most useful as a coastal defense weapon, as it lodged in the impact-smashed timbers of attacking ships where it smoldered until the dry wood burst into flame. As fire was one of the greatest dangers on wooden ships, hot shot was greatly feared by ships' crews during the Age of Sail.

Another flammable loading, the carcass, consisted of a spherical projectile covered in a flammable compound often made up of niter, sulfur, antimony, and rosin and wrapped in a wicker or cloth bag. Like hot shot it was highly destructive to wooden targets; as it did not require a furnace, with its attendant fire hazards for preparation, it could be fired safely by ships' gunners as well. Another form of carcass consisted of a hollow cast iron ball filled with flammable material and with four holes to allow the ignition of the internal charge and subsequent jetting of the flaming material into the target. A variation of the carcass, the self-descriptive spike shot, consisted of a round shot coated with an incendiary mixture and mounting a sharp spike that, with luck, allowed it to stick firmly to wooden targets.

The common shell, also known as simply "shell," was primarily a long-range antipersonnel howitzer and mortar projectile made up of a fused hollow cast iron ball filled with a bursting charge of gunpowder. Gunners most commonly cut the shell's fuse, to cause it to explode over enemy troop formations, raining down shell fragments over the target. The fuses could also be cut to allow the shell to ricochet along the ground, to explode within an enemy column or to detonate within a structure. The unreliable fragmentation of common shell, however, limited its effectiveness, leading to more experiments in explosive projectiles.

Shrapnel

In about 1783 combat veteran Lieutenant Henry Shrapnel (1761–1842) of the Royal Artillery began experiments to develop a more lethal alternative to the common shell. Although originally and officially recognized as spherical case shot, his new projectile inevitably was more popularly called shrapnel, in honor of its inventor. As originally submitted to the Ordnance Board, Shrapnel's device consisted of a thin-walled hollow iron shell fitted with a fuse and filled with musket balls and a bursting charge. Experiments proved that this arrangement was much more effective than simple shell, as it delivered the musket balls to the target at a high velocity and in a lethally efficiently cone-shaped pattern that covered a greater area. A later version of shrapnel incorporated a separate internal powder chamber to avoid dangerous friction between the loose musket balls and the bursting charge. Tests undertaken in the early nineteenth century indicated that the effective range of shrapnel fell between 300 and 1,100 yards. It also presented the decided advantage of performing well as ammunition for both guns and howitzers.

Shrapnel initially met with the typical bureaucratic resistance to his invention, but his persistence eventually won the board's approval: in 1803 he received orders to oversee the production of his spherical case at the Carron Iron Works. The first combat use of shrapnel occurred on 30 April of the next year against the Dutch in Surinam, where it proved so effective that the stunned defenders surrendered almost immediately. Shrapnel also gave the British artillery a great advantage over its French counterpart, as France never developed its own version of the projectile during the Napoleonic Wars. It accordingly played a significant role in the Allied victory at the 18 June 1815 Battle of Waterloo and was later adopted by most major powers. Henry Shrapnel reaped the benefits of his efforts, being appointed senior assistant inspector of artillery in 1804 and later retired with the rank of lieutenant general.

Antipersonnel Loadings

The earliest and crudest form of antipersonnel loading, langridge (or langrage), consisted of whatever scrap metal, stones, or other potentially dangerous material was available to cram down a cannon barrel, either loosely or in a bag. Although sometimes necessary as a field-expedient alternative to formal ammunition, langridge was frequently damaging to bores and was ballistically inefficient and thus useless at any but the closest ranges. One of the more novel uses of langridge occurred during the 1857 siege of Arrah during the Indian Mutiny, when the desperate defenders loaded their cannons with the doorknobs pulled from the local buildings.

An ideal close-range antipersonnel loading, the self-descriptive canister round consisted of a cylindrical metal container filled with either lead or iron balls and sealed at either end with a wooden or metal plate. More sophisticated canister rounds were fitted with a wood sabot to which a powder bag could be attached to create fixed canister ammunition. Upon firing, the metal canister would disintegrate upon leaving the muzzle, spreading the iron balls in a cone-shaped pattern in the same manner as a shotgun. The lethality of canister was often enhanced in desperate situations by double-shotting the piece with either two canister rounds or a canister loaded on top of a solid shot. Numerous experiments took place during the eighteenth and the nineteenth centuries to find the optimal loadings for English canister rounds, resulting in 1850 in the standard loads of 9-pounder gun (41 50-ounce bullets); 6-pounder gun (41 3.25-ounce bullets); and 24-pounder howitzer (100 20-ounce bullets).

Deriving its name from its grape-like appearance, grape shot was effective both for antipersonnel use and against the rigging of enemy shipping. A typical grape shot loading of the period, known as quilted grape, consisted of a round wooden or metal base to which a central wood or metal dowel was attached. Iron balls were then placed around the dowel and held in place with burlap or canvas and twine. Another form of grape shot, known as a "stand" of grape, eventually replaced quilted grape shot by the mid-nineteenth century. A stand of grape, also known as "tier grape," consisted of two circular iron plates secured by a central bolt fastened with a large square nut. Nine iron balls in three courses of three balls were then placed between the plates, where they, in turn, were held in place by two iron rings.

Both forms of grape shot flew apart upon leaving the muzzle in a manner similar to that of canister. The wood components of quilted grape shot tended to disintegrate completely upon firing, whereas the spinning metal plates, bolt, and rings of the stand of grape's framework added to the projectile's deadliness. The sharp edges of a stand of grape shot, however, tended to damage the bores of bronze pieces, and it was therefore used most often in iron cannons. As a general trend, canister eventually replaced grape shot for field use; grape shot, owing to its effectiveness in destroying rigging, became almost exclusively a naval loading.

Naval loadings also included other types of ammunition including chain shot and crossbar shot, designed specifically to spin in flight in order to destroy enemy ships' rigging. Crossbar shot (also called simply bar shot) consisted of two iron cannon balls connected by a short iron bar. Similar in function to crossbar shot, chain shot was made up of two iron cannon balls attached by a short length of chain. The jointed crossbar shot combined the basic ideas of the crossbar and chain shots, in that it was made up of two iron balls, each incorporating a loop at the end opposite the ball to attach to its mate. Another testament to the inventiveness of early ordnance designers, the expanding crossbar shot resembled the jointed crossbar shot, but its bars were designed to slide together as a compact unit for loading. Upon firing, however, the inertia of the balls theoretically pulled the balls away from one another, to increase the damage area caused by the whirling balls. Whether effective or not in their intended role, such projectiles certainly created an unnerving noise as they flew through ships' rigging.

Artillerists also used a variety of illumination projectiles, usually fired from mortars to take advantage of their high trajectories. One of the most sophisticated consisted of two metal hemispheres containing the flammable material and a small parachute. Once fired, the outer casing fell away, allowing the parachute to deploy and enable the flare to illuminate the enemy target.

Field artillerists eventually developed a relatively standardized procedure in their use of ammunition to meet specific situations. As enemy forces approached, gunners compensated for distance and type of target by their choice of projectiles. Solid shot was the most effective choice for long-range action against hard targets such as enemy artillery pieces, as well as troops and horses. It was, moreover, also useful for close-range actions, especially in enfilade fire, and thus made up the majority of ammunition chests' contents. As the target moved closer, gun crews next moved to explosive common shell, or later, spherical case (shrapnel); once the enemy was at 300 yards or less, the choice was canister.

The process of efficiently operating a muzzleloaded cannon, especially while under fire, required a series of precise actions to avoid dangerous misfires and premature discharges. Of chief concern were the twin necessities of keeping the gunpowder dry and away from sources of accidental ignition, such as friction or static electricity. To avoid this latter hazard, ammunition chests were scrupulously checked for loose powder; powder magazine personnel typically wore cloth slippers; and many of the implements used in direct contact with powder were of wood or copper. Gun crews also perfected procedures in which each member performed specific duties in a coordinated drill, so as to maintain a high rate of fire with minimal accidents. These drills were performed with specialized instruments known variously as implements or sidearms that, although sometimes stylistically different, were remarkably consistent in basic design from country to country.

The handspike was little more than a stout hardwood pole, usually about 3 to 4 feet long. Although also quite handy as a club for bludgeoning opponents in desperate situations, the crewman charged with aiming the piece inserted the handspike into metal rings at the end of the trail for leverage in traversing the piece from left to right. In some early instances the rammer and sponge were two separate implements, but these were replaced by the spongestaff or spongerammer, a much more efficient combination of the two into one tool. The spongestaff consisted of a pole fitted on one end with a sponge made up typically of wool, with the opposite end mounting a cylindrical wood block for ramming. The spongestaff was an essential loading implement, as the sponge end was soaked in water to remove any remaining sparks from the bore, and the rammer end was used to shove the powder charge and projectile back to the breech. A large, double-pronged corkscrew-like device mounted on a pole, the worm or wad hook was used to search the barrel and remove any remnants of wadding or fouling from the bore.

The processes of priming and firing artillery also evolved during the period. The simplest priming method consisted of merely pouring loose powder into the vent. Gunners using this method carried priming powder in either cow or ox horns—priming horns—or in priming flasks made of leather or wood. Many priming flasks were fitted with spouts that automatically measured the correct amount of powder for each use. Metal tubes or goose quills filled with priming powder eventually replaced the use of loose powder for priming. This innovation eliminated the inevitable spillage of the earlier method and also protected the vent from erosion caused by direct contact with the corrosive powder. Consisting of a 3-strand hemp cord soaked in a solution containing saltpeter and wrapped with hemp thread, the slow match burned at a steady rate of about 3 feet in 8 hours, providing the gunners a steady source of fire in the field. The linstock was a wooden staff with a pointed bottom end for securing in the ground; it was used to hold the slow match. Although some linstocks were drilled with a single hole at the top to hold the match, a twin fork to hold the match ends to either side surmounted most. The forked linstock was typically secured in the ground between two guns. The portfire consisted of a rigid paper tube filled with a combustible mixture that burned at the rate of about 1 inch a minute; it was secured in a portfire holder. Immediately before action the gunner lit the portfire from the linstock in preparation to applying it to the priming in the gun's vent. At the conclusion of action the gunner then cut off the burning end of the portfire with a portfire cutter, a bladed instrument attached to the cannon's trail.

The Gun Drill

To facilitate the most efficient loading, individual artillery crewmen were assigned specific tasks requiring precisely coordinated actions to ensure speed and safety. These procedures were outlined in various manuals, which differed only slightly in detail from country to country. In a grim acknowledgement of the inherent dangers of the profession, these manuals often included procedures for short-handed crews reduced by casualties or accidents. The basic English gun crew of the period was uniformed in a blue coat with red facings and generally consisted of a noncommissioned officer commanding the piece and known as Number One. The two crewmen stationed at the rear of the piece were known as the ventsman (Number Four) and the firer (Number Five) with the spongeman (Number Two) and loader (Number Three) serving the muzzle.

After the initial discharge the ventsman "served the vent" by placing his thumb, protected by a leather "thumbstall," over it to prevent the escape of air during the sponging and loading process. This was a critical action, as the tightly fitting sponge or rammer could act as a piston and create a bellows effect within the bore. That, in turn, could ignite smoldering powder or wadding from the earlier discharge and, in extreme cases, blow off the front crewmember's hand or arm. These crewmen were understandably sticklers for the observance of this procedure, and if the ventsman failed in performing it they could claim their time-honored right to wreak vengeance on him with their spongestaff.

Once the vent was served, the spongeman dipped his spongestaff into the water bucket and sponged the bore to eliminate any lingering sparks. He then stepped aside to allow the loader to insert the powder charge into the muzzle, reversed his implement, and rammed the charge home with its rammer end. The ventsman then removed his thumb from the vent and inserted the pricker, a sharpened wire to punch a hole in the powder bag before reapplying his thumb to the vent. This allowed the loader to place the projectile into the muzzle, so that the spongeman could seat it on top of the powder charge. With the charge firmly in place, the Number One directed the aiming of the piece and ordered the ventsman to prime the vent with either loose powder or a priming quill or tube. As the piece often recoiled several feet, all crewmen then stepped clear of the wheels and trail to avoid injury. When at last ready the fire, the firer, having lit his portfire from the linstock, touched it to the vent, discharging the piece. Although the flintlock mechanism as used with small arms was available to artillerists in the late eighteenth century, it was confined primarily to naval use. Crews sometimes modified this procedure in the heat of battle to achieve a higher rate of fire by combining the loading of the powder and ball into one procedure. In truly desperate cases they also skipped the sponging procedure, preferring the risk of accidental discharge to the total loss of the gun and crew.

Aiming

Artillerists relied mainly on "direct fire"—firing at targets within their line of sight. A key factor in obtaining accurate direct fire was determining "point-blank"—that is, the point at which the projectile again intersected the axis point of the line between the muzzle and the target. Although field artillery pieces were capable of ranges of more than 2,000 yards, most actions occurred within approximately 500 yards, with 300 yards about the absolute maximum for canister. The duty of the Number One crewman, the process of aiming artillery, known as laying the piece, consisted of a series of specific procedures to ensure hitting the target. Although trained in the use of the various sighting instruments, the Number One's skill and experience were critical: much of the aiming was done by eye alone, especially in combat situations requiring rapid action. Bronze cannons further complicated the aiming process, as they tended to become more accurate and to achieve longer ranges once heated by a number of discharges. Experienced gunners thus adjusted their sights and powder charges accordingly, a fine art that often eluded novice artillerists.

The basic laying procedure consisted of three main movements. The first, known in the British army as traversing and in the navy as training the piece, was the movement of the barrel on the horizontal plane to align with the target. The raising or lowering of the barrel on the vertical plane and then adjusting the tangent elevation on the vertical to compensate for the projectile's trajectory to the target completed the laying. These adjustments were accomplished with the positioning of a quoin beneath the breech or by way of a large, threaded elevating screw attached to the carriage at the rear of the barrel.

The earliest and simplest method of laying consisted of sighting down the top of the barrel from the base ring to the muzzle, along what was known as the "line of metal." This method, however, was rather inaccurate, as the line of metal was in some variance to the actual bore, owing to the barrel's outside taper, known as the dispart. Early gunmakers attempted to eliminate this problem, especially in howitzers, by the incorporation of a raised "dispart patch" cast on the top of the muzzle. The dispart patch thus raised the top of the muzzle to the same plane as the breech and served as a rudimentary front sight. The gunner's quadrant and level and the hausse rear sight were also used for more precise sighting, but in more intense combat situations requiring rapid fire they were often eschewed in favor of the gunner's practiced eye.

Smoothbore artillerists recognized three basic aiming categories. These included what the French termed *à toute volée,* or "random fire," the most inefficient and least used method of aiming. Random fire typically employed maximum powder charges to achieve the longest possible range. As actual aiming at such distances was virtually impossible, hits on targets were indeed random and could be obtained only by sustained fire by numerous pieces. The high expenditure of ammunition for such questionable results tended to make artillery officers discourage random fire, unless absolutely necessary.

Direct fire (*á plein fouet*)—in other words, firing directly at the target—and ricochet fire were by far the most effective methods of aiming and were thus the most commonly used. Whereas direct fire achieved the greatest possible velocity against the target, ricochet combined deadliness with a psychological effect. In ricochet fire, gunners aimed their pieces to achieve a glancing first strike on the ground in front of their target that would cause solid shot to carom somewhat erratically from the line of its original flight. Ricochet fire was particularly effective against advancing infantry, in that the bouncing shot was capable of knocking down numbers of men and was moreover unnerving, as it was unpredictable in its direction.

Under ideal conditions a seasoned gun crew could sponge, load, and fire their piece in five seconds and produce a rate of fire of 8 rounds a minute—a rate that could be extended to 9 shots a minute if sponging were omitted. Predictably, combat conditions including the need for accuracy greatly lowered the rate of fire. Relaying the piece after each shot was also complicated by the weapon's recoil: a light gun typically jumped backward some 3 to 4 feet after each firing. This required the crew to "run up" the gun and relay it during the loading process, thus reducing the firing rate to about 2 rounds a minute for round shot and 3 rounds for case or shrapnel. As a close-range loading, canister required minimal aiming and could be fired faster.

Spiking was one of the more common of the various methods used to deny enemy forces the use of artillery pieces. It was most often used to disable a piece when capture was inevitable or during raids on enemy gun positions. A simple procedure, it required merely the hammering of a metal rod, spike, or nail into the cannon's vent to render it incapable of firing. The most effective spikes were of soft iron, which would bend upon hitting the bottom of the breach and thus be more difficult to extract. The British apparently invented and issued a special spike with a split end that would splay out in two directions, making it even more difficult to remove.

MANUFACTURE OF
CANNONS IN ENGLAND

The vast majority of English cannons were cast by civilian gun founders such as the Carron Company, and Low Moor Ironworks in Bradford. They were then tested and proofed by ordnance inspectors. English gun founders created their cannon molds by building a model of the finished piece consisting of a wooden core over which they layered rope covered with a paste of clay, powdered brick, and grease. Upon drying they then lathed this rough form into its final shape. They then built a multisectioned clay mold from the model that was secured with iron straps for the final pouring. The guns were then cast in a vertical position, with the muzzle up and intentionally cast longer than the gun's final length. Known as a "deadhead," this extension both compressed the metal below it during the cooling process and acted to trap the lighter impurities in the metal. It was then sawn off in preparation to boring the piece. Later pieces employed the sand-casting method using a copper inner core.

Pioneered by Swiss-born gun founder Jean Maritz (1680–1743), the horse-driven bore drilling process first appeared in 1739. Maritz, who entered the French military in 1734, passed on his ideas to his son—also named Jean—who perfected his machine. Although France attempted to maintain a monopoly on the process, by 1775, Maritz-drilled bores had become almost universal in Western Europe. The new drilled cannons offered a number of advantages over earlier guns cast around a central mandrel, as they had truer, more precise bores with fewer imperfections in their inner surfaces.

Gun founding was at times a very dangerous occupation. One of the more disastrous incidents occurred on 10 May 1716 at the Windmill Hill foundry in London. On that date an assembly of eminent personages had met at the facility to observe the recasting of a number of cannons recently captured by the Duke of Marlborough. In the rush to meet the festivities' opening, however, the workmen failed to allow sufficient drying time for the molds to cure. As a result, when the molten metal came into contact with the wet molds, the ensuing steam generated an explosion that engulfed the audience. Among many other victims, the explosion killed Windmill Hill's master founder and his son, and gravely injured Colonel Albert Borgard, the future first colonel of the Royal Artillery.

Throughout the smoothbore period Britain issued cannons made of both iron and "gun-metal," a term that described both brass, an alloy of copper and zinc, and bronze, made of copper and tin. In its typically eccentric fashion, British Ordnance tended to refer to all of these alloy guns as brass pieces, although the vast majority were actually of bronze. Both iron and bronze guns carried advantages and disadvantages that dictated which metal was best used in the construction of particular types of cannons.

Although heavier than iron, bronze is more flexible and could be cast into guns with thinner barrels, making it more desirable for use in mobile field artillery. However, as bronze is a relatively soft metal, bronze guns were prone to greater bore wear from the iron projectiles. This wear resulted in excessive windage, with a subsequent loss of accuracy that increased with repeated use. In addition, bronze guns could not tolerate overly heavy charges, and rapid firing could heat the barrels to the point of warping.

The erosion of the vent from heat and the corrosive action of the burning powder was another problem resulting from frequent firings of cannons made of both metals. Such oversized vents allowed excessive energy to escape at the breech, and also created a safety hazard to crewmen. In some cases, artillerists in the field addressed the problem with what resources were at hand. During the 1811 siege of Badajoz, Lieutenant Colonel Alexander Dickson improvised a repair of his guns by having the eroded vents filled with melted copper and then redrilled. Another, more acceptable method of refreshing vents, known as "bouching," involved drilling an oversized vent, threading the new hole, and installing a threaded corrosion-resistant vented copper plug. This component could be easily replaced in the field and proved so practical that, after about 1820, most British guns were manufactured with bouched vents.

EIGHTEENTH- AND EARLY-NINETEENTH-CENTURY ENGLISH SMOOTHBORE ARTILLERY

The successes of Gustavus Adolphus's field artillery in the seventeenth century exerted a profound effect throughout Europe. The British army responded by differentiating between its large caliber siege and coastal "heavy equipments" and its "light equipments" for field use. The light equipments were of bronze or brass and incorporated guns as heavy as 12-pounders and howitzers up to 24-pounders. As early field carriages were heavy, ponderous affairs, English field artillery of the period was typically deployed in more or less static positions as "Artillery of the Park," to provide covering fire for infantry and cavalry units.

During the latter seventeenth and throughout the eighteenth centuries, the British army began detaching two light field pieces per infantry battalion and cavalry regiment. The remaining, typically heavier, artillery stayed centralized in the Artillery of the Park. Although that arrangement occasionally provided a tactical edge on the battlefield, the army ultimately found it organizationally impractical. As a result, at the beginning of the nineteenth century, Britain abandoned the earlier system in favor of an autonomous Artillery of the Park arrangement.

English as well as most other European smoothbore cannons were made of both iron and bronze, and in England they were classified into four major types: guns, mortars, howitzers, and carronades. The small swivel gun also saw extensive use during the period as well. The trunnions of early English field pieces were typically mounted somewhat below the barrel's centerline.

Britain's progress from the jumble of various earlier artillery types to a rational organization mirrored that of other European powers. The various calibers, established during the Elizabethan period, included 6-, 9-, 12-, 18-, 24-, 32-, and 42-pounders—sizes that remained in British service through the eighteenth and into the early nineteenth centuries. The country began the century fielding a cannon design known as the "Rose and Crown" after the raised decorative motif cast into the upper face of its second reinforce. Later cannons were decorated with the raised royal cipher of the individual monarch, the name of the founder, and the date of manufacture. In use from 1650 through the end of Queen Anne's reign in 1714, most if not all Rose and Crown pieces were of iron and exhibited a long, graceful profile with the trunnions situated below the tube's centerline and a rather plain, unadorned cascabel.

Despite his country's attempts at standardization, when General John Armstrong investigated Britain's ordnance inventories in the 1730s he found six sizes of 24-pounders then in service, ranging from 8 to 10.5 feet in length. After a series of tests, Armstrong attempted to correct the situation with what has come to be known as the Armstrong System, consisting of the optimal lengths of brass (bronze) and iron guns. Still, the situation was little better in 1764; Board of Ordnance records indicated, for example, three lengths of bronze 6-pounders and seven of iron. The board's official listings of recognized cannons of that year illustrate a dizzying array of artillery pieces then in British service.

However well intentioned, Armstrong's reforms proved short-lived as other theorists stepped into the debate. Chief among them was John Müller, the master gunner of Woolwich. Author of *Treatise of Artillery* (1768) and *Elements of the Science of War* (1811), Müller exerted considerable influence over European and U.S. artillery development and theory during the latter half of the eighteenth and early nineteenth centuries. Müller's main concern was to increase the efficiency of British cannons by eliminating all unnecessary weight without sacrificing their effectiveness or compromising their crews' safety.

He subsequently reduced barrel lengths and the amount of metal used in their construction. Whereas the shortening of the cannon barrels was a rather straightforward proposal, the limiting of actual gunmetal used in the tube presented a number of more complex issues. To ensure safety, earlier guns had often been overengineered, being cast in the form of a series of "reinforces" that stepped the outside diameter of the barrel downward from breech to muzzle. Müller favored a smoother exterior profile yet did somewhat reluctantly agree to allow the addition of more or less decorative bands around the tubes, at least to suggest added strength. He also reduced the windage in British guns, making them more efficient in harnessing the explosive power of the charge and thus reducing the actual powder needed.

By midcentury British guns were relatively consistent in style, with a cleaner exterior profile; they were distinguished by a raised band around the center of the cascabel. As the century progressed minor changes occurred, including a flattening of the surface of the breech face, straight rather than tapered trunnions, and the addition of rimbases to the trunnions. On bronze guns, a connecting ring at the breech for the elevating screw was added. Although iron was much less expensive and the most common metal for artillery, Müller also advocated the use of the more flexible and hence less brittle bronze for seacoast and shipboard use. To this argument he also added bronze's advantage in that it does not rust—a considerable problem for iron guns used near salt water or sea air.

THE BRITISH LIGHT EQUIPMENTS

As the century progressed, the British leadership gradually grew to appreciate the advantage of mobile artillery in the field. During the 1701–1713 War of the Spanish Succession, John Churchill, First

Duke of Marlborough (1650–1722), proved a pioneer in the tactical use of field artillery against the forces of Louis XIV. At the 13 August 1704 Battle of Blenheim, Marlborough, after four unsuccessful attacks, detached a number of pieces from the Artillery of the Park and ordered them forward with his infantry. Their added firepower at the pivotal moment of the battle proved a decisive factor in breaking the French lines. At the 11 September 1709 Battle of Malplaquet, Marlborough again proved himself when he moved his forty-gun Grand Battery forward with his infantry. Their fire devastated the French cavalry waiting in reserve and contributed to the French withdrawal from the field. A half-century later, at the 1759 Battle of Minden during the Seven Years' War, the Royal Artillery placed a 12-pounder battery in position to enfilade the French positions and then moved it forward with the infantry to provide fire support. Experience during the Napoleonic Wars prompted the Royal Artillery to refine its field artillery equipment and tactics still further.

As the gun drill was virtually identical for all British field pieces of the period, artillery companies were assigned the appropriate ordnance to suit the needs of individual campaigns. The standard field pieces included the light 3-pounder gun, the 6-pounder, 9-pounder, and 12-pounder guns, and the 4.4-inch and 5.5-inch howitzers. Of those weapons, the 9-pounder gun seems to have fallen in and out of favor before making a comeback in 1808 during the Peninsular Campaigns. Introduced in 1719, the excellent brass 9-pounder proved itself on numerous battlefields and saw extensive service during the Seven Years' War. It was, however, not included in the official lists of ordnance in 1753 and seems to have been dropped in favor of the 6- and 12-pounder guns and the howitzers.

The situation reversed itself when, in preparing for the Peninsular Campaigns, British artillery commanders deemed the 12-pounder gun too cumbersome to negotiate Spain's rough terrain and primitive roads. As a result, the 6-pounder was the heaviest British field gun at the beginning of the campaign. Unfortunately, however, having sacrificed firepower for mobility, British crews soon found themselves outgunned by the French, who fielded both 8- and 12-pounders. Significantly more powerful than the 6-pounder and lighter than the 12-pounders, the 9-pounder thus presented a logical compromise and was soon reintroduced into the British artillery train. To compensate for the 9-pounders' weight, their horse teams were increased from the normal six horses to eight. The 9-pounders went on to render such outstanding service that Lieutenant General Arthur

Wellesley, the Duke of Wellington (1769–1852), ordered that the majority of his horse artillery and later his field batteries be issued large numbers of the guns.

Prior to the duke's decision, the British Royal Horse Artillery went through a number of ordnance types in search of the ideal combination of mobility and firepower. As originally organized in 1793, each troop fielded two light 12-pounder guns, two 6-pounder guns, and two light 5.5-inch howitzers. Having proved too heavy, the 12-pounder was dropped by the end of the decade, and from about 1800 troops were issued five 6-pounder guns and one light 5.5-inch howitzer. Wellington's reform then altered the mix to five 9-pounder guns and one 5.5-inch howitzer.

Still more experiments took place following the 18 June 1815 Battle of Waterloo. The issue was somewhat complicated over the advisability of mixing guns and howitzers in a single troop or battery. Although opponents argued that the practice unnecessarily complicated ammunition issues, its proponents' argument that it provided needed flexibility eventually prevailed. A typical British field battery of the early nineteenth century thus fielded four to five 9-pounder guns and one or two 24-pounder howitzers. Horse artillery troops used four to five 6-pounders and one or two 12-pounder howitzers.

British howitzers were made of brass and originally mounted on double bracket carriages that, being somewhat shorter than the standard gun carriage, gave them a slight advantage in maneuverability. After 1815 the British army eventually began mounting its howitzers on the more advanced block trail carriage. Owing to their extremely short barrels, the lightest of the British howitzers—the 4.4-inch howitzer and the 5.5-inch model—were the shortest ranged and least accurate of the British light field pieces. Consequently, they were eventually phased out of service: the 4.4-inch by the turn of the century and the 5.5-inch after Waterloo. Still, despite their shortcomings, both types performed creditable service. The 5.5-inch howitzer's case shot's fifty-five bullets were one shot over double that of the 6-pounder gun, and the light weight of the 4.4-inch made it suitable for use as a mountain artillery piece, a service it performed until 1865.

Firing a 16-pound shell filled with 100 bullets, the heavy 5.5-inch howitzer was a much more effective weapon than its lighter cousin. At Waterloo, Bull's Troop of the Royal Horse Artillery spectacularly demonstrated not only the heavy howitzer's deadliness but also its potential accuracy. There, with British and French troops closely engaged in the thick woods of Hougoumont, Major Bull's gunners deftly lobbed their shells over the red-coated infantry's heads to clear the far woods of the French opponents.

BRITISH HORSE ARTILLERY AT WATERLOO

Although originally intended upon its inception in 1793 to move with cavalry units on the field, the British Royal Horse Artillery was used at Waterloo essentially as conventional field artillery. The eight troops participating in the battle thus fought from relatively fixed positions. These included A Troop, commanded by Lieutenant Colonel Sir Hew Dalrymple Ross; D Troop, under Major George Beane; E Troop, under Lieutenant Colonel Sir Robert Gardiner; F Troop, under Lieutenant Colonel James Webber Smith; Captain Alexander Cavalié Mercer's G Troop; Major William Norman Ramsay's H Troop; and I Troop, under Major Robert Bull. Despite Wellington's distrust of their new weapons, Captain Edward Whinyates's Rocket Troop also participated. The horse artillery was generally heavily engaged, with both Ramsay and Beane being killed and Bull and Whinyates wounded.

Shortly before the campaign Sir Augustus Frazer, the commander of the horse artillery, ordered four troops to be re-equipped with heavier armaments. Consequently, A, D, G, and H Troops each fielded five 9-pounder guns and one 5.5-inch howitzer. E and F Troops retained their five 6-pounders and one 5.5-inch howitzer, and I Troop fielded 5.5-inch howitzers only. As Wellington held little faith in Whinyates's beloved rockets, the Rocket Troop was also conventionally armed with five 6-pounders and a 5.5-inch howitzer.

Captain Alexander Cavalié Mercer, commanding G Troop, kept an account of the campaign. In addition to vivid battle scenes and accounts of daily army life, Mercer's journal provides a detailed list of his troop's personnel and the number of horses required to provide the mobility needed by a horse artillery troop:

The *personnel* consisted of—Second Captain, Mercer, commanding; Captain Pakenham (subsequently Newland) as Second Captain; Lieutenants Bell, Hinks, Ingleby, and Leathes—the former acting as adjutant to Sir A. Frazer, the latter as supernumerary; and before we left Strytem, Ingleby exchanged with Lieutenant Breton, and joined Sir Robert Gardiner's troop; so that, finally, it stood: Breton, Hinks, Leathes—surgeon, Hitchins; 2 staff-sergeants, 3 sergeants, 3 corporals, 6 bombardiers, 1 farrier, 3 shoeing smiths, 2 collar-makers, 1 wheeler, 1 trumpeter, and 1 acting do., 80 gunners, 84 drivers—the 1 acting trumpeter not included. The organization was in three divisions, of two subdivisions each—a subdivision being of one piece of ordnance, with its ammunition waggon and detachment. Each division had one spare ammunition waggon and a proportion of the other carriages, etc. The division was commanded by a lieutenant, and the subdivisions, the right of the division by a sergeant, the left by a corporal—a bombardier to each subdivision. On parade, the 5 1/2-inch howitzer was the right of the centre division. Perhaps at this time a troop of horse-artillery was the completest thing in the army; and whether broken up into half-brigades under the first and second captains, or into divisions under their lieutenants, or subdivisions under their sergeants and corporals, still each party was a perfect whole. (Mercer, 88–89)

Mercer also provides an accurate accounting of the number of horses needed to move a single horse artillery troop:

5 guns, 9-pounders, and 1 heavy 5.5-inch howitzer— 8 horses each	48
9 ammunition waggons—viz. 1 to each piece, and a spare one per division—6 horses each	54
1 spare-wheel carriage—6 horses	6
1 forge, 1 curricle-cart, 1 baggage-waggon—4 horses each	12
Total in draught	120
6 mounted detachments—8 horses each	48
2 staff-sergeants, 2 farriers, 1 collar-maker	5
6 officers' horses, lent them by the Board of Ordnance	6
6 officers' mules, for carrying their baggage	6
Total	185
Additional horses unaccounted for above, spare, etc.	30
General total of animals	215
Besides which, each officer had his own two horses, and the surgeon one, making 11 more—so that, including these, we had	226

(ibid., 88)

BRITISH HEAVY EQUIPMENTS

British heavy ordnance—guns heavier than the brass 12-pounder and howitzers above the 24-pounder—was classified as garrison and siege or battering artillery, as they were designed either to defend or to destroy fortifications. Heavy ordnance was originally made of brass or bronze, but after around 1808, Britain began using cast iron heavy ordnance with only the 32-pounder howitzer being made of brass.

Eighteen-, 24-, and 32-pounder guns were mounted on double bracket trail carriages with 5-foot wheels. These carriages resembled the conventional field models but were more stoutly constructed to support the weight of the heavy pieces, as well as their punishing recoil. As the heavy artillery's ammunition was transported in wagons, limbers were simple affairs with no ammunition box. They consisted merely of a limber pole and two wheels attached by the axletree, which mounted a pintle to accept the hole in the trails' bottom transom. The limber wheels themselves were smaller than the carriage's wheels, to aid maneuverability in turning. The massive 56- and 68-pounders were almost always mounted in fixed positions as fortification or seacoast defense weapons.

Artillery siege craft required meticulous preparation and execution to collapse specific sections of enemy fortifications and to provide a breach for an infantry assault. Such weapons as the 18-pounder gun and 8-inch howitzer would often begin the process by providing suppressing and counter-battery fire. This allowed the sappers to prepare the positions for the heavier pieces, as well as let their crews set up their pieces. The heavy mortars were also useful in that their high arcing trajectories enabled them to drop deadly explosive shells over the target's walls.

Also favored for naval use, the 24-pounder was the most popular and effective gun for siege work. Once positioned, the heavy guns began by firing solid shot at carefully surveyed points to create an inverted U-shaped pattern of weakened masonry in the wall's face. Howitzers then fired explosive shell at the section within the U to collapse it, and the process would repeat itself until the breach was effected. Although usually effective, the process consumed vast amounts of time and ammunition—the siege of strongly fortified Badajoz during the Peninsula Campaign consumed some 14,000 round shot alone. Crews of heavy pieces were generally capable of maintaining a firing rate of some 20 shots an hour, a respectable accomplishment taking in the pieces' 6-foot recoil and the need to laboriously run up the carriages after each shot.

The 8- and 10-inch heavy howitzers were rather stubby affairs but more modern in appearance than their field counterparts. The larger howitzer saw constant use throughout the period and fired a shell weighing 85 pounds and a case shot containing 258 bullets. The 8-inch heavy howitzer, however, proved much more popular with its crews and even at times saw deployment as a heavy field piece. It fired a 41-pound shell and a case shot containing 170 bullets.

The heavy howitzers employed unique carriages that were designed to reduce the effects of their considerable recoil. The forward part of the carriage was, in effect, an abbreviated flask trail. Its lower transom, however, mounted a short block trail known in British service as a "perch," which ended with a fitting for attachment to the limber's pintle. The lower transom also mounted two smaller naval-type truck wheels that, in conjunction with two wooden bars hinged to the transoms and engaged to the wheel hubs, acted to absorb recoil.

British mortars ranged in size from the small brass 4.4-inch coehorn to the massive iron 13-inch heavy siege mortar. Whereas the little coehorns were mounted on simple wooden blocks, the siege models used two stout wooden brackets secured to a base plate and a forward transom. The barrel's trunnions were fixed to appropriate cutouts in the brackets at a fixed 45-degree angle, the range being adjusted by the powder charge. Owing to their size, the heavy mortars of the eighteenth century were transported to their positions by wagons.

The poor performance of the bronze siege guns used by British forces during the Peninsular Wars of 1808–1814 graphically illustrated such weapons' deficiencies. The 1811 investments of Badajoz and Olivença exposed the limit of the bronze guns in firing only some 120 rounds in a 24-hour period, approximately one-third the firing rate of comparable iron cannons. As a result, the British army limited bronze cannons for field use to no larger than 12-pounder guns and 32-pounder howitzers. As weight and mobility were less of an issue in siege weapons, Britain, except in extreme situations, used only iron siege guns after 1811.

AUSTRIAN ARTILLERY:
THE LICHTENSTEIN SYSTEM

Austrian artillery performed poorly against the Prussians during the 1740–1744 War of the Austrian Succession. Whereas other European powers had taken a number of measures to modernize their organization and command structures, Austria's had proven ineffective in that it had not been fully integrated into its military system. It was further hampered by grave problems with mobility, as well as standardization of cannons and support equipment.

Appalled by the state of his country's artillery, a dragoon officer, Joseph Wenzel Prince Lichtenstein (1696–1772), set out to modernize Austria's system and ultimately created the first truly modern European artillery organization. Personally financing much of his efforts and a master of both organization and delegation, Lichtenstein methodically adopted and adapted the best ideas from a variety of sources. The best features of Swedish, Prussian, and French artillery thus found their way by means of the prince's genius into what became known as the Lichtenstein System.

A natural administrator, Lichtenstein lured the best artillery experts from Austria and abroad to help him establish a sound artillery program. These men made up the core of the Feld-Artillerie Stab (Field Artillery Staff), the organizational heart of his system, and they, in turn, oversaw the Feldzeugamt, or Ordnance Office. The field artillery itself, or Feld-Artillerie Haupt-Korps, was made up of three eight-company (by 1756 ten-company) artillery brigades. As originally organized Austrian company strength was 96 men including officers, but, owing to experience in the Seven Years' War, that was raised to 140 men in 1759. In addition to its Austrian component, Lichtenstein's organization also included the semiautonomous Niederlandische National-Artillerie, ultimately reaching a strength of twelve companies of Norwegian artillerymen. The final component of Lichtenstein's organization, the Artillery Fusilier Regiment of three eight-company battalions, provided infantry and other support services.

Lichtenstein's artillery educational program matched if not exceeded that of any other nation. Produced by Lichtenstein and his staff in 1757, the artillery *Regulation* became the basic Austrian artillerist's bible, which, following its revision in 1808, was used well into the nineteenth century. Noncommissioned officer schools were set up on the brigade level, and their best students were encouraged to attend the Artillery Corps School in the Bavarian city of Budweis. Still, despite such efforts, the officer corps above battery level remained a rather unimpressive lot. Other than the great exception, Josef Smola, few displayed any understanding or aptitude for massed fire and the aggressive, fast-moving tactics that won battles. It was not until the early nineteenth century that the Austrians truly managed efficiently to combine talented artillery commanders with Lichtenstein's system.

Lichtenstein redesigned Austrian cannons, eliminating their earlier decorations and architectural flourishes to produce more modern-looking bronze gun tubes with cleaner lines. He also standardized Austrian field calibers to 3-, 6-, and 12-pounders to match those of the Prussians and incorporated a screw quoin invented by a Lieutenant Colonel von Holtzman of the Prussian army. In addition, he went on to standardize artillery carriages, rolling stock including limbers and ammunition wagons, ammunition, and wheel sizes.

Displaying a personal understanding of the practical aspects of an artilleryman's duties and problems, Lichtenstein paid particular attention to artillery implements. He redesigned Austrian rammers, sponges, and handspikes, and also provided means to attach them by hooks to the artillery carriage—an imminently practical measure that allowed crews bring their pieces into action more quickly. Lichtenstein System carriages also originally mounted a coffret, a removable ammunition box attached between the trails' flasks. Originating in Sweden, the coffret provided crews with a readily available supply of ammunition during combat, although the boxes were later mounted on limbers. Other innovations included an extra pair of trunnion holes in the 12-pounder carriage to aid in balance during transport—an idea later copied by the Frenchman Gribeauval for his system.

Lichtenstein's concern for mobility also extended to the fitting of a saddlelike seat to caissons and the trails of some 6- and 7-pounder howitzers for crews attached to cavalry units. In addition, some ammunition wagons mounted the seats, and, owing to their elongated appearance, received the nickname "wurst wagons." These innovations met with decidedly mixed reactions from artillerists in the field. Practical usage soon indicated that the extra weight of crewmen on the gun carriages added to the fatigue of draft animals, and the gun carriage seats were eventually discarded. For its part, the wurst wagon must have been an exquisitely uncomfortable mode of transportation. A contemporary engraving of one going into battle shows it mounted by eight men, perched on its peaked cover—four facing forward and the rest rearward, with all holding on to one another's waist for dear life. The Lichtenstein System nevertheless provided the means for Austria's Kavallerie Battieren (Cavalry Batteries)—quick moving artillery units capable of providing on-the-spot fire support at decisive moments on the field.

The combination of the Lichtenstein System and a very few talented artillery officers such as Josef Freiherr von Smola (1764–

1820) eventually established Austria as a formidable force on Europe's battlefields. Although the Austrians did not at first grasp its potential and efficiently mass their artillery on a regular basis until 1809, they at times exhibited brilliance before that date. At the 1793 Battle of Neerwinden, von Smola devastated a French attack on the Austrian right with canister from his rapidly deployed fourteen guns. Austria's most aggressive artillery commander, von Smola developed as a master of rapid field movement and massed artillery fire. He rose rapidly from the rank of lieutenant to eventually become a general-major and received the Knight's Cross of the Order of Maria Theresa. He later became artillery chief of Hohenzollern's Austrian II Corps.

The mobility afforded by the new Austrian artillery was such that the French also used the Lichtenstein caisson with seats for a brief period. Although his artillery proved lighter and more maneuverable than its French counterparts during the Seven Years' War, the prince died before seeing his system fully integrated into the Austrian Army (the system was not completely in place until shortly after the Napoleonic Wars). Still, the Lichtenstein System served Austria well until 1859.

FRENCH ARTILLERY

Under the chief engineer to Louis XIV, Sébastian le Prestre de Vauban (1633–1707), seventeenth-century French artillery theory addressed mainly siege and fortification issues. Still, French artillery had made great strides during the reign of Louis XIV, although it was not until 1732 that the country's artillery officers received military standing on a par with their cavalry and infantry counterparts. For their part, French cannons at the beginning of the century were often as much works of art as instruments of war. Whether of bronze or iron, their slender, tapered barrels were cast with ornately sculpted cascabels and dolphins and were further adorned with scrollwork, inscriptions, and royal crests. Unfortunately, this artistic license also extended to caliber, and French guns of the period were as disparate as those of any other country of the time. Upon his appointment by the king as head of the French artillery in 1732, General Jean-Florent de Vallière (1667–1759) quickly set about remedying the confusion in his country's ordnance system.

The Vallière System

The 1732 Vallière System, as instituted by the general, standardized French calibers to 4-, 8-, 12-, 16-, and 24-pounder guns and included 8- and 12-inch mortars as well as a 16-inch mortar designed to throw stone balls. As French measurements were somewhat larger than those of other countries, that country's designations are somewhat misleading: the French 8-pounder, for example, was roughly equal to the English 9-pounder. The guns' trunnions were positioned below the centerline of the barrel. As with earlier French guns, Vallière's had graceful lines and were highly ornamented. His ornamentation, however, was not the result of artistic whim but provided a practical method of identifying individual pieces. Calibers were thus indicated by the motif decorating the breech face. These included a face within a sunburst on the rear of 4-pounders, and 8- and 12-pounders, respectively, graced with monkey and rooster heads. The heavier guns exhibited more classical themes, with 16-pounders featuring the head of Medusa and 24-pounders that of Bacchus.

Other flourishes cast into the top of the barrel provided further information. The individual gun's name appeared directly behind the muzzle and was followed by the Latin inscription *Ultima Ratio Regum* ("The Last Argument of Kings"). The French artillery's grand master's name and arms—most commonly that of Louis Auguste de Bouron, Duc de Maine—came next, and near the breech on the first reinforce appeared a sunburst, the royal crest of Louis XIV, and the motto *Nec Pluribus Impar* (Not Unequal to Many).

Although Vallière's reforms greatly advanced the French ordnance system, they were by no means comprehensive. Significantly, they did not differentiate between fortress, siege, and field artillery. In addition, although he achieved uniformity in ammunition and barrel manufacture, French carriages still retained regional differences—their only conformity being the dark red paint that was applied to their woodwork. Moreover, Vallière did not include howitzers in his system. This omission was most probably owing to the French gunners' lack of understanding of the finer points of firing explosive projectiles, the howitzer's most effective ammunition.

The loading and firing of explosive projectiles, or "bombs," did present a number of difficult and potentially deadly problems to early gunners. Consisting of hollow, cast iron spheres filled with bursting powder, bombs required burning fuses to explode—with luck—on or near their targets—and not within or near the cannon itself. The fuses themselves, made up either of short lengths of slow match or of powder held within wooden plugs or quills, thus required lighting to achieve their purpose. The earliest and most hazardous method was known as "firing in two strokes." Firing at two strokes was best applied to very short barreled weapons such as mortars, in that it required the gunner first to apply his portfire to the bomb's exposed fuse before quickly touching the priming in the vent. Although still relatively short, howitzer barrels of the time were still simply too long for such a procedure, thus prompting Vallière to omit the weapon from his system.

In contrast, the artillerists of many other European countries had already mastered the technique of firing at one stroke, the method of loading explosive projectiles that eventually became universal, even in France. Dependant upon the flames of the cannon's main discharge to wrap around the projectile and light the fuse, this technique was much faster and safer than firing at two strokes, but it still required attention to detail for safety's sake. It was of the utmost necessity that the projectile be placed so that the fuse pointed away from the main powder charge and toward the muzzle of the piece. That position allowed the flame of the cannon's discharge to wrap around the ball and thus light the fuse. Conversely, if the ball were reversed, the blast would force the fuse into the bomb, exploding it in the gun tube. Although a few brave French gunners did employ howitzers early in the eighteenth century, they did not come into common use until about the middle of the century.

The Vallière System served France well enough early in the century, but such conflicts as the 1756–1763 Seven Years' War eventually exposed its many shortcomings. Not the least of these lay in the general weight and lack of maneuverability of even the light Vallière pieces. Seeking a more maneuverable field piece, some enterprising French gunners went afar to obtain more appropriate weapons. As early as the 1740s they began using a number of the Swedish light 4-pounders as introduced by Gustavus Adolphus. Already proven as light, rugged weapons, the Swedish cannons also featured an advanced elevating screw mechanism activated by a hand crank mounted underneath the carriage below the barrel's breech. The Swedish cannons became so popular among the French gunners that, in 1756, France finally adopted the design and began its own domestic production.

The Gribeauval System

French artillery at last reached prominence under the direction of Jean Baptiste Vaquette de Gribeauval (1715–1789). Having entered the French army as a volunteer, Gribeauval rose in the ranks and gained a reputation as a skilled artillerist. He was impressed early in his career by Prussian artillery while on an inspection trip to that country before the Seven Years' War. During the Seven Years' War, Gribeauval served on detached duty with the Austrian army as a general of artillery, for which service he received the rank of lieutenant general and the Cross of Maria Theresa. His talents were so apparent during his service with the Austrians that none other than Frederick the Great, who had personally witnessed Gribeauval's handiwork against his own forces during the 1761 siege of Schweidnitz, offered him a commission in the Prussian army. Gribeuaval, however, remained loyal to France and was rewarded upon his return home in 1762 with the French rank of lieutenant general and the Order of Saint Louis.

Upon his return to active French service, he focused on rectifying the deficiencies of the Vallière System and pushed for more artillery reforms. Gribeauval also respected Lichtenstein's work immensely but wanted to carry his ideas to the logical conclusion of a totally integrated artillery system. Upon his elevation to inspector-general of the artillery by Louis XIV in 1776, Gribeauval at last undertook a complete overhaul of the French artillery system. Touching nearly every aspect of cannon design, construction, carriages, and deployment, the so-called Gribeauval System served France into the Napoleonic Era. It was so far-reaching that it also profoundly influenced artillery in other nations, including that of the emerging United States. The general also designated French cannons by their specific use, including field, siege, garrison, and seacoast, with each type mounted on the appropriately specialized carriage. These reforms in combination with Gribeauval's strong advocacy of close artillery support for infantry made France's the most advanced artillery during the late eighteenth and early nineteenth centuries.

Gribeauval began his task by redesigning the French gun tubes to produce lighter, more efficient barrels. Following the method already adopted by a number of other powers, he at last ordered that the bores of French gun tubes be drilled rather than cast around a mandrel. This procedure produced more exact tolerances within the bore and reduced the windage between the projectile and the bore's wall. That, in turn, reduced the loss of energy from the blow-by of the cannon's detonation around the ball. As this improvement made the weapon more efficient, less powder was needed, and thus the barrel's walls could be thinned to create a lighter piece, a goal that Gribeauval continued to seek by shortening the barrel tubes.

Gribeauval's gun tubes were, however, still somewhat heavier than their Prussian and Austrian counterparts; he nevertheless considered the extra weight acceptable, as it helped lengthen the service life of the pieces. The ratio of the weight of gun metal to that of an individual shot in the Gribeauval System was 150 pounds of gun metal to 1 pound of shot, whereas that of the Austrians was 120 to 1 and the Prussians, 100 to 1.

Gribeauval also did away with Vallière's ornate baroque embellishments in favor of a plainer, more businesslike appearance to his gun tubes. In the process the dolphins lost their ornamental sculpturing and instead became simple, functional handles. He also raised the trunnions to a point slightly below the barrel's centerline and increased their diameter where they met the barrel with reinforcements known as rimbases.

Gribeauval's extensive field service also influenced his introduction of one of the most practical field artillery accessories—the prolong. In effect nothing more than a thick, long rope, the prolong allowed artillerists to connect the piece to the limber without directly mounting the carriage to the limber. This gave the crews two significant advantages in combat—it still provided the pulling power of the horse team, yet allowed the piece to be more easily and quickly manipulated by the gun crew. In addition, it also allowed the horses and limber to be at a somewhat safer distance when under fire. To reduce the tendency of the rear of the carriage to dig into the ground when being dragged by prolong, Gribeauval also redesigned the lower end of the trail with a slight upward tilt.

His intimate understanding of the practical problems of field artillerists operating on rough, broken, or muddy ground was also evident in Gribeauval's introduction of the bricole. A leather cross-belt, the bricole allowed gun crews to harness themselves to metal rings on the gun carriage to help manhandle it over rough terrain. Gribeauval's other innovations included improved ammunition gauges to reduce windage and a better bore searcher. He also developed the hausse rear sight, a removable, highly accurate instrument that later saw adoption by numerous other powers.

Having worked with artillery and artillerists, Gribeauval also dictated that rather than drawing weapons from a general stockpile, individual artillery companies should be permanently assigned specific pieces. This innovation ensured that, as they were more invested in their cannons, crews would more properly maintain their pieces rather than perform any but the most perfunctory cleaning and repairs. Moreover, as all artillery pieces—regardless of the sophistication of manufacture—have unique quirks, crews would be more likely to understand and thus more efficiently serve their weapons.

Gribeauval System Field Guns

Field guns included 4-, 8-, and 12-pounders, and Gribeauval at last incorporated new 6-inch howitzers into the French army as regulation field weapons. The 8-inch howitzer already in service since 1749 was also retained but was used on a more limited basis. The earliest Gribeauval field howitzer was heavily based on Prussian models that he had studied, but his later designs were so modified that they were virtually an entirely new type.

Gribeauval also redesigned his gun carriages so as to be more durable than the Austrian Lichtenstein models, to compensate for the combined rear and downward recoil—an improvement that both strengthened their construction and produced a lighter and shorter carriage than earlier models. Carriages were originally painted various shades of blue until after the Revolution, when their color was changed to green. Field carriages were also improved by the addition of black-painted iron reinforcing straps to stress points in the woodwork as well as the leading edges exposed to damage. A coffret—a removable ammunition chest located between the flasks—enhanced the ability of the crews to more quickly put their pieces in action during combat. To improve balance and enhance the stability of the guns while on extended marches, Gribeauval, borrowing from Lichtenstein's 12-pounder carriage, added an extra pair of half-round trunnion cutouts toward the rear of the carriage. This feature, known as encastrement, did, however, require a rather laborious process involving levering and rolling with two handspikes to move the tube between the two positions. It was thus rarely if ever used in situations where combat was imminent.

Transportation was further improved with the introduction of a more efficient limber mounting a pole for the hitching of horses in side-by-side pairs. For transport, the reinforced hole in the transom at the end of the trail was passed over a pintle mounted over the limber's axle and secured to make a four-wheeled cart. A four-horse team was required for the 4- and 8-pounders, and six horses for the 12-pounders. Gribeauval also introduced the caisson, essentially a large, four-wheeled ammunition chest with a rounded or peaked lid and a compartmentalized interior for various types of ammunition and equipment. The combination of the new limber and caisson enabled French field gunners to arrive on the field with their ammunition and thus go into action more rapidly than their opponents.

Gribeauval's method of elevating his field guns' tubes was also somewhat different from that of other European systems. Although employing a vertical elevating screw, as did most other contemporary systems, his screw did not come into direct contact with the barrel's breech. It instead pushed against a wooden platform hinged to a transom beneath the barrel. Howitzers' trunnions remained below the centerline, as they had in the Vallière System, but they too differed in their aiming mechanism. Although still retaining a quoin, it was adjusted mechanically for elevation by way of a horizontally mounted screw attached to the transom beneath the breech.

Gribeauval System Siege Guns and Mortars

Other than eliminating their decoration and strengthening their carriages, Gribeauval left the 16- and 24-pounder quoin-elevated siege, or "battering," guns essentially unchanged. He also retained the old 8-inch and lesser-used 12-inch mortars but did contribute a new 10-inch mortar to French service. Gribeauval replaced the earlier solid-wood mortar beds with a new support composed of cast iron cheeks connected by bolts and wood cross-pieces. These new mortar beds were more durable than the earlier model and were positioned with the aid of handles on each corner.

Gribeauval System Seacoast Artillery

Intended to defend key coastal areas against enemy ships, seacoast fortifications presented their own unique artillery requirements. Chief among these were an accurate long-range capability and heavy ship-killing caliber. As a consequence, seacoast artillery was much larger than land-based cannons. Although mobility was not a major issue with these fixed pieces, their carriages did need enough maneuverability for loading and aiming, and also had to be able to bear the weight and recoil of the cannons themselves. Early garrison and seacoast carriages were essentially nothing more than large truck carriages as used for naval purposes. The barbette carriage, designed to fire over a fortification's parapet, was a specialized carriage for seacoast use. A typical barbette carriage mounted two wheels on the rear of the trail, often set on tracks that eased traversing the barrel to maintain aim against moving targets such as ships.

Despite the obvious advantages of the new system, the transition from Vallière's to Gribeauval's was far from smooth, and it was racked with political and personal animosity. While in Austria, Gribeauval had worked under the direct auspices of the French ambassador to Vienna, the Duc du Choiseul, who, in turn, lobbied tirelessly for the adoption of the new system by the French government. The Vallière System, however, still had its staunch champions in the form of a number of well-connected backers, including the inventor's son. The Vallière faction was further strengthened by the never-to-be-underestimated perennial lethargy so common to military bureaucracies.

Gribeauval and Choiseul gained an initial, although short-lived, victory following the latter's appointment as minister of war and lobbying on the part of the de Broglie brothers, intimates of the king. Although Choiseul put the adoption of his friend's system into effect, it was immediately shelved upon the assumption of his successor, a Vallière proponent. Bitter debates and further testing followed, during which supporters of the competing systems divided into two factions—Gribeauval's the Bleus ("Blues") and Vallière's the Rouges ("Reds")—named for the colors of the artillerists' breeches advocated by the systems.

The du Teil Brothers

Two talented brothers, Jean-Pierre du Teil (1722–1794) and Jean du Teil (1733–1820), dominated French artillery theory from 1763 to 1789 and ultimately exerted a profound influence upon Napoleon. The elder brother, Jean-Pierre, the Baron de Beaumont, was a veteran of the Seven Years' War and saw rapid advancement in French service. He went on in 1779 to command the Artillery School of Auxonne, where the Gribeauval System was taught to such students as the young future emperor. He later became inspector general of artillery in 1791, filling the position formerly occupied by Gribeauval, who had died in 1789. His life and career ended, however, in the turmoil of the French Revolution; he was arrested and executed by the Jacobins in 1794.

For his part, Jean du Teil fought on the side of the Revolutionary forces and rose to divisional command. He too had an influence upon Napoleon, who served as a captain under his command during the 1793 Siege of Toulon. As the author of the influential *De l'Usage de l'Artillerie Nouvelle dans le Guerre de Campaigne,* de Teil extended his theories to a wider audience. In it he promoted his convictions of the importance of coordinated infantry and artillery combined operations and the effectiveness of concentrated artillery fire—doctrines later taken to heart by Napoleon as he organized the Grande Armée.

Jacques Guibert

The works of another Frenchman, Jacques Guibert (1743–1790), further established France as a leader in artillery thinking. His two tactical treatises, *Essai Général de Tactique* of 1772 and the later *Défense du Système du Guerre Moderne* were far-reaching in their impact. Guibert was a firm proponent of the need for mobility, concentration of fire, and long-range accuracy. He was particularly insistent on designating the enemy's infantry the artillery's primary target and thus discouraged counter-battery fire if at all possible. His maxim concerning the concentration of fire against enemy infantry—"The object of artillery should not consist of killing men on the whole of the enemy's front, but to overthrow it, to destroy parts of his front. . . . [T]hen they obtain decisive effects; they create a gap"—became gospel for future artillery commanders (Mercer, 54).

The Year XI System

With the death of Gribeauval in 1789 and the turmoil of the Revolution, the position of inspector-general of the artillery fell into disuse. An Artillery Committee formed by the National Assembly the next year proved completely ineffective, leaving the country's artillery with almost no direction during the early revolutionary period. As a trained and experienced artillerist, Napoleon Bonaparte

(1769–1821), as first consul and later emperor, attempted to bring about sweeping reforms to make French artillery a decisive factor on Europe's battlefields.

In 1800, Napoleon reinstated the office of inspector-general of the artillery and appointed the aged yet competent General François-Marie, Comte d'Aboville, to the position. Two years later Napoleon replaced d'Aboville with the younger General Auguste Marmont. It was Marmont who, in 1803, assigned Colonel François de Fautrier ultimately to replace Gribeauval's system with what became known as the Year XI System, named according to the new French Revolutionary calendar.

Bureaucratic incompetence and the lack of communication between various parties eventually doomed the Year XI system to failure. Produced primarily between 1804 and 1809 and emblazoned with the Napoleonic "N," the bronze 6-pounder gun and 24-pounder howitzer were handsome pieces and also quite serviceable. The heavier weapons, however, were ill conceived, and very few were made. In the end, the French army continued to rely on the tried and tested Gribeauval artillery through the Napoleonic Wars.

Louis de Tousard

It was Louis de Tousard (1749–1817) who personally transplanted the latest French artillery theory and practice to the New World and helped found the American artillery establishment. Having earlier met Benjamin Franklin, the American minister to France, Tousard served with the American forces in 1777 and 1778 and lost an arm from wounds suffered at the 1778 Battle of Rhode Island. Returning to French service, he won a series of promotions at home as well as the title of Chevalier of St. Louis.

Briefly imprisoned during the French Revolution, Tousard returned to America in 1795 and accepted a commission as a major in the 2nd U.S. Artillery Regiment. By 1800 he was a lieutenant colonel and artillery inspector. Tousard moved in the highest military circles and exerted considerable influence over George Washington. It was largely owing to Tousard's efforts that the fledgling country established the U.S. Military Academy at West Point in 1802, primarily to train engineers and artillerists.

Having retired from U.S. service, Tousard returned to France yet continued to travel between the two countries as he continued his career, alternately in French military and diplomatic capacities. In 1809, Tousard published *The American Artillerist's Companion; or Elements of Artillery,* a work that became the basic manual of the U.S. artillery service.

AMERICAN ARTILLERY

Upon its declaration of independence in 1776, the United States found itself in desperate need of artillery with which to fight the Revolution. Although relatively plentiful, French cannons captured during the 1754–1763 French and Indian War and supplied by France during the Revolution were, for the most part, of the ungainly and thus unpopular Vallière System. Luckily, as a consequence of its founding as English colonies, the new nation did have at its disposal a preponderance of cannons of British origin, and as a result domestic manufacture tended to follow the designs of the mother country.

American gun founders were, however, influenced by the more advanced ideas put forth in John Müller's *Treatise of Artillery* (1768), which was reprinted in Philadelphia in 1779. In addition, cannons brought over by the French also influenced American designs, and American ordnance exhibited certain French characteristics well into the nineteenth century. Consequently, some American cannons of the period were better weapons than their British counterparts, being of lighter weight and fitted with trunnions along the center line. American made cannons of the period were typically identified with a "US" (or "UC," for United Colonies) monogram in script and the gun founder's name, the city of manufacture, and the date of casting. Carriages were painted a variety of colors, including British lead gray and French blue; at times they were not painted at all but oiled and treated with turpentine.

Before the Revolution the colonies boasted a number of militia artillery companies, including the oldest and most prestigious Ancient and Honorable Artillery Company of Boston, founded in 1638. Such companies had performed relatively well in the French and Indian War and had participated in the successful siege of the French fortress city of Louisbourg at the mouth of the St. Lawrence in 1758. Still, the new American commander-in-chief, George Washington (1732–1799), quickly realized that such scattered and independent-minded organizations would be no match for the excellent British artillery. To oppose the British successfully the general needed a centralized artillery arm and the organization and leadership to make it function effectively.

Henry Knox

To meet this daunting task, Washington was indeed fortunate to gain the services of the man who was to become the "Father of American Artillery," Henry Knox. The son of Irish immigrants, Henry Knox (1750–1806), was born on 25 July 1750 in Boston. An intelligent and well-read young man, Knox first worked as a book seller but soon embraced the patriot cause and was present at the 1770 Boston Massacre. In 1772, at the age of twenty-two, he began his military career by enlisting in the Boston Grenadier Corps, a local militia unit, and later fought at the June 1775 Battle of Bunker Hill. In what was to lead to a lifelong friendship, Knox met Washington on the outskirts of British-occupied Boston in 1775. There, Washington, desperate for artillery with which to besiege the British troops under General Sir William Howe (1729–1814), promoted Knox to colonel of the Continental Regiment of Artillery. He then charged the young colonel with moving the artillery captured at Fort Ticonderoga on Lake Champlain down to the Americans' siege works.

In one of the most remarkable feats of the war, Knox successfully transported the artillery pieces by ox sleds approximately 300 miles over the ice- and snow-covered landscape in December 1775 and January 1776. Although Knox had abandoned the carriages owing to their poor condition, he delivered to Washington possibly as many as forty-three brass and iron guns, including 18-pounders and the largest piece, an 1,800-pound brass 24-pounder. There were also two iron howitzers and six iron coehorns, and eight larger brass mortars. Knox then supervised the placement of the newly arrived ordnance on the commanding Dorchester Heights above Boston. Realizing the advantage of Knox's artillery, Howe abandoned the city on 17 March, and the Americans retook the city the next day.

After the reinvestment of Boston, Knox went on to supervise the defenses of Connecticut and Rhode Island before rejoining Washington in New York. There he commanded some 520 officers and men and an artillery train of approximately 120 pieces. Knox was with the outnumbered Continental Army during its retreat from the superior British forces and later, on Christmas night 1776, directed

Washington's famous crossing of the Delaware River. Promoted to brigadier general and chief of artillery of the Continental Artillery, in 1777 he set up Springfield Arsenal to produce and repair weapons and equipment and was with the army at Valley Forge. Knox later participated with distinction at the 1777 battles of Brandywine and Germantown and at Monmouth in 1778. His supervision of the American artillery at the siege of Yorktown was a critical factor in the surrender of Cornwallis's forces on 19 October 1789 and brought Knox further promotion to major-general.

Following the hostilities Knox, by then weighing some 300 pounds, continued to serve his country. Among other positions, he was elected secretary of war under the Confederation government in 1785 and was appointed four years later to the same post in Washington's cabinet. Knox died in Thomaston, Maine, on 25 October 1806 from complications arising from accidentally swallowing a chicken bone.

PRUSSIAN ARTILLERY:
FREDERICK THE GREAT

The Prussian artillery that so impressed Austria's Prince Lichtenstein during the War of the Austrian Succession ultimately suffered during the reign of Frederick the Great (b. 1712; r.1740–1786). Although Frederick occasionally exhibited flashes of inspiration in his use of artillery, he often neglected it in favor of his infantry and cavalry. Moreover, what attention he did pay it was usually more meddlesome than helpful and often proved detrimental to the arm in the long run. Napoleon attributed the Prussian artillery's poor showing to its king's indifference to the arm. The reason for Frederick's attitude, according to Napoleon, was its nature, being one of the "grubby bourgeois arts, demanding hard and unglamorous toil . . . alien to the temper of the old European military nobility." As the French emperor summed it up: "Frederick, great man though he was, did not understand artillery" (Mercer 146–147).

Napoleon's assessment of Frederick's use of his artillery arm was more than justified. By encouraging his gunners to concentrate their efforts in counter-battery fire, the Prussian king went against the prevailing military doctrine that saw massed infantry as the most profitable targets for their artillery. Still, even Frederick was forced at times grudgingly to acknowledge that "[a] cannon ball knocks down a man six feet tall just as well as one who is only five feet seven. Artillery decides everything, and infantry no longer do battle with naked steel" (ibid., 28).

Despite Frederick's neglect, the Prussian artillery was not without talented artillerists. Serving as Generalinspecteur, the overall commander of the Prussian artillery, General der Artillerie Christian von Linger (d. 1755) earned the sobriquet "Father of the Prussian artillery." It was under his tenure that the Prussian army standardized its field guns to 3-, 6-, 12-, and 24-pounders. During the 1830s and 1840s, Lieutenant Colonel Ernst von Holtzman of the 2nd Artillery Battalion invented the horizontally mounted screw quoin and an improved screw-operated rear sight. Another officer, the Hanover-born Gerhard Johann David Scharnhorst (1755–1813), even went so far as to press for the education of Prussian artillery officers. Although Scharnhorst ultimately attained the position of chief of the Prussian general staff, his suggestions concerning artillery reforms went largely unappreciated by his king.

Prussian artillery was further crippled by its primitive transportation. Almost alone among those of other powers, Frederick's cannons depended on the antiquated practice of employing hired civilian teamsters rather than a militarized transportation system for their movement to the battlefield. Moreover, Frederick's ill-informed interventions continued to make his gunners' lives more difficult. Possibly intending to improve efficiency and reduce powder consumption, he ordered that his 6- and 12-pounder guns be drilled with chambered breeches. This feature, although long-proven effective in short-barreled howitzers and mortars, was an unfortunate modification to Prussia's guns. Not only did chambered guns require more careful loading—thus slowing their rate of fire—but they were also less reliable and more difficult to maintain in the field.

Despite his general indifference to the subject, Frederick nevertheless made a significant contribution to the advancement of field artillery. Owing to heavy casualties among his beloved infantry, Frederick found it increasingly necessary to compensate for their losses by increasing his artillery arm. In 1759 this situation eventually led to his introduction of the first true horse artillery units. These batteries, their entire crews furnished with mounts, were able to move more rapidly than any other artillery of the day and proved quite effective against the Russians during the Seven Years' War. It was, however, typical of Frederick in his offhand treatment of his artillery that he did not fully recognize its potential or pursue the arm's development beyond his immediate needs.

Whereas Frederick soon abandoned his horse artillery batteries, other European powers grasped the potential of the Prussian king's invention and exploited it to their future advantage. As a result, by the time of the Napoleonic Wars, England and nearly every other Continental power fielded horse artillery batteries. Prussia had set the precedent for horse artillery with 6-pounders, but such other nations as Austria fielded 3-pounders and Denmark used diminutive 1-pounders—a striking contrast to the French 8-pounder guns and 6-inch howitzers.

RUSSIAN ARTILLERY

Russian artillery languished under the reign of Catherine the Great (1729–1796). At the time when her son, Czar Paul I (1754–1801), assumed the throne, crews received little training, the artillery train was virtually ignored, and the cannons themselves were generally overly heavy and ponderous to move on the battlefield. Paul initiated a series of artillery reforms the year of his coronation that, within a decade, made Russian artillery equal to that of any other European power. These efforts led, in 1804, to the establishment of the Provisional Artillery Committee. The committee eventually put into motion a comprehensive series of reforms, and in 1808 it began publishing the *Artillery Journal* to promote new ideas in artillery theory and practice. The reformers' goals were realized with the Artillery System of 1805. The new system set down the basic measures that resulted in the standardization of cannon tubes, their carriages, as well as their ancillary equipments and the organization of the artillery train. As a result, Russian artillerists during the first decade of the nineteenth century had at their disposal excellent cannons, carriages, and caissons.

For field use the new system dictated 6- and 12-pounder guns, as well as various sizes of the licorne, named for its unicorn shaped lifting handles. Essentially a hybrid between a howitzer and gun, thus a *gun-howitzer,* the licorne was capable of a flatter trajectory and longer range than the conventional howitzer. Russian cannons of the period shared many similarities with Prussian and Austrian models, showing particular influence from the Lichtenstein System. Carriages were fitted with coffrets, and elevation was adjusted with a screw quoin.

The lighter Russian cannons were attached to field units in much greater strength than those of other countries: Russian divisions, for example, matched the artillery arm of an entire French corps. The basic field artillery designations were light, horse, and position, with a foot artillery battalion made up of two light and two heavy companies. Light companies fielded four light 6-pounders, four medium 6-pounders, and four 10-pounder licornes, whereas heavy companies consisted of four light 12-pounders, four heavy 12-pounders, four 18-pounder licornes, and two 2-pounder licornes. Horse artillery companies had six light 6-pounders and six 10-pounder licornes. In the field, the Russians tended to place their licornes on the flanks of their batteries, with their guns in the center.

At the turn of the century the Russians fielded excellent cannons and equipment and had well-trained crews, noncommissioned officers, and field-grade officers. Still, the czarist artillery arm was seriously handicapped by lack of a clear doctrine and adequate leadership on the command levels. The practice of appointing often inexperienced or even incompetent generals to artillery commands often negated their effectiveness and led to tactical failures. Moreover, when nearly all other European powers discouraged counterbattery fire as inefficient and wasteful of ammunition, Russian commanders stubbornly clung to the practice, thus sparing the enemy's valuable infantry. The Russians were also rather timid in risking their guns in combat situations. That tendency at times led to their premature withdrawal when they were most needed for infantry support—although the execution of a number of field officers for losing their guns does make such decisions somewhat understandable.

Possibly the foremost Russian artillery figure of the Napoleonic period, General Aleksey Andreevich Arakcheev (1769–1834) attempted to correct the situation with what came to be known as the Artillery System of 1805. Sometimes titled the grand vizier of the Russia Empire, Arakcheev served in 1799 and 1803 as the inspector general of artillery, advised Czar Alexander, and was elevated to minister of war, serving from 1808 to 1810. Arakcheev's achievements, however, as a highly effective administrator and his Artillery System of 1805 were at times overshadowed by his abrasive personality and violent temper. In one case he was said to have ordered the execution of two junior officers by having them buried to their necks and left to die of starvation and thirst. In another incident it was reported that he cut another's head off with his sword for a perceived infraction.

Arakcheev's one-time adjutant, Count Alexander Ivanovich Kutaisov (1784–1812), managed to expand his former commander's reforms without displaying his homicidal tendencies. A highly decorated general at the age of twenty-two, Kutaisov wrote the influential *General Rules for Artillery in a Field Battle* and pressed for a well-trained and professional corps of artillery officers, including generals. To that end he was instrumental in forming the Artillery Reserve in 1812, but he was killed while leading an infantry counterattack at Borodino that same year.

SPANISH ARTILLERY

In general, Spanish artillery pieces of the period differed from English and French models only in their minor details. Iron guns reflect some influence of John Müller's theories but mounted trunnions below the centerline, as with earlier English cannons. They do differ in their Spanish markings and moldings. Bronze guns from as late as the 1760s retained some rather archaic features, such as sculpted dolphins and ringed, swelled muzzles, but these were superseded when Spain adopted the Gribeauval System in the next decade. The Spanish mortero de plancha, or "plate mortar," was manufactured into the late 1780s and consisted of the barrel and bed cast into one piece. Range was thus adjusted by the amount of powder used. Spanish mortars were often cast with the monogram of the reigning king as well as the date of manufacture. They were also often individualized with names such as *El Espanto* (The Terror) inscribed near the muzzle. The 16-inch pedrero, or stone mortar, firing baskets of rocks or even hand grenades, was also used during the period, as well as coehorns, known to the Spaniards as the cuernos de vaca, or "cow horns." Spain eventually adopted Gribeauval System mortars, with the main differences between theirs and the French model being the use of bronze rather than cast iron in the carriage construction and a single cross-mounted dolphin on top of the barrel.

OTTOMAN ARTILLERY

Following his assumption of power in 1789, Sultan Selim III (1761–1803) initiated an overall modernization of the by then grossly inefficient Ottoman army. In 1793, Selim named Mustafa Reshid Efendi head of the Ottoman artillery—the Topijis—as well as the royal ordnance foundries and arsenals. He also recruited a number of French and Prussian advisors to train and organize the Topijis in the latest European artillery practices. The Ottoman artillery was subsequently expanded and reorganized into 25 regiments, each consisting of 115 men and officers and placed under the overall command of an officer known as the Topiji Bashi.

Although Prussian advisors attempted to impose some form of standardization on the numerous calibers then in Ottoman service, they were only moderately successful. As a result, Ottoman artillerists at times struggled to obtain suitable ammunition—a situation often exacerbated by a chronic shortage of dependable gunpowder. Despite such shortcomings, the new Ottoman artillery was a marked improvement over the earlier system of the seventeenth century. A typical Ottoman foot artillery regiment was armed with four basic types of bronze ordnance, including a mix of older, somewhat obsolescent pieces and the latest French designs. Each piece was served by a ten-man crew. The heaviest and least maneuverable, the Balyemez, was a 120-pounder or higher in caliber and the longest range of the Ottoman field pieces. The next heaviest Ottoman gun, the Sahi, ranged from a 4- to 14-pounder in caliber and, like the Balymez, was generally placed in rear positions to support infantry. The lighter yet aging Abu howitzer ranged from 70mm to 100mm and accompanied the infantry. The Ottomans also fielded modern French-designed guns designated Surat Topcusu, or "fast artillery." To serve as protection from enemy infantry as well as replacement gunners, twenty specially trained infantrymen accompanied the Abu and Surat Topcusu crews in the field.

CHAPTER FIVE

Nineteenth-Century U.S. Artillery, 1800–1865

EARLY FEDERAL PERIOD U.S. ARTILLERY

Following the Revolution, economics and an innate distrust of retaining a large standing army led to a considerable reduction in the new republic's military forces. After the rapid postwar demobilization, the regular army maintained only one artillery battalion, thus making the militia batteries a key element in the nation's military structure. While typically contributing to the social needs of their often well-heeled members, these militia units maintained at least a modicum of military skill that could be called upon at times of emergency. The first and most prestigious of these, the Ancient and Honorable Artillery Company of Boston, was organized during colonial times. Some of the other well-known militia companies of the period included the New York Battalion of Artillery, the Jackson Artillerists of Philadelphia, and Rhode Island's Newport Artillery and United Train of Artillery. Southern militia batteries included units that later fought against their Northern counterparts during the Civil War. They included Richmond's La Fayette Artillery, the Norfolk Light Artillery Blues, the Portsmouth Light Artillery, and the Chatham Artillery of Savannah, Georgia.

These early batteries were originally armed with a variety of cannons, including primarily British and French models, although Spanish and other types were also used. Although there were some complaints concerning the quality of its products, domestic manufacture eventually developed at the new federal arsenal at Springfield, Massachusetts. Private foundries, known for manufacturing better-made weapons, supplemented Springfield's output. These included the Philadelphia foundry of J. Byers and that of Daniel King in Germanton, Pennsylvania. Silversmith, engraver, and Son of Liberty, Paul Revere (1734–1818) also played a role in the development of American artillery.

Before his 18 April 1775 "midnight ride," Revere gained some experience with ordnance when he served briefly as a militia artillery lieutenant during the French and Indian War. Later, in 1776, he resumed his militia career as a lieutenant colonel of artillery and took over command of Castle William in Boston Harbor. Whereas his service as a garrison commander was notably lackluster, Revere made significant contributions to the American cause by establishing a gunpowder works and cannon foundry in Connecticut. He also oversaw the salvage of the cannons from the grounded British warship *Somerset*, one of the ships that had guarded Boston Harbor the night of his famous ride. In 1788, Revere expanded his own considerable business enterprises by setting up a bell and cannon foundry in Boston.

Early American cannons reflected both British and French influence. Although somewhat simpler in lines, the cannon tubes were similar to contemporary British examples. After 1809, carriages, however, were of the advanced French Gribeauval System design and were fitted with iron axles and coffrets or penthouse ammunition boxes between the flasks. They were also painted blue in the French fashion or even at times red, rather than the dull British gray. The early pieces were generally cast of brass or bronze, but as copper and zinc were difficult to obtain, by 1800 most cannons were cast in iron.

American gunners, having proved themselves during the Revolution, continued to build upon their reputation during the War of 1812. Whereas the much-vaunted skills of the American militia riflemen received the lion's share of credit for the victory, the artillery played a critical role in the battle. One source, Captain George Robert Gleig of the British 85th Foot, later recounted that the American artillerists first spread panic among his troops by their use of hot shot to ignite houses on the battleground that had been previously filled with incendiary materials. This, he asserted, followed by accurate direct fire against the British troops, was a deciding factor in the U.S. victory.

The King Howitzers

During the 1790s, Daniel King's foundry cast some of the most distinctively American cannons of the early Federalist period. The King Howitzers, as they have come to be called, were of 2.75-inch bore and cast in brass in two sizes. The smaller size was 16 inches long and weighed a mere 38 pounds. Its diminutive size and weight made it an obvious choice as a pack cannon for use on the frontier, and in 1792, General "Mad Anthony" Wayne (1745–1796) obtained a number of pieces in Pittsburgh for his coming foray into the wilderness. These pieces proved, however, to have defective trunnions, and Wayne rejected them in favor of the heavier model.

The larger howitzer, at 17 inches in length and weighing 60 pounds, proved up not only to the rigors of campaigning but also as an ideal choice for frontier use—at a total weight with carriage of 224 pounds it could easily be disassembled and transported by horse or mule. Wayne, commanding elements of the Legion of the United States, the forerunner of the U.S. Army (the transition occurred in 1796), also received 3-pound solid shot, shell, and canister for the howitzers. Wayne's artillery commander, Lieutenant Percy Pope—known as "Crazy Pope" for his impetuous behavior—put the little howitzers to deadly use at the 10 August 1794 Battle of Fallen Timbers. There Pope's artillery spread havoc as they opened with shot before switching to shell and finally canister as the Indians approached to within 80 yards.

Following the appointment of Henry Dearborn (1751–1829) as secretary of war in 1801, the United States completed its transition from brass to iron ordnance. During Dearborn's tenure, American cannons became progressively more streamlined than their British models, yet retained their calibers. American cannons during the period were thus 6-, 12-, 18-, 24-, and 32-pounders.

Federal Period Cast Iron Field Guns

In 1818 the Americans finally overreached themselves in their desire to simplify and lighten their ordnance. The lightweight new model 6-pounder cannons first produced that year were graceful pieces and presented a profile so slim that they became popularly known as walking sticks. Unfortunately, in their rush to lighten the pieces, the founders cast the Pattern of 1818 cannons with only a 10-inch diameter reinforce and dangerously thin barrel walls. Such flimsy construction and uncertain metallurgy combined to create guns that tended to burst at an alarming rate. The Fort Pitt Foundry cast about 100 walking sticks before ceasing their production in favor of more substantial designs. Although later models were cast with thicker walls, the memory of the walking sticks lingered among artillerists, leaving some with a residual distrust of cast iron ordnance.

In an attempt to provide gunners with a more substantial 6-pounder, Fort Pitt followed the walking stick with the more robust cast iron Pattern of 1827. Fort Pitt and the Columbia Foundry then turned to producing the somewhat heavier Pattern of 1834, until both foundries ceased production of field guns to turn their production to heavier artillery. Despite the 1835 ordnance committee decision to switch from iron to bronze, in 1836, Cyrus Alger continued to cast thirteen iron gun tubes of an identical pattern to the recently approved Pattern of 1835 bronze guns.

Early Federal Period Heavy Artillery

Following the expulsion of foreign forces from their territory, the Americans saw little real need for siege and conventional garrison artillery. Most offensive operations were against the Indian tribes on the frontiers: there were no fortified cities to attack, and field artillery was sufficient to defend the small frontier forts. The new nation did, however, construct a series of fortifications along its extensive coastline, and thus seacoast artillery made up the vast majority of its heavy artillery. With none cast in bronze, all early American seacoast artillery was cast in iron, and its calibers were standardized according to the British system of 18-, 24-, and 32-pounders. Still, the cash-strapped republic continued to retain a few French and Spanish pieces out of necessity. Those pieces required either reboring or their own ammunition.

Whereas American seacoast guns followed more or less British patterns, their carriages were based on the French Gribeauval System. Still, the U.S. practice of building carriages on site to fit particular fortifications led to considerable variation on the French theme. U.S. casement carriages—designed for placement in the gun ports or casements of fortifications—and barbette carriages, used to fire over the top of fortifications or barbettes, were very similar in design and appearance.

They consisted of a main carriage much like a standard naval truck carriage, although the rear wheels were typically smaller than the front. This assembly, in turn, was mounted on a lower bed fitted with tracks along which the main carriage could recoil upon firing. The rearward upper slope of the lower bed aided in reducing the recoil of the gun's heavy charge. The forward section of the bed was attached to a pivot within the casement or barbette, with the rear trucks mounted so as to allow traversing side to side along iron tracks. U.S. carriages also differed from the French in materials. In 1818, Chief of Ordnance Colonel Decius Wadsworth issued orders that American seacoast carriages be constructed of cast iron, abandoning the French practice of using wood as a primary component. Still, wooden seacoast carriages remained in American service through the Civil War. The Americans also adapted the carronade for land use by mounting it on a modified casement carriage. Although short-ranged weapons, they were apparently effective as antipersonnel weapons when loaded with grape shot or canister to guard the gates of fortifications.

With a production totaling 1,125, the Pattern of 1819 24-pounder siege gun was one of the most widely used heavy artillery pieces. Such pieces were capable, at 100 yards, of battering through nearly 2 feet of stone fortification, 3 feet of brick, and 15 feet of new earthworks. Although of an older design, the Pattern of 1819 saw considerable service from its adoption through the Civil War, when some tubes were rifled by Confederate arsenals. In appearance it was distinguished from other 24-pounders by its rather abruptly flared muzzle swell.

The first U.S. 32-pounder seacoast guns were probably cast around the period of the War of 1812. They were cast with an apparently unique sighting arrangement with triple front and rear sights. Production of seacoast guns then began in earnest in 1829 and continued through the 1840s. The Bellona Foundry near Richmond, Virginia; the Columbia Foundry of Georgetown, District of Columbia; the Fort Pitt Foundry at Pittsburg, Pennsylvania; Tredegar Foundry of Richmond, Virginia; and the West Point Foundry at Cold Spring in New York also manufactured some 1,222 Pattern of 1829 32-pounders between 1829 and 1839. The Confederate government rifled a number of Pattern of 1829s during the Civil War. In addition to 32-pounders, the Bellona, Columbia, and West Point foundries also cast 167 Pattern of 1831 42-pounder gun tubes.

Although later famous during the Civil War as a descriptive for large seacoast guns, the enigmatic term "columbiad" was probably originally applied to a smaller type weapon. The word itself possibly referred to the Columbia foundry near Washington, D.C. As first used around 1809, the term "columbiad" was apparently applied to a type of U.S.-made long gun ranging in size from 6- to 18-pounders. Then, around 1811, the word seems to have attached itself to heavy 50- and even possibly 100-pounder guns that fired shells along a flat trajectory unlike the howitzer's—the traditional shell-firing cannon's—arcing path. Some also saw some naval use: while cruising the Great Lakes, for example, the sloop *President* shipped six 18-pounder columbiads in addition to her complement of four long 12-pounder guns.

George Bomford (1750–1848), then a major in the ordnance department, played a key role in columbiad development during the War of 1812 and continued as a proponent for the next three decades. The weapons seem to have lost favor, however, for a period of about twenty years. Army records from 1818 listed an inventory of sixty columbiads, including 18-, 24-, 32-, 50-, and 100-pounders, yet by 1834 they were officially declared obsolete. The term then faded from the records only to reappear in the 1840s to describe heavy seacoast shell guns.

U.S. FIELD, GARRISON, AND SIEGE ARTILLERY OF THE 1830s AND 1840s

The unfortunate reputation of the cast iron walking stick cannon of 1818 contributed in no small way to the return by the United States to less brittle bronze for cannon casting. Americans had originally switched from bronze to iron primarily because of iron's availability and subsequent lower cost, yet the walking stick had caused artillerists to re-examine that earlier decision. Having burst at an alarming rate in the field and during ordnance tests in 1827, the Pattern of 1818 spread a growing distrust in the use of iron in general. Political and economic issues complicated what became a growing debate during the 1830s. As artillerists began calling for bronze cannons, the domestic iron industry lobbied Washington for the retention of iron. Finally, an 1835 ordnance committee recommended the return to bronze for field use, but, owing to political maneuvering, that change was not put into full effect until 1841. As a result of the transition, the lighter field pieces were of bronze, but the heavier siege and garrison pieces and mortars, with the exception of the 24-pounder coehorn, were of iron.

Alfred Mordecai

Born into an Orthodox Jewish family in Warrenton, North Carolina, Alfred Mordecai (1804–1887) was instrumental in modernizing U.S. artillery during the 1830s and 1840s. Mordecai excelled at mathematics and, at fifteen, entered the U.S. Military Academy at West Point, where at nineteen he was graduated first in his class in 1823. He then remained at the academy for two years as an assistant professor of natural and experimental philosophy and as a principal assistant professor of engineering. Assigned to the Corps of Engineers, from 1825 to 1828 Mordecai went on to supervise various coastal fortification construction projects, including Forts Monroe and Calhoun in Virginia. From 1828 to 1832 he went on to serve as assistant to the chief engineer in Washington, D.C., and on 30 May 1832 was promoted captain of ordnance.

While touring Europe in 1833–1834, Mordecai, apparently on his own initiative, collected extensive data on the French stock trail carriage. Upon his return to the United States that information, including detailed drawings, became the basis for U.S. prototypes of the design. In 1836, Mordecai assumed command of the Frankford Arsenal. There he continued his campaign to improve the U.S. ordnance system, a process that included the adoption of the stock trail carriage, scientific testing of equipment, and standardization with interchangeable parts. Three years later, in 1839, he was appointed to the ordnance board charged with developing the first truly complete U.S. ordnance system.

In 1841 these efforts culminated in the *Ordnance Manual for the Use of Officers in the United States Army,* the first U.S. artillery manual and the basis for the System of 1841. Mordecai's other publications included his earlier 1833 *Digest of Military Laws,* the 1845 *Reports of Experiments on Gunpowder,* and *Artillery for the United States Land Service, as devised and arranged by the Ordnance Board,* published in 1849. Mordecai's distinguished military career ended in 1861, with the beginning of the Civil War. Owing to his divided loyalties, he resigned his commission and entered private life. He died on 23 October 1887 in Philadelphia.

U.S. Pattern of 1841 Artillery

The United States fought the Mexican War, as well as various early actions against the Indians, with Mordecai's 1841 System, which, by

1844, had standardized U.S. ordnance to a remarkable degree. The system incorporated earlier proven pieces as well as new types that were developed on or shortly after that date. The practice of designating very limited production prototypes by their year of casting at times suggests a move away from standardization, but these pieces usually corresponded closely in size and performance with regular production models. Although in many cases obsolete, Pattern of 1841 ordnance also saw service with Federal forces during the early stages of the Civil War and in some cases with the Confederate Army until the war's end.

In light of its obvious superiority, the Americans were surprisingly slow in abandoning Gribeauval's obsolete flask trail carriage for Congreve's stock or block trail design. Chief of Ordnance Decius Wadsworth was initially impressed by British examples captured during the War of 1812 and ordered test models made for trials. Although they performed well enough, the ordnance board held in 1818 (the same year that the notoriously flawed walking stick gun was approved) stubbornly rejected the design in favor of the older model. It was not until the French themselves adopted the block trail as part of their Valee System in 1827 that the Americans seriously began to reconsider their own position. In 1829, U.S. designers began fabricating stock trail prototypes from drawings of French examples provided by Lieutenant Daniel Tyler. Prodded by such proponents as Alfred Mordecai, Secretary of War Lewis Cass eventually approved its adoption in 1836, yet complications and bureaucratic delays kept the stock trail carriage from officially entering service until 1840.

The basic stock trail carriage, known as the No. 1 6-pounder gun carriage, weighed 900 pounds and was applied to the 6-pounder gun and the 12-pounder howitzer, the two most widely used field pieces. There was also a larger No. 2 24-pounder howitzer carriage weighing 1,128 pounds, as well as a rarely used 1,175-pound No. 3 carriage for the 12-pounder gun and 32-pounder howitzer. Gun carriage construction was carried out by the Watervliet Arsenal near Troy, New York; the Allegheny Arsenal in Pittsburgh, Pennsylvania; and the Washington Arsenal, in Washington, D.C.

Artillery rolling stock used the same size wheels as the cannon carriages, thus minimizing problems with interchangeability. The simple two-wheeled limber was the basic towing vehicle and mounted a pintle on the rear for the attachment of cannons, caissons, battery wagons, and forges. A limber pole for attaching the horse team was bolted to the front, under which was slung a wood pole prop and a tar bucket containing grease for lubricating the wheel hubs. The limber itself weighed 695 pounds unloaded, and although designed for a six-horse team, it could be drawn by four if necessary. During action the limber was parked some yards behind the piece to supply a ready source of ammunition.

The limber also carried a single removable ammunition chest weighing 185 pounds empty and almost 560 pounds full. An iron handle was bolted to each side, and it was topped with a copper covered lid to which were strapped two canvas water buckets and a tarpaulin. A printed range table was generally pasted to the interior of the lid. The chest could hold fifty rounds of 6-pounder or thirty-two rounds of 12-pounder ammunition. It also contained two extra powder cartridges, primers, and other assorted equipment. The top of the chest provided rather precarious and exceedingly uncomfortable seating for three crewmen, the two outside men gripping the handles while interlocking arms with the center man.

The limber-drawn, two-wheeled caisson carried two ammunition chests, an ax, pick, shovel, and a spare wheel and limber pole. Fully loaded, it weighed almost 2 tons. The combination of the caisson, its limber, and that of the piece would have provided each crew with four ammunition boxes for immediate use in the field—200 rounds of 6-pounder and 128 of 12-pounder. Caissons were generally parked in the safest position possible behind the battery during action and were used to replenish the ammunition in the piece's limber chest.

Each battery was assigned one limber-drawn, two-wheeled battery wagon. Essentially a long wooden chest, it was covered with a rounded lid and mounted a forage rack on its rear for extra horse fodder. It carried various supplies and tools to maintain and repair harness and other equipment. Fully loaded with spare harnesses, paint, tools, and lubricants, it weighed some 1,289 pounds. Rather than ammunition, the battery wagon limber carried smaller tools used for carriage and harness repair.

A two-wheeled limber-drawn forge also accompanied each battery. It consisted of a compact bellows and firebox and space to transport coal, an anvil, 250 pounds of extra iron stock, and 100 pounds of horse shoes. A vise was bolted to the forward stock ahead of the bellows. Rather than ammunition, the forge's limber box contained blacksmith tools, replacement iron components, 200 pounds of horseshoes, and fifty pounds of nails.

U.S. Pattern of 1841 Field Artillery
Guns and Howitzers

Pattern of 1841 field pieces were of bronze and, with the exception of the 12-pounder mountain howitzer, mounted on the new stock trail carriage. The most used of the pattern of 1841 series, the 6-pounder field gun, was mounted on the No. 1 carriage and was capable of firing solid shot, shell, and canister. As a gun it was a flat-trajectory weapon that saw extensive service in the Mexican War and the early months of the Civil War. It remained standard until the introduction of the heavier and more versatile Pattern of 1857 Napoleon gun-howitzer and rifled weapons in the early 1860s.

Three bronze 6-pounders entered Federal service after the decision to return to bronze and before the adoption of the Pattern of 1841. The Pattern of 1835 was the first of these transitional pieces, with fifty-seven manufactured by Cyrus Alger and N. P. Ames. The two founders then reduced the length of the first gun to manufacture the Pattern of 1838, which was then followed by the heavier Pattern of 1840, the final step in the evolution of the Pattern of 1841.

The pattern of 1841 barrel tube had a 3.67-inch bore, was 65.6 inches long, and weighed 884 pounds. Some 817 Pattern of 1841 6-pounder guns were manufactured for the U.S. Army by a number of contractors. Of those, the majority—540 guns—were cast by Ames Manufacturing Co. of Chicopee, Massachusetts, and were usually marked on the trunnion end *N.P. Ames, Founder, Springfield, Mass*, with the date of manufacture. Other makers included Cyrus Alger and Co. of Boston; Marshall and Co. of St Louis, Missouri; Henry N. Hooper and Co. of Boston; and the Revere Copper Co.

The Cyrus Alger Foundry also cast a very limited number of smaller-scaled 6-pounders for use by Southern military schools. The Virginia Military Institute received four in 1848, The Arkansas Military Institute two in 1851, and the Georgia Military Institute four in 1852. Mounted on red painted carriages, the Virginia Military Institute guns were named Matthew, Mark, Luke, and John. The Rockbridge Artillery took over the "Four Apostles" at the beginning of the Civil War, and they were eventually used in the defenses of Richmond, where they were captured by Federal forces when the city fell in 1865.

The U.S. Pattern of
1841 12-Pounder Gun

Another flat-trajectory piece, the Pattern of 1841 12-pounder gun saw much more limited production than either the 6-pounder gun or 12-pounder howitzer. It was eventually replaced by the lighter and more versatile Pattern of 1857 Napoleon gun-howitzer. The pattern of 1841 was preceded in Federal service by several heavy

12-pounders and was based directly on the heavy Pattern of 1835, differing only in the smaller-diameter rimbases of the latter model. The Pattern of 1841 12-pounder shared the same basic lines as the Pattern of 1841 6-pounder and was cast with dolphins, a rather obsolete feature not shared with the smaller piece. It was mounted on the No. 3 stock trail carriage.

The versatile and mobile Pattern of 1841 12-pounder howitzer was designed to fire a heavier, explosive shell at a higher trajectory than the 6-pounder gun. It shared the same No. 1 block trail carriage and limber as the 6-pounder. It also saw considerable use during the Mexican War; owing to its slightly longer range, ability to fire canister, and greater lethality than the smaller 6-pounder gun, it saw extensive use by both sides throughout the Civil War.

Owing to their weight, the 24- and 32-pounder Pattern of 1841 howitzers saw much less service than the 12-pounder. Although sharing the same general profile as the smaller howitzer, they, as were the 12-pounder gun, were cast with dolphins. The 24-pounder was mounted on the No. 2 and the 32-pounder on the No.3 stock trail carriages. Despite its weight, some Confederate artillerists, such as the famed E. Porter Alexander, valued the 24-pounder howitzer as a field piece for the effectiveness of its heavy shells and 48-ball canister against infantry.

Firing the same ammunition as the conventional 12-pounder howitzer, the diminutive Pattern of 1841 12-pounder mountain howitzer was designed to combine maximum firepower with minimal weight. The first test models were based on a French design, but the early carriages proved too fragile for field use. After minor modifications to the gun tube and a complete redesign of the carriage, it was first adopted in 1836 and later designated as the Pattern of 1841.

The mountain howitzer was essentially a thin-walled, straight bronze tube interrupted with slight muzzle and breech rings, only 37 inches long and weighing a mere 220 pounds. It was mounted on a special carriage weighing 157 pounds not including its two 38-inch-diameter, 65-pound wheels. The carriage and tube could be drawn by a single horse or mule or easily dismantled to be carried by pack animals. Three horses were required for packing—one for the tube itself, another for the carriage and wheels, and a third for its ammunition boxes.

Owing to its limited range, the mountain howitzer was vulnerable to counterbattery fire and was thus not suitable for open engagements, such as those of the Eastern theater during the Civil War. Sometimes known by its gunners as the "bull pup," it was, however, ideal for the mountainous and wild terrain of the frontier and Mexico. It was used in the Mexican War and saw use in the Indian Wars well into the second half of the nineteenth century. Production records are somewhat incomplete, but some 114 mountain howitzer tubes were cast by Ames Manufacturing Co. of Chicopee, Massachusetts (Nathan P. Ames), and another 328 by Cyrus Alger and Co. of Boston for the federal government. Some states and various militia units apparently ordered mountain howitzers as well. During the Civil War, Tredegar Iron Works in Richmond, Virginia, cast a limited number for the Confederate government.

PRE–CIVIL WAR
U.S. SIEGE AND GARRISON ARTILLERY

Mordecai's 1841 system incorporated earlier proven artillery types and was, itself, later modified in 1844 as new weapons became available. With the exception of mortars, siege and garrison artillery was usually mounted on large, robust carriages similar to those of the field artillery.

Mortars

The bronze U.S. Pattern of 1838 24-pounder coehorn was the smallest of the U.S. mortars and was incorporated into the 1841 system. The federal government cast 279 coehorns, and they saw use in the Mexican War and the Civil War, with copies being cast by the Confederate government. The coehorn tube weighed 164 pounds, was 16.32 inches in length, and was cast with a muzzle ring and broad reinforcing band around its center. Its total weight with its 132-pound solid wooden bed was just under 300 pounds. Four iron handles were bolted to the bed, and, although two men could maneuver the piece, a four-man crew was most efficient. The standard projectile was a 17-pound explosive shell that required a half-pound charge to reach 1,200 yards at 45-degree elevation.

The larger mortars were cast in iron and, as with the 10-inch siege mortar, the 8-inch model required transportation to its firing position by a two-wheeled mortar wagon fitted with a winch. It was mounted on a cast iron bed and elevated by way of a wooden block. Records indicate that Cyrus Alger, Fort Pitt, and West Point cast some forty-one Pattern of 1840 8-inch siege mortars for government use. The 10-inch Pattern of 1840 siege mortar was basically an enlarged 8-inch mortar, and ninety-eight were manufactured for the federal government by the Cyrus Alger, Fort Pitt, and West Point foundries.

The West Point Foundry also cast thirty-three 10-inch seacoast mortars between 1840 and the beginning of the Civil War. Production of 12- and 13-inch models was apparently very low, with possibly no more than one each being made for testing purposes. The 10- and 13-inch seacoast mortars were cast with their trunnions centered along the barrel rather than at the base and made use of Rodman's cooling process during casting. Both were cast with two vents, the second serving as a spare and only partially drilled upon leaving the foundry. Only eight Pattern 1861 seacoast mortars were apparently cast. Firing the same 91-pound shell as the 10-inch siege mortars, they required a crew consisting of a gunner and four men. Other than minor markings and the army's "US" stamping and the navy's anchor, the two versions of the 1861 pattern 13-inch seacoast model were identical. About 162 13-inch mortars, each weighing 17,250 pounds, were cast at the Fort Pitt Foundry.

The 1861 13-inch seacoast mortar required up to 20 pounds of powder to fire its 204-pound shell, including its 7-pound bursting charge. Army crews were the same as for the 10-inch model. Navy mortars, however, were usually mounted on circular rotating beds for shipboard use and required a crew of eleven to load, fire, and rotate the bed to train it on targets. During the Civil War, Federal forces used four Pattern of 1861 13-inch mortars against Island No. 10 on the Mississippi and twelve against Fort Pulaski near Savannah, Georgia. The most famous of the 13-inchers, dubbed the *Dictator*, was mounted on a railroad flatcar, from which it fired into the city of Petersburg, Virginia. Aiming was accomplished by rolling the flatcar to various locations along a curved section of track.

Siege Guns

Only twenty Pattern of 1840 12-pounder siege guns were produced. The Pattern of 1845 was almost identical in appearance to the earlier model, with production for the federal government reaching around fifty-two. Richmond's Tredegar Iron Works also cast a limited number for Confederate use during the Civil War. The Pattern of 1839 24-pounder siege gun reached the size and weight limits for practical mobility and was the basis for the Patterns of 1840 and 1845. Both Pattern of 1840 and Pattern of 1845 tubes weighed 5,750 pounds, differing only in that the 1840 was cast with one reinforce and the 1845 with two. The earlier gun apparently had a very limited production, with about sixty-six Pattern of 1845 tubes cast by the Alger, Tredegar, and West Point foundries.

The 24-pounder's sheer weight demanded a special carriage and limber for efficient transportation. Although similar in appearance, the 24-pounder carriage was proportionately larger and heavier than the standard stock trail models. It also required a different limbering arrangement, dispensing with the carriage's lunette and instead utilizing a hole bored into the bottom of the trail. That, in turn, fit over a pintle mounted on top of the limber and was secured by a hook and chain. Using the same principle as the French Gribeauval System, the 24-pounder barrel was also repositioned for traveling, redistributing its weight and thus reducing the strain on the horse team.

Unlike the Gribeauval System, the 24-pounder carriage was not cut with an extra set of trunnion holes but instead used two large restraining bolts screwed into the rear of the cheeks. The trunnions thus rested against these traveling bolts, with the breech supported by a contoured wood block bolted to the trail. The elevating screw was also removed and remounted under the trail, where it was secured with a leather strap. The combined gun, carriage, and limber required a team of ten horses and five drivers.

Both the Patterns of 1840 and 1861 siege howitzers required a 4-pound charge to fire a shell weighing 46 pounds, including a 2-pound, 9-ounce bursting charge. The Columbia, Fort Pitt, West Point, and Tredegar foundries cast fifty Pattern of 1840 barrels before the adoption of the Pattern of 1861. Tredegar also apparently cast about twenty simplified examples of the 1840 model for the Confederacy during the Civil War. The Fort Pitt and Cyrus Alger foundries later manufactured 171 Pattern of 1861 pieces utilizing the hollow casting and Rodman cooling technique. The 1861 howitzers were cast without muzzle swells or reinforces.

SEACOAST ARTILLERY

Seacoast cannons made up the largest and most powerful artillery pieces and were designed for permanent installation in coastal fortifications. They were thus mounted on either barbette or casement carriages, the latter being of either front- or center-mounted pintle design. The sheer size of such pieces required large crews and slowed loading time. The smallest projectiles necessitated two men for loading, with larger shells and shot requiring heavy mechanical hoists. Ramming very often required two men to push powder charges and rounds down the bore. The major types of seacoast weapons from 1840 until the Civil War were iron smoothbore pieces and included heavy guns, the new, heavier columbiads, and heavy mortars.

Bellona, Columbia, and West Point foundries manufactured fifty Pattern of 1840 32-pounder seacoast guns between 1841 and 1843. These pieces were then superseded by the somewhat heavier Pattern of 1845, with Alger, Fort Pitt, Tredegar, and West Point manufacturing 182 barrels. Originally intended as limited production prototypes for the Pattern of 1840, one Pattern of 1839 42-pounder barrel was cast by the Columbia Foundry and another by West Point. For some reason the Bellona Foundry overran its production to twelve tubes for a total of fourteen. Other than the more sophisticated lathing and finishing of the later model, the Patterns of 1840 and 1845 42-pounder seacoast guns were virtually identical. Columbia and West Point foundries cast forty Pattern of 1840s between 1841 and 1845, and Alger, Bellona, Fort Pitt, Tredegar, and West Point completed 318 Pattern of 1845 barrels. Both Federal and Confederate arsenals rifled large numbers of both models during the Civil War. Confederate founders such as Tredegar also cast 42-pounders during the Civil War and, along with other foundries, reinforced a number with heavy breech bands.

Seacoast Howitzers and Columbiads

Seacoast artillery made rapid technological advances from the 1840s through the Civil War. Originally, Alfred Mordecai listed a relatively few types—the 32- and 42-pounder seacoast guns, 8- and 10-inch seacoast howitzers, and 8- and 10-inch seacoast mortars—in his System of 1841—all excellent weapons for the period. Yet these were soon superseded by a number of much more sophisticated heavy weapons that saw far-reaching impact on future artillery trends. The most significant progress made during the period occurred in the development of heavy-caliber, long-range shell guns.

The term "columbiad" was apparently originally used as a rather general term to describe any large U.S.-made seacoast artillery pieces. It then dropped out of general use between about 1820 and

Columbiad gun (Courtesy Art-Tech)

1840 before re-emerging two decades before the Civil War. At that time it became a specific term for large-caliber artillery capable of firing long-range shell as well as solid shot at a flat trajectory.

The evolution of such weapons had begun earlier in the century, with the early columbiads and some larger howitzers. The U.S. government experimented with heavy chambered seacoast howitzers during the late 1830s and early 1840s, yet those efforts soon gave way under Chief of Ordnance George Bomford, with the development of the new columbiads. Early models were chambered, as were howitzers, yet they were capable of firing shells at a high trajectory, as well as solid shot at a flat trajectory. Later model columbiads were bored without powder chambers. A further improvement included the incorporation of an elevation ratchet mechanism running vertically along the center of the tube's breech face. This gave the columbiad a possible elevation of 39 degrees, rather than the 15 degrees typical with conventional guns. As the columbiad's potential became increasingly obvious, seacoast howitzer development, although valuable in information gained, was discontinued. All large seacoast howitzers and columbiads were of iron.

An example of one of Bomford's later designs, known as the Bomford gun, was cast for the army by Cyrus Alger and Company of South Boston in 1846. Of 12-inch bore, the Bomford gun weighed 25,510 pounds and was capable of firing a 225-pound solid shot or 181-pound shell 3.5 miles.

The seacoast howitzers were manufactured with chambered bores and designed to fire only spherical explosive shell at an arcing trajectory. Production of the first of the seacoast howitzers, the Pattern of 1839, numbered fifty-nine; it was followed the next year by the nearly identical Pattern of 1840. The Pattern of 1840 had a slightly smaller muzzle swell, and production totaled sixty-four pieces. Following the production of three experimental heavy 10-inch seacoast howitzers in 1839, the government officially adopted and received ten Pattern of 1840 10-inch seacoast howitzers. These were then followed by the last of the seacoast howitzers, the 8- and 10-inch Patterns of 1842. Thirteen 8-inch tubes were manufactured, and seven of the larger model. The two were similar in appearance, with the 8-inch model exhibiting a noticeably more streamlined profile.

The first new-style columbiads were of a transitional design, with a chambered bore; unlike later models, they fired only spherical shell. The 8-inch version's tube weighed 9,200 pounds, and production totaled 315. The tubes of the 159 10-inch Pattern of 1844s weighed 15,400 pounds. As with many large iron guns seized in Southern forts, a number of columbiads were rifled by the Confederates during the Civil War.

Intended to protect the land approaches to fortifications, the Pattern of 1844 flank howitzer used a 2-pound charge to fire a 21-pound canister round or a 17-pound shell, including its 12-ounce bursting charge. Seven major foundries cast 577 24-pounder flank howitzers, with additional tubes cast without reinforces by Tredegar for the Confederacy.

ARTILLERY IN THE MEXICAN WAR

Upon its independence in 1821, Mexico was initially relatively well supplied with Spanish artillery that followed the basic Gribeauval pattern. By 1846 its arsenal included some 150 field guns, including 4-, 6-, 8-, and 12-pounders, as well as a number of British iron 24- and 32-pounder garrison guns and some Congreve rockets. Although these pieces were reasonably up to date and their crews well trained, Mexican artillery suffered from issues of poor-quality ammunition that was both undependable and of low power. In addition to these deficiencies, the guns themselves tended to be heavier than U.S. pieces and their older carriages less maneuverable. Mexican horses also tended to be less robust than their U.S. counterparts, thus giving U.S. artillery batteries a distinct advantage in mobility during the war.

During the Mexican War, the United States held a distinct advantage in field artillery weapons and tactics. Whereas Mexico was forced to field ponderous, obsolete pieces and lacked both horse and mounted artillery, the United States had recently modernized with the 1844 system and boasted a number of innovative artillerists. The use of fully mounted artillery batteries had been pioneered in Europe years earlier yet was—for the Americans—the most far-reaching field artillery development to come from the war.

During most of the first quarter of the century, U.S. artillery was organized into four regiments, each composed of ten companies. Deployment was slow: their guns and rolling stock often pulled by mules or oxen, crews walked beside their pieces. In September 1830, Secretary of War Joel R. Poinsett cited the 1821 Army Reorganization Act in ordering that one company in each regiment be reorganized as light artillery. Such light artillery companies were to use faster horses rather than the plodding mules and oxen, with the gun crews mounted or riding the limbers and caissons.

Captain Samuel Ringgold assumed command of the first horse artillery unit in the United States, Company C, 3rd Artillery. Company C received the latest bronze 6-pounder guns, and, as every crewman was mounted, the company soon received the designation of "flying artillery" for its speed in the field. Ringgold's company was followed by Company K, 1st Artillery, commanded by Captain Francis Taylor; Company A, 2nd Artillery, under Lieutenant James Duncan; and Captain John Washington's Company B, 4th Artillery. As the crews of the latter three companies usually walked beside their pieces and rode the caissons and limbers only during fast maneuvers, they were designated "mounted artillery," rather than horse or flying artillery. Shortly before the war began, Captain Braxton Bragg's Company E, 3rd United States Artillery, also received the new 6-pounders, thus raising the light field artillery to five companies. Moving rapidly on the field and firing eight times to the Mexicans' one, U.S. field artillery proved key to such victories as those at Palo Alto and Buena Vista. Lessons learned during the war would also make the battlefields of the Civil War much bloodier.

The main duties of the U.S. Navy during the Mexican War consisted of assisting and protecting the transport of men and supplies and blockading Mexican territory. In March 1845, Secretary of the Navy George Bancroft ordered the organization of a board to examine current shipboard armaments and make recommendations for improving naval ordnance. At the beginning of the Mexican War, U.S. naval artillery was thus undergoing a transitional period from the use of primarily broadside battery smoothbores to more modern guns and battery systems. Although the new ordnance program dictated the use of mixed batteries of 32-pounder shot guns of various weights and 8- and 10-inch shell guns utilizing pivot mounts, many U.S. ships still mounted older weapons.

Long neglected by its various regimes, Mexico's navy was even less prepared for war. Most Mexican vessels were outdated and in poor repair, with most ships' batteries made up of 12- and 24-pounders and only a very few 32-pounders. To make matters worse, the country was forced to return its two most powerful warships, the steam frigates *Guadalupe* and the *Moctezuma*, to Britain shortly before the war began. The U.S. Navy thus dominated deepwater naval operations throughout the war. The greatest challenge to the navy centered on operations in the shallow waters of Mexico's rivers and along its coast.

Those operations made obvious the need for lighter weapons capable of suppressing shore opposition and in covering amphibious landing operations. Lacking such pieces naval officers improvised, using outdated carronades, as well as pressing 6- and 12-pounder field pieces into naval service. Lessons learned during the war eventually led to Dahlgren's innovative boat howitzer, a lightweight weapon easily adapted to shallow draft vessels as well as to land use.

ARTILLERY OF
THE AMERICAN CIVIL WAR

The battery was the basic field artillery unit during the Civil War. Although there were many variations owing to such factors as casualties and supply concerns, the standard Federal battery consisted of six pieces and their crews, whereas Southern batteries usually fielded four cannons. Batteries, generally commanded by a captain, were further subdivided into two-piece sections commanded by lieutenants. A single cannon, its limber, and caisson, along with its crew

Parrott Rifle seacoast battery (Courtesy Art-Tech)

and drivers, made up a platoon under two corporals and a sergeant known as the "chief of the piece."

Each crewman was assigned a number indicating his specific task, with most being cross-trained to perform multiple duties to compensate for casualties—a very real threat, owing to the long-range accuracy of the infantry's recently introduced rifled muskets. Equipped with a sponge-rammer at the right of the muzzle, Number 1 crewman sponged the piece to remove any residual sparks from the bore and then rammed the projectile and charge home. On the left of the muzzle, Number 2 used a worm to clear any obstructions from the bore and also placed the charge and projectile in the muzzle in preparation to ramming. During these procedures the Number 3, stationed to the right of the breech, "stopped" or covered the vent with his leather thumbstall-protected thumb and then pierced the powder bag by ramming a vent pick down the vent. Number 4, at the left of the breech, finally inserted a friction primer attached to his lanyard into the vent that he then pulled at the direction of the gunner. The gunner, usually a corporal, was responsible for aiming the piece and determining the range.

Other crewmen included the Number 5, who carried the ammunition from the limber to the piece; Number 6, who was in charge of the limber and who adjusted fuses; and the Number 7, who handed the rounds to the Number 5. After each discharge the crew manhandled the piece back into position, as typical recoil was about 3 to 4 feet. The loading and firing sequence was choreographed so that each crewman performed his duty simultaneously, to provide the fastest, most accurate fire possible.

Owing to the efforts of Mordecai and other dedicated ordnance officers, U.S. artillery development made numerous advances during the 1840s and 1850s. These advances were somewhat slowed, however, by the small peacetime army's lack of funding, the traditional conservatism of the military bureaucracy, and various other political and fiscal issues. Many of these impediments soon gave way with the inevitability of war. The American Civil War saw the final refinement of muzzleloaded, smoothbore artillery, as well as the introduction of modern rifled guns on a wide scale. Inventors, motivated by both patriotism and profit, also experimented with new cannon manufacturing techniques and types of ammunition. Ultimately, these developments established the foundations for U.S. artillery for the rest of the century.

U.S. and Confederate forces entered the war with what weapons were immediately at hand. The first shot fired at Fort Sumter during the early hours of 12 April 1861 was quite possibly fired by a 10-inch seacoast mortar cast by Henry Foxhall in the century's first decade. Other obsolete weapons, such as the Pattern of 1841 6-pounder, also saw use during the first stages of the war but proved outmoded when faced with such modern weapons as the new rifled guns. Whereas the 6-pounder was pulled from frontline Federal batteries in the East after a few months of fighting, it remained in some Confederate units and Western Federal units until the war's end. Still, the hard-strapped Confederates also managed to field some of the most modern weapons of the day, whether locally manufactured, captured, or imported from Europe.

The wide availability of advanced cannon designs inevitably sparked a debate among artillerists concerning the relative merits of smoothbore and rifled field guns. Conventional wisdom generally held that such pieces as the 12-pounder Napoleon gun-howitzer was the ideal weapon for field use. This view held—quite rightly—that 12-pounder smoothbores accepting fixed ammunition were faster to load than the rifled pieces, which required "semifixed" rounds with separate powder bags. The 12-pounder also fired a larger, more destructive projectile than the usual 10-pounder rifles, and their spherical shot could be ricocheted across hard ground with great effect.

Moreover, none could contest the 12-pounder's superiority as a close-range antipersonnel weapon. During the Civil War the 12-pounder Napoleon repeatedly proved its deadliness as a giant shot-gun when loaded with single and even double canister.

Although less effective at close range and as a ricochet fire weapon (the pointed projectiles of rifles tending to bury themselves harm-lessly in soft ground), the new rifled guns were unmatched for long-range accuracy. During the Civil War artillery commanders on both sides often arrived at the logical compromise by distributing both ri-fles and smoothbores in the field to exploit the advantages of both types of weapons.

Both the Union and Confederate armies were well served by tal-ented artillery officers. Union brigadier general Henry Jackson Hunt (1819–1889), chief of artillery of the Army of the Potomac, vigor-ously promoted the independence of artillery as a separate arm, equal to the cavalry and infantry. A West Point graduate, Hunt dis-tinguished himself in the Mexican War and was a coauthor of the 1858 *Field Artillery Manual*. During the Civil War he displayed re-markable organizational and technical expertise and advocated accu-rate, massed concentrated fire against specific targets. His use of methodical counterbattery fire against Confederate positions proved particularly effective. At Gettysburg, Hunt again proved his bravery at the climax of the Picket/Pettigrew Charge by defending the guns in the center of the Union line with his revolver until his horse was shot from under him.

As chief of artillery to the Army of Northern Virginia, Hunt's Southern counterpart, Brigadier General William Nelson Pendleton (1808–1883), served competently throughout the war. Colonel Ed-ward Porter Alexander (1835–1910), chief of artillery of Longstreet's I Corps, also played a major role in the Confederate victories at Fred-ericksburg and Chancellorsville. He directed the Confederate barrage preceding the Picket/Pettigrew Charge at Gettysburg and, promoted to brigadier general, served at Spotsylvania, Cold Harbor, and Peters-burg; he was also present at Appomattox. Both Pendleton and Alexan-der were overshadowed in the popular imagination by the brief career of the "boy major," John Pelham (1838–1863). Pelham left West Point to enter Confederate service at the beginning of the war and quickly won a reputation as a skilled and aggressive artillerist. As cap-tain he served as head of General J. E. B. Stuart's Horse Artillery; later, as major, he commanded the Horse Artillery Battalion, Cavalry Division, Army of Northern Virginia. Such exploits as Pelham's duel with one gun against twenty-four Federal pieces at Fredericksburg won him the personal admiration of General Robert E. Lee. The "Gallant Pelham," as he was by then known, was killed in a cavalry action at Kelly's Ford on 17 March 1863.

Improvements in Ammunition, Primers, and Fuses

Appearing about the time of the Mexican War, the friction primer presented gunners with a much more reliable ignition mechanism than the earlier linstock. It consisted of a copper tube about 2 inches in length filled with rifle powder and sealed with wax at its lower end. A shorter tube containing a friction-sensitive compound was soldered at a right angle to its upper end, and a twisted, serrated wire passed through the upper tube and ended in a loop. The whole arrangement was coated with varnish or lacquer as a form of water-proofing. For firing, the Number Four crewman, standing to the left-rear of the piece, inserted the long end of the primer into the piece's vent and placed a hook on the end of his lanyard through the primer's wire loop. A steady pull on the lanyard then dragged the rough wire through the friction composition, igniting it and sending flame through the main tube down to the piece's main powder charge. The new friction primer immediately gained popularity for its simplicity in use, reliability, and resistance to moisture.

Other than minor improvements, the basic smoothbore projectiles of the Civil War—solid shot, shell, grape shot, and canister—remained relatively unchanged from those of the Mexican War. Of those, the explosive projectiles, such as case shot and common shell, required fuses in order to detonate. The simplest form of fuse consisted of gunpowder bound with gum arabic and contained in approximately 2-inch-long tapered tubes made of thick paper. The paper fuses were color coded and stenciled with their burning time in seconds. Shells were fitted with either hammered-in wooden or screw-in brass or copper fuse plugs drilled with a tapered hole to hold the fuse firmly in place. In preparation to firing, a crewman stationed at the limber selected an appropriately timed fuse and inserted it into the fuse plug. The ignition of the piece would light the fuse, and it would then—in a best-case scenario—explode over the enemy target. For the most part, paper time fuses were phased out early in the war by the North, whereas, owing to their simplicity, the Confederates used them throughout the conflict.

The U.S. government adopted the Bormann fuse in the early 1850s. Invented by a Belgian artillery captain, Charles G. Bormann (1796–1873), the Bormann fuse was the most successful time fuse used during the Civil War. It consisted of a threaded zinc or pewter disk 0.5 inch thick and about 1.5 inches in diameter that screwed into a corresponding hole in the shell. A curving U-shaped channel cast into the interior of the fuse contained a trail of mealed powder that ended in a hole in the disk's base leading to the shell's main bursting charge. Raised marks on the face of the fuse were graduated up to 5.5 seconds, allowing for accurate time setting. To set the fuse, a crewman punched a hole in the fuse face at the appropriate setting with a special tool, thus allowing the piece's ignition to fire the powder trail. Both the Union and the Confederacy used Bormann fuses in spherical shells and, in rare cases, in rifled projectiles. Confederate-manufactured examples were predictably less reliable than their Northern counterparts.

In an effort to develop fuses capable of detonating on impact, numerous domestic inventors patented various types of percussion fuses. Charles James, inventor of the canons and projectiles that bore his name, also patented an early percussion fuse. The James fuse made use of a free-floating internal metal striker incorporating a nipple and percussion cap. Upon firing the forward movement of the projectile kept the striker to the rear of the fuse, whereas impact caused it to fly violently forward, firing the percussion cap against the brass "anvil" in the fuse's nose. The James fuse worked reasonably well under ideal circumstances, yet it was dangerously sensitive and could detonate prematurely from rough handling and during loading. This tendency was grimly highlighted in 1862, when James was accidentally killed when a shell detonated during a demonstration of his patents.

Despite some improvements to James's design, other percussion fuses proved much more reliable and safer to the gunners using them. Andrew Hotchkiss and his brother Benjamin patented a number of shells and fuses that proved very effective during the war, as did John P. Schenkl of Boston and Robert P. Parrott. All such improved fuses incorporated various devices, such as wires or screws, that held the striker in place before being sheared off upon impact.

The war sparked an unprecedented leap in the development of projectiles needed for the various types of rifled guns that proliferated during the period. In 1852, Captain Boxer of the British Royal Arsenal at Woolwich had furthered Shrapnel's explosive shell principle by fusing cylindrical rifle projectiles, and the idea was quickly applied in the United States. Dozens of projectile patents were registered in both the South and North and saw various degrees of use. Named for their inventors, these included Absterdam, Archer, Brooke, Braun, Burton, Dahlgren, Dyer, Ellsworth, Harding, Hotchkiss, James, Mullane, Read, Parrott, Sawyer, Schenkl, and Wiard projectiles. Although fusing and construction were key to such patents' claims, sabot design was very often their distinguishing feature.

Rifled artillery sabots performed a distinctly different role from that of smoothbore guns and howitzers. Smoothbore artillery projectiles were normally fitted with a wooden sabot to which the powder bag was tied to create a one-piece "fixed" cartridge. Their purpose accomplished, upon firing such wooden sabots usually disintegrated when leaving the muzzle. In contrast, the sabots of rifle projectiles were designed to grip the bore's rifling, to impart the stabilizing spin needed for accuracy and range. The two problems facing sabot designers were to create a sabot that would slide easily down the bore during loading yet would expand sufficiently to engage the rifling.

Robert Parrott first addressed the issue by incorporating a thin iron ring around his projectile's base, but he found that iron lacked the necessary flexibility and later turned to softer brass sabots. Other inventors used zinc and copper sabots with various success. Although soft, lead often created problems in that it tended to peal off the projectile upon firing, creating a hazard when firing over the heads of friendly infantry. The Hotchkiss-patent projectiles were the most successful of the lead saboted designs. Hotchkiss bolts and shells consisted of a main body connected to a lower base cup by a lead "driving band" sabot. Upon firing, the base cup slammed against the lead band, thus driving it into the bore's grooves. Hotchkiss projectiles worked particularly well in the 3-inch Ordnance Rifle, yet the rifling in Parrott guns tended to twist the sabot away after the round cleared the muzzle. The papier-mache Schenkl sabot avoided any such danger, as it disintegrated completely. It was, however, susceptible to moisture, as it would swell and not fit the muzzle when wet.

The Hale Rocket

In 1844, William Hale (1797–1870), an English civil engineer, patented an improved war rocket that was manufactured under license in the United States and saw limited service in the Mexican War and the Civil War. Two sizes were apparently used: 2.25-inch-diameter

6-pounders and 3.25-inch-diameter 16-pounders. Rather than using the unwieldy stabilizing stick of the earlier Congreve rockets, Hale originally incorporated angled vents or curved metal vanes around the main exhaust nozzle that imparted a stabilizing spin to the rocket's flight. Later designs employed a number of vents around the base of the rocket's nose section. The body was made of rolled sheet iron, and the fuel consisted of a compressed mixture of niter, sulfur, and charcoal, with the warhead being either solid, case shot, or incendiary. The launcher was an open-ended metal trough or tube supported by two metal legs. Hale rockets were fielded by both the Union and Confederate forces but were found to be largely ineffective.

CIVIL WAR FIELD ARTILLERY
The Napoleon

The Pattern of 1857 12-pounder Napoleon gun-howitzer was one of the most versatile and popular field pieces used during the Civil War. Based on a French design credited to Emperor Napoleon III, the bronze Pattern of 1857 was intended to replace the Pattern of 1841–1844 6-pounder gun and 12-pounder gun and howitzer. Although technically a gun, owing to its ability to fire canister and solid shot, the Napoleon was often referred to as a gun-howitzer for its ability also to fire explosive shell.

American Napoleon production began slowly. The first prototype, 3 inches shorter than subsequent pieces, was cast by the Ames foundry in 1857 and was eventually followed after some minor design improvements by another five tubes. These later five guns remained the only Napoleons in Federal service until production began in earnest in 1861. Four were assigned to Battery M, 2nd U.S. Artillery, commanded by Captain Henry Hunt at Fort Leavenworth, Kansas. Hunt's four pieces were later the only Napoleons fielded at First Manassas, and his skillful use of the new 12-pounders proved critical in covering the Union army's retreat.

Early U.S. Napoleons closely followed the French model, and the roughly twenty-nine cast before 1861 shared the dolphins of the earlier Pattern of 1841–1844 12-pounders. The new weapons were shorter and somewhat more than 500 pounds lighter than the earlier 12-pounders, factors making them much easier for gunners to handle in the field. Its 66-inch bronze tube was bored to 4.62 inches

1857 6-pounder Napoleon gun-howitzer (Courtesy Art-Tech)

and weighed 1,227 pounds. Loaded with a 2.5-pound charge the Napoleon could fire a 12.3-pound solid shot 1,619 yards. It was particularly prized for its ability to fire canister rounds packed with twenty-seven iron balls—a particularly lethal antipersonnel loading, especially when doubled at very close ranges.

During the Civil War the North produced some 1,156 Napoleons, with possibly as many as 630 being cast by Southern foundries. Such foundries as Alger, Ames, Revere, Henry N. Hooper, and Greenwood carried out Federal production. Napoleons cast by Alger, Ames, Hooper, and Revere exhibit a small flat area at the top of the breech for the attachment of a pendulum hausse sight, whereas the sights of Greenwood pieces were apparently screwed to the breech. The Phoenix Iron Company manufactured a possibly unique and experimental wrought iron Napoleon.

Owing to shortages of copper, Confederate manufacturers cast Napoleons of varying quality in both bronze and iron. The firm of

Leeds and Co. of New Orleans cast about twenty, and Quinby and Robinson of Memphis an unknown number of bronze Napoleons similar to the Federal guns. The more common Confederate Napoleons were cast without a muzzle swell and thus exhibit a sleeker profile than their Northern counterparts. Approximate production numbers suggest that Tredegar cast some 122 tubes, Augusta 100, Macon 60, Columbus 55, and Charleston possibly 10.

Following the loss of the Ducktown and other copper mining areas to Federal forces, Confederate founders began manufacturing cast iron 12-pounder "Napoleons." Such cast iron pieces were actually Napoleons in caliber, length, and name only. With their cast iron tubes and wrought iron reinforcing bands, they most closely resembled Parrott rifles. Tredegar manufactured some 121 cast iron Napoleons during the war, and in general they were well received by the gunners who used them. Some gunners actually declared the cast iron pieces superior, as they did not produce the ear-splitting ringing sound upon firing that was often so painful to crews of bronze pieces.

The Parrott Field Rifle

Between 1856 and 1859, Robert Parker Parrott and Dr. John Braham Read collaborated in developing what was to become the most used rifled field gun by either side during the Civil War. In 1849, Parrott, the superintendent of the West Point Iron and Cannon Foundry of Cold Spring, New York, became interested in rifled guns after the successes of Krupp in Germany. In the following years he applied his own skills to designing an American rifled gun and eventually joined with the Alabamian Read, who had an interest in designing the appropriate projectiles. Their joint venture proved successful, with both men receiving various federal patents; yet, with secession, Read sided with his native state and returned home. Parrott continued to manufacture his rifles and their ammunition in various calibers throughout the war, whereas Read aided the Southern cause by designing projectiles.

Parrott's design incorporated a cast iron gun tube strengthened at the breech by a broad wrought iron reinforcing band. During the manufacturing process the tube was cooled with water as the band was heated and then heat shrunk to the barrel as it expanded. The final result produced a relatively lightweight, economical gun and gave the Parrott rifle its distinctive profile. The Parrott rifle was not, however, without its defects. Although immensely strong at its breech, the

10-pounder Parrott rifle (Courtesy Art-Tech)

brittle cast iron forward of its reinforcing band was prone to burst, especially in larger caliber pieces. Nevertheless, its low cost and ease of manufacture dictated its land and naval use throughout the war, with almost 2,000 guns accepted by the federal government, as well as numerous pieces manufactured by Confederate foundries.

The first of the Parrott field rifles, the 2.9-inch Army Pattern of 1861 10-pounder, was eventually superseded by the 3-inch Pattern of 1863, which appeared in the latter part of that year and was cast without the earlier pattern's muzzle swell. The primary impetus for the change in caliber was to allow more interchangeability in ammunition between Parrotts and other rifled guns then in service. Although the Pattern of 1863 was capable of firing Pattern of 1861 ammunition, the reverse was not possible—a drawback apparently considered acceptable under the circumstances. The highly accurate 3-inch Parrott achieved a range of about 1,900 yards. The federal government purchased more than 500 Parrott 10-pounders during the war, with others going to various state units.

Confederate foundries including Tredegar also manufactured both 2.9-inch and 3-inch Parrott rifles. Southern Parrotts were somewhat longer and heavier than Northern guns and were also distinguished by a longer reinforcing band, often beveled on its leading edge.

As with the 10-pounder guns, early 3.67-inch, 20-pounder Parrotts were cast with a muzzle swell, that feature being omitted on later pieces. With a range of 1,900 yards, they were mounted on the #3 stock trail carriage. Federal purchases for both the army and navy totaled 507 pieces. Confederate 20-pounders were essentially identical to the Northern models, other than their longer and heavier band giving a somewhat greater total weight.

The Ordnance Rifle

Often incorrectly referred to in contemporary accounts as a "Rodman" (possibly owing to a similarity in appearance to the larger gun), the 3-inch Ordnance Rifle was generally considered the finest rifled field piece of the Civil War. It was patented by John Griffen in 1855 and, following minor modifications by Samuel J. Reeves, of the Phoenix Iron Company in Phoenixville, Pennsylvania, was adopted by the Ordnance Department in 1861.

Most Ordnance Rifles were manufactured at the Phoenix Iron Works and proved instantly popular among the gunners who received them. Some 1,000 entered Federal service, and Ordnance Rifles made up possibly 41 percent of all Federal pieces at Gettysburg. Unlike the cast iron banded Parrott rifles, the 10-pounder Ordnance Rifle was constructed of tougher wrought iron, consisting of iron bands welded together around a mandrel and then lathed to a sleek, modern profile. It was then bored and rifled. The Ordnance Rifle achieved a maximum range of 1,830 yards.

A versatile piece, the Ordnance Rifle was usually loaded with Hotchkiss and Schenkl-patent projectiles but also accepted 3-inch Parrott ammunition. Confederate gunners also appreciated captured Ordnance Rifles and its Southern-made copies. They found that it was also effective firing Southern projectile designs, including Archer, Mullane, Read, and Read-Braun patents.

The James Rifle

A one-term U.S. senator and major-general in the Rhode Island State Militia, Charles Tillinghast James, patented a unique rifle projectile as well as rifling system and the cannon that bore his name. The James rifling method consisted of deeply cut lands and grooves that gained in their right-hand twist as they neared the muzzle. The rifling could be applied to existing smoothbores, such as the Pattern of 1841 6-pounder, or to the limited number of rifles designed by James. James also patented a special projectile for his guns that incorporated a cylindrical hollow base section cast with eight or ten lengthwise slanting slots. These were filled with lead, and the whole base section was then covered with a tin cover and greased canvas sheath. In theory, the pressure generated by the gun's firing pushed the lead outward in their slots to grip the bore's rifling.

The standard James rifle was a bronze, 3.67-inch bore 14-pounder cast by the Ames Manufacturing Company of Chicopee, Massachusetts, in 1861 and 1862. Other than its pronounced blade-style front sight, the James was very similar in appearance to the sleek lines of the 3-inch Ordnance Rifle. Although heavier iron smoothbores rebored with James rifling performed very well, the bronze 14-pounder failed to gain popularity. A number of factors led to the failure of the James. When new, the deeply cut rifling was difficult to clean, and sometimes smoldering powder bag remnants remained in the bore after sponging—a dangerous situation while loading. The James rifle's comparatively soft bronze construction also played a role in its rejection by the army. Repeated firings rapidly wore down the lands, thus making the pieces increasingly inaccurate and negating the accuracy vaunted by the system's inventor.

The James's final downfall lay in the design of its patented projectile. In early actions the James projectile quickly evidenced a tendency to fling off its soft lead sabot soon after leaving the gun's muzzle. These fragments proved very dangerous to friendly troops when artillery batteries fired over infantry in preparation for assaults. Despite a switch to better-performing Hotchkiss patent projectiles, the James never escaped its earlier reputation and was eventually phased out of service. Unfortunately, James's demise preceded that of his invention. During a demonstration of James projectiles and rifles on 16 October 1862, an ordnance worker accidentally set off a James shell while attempting to manipulate its fuse with a pair of pliers. The worker was killed immediately, and James, who was attempting to assist him, was mortally wounded and died the next day.

The Wiard Rifle

The army's superintendent of ordnance stores, Norman Wiard, patented a unique rifled gun and carriage that saw only limited service during the Civil War. Cast of low-carbon "semi steel" and lacking a cascabel knob, the Wiard Rifle presented a distinctly odd appearance, having a straight, tubular profile from its hemispherical breech to the trunnions where it tapered dramatically to the muzzle. The Wiard performed well, however, and its carriage allowed a greater elevation than standard mounts of the period. Wiard supervised the casting of both 6- and 10-pounder guns of his design at his Trenton, New Jersey, foundry.

CIVIL WAR SEACOAST ARTILLERY

The last of the Bomford-style columbiads, the Pattern of 1857 "New Columbiads," were bored without a powder chamber and were thus true guns. Ninety-four 8-inch models were cast, with only seven of the larger 10-inch model being produced. Unfortunately, new designs and manufacturing techniques introduced by Thomas Jackson Rodman (1815–1871) made the Pattern of 1857 seacoast artillery almost instantly obsolete. Although the earlier models remained in service—often in modified form—the new pieces were superior in every aspect.

Rodman Guns

At the forefront of artillery development, Thomas Jackson Rodman invented both a new technique making possible the casting of the largest cannons of the period as well as a much improved form of gunpowder. Rodman graduated seventh in the U.S. Military Academy class of 1841 and was commissioned a lieutenant in the Ordnance Department. As an ordnance officer, Rodman directed his interests in metallurgy and casting toward improving the current techniques used in making big guns. The 28 February 1844 explosion of the heavy shell gun *Peacemaker* illustrated the grave problems encountered in casting such large pieces. During a demonstration aboard the steam frigate USS *Princeton* near Washington, D.C., the giant gun exploded, wounding and killing a number of the crew and visiting dignitaries. Those killed included Captain Beverly Kennon, the chief of the Bureau of Construction, Equipment and Repair; Secretary of the Navy Thomas Gilmer; and Secretary of State Abel P. Upshur.

In that year Rodman began a series of studies and experiments in the casting of large pieces of iron ordnance. Through these efforts he identified the inconsistent cooling inherent to the casting

1861 Rodman (Courtesy Art-Tech)

methods as the source of failure of such guns as the *Peacemaker*. Contemporary practice relied on casting the barrel with a solid core, allowing it to cool from the outside in, and then drilling and polishing the bore. This procedure led to weaknesses within the iron, as well as internal air pockets and fissures—all imperfections that could lead to cracking or bursting during firing or even transport.

Rodman proposed to cast large gun tubes vertically, with a pipe running through the center through which water continuously flowed. This permitted a controlled cooling of the metal from the inside out, allowing each successive layer to harden and compress the inner layers. The core would then be removed and the bore polished in the final finishing. This new method, theorized Rodman, would reduce the tube's internal flaws and create a consistent density throughout the casting.

The army authorized Rodman to conduct tests that he performed at Knapp, Rudd and Company's Fort Pitt Foundry in Pittsburgh, casting twin guns, one in the old-style conventional method and the other in the new technique. During Rodman's intensive trials the new method proved consistently more efficient in withstanding huge internal pressures without bursting. In 1859 the War Department approved the production of the largest cannon ever cast to that date—a 15-inch columbiad christened the *Lincoln Gun* that was cast the next year at the Fort Pitt Foundry.

Rodman's new columbiad was as radical in its appearance as its casting method. Although it did incorporate the breech-elevating ratchet of the old models, it lacked reinforces and instead exhibited a smooth, wine bottle-shaped profile foretelling later cannon designs. Weighing a staggering 49,099 pounds, the tube was 4 feet across at its widest point and 15 feet, 10 inches in length. Successful tests were carried out at Fort Monroe, Virginia, in March 1861 with 450-pound solid round shot and 330-pound explosive shell.

Conventional cannons would have required longer barrels than the relatively short Rodman tube to fire such large projectiles. This was owing to the inefficient burning of the standard gunpowder's irregularly shaped powder granules. The powder granules' tendency to burn from the outside in created the highest pressure in the breech, but, as the lessening powder charge continued to burn, pressure decreased as the projectile moved down the bore. Rodman addressed the problem by inventing a gunpowder consisting of perforated hexagonal grains. His new powder made possible almost instantaneous burning that maintained a consistent bore pressure for the entire length of the bore during firing. The results were so impressive that the Rodman was adopted in several calibers for seacoast and fortress use as the Pattern of 1861. Early model Rodmans incorporated the breech-elevating ratchets of the standard columbiads with those cast after 21 February 1861 having recessed elevating indents.

The Fort Pitt and West Point foundries cast the first 65 8-inch Rodmans with the old-style elevating ratchets in 1861. These were followed by another 148 standard models cast by Fort Pitt and Seyfert, McManus and Company of Reading, Pennsylvania, between 1861 and 1865. Fort Pitt also began casting 10-inch Rodmans in 1861, with later production also carried out by Cyrus Alger and Co. of Boston and West Point, and Seyfert, McManus and Company. Between 1876 and 1887 the bores of 210 10-inch Rodmans were sleeved with either wrought iron or steel inserts and converted to 8-inch rifles. A truly massive weapon, his 15-inch columbiad was based on Rodman's original Lincoln Gun. Able to fire at a flat trajectory and at long range, it required a 40-pound charge to fire a 302-pound shell 1,518 yards. It could also reach as far as 4,680 yards at 25 degrees elevation with a 315-pound shell and 50-pound charge. In addition to the original prototype, Cyrus Alger, Fort Pitt, and Seyfert, McManus and Company manufactured 322 tubes between 1861 and 1871.

Although Rodman claimed that his casting method could produce guns of almost infinite size, only three 20-inch tubes—the largest of the Rodmans—were made. Fort Pitt cast only two for the federal government—the first on 11 February 1864 and another in 1869. A third was exported to Peru. Although Fort Pitt was one of the largest foundries in the world, the casting of 20-inch Rodman No. 1 pushed its capacities to its limits. Six furnaces were required to melt the 80 tons of iron needed for its specially designed four-piece mold, as well as new lathing equipment designed by Rodman. When finished, the 20-inch Rodman was just over 20 feet long and weighed 58 tons. It was then transported on a specially made railroad car amid great fanfare to guard New York Harbor at Fort Hamilton, where it was mounted on an 18-ton iron front pintle carriage.

On 25 October 1864 huge crowds lined the waterfront to witness the gun's initial test firing, yet they were disappointed when the pull of the lanyard failed to detonate the gun's charge. The charge was then extracted, and a man crawled down the gaping bore to inspect the vent and breech for obstructions. As both the vent and bore were found to be clear, the crew realized that the narrow 23-inch vent was simply too long for the standard heavy artillery friction primer's flame to travel. On the second firing attempt they filled the vent with priming powder, and the gun functioned perfectly.

Despite Rodman's success, his largest guns ultimately proved impractical. The firing rate was greatly slowed by the weight of the ammunition and the special equipment needed to load the huge projectiles, as well as by the sheer mass of the gun itself. Although incredibly intimidating, the 20-inch Rodmans never saw combat use.

Heavy Parrott Rifles

Parrott also manufactured heavy 4.2-inch 30-pounder, 5.3-inch 60-pounder, 6.4-inch 100-pounder, 8-inch 200-pounder, and 10-inch 300-pounder rifles at the West Point Foundry. Both the Union army and navy obtained the large Parrotts for siege, seacoast, and shipboard use, but the guns' basic design flaws were amplified by the use of heavy powder charges. Although later tests indicated that the guns' failures were due to bore fouling and improperly lubricated projectiles, the heavy Parrotts quickly gained a reputation for exploding with alarming frequency. The navy thus ultimately removed the heavier pieces from service for safety reasons. For land use, heavy Parrotts were usually mounted on cast iron barbette carriages, whereas they were often mounted on pivot carriages or in monitor turrets aboard ships.

The 30-pounder Parrotts continued the trend of early guns cast with muzzle swells with later guns exhibiting straight muzzles. Owing to its weight and caliber, the standard army 30-pounder was generally classified as a siege or garrison piece, although some did see field use. With its larger reinforcing band and longer barrel, the Confederate 30-pounder Parrotts were somewhat heavier; as they were copies of the early Federal models, all Southern-made 30-pounders retained the muzzle swell.

The navy's 30-pounder Parrott was more compact than its army cousin and was fitted with a breeching ring rather than a cascabel knob. It was served by a nine-man crew with a powder boy and achieved a range of 6,700 yards. The Federal navy also purchased 110 60-pounder Parrotts in 1864 and 1865, and they were successfully used against Fort Fisher near Wilmington, North Carolina. They required an eleven-man crew including a powder boy and a 6-pound charge to fire 50- and 60-pound shells.

With the first deliveries beginning in late 1861, the federal government eventually purchased 585 100-pounder Parrott rifles for use by both the army and the navy. Early tests proved that, loaded with a 10-pound charge, it attained a range of more than 5 miles. The more common loading during the war, however, consisted of a reduced powder charge of 8 pounds and an 80-pound shell. The 100-pounder Parrott was used as a seacoast and siege weapon by the army and as both a side and pivot gun by the navy. When used as a side gun aboard ships, it required a crew of sixteen in addition to a powder boy.

Called the 150-pounder by the navy and the 200-pounder by the army, the disparity in the 8-inch Parrott rifle's designation arose when the weight of the gun's original 200-pound projectile was reduced to 150 pounds—a change officially noted only by the navy. Some 178 were delivered to the federal government. For shipboard use, the 8-inch Parrott was typically mounted on a pivot mount; owing to the weight of the piece and its ammunition, it required a crew of twenty-five. They were also mounted in monitor turrets where at times they were paired with Dahlgren smoothbores.

Known as the "Swamp Angel," the best known Parrott was a Union army 200-pounder that shelled Charleston, South Carolina, with incendiary shells on 22 and 23 August 1863. The construction of the Swamp Angel's firing platform—some 7,900 yards from the city—was one of the greatest engineering feats of the war. The so-called Marsh Battery was constructed using log pilings in the swamp between Morris Island and James Island, and despite dire warnings from detractors it successfully supported the 16,500-pound gun and its 4-ton carriage. The "Angel" itself was less successful. After a number of shots its gunners realized that defective fuses had possibly caused some of the projectiles to detonate prematurely in the bore. Later checks revealed that the reinforcing band had jarred loose from the barrel. Undeterred, the gun's captain spliced two lanyards together and continued firing from outside the gun's earthworks—only to have it explode at the breech on the thirty-sixth round, injuring four crewmen. Despite such efforts, Charleston suffered little real damage from the Swamp Angel, and the gun itself was sold as scrap. It was later recovered by the city of Trenton, New Jersey, where it is now displayed.

Heavy Mortars

The new mortar patterns of 1861 exhibited smooth exterior lines without reinforces, and had trunnions cast along the barrel's centerline rather than at the base. During the manufacturing process, they were hollow-cast and utilized Rodman's water bore-cooling technique. In addition, elevation was no longer effected with a quoin but by way of graduated rectangular sockets cast into the barrel. Pattern of 1861 mortars were also cast with twin vents, the right vent only partially drilled, so as to be easily made ready when the first became eroded and was plugged.

Cyrus Alger, Fort Pitt, and Seyfert and McManus cast 170 8-inch, and the latter two foundries 150 10-inch, Pattern of 1861 siege mortars. The 8-inch mortar required up to 2 pounds of powder to fire a 45-pound shell loaded with a 1-pound, 12-ounce bursting charge; it was served by a gunner and two-man crew. The 10-inch model used as much as 4 pounds of powder to launch its 91-pound shell filled with 3 pounds of powder; it was served by a gunner assisted by a four-man crew. The shells for the two sizes of mortars were cast with two indentions, or "ears," on either side of the fuse hole to accommodate a pair of shell tongs for carrying and loading by two crewmen.

U.S. NAVAL ARTILLERY TRENDS
Naval Artillery

In 1845 the United States joined the major European powers in making the 32-pounder its standard heavy naval gun. The navy also found that the new friction primers being used by the army were not well suited for shipboard use. Upon firing, the primers' hot spent tubes were ejected from the vent with great force, creating a danger to the crews cramped in the confines of the gun decks, as well as a fire hazard on wooden ships. The navy subsequently adopted a tubular percussion primer consisting of a 2.5-inch-long bird feather quill containing a small explosive wafer. As the percussion primer was almost totally consumed upon firing, it eliminated the inherent danger of the friction primer aboard ship. Both Enoch Hidden and John Dahlgren patented hammer mechanisms in the early 1830s to detonate the new primers. Dahlgren's bronze hammer device proved especially effective when mounted on his 12-pounder boat howitzer.

In 1839 and 1840, Commodore Matthew Perry, under orders from Secretary of the Navy James Paulding, tested the new French Paixhans shell guns against current U.S. naval ordnance. The tests were carried out at Sandy Hook, where the Paixhans guns proved accurate and reliable, leading to their adoption the following year. Other tests resulted in a recommendation to reduce the windage of American guns to increase their accuracy, and that a rust-resistant coating be applied to solid shot—a necessary precaution, as reduced windage required more precisely fitting shot. Earlier, unprotected ammunition rusted and flaked heavily in the salt air during long cruises and required chipping with hammers before use. Although such projectiles gave satisfactory use in guns with ample windage, their deformities were unacceptable for the newer guns.

In the United States naval artillery did not become fully autonomous until 1862, when the Bureau of Ordnance was established. Its predecessor, the Bureau of Ordnance and Hydrography, was set up in 1842 during a general reorganization of the naval bureaucracy, and as such it oversaw the initial testing and adoption of U.S. shell guns. One of the more pressing concerns facing the bureau involved the manufacture of gun tubes capable of withstanding the immense internal pressures generated by their large powder charges.

Daniel Treadwell (1791–1872), a talented inventor and professor at Harvard University, presented one of the more ingenious solutions to building large guns. Professor Treadwell advocated the use of wrought iron, as it was less brittle and roughly twice as strong as cast iron. His "built up" design incorporated successive layers of wrought iron bars coiled and welded around a thin cast iron central tube. To add more strength, he later added layers of steel bars welded laterally and longitudinally to the matrix, to reduce further the risk of the tube's cracking or bursting.

Twenty Treadwell guns were manufactured and tested by the army and navy between 1841 and 1845. After extensive trials, the navy finally rejected them, owing to concerns with the reliability of their new welded construction. Although more favorable to the guns, the army also did not adopt them for service. Treadwell's basic design, however, was sound and was later used in the British Armstrong guns. For his part, the professor continued to expound on his invention in 1856 with the publication of *On the Practicability of Constructing a Cannon of Great Calibre,* followed in 1864 by *On the Construction of Hooped Cannon.*

The Peacemaker Disaster

The rush to push experimental cannon manufacturing techniques beyond the technical expertise of the period presented its own dangers. In January 1844 the first screw-propelled U.S. steam warship, the USS *Princeton,* docked in New York to receive its guns. This revolutionary ship was commanded by the aggressive proponent of innovation Captain Robert Stockton (1795–1866), who was eager to demonstrate the *Princeton*'s superior speed and weaponry. Stockton had overseen the ship's construction and had also played a key role in the development of its main armament—two huge 12-inch wrought iron shell guns. He had originally intended for the guns to be of identical design, yet his own impatience, international political tensions, and flawed inspection practices led to his taking on two very different pieces, one of which would trigger disaster the next month.

Although Stockton played a role in the construction of the *Princeton* and its guns, the actual designs were the handiwork of Swedish-born John Ericsson of later *Monitor* fame. As he considered no foundries in the United States capable of such a large project, Ericsson had the first gun, christened the *Orator,* cast in England at the Mersey Iron Works near Liverpool. The gun was delivered in 1841 to the United States, where it was tested at Sandy Hook. Proof firings, however, produced a number of small cracks along the *Orator*'s welds; rather than condemn the gun, however, Ericsson reinforced its breech by banding it with large heat-shrunk iron hoops. With a 13-foot-long unchambered bore, the reinforced *Orator* weighed 27,390 pounds and fired a solid 225-pound shot as well as shell.

Political disputes between the United States and Britain over the Canadian border led to chilled relations between the two nations and temporarily denied Ericsson and Stockton the use of the Mersey Iron Works. In response, the Americans rather spitefully renamed the *Orator* the *Oregon* and turned to Ward and Company of New York to cast the second gun domestically. Rather than reinforce the second gun by banding, Ericsson and Stockton modified the original design by adding more metal to its breech. The resulting piece, named the *Peacemaker,* thus weighed the same as its mate.

Whereas the *Oregon* had undergone intensive testing, the impatient Stockton dismissed Ericsson's objections and apparently test fired the *Peacemaker* only five times before certifying it as accurate and fully proofed. Both guns were then mounted on the *Princeton* on new, wrought iron carriages designed by Ericsson, with the *Peacemaker* in the bow position. After a series of trial runs near Washington, D.C., on 28 February 1844, some 350 dignitaries, including President John Tyler, and their families boarded the *Princeton* to witness its capabilities. The *Peacemaker* generated much excitement, and Stockton gloried in firing it for the assembled crowd. After a number of firings, however, the huge gun suddenly exploded, hurling a 2-ton section of breech as well as smaller fragments into the audience, killing and wounding a number of the crew as well as civilians. Among the eight dead were Secretary of State Abel P. Upshur and Secretary of the Navy Thomas Gilmer. President Tyler, who was elsewhere on the ship at the time, was uninjured, but Stockton himself was wounded in the blast.

The *Peacemaker* disaster sparked a predictable and vociferous debate over the use of such large wrought iron guns. Stockton, like Ericsson, denied any responsibility for the explosion and was ultimately cleared by a court marshal. Still, despite Stockton's objections, the *Oregon,* along with the wreckage of the *Peacemaker,* was removed from the *Princeton,* never to fire again. The incident did have some positive effects, however, in that it spurred efforts to re-examine and improve metal casting techniques and proofing procedures—techniques and procedures that were later successfully used by such designers as Thomas Rodman.

Dahlgren Guns

The most influential U.S. naval ordnance expert of the period, John Adolph Bernard Dahlgren (1809–1870), entered the U.S. Navy at the age of seventeen as a common seaman in 1826 and was commissioned a midshipman in 1842. Although he preferred sea duty, in January 1847 then Lieutenant Dahlgren was assigned to the Washington Navy Yard for ordnance service. Although Dahlgren's tireless self-promotion and cultivation of political officials made him unpopular with many of his fellow officers, he applied his considerable intellect to improving the navy's armaments by instituting scientific research and development techniques. A prolific writer, he published his findings and views in a number of works including *System of Boat Armament in the United States Navy: Reported to Commodore Charles Morris, Chief of Bureau of Ordnance and Hydrography* (1852); *Form of Exercise and Manuvre for the Boat-Howitzers of the U. S. Navy* (1852); *Ordnance Memoranda: Naval Percussion Locks and Primers, Particularly Those of the United States* (1853); *Shells and Shell Guns* (1856); and *A Few Hints to Captains of the New IX Inch Shell Guns* (1856).

Dahlgren's career accelerated upon the resignation of his superior, Captain Franklin Buchanan (1800–1874), as commandant of the Naval Yard to enter Confederate service. On 18 July 1862, Dahlgren became the chief of the Bureau of Ordnance; and, with the direct intervention of President Abraham Lincoln, on 7 February 1863 he was promoted to rear admiral. Over the span of his distinguished career, Dahlgren designed improved gun locks, primers, and sights, as well as an excellent boat howitzer. He gained his greatest fame by improving the navy's heavy ordnance with his invention of the large shell guns that bore his name. His final legacy, however, was somewhat marred by his insistence on the superiority of smoothbore muzzleloader artillery for naval use—a doctrine followed by the U.S. Navy long after European powers such as Britain and France had converted to rifled breechloaders.

Coastal operations during the Mexican War revealed the need for a light artillery piece suitable for supporting amphibious landings and shallow water actions. Shortly after the war Dahlgren developed two sizes of 12-pounder howitzer, as well as a 24-pounder for both shipboard and land use. These were chambered pieces that exhibited straight lines without muzzle swells and were cast with a single bottom loop similar to that of the carronade for attachment to their carriages. Production was carried out by the Washington Navy Yard, Cyrus Alger, and Charles T. Ames.

Dahlgren designed a special sliding boat carriage allowing a 120-degree traversal to be mounted in the bows of ship launches. This arrangement allowed the navy's small boats to support amphibious assaults and operations along rivers and estuaries. For land use, Dahlgren provided a unique wrought iron field carriage that was stored in the launch's stern sheets. Once landed, the howitzer tube could quickly and easily be transferred from the boat to the field carriage. As the howitzer's crew was not expected to use horses for transport, the field carriage also mounted a small wheel on its trail to help the crew drag it over difficult terrain. A well-trained crew using fixed ammunition was capable of as many as ten shots a minute using the field carriage, and about half that rate firing from the boat carriage.

Dahlgren's light and medium 12-pounder bronze howitzers shared a 4.62-inch bore and the same ammunition, with most crews preferring the heavier, more robust piece. Designed for sloops' launches, the light howitzer's tube weighed just 432 pounds, and the piece with boat carriage 600 pounds. Relatively few were cast between 1848 and 1870. The Washington Navy Yard manufactured 183 tubes during that period, with another two being made by Cyrus Alger.

The excellent medium—sometimes referred to as heavy—12-pounder boat howitzer was intended for frigates' launches and was the most popular of the boat howitzers. The tube weighed 760 pounds, and the combined weight of the tube mounted on the boat carriage totaled 1,200 pounds. The barrel length was 55 inches, and a maximum range of 1,085 yards could be achieved with a 1-pound charge. Between 1849 and 1865, Alger manufactured 57, the Washington Navy Yard 197, and Ames 202.

Dahlgren also designed a larger 24-pounder, 5.82-inch-bore boat howitzer utilizing a 2-pound charge for use on the launches of ships-of-the-line and frigates. The 24-pounder had a 1,310-pound tube and, mounted on its boat carriage, weighed a total of 2,000 pounds. While at the Washington Navy Yard, Dahlgren continued to supervise the manufacture of rifled variations of his 12-pounder 3.4-inch-bore boat howitzers. The yard produced 411 bronze rifled howitzers during the Civil War, and in 1863 it cast 12 steel howitzers.

Dahlgren's little boat howitzers performed extremely well and were highly popular with their crews. Their most likely first combat use occurred in an 1856 action to protect U.S. trade interests in China. In November, Commander Andrew H. Foote (1806–1863) led a small force of sailors and marines against the "Barrier Forts" on the Pearl River below Canton. The howitzers provided much needed firepower as the Americans, under heavy fire, were able to maneuver them over the marshy ground surrounding the four strongholds to take them one by one. During the Civil War they were particularly useful to naval forces operating on the Mississippi River and the bayous and rivers of the Western Theater.

In 1845 the U.S. Navy standardized six weight classes of the 32-pounder as its basic armament, along with two weights of 8-inch shell guns. During this period Dahlgren continued to study British and French shell gun developments, as well as conducting extensive tests of the 32-pounders then in U.S. service. His efforts gained a new urgency in November 1849, after a 32-pounder exploded killing a gunner during tests at the Navy Yard's experimental battery. In January the next year Dahlgren, convinced that more powerful—and safer—guns were needed, offered designs for a 9,000-pound IX-inch gun and an 8,000-pound 50-pounder. (At this time the U.S. Navy had begun designating shell guns with their bore diameters in Roman numerals, to distinguish them from shot-firing guns.)

The two guns were quickly cast at the West Point Foundry, and Dahlgren began tests at the Washington Navy Yard that spring, where he soon deemed the heavier IX-inch gun the superior design. The new gun evolved over the following months to incorporate a bulbous breech area that narrowed dramatically toward the muzzle, giving it a distinct "soda bottle" shape. This design concentrated the gun's metal at the breech, where the internal pressure was greatest during firing, and reduced it toward the muzzle, thus lessening the gun's weight. Dahlgren also addressed the problem that repeated firings tended to erode vents. To extend the life of his guns, he incorporated twin vents in his later guns—one filled with zinc until the first wore out, at which point the second was cleared for use and the first zinc-sealed. Dahlgren, who distrusted Rodman's internal-cooling casting method, had his guns cast in the more traditional method involving external cooling followed by lathing to achieve the final profile. Although other models were manufactured, the IX- and XI-inch smoothbores were the most commonly used Dahlgrens by the U.S. Navy during the Civil War. As a further tribute to Dahlgren's contributions, none of his IX- or XI-inch guns were reported to have burst in action—an impressive record when compared with the notorious Parrotts also in use.

There were 1,185 IX-inch Dahlgren shell guns cast between 1855 and 1864 by Cyrus Alger and Company of South Boston; Pittsburgh's Fort Pitt Foundry; Seyfert, McManus and Company of Reading, Pennsylvania; West Point of Cold Spring, New York; and Tredegar and Bellona in Virginia. The IX-inch gun tube exhibited a slight muzzle swell and a breeching loop through the cascabel. It was often mounted for broadside use on a 5-ton Marsilly carriage utilizing a single pair of front truck wheels. Widely used by the U.S. Navy during the Civil War, it gained a reputation for reliability and accuracy. In 1861, Fort Pitt cast sixteen tubes for the army, but their service was limited.

Some 465 XI-inch Dahlgrens were manufactured between 1856 and 1864 by the following foundries: Alger; Zachariah Chafee's Builders Foundry in Providence, Rhode Island; Fort Pitt; Hinkley; Williams and Co.; Portland Locomotive Works of Maine; Seyfert, McManus and Co.; Trenton Iron Works; and the West Point Foundry. Similar in appearance to the IX-inch model, some XI-inch guns were also finished without muzzle swells. They shared the reputation of the smaller gun for effectiveness and safety. From 1862 through 1865, Seyfert, McManus and the West Point Foundry also cast 29 X-inch Dahlgren shell guns and an equal number of solid shot tubes.

Thirty-four XV-inch Dahlgren short cannons were cast by Fort Pitt Foundry between 1862 and 1864. As originally designed, they were 161 inches long and weighed 42,000 pounds. In 1864 the navy's Bureau of Ordnance, desiring a longer gun to extend farther out of gun turret ports, began orders for a new XV-inch Dahlgren Long Cannon. Also known as the "New Model," it was 177 inches in length and weighed 43,000 pounds. The production of eighty-six tubes was carried out by Cyrus Alger, Fort Pitt, and Seyfert, McManus & Co. from 1864 to 1866, as well as in 1871 and 1872.

Only four giant XX-inch Dahlgrens were cast by the Fort Pitt Foundry between 1864 and 1867. As muzzleloading smoothbores they were essentially obsolete from their inception and merely proved that Dahlgren's process was capable of matching Rodman's in the production of large guns. The gun tubes were 216 inches in length and weighed 97,300 pounds. As was the case with the 20-inch army Rodman, the XX-inch navy Dahlgren never saw active service.

Dahlgren also approached the government with a design for a rifled gun in 1856, but bureaucratic obstacles delayed the casting of a prototype until the spring of 1859. He later oversaw the casting of a number of rifles of various calibers according to his designs, of which none saw extensive service. These included 4.4-inch 30-pounders, 5.1-inch 50-pounders, 6-inch 80-pounders, and a 7.5-inch 150-pounder that never saw service. Dahlgren rifles were cast without trunnions and were instead mounted by way of a trunnion band wrapped around their gun tubes.

Heavy Guns and Armor Plate:
The USS *Monitor* vs. the CSS *Virginia*

The first battle between steam-driven, ironclad warships—the 275-foot, 3,200-ton CSS *Virginia* and the 172-foot, 776-ton USS *Monitor*—occurred on 9 March 1862 at Hampton Roads, Virginia. The two ships were radically different in their designs. The *Virginia* was built on the wooden hull of the steam frigate USS *Merrimack,* whose burned hulk had been salvaged, armed, and iron plated by the Confederates after their seizure of the Gosport Navy Yard in 1861. Such improvisation produced an ungainly vessel with poor handling qualities, overly deep draft, and unreliable propulsion. The *Virginia*'s armor, however, made it nearly invulnerable to conventional enemy artillery, and its battery was formidable—two 12-pounder howitzers on deck, with the gun deck mounting two Brooke 7-inch rifle pivots, two Brooke 6-inch rifles, and six IX-inch Dahlgren smoothbores. In contrast to its technological innovations, the *Virginia* was also fitted with a cast iron ram on its bow—a distinct anachronism harking back to Greco-Roman naval warfare.

For its part, the *Monitor* was designed by the famous Swedish-born engineer John Ericsson and represented the very apex of the naval technology of its day. Of a much shallower draft—about 10.5 feet as compared with the *Virginia*'s 22 feet—and mounting better engines, the *Monitor* was vastly more maneuverable than its adversary. Its hull was also much lower in the water, presenting a smaller target, in contrast to the *Virginia*'s high sloping sides. Its revolving turret, housing two XI-inch Dahlgrens, was both the *Monitor*'s most innovative feature as well as the source of observers' descriptions of it as a "cheese box on a raft."

The action began on 8 March, when the *Virginia*, commanded by Dahlgren's earlier superior, Captain Franklin Buchanan, steamed against the Union blockading fleet. In this first sortie, the armored *Virginia*'s heavy shell guns proved devastating against its wooden-sided opponents, inflicting heavy damage. It then rammed and sank the sloop USS *Cumberland* (losing its ram in the process) and eventually fired and exploded the frigate USS *Congress.* Having neutralized the *Cumberland* and *Congress,* the *Virginia* then forced the unarmored steam frigates USS *Minnesota* and *Roanoke,* as well as the sailing frigate *St. Lawrence,* helplessly aground. When the firing ceased, the Federal casualties totaled some 300 killed and another 100 wounded. For its part, the Confederate ironclad had incurred no crippling damage, as most of the Union ships' rounds bounced harmlessly off its sloping casements. Still, Federal strikes damaged the muzzles of two of the *Virginia*'s guns, and splinters from the armor's wood backing wounded some ten Confederate sailors. Buchanan exposed himself to Federal sniper fire and sustained a leg wound that forced him to turn over command to his executive officer, Lieutenant Catesby ap Roger Jones (1821–1877).

That evening the *Monitor,* commanded by Lieutenant John Lorimer Worden (1818–1897), completed a harrowing voyage from New York and anchored in a protective position near the grounded *Minnesota.* The first battle between steam-powered ironsides began at 8:00 AM on 9 March 1862, when the *Monitor* intercepted the *Virginia* as it steamed forward to finish off the helpless *Minnesota.* The battle continued for the next four hours as the two adversaries circled each other, firing steadily at close range. Despite the heavy firing, the encounter ended essentially in a draw—although the *Monitor* did manage to save the stranded Union ships, neither it nor the *Virginia* was able to inflict mortal damage to its armored opponent.

A number of factors contributed to the battle's less than decisive outcome. The *Virginia*'s fire, despite being heavy and sustained, was relatively inaccurate. Although a single shot did strike the *Monitor*'s tiny conning house, temporarily blinding its captain, only twenty-one shots struck home, with no other effect beyond denting the Union ship's armor. For its part, the *Monitor* scored fifty strikes on the *Virginia,* also inflicting little damage. Other than relatively poor gunnery, the Confederates' failure to cripple the *Monitor* was caused largely by their use of improper ammunition. Expecting to encounter only wooden ships, the Confederates had steamed into battle with only explosive shell rather than armor-piercing solid bolts on board. For their part, the *Monitor* gunners failed to concentrate their fire on the *Virginia*'s vulnerable waterline. Ironically, the very designer of the Union ship's guns also played a pivotal role in their failure to punch through the Confederate ironclad's sides. Whereas the *Monitor*'s designer, Ericsson, had advocated 30-pound powder charges for its XI-inch guns, Dahlgren ordered the charge halved, thus greatly reducing effectiveness.

CONFEDERATE ARTILLERY

Upon secession, the agrarian South faced numerous obstacles in procuring and manufacturing ordnance of any kind. The Southern states did appropriate some 1,750 artillery pieces early in the war when they seized local federal installations such as the Gosport Naval Yard and various fortifications within their borders. These included 52 new IX-inch Dahlgrens, yet the preponderance of those weapons was made up of older, often obsolete smoothbore seacoast and siege guns. Although adequate as a stopgap, the pieces were unsuited for field use and woefully inadequate for use against the soon to be emerging ironclads. The early Confederacy's only source of field pieces consisted of possibly as many as 400 equally outdated guns and howitzers owned by military schools and militia organizations. During the first months of the war the Southern armies were thus often forced to provide themselves with their own artillery through capture. Confederate forces gained somewhat more than 250 pieces during the 1862 Peninsula Campaign, at Second Manassas (Second Bull Run), Harpers Ferry, and Braxton Bragg's campaign in Kentucky and Tennessee.

Only one Confederate foundry—Tredegar Iron Works in Richmond, Virginia—had a production capacity comparable to those in the North. It, as well as the smaller Bellona Foundry, some 13 miles up the James River, had provided ordnance for the federal government before the war, yet it had relied heavily on Northern suppliers for machinery and raw materials. Still, despite few sources for the iron and copper necessary for cannon founding and a lack of modern machinery and skilled labor, Southern foundries made great strides in providing the Confederacy with cannons of all types. Soon after secession the Confederate government began setting up government-operated arsenals to modernize existing pieces and cast new artillery. For their part, civilian foundry owners, motivated by various combinations of profit and patriotism, turned from making farm equipment and frying pans to casting cannons. As domestic ordnance production slowly developed, purchasing agents also scoured Europe for artillery, ultimately providing Confederate gunners with some of the most sophisticated weapons of the day.

Despite such efforts, the Confederacy never approached the North in the number or quality of the artillery pieces it fielded during the war. The region's lack of a large skilled labor force and the capture of both foundries and mining areas by Union forces proved a crippling check to Southern cannon production. Moreover, foreign imports were also reduced to a trickle as the Union blockade of Southern ports tightened and European countries found other sources for cotton, the South's main trading commodity.

The daunting task of supplying the Confederacy with ordnance of all types fell to its talented chief of ordnance, Brigadier General Josiah Gorgas (1818–1883). A native of Pennsylvania and 1841 graduate of the U.S. Military Academy, Gorgas was assigned to the ordnance corps and served with distinction in the Mexican War. His marriage in 1853 to Amelia Gayle of Alabama apparently influenced his later decision to resign his commission as captain in the U.S. Army to join the Confederate cause.

Commissioned a brigadier general in the Confederate Army, Gorgas applied his considerable organizational genius to solving his adopted country's never-ending ordnance crises. Under his direction the Confederacy established four government foundries dedicated to the casting of field pieces, with a fifth assigned the manufacture of heavy ordnance. He also coordinated the efforts of dozens of private ordnance enterprises, as well as encouraging blockade running—all while struggling with the problems of crippling inflation and the chronic lack of materials and manpower.

Under optimal conditions, it took Southern foundries between two and four weeks to manufacture a complete field cannon and carriage. To finish a 10-inch columbiad required from 400 to 500 hours of labor, with the large Tredegar foundry capable of producing one such large gun a month. Still, Southern foundries seldom, if ever, operated under optimal conditions. Nevertheless, the determination and ingenuity of Gorgas and the Southern founders allowed the Confederacy to continue cannon production until the war's end. In November 1863, Federal forces captured the Ducktown copper mines near Chattanooga, Tennessee, thus depriving Southern foundries of 90 percent of their supply of the critical metal. Confederate founders responded by recasting condemned bronze guns and calling on churches to donate their bells and patriotic ladies their brassware as alternative sources of the metal. As copper became virtually unavailable, Southern makers, notably Tredegar, at last began producing such pieces as the versatile Napoleon gun-howitzer in iron rather than bronze.

Owing to a degree of bureaucratic inefficiency and conservatism, the Confederacy was initially somewhat slow in adopting rifled guns for general field use. This tendency was reinforced by the problems that the Southern ordnance system faced in developing and manufacturing the more complicated rifles, as well as reliable shells and fuses. The capture of a Federal 30-pounder Parrott rifle at the Battle of First Manassas provided the Confederates with a model from which to develop their own modern rifles. On 26 July 1862,

Tredegar began copying the Parrott, known by its new owners as "Long Tom," and they were able to deliver two 30-pounder Confederate Parrotts to the government in September. As a further move to modernize the South's ordnance, in late 1862, Gorgas mandated the end of the production of 6-pounder guns and restricted the army's field artillery gun types to 12-pounder Napoleons and 10- and 20-pounder Parrott rifles.

Confederate 6-Pounder Field Guns

A combination of necessity and conservatism led to the Confederate Army's continued use of 6-pounder guns after the Union army had abandoned them. Some officers who had seen their effectiveness in Mexico retained a respect for the older pieces and saw no reason to change from the tried-and-true earlier guns to something unfamiliar. On a more practical level, most field guns already in Southern hands were older types and available for immediate field service or to serve as pattern models for the nascent Confederate cannon industry.

Confederate founders cast both iron and bronze 6-pounder guns of varying quality and overall appearance. Confederate founders casting bronze guns included Tredegar Iron Works (34), John Clarke of New Orleans (approximately 50), and A. M. Paxton and Company of Vicksburg, Mississippi (14). Noble Bros. and Co. of Rome, Georgia, cast about 20 bronze and some iron 6-pounders. With a production of possibly as many as 40 guns, Tredegar also cast 6-pounders, as did T. M. Brennan of Nashville, Tennessee, a firm that cast around 30 guns. Other founders, such as Leach and Avery of Tuscaloosa, Alabama, and Ellis and Moore of Nashville, manufactured small numbers of iron pieces.

Tredegar Iron Works

Founded in the 1830s by Francis B. Deane, Jr., and named after a Welsh foundry, Virginia's Tredegar Iron Works was the largest and most productive Confederate cannon factory. Under the capable direction of Joseph Reid Anderson (1813–1892), Tredegar Iron Works overcame shortages in raw materials and manpower to produce nearly 50 percent of the more than 2,300 cannons manufactured in the Confederacy. Graduating fourth in the West Point class of 1836, Anderson served briefly as an artillery and engineer officer before resigning his commission in 1837 to become assistant engineer for his home state, Virginia. He then bought the failing Tredegar Iron Works in 1848 and reorganized it as the Joseph R. Anderson Company. Over the next decade his efforts led to the foundry's steady rise to become one of the country's most thriving businesses.

During the period from 1844 through 1860, Tredegar manufactured some 881 cannons for the federal government, and by 1860 it boasted a workforce of 800 employees, including slaves. The company's fortunes were threatened in 1859, when Anderson refused to adopt the new Rodman casting technique, a change that the federal government mandated that year for its heavy artillery contracts. Fortunately for Anderson, Tredegar was able to remain solvent over the following months, filling state contracts until the Civil War renewed orders for the Confederate government.

Following secession, Anderson, an ardent states' rights advocate, volunteered his services to the Confederacy and was commissioned brigadier general on 3 September 1861. Having initially commanded the defenses of Wilmington, North Carolina, Anderson commanded the Third Brigade of General A. P. Hill's Division at the Virginia battles of Mechanicsville, Gaines's Mill, and the 30 June 1862 Battle of Frayser's Farm, where he was wounded. The next month he resigned his commission to return to the supervision of Tredegar. By 1863, Anderson had increased the foundry's workforce from its 1861 total of 900 employees to some 2,500 workers. On 15 May 1863 the foundry was heavily damaged by fire, and until it was eventually reopened the government's Richmond Naval Ordnance Works continued to band and rifle older guns.

Despite Anderson's skilled leadership, the Confederacy's decline and a lack of materials and skilled labor led to a reduction of Tredegar's workforce to fewer than 500 employees in late 1864. As only three men possessed the skills making them absolutely critical to the foundry's operation, many of the white workers were often dispatched to Richmond's trenches when needed for the city's defense. As those employees displayed a growing tendency to desert, the white work force shrank to less than half its earlier level and the slave workers doubled in number. With the end of iron production in March 1865, Tredegar's cannon production ceased during the last weeks of the war. As Federal forces closed on Richmond, Anderson organized his company's defenses and, despite the general destruction of Richmond the next month, managed to save the foundry from looting and burning and eventually reopened it in 1867 as the Tredegar Company.

During the war Tredegar produced a variety of types of ordnance, including columbiads, Brookes rifles, 3-inch rifles, 6-pounder iron and bronze smoothbore guns, 2.25-inch mountain rifles, and 12-pounder mountain howitzers. It also rifled and reinforced by breech banding older weapons in an effort to modernize weapons captured at the time of secession. Other than markings, Tredegar ordnance was often distinguishable from Federal examples by a lack of final finish on noncritical exterior surfaces, with lathe marks remaining visible. Tredegar cannons were generally marked with the year of their manufacture on the left trunnion and, on the right: J.R.A. & CO. The foundry manufacturing number was stamped into the piece's muzzle face.

The Bellona Foundry

In 1816, Major John Clark established the Bellona Foundry some 13 miles above Richmond on the James River. He later sold the business in the 1840s to Dr. Junius L. Archer, who built up the foundry into a major supplier of heavy ordnance to the U.S. government. In the late 1850s, Archer, like Tredegar's Anderson, had refused to adopt the Rodman casting methods and thus also had lost his federal contracts. At the beginning of the Civil War the state of Virginia claimed all ordnance held at the foundry, and the company soon began production for the Confederate government. Bellona's 1862 production included fifteen 8- and 10-inch columbiads, three 24-pounder guns, two 7-inch guns, two 9-inch guns, and five 4.2-inch siege guns. Although damaged by fire in 1863, Bellona continued casting throughout the war, with a total production of approximately 135 pieces of ordnance, some finished by Tredegar. Bellona guns were typically identified on the trunnion with the stamping in two lines: B.F./ J.L.A. (for Junius L. Archer).

Confederate Government Foundries

In addition to private foundries, the Confederacy established five government arsenals for the production of artillery. These included installations in Georgia located in Augusta, Columbus, and Macon, the Charleston Arsenal in South Carolina, and the Selma Naval Gun Foundry in Alabama.

Originally a U.S. arsenal, the Augusta Arsenal, under the command of Colonel George Washington Rains, was one of the first Confederate arsenals to begin full production. Using copper from the Ducktown mines in Tennessee as well as metal from local mines, scrap, and melted down obsolete weapons, Augusta began production of 12-pounder Napoleons by the end of 1862. Those pieces were cast at the nearby Augusta Foundry and Machine Works, with some being completed at the Georgia Railroad Machine Shop. Made up of a new Austrian-developed alloy consisting of copper, tin, zinc, and iron, Augusta pieces were generally favorably received by their crews, with most being issued to the Army of Tennessee.

In 1863, Rains claimed that the arsenal could manufacture a Napoleon a day, yet the foundry probably completed no more than 130 of the gun-howitzers during the war. Augusta cannons were identified on the right trunnion face in three lines: GOVERT/ FOUNDRY & MACHINE WORKS/ AUGUSTA, with A. F. (for Augusta Foundry) stamped into the muzzle face.

With the Baton Rouge Arsenal under threat from Union forces after the fall of New Orleans in April 1862, Confederate authorities ordered the removal of its machinery to Columbus, Georgia. Captain F. C. Humphreys took command of the new facility, and production began in May 1863. The majority of the foundry's output was issued to the Army of Tennessee and the Army of Mississippi. Of the possible total of eighty pieces manufactured at Columbus, approximately fifty-two were 12-pounder Napoleons, distinguished from their Union counterparts by their lack of a muzzle swell, giving them a somewhat sleeker appearance. The arsenal also cast other types of cannons, including at least one 9-pounder. Columbus Arsenal cannons were usually marked on the muzzle face with their casting number, date, and F.C.H. C.S. ARSENAL COLUMBUS, GEO.

Before the Civil War, J. D. and C. N. Findlay manufactured railroad components at their Findlay Iron Works in Macon, Georgia. In April 1862 the Confederate government acquired the firm and, placing it under command of Captain Richard M. Cuyler, renamed it the Macon Arsenal. Cuyler expanded the original eleven-employee workforce and by early 1863 began producing bronze 12-pounder Napoleons for the Army of Tennessee and the Army of Mississippi. The Macon Napoleons, as was typical of the Confederate manufactured gun-howitzers, were cast without muzzle swells. As the Tennessee and Mississippi gunners turned in their obsolete 6-pounders and 12-pounder howitzers, Macon replaced them with more Napoleons as well as, beginning in 1864, 10-pounder Parrott rifles.

The total production at Macon included some 53 12-pounder Napoleons, 12 10-pounder Parrotts, 5 20-pounder Parrotts, and one 30-pounder Parrott. They were usually stamped on the muzzle face with their date of casting, inspector's initials, casting number, and MACON ARSENAL.

Originally a U.S. installation, the Charleston Arsenal was taken over by the state of South Carolina on 30 December 1860 and soon after turned over to the new Confederate government. By 1863 the facility employed 329 employees repairing small arms and manufacturing small arms ammunition, as well as friction primers and heavy artillery projectiles. The arsenal's surviving records indicate that the arsenal probably manufactured fewer than 20 12-pounder Napoleons, marked on the right trunnion face: CHARLESTON ARSENAL.

With the intention of producing heavy ordnance for the Confederate government, local businessman and politician Colin J. McRae set up a casting facility in Selma, Alabama. McRae, however, encountered numerous financial and construction difficulties, and the government somewhat reluctantly took over the operation of the partially finished foundry. In February 1863, Colonel George W. Rains briefly assumed command at Selma to oversee the production of ordnance for both the Confederate Army and Navy. Rains never warmed to his assignment and was tireless in his criticism of the entire operation. He was thus soon relieved, and on 1 June 1863 he was replaced by Commander Catesby ap R. Jones (1821–1877) of the Confederate Navy. Jones, who had served as acting commander of the CSS *Virginia* during its duel with the Federal ironclad USS *Monitor,* approached his new assignment with the efficiency and determination for which he had become known.

Jones's talents were immediately put to the test, as the facility was still under construction and no guns had yet been cast. The navy, moreover, was insistent that Selma begin casting some of the largest weapons attempted at that time—heavy rifles and smoothbores designed by John M. Brooke, the head of the Navy Bureau's Ordnance and Hydrography Department.

Although Richmond's Tredegar foundry had successfully cast a number of Brooke cannon, the Selma works had little access to resources comparable to those of the long-established firm. Jones found that the iron available locally was of poor quality, and skilled labor was in chronically short supply: arsenal records from early 1865 indicate that more than 300 of the 450 employees were unskilled slaves rented from nearby plantations and businesses. Multiple furnaces were required to melt the more than 7 tons of iron that went into a Brooke gun casting, and after eight days of cooling, it took over a thousand hours to bore, rifle, and band the finished tube. Still, in the summer of 1863, Jones began production of 7-inch Brooke guns; the results, however, were disappointing failures.

Jones continued to improve the casting techniques at Selma and eventually, in January 1864, completed and delivered two 7-inch Brooke rifles for installation on the new ironclad CSS *Tennessee*. In May, Selma completed two more Brookes for the ironclad CSS *Nashville* and later produced more guns for mounting on other Confederate ironclads and gunboats. In the summer of that year Selma also completed two 24,000-pound, 11-inch smoothbore pieces, with one each going to the defenses of Charleston, South Carolina, and Wilmington, North Carolina. Before its capture and destruction by Federal troops on 2 April 1865, Selma attained the production capabilities to manufacture large numbers of heavy artillery shells as well as at least 102 Brooke guns, 19 coehorn mortars, 20 6-pounders, and 12 30-pounder Parrott rifles.

Other Confederate Artillery Manufacturers

A number of Southern civilian foundries attempted with various degrees of success to manufacture cannons for the Confederate Army and Navy. Before its capture by Federal forces in April 1862, New Orleans boasted no fewer than five such ordnance facilities, including the firms of Bennett and Lurges, Bujac and Bennett, John Clark and Company, Leeds and Company, and S. Wolfe and Company. Other manufacturers included the two Memphis companies of Quinby and Robinson, and Street, Hungerford and Company; the Washington Foundry of Richmond, Virginia; T. M. Brennan and Company in Nashville, Tennessee; the Georgia concerns of Columbus Iron Works and Noble Brothers and Company in Rome; A. B. Reading and Brother in Vicksburg, Mississippi; and J. R. Young and Company in Huntsville, Alabama.

Confederate Brooke Rifles and Smoothbores

Upon Virginia's secession, Florida-born Lieutenant John Mercer Brooke (1826–1904) resigned his commission in the U.S. Navy to join the Confederate cause. An 1847 graduate of the U.S. Naval

Academy, Brooke helped supervise the refitting and conversion of the scuttled USS *Merrimack* into the ironclad CSS *Virginia*. Promoted commander in 1862, he then took over as head of the Confederate Navy Bureau's Ordnance and Hydrography Department. In that post he developed new types of artillery fuses, underwater mines, improved ratcheted sabots, and various projectiles, including flat-nosed, armor-piercing bolts. Brooke gained his greatest reputation for his alternative and in many ways improved counterpart to the North's heavy-caliber Parrott rifles.

Brooke's design, like Parrott's, made use of cast iron gun tubes reinforced at the breech with wrought iron bands. Unlike Parrott guns, however, the Brooke cannons were more typically fitted with two and sometimes three bands, giving them added strength. Other differences included the use of multiple welded sections in the construction of the Brooke bands, as opposed to the single one-piece band of the Parrott—a necessity imposed by the South's lack of heavy rolling machinery. Brooke rifles also incorporated a distinctive seven-groove rifling system similar to the English Blakely design. The majority of Brooke cannons were designed for naval use, with a small number being manufactured for coastal defense. Production was carried out at J. R. Anderson's Tredegar Iron Works in Richmond and the Selma Naval Gun Foundry in Alabama. Despite the relatively poor quality of iron available in the South, Brooke rifles earned a much higher reputation for safety than the large Parrotts used by the U.S. Navy. Following the war Brooke accepted a professorship at the Virginia Military Institute, where he taught until his retirement in 1899.

Tredegar manufactured the first 10 6.4-inch Brooke rifles with single bands giving them—other than their rounded breech faces—a very close resemblance to the Parrott rifle. Following the directive of Secretary of the Navy Stephen R. Mallory, Tredegar began double banding the breeches of Brooke rifles in late October 1862. The 6.4-inch Brooke was generally intended as a broadside naval weapon and typically fired either 65-pound shells or 80-pound solid bolts. Tredegar manufactured 25 double-banded pieces and probably added bands to some earlier single-banded cannons. The Selma Naval Gun Foundry encountered numerous difficulties in casting heavy pieces such as the big Brookes. The new instillation did finish 15 Brooke 6.4-inch rifles but found it necessary to rework five defective 6.4-inch rifle castings into 8-inch double-banded smoothbore guns.

Early 7-inch Brookes were also manufactured with a single breech band, with an extra band added after October 1862. Designed for pivot mounting, they fired either a 110-pound shell or 120-pound bolt. Tredegar produced a total of 23, and Selma 39. The ironclad CSS *Virginia*'s two 7-inch Brooke pivot guns were made up of unfinished IX-inch Dahlgren castings captured when Southern forces seized Federal naval facilities early in the war. Tredegar also made three 7-inch rifles reinforced with three bands, the innermost extending somewhat beyond the tube's midpoint. The triple-banded Brooke did not incorporate trunnions but was slung in its mounting by way of a breech strap and trunnion band wrapped around its circumference.

FOREIGN ARTILLERY USED IN THE AMERICAN CIVIL WAR

At the beginning of the Civil War, neither the Northern nor Southern logistics and ordnance organizations were prepared to supply and arm the vast influx of volunteers swelling their armies' ranks. To gain time, both sides dispatched agents to Europe to buy foreign military goods, including uniforms, accoutrements, small arms, and artillery. For their part, European arsenal commanders were more than happy to clear out stocks of obsolete and often defective equipment in exchange for U.S. gold, bonds, or cotton. Of all the foreign weapons used by either side, those obtained from Britain proved the most effective.

During the early months of the war the most famous of the Confederate agents, Major Caleb Huse, scoured Europe signing contracts for weapons ranging from pistols to cannons. Such weapons were usually sufficient until more modern weapons could be procured but often required some improvisation to use U.S. ammunition. One such example—the approximately 17 Austrian bronze 6-pounders obtained by Huse—were bored to 3.74 inches rather than the American 3.67 caliber. Although a seemingly minor detail, such disparities required extra effort on the part of ordnance crews, who had to wrap ammunition for the Austrian pieces in an extra layer of canvas for a proper bore fit.

The son of a Congregational minister, Sir Joseph Whitworth (1803–1887) was one of Britain's leading engineers and helped to revolutionize the country's precision tool making industry. He designed machine equipment and a highly accurate rifle, as well as advanced cannons. Whitworth designed various calibers of both muzzle- and breech loading artillery pieces, with both types sharing his unique rifling system. The bores of Whitworth cannons and small arms were precisely cut with distinctive spiraling hexagonal rifling that required a matching six-sided projectile. The odd shape of the projectile produced a weird, unnerving shriek as it traveled through the air.

Although rejected by the British army in favor of Armstrong weapons, Whitworth rifles were made of high-grade steel and iron and were capable of extremely accurate long-range fire of nearly six miles. Still, such accuracy was often negated by the period's lack of sophisticated sights, fouling problems, and the complicated loading procedure that often baffled poorly trained crews: in many cases Confederate gunners locked the breechloaders' mechanisms and simply used them as muzzleloaders. Moreover, the slender Whitworth projectile was too small to carry a significant bursting charge. Solid bolts did, however, prove highly effective against armored targets, owing to their high velocity at flat trajectories.

The breechloading 2.75-inch 12-pounder was the most commonly used Whitworth by both sides during the American Civil War. Other lesser used models included the 2.15-inch and 3.75-inch breechloaders, as well as the muzzleloading 5-inch 80-pounder seacoast rifle. With a 10-pound charge and an 80-pound projectile filled with a 3.17-pound bursting charge, the seacoast Whitworth had an astounding 13,665-yard range at 10-degree elevation. Although an impressive weapon, such large rifles were prone to fouling, and inexperienced crews often found loading difficult and at times dangerous: improperly handled shells were prone to detonate prematurely.

The Confederacy imported a small number of both muzzle- and breechloading British Armstrong rifles of various sizes during the Civil War. The most popular Armstrong for field use, the 3-inch model, fired a 12-pound projectile 2,200 yards. The 70-pounder 6.4-inch breechloading Armstrong fired a 79.8-pound projectile loaded with a 5.4-pound bursting charge 2,183 yards. Two large 8.5-inch (150-pounder) 120-inch-long muzzleloading Armstrongs were included in the defenses of Wilmington, North Carolina: a 15,737-pound cannon at Fort Fisher and a 15,786-pound gun at Fort Caswell. The 150-pounder required a 20-pound charge.

Although rejected by his own government, British captain Theophilus Alexander Blakely found the Confederacy a ready buyer of his muzzleloaded rifled cannons during the Civil War. Blakely contracted with various private firms to cast his heavy and field pieces under license. Most Blakely bores were cut with right-hand twist—the so-called saw tooth or hook-slant rifling—and were manufactured using a cast iron core reinforced at the breech with wrought iron bands. Sizes ranged from small 2.5-inch 6-pounders to 12.75-inch seacoast rifles. Several types of 3.5-inch 12-pounder Blakely field rifles saw Confederate service during the Civil War. Other less used types included the 3.75-inch 16-pounder and the 4.5-inch 20-pounder, classed as naval and siege weapons.

Larger Blakelys included 7-inch (120-pounder) navy rifles. The Confederate raiders CSS *Alabama* and CSS *Florida* each mounted a 7-inch Blakely on pivots. A number of Blakely 7.5-inch pieces were also made up from British 42-pounder smoothbores that were banded and rifled according to Blakely's patent. The barrels of the converted pieces utilized twelve-groove "hook-slant" rifling. On 22 May 1863 one such rifle—known as the Widow Blakely, as it was the only Blakely in the Vicksburg defenses—lost two feet of its muzzle when a shell exploded prematurely. Workmen repaired the remainder of the tube, and the Widow continued to defend the city until its fall on 4 July.

Other heavy pieces included 8.12-inch rifles made up from converted British 68-pounder smoothbores, 9-inch rifles, and 12.75-inch seacoast rifles. The 12.75-inch Blakely fired very heavy flanged projectiles, including 450-pound shells, to about 2,000 yards, and reportedly bolts as heavy as 700 pounds. Two 12.75-inch Blakelys were delivered through the blockade for the defense of Wilmington, North Carolina, in August 1863 but were rerouted to Charleston, South Carolina, by order of Secretary of War James Alexander Seddon and General Pierre Gustave Toutant Beauregard. Local gunners, however, were unfamiliar with the Blakelys' innovative air chamber. Some 7 inches in diameter and 30 inches long, the bronze air chamber was located at the breech below the guns' powder chamber and was intended to reduce the shock of the recoil. Baffled by the unexplained extra space, General Roswell Sabine Ripley ordered one of the guns' crews to load the air chamber with powder during its first firing, thus bursting the piece. When loaded correctly, however, the second gun functioned satisfactorily; after repairs, the damaged gun was returned to service.

CHAPTER SIX

Late-Nineteenth- and Early-Twentieth-Century Artillery

EUROPEAN DEVELOPMENTS, 1815–1914

During the first half of the 1800s, European and U.S. artillery equipment and doctrine remained essentially unchanged from that of the previous century. By the last quarter of the century, however, various conflicts—such as the American Civil War, the Crimean War, and the Franco-Prussian War—exposed the deficiencies of existing weapons and practice, as well as serving as proving grounds for new ordnance. The Industrial Revolution brought about a flood of artillery innovations, including the advent of rifled "quick-firing" breechloaders, smokeless powder, metallic cartridges, and advanced recoil-reduction mechanisms. Improved metallurgy also made possible the development of cast steel pieces, permitting the manufacture of larger, more powerful guns and howitzers capable of much longer range fire than previous bronze and iron artillery.

Such changes were both contemporary and necessitated by the advent and proliferation of rifled infantry small arms during the 1850s and 1860s. As the new rifled musket increased the infantryman's accurate killing range from roughly 100 yards to as much as 800 yards or farther, smoothbore artillerists found themselves at a dangerous disadvantage. Moreover, to achieve their maximum ranges, smoothbore artillery required such extreme elevation that the pieces' breeches at times recoiled into the ground and were eventually put out of action. The situation provided the impetus for more artillery innovations, and by the second half of the century gunners again gained the advantage in range and the deadliness of their projectiles.

Rifled Artillery

Long before the nineteenth century, designers knew that spiraling grooves cut into a gunpowder weapon's bore could impart a stabilizing spin to its projectiles' flight. That this spin also enhanced the projectile's accuracy and range added to the desirability of rifled weapons. By midcentury a host of rifle designs vied for dominance and acceptance by various governments' ordnance departments. One of the earliest pioneers of modern rifled artillery, the Italian major Giovanni Cavalli, unveiled his first design in 1846. A cast iron gun, its bore was cut with simple two-groove rifling to accept an elongated projectile fitted with corresponding lugs that mated with the gun's grooves. Cavalli's gun proved capable of accurately firing a 64-pound projectile 3,400 yards and so impressed a Sardinian ordnance committee that the government ordered 23 Cavalli rifled guns. Unfortunately, two of the Sardinian guns burst during practice firings, killing and injuring a number of their crews. Although the accidents were probably more owing to defective casting than to the guns' basic design, Cavalli reworked his drawings and in about 1854 offered a new rifled gun capable of a range of about three miles. Cavalli later commented that the new, more complicated artillery pieces would require more intelligent and educated gunners to operate both safely and effectively.

Other rifled cannon pioneers included Colonel Treuille de Bealieu of France and the Swedish baron Martin Wahrendorff. Bealieu began work in about 1840 and developed a rifled system that also made use of studded projectiles. His guns saw limited service in various colonial actions and showed promise against the Austrians in Italy in 1856. Also working in the 1840s, Baron Wahrendorff experimented with smaller, multiple-grooved rifling using lead-sheathed projectiles. The baron's lead-coated projectiles offered advantages that appealed to later inventors, yet they were not without serious defects. Although the soft lead caused minimal bore wear and expanded easily to engage the rifling and eliminate windage, it tended to peel off in the piece, fouling the lands and grooves. Later model Wahren-dorff projectiles incorporated copper coatings that were never completely satisfactory. Still, a 6.4-inch cast iron Wahrendorff exhibited at the 1851 Great Exposition in London generated a certain degree of interest, and the guns saw limited garrison use by England, Sweden, and Prussia. These early designs, however, were soon overshadowed by the rapid advancements of later systems such as those by the Englishmen Sir Joseph Whitworth, Sir William Armstrong, and Americans including Robert Parrott.

Two British engineers, Charles Lancaster and Joseph Whitworth, designed unique rifling systems that saw limited use by Britain and other countries. Rather than a grooved, round-profile bore, the Lancaster system utilized an oval bore that twisted gradually along its length, thus causing its corresponding oval cross-section projectile to spin. For its part, the Whitworth system relied on a hexagonal twisting bore and a matching hexagonal projectile. Cannons of both systems were highly accurate at long ranges yet ultimately proved impractical for general use. The extremely precise tolerances used in the manufacture of the two systems required meticulous maintenance by gun crews to avoid malfunctions, and even moderate bore wear led to projectiles jamming in the bores. British forces used a few Lancaster guns during the Crimean War at the siege of Sevastopol, but they proved failures; a limited number of Whitworth pieces, however, although temperamental, gained a reputation for accuracy in Confederate hands during the American Civil War.

Originally trained as a lawyer, Sir William George Armstrong (1810–1900) turned his talents to engineering, inventing hydraulic engines and cranes. In 1854 he patented a wrought iron rifled cannon that incorporated a number of graduated reinforcing bands, giving it a distinctive stepped profile. Armstrong also developed a unique "shunt" type of rifling, with each groove cut to two depths to accommodate the system's special studded projectiles. The deeper half of the groove provided extra space to ease loading, whereas, upon firing, the studs shifted to the shallow side to provide the close fit within the bore necessary for accuracy. The powder charge was contained in a separate bag. The breech mechanism consisted of a separate wrought iron vent piece that was inserted into a slot in the top of the piece and locked into position by way of a large screw in the rear of the gun. A copper ring in the face of the vent piece expanded on firing to seal the breech and prevent the escape of gasses and subsequent loss of energy.

In July 1855, Armstrong submitted a 3-pounder breechloader for tests to the master general of the ordnance, and after a series of trials against other designs a special committee approved it for the British service on 16 November 1858. Upon the acceptance of his design, Armstrong relinquished all patent rights to the Crown and was subsequently appointed superintendent of the Royal Gun Factory at Woolwich in November 1859. By March 1861, Armstrong had overseen the manufacture of 941 of his guns for the British army, as well as guns for the Royal Navy.

The most popular Armstrong for field use, the 3-inch 12-pounder, had a range of some 2,200 yards. One of the more long-lived Armstrongs, the Model 1862 "Pattern G" 40-pounder, remained in service until 1920. Production of the Pattern G totaled some 810 guns. The 70-pounder 6.4-inch breechloading Armstrong fired a 79.8-pound projectile loaded with a 5.4-pound bursting charge 2,183 yards. Examples of large 8.5-inch (150-pounder) 120-inch-long muzzleloading Armstrongs weighed up to about 15,790 pounds and required a 20-pound charge.

MID-NINETEENTH CENTURY EUROPEAN WARS
The Crimean War

The Crimean War of 1854–1856 was initiated by a Russian incursion into Ottoman territory that prompted Great Britain, France, and the Kingdom of Piedmont to ally themselves with the Turks to prevent Russian expansion. Most of the fighting concentrated around the strategic Russian Black Sea naval base at Sevastopol, with major actions occurring at the Alma River (20 September 1854), Balaclava (25 October 1854), and Inkerman (5 November 1854). Most notable for incompetent leadership and abysmally inefficient logistics among all the combatants, the war eventually ended following the Russians' surrender of Sevastopol on 11 September 1855.

For the most part, the British artillery used in the Crimean War was essentially the same as that of the Napoleonic period. Although the friction primer had recently been introduced, British gunners also used the earlier percussion primers and, at times, the even more outdated portfires. The Rocket Troop and the Royal Horse Artillery fielded the excellent light 6-pounder gun with the field batteries, putting the 9-pounder gun to deadly use at Alma and Inkerman.

Somewhat ironically, two 18-pounder siege guns employed as field pieces provided the decisive firepower at the fog-shrouded battle of Inkerman. At the critical point of the battle, their crews dragged the two heavy pieces to an exposed position within range of a large Russian battery bombarding the English infantry. Despite heavy enemy fire, the two guns systematically destroyed the Russian guns one by one, thus depriving their infantry of covering fire.

Consisting of six major bombardments, the allied siege of Sevastopol saw possibly the largest use of siege artillery of the period. Although no heavy howitzers were used, the British made extensive use of mortars and heavy siege guns, including 18-, 24-, and 32-pounders. Naval personnel also crewed a lesser number of heavier 68-pounders, and a few new naval shell guns also saw use.

French field gunners held a distinct advantage in their newly issued pieces. Adopted in 1853 and the invention and namesake of the French emperor, the light 12-pounder Napoleon gun-howitzer was the most versatile field artillery piece of the era. The Napoleon was highly maneuverable and was equally capable of firing solid round shot and canister at the gun's flat trajectory, as well as the howitzer's explosive shell and shrapnel.

The Russian artillery consisted of comparatively better-educated officers and better trained and paid noncommissioned officers and enlisted men than the czarist infantry. The Russian light batteries and horse artillery fielded a fine 6-pounder gun and 9-pounder howitzer with field batteries having 12-pounder guns and 18-pounder howitzers, with rocket batteries also seeing service. Many Russian gun carriages were also of an innovative design, utilizing wrought iron tubular construction. The new carriages were very maneuverable, resistant to harsh weather, and less prone to breakage.

Ultimately, the Crimean War proved to many of its participants and observers that the existing artillery and the training of all its participants were deficient on many levels. The war was also intensely covered by war correspondents, who reported on the limitations of the combatants' artillery. Their reports, in conjunction with the intensifying Industrial Revolution, led to a renewed impetus to develop new artillery pieces and doctrines.

The Prusso-Danish War

The five-month-long Prusso-Danish War of 1864 arose over the two powers' competing claims upon the duchies of Schleswig and

Holstein. The conflict tended to confirm the contemporary American Civil War findings concerning the limits of even the most modern artillery against earthwork rather than masonry fortifications. During the sixty-five-day siege of Duppel, the Danish defenders, armed with 92 older smoothbores and a few mortars, faced a superior Prussian force with some 144 artillery pieces including a high percentage of modern Krupp rifled breechloaders. Despite continuous barrages, however, the Prussian artillery proved largely ineffectual; Duppel's earthen defensive works absorbed the besiegers' shells, whereas masonry walls would have shattered easily. In the end the Prussians took the city not because of an advantage in artillery but by an overwhelming and costly infantry assault.

The Austro-Prussian War

The 1866 "Seven Weeks' War" between Austria and Prussia saw both belligerents fielding significant numbers of rifled artillery. Although the Prussians again bettered their opponents, the war exposed numerous deficiencies in their training and the integration of their artillery into their overall command structure. Prussia soon established its School of Gunnery, which espoused professionalism, training in the use of rifled ordnance, and the aggressive deployment of artillery in battle. The Prussian lead in the use of mobile, aggressive artillery tactics was later furthered by Prinz Kraft zu Höhenlohe-Ingelfingen, whose series of *Military Letters* was published and widely read in Prussia and abroad.

The Franco-Prussian War

The Franco-Prussian War of 1870–1871 served as the proving ground for a new generation of quick-firing, breechloading rifled field artillery. The two belligerents, as well as other nations, later applied the lessons learned during the brief conflict—with widely varying degrees of success—to form the doctrines that dominated artillery theory for nearly half a century. The French army entered the war with few, although significant, technological advantages. These included the Chassepôt infantry rifle, a much better weapon than the German's outdated Dreyse "needleguns," and a number of new types of machine guns, including a small number of American Gatling guns. French artillery, however, was undergoing a rather slow modernization process and was still composed primarily of obsolescent smoothbore muzzleloaders.

French artillery thus included 4- and 12-pounder field guns, as well as 8-pounder smoothbore muzzleloaders that were rifled to take modern ammunition. In 1869 the government began the development and testing of a bronze 7-pounder breechloader, and despite a number of setbacks production began almost immediately. Achieving a range of about 5,500 yards, at least 230 saw service during the war. In addition to domestic field pieces, France also purchased 330 Civil War–surplus U.S. Parrott rifles.

The French army also lacked enough heavy guns to defend its cities and fortifications adequately from the invaders. Two of the more common pieces—the heavy 12-pounder bronze muzzleloaded rifle and a 24-pounder of similar design—shared a maximum range of 5,570 yards. Howitzers and mortars were also available, but their limited range hampered their effectiveness. These deficiencies were somewhat countered by the pressing of naval artillery into land service. More modern heavy naval breechloaders thus saw service in the defense of Paris, as did various gunboats stationed on the Seine.

For its part, the German field artillery entered the war with a distinct technological advantage. Whereas the standard French field piece was already obsolete, the Germans had advanced Krupp 4-pounder 80mm breechloaders. The Krupp pieces were lightweight, dependable, and accurate. Moreover, the German gun's maximum range of 4,156 yards was also superior to the average French piece's 3,445 yards. They were manufactured with steel barrels; metal parts were painted black and the carriages a medium blue. German time fuses were also more reliable, although the French later switched to an improved percussion detonator.

More significantly, German artillery tactics proved far superior to those of the French. During the war the Germans introduced the use of grand batteries such as that used at the decisive 1 September 1870 Battle of Sedan, where they massed some 540 guns under one commander. The tactics used at Sedan, championed by Prince Krafft zu Höhenlohe-Ingelfingen, initially called for the destruction of the enemy's artillery batteries with a long-range concentrated barrage. The artillery would then turn its attention to the French infantry and advance during the German infantry attack, providing covering fire. Although such tactics exposed the German artillery to enemy rifle fire, their effectiveness proved such that they became official German doctrine by 1876 and were soon copied by France and Austria.

POST FRANCO-PRUSSIAN
WAR DEVELOPMENTS:
GERMANY, FRANCE, AND AUSTRIA

With Germany taking the lead, three of the four major European powers (Russia was the exception) reorganized their artillery organizations according to the tactics employed by the Prussians during the Franco-Prussian War. These reorganizations led to larger units consisting of batteries of two, four, six, or eight guns, concentrated into "groups" or battalions. Two battalions then made up a regiment, with two regiments becoming a brigade. Artillery brigades were, in turn, attached to army corps and could be subdivided into their components as needed.

Rapid advances in metallurgy, manufacturing techniques, and ammunition also provided artillerists with more accurate, longer-range, and faster-loading cannons. Although field artillery was still drawn by six-horse teams, it became lighter and thus more maneuverable. The average field gun caliber also dropped, from about 87mm to 75mm, as the guns' maximum ranges increased from about 4,375 yards to approximately 8,750 yards and the rate of fire increased from about two rounds per minute to as many as seven.

Advances in ammunition were a major factor in the development of the new breechloading quick-loaders. The period saw the elimination of a separate powder bag in favor of one-piece fixed rounds utilizing a metallic powder cartridge. The metallic cartridges were more moisture resistant than the earlier powder bags and were much faster to load. Fuses for shrapnel, the favored explosive projectile, as well as high-explosive shell continued to evolve from the earlier simple burning paper fuse to various types of mechanical time and percussion models.

Advances in Propellants

New propellants played no small role in the late-nineteenth-century artillery revolution. The traditional black powder used since the Middle Ages had a number of disadvantages, including a tendency to foul bores with often dangerously smoldering residue after each shot. That made each subsequent loading more difficult, unless the bore were carefully searched and sponged—a time-consuming process. Moreover, as black powder residue was also corrosive, guns required meticulous cleaning and oiling soon after firing. From a tactical standpoint, the thick and acrid white smoke produced by black powder quickly obscured commanders' and gunners' views, making accurate aiming difficult if not impossible, as well as revealing the position of masked batteries.

First appearing in the mid-1840s, new smokeless propellants addressed nearly all of the deficiencies of black powder: they were less corrosive, more powerful, and produced almost no smoke or fouling upon ignition. Introduced around 1846, one of the earliest forms, known as guncotton, was based on nitrocellulose. In 1886 the Frenchman Paul Vielle (1854–1934) improved the formula by gelatinizing guncotton and adding ether and alcohol to create *Poudre B,* now known as pyrocellulose. The next year, the Swedish-born Alfred Nobel (1833–1896) invented ballistite, another form of smokeless powder, which was soon improved upon in 1889 by an Englishman, Sir Frederick Abel (1826–1902), and a Scot, Sir James Dewar (1842–1923), to become cordite.

Recoil Reduction

During the same period other designers were also addressing the problem of reducing the recoil of artillery pieces. Recoil had plagued gunners since the very beginning of gunpowder artillery, as it tended to make the piece jump backward at every firing. In the case of many field pieces, recoil often made guns jerk back violently as much as 3 or 4 feet, creating a danger to the crew and requiring it to be rolled back into position and relaid. By the end of the century designers had developed recoil systems employing various combinations of springs and hydraulic pistons that allowed the barrel to recoil but virtually eliminated the backward movement of the carriage. Thus, by the twentieth century, some new breechloaders were capable of firing as many as 20 rounds per minute with reasonable accuracy. As a further improvement, designers also incorporated steel-plate shields mounted to gun carriages to provide crews protection from enemy rifle fire and shrapnel. Leading artillery designers included Germany's Heinrich Ehrhardt (1840–1921), Putilov in Russia, and Thorsten Nordenfelt, the developer of the famous French 75mm Model 1897.

Krupp

The Krupp arms-making dynasty was founded in Essen upon the fortune amassed by Arndt Krupp, who settled in that city in 1587. His son Anton expanded the family's endeavors into making firearms during the Thirty Years' War of 1618–1648, and the family progressively expanded its operations over the ensuing decades. In 1811, Friedrich Krupp (1787–1826) established a steel casting facility, and, although he successfully began casting steel in 1816, he expended considerable funds in the process. His son, Alfried (1812–1887), continued his father's work and eventually re-established the family fortune. By its nature steel was very difficult to cast, and internal faults were often impossible to detect through existing testing procedures. Defective cast steel pieces were also much more dangerous to crews than iron cannons, as the softer iron tended to split or burst with less energy than the harder steel, which more often ruptured with deadly violence. The Krupp firm's success in casting steel was considered one of the major metallurgical achievements of its day.

Beginning in 1844, Alfried Krupp began experimenting in machining guns from solid cast steel blanks and in 1847 produced his first steel cannon. That same year he presented a steel gun to the King of Prussia, Frederick Wilhelm IV (1795–1861)—an act of entrepreneurial generosity that later won an order for 300 field guns. He went on to display a 6-pounder muzzleloading gun at the Great Exhibition of 1851 and began experiments in developing breechloading weapons. In 1856, Krupp introduced a 90mm field gun fitted with a transverse sliding breechblock that fit through a corresponding slot in the rear of the barrel.

Germany subsequently made the transition to rifled breechloaders during the 1860s, a move that gave it a distinct artillery advantage during the 1870–1871 Franco-Prussian War. Shortly after the war it adopted 78.5mm guns for its horse artillery and 88mm pieces for field use. The logistical difficulties associated with supplying two sizes of ammunition in the field and recent advances in metallurgy and gun design then led to the Model 73/88 system, which used the 88mm caliber for both horse artillery and field use and the later Model 73/91 system, utilizing nickel steel barrels. The Model 73/91 was finally superseded by Germany's answer to the French 75—the Model 96 or Feldkanone 96 neur Art.

Rheinmetal

One of the premier German ordnance concerns, Rheinische Metallwaaren und Maschinenfabrik, was established in 1889 and began operations manufacturing small arms ammunition. Soon afterward,

Dr. Heinrich Ehrhardt assumed the firm's directorship and expanded its operations to include artillery development and production. As a response to the French 75, Einhardt designed an excellent 15-pounder QF (Quick-Fire) gun that was adopted by Britain in 1901, thus establishing Rheinmetal as a major international arms manufacturer.

French Advances

The French industrialist Eugène Schneider began cannon production in 1870 and by the turn of the century commanded an arms empire to rival the German industrial giant Krupp. The Schneider concern employed some 14,000 employees and incorporated company-owned railways and mines as well as a huge factory complex. By the advent of the twentieth century, it could boast more than twenty-five powers across the globe as customers for its output of advanced artillery.

Ironically, the Germans' confiscation of nearly the entire French artillery arsenal following the Franco-Prussian War forced France to rearm from scratch with the very latest cannon designs. Therefore, by 1875, France boasted some of the best artillery ever fielded. Although a national fervor to avenge the country's humiliating defeat played no small role in its rapid modernization, France also benefited from the efforts of a number of talented designers. The culmination of these engineers' experiments along various artillery avenues was eventually combined to create a masterpiece of artillery—the famous "French 75."

Vechere de Reffye, the commandant of the Meudon Arsenal, played a critical role in the evolution of modern, rapidly loaded field pieces. Basing his efforts on an earlier U.S. model, Reffye worked extensively in perfecting a breech mechanism using the interrupted screw principle. Reffeye's breech consisted of a heavy steel block threaded to mate with the rear of the gun barrel. The incorporation of a number of smooth slots milled through the screw threads of both the block and the breech of the piece then allowed the hinged block to fit snugly into the breech, where it was locked by a quick one-quarter turn of the breech handle. Reffye also advocated the use of metallic cartridges containing powder, primer, and projectile in one unit. The advantages of such a cartridge, he maintained, were numerous, including consistently measured and waterproof powder, as well as ease of loading. The brass cases he recommended also expanded when fired, providing effective obturation; also, as the cases incorporated a self-contained primer, there was no need to drill a vent in the breechblock, weakening it structurally. During the 1870s, Colonel C. Ragnon de Bange, head ordnance engineer of the Société des Anciens Établissements Cail in Paris, built on Reffeye's work in designing breech mechanisms more suitable for heavier artillery pieces. De Bange's breech mechanism also relied on the interrupted screw principle yet did not employ fixed metallic cases, as the French saw them as overly expensive for use in heavy guns and howitzers. As de Bange's system used powder bags, he addressed the obturation problem by using an asbestos pad on the breech face that compressed upon firing, thus sealing the gap between the block and rear of the barrel.

During the last quarter of the century, General Hippolyte Langlois emerged as a visionary theorist who expounded on the possibilities of maneuverable quick-firing field artillery. In his 1892 book *Field Artillery in Cooperation with Other Arms,* Langlois advocated the development and deployment of relatively small caliber rifled breechloaders using metal cartridges that could be deployed rapidly to deliver a *rafale,* or "squall," of intense fire at decisive moments on the field.

Other technological breakthroughs also contributed to the French advances during the period that, when combined, would culminate in a true masterpiece of artillery design. These included the invention of a safer and more powerful nitrocellulose-based smokeless powder by Paul Eugene Vielle. Christened *Poudre B* in honor of France's minister of war, General Boulanger, it was, in turn, followed by the improved *BN,* or *Blanche Nouvelle* (New White), powder. By 1898, General George-Raymond Desaleux had also developed a high-explosive, more aerodynamically stable "boat-tailed" projectile code-named *Obus D,* or "Shell D." The combination of *Poudre B* with a metal case and the Shell D afforded the French a highly efficient round suitable for Langlois's ideal field gun—the French 75.

QUICK-FIRING GUNS IN PRE–WORLD WAR I ARTILLERY ACTIONS

The new quick-firers proved themselves in the 1899–1902 Second Anglo-Boer War, the 1904–1905 Russo-Japanese War, and the Balkan Wars of 1912–1913. These preludes to the Great War served as testing grounds for the more advanced weapons then appearing and allowed the participants and observers to modify their tactical doctrines accordingly.

The Second Boer War 1899–1902

British forces consistently held seemingly overwhelming numerical artillery superiority over their Boer opponents during the fighting in South Africa at the turn of the century. At such battles as the 15 December 1899 action at Colenso, the British fielded 44 guns against the Boers' 5; at Paardeberg (19–27 February 1900), the odds were 91 to 6 in Britain's favor. The ever-resourceful Boers, however, compensated for their numerical deficiencies with better weapons and more adaptable tactics.

The Boers used fixed ammunition and fielded light quick-firers obtained from France, Germany, and—ironically—Britain itself, whose gunners in South Africa still manned older and slower-firing 15-pounders. Moreover, the British ammunition left much to be desired. Whereas British shrapnel was deadly, it was a relatively short-range round; the longer ranged high-explosive shells' lyddite bursting charges were so weak that the Boers often ignored long-range British bombardments.

The 5 February 1900 battle at Brakfontaine illustrated the effectiveness of the Boer artillery and tactics over numerically superior British forces. At Brakfontaine a relatively small Boer force, with only three 75mm quick-firers, faced a British infantry brigade supported by 36 field pieces. Discarding current theory, the Boers did not mass their guns but instead fired from concealed positions, taking advantage of their guns' longer ranges and higher firing rates. The British, for their part, failed to coordinate their infantry and artillery, thus allowing the Boers essentially to snipe at will.

The Russo-Japanese War (1904–1905)

Both the Japanese and Russian forces fielded modern quick-firing field pieces during the 1904–1905 Russo-Japanese War. Although the Russian cannon proved slightly superior to its Japanese counterpart, the Japanese commanders—who apparently, unlike the Russians, had learned much from observing the Franco-Prussian War—employed much more effective tactics.

The Japanese 75mm Arisaka field gun was a light and maneuverable piece capable of firing about 6 to 7 rounds per minute. It had a maximum range of 4,921 yards firing shrapnel and 6,015 yards using high-explosive rounds. The Russian 76.2mm Model 1900 Putilov was superior to the Japanese gun in its range, rate of fire, and the weight of its projectiles. Capable of firing as many as 20 rounds per minute, it had a maximum range of 7,000 yards with high-explosive rounds and 6,124 yards with shrapnel. The Putilov, however, did have some problems with its recoil mechanism that affected its ability to fire both rapidly and accurately simultaneously.

The Japanese organizational structure and tactics proved critical elements in their successful prosecution of the war. Although lacking field telephones, Japanese artillery officers were highly motivated to achieve common goals and well trained to anticipate one another's actions and cooperate accordingly. The Japanese assigned six six-gun batteries to each division, with a reserve of two eighteen-battery artillery brigades. This system allowed them to mass guns quickly at key moments to support infantry offensives. In some instances it also enabled single well-handled batteries to annihilate massed Russian batteries by systematically concentrating and neutralizing individual targets one by one. As the protection and support of the infantry was the artillery's primary goal, the Japanese gunners often pushed their guns along with assaults to divert enemy fire from the infantry, as well as to provide close fire support.

In contrast, Russian artillery officers were much less aggressive and less inclined to risk their guns in fully committed engagements. Although the Russians employed field telephone communications and their eight-gun batteries were capable of delivering more firepower than could the Japanese, they tended to mask their batteries and not mass them as effectively as the Japanese. Russian artillery officers did show some ability to learn from their experiences fighting the Japanese, but rarely did they apply their experience as decisively. More significantly, the Russo-Japanese War proved the effectiveness of high-explosive shells against entrenched troops, as well as the use of plunging indirect fire against concealed targets—two developments that would help define the artillery's role during World War I.

NAVAL ARTILLERY TRENDS

The second quarter of the nineteenth century saw far-reaching changes in naval artillery. During that period the U.S. and European navies followed very similar paths in the development of naval artillery, gunnery, and theory. Technical advances were also speeded by the establishment of ordnance research and testing facilities such as Britain's HMS *Excellent* at Portsmouth and the Sandy Hook proving grounds in New Jersey. With France tending to lead the way, guns generally became standardized aboard ships to single calibers of various sizes. More important, the introduction of shell guns led to fewer but heavier guns aboard ships, as well as the eventual demise of wooden sailing ships and the introduction of armored, steam-powered vessels.

Beginning in 1820, the French navy officially eliminated its heavier guns in favor of 30-pounders of various weights and lengths dependant on their shipboard placement. Britain followed in 1839 by dropping the 42-pounder, thus making the 32-pounder its standard heavy caliber gun. After studying the French and British systems, the United States made the 32-pounder its standard heavy gun in 1845. Although the heavy pieces such as the 42-pounder had outspoken proponents who argued for their greater smashing power, standardization greatly simplified shipboard magazine logistics. In practice, however, such standardization was not always achieved. As a matter of sheer economic necessity older weapons often remained in service, as the new shell guns required their own explosive ammunition and fuses.

The change from traditional solid shot to explosive shell as the primary naval loading was a major factor in the transition from wooden to iron ship construction. Whereas solid shot was capable of punching holes through wooden ships' sides, wrecking rigging and killing and wounding crews, it usually required large numbers of accurate strikes to sink an enemy vessel or force it to surrender. Following the invention of shrapnel, a number of theorists saw that the potential of large-caliber explosive projectiles for naval use was enormous.

The Danes set something of a precedent for explosive naval ordnance following the loss of most of their large ships to the British at Copenhagen in 1807. Denied a blue-water fleet, Denmark relied on a creative innovation in challenging the world's most powerful navy. Having mounted howitzers on a number of smaller ships and oared gunboats, the Danes developed a strategy of attacking larger British ships en masse. During several engagements the howitzers' explosive shells inflicted heavy damage and sank larger British warships operating in the Baltic.

Paixhans Shell Guns

A French army officer, Colonel Henri-Joseph Paixhans (1783–1854), later advocated the flat trajectory of the gun rather than the arcing howitzer trajectory as the ideal delivery system for explosive projectiles against ships. A veteran of the Napoleonic Wars, Paixhans expounded on his theories in 1822 with *Nouvelle force maritime et artillerie,* which he followed in 1825 with *Experiences faites sur une arme nouvelle.* The French navy, with a smaller fleet than Britain's, saw the advantage of more advanced and destructive ordnance as the answer to its numerical disadvantage.

In 1823 and 1824, two 86.5-pounder (80-pounder by French measurement) prototype Paixhans shell guns were cast and put through rigorous tests. The accuracy and destructiveness of the two pieces convinced the French navy to adopt the design in 1824. The Paixhans shell gun was first officially standardized as the *canon-obusier* of 80, no. 1, 1841. It was 9 feet, 4 inches long and could fire a 60.5-pound (English weight) shell, as well as an 86.5-pound (English weight) solid shot. The Paixhans was drilled with a powder chamber and had a bore of 8.95 inches. A number of improvements the next year included the enlargement of the powder chamber and the shortening of the barrel to 9 feet. The improved Paixhans was then redesignated the *canon-obusier* of 80, no. 1, 1842. The United States and Britain soon began experimenting with Paixhans's designs, leading to a general arms race to develop the most effective shell guns.

English and American Shell Guns

A continuous controversy between proponents of breechloading and muzzleloading naval guns complicated the issue in Great Britain and the United States. In the United States, Dahlgren's continued influence was manifested in that country's reluctance to abandon its large muzzle loaders. In Britain, Armstrong breechloaders demonstrated excellent long-range accuracy but once in service did manifest a number of problems. Poorly trained crews at times found the breech mechanism difficult to operate, and if not properly locked the mechanism itself was prone to excessive wear and subsequent malfunction. For safety reasons apprehensive naval crews also often loaded breechloading Armstrongs with reduced charges, thus greatly reducing their effectiveness against ironclad warships. These concerns eventually led to new trials that resulted in the reversion to muzzleloading Armstrongs that, although accurate and hard-hitting, were much slower to load.

During the 1860s and 1870s, Woolwich manufactured several marks of large naval and seacoast Armstrong muzzleloaders, ranging from the 12-ton, 9-inch Mk IV to the 81-ton, 16-inch Mk I. Other big Armstrongs included the 38-ton, 12.5-inch Mk I; the 35-ton, 12-inch Mk I; the 25-ton, 12-inch Mk II; the 25-ton, 11-inch Mk II; and the 18-ton, 10-inch Mk II. The largest rifled muzzleloaders in British service were 17.72-inch, 100-ton giants that, with a 460-pound charge, fired a 1-ton projectile at a muzzle velocity of nearly 1,700 feet per second. Four were manufactured and were mounted in the defenses of Gibraltar and Malta.

In 1879 a devastating disaster aboard the HMS *Thunderer* at last provided the impetus for the Royal Navy to end the use of muzzle-loaded artillery. During gunnery practice, one of the *Thunderer*'s 12-inch turret-mounted Armstrongs misfired—a mishap that went unnoticed owing to the heavy recoil and the report of its twin. The gun was subsequently reloaded with a second charge and exploded, killing 11 and wounding 35 of the ship's crew. Spurred by public outcry, advocates for modernizing naval guns cited the accident to argue that, had the piece been a breechloader, the unfired charge would have been readily detected and the disaster averted.

Naval Gun Turrets

The *Thunderer* disaster occurred in the midst of a general move away from multiple, side-mounted "broadside" mountings, toward fewer yet larger turret-mounted ordnance aboard ships. Ships' masts presented an early obstacle to gun turrets, but as navies gradually modernized and shifted to steam power, turrets became much more practical for shipboard use. In Britain, Captain Cowper Coles of the Royal Navy introduced what he termed a gun "cupola" armored turret in 1861. Denmark quickly followed with the launching of the *Rolf Krake,* mounting a pair of turrets, each with two 8-inch guns, and Brazil, Italy, Prussia, and Russia soon followed suit with their own turreted warships.

As the guns and turrets grew ever heavier, their internal driving mechanisms became more complex. The earliest turrets were hand-cranked affairs that were soon made obsolete by such vessels as the USS *Monitor,* the U.S. ironclad that utilized a steam-driven turret-rotating mechanism. Steam eventually gave way to hydraulic mechanisms that made possible even larger gun turrets. By the end of the century capital warships boasted hydraulic turrets containing multiple heavy breechloaders mounted on massive hollow pivots. Such pivots, in turn, passed through several decks, giving the turret stability and providing a means of internal loading from lower magazines.

As the *Thunderer* had illustrated, naval turret gunnery was an often dangerous affair and continued to present safety problems for designers. A number of deadly accidents, such as the 13 April 1904 explosion within one of the USS *Missouri's* 12-inch gun turrets, led to more sophisticated safety measures. During the following decades, such firms as Krupp in Germany, Britain's Vickers-Armstrong, Schneider in France, and Italy's Ansaldo became leaders in turret construction. Their designs incorporated such modern innovations as automated loading and electrical ignition. They also included multiple safety measures such as sealed internal hatches and pressurized gun compartments, to reduce fire hazards.

The New Ironclads

The proliferation of new armored warships necessitated the development of powerful new ordnance. In 1858, France laid the keel of the first ironclad steamship, *La Gloire,* and the following year Britain began the construction of its own steam-driven ironclad, HMS *Warrior.* During the American Civil War the USS *Monitor* and the CSS *Virginia,* two ironclads of radically different design, fought to a draw at Hampton Roads owing to the effectiveness of their armor and the ineffectiveness of their guns.

During the ensuing years two main theories emerged as to how to defeat the ironclads' wooden-backed armor plate. The Americans, possessing large numbers of heavy smoothbores, favored racking, the method of firing large-caliber projectiles at relatively low velocity, to pound repeatedly (or "rack") the armor plate until it lost its structural integrity. One of racking's greatest merits lay in that, as the iron plates were backed by wood planking, strikes tended to shatter the backing into deadly splinters that could kill or otherwise incapacitate an enemy crew.

Other navies, most notably Britain's, followed the punching school of thought. Punching required a high-velocity, pointed projectile that would pierce directly through the armor and destroy whatever it was designed to protect. British tests conducted in 1863 by Lieutenant W. H. Noble indicated the effectiveness of lighter, high-velocity rounds, and more tests followed to determine the most efficient design for such a projectile. Captain (later Major) William Palliser created the so-called chilled nose punching round, when he found that casting a pointed projectile nose down to increase its density and then rapidly cooling it with water created a very hard armor-piercing round. By the end of the century projectiles filled with high explosives that could penetrate a ship's protective plate were the preferred loading for naval and coastal artillery weapons.

PRE–WORLD WAR I ARTILLERY TRENDS

At the beginning of the century, artillery construction fell under three basic techniques. Armstrong's built-up method of heat shrinking progressively larger reinforcing bands around a central tube remained a viable method for manufacturing large guns and howitzers as did, to a lesser degree, wire-wound pieces. Wire-wound cannons consisted of a central tube wrapped in tremendous lengths of flat wire that were, in turn, secured and reinforced by heat-shrunk bands, much like built-up guns. Although in some cases more economical than other methods of cannon construction, wire-wound guns were difficult to rebore and eventually fell out of use. The third technique, as pioneered by Krupp, relied on machining the piece's barrel out of a single blank stock; as technology improved, that soon became the preferred of the three construction methods.

The major powers interpreted the artillery lessons of the Franco-Prussian War, Second Boer War, and Russo-Japanese War according to their own inclinations and command structures. Still, by 1910, France and Germany viewed artillery duels as ineffective, and the protection of one's own and the destruction of the enemy's infantry their artillery's primary purpose. Following its defeat by the Germans, France initially modified its doctrine to mimic some aspects of its enemy's, yet it still retained a reluctance to expose its gun crews to opposing infantry or artillery fire. For a brief period the use of field pieces with armored shields did encourage the French into more aggressive infantry support, yet by 1910, French doctrine had reverted to providing indirect fire support from less exposed positions.

Artillery Organization

France and Germany developed profoundly different approaches to their artillery organizations during the new century's first decade. The differences in their command structures were particularly apparent. As its primary purpose was to provide fire support, the French artillery was considered essentially subordinate to the infantry and was thus subject to rigid control and had little autonomy. It was divided into infantry batteries subordinate to the infantry commander and into counter-batteries to provide antiartillery fire. German artillery batteries, in contrast, were allowed much more freedom of action in the field, allowing individual commanders to operate as they saw fit. The French officers themselves received rigorous technical and theoretical training at the École Polytechnique, whereas German officers concentrated on tactics and the other more practical aspects of their profession.

In 1910, French field artillery batteries were made up of four guns, whereas the Germans favored larger six-gun batteries. By 1914 the French organized its field artillery regiments into battalions consisting of three four-gun batteries armed with the French 75mm gun. Divisional regiments were made up of three battalions and operated with infantry divisions while in the field, whereas the four-battalion corps regiments acted as an artillery reserve. A German artillery brigade of the same period consisted of three battalions armed with the 77mm light field gun and one battalion of 105mm light field howitzers.

Field Howitzers

By 1914 only Germany had invested in building a sizable and modern field howitzer capability. Much of Germany's impetus in expanding its field howitzer arsenal began in 1891, when Count Alfred von Schliefen (1833–1913) became chief of the German Imperial General Staff, a position he held until 1905. The architect of the Schliefen Plan, he saw it as essential that Germany field large numbers of mobile heavy-caliber siege pieces capable of reducing French and Belgian fortifications in rapid succession. To that end Germany adopted a new 105mm field howitzer in 1898 that was further improved in 1909 by the addition of a number of refinements, including an improved recoil mechanism. The German 105mm field howitzer and an even heavier 150mm model eventually proved very effective against trenches when war commenced in 1914.

Other European powers including Italy and Belgium were much slower in appreciating the advantages offered by field howitzers; although Russia and Britain each had developed relatively good pieces—122mm (4.8-inch) and 114mm (4.5-inch), respectively—neither country had numbers comparable to those of Germany. Germany's archrival, France, was so enamored of *Mademoiselle*

Soixante-Quinze that it failed to boost production of its own 155mm field howitzer, already being manufactured, and instead relied more on obsolete De Bange system pieces. Such shortsightedness among its rivals gave Germany a distinct artillery advantage in the early stages of trench warfare during World War I. Whereas flat-trajectory weapons such as the French 75 were excellent against exposed targets, they were virtually useless against dug-in troops or enemy artillery in defilade positions.

Still, the French were so stubborn in their attachment to guns that they attempted to alter their ammunition so that it would produce a rough simulation of the howitzer's plunging trajectory. To that end they developed *plaquettes*, washer-shaped devices that, when attached around explosive shells, caused them to arc in flight. As with many such improvisations, the *plaquettes* proved a failure and were eventually abandoned. Beginning in 1905 the Germans also unsuccessfully experimented with ammunition in attempt to produce a single howitzer round with both high-explosive and shrapnel capabilities. The warhead of the resulting "unitary shell" thus contained a high-explosive compound in addition to round case shot; it could be detonated by time, impact, or delayed impact fuses. As with many such hybrids, the unitary shell proved inefficient as well as expensive to manufacture and was soon replaced by conventional high-explosive and shrapnel rounds.

WORLD WAR I

The Allied and Central Powers entered World War I in various states of readiness and with a number of artillery doctrines. Confident in its much vaunted 75mm field gun, France based much of its faith in mobile, relatively light-caliber, rapid-fire tactical artillery. By 1914, Germany and Britain, as well as Russia, had also developed reasonably efficient quick-firers. In addition, Germany also saw heavy yet mobile guns and howitzers as the key to rapidly neutralizing Belgian and French fortifications in accordance with their Schlieffen Plan. Other belligerents, such as the United States, were less prepared and were forced in many cases to improvise rapidly to meet the challenges of a world war. The United States thus fought the war with predominantly foreign-designed and -manufactured ordnance.

The war also saw the introduction of new, more lethally efficient projectiles. In their search for a compound stable enough to withstand the shock of firing yet explode violently on target, British scientists experimented with picric acid, a chemical used in the dyeing industry. Using picric acid, they ultimately developed lyddite, to create a practical high-explosive (HE) shell for British service. The other major powers quickly followed suit, and high-explosive shells became a standard component in the world's arsenals. In 1914, Germany began using even more explosive TNT as a high-explosive bursting charge. Other new projectiles included smoke shells containing white phosphorus, to obscure troop deployments, and, as World War I progressed, shells containing poison gas.

In an effort to produce inexpensive cast iron projectiles capable of inflicting maximum casualties, Germany's Kaiser Wilhelm Institute for the Advancement of Science developed a xylyl bromide gas shell in 1914. Although the first German shells proved largely ineffective on the Eastern Front the following January, other, more lethal shell designs followed. The French replied with much improved, larger shells filled with just enough explosive to crack the shell casing and release their deadly phosgene gas. First used at Verdun, the French shells set the standard for future developments. Soon after Germany fielded an array of gas shells, including the so-called Blue Cross projectile containing arsenic-based smoke, phosgene-filled Green Cross, and the insidious Yellow Cross, containing mustard gas. As the war progressed, gas became an everyday threat to frontline troops of all sides.

Although both the French and German artillery saw limited success during the early stages of the war, the realities of trench warfare forced both sides to modify their initial doctrines. Because entrenched troops were protected from the flat trajectory of direct-fire guns such as the French 75, the war saw the ascendancy of the indirect fire of the howitzer, with its arcing trajectory and heavy shells. Other new weapons also arose during the war, including antiaircraft artillery and self-propelled and antitank weapons, as well as the super heavy long-range railroad gun.

Long-range indirect fire also necessitated advances in fire control. Although notoriously unreliable, field telephones gave forward observers unprecedented communication with artillery officers far to the rear. Artillery officers also learned to formulate timetables to coordinate preparatory barrages before infantry assaults to avoid casualties from "friendly fire" and yet disrupt the enemy's defensive capabilities.

During the September 1917 siege of the Russian-held Baltic city Riga, General Oskar von Hutier, commander of the German 8th

Army, demonstrated a degree of originality rarely matched by Allied commanders. Aided by his artillery commander, a Colonel Bruchmuller, he proved the effectiveness of coordinating the infiltration of the enemy's lines by specially trained storm troops combined with flexible artillery deployment. At Riga, von Hutier divided his 750 guns and 550 mortars to perform two distinct roles. These included the Infantrie Kampfzug Abteilung, or IKA, to provide direct infantry support, firing high-explosive and gas shells, and the Artillerie Kampfzug Abteilung, or AKA, which provided long-range fire to suppress the Russian artillery and disrupt their reserves and command structure. Von Hutier's tactics proved so successful at Riga that he and Bruchmuller were reassigned to the Western Front, where they successfully applied them during the German April 1918 offensive.

Having apparently originated during the American Civil War, railway artillery also reached a high state of development during World War I. Driven by necessity owing to its lack of heavy land ordnance, the French pioneered the practice of mounting unused naval and coastal artillery guns on railroad cars. This practice enabled them to deploy high-caliber weapons rapidly to the front, where aiming was accomplished by their positioning on specially laid sections of curved track. Britain followed a similar course, and Germany experimented with placing standard pieces, such as the 170mm field gun, on railroad gondolas. They also, like the late-entering Americans, produced large and effective railroad guns that saw service during the war.

United States Artillery

Following the Civil War only a few private U.S. firms, such as the Driggs-Seabury Company and Bethlehem Steel, remained in the ordnance business. Their production, however, was limited to filling export orders and a few supplemental contracts for the U.S. government. The vast majority of artillery production was apportioned by the Ordnance Department to two major government arsenals. Originally established in 1812 near Albany, New York, the Watervliet Arsenal assumed its role as the primary government cannon barrel foundry in 1889. Carriage production was carried out in Illinois at the Rock Island Arsenal.

Still, U.S. artillery lagged behind Europe's during the late nineteenth century. During the Spanish American War the artillery's command structure lacked effective organization, and its continued use of black powder revealed the positions of field guns, making them easy targets for the Spanish gunners. By 1901 it was obvious that a complete reorganization was necessary, thus leading to the Military Reorganization Act of 1907. The new act at last formally differentiated between coast and field artillery and reaffirmed the field artillery's identity as a separate and necessary arm.

Nevertheless, the U.S. entry into World War I caught the Ordnance Department unprepared to provide a domestically produced quick-firing field gun to meet the needs of the rapidly mobilizing army. As its own M1916 3-inch field gun was still in a developmental stage, the United States was forced to obtain much of its field artillery from its allies or manufacture foreign designs under license agreements. These included the excellent French 75 as well as the British 18-pounder field gun, which U.S. manufacturers modified to accept the French 75's ammunition, an adaptation that they also eventually applied to their own M1916. In addition to these lighter pieces, the United States also used French 155mm howitzers and guns and British 6-inch guns and 8- and 9.2-inch howitzers.

Despite such technological advances as tanks, railroad, and motorized antiaircraft guns, World War I was essentially a horse-drawn artillery war. Although automobiles, trucks, and tracked vehicles were available, their technology was still relatively new, production was limited, and few soldiers had the mechanical skills to maintain them in the field. As a result, the World War I artillerist typically walked beside his piece to battle at 2.5 miles per hour, as had his predecessors centuries earlier.

FIELD ARTILLERY TO 1920
The French 75

Affectionately christened *Mademoiselle Soixante-Quinze* (Miss Seventy-five) by the French and later U.S. gunners who crewed it, the French 75 became one of the most famous artillery pieces of all time. It was adopted by France in 1897, by the United States in 1917, and remained in service with the former until that country's fall in 1943; it was used by other, smaller nations into the 1950s. Having learned that recent Krupp recoil reduction experiments had proved unsuccessful, the French director of artillery, General Charles P. Mathieu, directed that a development program be set up to design a quick-fire 75mm gun as envisioned by Langlois. He subsequently assigned the project to Colonel Albert Deport, director of the Chatillon-Commentry Gunfoundry at Puteaux, where the development process was carried out in strictest secrecy.

Deport began by appropriating a number of features from an earlier 57mm gun developed in 1889 by Captain Sainte-Claire Deville. These included an improved caisson, seats for the crew, a steel gun shield to protect crewmen from small arms fire and shrapnel, a removable rear sight, and a collimator—a telescopic direct-fire sight. For the breech mechanism, the design team adopted a design incorporating a simple rotating eccentric disk-shaped breechblock designed by Thorsten Nordenfelt of Société Nordenfelt. The block itself was manufactured with a milled cutout that, when the unit was rotated up, allowed loading. A one-half turn downward then closed the breech, with the metallic cartridge providing self-obduration.

Although they had been ingeniously combined, the French 75 thus incorporated features that were already available and used in various other artillery pieces. The greatest obstacle facing the designers lay in neutralizing the gun's recoil and automatically returning its barrel to its original position. They approached the problem with what came to be known as the "long recoil" system, consisting of a piston attached to the lower rear of the gun barrel and two gas and oil-filled piston tubes mounted to the carriage. Upon firing, the barrel and its piston moved violently rearward to compress the oil in the upper tube, or "buffer," to force oil into the lower tube, or "recuperator," and thus control its recoil. At the point of extreme recoil, the tapered "throttling rod" attached to the rear of the floating piston in the recuperator sealed a diaphragm to shut off the oil flow to the lower piston. This action also further compressed nitrogen gas contained under pressure in the recuperator, thus providing the energy to return the gun barrel to its firing position.

The first prototypes were finished in 1894, but tests revealed that their recoil systems did not perform as originally desired. Captain Emile Rimailho and Captain Sainte-Claire Deville, however, continued to perfect the recoil system until the project culminated in 1897. In addition to its many advanced features and recoil system, the new Model 1897 also incorporated carriage innovations that further lessened its recoil. Although still mounted on conventional wood-spoked, iron-tired wheels, its three-point suspension's wheel brakes and trail spade (a blade attached to the end of the trail as an anchor) provided unprecedented stability. It was also capable of independent tube traversal and elevation.

The Schneider concern and the Bourges Arsenal, the primary French ordnance facility southeast of Paris, manufactured the French 75 for the French government and its allies. It entered service in 1898, and some 1,100 were in use by 1914. Its hydraulic long-recoil system virtually eliminated recoil, and with its eccentric screw breech it made possible a firing rate of up to 20 rounds a minute—a rate that increased to 30 when fitted with a semiautomatic breech mechanism. Moreover, the Model 1897's maximum range approached 5 miles.

The French 75mm barrel was 106 inches in length, and the weapon's overall weight was 2,560 pounds. It was capable of elevation ranging from -11 to +18 degrees and could traverse up to 6 degrees. It fired a 15.9-pound shrapnel shell at a muzzle velocity of 1,735 feet per second to a maximum range of 9,300 yards.

The French 75 was first used by French forces in China during the 1900 Boxer Rebellion and quickly proved its superior mobility and high rate of fire. Its success alarmed the other major powers, initiating an arms race that resulted in their development and adoption of quick-fire field pieces of 75mm to 77mm calibers by 1906. France and the United States later improved the original design by replacing its early stock trail carriage with a split trail and adding pneumatic rubber tires. These additions boosted the gun's maximum range up to 7 miles.

Belgian Artillery

Belgium, for centuries a major center of small arms production, also boasted the Cockerill and FRC ordnance foundries. Both firms, however, directed the majority of their sales to foreign clients, thus placing the Belgian army in the rather odd situation of obtaining cannons from outside sources. Before and during World War I, Belgium consequently fielded French and German designs either obtained from abroad or manufactured under license by Cockerill and FRC. During World War I the Belgians fielded a variety of field guns, such as the 75mm M05, the 75mm Model TR, the 105mm M13, the 75mm M18, and the 120mm field howitzer.

German Field Artillery

Germany was decidedly behind France in field artillery development during the immediate prewar years. Constructed of steel and designed for use by the horse artillery, the light 80mm Model 73 field gun was an early attempt at producing a modern field piece. It employed a breech mechanism consisting of an expanding steel ring in the breech face against which a removable cylindrical breech-block pressed a steel plate to create a gas seal. Although a good weapon for its time, the Model 73's breech mechanism wore out rapidly, it lacked a recoil mechanism other than wheel brakes, and it lacked sufficient range when loaded with shrapnel. Improvements in metallurgy and experimentation later allowed German designers to lighten the Model 73's barrel. The result was the 90mm Model 73/88, which was then issued to both horse artillery and field batteries. After being refitted with nickel steel barrels, the design was finally redesignated the Model 73/91.

Although by no means a match for many more advanced foreign breechloaders, the 77mm Field Gun Model 96 (the Americanized form of the German Feldkanone M96) was at least an improvement over the Model 73/91 that it replaced. Adopted in 1896, it had improved horizontal sliding block and case extraction mechanisms as well as better sights and a capability of traversing 4 degrees to either side. Its design, however, did not adequately address controlling recoil, as it utilized only a wire-rope brake and a spade at the end of its trail that anchored it to the ground.

As the leading German arms producers, such as Krupp and Ehrhardt, found it more profitable to market their latest designs to Asian and Latin American governments, the German army found itself in the ironic position of fielding essentially obsolescent artillery. Rushed to provide a stopgap weapon in the face of foreign quick-firing advances, German engineers radically redesigned the Model 96 to produce the Model 96 New Model, the basis for German field guns for the next twenty years.

The New Model 96 shared the caliber, elevation capabilities, and range of the earlier model yet did incorporate a number of significant improvements. Weighing one ton, it had the ability to traverse to the left and right on its carriage, and it was equipped with a more efficient one-movement breechblock. More significantly, the barrel itself rode in a trough-like cradle, its recoil buffered by a hydraulic and spring-operated recoil device. The combination of the new model's breechblock, fixed ammunition, and recoil system at last provided the German army with its own quick-firing field piece capable of a firing rate of about 20 rounds per minute. To protect the crew, who could now remain behind the piece during firings, the New Model also mounted a 4-millimeter-thick steel shield on either side of the barrel.

In addition to the M96, Germany also issued the 135mm FK 13, the 77mm FK 96/15, the heavy yet excellent 77mm FK16, and the 105mm K17. The improved 105mm Model FH98/09 howitzer incorporated an improved recoil system over the earlier FH98, and its box trail was fitted with an opening directly behind the breech to allow higher elevation of the barrel. Other field howitzers included the 105mm 1eFH16 and the 105mm FH 17.

Austro-Hungarian Field Artillery

The Artillerie Zeugfabrik in Vienna served as the principal state artillery manufacturer for the Austro-Hungarian Empire during the nineteenth century. In the years prior to World War I two private firms—the Böhler Company and Skoda in Pilsen—also emerged as major arms suppliers that produced ordnance for Austria-Hungary as well as other countries. Skoda eventually established itself as a major international supplier of excellent artillery pieces for numerous clients, and it continued operations in the newly formed Czechoslovakia after World War I.

Standard Austrian World War I–era field pieces included the 75mm FK M05 field gun, the 76.5mm FK M05 field gun, the 75mm FK M12, the 76.5mm FK M17, and the 76.5mm FK M18. Although its exceptionally long trail made it somewhat unwieldy, the effectiveness of the 104mm field howitzer M99 made it popular with its crews. Other field howitzers included the 100mm M14, the 104mm M17, and the 105mm M15/T.

British Field Artillery

The success of the French 75 and combat experience against the Boers in South Africa prompted Great Britain to modernize its field artillery with the introduction of its own quick-firers. The accurate Boer rifle fire was also a particular incentive to add bulletproof steel shields to field weapons for the protection of the crews. The new quick-firers were also equipped with improved and easily accessible limbers that were compartmentalized into sections for fuses, small implements, and ammunition.

During World War I Britain issued a variety of quick-firers, including the 4.7-inch Mk 1 field gun, the 12-pounder (pdr) 6-cwt (hundredweight) Mk4, and the 15-pdr Mk1, the latter mounted on a steel carriage with seats on either side of the trail for the crew and fitted with protective shields. Following the South African Wars the British at last recognized the need for a powerful, rapid-firing modern field gun. With a Vickers gun tube and a carriage designed by the Woolwich Arsenal, the quick-firing 18-pdr Mk1 was adopted in 1904 and achieved a 6,523-yard maximum range firing an 18.5-pound shell. Designed as a companion piece to the 18-pdr M1 Gun, the 4.5-inch Howitzer Mk1 was developed by the private firm of Coventry Ordnance works and also entered service in 1904. At its maximum 45 degree elevation, the Mk1 fired a 35-pound shell 7,300 yards.

United States Field Artillery

Caught in a race to obtain a quick-firing field gun, in 1902 the United States adopted the 3-inch M1902, a slightly modified German Erhardt design. The M1902 fired a 15-pound shell to a maximum range of 7,477 yards and was mounted on the Model 1902 single trail carriage developed by Captain Charles B. Wheeler. Although the M1902 was a serviceable weapon, the U.S. Army desired a domestically designed gun for issue to its field batteries. The Ordnance Department thus began development of the 3-inch M1916, a modern weapon with a split trail carriage and a hydrospring recoil system. As adopted in 1918, it fired a 13.7-pound shell up to 9,592 yards. The Ordnance Department had some difficulty, however, in producing enough 3-inch ammunition to meet the needs of the rapidly mobilizing army. It thus ordered the rechambering of the M1916 to accept the ammunition used by the French 75. The Ordnance Department's decision thus brought into being the 75mm M1916. Officially adopted in 1917, it was capable of firing a 13.5-pound shell to a maximum range of 12,448 yards.

Before the entry of the United States into World War I, U.S. firms were already manufacturing considerable amounts of ordnance, including the British 18-pounder for the Allied powers. Another wartime expedient, the 75mm M1917 quick-firing gun, was essentially the British 18-pounder adapted to accept the French 75 loading, the standard field gun cartridge used by the United States during the war. It was adopted in 1918 and fired a 15-pound shell to a maximum range of 8,720 yards. The 4.7-inch Howitzer M1908, the army's standard high-trajectory field piece during World War I, fired a 60-pound shell to a maximum range of 6,875 yards.

Italian Field Artillery

Although its Turin Arsenal manufactured a limited number of mountain guns, before World War I, Italy acquired its artillery from foreign sources, including Krupp of Germany, the Austro-Hungarian Skoda factory, and the French Deport firm. These included the Krupp-designed 75mm 75/27 Mo.06, which also saw service in World War II, and the 75mm Gun Mo.12 Deport. Designed by the prolific Colonel Albert Deport of France and adopted in 1912, the 75mm Gun Mo.12 Deport introduced a dual recoil system as well as the split trail carriage. The latter innovation incorporated twin hinged trails that could be closed for limbering and then spread apart to stabilize the piece and allow greater recoil at higher elevation. The Mo.12 was acquired by other powers as well as Italy, and the split trail carriage quickly became the standard for nearly all field pieces worldwide.

Italy also fielded the 75mm Gun Mo.06/12 and a howitzer designated the Obice da 100/17 Mo.14. An Austro-Hungarian design, the quick-firing caliber 100mm Mo.14 howitzer was adopted in 1914, and numbers were also captured from the Central Powers at the end of World War I. The 100/17 saw extensive Italian service during World War II and was also used by Polish and Romanian forces.

Japanese Field Artillery

Japan, the rapidly emerging Eastern power, plunged into the development of modern quick-firing field pieces. Designated by their year of production according to the Japanese calendar, the Japanese pieces were equal if not superior to many of their European and U.S. counterparts. The standard Japanese pieces of the period included the 75mm Meiji 38 and 105mm Meiji 38 guns adopted in 1905, and the 75mm Meiji 41 gun adopted in 1908. In 1917, the improved Meiji 38 replaced the earlier model's quick-firing breech mechanism with a horizontal sliding block.

Russian Field Artillery

Russia began the century and fought the Russo-Japanese War with a 76.2mm quick-firing, screw-breech field gun designed by General Engelhardt. The Model 1900 (76 K/00) was mounted on a wooden block trail carriage with conventional iron-tired wood-spoked wheels with traveling seats for crewmen on each axletree. The hydraulic and spring-activated recoil mechanism was mounted within the carriage. Production was carried out at various government factories including Putilov, Obuhov, and Perm.

The Model 1900 was soon followed by the 76.2mm quick-fire Model 1902 (76 K/02). Apparently influenced by the French 75, Putilov Arsenal engineers L. A. Bishjakov, K. I. Lipinski, and K. M. Sokolovski redesigned General Engelhardt's original model to produce the most used Russian field gun of World War I. Later models were fitted with shields manufactured with upper and lower folding sections. Other Russian field pieces included the 85mm M02 and the 3-inch (76.2mm) M13 guns, and the quick-firing 122mm M04 howitzer.

Swedish Field Artillery

Bofors, Sweden's primary ordnance manufacturer, began arms manufacturing in 1883 and remains in operation today. During the 1920s the German arms giant Krupp acquired interest in Bofors and installed a number of German technicians in Sweden to develop ordnance without the restrictions imposed under the Versailles Treaty. The company gained its greatest fame with its 40mm L/60 antiaircraft gun, which it introduced in 1929. Undergoing continuous improvements, the L/60 remained in service with various nations well into the 1950s. Other Swedish field pieces included the 75mm M1902 gun and the 105mm M1910 howitzer.

MOUNTAIN ARTILLERY
Austria

To provide their troops with lightweight yet potent artillery pieces for mountain warfare, the majority of the major powers involved in World War I adopted mountain howitzers and guns. Mountain pieces were typically designed for ease of disassembly for pack transport over difficult terrain. Austria, with its extensive Alpine region, was one of the most prolific manufacturers of such efficient little weapons. These included the 72.5mm M08, the 104mm M08 howitzer, the 72.5mm M09, the 104mm M10 howitzer, the 75mm M13 howitzer, the 75mm M15 mountain howitzer, the 100mm M16 howitzer, and the 150mm M18 mountain howitzer.

Germany

Germany adopted the 75mm Geb K08 in 1908. Firing an 11.6-pound shell up to 6,288 yards, the K08 required up to five mules to transport when disassembled and incorporated a lightweight differential spring recoil system that allowed the firing pin to strike as the barrel traveled forward. The 105mm Geb H L/12 howitzer entered service in 1910. It was followed in 1914 by the 75mm Geb G14, a horizontal sliding block weapon that fired an 11.5-pound shell to a maximum range of 5,140 yards.

France

France also fielded considerable numbers of mountain pieces, such as the 65mm Gun Mle 06, the quick-firing 70mm Schneider Mle 08, and the postwar 75mm quick-firing Mle 19 and 105mm Howitzer Mle 19. Easily distinguished by its large recoil spring wrapped around its barrel, the 75mm Deport mountain gun was accepted in 1910. It also had a semiautomatic, horizontal sliding block breech mechanism and fired a 14-pound shell.

Great Britain

Great Britain, owing to its numerous operations in the mountainous regions of its colonies, issued several fine mountain pieces. Adopted in 1901, the 10-pdr Jointed Mk1 fired a 10-pound shell up to 5,993 yards. Also known as the "screw gun," the barrel of the Mk1 could be dismantled for easier transport in difficult terrain. The 2.75-inch Mk1 gun was adopted in 1912. Designed to be disassembled and transported by mules, it replaced the earlier Mk1 and was the primary weapon of the Indian Mountain Artillery. The quick-firing 3.7-inch Howitzer Mk1 was adopted in 1915 and eventually replaced the 2.75-inch Mk1. It had a 44.4-inch two-piece barrel that was joined by a large junction nut. The Mk1 fired a 20-pound shell to a maximum range of 5,900 yards and required two mules to transport the barrel and six for the carriage.

Other Mountain Artillery

Italy, Japan, Russia, and the United States also produced quantities of mountain artillery. In 1903, Italy adopted the quick-firing 70mm Mo.2, which was superseded in 1910 by the 70mm Mo.08 and the 65mm Canone da 65/17 in 1913. Japan adopted the quick-firing 75mm Meiji 41 in 1908 and later improved it in 1917. The improved Meiji 41 shared the basic 1908 model's characteristics, apart from a slightly greater range and traversal capability. World War I–era Russian mountain artillery included the 76.2mm quick-firing Gun M04 and the quick-firing 105mm Howitzer M09, whereas in 1903 the United States fielded the quick-firing 2.95-inch Gun M1903, a gun owing many of its features to a German Erhart design. In 1912 the United States adopted the 3-inch Howitzer M1911, a weapon that fired a 15-pound shell to a maximum range of 5,668 yards.

TRENCH MORTARS AND CANNONS

In 1910, Rheinmetall introduced its first type of *Minenwerfer,* a short-range, high-trajectory mortar intended to destroy barbed wire barriers and machine gun emplacements in preparation for assaults. The first model was a 250mm weapon capable of firing a 214-pound bomb up to 437 yards. A second 170mm version followed that and threw a 125.5-pound shell to a maximum range of 820 yards. Both models quickly proved their value in the early stages of World War I trench warfare, spurring Great Britain and France to develop their own counterparts.

Prompted by the effectiveness of the Germans' *Minenwerfer,* the French responded with their own improvised trench mortars designed to throw small bombs—often little more than grenades—at high trajectories into enemy positions. They at first rushed small, obsolete muzzleloaded mortars to the front, followed by modified De Bange mountain guns. These were later supplemented by the more conventional M1916TR. The 37mm Nordenfelt screw breech M1916TR trench cannon was adopted in 1916. It weighed 258 pounds, had a simple tripod carriage with two long trails to the rear and a shorter front support leg, and fired a 1-pound shell to a maximum range of 2,625 yards.

ANTIAIRCRAFT ARTILLERY

The development of specialized antiaircraft artillery also intensified during the war. The first documented use of antiaircraft artillery occurred as early as the siege of Paris during the Franco-Prussian War in 1870. At Paris, the Prussian commander von Moltke ordered weapons from Krupp in order to shoot down balloons in which the French were trying to sail over the Prussian lines. Krupp eventually delivered a number of single-shot, caliber 1-inch rifles that were mounted on pedestals bolted to the beds of two-horse wagons; they theoretically could follow the balloons on the ground while maintaining a steady firing rate. The Krupp pieces were relatively ineffective, yet at least one French balloon was apparently downed by their fire.

The rapid proliferation of powered military aircraft at the turn of the century, however, spurred an equally dedicated effort to neutralize the threat of air attacks. During the 1909 Frankfurt International Exhibition, Krupp unveiled three antiaircraft guns in a bid to monopolize the emerging market. These included a caliber 65mm 9-pounder and a 75mm 12-pounder. Krupp claimed that the largest, a pedestal-mounted 105mm gun intended for shipboard use, achieved a maximum ceiling of 37,730 feet. The caliber 65mm gun had an 18,700-foot range, could elevate 75 degrees, and its carriage had unique hinged axles that allowed the wheels to be pivoted to a position perpendicular to their traveling position. With the trail spade acting as its axis, this arrangement enabled the crew to traverse the piece 360 degrees to track enemy aircraft. With a claimed maximum ceiling of 21,326 feet, the caliber 75mm gun was mounted on a truck bed, thus giving it a high degree of mobility. Not to be outdone, Erhardt, Krupp's closest domestic competitor, also exhibited a 50mm quick-firing antiaircraft gun mounted in an armored car's turret.

The period also witnessed considerable experimentation in antiaircraft shells and fuses. Krupp introduced a high-explosive shell for its 3-pounder equipped with a "smoke-trail" fuse, an early tracer round that both aided the crews in sighting and was an effective incendiary against the hydrogen-filled airships of the period.

In 1914, French designers responded to the new menace posed by German aviators with the Autocannon, a standard French 75 on a special mounting bolted to a De Dion Bouton automobile chassis. As a timely expedient, the affair proved effective enough that some

Autocannons were also used in London's air defenses. Another application of the 75 to an antiaircraft role incorporated a two-wheeled carriage on a 360 degree rotating base with four stabilizing outriggers.

During World War I the Germans continued to experiment in antiaircraft weaponry, beginning in 1914 with the 77mm Ballonen-AK. The Ballonen-AK was then, in turn, followed in 1915 by the 77mm Luftkanone, a basic 77mm field cannon barrel mounted on a rotating scaffolding. The more effective Krupp 88mm FlaK entered service in 1918 and eventually became the inspiration for the famous World War II German "Eighty-Eight."

As a response to the new threat from the air, in 1914, Britain adopted the 3-inch, 20-cwt Mk 1 antiaircraft gun. The following year the 2.9-inch, 10-pounder quick-fire "Russian" antiaircraft gun and the quick-firing 12-pounder, 12 cwt, 3-inch Mk1 also entered service. Other British antiaircraft artillery included the quick-firing, 3.3-inch, 13-pounder 9-cwt antiaircraft gun, the semiautomatic 4-inch Mk5 capable of firing a 30.8-pound shell to a maximum ceiling of 29,987 feet, and the quick-firing, 3.3-inch 18-pounder Mk2, adopted in 1916.

Italy began fielding the 76.2mm 76/40 Ansaldo and the 76.2mm 76/45 Mo.11 in 1912. In 1915, the same year as Russia began issuing its 76.2mm M15, the Italians adopted the semiautomatic 75mm 75/27 Mo.06/15. The United States issued a modification of the French 75 for use against the new aircraft that were appearing over World War I battlefields. The 3-inch M1917A2 was fitted with a semiautomatic loading system, and its special mounting made possible a full 360 degree traversal and an elevation of 85 degrees. At full elevation its 12.8-pound shells attained a maximum ceiling of 29,389 feet.

SELF-PROPELLED ARTILLERY

In an attempt to provide more mobile artillery to its trench-bound troops, France pioneered the mounting of artillery to tracked carriages. Although self-propelled artillery was a relative rarity during World War I, it became an integral part of postwar armies. In 1918, French designers at St. Chamond mounted a nontraversing caliber 240mm barrel on a specially modified tracked tank chassis, whereas the self-propelled gun produced by Schneider incorporated a 220mm nontraversing caliber 220mm barrel on a tracked chassis.

ANTITANK ARTILLERY

The Allied introduction of tanks during World War I forced Germany to counter with effective antitank artillery. As the first tanks were relatively lightly armored, German gunners initially found field guns firing high-explosive ammunition at close range to be effective. As the Allied armor increased, the Germans answered with specialized weapons firing armor-piercing ammunition. Adopted in 1918 to counter the new Allied weapons, the 37mm PaK 1918 weighed just 386 pounds and had a horizontal sliding block and a 31.9-inch barrel. It fired a 1.3-pound shell to a maximum range of 2,843 yards.

MEDIUM AND HEAVY ARTILLERY

At the turn of the century massively constructed fortifications were a common feature of strategic locations around the globe. It was thus necessary to develop and build suitable weapons both to defend and to reduce such positions. As World War I entered its static phase of trench warfare, it also became necessary to continue the development of large ordnance to neutralize well-prepared defenses, as well as opposing batteries in preparation for the grand and costly assaults that marked the conflict. As a result World War I was in many ways a heavy artilleryman's fight, and the world's factories worked overtime to keep them supplied with the tools of their trade.

Austria and Germany

Austria and Germany were particularly prolific in manufacturing such massive weapons. Owing to the design and production capabilities of the Krupp facilities, Germany produced the most famous heavy weapons of the war. During the 1890s, Krupp began a program to produce a heavy howitzer capable of destroying the massive concrete fortifications then being constructed in Belgium and France. "Alpha," the first of a series of prototypes, was a 204mm weapon; it was followed in 1900 by the 305mm "Beta." Completed in 1911, the 420mm "Gamma" H was the culmination of the firm's program; weighing 175 tons, it required dismantling for transport on ten railroad cars and fired a 2,535-pound shell up to 8.8 miles. By 1914 the Gamma series had evolved into the more mobile Gamma M, also known as the "Big Bertha" gun.

Popularly named after Alfred Krupp's daughter, the 41.3-ton, 420mm "Big Bertha" had a horizontal sliding block and fired a 1,719-pound shell up to 10,253 yards. Big Bertha required five tractors to transport its components, and it had to be assembled on site. In conjunction with a number of Austrian Skoda 305mm howitzers, the L/14 was first used with devastating effect against Liège in August 1914; it saw other action on both the Western and Eastern fronts. Owing to its relatively short range and vulnerability to Allied fire, Big Bertha was obsolete by 1917. Another heavy piece, the 211mm Mörser was adopted in 1916. It weighed 14,727 pounds and fired a 250-pound shell up to 12,139 yards.

Designed by Krupp engineers and adopted in 1918, the Paris Gun used the basic 380mm Max railroad gun barrel fitted with a barrel liner and lengthened 20 feet. The 210mm Paris Gun weighed 1,653,470 pounds and mounted a 2,550-inch barrel with a horizontal sliding block. It fired a 264-pound shell up to 82 miles. Crewed by naval personnel, the Paris Gun was so powerful that it fired its shells into the stratosphere, where the thinner atmosphere exerted less resistance, allowing such long ranges. The stress on the bore, however, wore the barrel significantly, and each succeeding projectile had to have progressively larger driving bands and heavier powder charges to compensate for the increasing windage. Although hugely inefficient in the final analysis, the Paris Gun's greatest value lay in its use as a propaganda tool rather than an artillery piece.

Although less dramatic in appearance and effect than its heavy artillery, Germany's medium ordnance played a critical role in the country's war effort. The 150mm sFH02 was adopted in 1902, and was followed by the 150mm sFH113 and 150mm K16 in 1917.

The year 1880 was a watershed for Austria's production of a variety of precursors to its twentieth-century medium and heavy arsenal. That year the nation adopted the 120mm siege gun M80, the 149mm siege gun M80, the 180mm siege gun M80, and the 149mm M80 siege howitzer. These pieces were then followed by the even more formidable 150mm Field Howitzer M94 and in 1898 the 250mm "Gretel" Howitzer, capable of firing a 292-pound shell 7,108 yards.

As World War I ground on, Austria continued to develop ever more powerful medium and heavy pieces. In 1914 the excellent 149mm M14 field howitzer replaced the aging Model 1899. It was then supplemented the following year by the 152.4mm M15 gun firing a 124.5-pound shell up to 20,779 yards, the 149mm Field Howitzer M15 that achieved a range of 12,577 yards with a 92.5-pound shell, and the 149mm Howitzer M15 firing an 84-pound shell to a maximum range of 8,858 yards.

A counterpart to the heavy German "Bertha" howitzers, the 305mm "Emma" howitzer was adopted in 1913 and achieved a 13,123-yard maximum range with an 838-pound shell. The 280mm howitzer was accepted the following year and fired a 745-pound shell up to 12,030 yards. In 1916, Austria introduced both the 305mm Howitzer M16, with a maximum range of 32,808 yards with a 1,543-pound shell, and the 380mm Howitzer M16, which fired a massive 2,205-pound shell to a maximum range of 16,404 yards. These weapons were followed in 1917 by the nearly 117-ton, 420mm L/15 Howitzer, firing a 2,205-pound shell up to 15,967 yards.

Belgium and France

For their part, Allied foundries also manufactured a variety of effective medium and heavy artillery pieces to counter those of the Central Powers. Long a center of arms production, Belgium in 1917 adopted the 155mm Gun M17, firing a 95-pound shell up to 16,951 yards, and the 150mm Howitzer M17, a high-trajectory piece that fired a 91-pound shell to a maximum range of 9,405 yards.

Although prone to rest on the laurels won by its famous 75, France also plunged into modern heavy ordnance production. In 1885 it adopted the high-trajectory 270mm Howitzer, an interrupted screw breech weapon that fired a 335-pound shell up to 8,749 yards. Adopted in 1890, the 120mm Short Gun Mle 90 fired a 40-pound shell to a maximum range of 6,343 yards. The Mle 90 used a hydraulic recoil buffer attached to its carriage and the firing platform; for transport it was fitted with an extra rear pair of traveling trunnion holes in much the same manner as the eighteenth-century Gribeauval system. In 1885, the Mle 90 was joined by the high-trajectory 270mm Howitzer, an interrupted screw breech weapon that fired a 335-pound shell up to 8,749 yards.

The French army next accepted the 220-pounder, 220mm Howitzer Mle 01 in 1903 and followed it in 1905 with the 155mm Howitzer Rimailho Mle 04, a more versatile weapon that fired an 89-pound shell up to 6,562 yards. Each army corps was assigned four Mle 04s, and they remained in service through the majority of World War I. Adopted in 1912, the 139mm Gun Mle 10 fired a 67-pound shell up to 19,029 yards, and the 1914-issued 155mm Gun Mle 77/14 had a maximum range of 12,467 yards with a 95-pound shell. As the war progressed the French continued to field new designs.

The 120mm Howitzer Mle 15TR howitzer was adopted in 1915, as was the 220mm Howitzer Mle 16 that was, in turn, followed in 1916 by the 145mm Gun Mle 16.

The year 1917 saw the greatest number of new French designs during the war. The 155mm Gun Mle 17LS appeared that year, as did the famed 155mm Gun Mle 17 GPF. The 155mm Mle 17 GPF (Grand Puissance Filloux, or High Powered gun designed by Lieutenant Colonel Filloux of the Puteaux Arsenal) weighed 23,700 pounds and had a maximum range of 17,717 yards firing a 95-pound shell. The Mle 17 GPF was also adopted by the United States and stayed in that country's service into World War II, when it was adapted for self-propelled use by mounting on a tank chassis.

Other 1917-issued weapons included the 220mm Gun Mle 17, the 279mm Mortar Schneider, a massive weapon that fired a 452-pound shell, and the 155mm Howitzer Mle 17, which replaced the obsolete 155mm Rimailho. A Schneider design, it achieved a 12,577-yard maximum range firing a 96-pound shell. Also manufactured in the United States under license, the Mle 17 served as that country's medium howitzer from World War I to World War II. Accepted in the last year of the war, the 155mm Gun Mle 18 fired a 95-pound shell to a maximum range of 13,123 yards.

Great Britain

Great Britain adopted the stubby 5-inch Howitzer Mk1 in 1895. Having an interrupted screw breech mechanism, it fired a 50-pound shell to a maximum range of 4,801 yards. It was first used in the 1897 Nile Campaign, and, although by then obsolescent, out of necessity it also saw service in World War I. It was later replaced by the 4.5-inch howitzer. The 6-inch, 30-cwt Howitzer Mk1 entered service the year after its 5-inch cousin; it fired a 118-pound round up to 5,200 yards. Its barrel could be removed and, placed on a special mounting in a siege role, it could reach a range of up to 7,000 yards. Practical use, however, proved it to be overly complicated, and it was later replaced by the 26-cwt model. The 5-inch, 60-pdr Gun Mk 1 fired a 60-pound shell to a maximum range of 13,889 yards. It was adopted in 1904 and, improved in 1918 as the Mk2, remained in service until it became obsolete in 1944. Also adopted in 1904, the 9.5-inch Howitzer Mk1 fired a 280-pound shell up to 7,650 yards.

Britain steadily intensified its heavy armaments development as World War I continued its deadly progress. Designed and manufactured by Coventry Ordnance Works, the 9.2-inch Howitzer Mk1 was adopted in 1914 and first used at the Battle of Neuve Chapelle. Its 15 tons required its dismantling for transport by tractor-powered wagons. The Mk1 achieved a maximum range of 10,061 yards with a 290-pound shell. The 6-inch, 26-cwt Howitzer Mk1 entered service the next year; firing a 100-pound shell to a maximum range of 9,499 yards, it proved easier to maneuver, and had a greater range, than earlier 6-inch models. It remained in British service well into World War II.

The 8-inch Howitzer Mk1 also entered British service in 1915, as did the 15-inch Howitzer Mk1. Although Coventry Ordnance Works initially failed to gain the army's interest in its huge 15-inch heavy howitzer, its director, a retired admiral, did convince Sir Winston Churchill, First Lord of the Admiralty, that it would make a splendid weapon for land-based naval personnel. The 15-inch Mk1 was thus adopted in 1915, and a number, manned by Royal Marine crews, saw some service in France. The marines were, however, subsequently reassigned to other duties, and the howitzers ultimately were given to reluctant army crews. Although forced to use the Mk1s owing to wartime expediency, the army never warmed to them; it quickly abandoned them after the Armistice. The 15-inch Mk1 howitzer fired a 1,400-pound shell to a maximum range of 10,794 yards. Other British pieces that entered service during the war included the 6-inch Gun Mk19 of 1916, and the 8-inch Howitzer Mk7, 9.2-inch Howitzer Mk2, and the 12-inch Howitzer Mk1, all adopted in 1917.

United States

The United States steadily increased its production, supplemented by some foreign designs, during the late nineteenth and early twentieth centuries. Adopted in 1893, the 7-inch Howitzer M1890 fired a 105-pound shell as far as 5,995 yards. As part of its recoil system, the trunnions were flanked by Belleville springs behind to absorb recoil, as well as hydraulic buffers in front. These were supplemented by another hydraulic return buffer connecting the carriage to its firing platform. The M1890 was followed in 1900 by the 5-inch Gun M1898, which fired a 45-pound shell up to 9,810 yards. The more efficient quick-firing 4.7-inch Gun M1906 was adopted in 1906 and fired a 60-pound shell to a maximum range of 9,537.5 yards. The 6-inch Howitzer M1908 followed and fired a 120-pound shell up to 6,703.5 yards.

Despite its efforts, upon its entry into the war, the United States found itself seriously lacking in ordnance of all kinds; it relied heavily on foreign—more specifically, French—designs to supplement its output. In 1917 the United States accepted a number of medium and heavy pieces, including the quick-firing 4.7-inch Gun M1917. Designating it the 155mm Howitzer M1917, the United States also adopted the Schneider-designed French 155mm Mle 17 howitzer as a counterpart to its 155mm GPF gun. It fired a 95.5-pound shell to a maximum range of 12,535 yards. The M1917 remained the standard medium howitzer of the United States until Word War II.

In 1918 the U.S. Army adopted the French 155mm GPF Gun as the 155mm Gun M1918M1. It fired a 95-pound shell to a maximum range of 20,034 yards. The 5-inch Gun M1918 was also adopted in the last year of the war; it fired a 60-pound shell up to 11,990 yards. The last French design, adopted in 1920, the 240mm Howitzer M1918, weighed 41,402 pounds could fire a 346-pound shell as far as 16,350 yards.

Italy

Italy fielded a wide array of medium and heavy artillery during World War I and the interwar years. It introduced the 155mm Canone da 155/25 in 1908, following it in 1910 with the 149mm Canone da 149/35, which could fire a 101-pound shell to a maximum of 10,608 yards. The 152.4mm Canone da 152/37 Mo.15 entered the war in 1915 and fired a 120-pound shell up to 26,794 yards. It, in turn, was followed in 1935 by the 149mm Canone da 149/40 Mo.35, firing a 112-pound shell to a maximum range of 24,060 yards.

The 149mm Obice 149/12 incorporated a Krupp-designed horizontal sliding block and was mounted on a heavy wooden base that was transported on a two-wheeled carriage connected to a two-wheeled limber. The 210mm Mortaio da 210/8 could elevate to fire a 222-pound shell up to 8,449 yards. Other Italian pieces included the 149mm Obice da 149/13 and 305mm Obice da 305/17DS of 1915, and the 260mm Mortaio da 260/9 Mo.16 and 305mm Mortaio da 305/8 Mo.11/16, adopted in 1916. The 210mm Obice da 210/22 Mo.35 was adopted in 1934. It fired a 225-pound shell to a maximum range of 17,500 yards.

Japan

Japan, too, continued its development of modern weaponry—a trend that it later intensified in its preparation for World War II. The quick-firing 120mm Field Howitzer Meiji 38 was adopted in 1905, as was the 105mm quick-firing Howitzer Meiji 38. The heavy 240mm Howitzer Meiji 45 then entered service in 1912, and the 150mm Howitzer Taisho 4 was adopted in 1915.

Czechoslovakia

Following the war, in 1919 the newly formed Czechoslovakia produced a number of medium and heavy weapons, including the 150mm vz15/16 Gun, the 149mm vz14/15 Howitzer, the 150mm vz15 Howitzer, and the caliber 210mm vz18 Howitzer.

COASTAL ARTILLERY

During the second half of the nineteenth century, the threat of heavy, armored warships as well as fast, shallow-draft raiders necessitated a variety of types of coastal artillery. Some of the largest guns ever built, heavy coastal artillery guns fired armor-piercing shells sometimes weighing more than a ton miles out to sea. Shorter-ranged coastal mortars were also included in coastal defenses to provide plunging fire to the less heavily armored decks of hostile vessels, and lighter caliber quick-firing guns proved useful in countering smaller craft. Early seacoast pieces were fitted with simple telescopic sights for direct fire, a practice that remained in use for the lighter caliber short-ranged weapons. Later, heavier pieces utilized more sophisticated range-finding techniques relying on distant observers on higher ground who communicated with the gun crews via field telephones.

Such weapons were mounted on specialized carriages suitable to their particular needs. These included much-enlarged versions of the traditional barbette carriage, as well as massive pivoting supports anchored into the concrete fortifications. The "disappearing carriage" also enjoyed a brief popularity during the period, as it enabled large guns to recoil below the parapet of a fortress to enable the crew to reload in relatively safety. The disappearing carriage, however, eventually faded from service, owing to its complexity and the general obsolescence of fixed coastal artillery.

Germany

Germany tended to use modified naval ordnance, such as the 210mm Schiffskanone SK L/40 (ship's canon L/40), adopted in the 1890s, for its coastal defenses. The country's heavy ordnance facilities, most notably Krupp, manufactured large numbers of these heavy, long-range coastal guns. These also included the 283mm SK L/40 adopted in 1901, the 283mm Küsten Haubitze of 1903, the 283mm SK L/45 mounted on a retractable "disappearing mount" adopted in 1907, the 173mm SK L/40 of 1908, the 240mm SK L/35, which entered service in 1910, and the 283mm SK L/50, adopted the same year. The year 1914 saw the adoption of the 149mm SK L/40, the 240mm SK L/40, and the massive 356mm SK L/52.5, which fired a 1,180-pound shell to a maximum range of 55,665 yards.

Great Britain

An island nation with numerous colonial holdings, Great Britain put considerable energy into the design and construction of coastal artillery. Much of this effort was directed into the development of advanced gun carriages that supported the massive weight of the guns, absorbed their recoil, and allowed them to elevate and traverse. The most advanced—and complicated—of these designs, the disappearing carriage, also provided protection for its crew as it served the piece between firings.

Up until the mid-nineteenth century, coastal artillery was typically mounted on either metal or wooden garrison carriages very similar in design to standard naval truck carriages. By mid-century, however, artillerists began to see the need for improvements that would allow gunners to reload safely, out of an enemy's line of fire. To that end, a captain (later colonel) of the Edinburgh Militia Artillery, Alexander Moncrief (1829–1906), designed the first successful "disappearing carriage."

Twenty of the first carriages designed by Moncrief went into service in 1871. The so-called first model Moncrief carriage incorporated a 7-inch rifled muzzleloader mounted to an upper assembly that was, in turn, hinged to a lower carriage counterbalanced by a stone-filled iron box. Upon firing, the design harnessed the gun's recoil to force the barrel back and downward, where it was secured by a catch to allow reloading. After reloading the piece in the relative safety below the parapet, the crew then released the catch, permitting the counterweight to return the gun tube to firing position.

Later, while working at Woolwich, Moncrief simplified his basic design by discarding the lower carriage assembly and replacing the gravel box with solid iron blocks. Some eighty Mark II Moncrief carriages were made and issued, eventually leading to a knighthood for their inventor in 1890. The Elswick Ordnance Company subsequently modernized Moncrief's design by adding a hydropneumatic mount that subsequently became the standard for British coast artillery pieces.

Britain's coastal artillery consisted of a wide variety of weapons ranging from light, quick-firing guns to some of the heaviest guns ever fielded. Some of the lighter weapons were adopted in 1885, such as the 3-pdr Hotchkiss Mk1, which fired a 3.3-pound shell to a maximum range of 7,491 yards, the 6-pdr Hotchkiss Mk1, and the 6-pdr Nordenfelt Mk1. Adopted in 1889, the 3-pdr Nordenfelt Mk1 had a caliber 1.8-inch bore and range of up to 7,491 yards. One of the most long lived of British guns, the 12-pdr 12-cwt Mk1, was adopted in 1894 and remained in service until 1957. The caliber 3-inch quick-firing Mk1 was equipped with an armored shield, mounted on a central pivot providing 360 degree traversal, and fired a 12.5-pound shell up to 10,100 yards. The heavier 4.7-inch Mk2 was adopted in 1888, had a quick-firing breech mechanism, and could fire a 45-pound shell up to 12,992 yards.

Heavy British coastal artillery included the 13.5-inch Mk3F, adopted in 1892, which fired a 1,250-pound shell; the 10-inch Mk3, which was adopted in 1888 and fired a 500-pound shell to a maximum range of 11,483 yards; and the 6-inch Mk7 of 1898, which fired a 100-pound shell up to 12,598 yards. In 1900, Britain began fielding both the 4.7-inch Mk5, a 45-pounder, and the 9.2-inch Mk10. The latter fired a 379-pound shell to a maximum range of 36,691 yards. The Mk10 also utilized a hydraulic loading system as well as a Vavasseur mount, incorporating a rearward, upward-inclined plane with hydraulic buffers.

Adopted in 1905, the 7.5-inch Mk2 fired a 200-pound shell up to 21,708 yards, and the 9.2-inch "High Angle" could elevate up to 45 degrees to provide plunging fire of its 289-pound shells into ships' decks at a range of up to 16,601 yards. The lighter 4-inch Mk3 entered service the next year and fired a 25-pound shell to a maximum of 11,200 yards; the wartime 4-inch Mk5 of 1915 achieved a range of 14,797 yards with a 31-pound shell.

United States

During the last decades of the nineteenth century, the United States developed a number of long-range coastal defense guns to replace the aging muzzleloaded Rodmans and columbiads of the Civil War period. The manufacture of these heavy breechloaders continued into the 1920s and was supplemented by the introduction of smaller caliber rapid-fire (the American term for quick-fire) weapons to defend against fast coastal-raiding vessels.

The United States also experimented with a number of innovative carriage designs, including types of disappearing carriages such as those being used by British coastal defense guns. The standard U.S. disappearing carriage, the Buffington-Crozier System, was applied to guns up to 16 inches in caliber; it relied on a combination of counterweights and hydraulic buffers to lower the barrel below the parapet for safe loading. The system, however, did not allow for sufficient elevation for extreme long-range fire, and its slow operation limited its rate of fire. During the 1880s, in an attempt to produce a more effective coastal defense weapon, the United States also developed the Zalinski Dynamite Gun, a truly ingenious yet ultimately impractical weapon that saw limited use just prior to the turn of the century.

In an attempt to safely fire a high-explosive shell that did not burst in the barrel, a Mr. Mefford invented a giant air rifle to project dynamite-filled shells. For propulsion, Mefford's gun utilized highly compressed air to force the projectile through a very long barrel that allowed it to build up sufficient velocity to attain a reasonable range. In 1884 he demonstrated his invention at Fort Hamilton, New York, where it showed some promise as a coastal defense gun.

Although a talented inventor, Mefford was apparently a poor businessman, and he neglected to protect his patents. Soon after his demonstration at Fort Hamilton, one of the observers, a Lieutenant Edward Louis Zalinski of the U.S. Artillery, found employment with the newly organized Pneumatic Dynamite Gun Company. Having circumvented Mefford's patents, the firm soon began manufacturing an 8-inch gun based almost entirely on his prototype and firing a finned projectile with an electric fuse designed by Zalinsky. The U.S. government subsequently acquired a limited number of the new guns—by then known as Zalinsky Dynamite Guns—and they were placed in the defenses of San Francisco and Fort Hancock, New York. Three others were included in the armament of the USS *Vesuvius*. The guns' maximum range was approximately 3 miles. Ironically, Zalinsky never intended his namesake as a true artillery piece but rather, as he called it, an "aerial torpedo projector," intended as a long-range mine layer. As such, it soon became obsolete as new designs became available; the project was ultimately scrapped.

The last decade of the nineteenth century saw the adoption by the United States of a wide range of coastal weapons. The 10-inch Gun

M1888M1 was adopted in 1891; intended to deliver its 1,050-pound shells in plunging fire onto the decks of attacking ships, the 12-inch Mortar M1890 mortar entered service the following year. In 1895 the U.S. government adopted the British-designed 4.72-inch Armstrong quick-firing 45-pounder gun, as well as the heavy 12-inch Gun M1888, which fired a 977-pound shell up to 18,339 yards.

The U.S. government adopted another British design, the 6-inch quick-firing Armstrong coastal gun, in 1896, as well as the 8-inch Gun M1888, a piece capable of firing a 324-pound shell up to 16,241 yards. The 12-inch Gun M1895 was adopted in 1898 and was followed by numerous guns entering service in 1900. Among these were the rapid-fire 2.24-inch RF Gun M1900, designed to defend against fast-moving shallow-draft vessels, the rapid-fire 4-inch Driggs-Schroeder, the 5-inch Gun M1900, and the 6-inch M1897.

The year 1902 also saw a burst of adoptions that included the rapid-fire 3-inch Gun M1902, which was intended for the same purpose as the M1900; the 10-inch Gun M1900; and the 12-inch Gun M1900, which fired a 1,072-pound shell to a maximum range of 17,277 yards. An improvement over the 3-inch coastal artillery gun adopted the previous year, the 3-inch gun M1903 fired a 15-pound shell to a maximum range of 11,282 yards. The 6-inch gun M1900 was also adopted in 1903; it could deliver a 90-pound shell out to 16,459 yards. The 6-inch gun M1903 was adopted in 1905, and the 6-inch gun M1905 and the 14-inch M1907M1, firing a 1,662-pound shell to a maximum range of 22,727 yards, in 1908.

In 1910 the United States adopted the 6-inch gun M1908, as well as the plunging-fire 12-inch mortar M1908, capable of launching a 1,050-pound shell up to 9,156 yards. Used in twin-gun turrets, the 14-inch M1909 was adopted in 1913, as was the 12-inch mortar M1912. Heavier and longer than its predecessors, the M1912 fired a 700.5-pound shell 19,255 yards. Also entering service in 1913, the 14-inch M1910 chambered a 1,662-pound shell; its maximum range was 22,727 yards. The largest and most potent U.S. coastal gun, the 16-inch gun M1895, was adopted in 1917; it was mounted on a barbette carriage. This piece weighed 1,277,119 pounds and fired a 2,404-pound shell to an extreme range of 27,277 yards. M1895s were used to defend the Panama Canal and other strategic coastal installations.

Japan

Japan's World War I–era coastal pieces included the quick-firing 149mm Gun Meiji 45 of 1912 and the quick-firing, dual-purpose

127mm antiaircraft and coastal-defense Taisho 3 of 1914. In 1918 the country adopted the 105mm Gun Taisho 7, as well as the massive 305mm Howitzer Taisho 7 (Long), which fired a 1,098-pound shell to a maximum range of 16,678 yards, and its sister, the 305mm Howitzer Taisho 7 (Short), which fired an 882-pound shell up to 12,000 yards.

RAILWAY ARTILLERY

Although artillerists had mounted pieces on railroad cars since at least the 1860s, it was not until World War I that railroad artillery saw its true potential. Strategists saw the new weapons as a convenient mode for delivering heavy fire against enemy positions while also exploiting the mobility provided by the sophisticated rail networks of Europe and the United States.

In 1916, Germany adopted the 17cm (173mm) K (E) "Samuel" as a wartime expedient. Basically a standard field piece bolted to a railroad gondola, the 173mm Samuel fired a 138-pound shell to a maximum range of 26,270 yards. The 21cm (209mm) SKL/40 "Peter Adalbert" also entered service that same year, as did the 38cm (381mm) SK L/45 "Max." One of the most successful railway guns, the 595,248-pound Max fired an 882-pound shell up to 51,950 yards. For 360 degree traversal it could be raised from its railroad gondola and bolted to a turntable bed. The Max was used at Verdun and saw the majority of its service in Belgium, using railroad tunnels for concealment and firing at long range at Allied positions. Adopted in 1917, the 35cm (350mm) K (E) railroad gun could also traverse 360 degrees and fired a 1,543-pound shell up to 32,808 yards.

Germany's ally Austria also fielded potent railway guns. The 350mm M16 railroad gun was adopted in 1916, traversed 360 degrees, and had a maximum range of 32,808 yards with a 1,543-pound shell. Adopted in 1917, the 380mm "Lulo" fired a 1,874-pound shell to a maximum range of 41,557 yards.

For its part, France was possibly the most prolific nation in the production of railroad artillery types during the period. The 164.7mm Matériel de 164 Mle93/96 was adopted in 1912 and was followed in 1914 by the 194.4mm Matériel de 194 Mle70/94. France then quickly accelerated railroad artillery development following its entry into the war. During 1915 it fielded the 240mm Canon de 240 Mle 84, the 240mm Canon de 240 Mle 93/96, the 305mm Matériel de 305 Mle 93/96, the 320mm Matériel de 320

Mle 74, the 340mm Matériel de 340 Mle 12, and the 370mm Canon de 370 Mle 75/79, capable of reaching a range of 26,247 yards firing a 1,563-pound shell.

Production continued into the following war years, and 1916 saw the introduction of the 274mm Matériel de 274 Mle 87/93, the 305mm Canon de 305 Mle 06, and the 305mm Matériel de 305 Mle 06/10. In 1917, France adopted the 285mm Canon de 285 Mle 17, the 320mm Canon de 320 Mle 17, the 340mm Canon de 340 Mle 84, the 340mm Canon de 340 Mle 93, the 370mm Matériel de 370 Mle 15, and the 400mm Matériel de 400 Mle 15/16, which fired a 1,413-pound shell up to 17,498 yards. The last French railroad gun of the war, the 520mm Obusier de 520 of 1918, fired a truly enormous 3,645-pound shell to a maximum range of 15,967 yards.

Great Britain adopted the 9.2-inch gun Mk3 and the 12-inch gun Mk9 in 1915. These were followed in 1916 by the 9.2-inch gun Mk10, the 12-inch Howitzer Mk1, and the 12-inch Howitzer Mk3. Originally built by the Elswick Ordnance Company for Japan in 1916, the 14-inch Mk3 entered British service because of the war: it was christened the "Boche-Buster." The piece was subsequently assigned to the 471 Siege Battery, Royal Garrison Artillery, stationed at Arras. It was capable of firing a 1,653-pound shell up to 21.6 miles. The Boche-Buster was ultimately scrapped in 1926. The last British designs of the period included the 12-inch gun MkII of 1918 and the 18-inch Howitzer Mk1, adopted in 1920 and capable of firing a 2,500-pound shell up to 22,720 yards.

The United States adopted a number of railroad artillery pieces in 1918. These included the 8-inch gun M1888M1, the 10-inch gun M1888M1, the 12-inch mortar M1890, and the 12-inch gun M1895. Following the war, the 14-inch gun M1919 then entered service in 1919; in 1920 it was followed by the 14-inch M1919M1 and the 14-inch M1920M1. The latter could fire a 1,000-pound shell up to 48,228 yards. Four were manufactured, with two guns being placed in the defenses of Panama and the other pair going to San Francisco.

CHAPTER SEVEN

The Interwar Years and World War II, 1921–1945

IN RESPONSE TO LESSONS LEARNED during World War I, ordnance designers initiated a number of innovations during the interwar years. Despite the financial limitations imposed by the depressions of the 1920s and 1930s, new or improved types of antitank, antiaircraft, and self-propelled artillery entered development in time to see use in World War II. After World War I a U.S. ordnance committee recommended the replacement of the French 75 with a 105mm howitzer capable of firing shrapnel and high-explosive ammunition up to about 12,000 yards. In 1922 the cost-conscious British began an extensive research and development program but committed to little actual production. For its part, Germany circumvented the strict restrictions of the Versailles Treaty by having private armament companies develop and test new designs abroad. To that end Krupp engineers worked in Sweden at the Bofors firm, while Rheinmettall acquired control of a Swiss company as well as installed workers in Austria.

FIELD ARTILLERY

During the 1920s and 1930s, Britain faced the dilemma of replacing its aging 18-pounders under the financial constraints of an uncertain interwar economy. The 25-pounder Mk1 was an attempt to solve the problem by mating a 3.45-inch, 25-pounder barrel to the old 18-pounder carriage. The Mk1 saw some service in 1940 and 1941, but the carriage proved too light for the new gun tube; thus the more robust 25-pounder Mk2 soon replaced it. Adopted as the primary divisional gun in 1940, the Mk2 had a vertical sliding breech mechanism. Fitted with a muzzle brake and other improvements, it remained in service until 1967. Later models had hinged trails that allowed greater elevation, and the Mk2 achieved a maximum range of 13,400 yards with a 29-pound shell. The 25-pounder Short Mk1 had an abbreviated barrel and was developed by the Australians for jungle use. It was also known as the "Jungle 25-pounder" and was fitted with a small wheel on its trail for easier manhandling in dense foliage. It was adopted in 1944 and fired a 25-pound shell to a maximum range of 11,811 yards.

Named after its inventor, a toy designer at the Trianco Engineering Company, the unique Smith Gun was intended as an emergency weapon with which to arm the Home Guard. It was a 3-inch smoothbore weapon with a 54-inch-long barrel designed for ease of manufacture. Weighing only 604 pounds it was mounted on a very light carriage supported by two solid-steel wheels and could be towed behind a civilian automobile. For action, the crew of the Smith Gun flipped the piece over so that one wheel acted as its base and thus allowed it to traverse a full 360 degrees. It could elevate 40 degrees and fired an 8-pound shell up to 550 yards. Although some Smith Guns were also issued to regular British troops guarding airfields, none saw combat use, and they were retired in 1945.

To the detriment of its field artillery development, during the interwar years France expended a tremendous amount of effort and resources in constructing and arming the Maginot Line. As a result, the aging Mle1897, recently modernized with the addition of pneumatic tires, remained the standard French field gun. Intended as a replacement for the Mle1897, the promising 105mm Cannon Court Mle35B appeared too late, and only 410 were produced before France's surrender. France also continued to manufacture trench cannons such as 45mm Nordenfelt M1923 as well as the 75mm St. Chamond, which entered service the same year. The 105mm Mle 36 and the 105mm Howitzer Mle 35 were adopted in 1937.

An update of the Model 1916, the 75mm Gun Model M1920 MII entered U.S. service in 1920. It was fitted with the French St. Chamond recuperator, a single box trail carriage, and, with a range of 15,100 yards, proved popular with its crews. After a series of experiments the M1920 MII was eventually replaced in 1926 with the split trail carriage 75mm Model 1923 E, the standard U.S. field gun of the period. Beginning in 1933, the United States underwent the process of adapting its 75mm field guns for high-speed towing. That involved replacing their wooden-spoked, iron-tired carriages with the Carriage M2A2, fitted with rubber pneumatic tires. Despite upgrades of the basic M1897 design, during the early stages of World War II the various types of 75mm field guns proved ineffective against German armor, ultimately leading to their retirement.

U.S. field howitzers included the 75mm Howitzer M1 on Carriage M3A1, which fired a 15-pound shell to a maximum range of 9,625 yards, and an update from the earlier horse-drawn M1, the 105mm Howitzer M101 (M2A1). The M101 howitzer was accepted in 1940 and was the workhorse field howitzer of the United States until 1943, when it was replaced by the improved M102. Manufactured by the Rock Island Arsenal, it was mounted on a split trail carriage with high-speed pneumatic tires and was capable of firing a 33-pound shell 12,250 yards. For high-angle firing, crews often dug a pit beneath the breech to prevent damage during recoil. The M101 was served by a crew of eight and had a maximum firing rate of 10 rounds per minute. The United States adopted the 105mm Howitzer M3A1 in 1942. It fired a 33-pound shell up to 8,295 yards.

Russian artillery production was interrupted by the Revolution and finally resumed in the late 1920s with the manufacture of slightly modified versions of earlier czarist models. The first Russian field gun designed under the communist regime, the 76.2mm Regimental Gun M27, was adopted in 1927; it fired a 14-pound shell up to 14,873 yards. It was followed in 1930 by the quick-firing 76.2mm M02/30 and the heavier 107mm M10/30. The M02/30 fired a 14-pound shell to a maximum range of 14,217 yards, and the M10/30 fired a 38-pound shell to a maximum range of 17,880 yards.

The Soviets adopted the 122mm Howitzer M38 in 1938 and the 76.2mm Divisional Gun USV in 1939. The USV fired a 13.5-pound shell up to 13,326 yards. Large numbers were captured by the Germans during the 1941 invasion and were reissued to Nazi units as the 76mm PaK 39(r). Other Soviet field guns included the 107mm Gun M40, adopted 1940, and the 76.2mm Gun M41, adopted in 1941. Following the Nazi invasion, the Soviet Union initiated a new development program to produce weapons powerful enough to counter heavy German armor yet of simple enough design to speed production. Such pieces included the 76.2mm Gun ZIS-3 of 1942, and the 85mm Divisional Gun D-44. Designed by the FF Petrov bureau to replace the 76mm ZIS-3, the D-44 was adopted in 1944 but did not enter service until after World War II. It is now obsolete. It was served by a crew of eight, had a semiautomatic vertical sliding breech mechanism, and attained a firing rate of up to 20 rounds per minute. The D-44 fired a 21-pound shell up to 16,951 yards. The 85mm Divisional Gun D-48 was adopted in 1945 and fired a 21-pound shell to a maximum range of 17,498 yards. Soviet field howitzers also included the 122mm Howitzer M1938 (M30), a weapon that also saw extensive post-war use.

Both Belgium and Czechoslovakia produced field pieces during the interwar years, and after their fall to the Nazis, these weapons, such as the Belgian 120mm Gun M32, saw at least limited use by German forces. Following the formation of Czechoslovakia in 1919, the venerable Skoda factory in Pilsen continued to update prewar ordnance until turning to new designs in the 1930s. It continued operations after the German occupation during World War II and developed and produced weapons for the German forces, including the 105mm leFH43 field gun. After 1945 the company remained in operation as the V.I. Lenin Works; it manufactured Soviet designs for the Warsaw Pact until the fall of the Soviet Union and subsequent breakup of the pact. One of the earliest Czech pieces, the 100mm Field Howitzer vz14/19, was adopted in 1923. In 1934, Skoda produced a wide range of weapons, including the 75mm Field Gun vz35, the 76.5mm vz30, the 100mm Field Gun vz35, and the 100mm Field Howitzer vz30/34. The 76.5mm Field Gun vz39 and the 100mm Field Howitzer H3 entered service in 1939.

Following the Nazi assumption of power, Germany escalated its efforts to circumvent the Versailles Treaty restrictions and develop new field guns and howitzers. These included the 75mm field gun FK15Na, adopted in 1933, and the field howitzer 105mm leFH18 of 1935. The 105mm field howitzer leFH18M entered service in 1940. It shared the same specifications as the earlier leFH18 yet fired a 31-pound projectile to a maximum range of 13,479 yards. The 105mm leFH18/40 was adopted in 1941, and the following year the 105mm leFH42 entered German service. It fired a 33-pound shell to a maximum range of 14,217 yards. Initially designed for Brazil and diverted to German use at the beginning of World War II, the 75mm FK38 was adopted in 1942. The versatile and maneuverable 75mm FK7M85 entered service in late 1944. Designed to serve as both an antitank and field gun, it incorporated a 75mm PaK40 barrel on a leFH18/40 carriage with tubular split trails. The FK7M85 fired a 13-pound shell to a maximum range of 12,577 yards. Developed and manufactured at the Skoda factory in occupied Czechoslovakia, the 105mm leFH43 was also adopted in 1944. It fired a 33-pound shell to a maximum range of 16,404 yards.

During the interwar years, Germany also began the development of the "IG" Infanterie Geschutz Geschütz, or "Infantry Gun." Manned by infantrymen, infantry gun platoons were assigned on the regimental level to provide close artillery support in the field when needed. Lighter than conventional artillery, infantry-accompanying artillery was of limited use against armor yet highly effective against opposing infantry. In addition to the standard infantry gun, for added firepower on the front lines, Germany also produced the "sIG" Schwer Infanterie Geschütz, or "Heavy Infantry Gun."

Adopted in 1927 and used extensively throughout World War II, the 75mm IG18 weighed just 882 pounds and had a 33-inch-long barrel with a vertical sliding breech. It fired a 13-pound shell to a maximum range of 3,700 yards. The largest of the German infantry-manned guns and also used in self-propelled applications, the 150mm, horizontal sliding block sIG33 was adopted in 1933. Developed clandestinely to avoid the Versailles restrictions, it fired an 84-pound shell to a maximum range of 5,140 yards. Adopted in 1936, the 75mm IG L/13 was 52 pounds lighter than the IG18 and fired a 14-pound shell up to 4,200 yards. The 75mm IG13 and slightly heavier IG42 were adopted in 1944. Both guns fired a 12-pound shell, with the IG13 achieving a range of 5,632 yards and the IG42 5,030 yards.

During World War II Italy continued to field World War I–vintage weapons, many of which were obtained from foreign sources. In the 1930s the country began more intensive domestic production. The 75mm Obice da 75/18 Mo.35 was an adaptation of the 75/18 mountain howitzer for field use and was adopted in 1935. The 75mm Ansaldo-designed 75/32 Mo.37 was adopted in 1937 and was mounted on the same carriage as the 75/18 Mo.35. It fired a 14-pound shell to a maximum range of 13,670 yards and also saw service in antitank and self-propelled roles. Adopted in 1942, the 105mm 105/40 Mo.42 fired a 38.5-pound shell to a maximum range of 19,248 yards.

Japan fielded a variety of field guns, including the 37mm Infantry Gun Taisho 11, adopted in 1922, a diminutive piece weighing only 207 pounds and firing a 1.3-pound shell to a maximum range of 5,468 yards. Adopted in 1925, the quick-firing 105mm Gun Taisho 14 was a much more powerful weapon and fired a 35-pound shell up to 16,404 yards. Other Japanese field pieces included the 75mm

Field Gun Model 90, adopted in 1930, the 105mm Howitzer Model 91, adopted the following year, and, adopted in 1932, the 70mm Infantry Howitzer M92 and the 105mm Gun Model 92. The 75mm Field Gun Model 95 was adopted in 1935 and fired a 14-pound shell to a maximum range of 12,000 yards.

Despite Sweden's neutrality, its arms giant Bofors produced a wide variety of excellent weapons for both domestic use and export. The quick-firing 105mm Gun M28 was adopted in 1927 and was typical of such weapons, as were the 75mm Gun M02/33 and 105mm Gun L/42 of 1934. The 75mm Light Gun entered service the following year, and the 105mm Gun M37 in 1937. The 75mm Gun M40 and 105mm Howitzer M40 were adopted in 1940. Prior to World War II, Switzerland acquired artillery from foreign sources. Following the war the Federal Gun Factory at Thun began manufacturing numerous types of excellent pieces for the Swiss army. The 75mm Gun M03/22 entered service in 1923 and fired a 14-pound shell to a maximum 10,936 yards. Adopted in 1935, the 105mm Gun M35 fired a 33-pound shell up to 19,138 yards.

MOUNTAIN ARTILLERY

Favored for their combination of ease in transport over rough terrain and relatively high destructive power, mountain artillery continued to see continued development and use during the period. The United States adopted one of the best of such weapons—the 75mm Pack Howitzer M1—in 1927. During the 1930s it was slightly modified to be more easily transported by glider for airborne operations and was thus redesignated the 75mm Pack Howitzer M8 (airborne). It could also be disassembled into six components for pack transport and was first used in the Philippines in 1942. The M1 fired a 15-pound shell as far as 9,186 yards.

Other future Allied and neutral powers also produced mountain pieces. In 1920, Czechoslovakia adopted the 100mm Mountain Howitzer vz16/19; France adopted the quick-firing 75mm Schneider in 1932; and six years later the Soviet Union began fielding the 76mm Gun M38. In 1933 neutral Switzerland adopted the 75mm Gun M33, and Sweden adopted the 90mm Howitzer Bofors in 1935.

Future Axis mountain artillery included Germany's 75mm Geb K15, adopted in 1925, and the improved 75mm Geb G36. Designed by Gebrüder Böhler AG of Austria, the 105mm Geb H40 was adopted by Germany in 1942 and fired a 32-pound shell up to 18,307 yards. An excellent weapon, the H40 remained in service with various armies into the 1960s. The Skoda-designed Canone da 75/13 Skoda was adopted by Italy in 1922 and was the main mountain gun used by the Italian Alpini troops. The Italians intended to replace it with the 75mm Obice da 75/18 Mo.34 in 1935, yet, although an excellent weapon, production was limited owing to manufacturing delays. Japan adopted its own 75mm Model 94 in 1934. Fitted with a relatively long trail, the Model 94 could be dismantled for transport by a team of eight mules.

ANTITANK ARTILLERY

The rapid development and proliferation of tanks during the interwar years and during World War II necessitated weapons to counter their threat. Germany introduced special antitank artillery and armor-piercing rounds during the latter half of World War I, and by World War II all major powers fielded similar weapons. Such ordnance required powerful armor-piercing capabilities to defeat ever-improving armor, yet also had to be concealable. To address these twin problems, some engineers turned to extremely high velocity projectiles or other types of unique design.

Of those, saboted projectiles emerged as an alternative to larger caliber, high-velocity rounds. They consisted of a larger jacket, or "sabot," that would fall away from a smaller projectile as it left the bore. As such a projectile utilized a large powder charge in relation to its weight; it had greater range and penetration than a conventional round. Although some sabot patents appeared during the 1870s, they were virtually ignored until French ordnance expert Edgar Brandt renewed experiments with the principle in the 1930s. German and British technicians also explored the use of sabots for antitank use, yet they soon found their efforts frustrated by the continual improvement in armor, thus requiring much larger and heavier antitank guns. As a key element to an antitank weapon's effectiveness—and survival—is stealth, designers were again forced to explore other, more concealable, options.

Projectile designers thus turned to the hollow charge principle to create more efficient antitank rounds. Utilizing a typically copper-lined conical depression in its nose, the hollow charge projectile was fused to explode a fraction of a second before hitting its target. Its detonation subsequently ejected the then molten copper forward with terrific force through the armor, thus facilitating the shell's penetration into the armored vehicle's interior. As the hollow charge principle was effective with even relatively low velocity guns, it soon found numerous proponents among both Allied and Axis ordnance designers.

Great Britain continued to increase the caliber of its antitank guns in a constant race to counter German armor. Fitted with a short trail and large armored shield, the 40mm British 2-pdr Mk9 antitank gun was adopted in 1936. It was subsequently replaced in 1941 by the semiautomatic 57mm 6-pdr 7-cwt Mk2. Used as both tank armament and in an antitank role, the Mk2 was still outclassed by the German 75; it was replaced the next year by the more potent caliber 3-inch (76.2mm) 17-pdr Mk1, which fired a 17-pound shell to a maximum range of 10,000 yards.

The United States also steadily continued to increase its calibers to defeat German armor. Adopted in 1938, the 37mm Gun M3 antitank gun was followed in 1941 by the 57mm Gun M1 and the 3-inch M5. Originally intended as an antiaircraft design, the semiautomatic 90mm T8 Antitank Gun was adopted in 1944. Although some attempts were made to mount it on various two-wheeled split trail carriages, it saw significant combat only as either a self-propelled or tank gun. The T8 fired a 24-pound projectile to a maximum range of 21,435 yards.

Beginning in 1932 with the 45mm M1932 and the 45mm M1937, the Soviet Union followed the same path of caliber escalation. Adopted in 1942, the 45mm M42 was essentially a larger-bore copy of the German 37mm antitank gun. The M42 was quickly superseded in 1943 by the more potent caliber 57mm ZIS-2. The excellent ZIS-2 was, in turn, superseded in 1944 by the semiautomatic 100mm Field Gun M1944 (BS-3). Originally based on a naval design and mounted on a dual-tire split trail carriage, the M1944 fired a 35-pound high-explosive shell to a maximum range of 22,966 yards and an antitank projectile to an effective range of 1,093 yards. With a crew of six, the M1944 was capable of firing up to 10 rounds per minute. Although the 100mm T-12 eventually replaced the M1944 in Soviet service, many remain in use around the world.

France, Belgium, and Czechoslovakia also developed antitank weapons during the interwar years that, following their fall, also saw at least some use by the Nazis during World War II. These included the French semiautomatic 25mm Hotchkiss Mle 34 of 1934 and the 47mm Puteaux antitank gun, which was mounted on a carriage fitted with wheels that could be raised to allow the gun to sit on its 360-degree traversing mount with three supporting legs. Belgium issued the 47mm FRC antitank gun in 1932, and Czechoslovakia developed numerous antitank weapons before its fall to the Nazis. The 40mm vz30 was adopted in 1930 and was followed in 1934 by the 37mm vz34, in 1937 by the 37mm vz37, and its successor, the 47mm vz38.

Following Hitler's assumption of power in 1933, Germany began an intensive antitank gun development program that continued through the war years. Adopted in 1936, the 37mm PaK36 was the primary Nazi antitank gun until it was superseded in 1940 by the semiautomatic 50mm PaK38, which fired a 4.8-pound shell up to 2,898 yards. The still more powerful 75mm PaK40 and 75mm PaK97/38 were adopted in 1941. Germany also fielded numerous captured Allied weapons, such as the Soviet M30, designated the 76.2mm PaK36(r) in German service.

German engineers also explored a variety of unconventional designs that, although often effective, were rendered impractical owing to wartime shortages in materials. The principle of incorporating a tapered bore—reducing its internal diameter from breech to muzzle in order to increase its projectile's velocity—was first put forward in 1903 by Karl Puff. It was later reintroduced by a German engineer named Gerlich and at last applied by Rheinmetall-Borsig. The highly unique Gerlich projectile consisted of a solid tungsten carbide core enclosed by a more malleable iron outer shell. To allow shrinkage, it was also fitted with soft metal base and shoulder skirts that folded rearward along its length as it traveled down the tapered bore. Also known as "squeezebores," taper-bore guns achieved the very high velocities that made them ideal for use against armored targets.

The 42mm LePaK41 was adopted in 1941; it fired a 0.7-pound projectile at a muzzle velocity of 4,150 fps to a maximum range of 1,094 yards. The semiautomatic 75mm PaK41 Squeezebore entered service in 1942 and incorporated a tapered—75mm to 55mm—barrel that produced a muzzle velocity of 3,691 fps and had a maximum range of 4,593 yards, firing a 16.5-pound shell. The final form of the German squeezebore guns, the 28mm Schweres Panzerbuchse 41, tapered from a 28mm breech to its 21mm muzzle. With a muzzle velocity of 4,590 fps, it could punch through 2.6 inches of armor at 500 yards. Although it was used successfully to a limited extent in North Africa in 1941, the Germans were forced to abandon taper-bore guns owing to wartime shortages of tungsten.

Other higher caliber but yet more conventional German antitank guns also saw extensive use. Krupp designed the semiautomatic 88mm PaK43 Panzer Abwehr Kanone after the firm turned its efforts from producing antiaircraft guns in favor of tank and antitank ordnance. It was adopted in 1943, and, with its wheels removed prior to action, the Pak43 presented a very low profile, making it ideal for ambushing enemy armor from concealed positions. Its 23-pound armor-piercing shell was capable of piercing 6.5 inches of armor at 2,187 yards, and its special tungsten-core round, reaching a velocity of 3,707 fps, could penetrate 7 inches of armor. The Pak43 also fired a high-explosive shell up to 11 miles.

The 88mm PaK43/41 was based on the famous "Eighty-Eight" FlaK gun and was hurried into service in 1943 as an antitank weapon to counter the Russian T-34 tank on the Eastern Front. Mounted on a standard two-wheeled, split-trail carriage, it attained a maximum range of 19,138 yards firing a 23-pound shell. Nicknamed the "Scheunetor" (Barn Door) by its crews, it was an awkward weapon to maneuver yet highly effective: in one action a single PaK43/41 was credited with destroying six T-34s at a range of 2 miles.

Designed by Rheinmetall-Borsig in 1943, the 81mm Panzer Abwher Werfer 600 (PAW600) incorporated the high-low principle in an attempt to provide a powerful yet lightweight antitank gun. As a high-low principle weapon, the PAW600 used a very light, smoothbore barrel with a reinforced chamber to absorb the high pressure of its special cartridge. The chamber itself delayed the launching of its special 6-pound finned projectile until the pressure equalized, and then it allowed it to blast free of the muzzle at between 1,365 and 1,706 fps. Although relatively inaccurate at its maximum 6,780-yard range, the PAW600 did prove effective as a short-range antitank weapon, and some 260 were built during the war. Mounted on a light carriage with tubular trails, it weighed just 1,323 pounds. Developed by Rheinmetall, the highly potent 128mm PaK44 entered service in 1945, too late to make an effective impact on the German war effort. Mounted to a four-wheeled carriage with cruciform stabilizers, it could traverse 360 degrees and fired a 62-pound shell to a maximum range of 26,684 yards.

Germany's allies also fielded antitank weapons. Manufactured in Italy from a German Böhler design and adopted in 1935, the Italian 47mm Canon da 45/30 Modello 35 was an excellent weapon that was used in both field and mountain applications. In 1939, Italy also began fielding the 47mm Canon da 47/32 Mo.39. The

Japanese 37mm Model 94 was adopted in 1934, the semiautomatic 37mm Model Ra-97 in 1937, and the semiautomatic 47mm Model 01 in 1941.

ANTIAIRCRAFT ARTILLERY

The rapid improvement of aircraft performance during the 1930s forced European antiaircraft gun designers into a continuous race to counter their threat. Although neutral, Sweden, through its famous Bofors factory, emerged as a leader in exporting advanced antiaircraft weapons to the future belligerents of World War II. These included the widely exported 40mm L/60 (also known as the M33), introduced in 1933, and the 80mm L/50 and 75mm L/52 of 1936. For its part, the United States made little real progress in developing antiaircraft artillery during the interwar period. At the time of the Pearl Harbor attack, most U.S. antiaircraft batteries were still armed with the antiquated 3-inch gun first adopted in 1917.

As the war progressed, three classes of antiaircraft artillery evolved. Introduced in 1929, the Swedish-made Bofors 40mm gun exemplified the best of the light category. Typically used in a twin mounting, the Bofors was easily traversed and had a high rate of fire, yet its shells were fused to detonate after 7 seconds of flight. Although that setting lessened the danger of live shells falling back to earth, it did limit the gun's combat range to only about 7,200 feet. As heavier antiaircraft weapons were effective at only about 15,000 feet or higher, a third, intermediate, class emerged to fill the gap between the two.

During the late 1930s, British technicians began experiments in producing a radar-guided proximity fuse that would detonate without actually striking its target yet close enough to cause damage. The United States continued explorations in the field after 1941 and soon perfected a fuse that was first used in an antiaircraft role aboard the USS *Helena* in 1943. The proximity fuse was so successful that it was quickly distributed to U.S. forces in both the Pacific and European theaters, where it was also applied to ground use. Other World War II antiaircraft innovations included improved automatic loading mechanisms, automatic fuse setters, and mechanical time fuses.

Britain adopted the 4.5-inch Mk2 antiaircraft gun in 1936. Originally designed as a naval gun and pressed into an antiaircraft role, it had a semiautomatic horizontal sliding block and fired a 54.4-pound shell to a maximum ceiling of 42,585 feet. Its firing rate, however, was a relatively unimpressive 8 rounds per minute. Later models relied on a 4.5-inch cartridge necked down to accommodate a 3.7-inch shell and incorporated an appropriately relined barrel to accept the new ammunition. The improved gun, equipped with a mechanical loader and firing a 28-pound shell to a 45,000-foot ceiling, produced a much more acceptable firing rate of 19 rounds per minute.

One of the finest antiaircraft guns of World War II, the British 3.7-inch Mk1 antiaircraft gun was first adopted in 1937. As originally designed, it fired a 25-pound shell to a ceiling of 28,000 feet. Later, improved models fired a 28-pound shell up to a maximum ceiling of 59,300 feet. Mounted on a four-wheeled carriage and with a semiautomatic horizontal sliding block, the Mk1 also saw service during the Korean War.

Adopted by Great Britain in 1939, the Swedish-designed Bofors 40mm Mk8 twin-mounted antiaircraft gun had an automatic breech mechanism that, at a rate of 120 rounds per minute, fired a 2-pound shell to a maximum ceiling of 20,000 feet. Very mobile and widely used by nearly every European power, the Bofors's actual effective range was, however, limited to only about 7,200 feet, as its shells were fused to detonate after a 7-second flight. Great Britain also defended its skies with the semiautomatic 3.7-inch Mk6 and the 5.25-inch Mk2, adopted in 1942, and the semiautomatic 6-pounder, 6-pdr, 6-cwt Mk1, adopted in 1944. Intended as an intermediate range gun, the Mk1 incorporated a coastal artillery barrel but proved unsuccessful, owing to difficulties in converting it to semiautomatic loading.

In 1927 the United States introduced the semiautomatic 105mm AA M3 antiaircraft gun, which fired a 33-pound shell to a ceiling of 42,000 feet. The next year the 3-inch M3 Antiaircraft Gun appeared on the scene, and in 1931 it, in turn, was superseded by the 3-inch M4 Antiaircraft Gun, with a maximum ceiling of 29,035 feet. The U.S. government adopted the semiautomatic 37mm M1 Antiaircraft Gun in 1938. It fired a 1.3-pound shell to a maximum ceiling of 18,602 feet. The semiautomatic 90mm M1 Antiaircraft Gun was adopted in 1940. The M1, like the improved M2 version, utilized an automatic fuse setter and power rammer. During the Korean War the M2 also proved effective as an antipersonnel weapon capable of firing 28 rounds per minute up to 19,560 yards. The 120mm Gun M1 came into service in 1943 and, with a semiautomatic vertical sliding breech, fired a 50-pound shell to a maximum ceiling of 57,415 feet. Primarily installed as a home defense weapon, the 120mm M1 saw little combat use.

The Soviet Union adopted the 76.2mm M31 in 1931 and, with the introduction of the semiautomatic 76.2mm M38 in 1938, began a continual development of antiaircraft weapons to counter the German Luftwaffe. The following year the Soviets adopted the 37mm Gun M39, a nearly exact copy of a Swedish Bofors design, and the semiautomatic 85mm M39. The Soviets, acting on the success of the German Eighty-Eight as an antitank gun, also adapted the M39 to a similar role. The M39 fired a 20-pound shell to a maximum ceiling of 27,165 feet and, when employed as an antitank weapon, was fitted with armored shields to protect its crew. Adopted in 1944, the 85mm M44 had a semiautomatic breech mechanism and fired a 20-pound shell up to a 33,465-foot ceiling.

Czech antiaircraft weapons included the 83.5mm Kan PL vz22 of 1925, the 76.2mm Kan PP Let vz28, adopted in 1928, and the 75mm Kan PP Let vz32 of 1932. The semiautomatic 37mm vz37 was adopted in 1938 and fired a 3.3-pound shell to a maximum ceiling of 23,294 feet.

Although initially hampered by the restrictions imposed by the Versailles Treaty, Germany rapidly developed a system of highly effective antiaircraft weapons. An early attempt, adopted in 1928, the 75mm FlaK38 fired a 14-pound shell to a maximum ceiling of 37,730 feet. In the decade following World War I, Krupp arranged with the Swedish arms giant Bofors to allow its engineers to work secretly on new designs in Sweden. One of the most successful artillery pieces of all time came about as a result of that arrangement—the famous German Eighty-Eight. Originally designed as an antiaircraft gun, combat experiences in the Spanish Civil War and early World War II proved the Eighty-Eight's versatility in other applications. By war's end, German designers had also adapted it to antitank, tank, and conventional field applications. The first test model was assembled in 1931, and after trials the new gun went into service in 1933 as the caliber 88mm FlaK18. With a veteran crew it achieved a firing rate of 15 rounds per minute. The FlaK18 fired a 21-pound shell to a maximum ceiling of 26,247 feet, and in a ground role it achieved a range of 9.2 miles.

Krupp engineers continued to improve the FlaK18 and also redesigned it to ease its manufacture. The redesigned Eighty-Eight entered service in 1937 as the Flak36 and saw considerable service with Germany's Condor Legion in the Spanish Civil War. Having proved the gun's effectiveness as a ground weapon in Spain, Krupp again improved the Eighty-Eight, by adding ground sights and providing high-explosive shells for field use. Firing high-explosive and armor-piercing ammunition, the Eighty-Eight further proved itself against British armor in North Africa in 1941–1942. As the war progressed, it became increasingly necessary to increase German tank armament to match the heavy guns and armor of the new Soviet tanks on the Eastern Front. That necessity resulted in slight modifications to the basic Eighty-Eight design, which resulted in the Kwk36 (Kampfwagen Kanone) and the Kwk43, for use in Tiger tanks and self-propelled guns.

Other German antiaircraft guns included the 37mm Flak18 and 36/37 series, which entered service in 1935 and, at 160 rpm, fired a 1.5-pound shell to a maximum ceiling of 15,750 feet. First introduced in 1938 as the Flak38 and improved in 1939 as the Flak39, the semiautomatic 105mm antiaircraft gun fired a 33-pound shell to a maximum ceiling of 37,400 feet. More than 2,000 Flak39s were manufactured during World War II. Adopted in 1941, the automatic 50mm FlaK41 was an intermediate antiaircraft gun effective at 18,000 feet and reaching a maximum ceiling of 59,528 feet firing a 4.8-pound shell. Despite a relatively unstable carriage, the FlaK41 was a good weapon and was popular with its crews. It later became the starting point for a more advanced 55mm gun that incorporated a comprehensive fire control system yet did not reach production by the war's end.

Heavy German antiaircraft weapons also included the semiautomatic 88mm FlaK41, a Rheinmetall-Borsig variation of Krupp's famous Eighty-Eight designed primarily for antiaircraft use. It entered service in 1943 and, mounted on a revolving base, traversed 360 degrees and fired a 21-pound shell to a maximum ceiling of 36,213 feet. In a ground role it achieved a range of 21,544 yards. Adopted in 1942, the FlaK40 had a 128mm barrel with a semiautomatic horizontal sliding block. The Flak40 fired a 57-pound shell to a maximum ceiling of 48,556 feet.

Italian antiaircraft artillery included the 37mm Breda 37/54, adopted in 1925, and the 75mm 75/46 Mo.35 Ansaldo of 1935. A versatile weapon also used in a ground role, the semiautomatic 75/46 Mo.35 was adopted in 1935 and had a maximum ceiling of 30,500 feet with a 14-pound shell. A Czech design, the 75mm 75/49 Skoda fired a 14-pound shell to a maximum ceiling of 30,000 feet, and the semiautomatic 75mm 75/50 Ansaldo was adopted in 1938 and also fired a 14-pound shell, to a ceiling of 27,559 feet. The

90mm 90/53 Ansaldo was adopted in 1938 and fired a 22-pound shell to a maximum ceiling of 39,370 feet, whereas the 102mm 102/35 was adopted in 1938 and fired a 29-pound shell; it had a maximum ceiling of 31,168 feet.

Japan adopted the 80mm Taisho 10 in 1921 and the semiautomatic 105mm Taisho 14 in 1925. The semiautomatic 75mm Model 88 was adopted in 1928 and was the standard Japanese field antiaircraft gun during World War II. It fired a 14-pound shell to a maximum ceiling of 29,000 feet. A British Vickers design and produced in single- and twin-mounting configurations, the 40mm Model 91 was adopted in 1931, whereas the semiautomatic 80mm Model 99 entered service in 1939 and reached a maximum ceiling of 32,000 feet firing a 20-pound projectile. The 120mm Type 3 was adopted in 1943. Firing a 57-pound shell, it achieved a maximum ceiling of 48,000 feet. The 75mm Type 4 was adopted in 1944, and a 150mm prototype antiaircraft gun appeared the same year. Firing a 98-pound shell, it reached a maximum ceiling of 62,336 feet.

MEDIUM AND HEAVY ARTILLERY

The United States adopted the long-range 155mm Gun M1 "Long Tom" in 1938. Firing a 96-pound shell, it had a range of 25,700 yards. It shared the same split-trail carriage as the U.S. 8-inch and British 7.2-inch howitzers. The 8-inch Howitzer M1 (M115) was accepted in 1940 and after World War II underwent a number of design changes, resulting in its redesignation as the Howitzer, Heavy, Towed, 8-inch, M115. The basic M115 fired a standard 95-pound M107 projectile to a maximum range of 19,794 yards. With a fourteen-man crew, it attained a maximum firing rate of 1 round per minute.

The year 1941 witnessed the introduction of both the 4.5-inch Gun M1 and the 155mm Howitzer M1 (M114). The Gun M1 fired a 55-pound shell to a maximum range of 20,505 yards, whereas the howitzer M1 fired the 95-pound M107 shell to a maximum range of 15,966 yards. The Howitzer M1 was upgraded after World War II as the M114 and was widely exported. Mounted on a split trail carriage, it was served by a crew of eleven and capable of a sustained firing rate of 40 rounds per hour. The 8-inch Gun M1 and its counterpart, the 240mm Howitzer M1, entered U.S. service in 1943. The two pieces shared the same heavy twin-trailed carriage that for transport required the howitzer barrel to be removed for towing by a High-Speed Tractor M8. The Gun M1 could fire a 240-pound shell up to 35,357 yards; the heaviest combat U.S. artillery piece of World War II, the Howitzer M1, fired a 360-pound shell and had a 25,224-yard range.

Officially designated the Bomb Testing Device T1, the largest-bore World War II artillery piece, the caliber 914mm muzzleloaded rifled mortar was originally designed to fire aerial bombs for testing purposes. More commonly known as "Little David," it was re-designed as a heavy artillery piece in anticipation of attacking forti-fied strongholds during the planned invasion of Japan. Although never seeing combat use, the Little David was an intimidating piece of ordnance. It required 553 pounds of propellant to fire a shell filled with a 1,598-pound high-explosive bursting charge to a maximum range of 9,498 yards.

The British government accepted the 4.5-inch Gun Mk2 in 1939, and the 5.5-inch Gun Mk3 in 1941. The Mk3 was widely exported and remained in service as the standard British medium gun until 1980. It fired a 100-pound shell to a maximum range of 16,196 yards. The Mk3 was easily distinguished by tall vertical projections on either side of the tube housing springs to balance the barrel. Served by a crew of ten, it had a firing rate of 2 rounds per minute. The 7.2-inch Howitzer Mk1 was adopted in 1941, and the 7.2-inch Howitzer Mk6 in 1943. The Mk6 fired a 202-pound shell to a maxi-mum range of 19,603 yards.

In 1930 and 1931, respectively, the Soviet Union adopted the 152mm Gun M10/30 and the 203mm Howitzer L-25. The L-25 fired a 217-pound shell to a maximum range of 19,685 yards. The Soviets continued to develop a range of medium and heavy pieces throughout the decade, including the 152mm Gun M10/34, adopted in 1934, the 152mm Gun Howitzer BR-2 of the following year, and the 152mm Gun ML-20, adopted in 1937. The ML-20 fired a 95.5-pound shell to a maximum range of 18,898 yards and following World War II saw wide use among the Warsaw Pact members, as well as other Soviet satellites and allies.

In 1938 the Soviet Union adopted the 122mm Corps Gun M31/37 (A-19) and the 152mm Howitzer M-10, followed by the 122mm Howitzer M1938 (M-30) in 1939. Developed by the FF Petrov design bureau at the Artillery Plant No 172 at Perm, the 122mm Howitzer M1938 (M-30) remained in service with the War-saw Pact until superseded by the 122mm D-30. It was also manufac-tured by China as the Type 54 and the Type 54-1. The M-30 utilized the same split trail carriage as used with the 152mm Howitzer

M1943, was manned by a crew of eight, and achieved a maximum firing rate of 6 rounds per minute.

The Soviet Union adopted the 210mm Gun M39/40 and the 305mm Howitzer BR-18 in 1940. The latter fired a massive 727.5-pound shell to a maximum range of 17,935 yards. Intended to replace the M1938 (M-10), the 152mm Howitzer D-1 was adopted in 1943. It was developed at the Artillery Plant No. 9 at Sverdlovsk and incorporated a modified M-10 barrel mounting a large muzzle brake mated to a strengthened M1938 (M-40) split trail box carriage and recoil system. With a crew of six, the D-1 was capable of firing an 88-pound shell up to 13,561 yards. The D-1 was widely exported and is still in use by former Soviet satellites; it was used as a reserve weapon and for training in Russia into the 1990s.

France, Belgium, and Czechoslovakia also manufactured medium and heavy pieces during the interwar years—pieces that saw some German use after their respective countries' fall to the Nazis in World War II. France adopted the 155mm Howitzer Mle 29 in 1930 and followed it with the 155mm Gun Mle 32 in 1933. Belgium also began fielding the 155mm Howitzer M24, with a maximum range of 18,591 yards with a 95-pound shell. Czechoslovakia's arsenal included the 149mm Howitzer vz25, adopted in 1925, and the 149mm Howitzer vz37 of 1937. The vz37 had a maximum range of 16,514 yards firing a 92.5-pound shell.

Germany continued to pour tremendous amounts of money and resources into the production of advanced heavy weaponry. Such effort, however, ultimately proved detrimental to its overall war effort, as the results were often impractical and diverted production away from more useful ordnance. The 105mm sK18 gun was adopted in 1934, as was the 150mm sFH18 (heavy field howitzer). Serving as the primary divisional medium howitzer during World War II, the sFH18 fired a 96-pound shell up to 14,490 yards. Intended as a lighter alternative to the sFH18, the 150mm sFH36 incorporated light alloys in its construction and could be horse-drawn if necessary. Designed by Rheinmetall, it was manufactured from 1938 until wartime metal shortages ended its production in 1942. The 150mm K18, adopted in 1938, fired a 95-pound shell up to 26,794 yards.

Adopted in 1937, the caliber 238mm KL/46 fired a 397-pound shell up to 35,000 yards, whereas the 240mm K3 entered service in 1938 and fired a 334-pound shell to a maximum range of 19,138 yards. Other heavy pieces adopted in 1939 included the 211mm Mörser 18, which fired a 293-pound shell up to 18,263 yards; the 356mm H M1, firing a 1,268-pound projectile to a maximum range of 21,872 yards; the 538mm SP Mrs Karl, firing a 2,749-pound shell to a maximum range of 13,670 yards; and the even heavier caliber 598mm SP Mrs Karl with a maximum range of 7,300 yards firing a 3,475-pound projectile. In 1940, Germany introduced the 240mm H39, as well as the 149mm K39, and in 1941 it adopted the 105mm sK18/40, the 149mm SKC/28, and the 173mm K18. In 1943 both the 211mm K38 and the 210mm K39 entered German service.

A German engineer by the name of Conders at the Röchling Steel Company developed one of the more bizarre weapons of the war— the 150mm so-called Hochdruckpumpe (HDP), or High Pressure Pump. It revived a principle first introduced in the earlier 1867 Lyman and Haskell Gun, which had incorporated a long barrel with multiple side powder chambers along its length to boost the projectile's velocity as it successively passed each chamber. Conders's success with a 20mm test gun eventually led, in 1944, to a full-scale, 492-foot-long 150mm gun with fifty side chambers. Intended for use with a special, dart-like projectile, the full-scale prototype was captured before entering service.

Other Axis medium and heavy ordnance included Italy's 210mm Obice da 210/22 Mo.35 howitzer, adopted in 1934, and the 149mm Canone da 149/40 Mo.35, adopted the following year. In 1929, Japan adopted the 150mm Gun Model 89; the 150mm Howitzer Model 96 was adopted in 1936. The caliber 410mm Siege Howitzer weighed 179,192 pounds and had a maximum range of 21,194 yards firing a 2,198-pound shell.

COASTAL ARTILLERY

The various powers invested less in coastal artillery development during the 1920s than in the previous decades. Such diplomatic moves as the 1921 Washington Conference limited naval gun sizes, thus leading to a general reduction in coastal armament. There was, however, a renewed impetus to modernize coastal artillery following Japan's 1934 rejection of the treaty. After World War II, the decline of the battleship and the ascendancy of air power and missile artillery led to a reassessment of the viability of large, fixed coastal weapons. The United States decommissioned its coastal artillery in 1948; it was followed by Great Britain in 1956.

Adopted in 1936, Great Britain's 15-inch Mk1 had a maximum range of 42,000 yards firing a 1,940-pound shell, whereas its 6-inch Mk24, adopted in 1939, fired a 100-pound shell up to 21,708 yards;

the 8-inch Mk8 of 1942 had a maximum range of 29,200 yards firing a 256-pound shell. Adopted in 1937 and designed for defense against smaller and faster vessels, the dual-mounted 6-pdr, 10-cwt Mk1 Twin had caliber 57mm barrels with semiautomatic vertical sliding breech mechanisms. The Mk1 fired a 6-pound shell up to 5,151 yards. The United States defended its coasts with the 16-inch Gun M1919 and the improved 16-inch Gun M1919 MII, adopted in 1923. The MII fired a 2,339-pound shell up to 41,601 yards. The 16-inch Howitzer M1920 was adopted in 1927 and fired a 2,099-pound shell to a 73,491-yard maximum range.

Adopted in 1932, Germany's heavy 305mm SK L/50 could fire a 551-pound shell up to 55,774 yards. Designed for use against lighter craft, the semiautomatic 37mm SK C/30 entered service in 1934 and could fire a 1.5-pound shell up to 7,201 yards. The 105mm SK C/32 was also adopted in 1934 and fired a 33-pound shell to a maximum range of 16,678 yards. Other German coast artillery pieces adopted in 1934 included the 150mm Ubts and Tbts K L/45 and the 203mm SK C/34. The 88mm C/35 entered service the following year and was followed in 1936 by the semiautomatic 149mm SK C/28, in 1937 by the 149mm Tbtsk C/36, and in 1938 the semiautomatic SK L/60. The 406mm SK C/34 was adopted in 1939 and fired a 2,271-pound shell up to 61,242 yards.

Originally intended for a class of battleships that were never produced, Krupp manufactured seven caliber 406mm barrels by 1937 that were accepted in 1940. Although none entered service, three were mounted in the coastal defenses in Narvik, Norway, and the others, after a brief stint as railway guns, were positioned in the defenses of the Pas de Calais. Mounted in a protective turret, the so-called Adolf could fire both a 1,345-pound shell with an 800-pound charge and a 2,271-pound shell using a 664-pound charge; at its maximum 45-degree elevation, it realized a maximum range of 35 miles. After the war Norway continued to use its three Adolfs in its coastal defenses well into the 1960s.

RAILROAD ARTILLERY

Its sheer size, reliance on rail systems for movement, and vulnerability to aircraft led to the eventual demise of the railroad gun. Still, a number of such weapons, such as the U.S. 8-inch Gun Mk VI Model 3A2, were adopted during the period. It was, however, Germany that expended the most energy on railway artillery development during World War II. During the 1930s, German engineers adapted a number of naval guns of World War I design to a railroad configuration known collectively as Bruno guns. Six caliber 238mm K (E)s were manufactured between 1936 and 1939. The 238mm Theodor Bruno had a maximum range of 12.5 miles firing a 327-pound shell. Three examples of the caliber 283mm K (E) Lange Bruno (Long Bruno) were produced in 1937 and had a maximum range of 22.4 miles firing a 626-pound shell. In addition, eight 283mm K (E) Kurz Brunos (Short Brunos) were manufactured in 1937 and 1938. The Kurz Bruno fired a 529-pound shell to a maximum range of 32,262 yards. Two 283mm K (E) Schwerer Bruno guns were produced in 1937 and 1938 and fired a 626-pound shell to a maximum range of 22 miles. Krupp also manufactured three improved 147-ton 283mm Neue Brunos (New Brunos) between 1940 and 1942. The Neue Bruno fired a 584-pound shell to a maximum range of 23 miles.

Germany also produced the 149mm K in Eisenbahnlafette in 1937 and the 173mm K (E) railroad gun in 1938. Its design inspired by the World War I Paris Gun, the 211mm K12 (E) was completed in 1939. It weighed 98 tons, and its 1,260-inch-long barrel launched a 237-pound shell up to 93 miles. Possibly fired twice in 1940 at Kent across the English Channel, the K12 ultimately proved a failure and the project was abandoned. The 203mm K (E) entered service in 1941, as did the 800mm K (E) Gustav ("Dora Gerat"). Designated "Gustav" by Krupp after Gustav von Bohlen und Krupp, the massive 1,329-ton caliber 800mm K (E) was more popularly known to its crew as "Dora." Only one Gustav was completed. At its maximum 65-degree elevation and with a 2.2-ton charge, Gustav fired a 4.7-ton high-explosive shell up to 51,400 yards and a 7-ton concrete-piercing projectile to a maximum range of 24 miles. Owing to its tremendous size, the Gustav had to be transported in sections and required three weeks to be assembled on site, with an extended crew of gunners, guards, and auxiliaries of 1,420 men. Although originally intended to attack the Maginot Line, the Gustav's only combat use occurred during the siege of Sevastopol, where it fired forty rounds, and during the 1944 Warsaw Uprising, where it expended thirty shells.

Originally designated the 38cm SK C/34, a gun designed by Krupp to arm Bismarck-class battleships, development began on the 380mm K (E) Siegfried in 1938. Three were eventually completed in 1943. Mounted on a revolving turntable, the Siegfried had a horizontal sliding block and a 703-inch-long barrel requiring a metal support structure that elevated 45 degrees. Firing a 1,091-pound shell, it had a maximum range of 26 miles. More commonly known as "Anzio Annie" from one example's use against Allied forces in the 1944 invasion of Italy, the 283mm K5 (E) was also known to the Germans as "Leopold." Entering service in 1940, it weighed 480,607 pounds and mounted a horizontal sliding block and 802-inch-long barrel. Firing a special 561-pound splined shell, it had a maximum range of nearly 39 miles. The Germans fielded some twenty-five K5 (E)s during World War II, with one survivor now held at Aberdeen Proving Ground in Maryland and another in France.

The K5 (E) also provided the basis for a number of experimental weapons and projectiles that were developed at the Rocket Research Establishment at Peenemunde. There, German scientists developed a special rocket-assisted projectile fitted with a motor that ignited at the apex of its trajectory. Although the rocket boosted the projectile's range to some 53 miles, its accuracy was poor, and the motor reduced the internal space available for its explosive charge. Another attempt to extend the gun's range, the self-descriptive Peenemunde Arrow Shell, saw limited use in late 1944. Brilliant in concept yet poor in performance, the Arrow Shell was 70 inches long, guided by four fins, and had a 310mm driving band around its 120mm body. Fired from a 310mm smoothbore barrel at a velocity of 5,000 fps, the shell's driving band dropped away after leaving the muzzle, giving it the astounding range of more than 90 miles. Although ultimately crippled by poor accuracy and a small explosive payload, most of the experimental guns saw at least some use during the war.

RECOILLESS ARTILLERY

During the 1930s various technicians attempted to solve the problem of providing a powerful, lightweight weapon that did not require a heavy recoil system and carriage. To that end, they experimented with various methods of bleeding off a percentage of the cartridge's exhaust gas in order to reduce its recoil and thus eliminate the need for a heavy barrel and cumbersome recoil mechanism. By redirecting the gun's blast through holes or venturis at the barrel's breech, they eventually found that they could produce a more portable and concealable weapon suitable for mounting on light vehicles and for airborne use. The Germans first used such recoilless artillery during their 1941 airborne assault on Crete, where they used them as lightweight field guns. For their part, British designers saw their potential as antitank weapons. Although the British recoilless guns were developed too late to see combat service, the United States did deploy a very few in the Pacific Theater, where they saw limited action. Within five years recoilless artillery, firing hollow- or squash-head projectiles, superseded conventional artillery in most antitank applications.

Germany adopted recoilless rifles in 1941. Mounted on a light, two-wheeled carriage, the 75mm LG40 saw considerable service in World War II. It had a horizontal sliding block and weighed 320 pounds. Firing a 1.8-pound shell to a maximum range of 7,436 yards, a number were issued to German parachute troops during the 1941 invasion of Crete. The heavier 105mm LG40 and LG42 fired a 32.6-pound shell to a maximum range of 8,694 yards. The 75mm RFK43 weighed just 95 pounds and was adopted in 1944. It fired a 9-pound shell up to 2,187 yards.

Sir Denis Burney, the father of British recoilless artillery, began development of such a system with the Broadway Trust Company in 1941. The Burney Guns, as his several designs were called, utilized a chamber and special cartridge casing, both of which were manufactured with holes to allow a portion of the gas caused by detonation to escape. The gas was then directed rearward by venturis that reduced recoil to a negligible level. The Burney Guns were essentially experimental weapons and were not adopted by the British government. They did, however, lead the way to more advanced recoilless weapons; his "Wall-Buster" shell, filled with plastic explosives, became the basis for future antitank projectiles. A shoulder-fired weapon, the 3.45-inch P1 Burney Gun, appeared in 1944 and fired a 3.7-pound projectile up to 547 yards. Also introduced in 1944 for antitank use, the 3.7-inch Mk1 had six exhaust venturis, weighed 375 pounds, and could fire a 22.5-pound shell up to 1,996 yards. The 7.2-inch P1 appeared the same year yet did not see combat. With four venturis, it fired a 120-pound shell up to 3,401 yards. The 95mm Mk1 debuted in 1945, too late to see use in World War II. It fired a 25-pound shell up to 10,800 yards.

The United States adopted the 57mm RCL Rifle M18 recoilless rifle in 1945. It weighed only 44 pounds—light enough to be mounted on a machine gun tripod—and could fire a 2.5-pound projectile 4,921 yards. The Communist Chinese also produced large numbers of copies of the M18. Also adopted in 1945, the tripod-mounted 75mm RCL Rifle M20 weighed 167.5 pounds and fired a

14-pound projectile to a distance of 7,300 yards. The M20 saw considerable service in the Pacific Theater during World War II and during the Korean War.

SELF-PROPELLED ARTILLERY

Following World War I numerous designers approached the problem of motorizing artillery pieces to make them more mobile in the field. Although tanks had made their debut during the war, military planners also saw the need for a distinct type of self-propelled field artillery to accompany and support infantry. In 1919, the noted U.S. tank designer J. Walter Christie (1856–1944) mounted a 155mm gun on a special chassis equipped with tracks for cross-country use and wheels for road transportation. Although Christie's designs found little favor at home (he later worked extensively for the British and the Soviets), he did set the groundwork for later developments.

As self-propelled gun and tank crews were required to operate in confined spaces, it also became necessary to find some method of reducing the choking fumes released at the breeches of their pieces after firing. To prevent such leakage, designers often incorporated fume extractors into their barrel designs. The fume extractor was a barrel-shaped compartment around the cannon tube somewhat past its midsection. As the fired shell passed the fume extractor, holes drilled through the barrel allowed a portion of the highly pressurized gas to enter its outer chamber. Once the projectile cleared the muzzle the pressure was then released, thus forcing the majority of the propulsive gasses toward the muzzle rather than the breech.

Although the proponents of the opposing schools altered their basic doctrines to suit the situation, during World War II two main schools of thought emerged concerning the proper use self-propelled artillery. The United States and Britain generally utilized their self-propelled guns in a conventional, indirect-fire infantry support role. In contrast, the Soviets and Germans tended to use theirs as rapidly advancing, infantry-accompanying direct-fire weapons. Britain's first attempt at building a self-propelled artillery piece, the Birch Gun, was an 18-pounder field gun mounted on a Vickers "C" tank chassis. It was named in honor of Sir Noel Birch, Master-General of the Ordnance, and first appeared in 1925. An improved version, debuted in 1926, discarded the earlier model's restrictive turret and allowed for a much greater 85 degree elevation for antiaircraft use.

Lacking the capacity to mass produce suitable chasses, Britain continued to improvise during the first years of the war. The Bishop was adopted in 1942 and saw service in North Africa, Sicily, and the invasion of Italy. Essentially a 25-pounder field gun mounted in an awkward-looking, cramped turret on a Valentine tank chassis, the Bishop served Britain until suitable alternatives became available. It was phased out of combat service in 1943 and was later used for training self-propelled gun crews. Another early attempt at providing self-propelled field artillery equipment, the Priest consisted of a U.S. M2A1 field howitzer mounted on a M3 Grant tank chassis. Owing to the pulpit-like appearance of the Grant's machine gun cupola, British crews quickly christened the weapon "Priest," thus beginning their nation's tradition of giving self-propelled field guns names with religious connotations. Also known as the 105mm Self-Propelled Howitzer M7 in U.S. service, some 3,500 Priests were manufactured and entered service between 1941 and 1943. The Priest saw action with British forces during the October 1942 Battle of El Alamein and was finally replaced in British service by the Sexton and in the United States by the M37 in 1945.

The Deacon was adopted in 1942. Its 57mm barrel was mounted on an AEC truck, and, firing antitank projectiles, it achieved a maximum range of 1,094 yards. A Canadian development, and used by British and Commonwealth forces, the Sexton entered service in 1943. With a crew of six, the Sexton utilized a 25-pounder gun mounted on a Canadian Ram tank chassis. Its caliber 87mm barrel realized a maximum range of 13,402 yards. Intended to replace the Bishop, some 2,250 Sextons were manufactured with a number remaining in service with other nations into the 1970s.

Classified as tank destroyers and not mobile field artillery, the Achilles and Archer escaped the British practice of giving self-propelled artillery religious-themed names. Adopted in 1944 and used up until 1950, the excellent caliber 76mm Achilles was mounted on an M4A2 U.S. Sherman. It had a maximum range of 2,187 yards firing antitank ammunition. The 75mm Archer was adopted in 1944. Mounted on a Valentine tank chassis, its 17-pounder gun had a maximum range of 18,591 yards. The Archer served well in the European Theater and remained in limited service until the end of the decade.

As World War II progressed, Germany expended a tremendous amount of effort and resources to develop and field ever larger and more powerful self-propelled weapons. The early 75mm Sturmgeschütz 40 and 150mm sIG auf PzkwI were adopted in 1940. The

Sturmgeschütz 40 was mounted on a Panzer III tank chassis and had a maximum range of 5,468 yards, whereas the sIG auf PzkwI incorporated a Panzer I chassis and had a maximum range of 5,140 yards. Both, however, were dwarfed by another self-propelled weapon that appeared the same year.

Named in honor of its research and development program's chief, General Karl Becker, the 600mm Karl 040 began production in 1940, with six being completed by the end of 1941. Dispatched to the Eastern Front, each received a distinctive name, such as Adam, Eve, Odin, Loki, Thor, and Ziu. The Karl was manufactured by Rheinmetall-Borsig and, mounted on a tracked chassis, was more flexible than a railroad gun; yet, at 122 tons, it was still a ponderous weapon. It was typically lowered from its driving carriage in preparation to firing and incorporated a hydropneumatic recoil system. The Karl fired a 4,839-pound concrete-piercing projectile up to 4,921 yards and a 3,472-pound high-explosive shell up to 7,300 yards. In 1943, Rheinmetall-Borsig provided the Karls' crews with alternative caliber 540mm barrels that fired a 2,756-pound shell to a maximum range of 6.5 miles.

Lighter, self-propelled artillery, however, proved much more effective for field service. Adopted in 1941, the 150mm sIG auf PzKwII was mounted on a Panzer II tank chassis and had a maximum range of 5,140 yards. The sIG auf PzKw 38(t) incorporated the German 150mm siG33/1 L/12 howitzer mounted on a Czech 38(t) tank chassis. It was adopted in 1943 and had a maximum range of 5,140 yards. Crewed by five, the Wespe ("Wasp") incorporated the 105mm leFH 18 howitzer with a maximum range of 11,674 yards on a Panzer II chassis. Following its first combat appearance at the July 1943 Battle of Kursk, the Wespe saw extensive service on all fronts during World War II. Armed with a short 150mm StuH43 L/12 howitzer and mounted on a Panzer IV tank chassis, the Sturmpanzer IV Brummbär (Grizzly Bear) was adopted in 1943; 306 were produced before the end of World War II. Crewed by five men, it had a maximum range of about 4 miles.

Some 90 Schweres Infantriegeschütz 33 (Sf) auf PzKpfw 38(t) Ausf. H, Grille self-propelled guns were manufactured between February and April of 1943. With a five-man crew, it originally mounted a 150mm alG33/1 L/12 gun on a Czech 38(t) tank chassis and had a maximum range of 5,140 yards. Also adopted in 1943 and intended as an infantry support weapon, the Schwere Panzerhaubitze auf Fahrgestell Panzerkampfwagen III/IV (Sdkfz 165) Hummel ("Bumblebee") incorporated a 150mm sFH18 howitzer mounted on a modified Panzer IV tank chassis. Its ammunition replenished from an accompanying armored support vehicle, it was served by a six-man crew and had a maximum range of 7.8 miles firing a 96-pound shell. Approximately 100 Hummels were manufactured, with most seeing service on the Eastern Front.

Spurred by ever more effective Soviet armor, Germany continued its own development of potent self-propelled antitank guns. Known variously as the Nashorn (Rhinoceros) and Hornisse (Hornet), the PaK43/1 (L/71) auf Fahrgestell Panzerkampfwagen III/IV (Sf) self-propelled tank destroyer entered service in 1943. Its 88mm PaK43/1 L/71 gun was mounted on a Panzer IV tank chassis and had a maximum range of 3,280 yards. Crewed by four men and maneuverable, the Nashorn proved an excellent weapon, and some 494 were manufactured by the end of the war. Also known as the "Ferdinand" in honor of its designer, Dr. Ferdinand Porsche, the Sturmgeschütz m/8.8cm Pak43/2 Sd Kfz 184 "Elefant" was rushed into service in 1943, with some 90 being built prior to the Battle of Kursk. Manned by a crew of six, it was mounted on a Tiger tank chassis and armed with the potent German 88 FlaK gun. Although its 9 inches of forward armor provided an extreme degree of protection, the 143,300-pound Elefant, owing to its slow speed and lack of machine guns on early models, was vulnerable to infantry.

The Jagdpanzer 38(t) Hetzer Sd. Kfz. 138/2 tank destroyer entered service in the spring of 1944, and some 2,584 were completed before the war's end. It mounted a 75mm PaK39 L/48 gun on a Czech 38(t) tank chassis and achieved a 2,187-yard maximum combat range. Although the Hetzer's interior was very confining for its four-man crew, its low profile and potent gun proved it an effective weapon. The Hetzer underwent several design changes through its production, and a number remained in Swiss and Swedish service through the 1950s. Also known as the Jagdpanzer IV and the Jagdpanzer 39, Sturmgeschütz IV consisted of a 75mm PaK42 l/70 antitank gun mounted on a Panzer IV tank chassis. Entering service in 1944, it was served by a four-man crew and had a combat range of up to 8,393 yards.

Owing to manufacturing difficulties, the Sturmgeschütz IV underwent a number of variations throughout its production run, with early models, owing to their ungainly handling characteristics, earning the nickname "Guderian's Ducks." Later versions of the tank destroyer, with improved drive trains and a low profile, proved quite popular with their crews. The Jagdpanzer IV first saw combat with the Herman Goring Division in Italy and later performed well on the Eastern Front, at Normandy, and during the Ardennes Offensive. The most celebrated Jagdpanzer IV commander, SS Oberscharfueher Rudolph Roy of the 12th SS Panzer Division, Hitler Jugend, was credited with destroying thirty-six Allied tanks following the invasion of Normandy. Having won the Knight's Cross for his exploits, Roy was later killed in the Ardennes in December 1944 by a U.S. sharpshooter.

Mounted on a Panther tank chassis, the Jagdpanther mounted an 88mm Pak 43/3 L/71 gun and weighed 100,310 pounds. It was adopted in 1944, and 392 were completed before production ceased in March 1945. With a crew of five, the Jagdpanther had a maximum range of 3,281 yards. First appearing in 1944, the massive 158,071-pound, Jagdpanzer VI was designed as a heavy tank destroyer and infantry-support weapon. Later redesignated Jagdtiger ("Hunting Tiger"), it incorporated a 128mm Pak 44 L/55 gun mounted on a Tiger II tank chassis. It had a crew of six and a maximum effective combat range of 4,374 yards. Although the most potent and long-ranged antitank weapon of the war, the Jagdtiger suffered many mechanical problems, and its high profile made it an easy target for enemy gunners. In addition, manufacturing and technical difficulties resulted in a limited production of no more than 85 examples.

Germany also developed and fielded mobile platforms for antiaircraft protection: 86 Wirbelwind ("Whirlwind") antiaircraft self-propelled guns were manufactured in 1944 to accompany and defend armored columns from air attack. Mounting four caliber 20mm barrels on a Panzer IV tank chassis, the Wirbelwind achieved a maximum ceiling of 10,500 feet. The Wirbelwind was superseded by the more potent Möbelwagen and Ostwind. The Ostwind mounted a 37mm FlaK 43 gun in a rotating turret attached to a Panzer IV tank chassis and was adopted in 1944, with 40 manufactured before the end of the war. It achieved a maximum 13,123-foot ceiling. Manufactured in 1944 and 1945, the Möbelwagen, or "Furniture Truck," received its name from its boxy appearance. It, too, was designed to accompany armored columns and mounted a 37mm FlaK 43 gun on a Panzer IV tank chassis.

Italy produced approximately 30 Semovente 90/53 self-propelled guns utilizing antiaircraft guns modified for antitank use in 1942 and 1943. They subsequently saw some use against Allied forces in North Africa and Sicily. The Semovente 90/53 incorporated a 90mm antiaircraft gun mounted on an M14/41 tank chassis and had a maximum range of 20,779 yards. It fired a 22-pound armor-piercing projectile at 2,760 fps and could pierce 5.5 inches of armor at 547 yards. Semoventes confiscated by German forces following Italy's capitulation were redesignated in German service as the Sturmgeschütz M42 mit 75/18 850(i) and the Sturmgeschütz M42 mit 75/34 851(i). Apparently only one self-propelled Semovente 149 self-propelled gun was manufactured before Italy's capitulation. Mounted on an M13/40 tank chassis, it incorporated a 149mm Model 35 gun that fired a 110-pound shell to a maximum range of 14.8 miles.

The Soviet Union's 76.2mm SU76 was adopted in 1943 and was mounted on a T70 tank chassis. Adopted in August of the same year, the 85mm SU85 The SU85 tank destroyer was served by a crew of four, and 2,050 were produced until July of 1944. It had an 85mm Gun D-5S mounted on a T34 tank chassis. Other Soviet self-propelled ordnance fielded by the Soviets in 1943 included the 122m SU122 and the SU152 assault gun. Both pieces were mounted on the Stalin tank chassis, with the SU122 incorporating a 122mm gun and the SU152 the 152.4mm Howitzer ML-205S. Crewed by five men, a total of 704 SU122 assault guns were manufactured in 1943. The SU100 tank-destroyer was adopted in 1944, and approximately 1,675 were manufactured into June of 1945. With a crew of four, it had a 100mm Gun D-10S mounted on a T34 tank chassis. The SU100 had a maximum combat range of 3,281 yards.

During the first months of World War II, the United States was forced to improvise to provide its forces with self-propelled artillery. In an early attempt to provide a self-propelled gun, in June 1940, U.S. engineers adapted the venerable 75mm M1897A gun to the M3 halftrack chassis. Adopted in 1941 and obsolete in 1944, the 75mm Gun Motor Carriage M3 had a mere 1,933-yard range, firing up to 15-pound projectiles. U.S. forces used the M3 in all theaters of the war, and, although sometimes used as a tank destroyer, it was more effective as a mobile infantry support weapon.

As the 75mm gun was found deficient against modern armor, in 1941 the higher-powered 105mm M1A2 howitzer was mounted on an M3 or M4 tank chassis to create the 105mm Howitzer Motor Carriage M7. The first M7s saw service with U.S. forces in the Philippines in 1941, and they proved particularly effective in British hands against Afrika Korps panzers at El Alamein in 1942. An adaptation of the French 155mm GPF gun to motorized use, the 155mm Gun Motor Carriage M12 was mounted on an M3 tank chassis. With a crew of six, it was adopted in 1941 and proved very effective in the European Theater during World War II. It was capable of a maximum range of 21,982 yards.

Introduced in 1942, the 37mm Gun Motor Carriage M6 was an unsuccessful early war attempt to quickly provide a mobile antitank gun. It consisted of a 37mm gun mounted to the bed of a Dodge WC-51 three-quarter-ton 4x4 truck chassis and was crewed by four men. The M6 had a maximum range of 1,094 yards firing a 1.9-pound antitank round. At best a stopgap, the M6 proved almost completely ineffective against German armored vehicles and was withdrawn from service. The 57mm Gun Motor Carriage T48 was also originally intended as a temporary expedient weapon at the beginning of the war. It saw combat service only with British forces and—with a more powerful gun—the Soviet Army. Production of the 19,000-pound T48 began in 1942, and it incorporated a 57mm M1 gun mounted to the bed of an M3 half-track chassis. With a crew of five, it fired 6-pound antitank projectiles to an effective combat range of 2,625 yards.

With a crew of four, the 75mm Howitzer Motor Carriage M8 mounted a 75mm M2/M3 howitzer on an M5 light tank chassis and was adopted in 1942. Secondary armament consisted of a caliber .50 machine gun mounted at the rear of its open-top turret. The M8 had a maximum range of 9,613 yards and saw extensive service during World War II, with a total of 1,778 being manufactured by the end of the war. The 3-inch Gun Motor Carriage M10 antitank gun was adopted in 1942, and 4,993 were manufactured through 1943. It mounted a 3-inch Gun M7 in a semi-enclosed turret on an M4 tank chassis. With a crew of five, it proved a much more successful U.S. attempt to produce a self-propelled antitank gun. The M10 fired a 15-pound shell to a maximum range of 15,967 yards.

Also known as the "Hellcat," the 76mm Gun Motor Carriage M18 tank destroyer mounted a 76.2mm M1 gun in an open-top turret on a tracked chassis. Entering service in 1944, it was crewed by five men and fired 15-pound antitank projectiles to a maximum range of 3,281 yards. The M18 proved a fast, nimble, and powerful antitank weapon, and it saw service until the end of World War II. The 90mm Gun Motor Carriage M36 incorporated an open-top turret on a M4A3 Sherman tank chassis. Also known as the "Jackson," 1,413 M36 tank destroyers were manufactured in 1944 and 1945. It was crewed by five men, and its modified antiaircraft 90mm Gun M3 achieved a maximum range of 17,060 yards. The M36 proved highly effective against heavy German armor and saw extensive action during the 1944 Ardennes Offensive.

Designed as an antiaircraft weapon to accompany mobile columns and with a total production of 285, the Twin 40mm Gun

Motor Carriage M19 entered service at the end of 1944. It incorporated twin 40mm Bofors antiaircraft guns in an open-top, rear-
mounted turret on an M24 tank chassis. With a crew of six, the
M19 also proved effective in a ground-support role. The M19 had a
cyclic rate of 240 rpm and, firing armor-piercing ammunition, had
a maximum range of 9,475 yards. In an antiaircraft role, it achieved
a ceiling of 22,875 feet.

With a crew of seven, the 105mm Howitzer Motor Carriage M37
incorporated the 105mm M4 howitzer mounted on a modified M24
Chaffee light tank chassis. Adopted in September 1945, only 150
were accepted by the government. The M37 had a maximum range
of 12,000 yards, and a caliber .50 machine gun was mounted in a
cupola to the right of the howitzer as secondary armament.

Adopted in February 1945 and used in the Korean War, the
155mm Gun Motor Carriage M40 mounted either a 155mm Gun
M1A1 or M2 mounted to the rear deck of a modified M4 medium
tank chassis. Crewed by eight men, it had a range of 25,722 yards
firing a 95-pound projectile. The 155mm Howitzer Motor Carriage
M41 was adopted in June of 1945, and a total of 85 were accepted
by the army. It incorporated a 155mm Howitzer M1 with a maximum range of 16,360 yards on the rear of an open M24 Chaffee
light tank chassis. The M41 saw service in both World War II and
the Korean War.

Adopted in June 1945 and with a limited production of only 48,
the 8-inch Howitzer Motor Carriage M43 incorporated an 8-inch
Howitzer M1 or M2 barrel that had a maximum range of 18,515
yards firing a 200-pound shell. Mounted to the rear deck of an M4
medium tank chassis and with a crew of eight, it was used extensively in the Korean War. Anticipating the need for heavy, self-
propelled artillery for the invasion of Japan, the U.S. Army also
adopted the 240mm Howitzer Motor Carriage T92 and 8-inch Gun
Motor Carriage T93 in 1945. The heaviest U.S. self-propelled
weapons of the war, both were mounted on a M26E3 Pershing heavy
tank chassis and were manned by a crew of eight. The T92 used the
240mm Howitzer M1, whereas the T93 mounted the 8-inch Gun
M1s. The T92 had maximum range of 25,262 yards firing a 360-
pound shell. A large spade mounted to the rear of the chassis absorbed recoil, and a T31 cargo carrier provided ammunition. Owing
to Japan's surrender, only five T92s and two T93s were delivered.

CHAPTER EIGHT

Post–World War II and Late-Twentieth-Century Developments

ALTHOUGH THE KOREAN WAR was fought with World War II weapons, the introduction of atomic weapons forced tacticians to rethink the role of conventional artillery in future conflicts. Following World War II, the Soviet Union and its Warsaw Pact allies generally continued to follow the strategic and tactical models that had proved successful against the German army. Its field artillery thus remained an integral part of its ground forces. Yet, owing to their perceived vulnerability to tactical nuclear weapons, the Soviets put less emphasis on self-propelled artillery. Conversely, the new North Atlantic Treaty Organization (NATO) forces maintained their self-propelled artillery and decreased their conventional artillery, with an eye toward increasing missile and tactical nuclear weapon capabilities.

In an effort to standardize weapons and calibers, NATO specifications limited field guns to caliber 105mm and medium weapons to 155mm. Britain thus initially adopted the Italian 105mm M56 Pack Howitzer, as well as the U.S. 155mm M44 self-propelled howitzer. Later, in the 1960s, the British army adopted the domestic self-propelled 105mm "Abbott" and the heavier U.S. 155mm M109 and 8-inch howitzer, before finally moving to its 105mm Light Gun and the advanced 155mm FH70 howitzer. During the 1980s the United States also began moving away from the development of heavy ordnance in favor of lighter weapons suitable for air transport for use by its Rapid Deployment Force.

Following World War II, the growing sophistication of antiaircraft rockets seemed to foretell the demise of conventional antiaircraft artillery. Still, the proximity fuse in conjunction with rapidly traversing artillery with a high rate of fire showed promise as an effective counter against low-flying attack planes and helicopters. As a result, most major powers continued to develop such weapons after World War II. The 75mm M51 "Skysweeper" Antiaircraft Gun was adopted in 1951 and remained in service into the early 1970s. Developed at the Watervliet Arsenal in the mid-1940s, it incorporated an onboard radar system, optical director, and fire control computer. It mounted a caliber 75mm barrel served by an autoloader fed by two revolving ammunition drums. With a firing rate of 45 rounds per minute, the Skysweeper fired a 15-pound projectile armed with a proximity fuse to a 30,020-foot maximum ceiling.

TOWED FIELD ARTILLERY
The United States and Great Britain

The United States adopted the 75mm Pack Howitzer M116 in 1955 to replace the earlier 75mm Pack Howitzer M8 (airborne). The M116 fired a 15-pound shell to a maximum range of 9,055 yards. Additionally, the United States adopted the 105mm Howitzer M102 in 1965, to replace the World War II–era 105mm M101 for airborne use. Manufactured by the Rock Island Arsenal, it was mounted on an aluminum carriage with a wishbone-shaped trail and fired the standard M1 high-explosive (HE) 33-pound shell to a maximum range of 12,577 yards. The M102 was first used in Vietnam in 1966 and was replaced in U.S. service by the British Light Gun M119. The Rock Island Arsenal began producing the 155mm Howitzer M198 in 1978 as a replacement for the M114A1. Used by the United States, it is also widely exported. It is mounted on a split-trail carriage with a retractable firing base. With a crew of eleven, the M198 chambers a full range of ammunition and fires the 95-pound M107 high-explosive shell to a maximum range of 19,794 yards.

Great Britain also modernized its towed arsenal following the Korean War. The Royal Armament Research and Development Establishment at Fort Halstead designed the 105mm Light Gun

L118 to replace the Italian Oto Melara 105mm Model 56 Pack Howitzer, which had then been in British service with the designation 105mm L110A1. It was soon adopted by numerous other countries, including Australia in 1981. In 1986 the United States adopted the Light Gun as the M119 and began its domestic production at the Watervleit and Rock Island arsenals. The Light Gun has a maximum range of 16,480 yards firing a 35.5-pound projectile. It has a semiautomatic vertical sliding breech and is mounted on a lightweight carriage with tubular trails. The Light Gun weighs 4,008 pounds and is capable of traversing 11 degrees when raised on its firing base. Using the same ammunition as the self-propelled Abbot, it is a versatile, lightweight weapon designed to be transported to the battlefield by helicopter.

First developed by the Armaments Group of Vickers Shipbuilding and Engineering, the 155mm Ultralightweight Field Howitzer (UFH) incorporates a number of titanium castings in its construction to reduce its weight. It is thus ideal for airlift delivery and has been tested by Great Britain and Italy; in 1997 the United States chose it to replace the 155mm M198 howitzer, designating it the M777A1. Served by a crew of six, the UFH chambers all types of NATO 155mm ammunition and fires up to 5 rounds per minute. It has a maximum range of 29,528 yards with standard high-explosive projectiles.

During the 1960s, Great Britain joined in a program with the United States and West Germany to develop and manufacture the "Field Howitzer of the 1970s," otherwise known as the 155mm Howitzer FH70. The United States dropped out of the program soon after and, in 1970, were replaced by Italy, with the first pieces entering service in 1978. As participants in the joint venture, each country contributed to the FH70's design; Great Britain developed the carriage, traversing mechanism, and high-explosive ammunition. West Germany was responsible for the barrel, loading mechanism, auxiliary propulsion unit (APU), sights, and illuminating ammunition. Italy contributed the cradle, recoil system, and elevating gear. The FH 70 was mounted on a split-trail carriage fitted with small guiding wheels on the trail ends and a Volkswagen gas-powered engine (APU) that was capable of driving the two main wheels for short distances. It fired a 96-pound shell to a maximum range of 26,247 yards. By the end of the 1970s other powers, including Japan and Saudi Arabia, had also adopted the FH70.

Based on the British 105mm L13 gun, the Indian Light Field Gun first appeared in the early 1990s. It is mounted on an aluminum alloy carriage with a shield and bow-shaped trail. The Light Gun traverses 360 degrees when using its firing base, and owing to its light weight, it can be airlifted or parachuted into action. It can fire up to 6 rounds per minute and has a maximum range of 18,810 yards.

France

Having relied on U.S. and other ordnance in the immediate postwar years, France began to regain its manufacturing capabilities by the early 1950s. Entering service in 1952, the 155mm Howitzer Model 50 was also manufactured by Bofors for Sweden and was exported to Israel and other nations. It was eventually replaced in France by the 155mm Towed Gun TR. The Model 50 was mounted on a four-wheel split-trail carriage with a forward-mounted base plate. It fired a 96-pound high-explosive round up to 19,412 yards.

Originally organized in 1973 and nationalized in 1991, Giat Industries emerged as a major international arms manufacturer. Giat's Le Canon de 155mm Tracte (155mm Towed Gun TR) debuted in 1979 and entered production in 1989, with a number seeing service in 1991 in Operation Desert Storm. Its split-trail carriage is fitted with a 39 horsepower APU and firing jack. With a crew of seven it takes only 90 seconds to go into battery, and emergency backup systems allow it to remain in action following a moderate degree of battle damage. It is fitted with a hydraulic rammer and accepts a wide variety of French and NATO ammunition. The 155mm TR is capable of high-speed loading and can fire an extended-range projectile to a maximum distance of 35,000 yards.

An improved version of the aging M114, the Giat Industries 155mm Howitzer M114F appeared in 1987 and was manufactured mainly for export sales. It fires the standard NATO 155mm M107 projectile up to 20,231 yards at a rate of 4 rounds per minute. In 1990, Giat began deliveries to Singapore, Canada, and Indonesia of the semiautomatic 105mm LG1 MKII Light Gun, a weapon also designed for export. It weighs only 3,351 pounds and is thus highly mobile; it can be put into firing order in a mere 30 seconds. It is mounted on a split-trail carriage with a protective shield. With a full crew of five, it is capable of firing 12 rounds per minute and uses a wide range of both French and NATO ammunition; it achieves a maximum range of 20,000 yards.

Austria

During the 1980s the Austrian ordnance manufacturer Noricum began producing both APU-equipped and conventional towed models of its semiautomatic 155mm GH N-45. It is mounted on a four-wheel split-trail carriage and is equipped with a pneumatic rammer. The GH N-45 can fire bursts of 3 rounds in 16 seconds, or 7 rounds per minute; firing high-performance ammunition, it can attain a maximum range of 43,307 yards. Austria, Thailand, and a number of Middle Eastern governments have procured the GH N-45. In the early 1990s the Austrian government convicted several Noricum executives of selling 200 GH N-45s to Iran in violation of neutrality laws, and the company later came under suspicion of selling weapons to Iraq.

Italy

Production of the Oto Melara 105mm Model 56 Pack Howitzer for the Italian army began in 1957. Also sold widely abroad, it is served by a seven-man crew and can fire up to 8 rounds per minute. Mounted on a split-trail carriage, it is fitted with a semiautomatic vertical sliding breech mechanism. Easily transported by air, the Model 56 can also be disassembled for land transport, and its wheels can be lowered for concealment in an antitank role. Firing the same ammunition as the U.S. 105mm M1, the Model 56 fires a 33-pound high-explosive projectile up to 11,565 yards.

Spain

Spain used both Soviet and German ordnance following World War II and later added a number of U.S. weapons, before revitalizing its own cannon industry. First manufactured by the Sociedad Española Construction Naval in the early 1950s, the 105mm M/26 Field Howitzer has undergone continuous improvements over its service life. It is mounted on a split-trail carriage and, with a crew of six, fires both U.S. and Spanish high-explosive and antitank ammunition at 6 rounds per minute for up to 12,522 yards.

Designed by Fabrica de Artilleria de Sevilla, a subsidiary of the Santa Barbara arms firm, the Santa Barbara 155mm SB 155/39

Towed Howitzer was introduced in 1994 as a potential replacement for the U.S. 155mm M144 howitzer currently in Spanish service. Served by six men, it is equipped with a power rammer and fires a 96-pound shell up to 26,247 yards. The SB155/39 is mounted on a split-trail carriage with retractable wheels and circular firing base; it is also available with a 70-horsepower diesel APU.

South Korea

South Korea was originally supplied with predominately U.S. ordnance. It has steadily become self-sufficient in the production of artillery and has entered the export market. The Daewoo Corporation has manufactured copies of the U.S. 105mm M101A1 and the 155mm M114A2 howitzers for the South Korean army and for foreign sales. The Kia Machine Tool Company Ltd. began manufacturing the 105mm KH178 Light Howitzer in 1984. It is based on the U.S. 105mm M101 howitzer and the British 105mm Light Gun and fires all standard 105mm ammunition. It is mounted on a two-wheel, split-trail carriage and fires a high-explosive shell up to 16,076 yards. Also manufactured by Kia and with a firing rate of 4 rounds per minute, the 155mm KH179 Howitzer was adopted in 1983. It can be transported by helicopter and is mounted on a split-trail carriage. The KH179 fires a high-explosive shell up to 24,060 yards.

Soviet Union and Russia

During the Cold War the Soviet Union continued an extensive ordnance production to counter the perceived Western threat. As a result, the Soviets began fielding a wide array of new weapons during the 1950s. These included the 57mm M50 antiaircraft gun, which was adopted in 1950; it could fire a 6-pound shell to a maximum 13,123-foot ceiling. Adopted in 1953 and later replaced by the 240mm 2S4 self-propelled mortar, the 240mm Mortar M-240 was manned by a crew of up to eleven and had a smoothbore barrel. With a firing rate of only 1 round per minute, it fired a 288-pound high-explosive projectile up to 10,608 yards.

   The excellent 130mm Field Gun M-46 (M1954) entered Soviet service in 1954 and superseded the 122mm M1931/37 (A-19). It was capable of firing a wide range of ammunition, including armor-piercing and chemical projectiles, and a number of variants of the basic gun were produced by the Soviet state arsenals. The M-46 was widely exported by the Soviet Union and saw extensive use around the globe. It was mounted on a split-trail carriage fitted with large recoil spades. It was manned by a crew of eight and fired a 74-pound high-explosive shell up to 29,690 yards. The Israelis captured large numbers of M-46s from the Egyptians in the 1973 war.

Originally introduced in 1955 with the 2A19 gun tube to replace the 100mm M1944, the 100mm Antitank Gun T-12 antitank gun underwent a number of improvements in 1970. These included the mounting of the smoothbore 100mm 2A29 gun and modifications to its split-trail carriage. It was subsequently redesignated the MT-12. Both versions require a crew of six and mount a smoothbore barrel with a semiautomatic vertical sliding breech block. Capable of chambering a number of types of ammunition, the 2A29/MT-12 fires a 50.7-pound high-explosive antitank (HEAT) projectile up to 6,512 yards. Both are also capable of firing a maximum of 14 rounds per minute. A further improvement, the MT-12R is fitted with radar aiming equipment.

The 122mm Field Gun M1955 (D-74) was designed by the FF Petrov design bureau at the Artillery Plant No. 9 and adopted in 1955. Although intended to replace the aging 122mm Corps Gun M1931/37, it was outperformed by the 130mm Field Gun M-46 and thus relegated to reserve status in Soviet service and issued widely to Warsaw Pact members. Mounted on a split box-trail carriage with a retractable firing base, it was manned by a crew of ten and fired up to 7 rounds per minute. The D-74 was capable of firing an array of ammunition including armor-piercing and illumination rounds. It fired a 56-pound high-explosive shell up to 22,966 yards.

Based originally on a naval gun and introduced in 1955, the 180mm Gun S-23 was also provided to other Warsaw Pact countries as well as Egypt, India, Iraq, Somalia, and Syria. It was mounted on a split-trail carriage with a retractable firing base. The S-23 could maintain a firing rate of 1 round per minute with a 194-pound high-explosive projectile to a maximum range of 33,246 yards. The same year the 152mm Gun-Howitzer D-20 entered Soviet and Warsaw Pact service and was also widely exported around the world. It was mounted on a split-trail carriage with a forward-mounted, retractable firing base. With a crew of ten, it had a maximum firing rate of 6 rounds per minute and could chamber a variety of loadings, including chemical and tactical nuclear projectiles. With a conventional 96-pound high-explosive shell, the D-20 had a maximum range of 19,040 yards.

Also known as the Sprut-B ("Octopus-B"), the 125mm 2A45M Antitank Gun was developed at the Artillery Plant No. 9 and adopted in 1955. Intended as a defensive weapon, it incorporated a smoothbore gun mounted on a modified 122mm D-30 howitzer carriage with an auxiliary power unit (APU). In firing position, the carriage's three trails were extended for stability and allowed full 360-degree traversal. With a crew of seven, the 2A45M was capable of firing up to 8 rounds per minute. It fired a 15.5-pound armor-piercing antitank projectile to a maximum effective range of 2,296 yards and a 50.7-pound high-explosive shell up to 13,342 yards

Developed by the FF Petrov design bureau in the early 1960s to replace the semiautomatic 122mm M-30, the 122mm Howitzer D-30 has undergone a number of upgrades, resulting in the D-30M and D30A model designations. It was widely used in the Soviet army and has been manufactured by China, Egypt, and Iraq, where it became known as the 122mm Saddam Howitzer. When placed in firing position on its retractable base plate and double trail carriage, it is capable of traversing 360 degrees. The D-30 can chamber numerous types of ammunition, including armor-piercing, chemical, and illumination rounds. It has a maximum range of 16,732 yards and fires a 48-pound high-explosive fragmentation (FRAG-HE) shell and an armor-piercing high-explosive (HEAT) round.

Introduced in 1966 and used by Soviet forces in Afghanistan, the 76mm Mountain Gun GP (M1966) is mounted on a split-trail carriage. Manned by a crew of seven it is capable of firing many types of ammunition up to 12,576 yards. The 76.2mm Gun M69 mountain gun was adopted in 1969 and fires a 14-pound shell up to 12,030 yards.

The 82mm Vasilyek ("Cornflower") Automatic Mortar (2B9) entered service in the early 1970s and saw service with Soviet forces in Afghanistan. Although superseded by the 120mm 2B11 mortar, the 2B9 was also manufactured in Hungary and is still used by some Russian airborne units. The 2B9 is a semiautomatic breechloader fed by four-round clips; it is mounted on a split-trail carriage with retractable wheels. In firing position, it can traverse a total of 60 degrees; it elevates 85 degrees and fires a 7-pound high-explosive round up to 4,670 yards. Entering service in 1981, the 152mm Gun 2A36 (M1976) Giatsint ("Hyacinth") replaced the 130mm M-46 in Soviet service and was also provided to Finland and Iraq. It is mounted on a split-trail carriage with large rear spades and a forward-mounted retractable firing base. The M1976 is served by a crew of eight and fires a 101-pound high-explosive shell up to

29,528 yards. With rocket-assisted projectiles, it attains a range of 43,745 yards.

Designed at Perm and adopted in 1986 for airborne service, the 120mm 2B16 (NONA-K) Combination Gun combines the capabilities of both a howitzer and a mortar. With a crew of five, it is mounted on a split-trail carriage with a forward-mounted retractable base plate. It achieves a firing rate of up to 10 rounds per minute. The 2B16 can fire a high-explosive shell up to 9,514 yards or a high-explosive mortar bomb up to 7,765 yards. The 152mm Howitzer 2A65 (M1987) is mounted on a split-trail carriage with a retractable, forward-mounted firing base. It is manned by a crew of eight, is fitted with a semiautomatic breech and automatic rammer, and can achieve a firing rate of 7 rounds per minute. Capable of firing a wide variety of ammunition, the 2A65 fires a 96-pound high-explosive shell up to 27,012 yards.

Developed by the FF Petrov design bureau at Artillery Plant No. 9 in the early 1990s, the lightweight 152mm 2A61 Howitzer is crewed by seven and achieves a maximum range of 16,404 yards. Its barrel is fitted with a large muzzle brake, and it is mounted on a modified 122mm D30A (2A18M) carriage with retractable wheels and a three-piece trail that can be extended to form a stable firing base. Also designed by the FF Petrov facility, the 85mm Auxiliary-Propelled Field Gun SD-44 is essentially the 85mm D-44 fitted with a 14-horsepower, two-cylinder APU on a split-trail carriage. With many seeing service with airborne units, the D-44 is served by a crew of seven and achieves a maximum range of 17,115 yards. It fires an 8-pound high-explosive shell and a 16-pound HEAT projectile at a rate of between 10 and 15 rounds per minute.

Former Warsaw Pact Artillery

Czechoslovakia adopted the 85mm Field Gun vz52 in 1953 and also manufactured it for other members of the Warsaw Pact. It was mounted on a split-trail carriage with a protective shield and was crewed by seven men. The vz52 had a semiautomatic breech mechanism and could fire up to 20 rounds per minute. It accepted the same ammunition as the Soviet Divisional Gun D-44 and thus fired a 20.5-pound shell up to 16,160 yards. The 100mm Field Gun vz53 entered service the following year. Used in both field artillery and antitank applications, it had a split-trail carriage with a protective shield. Using the same 100mm ammunition as contemporary Soviet weapons, it fired a 35-pound high-explosive shell up to 21,000 yards and had an effective antitank range of 1,000 yards. The vz53 was served by a crew of six and attained a maximum firing rate of 10 rounds per minute.

Following World War II, Yugoslavia produced and issued numerous ordnance pieces of both foreign and domestic design. Early pieces included the 155mm Howitzer M65, a nearly exact copy of the U.S. 155mm Howitzer M114A1, and the 122mm Howitzer D-30, a copy of the Soviet 122mm Howitzer D-30. Widely exported and also known as the Tito Gun, the 76mm Mountain Gun M48 was fitted with a prominent muzzle brake and was mounted on a two-wheel split-trail carriage with folding trails. It was manufactured in several variants, including one that could be disassembled into eight components for transport by pack animals. The M48 was served by a six-man crew and had a maximum firing rate of 25 rounds per minute. It chambered a range of ammunition, including high-explosive and antitank rounds, and fired the M55 13.5-pound shell up to a maximum range of 9,569 yards.

Essentially a Soviet 130mm M46 converted to 155mm with improved sights, the Czech 155mm Converted Gun M46/84 is mounted on a split-trail carriage with a protective shield. It is manned by a crew of eight and achieves a maximum firing rate of 6 rounds per minute. The M46/84 fires standard M107 high-explosive shell to a maximum of 19,521 yards and, with extended-range ammunition, has a range of up to 42,650 yards. The 152mm Gun-Howitzer M84 series shares some characteristics of the Soviet 152mm Gun-Howitzer D-20. It has a semiautomatic breech and is mounted on a split-trail carriage with a protective shield. With a crew of eight, the M84 has a maximum firing rate of 6 rounds per minute; with standard ammunition, it achieves a range of 26,422 yards. The more advanced M84B1 and M84B2 models achieve a maximum range of 29,528 yards with extended-range ammunition.

Of Yugoslavian design and manufacture, the widely exported 105mm Howitzer M56 is fitted to a split-trail carriage with a protective shield. It is manned by a crew of seven and achieves a maximum firing rate of 16 rounds per minute and a range of 14,217 yards. Another modern Yugoslav design, the 100mm M87 Antitank Gun TOPAZ is based on a combination of features derived from the Soviet 122mm D-30J howitzer and 100mm T-12 antitank gun. The TOPAZ incorporates a split-trail carriage with shield that can be extended to form a cruciform firing base, providing a traversal of 360 degrees. Crewed by between five and seven men, it has a maximum firing rate of 14 rounds per minute and achieves a maximum effective range with HEAT ammunition of 1,312 yards.

People's Republic of China

Before the communist takeover in 1949, China procured its ordnance from foreign suppliers, primarily the German Krupp firm and Schneider in France. The communist regime later relied on the USSR for its artillery whereas the government in Taiwan turned to the United States for its weaponry. China North Industries Corporation (NORINCO) later began domestically manufacturing copies of Soviet artillery pieces and by the end of the 1970s began production of its own designs both for Chinese use and for export. The Communist Chinese Type 83 Gun-Howitzer is essentially a variant of the Soviet caliber 122mm D-30 Howitzer. Another copy of a Soviet design, the Type 66 Gun-Howitzer is basically a Soviet caliber 152mm D-20. Mounted on a split-trail carriage, the Type 66 has a semiautomatic breech and is manned by a ten- to twelve-man crew. It achieves a firing rate of up to 8 rounds per minute and fires a 96-pound shell up to 13,375 yards.

Based on the Soviet D-74, the semiautomatic NORINCO 130mm Field Gun Type 59-1 is crewed by up to ten men. It is capable of firing up to 10 rounds per minute and is mounted on a split-trail carriage. It can fire a number of projectile types and fires a 73.5-pound high-explosive shell up to 30,063 yards. The Type 59-1 is in service with numerous countries including North Korea, Vietnam, Egypt, and Pakistan. A copy of the Soviet D-30, the NORINCO 122mm Howitzer D-30 fires a 48-pound high-explosive projectile up to 16,732 yards. It has a maximum firing rate of 8 rounds per minute and is also mounted on a self-propelled chassis. A copy of the Soviet 122mm Howitzer M1938, the NORINCO 122mm Howitzer Type 54-1 is mounted on a split-trail carriage. It has a crew of eight and fires a variety of projectiles, including a 48-pound high-explosive shell, with which it attains a maximum range of 12,905 yards. China also exports the Type 54-1 to a number of other countries. The NORINCO 100mm Field Gun is a copy of the Soviet BS-3 (M1944) gun and is used primarily in antitank and counter-battery roles. With a six-man crew, it has a semiautomatic breech and fires a 66-pound antitank shell to a maximum effective range of 1,137 yards, or a 59.5-pound high-explosive round up to 21,872 yards.

A copy of the Soviet D1 howitzer, the NORINCO 152mm Type 54 Howitzer has a firing rate of up to 4 rounds per minute and achieves a maximum range of 13,560 yards. First produced in the 1960s for the Chinese army, the NORINCO 85mm Field Gun Type 56 is a copy of the Soviet 85mm Divisional Gun D-44 and is also widely exported. It has a semiautomatic breech and is mounted on a tubular split-trail carriage. The Type 56 has a maximum range of 17,115 yards firing a variety of ammunition types. With a crew of between six and eight, the Type 56 can fire up to 20 rounds per minute. The NORINCO 122mm Type 60 Field Gun is a copy of the Soviet D-74. It has a maximum range of 26,247 yards.

Intended for reserve batteries, the NORINCO 152mm Gun Type 83 is mounted on a split-trail carriage fitted with a centrally mounted firing platform. The Type 83 can fire up to 4 rounds per minute and has a maximum range of 41,557 yards firing a 106-pound extended-range projectile. The NORINCO 122mm Type 83 Howitzer was introduced in 1984 and has a maximum range of 19,685 yards. The Type 83 has a maximum firing rate of 8 rounds per minute. The smoothbore NORINCO 100mm Antitank Gun Type 86 is mounted on a split-trail carriage. It can fire a number of armor-piercing ammunition types at a rate of up to 10 rounds per minute The Type 86 has a maximum range of 14,932 yards.

During the early 1990s, NORINCO began development of a long-range 203mm howitzer with some design elements derived from Dr. Gerald Bull's 155mm/45 caliber system. It thus has many similarities with the South African G5 and the Austrian GH N-45 artillery systems. The NORINCO 203mm Howitzer is mounted on a split-trail carriage with large recoil spades and has a hydraulic-operated vertical sliding breech and prominent muzzle brake. With a firing rate of 2 rounds per minute it can fire standard 95.9-pound ammunition to a range of 43,745 yards or 100-pound extended-range full-bore-base-bleed (ERFB-BB) projectiles up to 54,680 yards. Another Chinese weapon sharing characteristics derived from Dr. Gerald Bull's work and the Austrian Noricum GH N-45 gun-howitzer, the NORINCO 155mm Gun-Howitzer Type WA 021 entered service in 1991 after a five-year development program. The WA 021 is mounted on a split-trail carriage with a center-pivot base capable of raising the piece off its wheels for firing. The WA 021 is capable of a sustained rate of 2 and a maximum of 5 rounds per minute. It achieves a maximum range of 42,650 yards firing extended-range ammunition, and some pieces are equipped with a four-cylinder diesel auxiliary propulsion unit (APU) for maneuvering short distances. An adaptation of the WA

021 barrel to the 130mm Gun Type 59-1 carriage, the 155mm Gun-Howitzer Type GM-45 is capable of firing 4 rounds per minute. In 1993, China produced the NORINCO 155mm Gun XP52, a prototype based on another Gerald Bull design. The XP52 achieves a rate of fire of up to 4 rounds per minute.

Finland

Finland has issued numerous weapons captured from the Soviet Union, as well as ordnance obtained from other foreign sources. These have included the Soviet 152mm M1937 (ML-20) gun-howitzer, called in Finnish service the 152H37 and later updated by the VAMMAS factory to become the 152H37A. The Finns originally designated another Soviet weapon, the 122mm Corps Gun M1932/37 (A-19), the 122K31 and later improved it to become the 152H88-31. Finland also obtained a number of 105mm sFH18 howitzers from Germany, known as the 150H40 in Finnish service, with improved models being redesignated the 152H88-40. Finland also fielded the more modern Soviet 152mm 2A36 (M1976) as its 152K89. Shortly after World War II the domestic Tampella firm emerged as a leader in modern weapon manufacturing and in 1991 reorganized as VAMMAS, to continue the development and production of superior ordnance.

Production of the semiautomatic Tampella 122mm M-60 Field Gun began in 1964. Served by a crew of eight, it was mounted on a four-wheel split-trail carriage. The M-60 fired a 55-pound high-explosive shell to a maximum of 27,340 yards. Obsolete by the 1990s, the Tampella 155mm Gun-Howitzer M-74 was mounted on a four-wheel, split-trail carriage and with standard ammunition achieved a maximum range of 26,247 yards. In 1991 the newly reorganized VAMMAS introduced the semiautomatic 155mm M-83 Howitzer. Both Tampella and VAMMAS have claimed that their weapons can be rapidly put into action with reduced crews of only two men. The M-83 has a split-trail carriage and is capable of accepting both the standard NATO M107 round as well as high-performance Finnish ammunition. The shorter-barrel M-83 achieves a maximum range of 32,808 yards, and the longer version 43,307 yards. Fitted with a high-speed rammer, the M-83 is capable of firing bursts of 3 rounds in 12 seconds and up to 10 rounds per minute. In 1991, VAMMAS collaborated with the Finnish Defense Forces to introduce the VAM-MAS 155mm 155GH52 APU. Based on the earlier 155mm M-83 howitzer, it is mounted on a four-wheel split-trail carriage with a forward hydraulic-powered firing base and APU. It is fitted with a semiautomatic breech and pneumatic rammer; with a crew of nine, it has the capability of firing bursts of 3 rounds in 12 seconds and a maximum of 10 rounds per minute. The GH52 APU fires a wide variety of ammunition, achieving a maximum range of 29,527 yards with standard high-explosive rounds.

Israel

Established in 1948, the Israeli Defense Force initially fielded whatever surplus foreign ordnance it could obtain. It eventually adopted the U.S. 105mm Howitzer M1 and the 155mm Howitzer M114. These were later supplemented with captured Soviet weapons obtained in conflicts with the Arab League. During the 1960s the Soltam firm began a project based on a Finnish design that eventually resulted in the 155mm M68 howitzer, which, following improvements, eventually became the M71 Gun-Howitzer. Further modifications led to the Soltam Models 839P and 845P weapons, which were also exported to Singapore and Thailand. First manufactured in 1970, the Soltam 155mm M68 Gun-Howitzer has a semiautomatic horizontal sliding block breech, muzzle brake, and fume extractor. Its four-wheel split-trail carriage is very similar to the Finnish Tampella M-60 and mounts a retracting firing base. The M-68 accepts the entire array of 155mm NATO ammunition and fires a 97-pound shell up to 22,966 yards. With a crew of eight, the M68 is capable of a maximum firing rate of 4 rounds per minute. It has been discontinued in Israeli service. With an improved rammer and longer barrel, the Soltam 155mm M-71 Gun-Howitzer is an improved version of the M-68 and entered production in 1975. It achieves a maximum range of 25,153 yards with conventional ammunition. With a crew of eight, the M71 can achieve a maximum rate of 5 rounds per minute. It is also in service with Singapore, Thailand, and South Africa, where it is designated the G4.

A further improvement over existing weapons, the Soltam 155mm Model 839P was introduced in 1983 and is fitted with a muzzle brake, fume extractor, and horizontal sliding block. It fires a 97-pound shell up to 33,900 yards. The Model 839P is mounted on a four-wheel split-trail carriage with a hydraulic-powered retractable firing base. It differs from the standard Model 839 in that it is equipped with an 80-horsepower diesel APU. The Soltam 155mm

Model 845P was adopted in 1984 and is basically the standard Model 845 fitted with an APU. The 845P fires a 97-pound shell up to 42,650 yards. Both the Models 839P and 845P can achieve a maximum firing rate of 5 rounds per minute. Soltam has also developed an upgrade package to modernize the Soviet 130mm field gun by fitting it with an improved 155mm semiautomatic horizontal sliding block barrel. The upgrade includes a pneumatic rammer and enables the 155mm M-46 to chamber all types of modern 155mm ammunition. The upgraded M-46 fires conventional rounds up to 32,808 yards and high-performance ammunition up to 42,650 yards. The company also manufactures a package to upgrade the U.S. 155mm M114 howitzer. The Soltam kit provides a 201-inch barrel that boosts its range to 19,794 yards.

South Africa

Following independence, South Africa continued to use British artillery equipment. The South African Defense Force (SADF) also issued the 40mm Bofors antiaircraft gun, as well as the Oerlikon 20mm and 35mm antiaircraft guns. South Africa began an intensive program to develop its ordnance industry following its combat experiences in 1975 against Angolan forces armed with superior Soviet weaponry. The country also adopted and designated the Israeli SOLTAM 155mm howitzer as the G4. Tests of the G5 as well as other ordnance systems eventually resulted in the South African 155mm G5 Gun-Howitzer. Manufactured by the LIW firm, a subsidiary of the Denel Group, the Denel 155mm G5 Gun-Howitzer entered service in 1983. It has since been used by South Africa against Southern Angola and South West Africa, as well as by Iraq in its war with Iran. Many were also captured by Coalition forces in Kuwait during Operation Desert Storm in 1991. The semiautomatic G5 is mounted on a four-wheel split-trail carriage fitted with a 79-horsepower APU. With a crew of five and firing a maximum of 3 rounds per minute, it fires a standard high-explosive round up to 32,808 yards. The G5 is also mounted on a six-wheeled G-6 chassis.

Sweden and Switzerland

Despite their neutrality, both Sweden and Switzerland have maintained extensive ordnance development and production. Sweden adopted the 105mm Howitzer Bofors 4140 in 1955. The 4140 was fitted with a semiautomatic mechanism and a cruciform firing base. With a crew of four, it had a maximum firing rate of 25 rounds per minute and an extreme range of 17,060 yards firing a 34-pound shell. Bofors later introduced the Swedish version of the 155mm Field Howitzer 77A in 1973 and followed it with the improved 77B in 1986. Used by Sweden, India, and Nigeria, the 77B is mounted on a split-trail carriage equipped with an APU. The 77B is served by a six-man crew and with an automatic rammer achieves a maximum firing rate of 10 rounds per minute. It can chamber all types of 155mm NATO ammunition and has a range of 26,247 yards

Manufactured by the K&W Thun concern between 1943 and 1953, Switzerland's 105mm Field Howitzer M46 was later modernized in the mid-1990s. It has a horizontal sliding block and is mounted on a split-trail carriage. The M46 fires a 33-pound shell up to 10,936 yards. It is served by a crew of seven and achieves a maximum firing rate of 10 rounds per minute. Switzerland has also produced the 90mm M50 and 90mm M57 antitank guns. Adopted in 1950, the M50 fired a 4-pound shell to a maximum of 3,281 yards; the M57, adopted in 1957, achieved a range of 3,281 yards firing a 6-pound projectile.

SELF-PROPELLED ARTILLERY
United States

Armored self-propelled artillery offers the advantages of being capable of rapidly moving into or out of combat with infantry units to provide both indirect and direct fire as needed. It also provides gun crews with a degree of protection against small arms and shell splinters unavailable to conventional towed artillerymen. The United States adopted a number of new self-propelled artillery designs in the decade following World War II, with many seeing service in the Korean War. Adopted in 1951, the 105mm Howitzer Motor Carriage M52 utilized the 105mm Howitzer M49 mounted in a large turret on the rear of an M41 tank chassis. Crewed by five men, the M52 had a range of 12,325 yards. Despite a number of production delays, 684 M52s were eventually manufactured. Numerous other U.S. self-propelled ordnance pieces were also debuted in 1951. The 155mm Gun Motor Carriage M53 was armed with a turret-mounted 155mm Gun M46 located to the rear of a highly modified M48

Patton tank chassis. Crewed by six men, the M53 had a maximum range of 25,400 yards. The 203mm Howitzer Motor Carriage M55 self-propelled howitzer mounted the 8-inch Howitzer M47 on the same chassis as the M53. The M55 had a maximum range of 18,373 yards. With a crew of six, the 40mm Self-Propelled Gun M42A1 "Duster" incorporated twin 40mm M42A1 antiaircraft guns mounted in an open turret on an M41 tank chassis. The Duster had a range of 5,468 yards.

The United States accepted the 155mm Howitzer Motor Carriage M44 in 1952. With a crew of five, it mounted a 155mm Howitzer M45 on an M41 tank chassis. It had a maximum range of 15,967 yards. Britain also adopted the M44 to replace its aging Sexton self-propelled 25-pounders. The 90mm Gun Motor Carriage M56 "Scorpion" self-propelled antitank gun entered service the following year. It was manned by a crew of four and mounted a 90mm Gun M54 on an unarmored aluminum M88 chassis. It had a range of up to 2,734 yards. The lightweight M56, also known as the SPAT (Self-Propelled Anti-Tank) gun, was intended primarily for rapid airborne delivery to the battlefield.

Adopted in 1961, the 105mm Self-Propelled Howitzer M108 was armed with a 105mm Howitzer M103 mounted in a large turret on a special amphibious chassis. With a crew of five, it was protected by lightweight aluminum armor. The M108 fired a 33-pound shell up to 12,577 yards. The lightweight aluminum-armored 155mm Self-Propelled Howitzer M109 was first accepted in November 1962, with production totaling 2,111. The M109 was armed with either the turret-mounted 155mm Howitzer M126 or M126A1 barrels. It incorporated a special amphibious chassis. Maximum range was 15,967 yards firing a 95-pound projectile. With a crew of four, a number of M109s were used by U.S. forces in Viet Nam.

Intended to be air-mobile, the 8-Inch Self-Propelled Howitzer M110 was adopted in 1962. It was armed with the 8-Inch Howitzer M2A2, which had a maximum range of 18,373 yards. The M110 incorporated a hydraulic loading lift as well as a hydraulic rear spade for stability. Adopted in 1978, the M110A2 was an updated version of the basic M110 fitted with the longer M201 howitzer barrel with an improved muzzle brake; maximum range was 23,294 yards. Manned by a crew of thirteen and used by NATO forces as a long-range divisional weapon, the nimble, self-propelled 175mm SP Gun M107 was adopted in 1963. It mounted a 175mm Gun M113 on the same chassis as the M110 howitzer. The M107 fired a 147-pound shell up to 35,761 yards. Fitted with a power rammer and large, rear-mounted stabilizing spade, the M107 saw service with U.S. forces during the Vietnam War. Entering service in 1978, the 155mm Self-Propelled Howitzer M109A2 was an improved version of the M109 with a longer M185 barrel. The M109A2's barrel is equipped with fume extractor and muzzle brake. It has a maximum range of 19,795 yards and has been issued both to U.S. and British forces. A further improvement of the M109 series, the M109A6 "Paladin," was first accepted in April 1992, and some 957 were produced. The Paladin is armed with the 155mm Howitzer M284.

Great Britain and France

Following six years in development, Britain's Rolls-Royce–powered 105mm L13 "Abbott" entered service in 1964. Used by the British and Indian armies, it had a semiautomatic vertical sliding breech mechanism and was mounted in an enclosed turret. It was fast and maneuverable and had a maximum range of 18,920 yards with a 35.3-pound shell; the maximum firing rate was 12 rounds per minute.

France adopted the 105mm Howitzer Modèle 50 sur affût Automoteur self-propelled howitzer in 1952. Remaining in service into the 1980s, the M 50 was intended as a close-support weapon, had a maximum range of 16,404 yards, and was mounted on an AMX-13 light tank chassis. Also incorporating the AMX-13 chassis, the antiaircraft 30mm, twin-mounted AMX-13 DCA was adopted in 1964. It had a maximum ceiling of 11,483 feet. Development of the 155mm Giat Industries Self-Propelled Gun F3 (Cn-155-F3-Am) began in the early 1950s, and it was adopted by France as well as many South American and Middle Eastern countries. It incorporates an AMX-13 light tank chassis and fires a 96-pound high-explosive shell up to 21,927 yards.

The 155mm SP Gun GCT (Grande Cadence de Tir) entered production in 1977 and was intended to replace the aging 105mm and 155mm guns mounted on the AMX-13 chassis. It was adopted by France in 1979 and was also exported to Saudi Arabia, Iraq, and Kuwait. Utilizing an AMX-30 MBT chassis and turret, it is crewed by four men. The GCT has two prominent rear spades for stability and fires a 95-pound shell up to 25,514 yards. Equipped with a vertical sliding breech mechanism and automatic loader, the GCT is capable of firing an average of 8 rounds per minute and bursts of 6 rounds in 45 seconds.

Giat Industries first introduced the CAESAR (CAmion Equipe d'un Systèm d'ARtillerie) Self-Propelled Gun in 1994. Designed to be easily transported by air for rapid deployment units, the high-speed CAESAR utilizes a modified Mercedes-Benz 6x6 U2450 L chassis equipped with a rear stabilizing spade. It is served by a crew of six and fires the full range of 155mm ammunition; it is capable of 15-second 3-round bursts and a sustained rate of fire of 6 rounds per minute. Firing ERFB-BB ammunition, it has a maximum range of 46,000 yards. A cooperative venture between France and Sweden, the Giat Industries/Hägglunds Vehicle CV 90105 TML Tank Destroyer employs a turret-mounted vertical sliding breech 105mm GT gun on a Häglunds CV 90 chassis. It was introduced to the export market in 1994. It is crewed by four men.

Germany

Production of West Germany's low-profile 90mm Thyssen Hhenschel Jagdpanzer Kanon (JPZ 4-5) tank destroyer began in 1965. With a crew of four, it used the same ammunition as the M47 and M48 tanks. The JPX 4-5 had a maximum firing rate of 12 rounds per minute and fired a standard HEAT projectile up to 2,187 yards. Also used by Belgium, the JPZ 4-5 is no longer in service with the German army. Mounted on a Leopard tank chassis, the antiaircraft Gepard was adopted in 1973. It mounted twin-caliber 35mm guns and achieved a maximum ceiling of 11,483 feet.

Following the cancellation of the SP70 program in 1986, Wegmann and Co. collaborated with the MaK System and Rheinmetall firms to develop a replacement suitable for both German service and export. The resulting 155mm Wegmann/MaK Panzerhaubitze 2000 (PzH2000) Self-Propelled Howitzer incorporates numerous computer systems and a turret-mounted Rheinmetall howitzer mounted on a tracked MaK chassis. With a crew of five, its ammunition is made up of separate projectiles and their bagged propellant charges. It is capable of three-round bursts in 10 seconds and a sustained rate of 8 rounds in less than one minute. The PzH2000 fires a conventional 155mm projectile up to 32,808 yards and extended-range projectiles to a maximum of nearly 43,745 yards. During the mid-1990s, Rheinmetall Defense Engineering initiated a program to modernize the U.S.-designed M109G self-propelled howitzers then in German service. The resulting 155mm Rheinmetall M109A36 retains the basic M109 chassis and employs numerous electronic and mechanical updates, including the mounting of the basic ordnance developed for the PzH2000. It fires conventional HE up to 27,012 yards and extended-range ammunition to a maximum of 32,808 yards.

Italy and Japan

Italy and Japan have also produced self-propelled ordnance. Manufactured by the OTO-Melara company and adopted in 1984, the antiaircraft 76mm OTO-Melara 76 was mounted on a Palmaria chassis and achieved a maximum ceiling of 19,686 feet. Japan accepted the Type 60 Self-Propelled Recoilless Gun in 1960. The Type 60 mounted twin 106mm Nihon Seikojyo recoilless guns on a Komatsu chassis. The Model B replaced the original version in 1967 and was in turn superseded by the Type C in 1975. Production ended in 1979. With a crew of three, the Type 60 had an effective maximum range of 1,203 yards firing HEAT ammunition.

Soviet Union

The Soviet Union adopted the self-propelled antiaircraft ZSU-57-2 in 1954. With a maximum 13,123-foot ceiling, the ZSU-57-2 mounted twin 57mm guns, whereas the antitank ASU57 was adopted in 1957 and mounted a caliber 57mm gun with a maximum range of 1,094 yards. Another antitank weapon adopted in 1961, the caliber 85mm ASU85 was mounted on a PT76 tank chassis. It had a maximum range of 3,281 yards. Also known as the Akatsiya ("Acacia"), the 152mm Self-Propelled Gun-Howitzer M-1973 (SO-152) entered Soviet service in 1971 and was also used by Hungary, Iraq, Libya, and Syria. It mounts a 2A33 gun-howitzer in a large 360-traversing turret on an Izdelie 303 tracked chassis. The SO-152 is served by a crew of four and can fire many ammunition types, including incendiary, nuclear, and laser-guided projectiles at up to 4 rounds per minute. The SO-152 fires a conventional 96-pound OF-540 high-explosive round to a maximum of 20,232 yards. It has since been replaced by the 152mm self-propelled 2S19 system.

The 122mm Self-Propelled Howitzer M1974 (SO-122) Gvozdika ("Carnation") was designed by the Khar'kov Tractor Works, and more than 10,000 were manufactured between 1971 and 1991. A low-profile, amphibious weapon and with a crew of six, it has seen service with the Warsaw Pact and numerous other nations including Finland, Iraq, and Syria. It mounts the 122mm 2A31 howitzer, a modification of the D-30 towed howitzer, in a fully traversing turret. The SO-122 chambers a wide variety of ammunition, including smoke, HEAT, chemical, and the 55-pound Kitolov-2 laser-guided projectile, which achieves a maximum range of 13,123 yards. It also fires the standard 48-pound OF-462 HE projectile up to 16,732 yards. Also known as the Tyul'pan, or "Tulip Tree," the 240mm Self-Propelled Mortar M-1975 (SM-240) was developed by the Uraltransmash facility and the Perm Machine Construction Works. It entered Soviet service in 1975 and has also been used by the Czech Republic, Iraq, Lebanon, and Slovakia. With a crew of five, it incorporates a 240mm 2B8 smoothbore mortar fed by twin 20-round drum magazines. The M-1975 chambers conventional, chemical, concrete-piercing, and nuclear projectiles. It fires a standard 286.5-pound HE fragmentation bomb up to 10,553 yards and a rocket-assisted 502.5-pound shell to a maximum of 19,685 yards. During the 1980s the M-1975 saw service in Afghanistan, where it proved successful firing the Smel'chak ("Dare Devil") laser-guided projectile.

Developed at the Kirov Plant in Leningrad, the 203mm Self-Propelled Gun M-1975 (SO-203) entered Soviet service in 1975 and has also been used by Czechoslovakia and Poland. It incorporates twin hydraulic rear spades and a 203mm 2A44 gun. Also known as the Pion ("Peony"), it can fire up to 2 rounds per minute and incorporates a power-assisted mechanism to load its separate powder charges and projectile. It fires a standard 242.5-pound HE shell up to 41,010 yards and a 225-pound rocket-assisted projectile to a maximum of 51,400 yards. The M-1975 has a crew of seven and carries four rounds of ammunition, with additional rounds and charges provided by an accompanying truck.

The 152mm Self-Propelled Gun (2S5) Giatsint ("Hyacinth") was designed and manufactured by the Uraltransmash Works and entered Soviet service in 1976. It saw service with Soviet forces in Afghanistan and was also adopted by Finland and Iraq. The 2S5 is equipped with a front mounted dozer blade to prepare firing positions and a rear stabilizing spade. It is served by between five and seven crewmen and, aided by a partially automated loading system, achieves a firing rate of up to 6 rounds per minute. The 2S5 utilizes a separate powder charge and projectile and accepts conventional, chemical, concrete-piercing, laser-guided, and tactical nuclear warheads. It fires a conventional 101-pound HE round up to 31,059 yards and a rocket-assisted projectile to a maximum of 43,745 yards. Adopted for service in 1981, the amphibious 120mm SO-120 Self-Propelled Howitzer/Mortar (2S9) Anona ("Anemone") was developed for air assault units and was used in Afghanistan. With a crew of four, it employs a turret-mounted 120mm 2A51 breechloaded mortar on an aluminum-hulled BTR-D APC chassis. It fires armor-piercing projectiles as well as conventional high-explosive mortar bombs up to 9,684 yards.

The Uraltransmash Works developed and built the 152mm Self-Propelled Artillery System 2S19 to replace the 152mm 2S3 weapon system. It entered service in 1989, and its long 2A64 152mm gun is mounted in a large 360-degree traversing turret on a T-80 chassis fitted with a front dozer blade. Equipped with an automated loading system, it achieves a rate of fire of up to 8 rounds per minute. It chambers a wide variety of ammunition, including tactical nuclear and the fin-guided Krasnopol laser-directed projectile. The 2S19 fires the conventional OF-45 high-explosive fragmentation shell up to 27,000 yards and the OF-61 base bleed projectile up to 31,605 yards. Entering Soviet service in 1990 and also exported, the 120mm 2S23 Self-Propelled Gun-Mortar System incorporates a turret-mounted 120mm 2A60 rifled gun-howitzer on an eight-wheeled BTR-80 chassis. With a crew of four, it has an automatic loading mechanism that allows a maximum rate of fire of up to 10 rounds per minute and fires HE, HEAT, and HE-RAP (rocket-assisted) ammunition. The 2S23 fires a 41.5-pound HE and HE-RAP shell to a maximum of 9,678 and 14,217 yards, respectively, and a 29-pound HEAT projectile to an effective maximum range of 875 yards.

The 152mm ZTS Self-Propelled Gun-Howitzer DANA (vz.77) entered Czech service in 1981 and has also been used by Libya, Poland, and Slovakia. Manufactured by Zavody Tazkeho Strojarsva (ZTS), it incorporates a turret-mounted barrel on an eight-wheeled Tatra 815 truck chassis. It is served by a crew of five and with a semiautomatic horizontal sliding block can fire up to 5 rounds per minute. The vz.77 chambers a variety of ammunition and fires the standard 96-pound EOF D-20 HE shell up to a maximum of 20,450 yards. Also manufactured by ZTS, the 120mm ZTS PRAM-S Self-Propelled Mortar System entered service in 1992 and is based on the amphibious BMP-Z tracked chassis. Manned by a crew of four, its breechloaded barrel has a maximum range of 8,788 yards and can fire up to 20 rounds per minute.

China

The Peoples' Republic of China's main ordnance producer, NORINCO, originally relied heavily on existing foreign models for its self-propelled ordnance and has since moved toward more original designs. The NORINCO 122mm Self-Propelled Howitzer Type 54-1 incorporated a type 54-1 122mm howitzer on a Type 531 APC chassis and was served by a crew of seven. Essentially a copy of the Soviet M-30, it fired a 48-pound HE shell to a maximum of 12,905 yards. With a crew of six, the NORINCO 122mm Self-Propelled Howitzer Type 85 mounts a 122mm D-30 howitzer in a partially enclosed firing compartment on an amphibious Type 85 armored personnel carrier chassis. It fires a 48-pound high-explosive shell up to 16,732 yards and an ERFB projectile up to 22,966 yards.

In service by 1984, the NORINCO Type 83 152mm Self-Propelled Gun-Howitzer and 130mm Self-Propelled Gun are based on the towed 152mm Type 66 gun-howitzer fitted with a fume extractor and mounted in a 360-degree revolving turret on a tracked chassis. It is manned by a crew of five and attains a maximum range of 18,843 yards. The 130mm self-propelled gun is essentially the Type 83 fitted with the 130mm Type 59 gun. First introduced in 1988, the NORINCO 155mm 45 Caliber Self-Propelled Gun exhibits many similarities to the U.S. M109 system. It mounts a semi-automatic horizontal sliding block barrel in a large turret and has twin retractable spades mounted on the rear of the chassis. It is served by a five-man crew and can fire up to five extended-range ERFB-BB projectiles to a maximum of 42,651 yards.

Israel

Upon its formation in 1948, the modern state of Israel initially relied on various surplus self-propelled weapons from foreign sources. As the country's industrial base solidified, Israel began producing progressively more original weapons for both its own use and the export market. Mounted on a U.S. Sherman tank chassis, the caliber 155mm M50 was adopted in 1958 and had a maximum range of 19,248 yards. In 1967 the Israeli armaments firm of Soltam Systems introduced the Soltam L33, incorporating a 155mm howitzer mounted on a U.S. Sherman tank chassis. Soltam then followed the L33 with the Soltam M72 in 1985. The M72 mounted a 155mm howitzer on a British Centurion tank chassis. It had a maximum range of 25,700 yards. Soltam has recently introduced the light-weight and nimble "Rascal," another 155mm howitzer mounted on a tracked chassis. The company has also adapted the Rascal's ordnance to a truck mounting known as the SPWH 2052.

RECOILLESS ARTILLERY

The United States continued to develop recoilless artillery during the Cold War. The 90mm RCL Rifle M67 recoilless rifle was adopted in 1955 and fired a 6.8-pound projectile up to 820 yards. It was followed in 1958 by the 120mm RCL M28 "Davy Crockett" recoilless rifle with a 2,187-yard range, and the still larger 155mm RCL M29 Davy Crockett adopted the same year. The M29 had a maximum range of 4,375 yards. The 106mm RCL Rifle M40A1 recoilless rifle entered service in 1965 and achieved a 7,518-yard range with a 17-pound projectile. The M40A1 was mounted on a simple trail with a single forward wheel and twin adjustable trails and was fitted with a caliber .50 spotting rifle on the right side of the barrel to aid in range finding. Numbers of the M40A1 were also mounted on light vehicles to add to their mobility.

In Britain the 120mm Battalion Anti-Tank gun (BAT) was developed at the end of the 1940s and adopted in 1952 as the 120 BAT L1. Developed at the Royal Armament and Research Establishment at Fort Halstead, it discarded Burney's original perforated cartridge case in favor of a German design incorporating a plastic seal that blew out upon firing. With a vertical sliding breech mechanism, the L1 fired a plastic, explosive-filled, 28-pound antitank "Squash-head" shell up to 1,094 yards. The "Wombat" and "Mobat" were later improved and lighter models of the BAT.

REFERENCE SECTION

CHAPTER SIX SPECIFICATIONS:

LATE-NINETEENTH- AND

EARLY-TWENTIETH-CENTURY ARTILLERY

Field Artillery
UNITED STATES

3-inch M1902

ADOPTION DATE: 1902
CALIBER: 3-inch
WEIGHT: 2,144 pounds
BREECH: quick-firing
BARREL LENGTH: 87 inches

ELEVATION: 15°
TRAVERSAL: 8°
PROJECTILE WEIGHT: 15 pounds
MUZZLE VELOCITY: 1,699 fps
MAXIMUM RANGE: 7,477 yards

3-inch M1916

ADOPTION DATE: 1918
CALIBER: 3-inch
WEIGHT: 3,050 pounds
BREECH: quick-firing
BARREL LENGTH: 84 inches

ELEVATION: 53°
TRAVERSAL: 45°
PROJECTILE WEIGHT: 13.7 pounds
MUZZLE VELOCITY: 1,968 fps
MAXIMUM RANGE: 9,592 yards

75mm M1916

ADOPTION DATE: 1917
CALIBER: 75mm
WEIGHT: 3,218 pounds
BREECH: quick-firing
BARREL LENGTH: 252 inches

ELEVATION: 53°
TRAVERSAL: 45°
PROJECTILE WEIGHT: 13.5 pounds
MUZZLE VELOCITY: 1,899 fps
MAXIMUM RANGE: 12,448 yards

75mm M1917

ADOPTION DATE: 1918
CALIBER: 75mm
WEIGHT: 2,873 pounds
BREECH: quick-firing
BARREL LENGTH: 270 inches

ELEVATION: 16°
TRAVERSAL: 8°
PROJECTILE WEIGHT: 15 pounds
MUZZLE VELOCITY: 1,738 fps
MAXIMUM RANGE: 8,720 yards

4.7-inch Howitzer M1908

ADOPTION DATE: 1908
CALIBER: 4.7-inch
WEIGHT: 4,807 pounds
BREECH: —
BARREL LENGTH: —

ELEVATION: 40°
TRAVERSAL: —
PROJECTILE WEIGHT: 60 pounds
MUZZLE VELOCITY: 902 fps
MAXIMUM RANGE: 6,875 yards

AUSTRO-HUNGARIAN

75mm FK M05

ADOPTION DATE: 1905
CALIBER: 75mm
WEIGHT: 2,094 pounds
BREECH: —
BARREL LENGTH: 87 inches

ELEVATION: 18°
TRAVERSAL: 6°
PROJECTILE WEIGHT: 14.7 pounds
MUZZLE VELOCITY: 1,640 fps
MAXIMUM RANGE: 6,015 yards

76.5mm FK M05

ADOPTION DATE: 1905
CALIBER: 76.5mm
WEIGHT: 2,249 pounds
BREECH: —
BARREL LENGTH: 90 inches

ELEVATION: 18°
TRAVERSAL: 8°
PROJECTILE WEIGHT: 14.7 pounds
MUZZLE VELOCITY: —
MAXIMUM RANGE: 7,983 yards

75mm FK M12

ADOPTION DATE: 1912
CALIBER: 75mm
WEIGHT: 2,072 pounds
BREECH: —
BARREL LENGTH: 76 inches

ELEVATION: 16°
TRAVERSAL: 7°
PROJECTILE WEIGHT: 14 pounds
MUZZLE VELOCITY: —
MAXIMUM RANGE: 6,562 yards

Note: — indicates the information is unavailable.

76.5mm FK M17

ADOPTION DATE: 1917
CALIBER: 76.5mm
WEIGHT: 3,056 pounds
BREECH: —
BARREL LENGTH: 90 inches

ELEVATION: 45°
TRAVERSAL: 8°
PROJECTILE WEIGHT: 14.7 pounds
MUZZLE VELOCITY: 1,640 fps
MAXIMUM RANGE: 10,827 yards

76.5mm FK M18

ADOPTION DATE: 1918
CALIBER: 76.5mm
WEIGHT: 2,932 pounds
BREECH: —
BARREL LENGTH: 90 inches

ELEVATION: 45°
TRAVERSAL: 8°
PROJECTILE WEIGHT: 17.7 pounds
MUZZLE VELOCITY: 1,640 fps
MAXIMUM RANGE: 11,483 yards

104mm Field Howitzer M99

ADOPTION DATE: 1899
CALIBER: 104mm
WEIGHT: 2,187 pounds
BREECH: —
BARREL LENGTH: 52 inches

ELEVATION: 42.5°
TRAVERSAL: 6°
MUZZLE VELOCITY: 951 fps
PROJECTILE WEIGHT: 31.5 pounds
MAXIMUM RANGE: 6,097 yards

100mm Field Howitzer M14

ADOPTION DATE: 1914
CALIBER: 100mm
WEIGHT: 3,131 pounds
BREECH: —
BARREL LENGTH: 76 inches

ELEVATION: 48°
TRAVERSAL: 5°
PROJECTILE WEIGHT: 25 pounds
MUZZLE VELOCITY: 1,378 fps
MAXIMUM RANGE: 8,749 yards

104mm Field Howitzer M17

ADOPTION DATE: 1914
CALIBER: 104mm
WEIGHT: 2,756 pounds
BREECH: —
BARREL LENGTH: 72 inches

ELEVATION: 45°
TRAVERSAL: 7°
PROJECTILE WEIGHT: 32 pounds
MUZZLE VELOCITY: 1,050 fps
MAXIMUM RANGE: 8,530 yards

105mm Field Howitzer M15/T

ADOPTION DATE: 1915
CALIBER: 105mm
WEIGHT: 3,080 pounds
BREECH: —
BARREL LENGTH: 73.8 inches

ELEVATION: 70°
TRAVERSAL: 6°
PROJECTILE WEIGHT: 35 pounds
MUZZLE VELOCITY: —
MAXIMUM RANGE: 8,475.5 yards

BELGIUM

75mm M05 Gun

ADOPTION DATE: 1915
CALIBER: 75mm
WEIGHT: 2,271 pounds
BREECH: —
BARREL LENGTH: 87 inches

ELEVATION: 15°
TRAVERSAL: 7°
PROJECTILE WEIGHT: 14.3 pounds
MUZZLE VELOCITY: 1,640 fps
MAXIMUM RANGE: 8,749 yards

75mm Gun Model TR

ADOPTION DATE: 1912
CALIBER: 75mm
WEIGHT: 2,315 pounds
BREECH: —
BARREL LENGTH: 87 inches

ELEVATION: 16°
TRAVERSAL: 7°
PROJECTILE WEIGHT: 14.3 pounds
MUZZLE VELOCITY: 1,640 fps
MAXIMUM RANGE: 8,749 yards

105mm M13 Gun

ADOPTION DATE: 1913
CALIBER: 105mm
WEIGHT: —
BREECH: —
BARREL LENGTH: 114.8 inches

ELEVATION: 37°
TRAVERSAL: 6°
PROJECTILE WEIGHT: 36 pounds
MUZZLE VELOCITY: —
MAXIMUM RANGE: 1,361.5 yards

75mm M18 Gun

ADOPTION DATE: 1918
CALIBER: 75mm
WEIGHT: 3,197 pounds
BREECH: —
BARREL LENGTH: 101.5 inches

ELEVATION: 43°
TRAVERSAL: 20°
PROJECTILE WEIGHT: 16 pounds
MUZZLE VELOCITY: 1,969 fps
MAXIMUM RANGE: 12,030 yards

120mm Field Howitzer

ADOPTION DATE: 1914
CALIBER: 120mm
WEIGHT: 2,866 pounds
BREECH: —
BARREL LENGTH: —

ELEVATION: 40°
TRAVERSAL: —
PROJECTILE WEIGHT: 44 pounds
MUZZLE VELOCITY: 984 fps
MAXIMUM RANGE: —

GREAT BRITAIN

4.7-inch Gun Mk1

ADOPTION DATE: 1895
CALIBER: 4.7-inch
WEIGHT: 8,417 pounds
BREECH: quick-firing
BARREL LENGTH: 188 inches

ELEVATION: 20°
TRAVERSAL: —
PROJECTILE WEIGHT: 46 pounds
MUZZLE VELOCITY: 2,149 fps
MAXIMUM RANGE: 10,007 yards

4.5-inch Howitzer

ADOPTION DATE: 1909
CALIBER: 4.5-inch
WEIGHT: 3,016 pounds
BREECH: sliding block
BARREL LENGTH: —

ELEVATION: 45°
TRAVERSAL: 3°
PROJECTILE WEIGHT: 35 pounds
MUZZLE VELOCITY: —
MAXIMUM RANGE: 8,202 yards

12-pdr 6 cwt Mk4

ADOPTION DATE: 1900
CALIBER: 4.7-inch
WEIGHT: 2,006 pounds
BREECH: quick-firing
BARREL LENGTH: 264 inches

ELEVATION: 16°
TRAVERSAL: —
PROJECTILE WEIGHT: 12.5 pounds
MUZZLE VELOCITY: 1,585 fps
MAXIMUM RANGE: 5,998 yards

15-pdr Mk1

ADOPTION DATE: 1901
CALIBER: 3-inch
WEIGHT: 2,271 pounds
BREECH: quick-firing
BARREL LENGTH: 450 inches

ELEVATION: 16°
TRAVERSAL: 6°
PROJECTILE WEIGHT: 14 pounds
MUZZLE VELOCITY: 2,493 fps
MAXIMUM RANGE: 6,398 yards

18-pdr Mk1

ADOPTION DATE: 1904
CALIBER: 3.3-inch
WEIGHT: 2,820 pounds
BREECH: quick-firing
BARREL LENGTH: 504 inches

ELEVATION: 16°
TRAVERSAL: 8°
PROJECTILE WEIGHT: 18.5 pounds
MUZZLE VELOCITY: 1,614 fps
MAXIMUM RANGE: 6,523 yards

GREAT BRITAIN: 4.5-INCH HOWITZER MK1
(Courtesy Art-Tech)

4.5-inch Howitzer Mk1

ADOPTION DATE: 1904
CALIBER: 4.5-inch (114mm)
WEIGHT: 3,009 pounds
BREECH: —
BARREL LENGTH: 58.5 inches

ELEVATION: 45°
TRAVERSAL: 6°
PROJECTILE WEIGHT: 35 pounds
MUZZLE VELOCITY: —
MAXIMUM RANGE: 7,300 yards

FRANCE

FRANCE: CANON DE 75 MODÈL 1897
(Courtesy Art-Tech)

Canon de 75 Modèl 1897

ADOPTION DATE: 1897
CALIBER: 75mm
WEIGHT: 2,560 pounds
BREECH: quick-firing
BARREL LENGTH: 106 inches
ELEVATION: 18°

TRAVERSAL: 6°
PROJECTILE WEIGHT: 15.9 pounds
  shrapnel
MUZZLE VELOCITY: 1,735 fps
MAXIMUM RANGE: 9,300 yards

37mm M1916TR Trench Cannon

ADOPTION DATE: 1916
CALIBER: 37mm
WEIGHT: 258 pounds
BREECH: Nordenfelt screw
BARREL LENGTH: 31.9 inches

ELEVATION: 21°
TRAVERSAL: 40°
PROJECTILE WEIGHT: 1 pound
MUZZLE VELOCITY: 1,319 fps
MAXIMUM RANGE: 2,625 yards

GERMANY

77mm Feldkanone M 96 (7.7cm Field Gun Model 96)

ADOPTION DATE: 1896
CALIBER: 77mm
WEIGHT: 3,400 pounds (with limber)
BREECH: quick-firing
BARREL LENGTH: —

ELEVATION: 15°
TRAVERSAL: 4°
PROJECTILE WEIGHT: 15.04 pounds
MUZZLE VELOCITY: 1,525 fps
MAXIMUM RANGE: 8,750 yards

GERMANY: 77MM FK96/15
(Courtesy Art-Tech)

77mm FK96/15

ADOPTION DATE: 1915
CALIBER: 77mm
WEIGHT: 2,249 pounds
BREECH: horizontal sliding block
BARREL LENGTH: —

ELEVATION: 15°
TRAVERSAL: 4°
PROJECTILE WEIGHT: 13.6 pounds
MUZZLE VELOCITY: 1,565 fps
MAXIMUM RANGE: 9,186 yards

77mm FK16

ADOPTION DATE: 1916
CALIBER: 77mm,
WEIGHT: 2,921 pounds
BREECH: horizontal sliding block
BARREL LENGTH: 105 inches

ELEVATION: 40°
TRAVERSAL: 4°
PROJECTILE WEIGHT: 13.5 pounds
MUZZLE VELOCITY: 1,969 fps
MAXIMUM RANGE: 11,264 yards

105mm K17

ADOPTION DATE: 1917
CALIBER: 105mm
WEIGHT: 7,275 pounds
BREECH: horizontal sliding block
BARREL LENGTH: —

ELEVATION: 45°
TRAVERSAL: 6°
PROJECTILE WEIGHT: 41 pounds
MUZZLE VELOCITY: 2,133 fps
MAXIMUM RANGE: 18,046 yards

105mm FH 98/09

ADOPTION DATE: 1909
CALIBER: 105mm
WEIGHT: 2,701 pounds
BREECH: horizontal sliding block
BARREL LENGTH: 65.6 inches

ELEVATION: 40°
TRAVERSAL: 4°
PROJECTILE WEIGHT: 35 pounds
MUZZLE VELOCITY: 991 fps
MAXIMUM RANGE: 6,890 yards

105mm 1eFH 16

ADOPTION DATE: 1916
CALIBER: 105mm
WEIGHT: 3,197 pounds
BREECH: horizontal sliding block
BARREL LENGTH: 69.7 inches

ELEVATION: 40°
TRAVERSAL: 4°
PROJECTILE WEIGHT: 33 pounds
MUZZLE VELOCITY: 1,296 fps
MAXIMUM RANGE: 10,089 yards

105mm FH 17

ADOPTION DATE: 1917
CALIBER: 105mm
WEIGHT: 3,307 pounds
BREECH: horizontal sliding block
BARREL LENGTH: 82 inches

ELEVATION: 43°
TRAVERSAL: 4°
PROJECTILE WEIGHT: 35 pounds
MUZZLE VELOCITY: 1,411 fps
MAXIMUM RANGE: 9,788 yards

170mm Minenwerfer

ADOPTION DATE: —
CALIBER: 170mm
WEIGHT: 1,157 pounds
SHELL WEIGHT: 125.5 pounds
BREECH: —
BARREL LENGTH: 25 inches

ELEVATION: —
TRAVERSAL: —
PROJECTILE WEIGHT: —
MUZZLE VELOCITY: —
MAXIMUM RANGE: 820 yards

250mm Minenwerfer

ADOPTION DATE: 1910
CALIBER: 250mm
WEIGHT: 1,455 pounds
BREECH: —
BARREL LENGTH: —

ELEVATION: —
TRAVERSAL: —
PROJECTILE WEIGHT: 214 pounds
MUZZLE VELOCITY: 656 fps
MAXIMUM RANGE: —

ITALY

75mm Mo.06

ADOPTION DATE: 1907
CALIBER: 75mm
WEIGHT: 2,216 pounds
BREECH: horizontal sliding block
BARREL LENGTH: —

ELEVATION: 17°
TRAVERSAL: 7°
PROJECTILE WEIGHT: 14 pounds
MUZZLE VELOCITY: 1,673 fps
MAXIMUM RANGE: 7,437 yards

75mm Gun Mo.12 Deport

ADOPTION DATE: 1912
CALIBER: 75mm
WEIGHT: 2,372 pounds
BREECH: Nordenfelt screw
BARREL LENGTH: 78.3 inches

ELEVATION: 65°
TRAVERSAL: 52°
PROJECTILE WEIGHT: 14 pounds
MUZZLE VELOCITY: 1,673 fps
MAXIMUM RANGE: 8,311 yards

75mm Gun Mo.06/12

ADOPTION DATE: 1913
CALIBER: 75mm
WEIGHT: 2,112 pounds
BREECH: horizontal sliding block
BARREL LENGTH: 87 inches

ELEVATION: 19°
TRAVERSAL: 7°
PROJECTILE WEIGHT: 14 pounds
MUZZLE VELOCITY: 1,673 fps
MAXIMUM RANGE: 8,311 yards

Obice da 100/17 Mo.1

ADOPTION DATE: 1914
CALIBER: 100mm
WEIGHT: 3,197 pounds
BREECH: —
BARREL LENGTH: 70.8 inches

ELEVATION: 48°
TRAVERSAL: 5°
PROJECTILE WEIGHT: 27.5 pounds
MUZZLE VELOCITY: 1,345 fps
MAXIMUM RANGE: 10,127 yards

JAPAN

75mm Meiji 38 Field Gun
ADOPTION DATE: 1905
CALIBER: 75mm
WEIGHT: 2,083 pounds
BREECH: quick-firing
BARREL LENGTH: 87 inches

ELEVATION: 16°
TRAVERSAL: 7°
PROJECTILE WEIGHT: 13 pounds
MUZZLE VELOCITY: 1,673 fps
MAXIMUM RANGE: 9,020 yards

105mm Meiji 38 Gun
ADOPTION DATE: 1905
CALIBER: 105mm
WEIGHT: 7,959 pounds
BREECH: quick-firing
BARREL LENGTH: 131.2 inches

ELEVATION: 35°
TRAVERSAL: 6°
PROJECTILE WEIGHT: 39.6 pounds
MUZZLE VELOCITY: 1,772 fps
MAXIMUM RANGE: 10,991 yards

75mm Meiji 41 Field Gun
ADOPTION DATE: 1908
CALIBER: 75mm
WEIGHT: 2,161 pounds
BREECH: quick-firing
BARREL LENGTH: 87 inches

ELEVATION: 16°
TRAVERSAL: 12°
PROJECTILE WEIGHT: 12.5 pounds
MUZZLE VELOCITY: 1,673 fps
MAXIMUM RANGE: 11,920 yards

75mm Meiji 38 Improved Field Gun
ADOPTION DATE: 1917
CALIBER: 75mm
WEIGHT: 2,502 pounds
BREECH: horizontal sliding block
BARREL LENGTH: 87 inches

ELEVATION: 43°
TRAVERSAL: 7°
PROJECTILE WEIGHT: 14.5 pounds
MUZZLE VELOCITY: 1,969 fps
MAXIMUM RANGE: 13,080 yards

RUSSIA

RUSSIA: 76MM CANNON MODEL 1900 (76 K/00)
(Courtesy Art-Tech)

76.2mm Model 1900 (76 K/00) Cannon

ADOPTION DATE: —
CALIBER: 76.2mm
WEIGHT: 2,293 pounds
BREECH: quick-firing
BARREL LENGTH: —

ELEVATION: 17°
TRAVERSAL: 2.5°
PROJECTILE WEIGHT: 14.5 pounds
MUZZLE VELOCITY: 1,936 fps
MAXIMUM RANGE: —

76.2mm Model 1902 (76 K/02) Cannon

ADOPTION DATE: 1902
CALIBER: 76.2mm
WEIGHT: 2,425 pounds
BREECH: quick-firing
BARREL LENGTH: —

ELEVATION: 17°
TRAVERSAL: 3°
PROJECTILE WEIGHT: 14.5 pounds
MUZZLE VELOCITY: 1,985 fps
MAXIMUM RANGE: —

85mm M02 Gun

ADOPTION DATE: —
CALIBER: 85mm
WEIGHT: 4,255 pounds
BREECH: —
BARREL LENGTH: —

ELEVATION: 16°
TRAVERSAL: 5°
PROJECTILE WEIGHT: 14 pounds
MUZZLE VELOCITY: 1,821 fps
MAXIMUM RANGE: 6,999 yards

3-inch M13

ADOPTION DATE: 1913
CALIBER: 76.2mm
WEIGHT: 22,112 pounds
BREECH: quick-firing
BARREL LENGTH: 93 inches

ELEVATION: 16°
TRAVERSAL: 6°
PROJECTILE WEIGHT: 14.5 pounds
MUZZLE VELOCITY: 1,673 fps
MAXIMUM RANGE: —

122mm M04 Howitzer

ADOPTION DATE: 1904
CALIBER: 122mm
WEIGHT: 2,701 pounds
BREECH: quick-firing
BARREL LENGTH: 57.6 inches

ELEVATION: 42°
TRAVERSAL: 5°
PROJECTILE WEIGHT: 46 pounds
MUZZLE VELOCITY: 958 fps
MAXIMUM RANGE: 7,327 yards

SWEDEN

75mm M1902 Gun

ADOPTION DATE: 1902
CALIBER: 75mm
WEIGHT: 2,145.5 pounds
BREECH: horizontal sliding block
BARREL LENGTH: 90 inches

ELEVATION: 16°
TRAVERSAL: 7°
PROJECTILE WEIGHT: 14 pounds
MUZZLE VELOCITY: 1,640 fps
MAXIMUM RANGE: 7,655

105mm M1910 Howitzer

ADOPTION DATE: 1912
CALIBER: 105mm
WEIGHT: 2,701 pounds
BREECH: horizontal sliding block
BARREL LENGTH: 65.6 inches

ELEVATION: 43°
TRAVERSAL: 4°
PROJECTILE WEIGHT: 31 pounds
MUZZLE VELOCITY: 1,000 fps
MAXIMUM RANGE: 6,780 yards

Mountain Artillery
UNITED STATES

2.95-inch M1903 Gun

ADOPTION DATE: 1903
CALIBER: 2.95-inch
WEIGHT: 829 pounds
BREECH: quick-firing
BARREL LENGTH: 53.4 inches

ELEVATION: 27°
TRAVERSAL: —
PROJECTILE WEIGHT: 12 pounds
MUZZLE VELOCITY: 918 fps
MAXIMUM RANGE: 4,883 yards

3-inch M1911 Howitzer

ADOPTION DATE: 1912
CALIBER: 3-inch
WEIGHT: 1,105 pounds
BREECH: —
BARREL LENGTH: —

ELEVATION: 40°
TRAVERSAL: —
PROJECTILE WEIGHT: 15 pounds
MUZZLE VELOCITY: 902 fps
MAXIMUM RANGE: 5,668 yards

AUSTRIA

72.5mm Mountain Howitzer M08

ADOPTION DATE: 1908
CALIBER: 72.5mm
WEIGHT: 886 pounds
BREECH: —
BARREL LENGTH: 60 inches

ELEVATION: 34°
TRAVERSAL: 8°
PROJECTILE WEIGHT: 10.5 pounds
MUZZLE VELOCITY: 1,017 fps
MAXIMUM RANGE: 5,687 yards

104mm Mountain Howitzer M08

ADOPTION DATE: 1908
CALIBER: 104mm
WEIGHT: 2,718 pounds
BREECH: —
BARREL LENGTH: 60 inches

ELEVATION: 42°
TRAVERSAL: 5°
PROJECTILE WEIGHT: 31 pounds
MUZZLE VELOCITY: 984 fps
MAXIMUM RANGE: 6,562 yards

72.5mm Mountain Howitzer M09

ADOPTION DATE: 1909
CALIBER: 72.5mm
WEIGHT: 1,005 pounds
BREECH: —
BARREL LENGTH: 38.64 inches

ELEVATION: 35°
TRAVERSAL: 8°
PROJECTILE WEIGHT: 10.5 pounds
MUZZLE VELOCITY: 1,017 fps
MAXIMUM RANGE: 5,796 yards

104mm Mountain Howitzer M10

ADOPTION DATE: 1910
CALIBER: 104mm
WEIGHT: 2,668 pounds
BREECH: —
BARREL LENGTH: 60 inches

ELEVATION: 70°
TRAVERSAL: 6°
PROJECTILE WEIGHT: 32 pounds
MUZZLE VELOCITY: 984 fps
MAXIMUM RANGE: 6,562 yards

AUSTRIA: 75MM MOUNTAIN HOWITZER M13
(Courtesy Art-Tech)

75mm Mountain Howitzer M13

ADOPTION DATE: 1914
CALIBER: 75mm
WEIGHT: 1,083 pounds
BREECH: —
BARREL LENGTH: —

ELEVATION: 36°
TRAVERSAL: 5°
PROJECTILE WEIGHT: 11.5 pounds
MUZZLE VELOCITY: 984 fps
MAXIMUM RANGE: 6,124 yards

75mm Mountain Howitzer M15

ADOPTION DATE: 1915

CALIBER: 75mm

WEIGHT: —

BREECH: —

BARREL LENGTH: —

ELEVATION: —

TRAVERSAL: —

PROJECTILE WEIGHT: 14 pounds

MUZZLE VELOCITY: —

MAXIMUM RANGE: 8,530 yards

100mm Mountain Howitzer M16

ADOPTION DATE: 1916

CALIBER: 100mm

WEIGHT: 2,723 pounds

BREECH: —

BARREL LENGTH: 74.1 inches

ELEVATION: 70°

TRAVERSAL: 5°

PROJECTILE WEIGHT: 35 pounds

MUZZLE VELOCITY: 1,115 fps

MAXIMUM RANGE: 8,475 yards

150mm Mountain Howitzer M18

ADOPTION DATE: 1918

CALIBER: 150mm

WEIGHT: 6,173 pounds

BREECH: —

BARREL LENGTH: 76.9 inches

ELEVATION: 70°

TRAVERSAL: 7°

PROJECTILE WEIGHT: 92.5

MUZZLE VELOCITY: 1,115 fps

MAXIMUM RANGE: 8,749 yards

GREAT BRITAIN

10-pdr Jointed Mk1

ADOPTION DATE: 1901

CALIBER: 2.75-inch

WEIGHT: 882 pounds

BREECH: —

BARREL LENGTH: 270 inches

ELEVATION: 25°

TRAVERSAL: —

PROJECTILE WEIGHT: 10 pounds

MUZZLE VELOCITY: —

MAXIMUM RANGE: 5,993 yards

2.75-inch Mk1

ADOPTION DATE: 1912

CALIBER: 2.75-inch

WEIGHT: 1,290 pounds

BREECH: —

BARREL LENGTH: 74.25 inches

ELEVATION: 22°

TRAVERSAL: 8°

PROJECTILE WEIGHT: 12 pounds

MUZZLE VELOCITY: —

MAXIMUM RANGE: 6,999 yards

3.7-inch Howitzer Mk1
ADOPTION DATE: 1915
CALIBER: 3.7-inch
WEIGHT: 1,609 pounds
BREECH: quick-firing
BARREL LENGTH: 44.4 inches

ELEVATION: 40°
TRAVERSAL: 40°
PROJECTILE WEIGHT: 20 pounds
MUZZLE VELOCITY: 971 fps
MAXIMUM RANGE: 5,900 yards

FRANCE

65mm Gun Mle 06
ADOPTION DATE: 1908
CALIBER: 65mm
WEIGHT: 882 pounds
BREECH: Nordenfelt screw
BARREL LENGTH: 50 inches

ELEVATION: 35°
TRAVERSAL: 6°
PROJECTILE WEIGHT: 8 pounds
MUZZLE VELOCITY: 1,083 fps
MAXIMUM RANGE: 6,015 yards

70mm Schneider Mle 08
ADOPTION DATE: 1908
CALIBER: 70mm
WEIGHT: 1,120 pounds
BREECH: quick-firing
BARREL LENGTH: 46.75 inches

ELEVATION: 20°
TRAVERSAL: 4.5°
PROJECTILE WEIGHT: 11.5 pounds
MUZZLE VELOCITY: 984 fps
MAXIMUM RANGE: 5,468 yards

75mm Deport
ADOPTION DATE: 1910
CALIBER: 75mm
WEIGHT: 727.5 pounds
BREECH: semiautomatic horizontal
    sliding block
BARREL LENGTH: 49.3 inches

ELEVATION: 45°
TRAVERSAL: 6°
PROJECTILE WEIGHT: 14 pounds
MUZZLE VELOCITY: 935 fps
MAXIMUM RANGE: —

75mm Mle 19
ADOPTION DATE: 1919
CALIBER: 75mm
WEIGHT: 1,453 pounds
BREECH: quick-firing
BARREL LENGTH: 52.2 inches

ELEVATION: 40°
TRAVERSAL: 10°
PROJECTILE WEIGHT: 14 pounds
MUZZLE VELOCITY: 1,476 fps
MAXIMUM RANGE: 10,499 yards

105mm Howitzer Mle 19

ADOPTION DATE: 1919
CALIBER: 105mm
WEIGHT: 1,653.5 pounds
BREECH: quick-firing
BARREL LENGTH: 49.2 inches

ELEVATION: 43°
TRAVERSAL: 9°
PROJECTILE WEIGHT: 26 pounds
MUZZLE VELOCITY: 1,148 fps
MAXIMUM RANGE: 8,311 yards

GERMANY

75mm Geb K08

ADOPTION DATE: 1908
CALIBER: 75mm
WEIGHT: 1,166 pounds
BREECH: horizontal sliding block
BARREL LENGTH: 49.3 inches

ELEVATION: 38°
TRAVERSAL: 5°
PROJECTILE WEIGHT: 11.6 pounds
MUZZLE VELOCITY: 984 fps
MAXIMUM RANGE: 6,288 yards

105mm Geb H L/12 Howitzer

ADOPTION DATE: 1910
CALIBER: 105mm
WEIGHT: 3,660 pounds
BREECH: horizontal sliding block
BARREL LENGTH: 49.2 inches

ELEVATION: 40°
TRAVERSAL: 51°
PROJECTILE WEIGHT: 32 pounds
MUZZLE VELOCITY: 1,854 fps
MAXIMUM RANGE: 18,307 yards

75mm Geb G14

ADOPTION DATE: 1914
CALIBER: 75mm
WEIGHT: 1,082 pounds
BREECH: horizontal sliding block
BARREL LENGTH: 46 inches

ELEVATION: 36°
TRAVERSAL: 5°
PROJECTILE WEIGHT: 11.5 pounds
MUZZLE VELOCITY: 920 fps
MAXIMUM RANGE: 5,140 yards

ITALY

70mm Mo.2

ADOPTION DATE: 1903
CALIBER: 70mm
WEIGHT: 853
BREECH: quick-firing
BARREL LENGTH: 78.3 inches

ELEVATION: 21°
TRAVERSAL: —
PROJECTILE WEIGHT: 10.5 pounds
MUZZLE VELOCITY: 1,158 fps
MAXIMUM RANGE: 7,251 yards

70mm Mo.08

ADOPTION DATE: 1910
CALIBER: 70mm
WEIGHT: 1,120 pounds
BREECH: horizontal sliding block
BARREL LENGTH: 47.26 inches

ELEVATION: 20°
TRAVERSAL: 5°
PROJECTILE WEIGHT: 11.5 pounds
MUZZLE VELOCITY: 984 fps
MAXIMUM RANGE: 5,468 yards

65mm Canone da 65/17

ADOPTION DATE: 1913
CALIBER: 65mm
WEIGHT: 1,226 pounds
BREECH: quick-firing
BARREL LENGTH: 42.5 inches

ELEVATION: 20°
TRAVERSAL: 8°
PROJECTILE WEIGHT: 9.5 pounds
MUZZLE VELOCITY: —
MAXIMUM RANGE: 7,437 yards

JAPAN

75mm Meiji 41

ADOPTION DATE: 1908
CALIBER: 75mm
WEIGHT: 1,199 pounds
BREECH: quick-firing
BARREL LENGTH: 55.1 inches

ELEVATION: 40°
TRAVERSAL: 7°
PROJECTILE WEIGHT: 13 pounds
MUZZLE VELOCITY: 1,427 fps
MAXIMUM RANGE: 7,677 yards

RUSSIA

76.2mm Gun M04

ADOPTION DATE: 1904
CALIBER: 76.2mm
WEIGHT: —
BREECH: quick-firing
BARREL LENGTH: 39 inches

ELEVATION: 35°
TRAVERSAL: 5°
PROJECTILE WEIGHT: 14 pounds
MUZZLE VELOCITY: 971 fps
MAXIMUM RANGE: 4,549 yards

105mm Howitzer M09

ADOPTION DATE: 1909
CALIBER: 105mm
WEIGHT: 1,609 pounds
BREECH: quick-firing
BARREL LENGTH: 41 inches

ELEVATION: 60°
TRAVERSAL: 5°
PROJECTILE WEIGHT: 26.5 pounds
MUZZLE VELOCITY: 984 fps
MAXIMUM RANGE: 6,562 yards

Antiaircraft Artillery
UNITED STATES

3-inch M1917A2

ADOPTION DATE: —
CALIBER: 3-inch
WEIGHT: 15,028 pounds
BREECH: semiautomatic
BARREL LENGTH: 165 inches

ELEVATION: 85°
TRAVERSAL: 360°
PROJECTILE WEIGHT: 12.8 pounds
MUZZLE VELOCITY: 2,798 fps
MAXIMUM CEILING: 29,389 feet

GREAT BRITAIN

GREAT BRITAIN: 3-INCH 20-CWT MK1
(Courtesy Art-Tech)

3-inch 20-cwt Mk1

ADOPTION DATE: 1914
CALIBER: 3-inch
WEIGHT: 5,997 pounds
BREECH: semiautomatic horizontal
  sliding block
BARREL LENGTH: 270 inches

ELEVATION: 90°
TRAVERSAL: 360°
PROJECTILE WEIGHT: 16 pounds
MUZZLE VELOCITY: 2,500 fps
MAXIMUM CEILING: 37,172 feet

3-inch 12-pdr, 12-cwt Mk1

ADOPTION DATE: 1915
CALIBER: 3-inch
WEIGHT: 1,344 pounds
BREECH: quick-firing
BARREL LENGTH: 120 inches

ELEVATION: 85°
TRAVERSAL: 360°
PROJECTILE WEIGHT: 12.5 pounds
MUZZLE VELOCITY: 2,198 fps
MAXIMUM CEILING: 20,013 feet

3.3-inch 13-pdr, 9-cwt AA

ADOPTION DATE: —
CALIBER: 3.3-inch
WEIGHT: 1,008 pounds
BREECH: quick-firing
BARREL LENGTH: 105.6 inches

ELEVATION: 80°
TRAVERSAL: 360°
PROJECTILE WEIGHT: 12.5 pounds
MUZZLE VELOCITY: 2,149 fps
MAXIMUM CEILING: 18,996 feet

4-inch Mk5

ADOPTION DATE: 1915
CALIBER: 3.9-inch
WEIGHT: —
BREECH: semiautomatic horizontal
   sliding block
BARREL LENGTH: 180 inches

ELEVATION: 80°
TRAVERSAL: 360°
PROJECTILE WEIGHT: 30.8 pounds
MUZZLE VELOCITY: 2,349 fps
MAXIMUM CEILING: 29,987 feet

3.3-inch 18-pdr Mk2

ADOPTION DATE: 1916
CALIBER: 3.3 inches
WEIGHT: —
BREECH: quick-firing
BARREL LENGTH: 92.4 inches

ELEVATION: 80°
TRAVERSAL: 360°
PROJECTILE WEIGHT: 18.5 pounds
MUZZLE VELOCITY: 1,614 fps
MAXIMUM CEILING: 17,995 feet

GERMANY

77mm Ballonen-AK

ADOPTION DATE: 1914
CALIBER: 77mm
WEIGHT: —
BREECH: horizontal sliding block
BARREL LENGTH: —

ELEVATION: —
TRAVERSAL: —
PROJECTILE WEIGHT: 17 pounds
MUZZLE VELOCITY: 1,598 fps
MAXIMUM CEILING: —

77mm Luftkanone

ADOPTION DATE: 1915
CALIBER: 77mm
WEIGHT: 2,756 pounds
BREECH: Nordenfelt screw
BARREL LENGTH: 90 inches

ELEVATION: 80°
TRAVERSAL: 360°
PROJECTILE WEIGHT: 17.5 pounds
MUZZLE VELOCITY: 1,598 fps
MAXIMUM CEILING: —

GERMANY: 88MM FLAK
(Courtesy Art-Tech)

88mm FlaK

ADOPTION DATE: 1918
CALIBER: 88mm
WEIGHT: 16,094 pounds
BREECH: horizontal sliding block
BARREL LENGTH: —

ELEVATION: 70°
TRAVERSAL: 360°
PROJECTILE WEIGHT: 34 pounds
MUZZLE VELOCITY: 2,575 fps
MAXIMUM CEILING: 12,631 feet

ITALY

76.2mm 76/40 Ansaldo
ADOPTION DATE: 1912
CALIBER: 76.2mm
WEIGHT: —
BREECH: quick-firing
BARREL LENGTH: 120 inches

ELEVATION: 80°
TRAVERSAL: 360°
PROJECTILE WEIGHT: 14 pounds
MUZZLE VELOCITY: 1,264 fps
MAXIMUM CEILING: 16,404 feet

76.2mm 76/45 Mo.11
ADOPTION DATE: 1912
CALIBER: 76.2mm
WEIGHT: 4,927 pounds
BREECH: quick-firing
BARREL LENGTH: 135 inches

ELEVATION: 80°
TRAVERSAL: 360°
PROJECTILE WEIGHT: 14 pounds
MUZZLE VELOCITY: 2,460 fps
MAXIMUM CEILING: 20,997 feet

ITALY: 75/27 MO.06/15
(Courtesy Art-Tech)

75mm 75/27 Mo.06/15
ADOPTION DATE: 1915
CALIBER: 75mm
WEIGHT: 10,307 pounds
BREECH: semiautomatic horizontal
  sliding block
BARREL LENGTH: 78.3 inches

ELEVATION: 70°
TRAVERSAL: 360°
PROJECTILE WEIGHT: 14 pounds
MUZZLE VELOCITY: 1,673 fps
MAXIMUM CEILING: 15,092 feet

RUSSIA

76.2mm M15

ADOPTION DATE: 1915
CALIBER: 76.2mm
WEIGHT: 22,399 pounds
BREECH: vertical sliding block
BARREL LENGTH: 90 inches

ELEVATION: 75°
TRAVERSAL: 360°
PROJECTILE WEIGHT: 14 pounds
MUZZLE VELOCITY: 1,929 fps
MAXIMUM CEILING: 18,045 feet

Self-propelled Artillery
FRANCE

St. Chamond

ADOPTION DATE: 1918
CALIBER: 240mm
WEIGHT: 61,729 pounds
BREECH: —
BARREL LENGTH: —

ELEVATION: 35°
TRAVERSAL: 0°
PROJECTILE WEIGHT: —
MUZZLE VELOCITY: —
MAXIMUM RANGE: 18,920 yards

Schneider

ADOPTION DATE: 1918
CALIBER: 220mm
WEIGHT: 57,320 pounds
BREECH: —
BARREL LENGTH: —

ELEVATION: 20°
TRAVERSAL: 0°
PROJECTILE WEIGHT: —
MUZZLE VELOCITY: —
MAXIMUM RANGE: 24,934 yards

Antitank Artillery
GERMANY

37mm PaK 1918

ADOPTION DATE: 1918
CALIBER: 37mm
WEIGHT: 386 pounds
BREECH: horizontal sliding block
BARREL LENGTH: 31.9 inches

ELEVATION: 9°
TRAVERSAL: 21°
PROJECTILE WEIGHT: 1.3 pounds
MUZZLE VELOCITY: 1,132 fps
MAXIMUM RANGE: 2,843 yards

Heavy Artillery
UNITED STATES

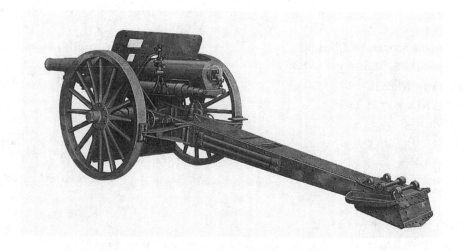

UNITED STATES: 4.7-INCH GUN M1906
(Courtesy Art-Tech)

4.7-inch Gun M1906
ADOPTION DATE: 1906
CALIBER: 4.7-inch
WEIGHT: 7,182.5 pounds
BREECH: quick-firing
BARREL LENGTH: 134.5 inches

ELEVATION: 15°
TRAVERSAL: 8°
PROJECTILE WEIGHT: 60 pounds
MUZZLE VELOCITY: 1,706 fps
MAXIMUM RANGE: 9,537.5 yards

4.7-inch Gun M1917
ADOPTION DATE: 1917
CALIBER: 4.7-inch
WEIGHT: 8,089 pounds
BREECH: quick-firing
BARREL LENGTH: 134.5 inches

ELEVATION: 40°
TRAVERSAL: 8°
PROJECTILE WEIGHT: 45 pounds
MUZZLE VELOCITY: 2,329 fps
MAXIMUM RANGE: 16,350 yards

5-inch Gun M1898
ADOPTION DATE: 1900
CALIBER: 5-inch
WEIGHT: 3,846.5 pounds
BREECH: —
BARREL LENGTH: 135 inches

ELEVATION: 31°
TRAVERSAL: —
PROJECTILE WEIGHT: 45 pounds
MUZZLE VELOCITY: 1,804 fps
MAXIMUM RANGE: 9,810 yards

155mm Gun M1918M1

ADOPTION DATE: 1918
CALIBER: 155mm
WEIGHT: 24,973 pounds
BREECH: —
BARREL LENGTH: 228 inches

ELEVATION: 35°
TRAVERSAL: 60°
PROJECTILE WEIGHT: 95 pounds
MUZZLE VELOCITY: 2,411 fps
MAXIMUM RANGE: 20,034 yards

5-inch Gun M1918

ADOPTION DATE: 1918
CALIBER: 5-inch
WEIGHT: 9,890 pounds
BREECH: —
BARREL LENGTH: 170 inches

ELEVATION: 21°
TRAVERSAL: 8°
PROJECTILE WEIGHT: 60 pounds
MUZZLE VELOCITY: 2,132 fps
MAXIMUM RANGE: 11,990 yards

155mm Howitzer M1917

ADOPTION DATE: 1917
CALIBER: 155mm
WEIGHT: 8,288 pounds
BREECH: interrupted screw
BARREL LENGTH: 91.5 inches

ELEVATION: 43°
TRAVERSAL: 6°
PROJECTILE WEIGHT: 95.5 pounds
MUZZLE VELOCITY: 1,476 fps
MAXIMUM RANGE: 12,535 yards

6-inch Howitzer M1908

ADOPTION DATE: 1908
CALIBER: 6-inch
WEIGHT: 7,404 pounds
BREECH: quick-firing
BARREL LENGTH: 78 inches

ELEVATION: 40°
TRAVERSAL: 6°
PROJECTILE WEIGHT: 120 pounds
MUZZLE VELOCITY: 902 fps
MAXIMUM RANGE: 6,703.5 yards

7-inch Howitzer M1890

ADOPTION DATE: 1893
CALIBER: 7-inch
WEIGHT: —
BREECH: —
BARREL LENGTH: 88.9 inches

ELEVATION: 40°
TRAVERSAL: —
PROJECTILE WEIGHT: 105 pounds
MUZZLE VELOCITY: 1,082 fps
MAXIMUM RANGE: 5,995 yards

240mm Howitzer M1918

ADOPTION DATE: 1920
CALIBER: 240mm
WEIGHT: 41,402 pounds
BREECH: —
BARREL LENGTH: 175.78 inches

ELEVATION: 60°
TRAVERSAL: 20°
PROJECTILE WEIGHT: 346 pounds
MUZZLE VELOCITY: 1,699 fps
MAXIMUM RANGE: 16,350 yards

AUSTRIA

120mm Siege Gun M80

ADOPTION DATE: 1880
CALIBER: 120mm
WEIGHT: 8,025 pounds
BREECH: —
BARREL LENGTH: 126.9 inches

ELEVATION: 30°
TRAVERSAL: —
PROJECTILE WEIGHT: 38.5 pounds
MUZZLE VELOCITY: —
MAXIMUM RANGE: 8,749 yards

149mm Siege Gun M80

ADOPTION DATE: 1880
CALIBER: 149mm
WEIGHT: 12,147 pounds
BREECH: —
BARREL LENGTH: 139.2 inches

ELEVATION: 28°
TRAVERSAL: —
PROJECTILE WEIGHT: 73 pounds
MUZZLE VELOCITY: 1,575 fps
MAXIMUM RANGE: 9,296 yards

180mm Siege Gun M80

ADOPTION DATE: 1880
CALIBER: 180mm
WEIGHT: 9,590 pounds
BREECH: —
BARREL LENGTH: 84 inches

ELEVATION: 35°
TRAVERSAL: —
PROJECTILE WEIGHT: 128 pounds
MUZZLE VELOCITY: —
MAXIMUM RANGE: 5,577 yards

152.4mm M15 Gun

ADOPTION DATE: 1915
CALIBER: 152.4mm
WEIGHT: 26,896 pounds
BREECH: —
BARREL LENGTH: 204 inches

ELEVATION: 32°
TRAVERSAL: 6°
PROJECTILE WEIGHT: 124.5 pounds
MUZZLE VELOCITY: 2,297 fps
MAXIMUM RANGE: 20,779 yards

149mm Siege Howitzer M80

ADOPTION DATE: 1880
CALIBER: 149mm
WEIGHT: 4,409 pounds
BREECH: —
BARREL LENGTH: 46.8 inches

ELEVATION: —
TRAVERSAL: —
PROJECTILE WEIGHT: —
MUZZLE VELOCITY: 673 fps
MAXIMUM RANGE: 11,483 yards

150mm Field Howitzer M94
ADOPTION DATE: 1895
CALIBER: 149mm
WEIGHT: 5,445 pounds
BREECH: —
BARREL LENGTH: 75.4 inches

ELEVATION: 65°
TRAVERSAL: —
PROJECTILE WEIGHT: 84 pounds
MUZZLE VELOCITY: 984 fps
MAXIMUM RANGE: 6,780 yards

250mm "Gretel" Howitzer
ADOPTION DATE: 1898
CALIBER: 250mm
WEIGHT: 15,521 pounds
BREECH: —
BARREL LENGTH: 84.6 inches

ELEVATION: 65°
TRAVERSAL: —
PROJECTILE WEIGHT: 292 pounds
MUZZLE VELOCITY: —
MAXIMUM RANGE: 7,108 yards

305mm "Emma" Howitzer
ADOPTION DATE: 1913
CALIBER: 305mm
WEIGHT: 44,092 pounds
BREECH: —
BARREL LENGTH: 168 inches

ELEVATION: 70°
TRAVERSAL: 120°
PROJECTILE WEIGHT: 838 pounds
MUZZLE VELOCITY: 1,115 fps
MAXIMUM RANGE: 13,123 yards

149mm Field Howitzer M14
ADOPTION DATE: 1914
CALIBER: 149mm
WEIGHT: 6,096 pounds
BREECH: —
BARREL LENGTH: 81.2 inches

ELEVATION: 70°
TRAVERSAL: 8°
PROJECTILE WEIGHT: 92.5 pounds
MUZZLE VELOCITY: 1,148 fps
MAXIMUM RANGE: 8,749 yards

280mm Howitzer
ADOPTION DATE: 1914
CALIBER: 280mm
WEIGHT: 34,756 pounds
BREECH: —
BARREL LENGTH: 132 inches

ELEVATION: 65°
TRAVERSAL: 10°
PROJECTILE WEIGHT: 745 pounds
MUZZLE VELOCITY: 1,115 fps
MAXIMUM RANGE: 12,030 yards

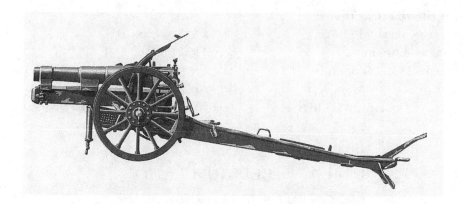

AUSTRIA: 149MM FIELD HOWITZER M15
(Courtesy Art-Tech)

149mm Field Howitzer M15

ADOPTION DATE: 1916
CALIBER: 149mm
WEIGHT: 12,258 pounds
BREECH: —
BARREL LENGTH: 116 inches

ELEVATION: 65°
TRAVERSAL: 8°
PROJECTILE WEIGHT: 92.5 pounds
MUZZLE VELOCITY: 1,673 fps
MAXIMUM RANGE: 12,577 yards

149mm Howitzer M15

ADOPTION DATE: 1915
CALIBER: 149mm
WEIGHT: 5,512 pounds
BREECH: —
BARREL LENGTH: 81.2 inches

ELEVATION: 70°
TRAVERSAL: 8°
PROJECTILE WEIGHT: 84 pounds
MUZZLE VELOCITY: 1,115 fps
MAXIMUM RANGE: 8,858 yards

305mm Howitzer M16

ADOPTION DATE: 1916
CALIBER: 305mm
WEIGHT: 451,947 pounds
BREECH: —
BARREL LENGTH: 144 inches

ELEVATION: 75°
TRAVERSAL: 360°
PROJECTILE WEIGHT: 1,543 pounds
MUZZLE VELOCITY: —
MAXIMUM RANGE: 32,808 yards

380mm Howitzer M16

ADOPTION DATE: 1916
CALIBER: 380mm
WEIGHT: 182,984 pounds
BREECH: —
BARREL LENGTH: 253.3 inches

ELEVATION: 75°
TRAVERSAL: 360°
PROJECTILE WEIGHT: 2,205 pounds
MUZZLE VELOCITY: 1,506 fps
MAXIMUM RANGE: 16,404 yards

420mm Howitzer L/15

ADOPTION DATE: 1917
CALIBER: 420mm
WEIGHT: 233,690 pounds
BREECH: —
BARREL LENGTH: 247.5 inches

ELEVATION: 70°
TRAVERSAL: 360°
PROJECTILE WEIGHT: 2,205 pounds
MUZZLE VELOCITY: 1,362 fps
MAXIMUM RANGE: 15,967 yards

BELGIUM

155mm Gun M17

ADOPTION DATE: 1917
CALIBER: 155mm
WEIGHT: 19,489 pounds
BREECH: —
BARREL LENGTH: 195.2 inches

ELEVATION: 42°
TRAVERSAL: 6°
PROJECTILE WEIGHT: 95 pounds
MUZZLE VELOCITY: 2,188 fps
MAXIMUM RANGE: 16,951 yards

150mm Howitzer M17

ADOPTION DATE: 1917
CALIBER: 150mm
WEIGHT: 5,040 pounds
BREECH: —
BARREL LENGTH: 100.3 inches

ELEVATION: 40°
TRAVERSAL: 5°
PROJECTILE WEIGHT: 91 pounds
MUZZLE VELOCITY: 1,099 fps
MAXIMUM RANGE: 9,405 yards

GREAT BRITAIN

5-inch 60-pdr Gun Mk1

ADOPTION DATE: 1904
CALIBER: 5-inch
WEIGHT: 9,855 pounds
BREECH: —
BARREL LENGTH: 160 inches

ELEVATION: 21°
TRAVERSAL: 8°
PROJECTILE WEIGHT: 60 pounds
MUZZLE VELOCITY: 2,077 fps
MAXIMUM RANGE: 13,889 yards

6-inch Gun Mk19

ADOPTION DATE: 1916
CALIBER: 6-inch
WEIGHT: 20,671 pounds
BREECH: interrupted screw
BARREL LENGTH: 210 inches

ELEVATION: 38°
TRAVERSAL: 8°
PROJECTILE WEIGHT: 100 pounds
MUZZLE VELOCITY: 2,349 fps
MAXIMUM RANGE: 18,750 yards

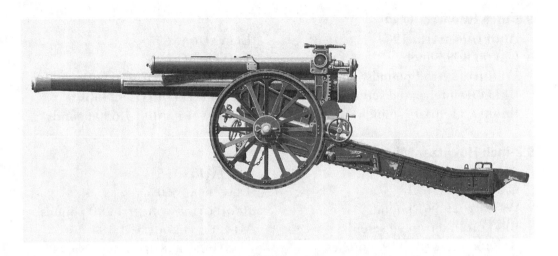

GREAT BRITAIN: 60-PDR GUN MK2
(Courtesy Art-Tech)

60-pdr Gun Mk2
ADOPTION DATE: 1918
CALIBER: 127mm
WEIGHT: 12,046 pounds
BREECH: interrupted screw
BARREL LENGTH: 185 inches

ELEVATION: 35°
TRAVERSAL: 8°
PROJECTILE WEIGHT: 60 pounds
MUZZLE VELOCITY: 2,123 fps
MAXIMUM RANGE: 16,404 yards

5-inch Howitzer Mk1
ADOPTION DATE: 1895
CALIBER: 5-inch
WEIGHT: 2,672 pounds
BREECH: interrupted screw
BARREL LENGTH: 40

ELEVATION: 45°
TRAVERSAL: —
PROJECTILE WEIGHT: 50 pounds
MUZZLE VELOCITY: 2,707 fps
MAXIMUM RANGE: 4,801 yards

6-inch, 30-cwt Howitzer Mk1
ADOPTION DATE: 1896
CALIBER: 6-inch
WEIGHT: 7,727 pounds
BREECH: interrupted screw
BARREL LENGTH: 84 inches

ELEVATION: 35°
TRAVERSAL: —
PROJECTILE WEIGHT: 118 pounds
MUZZLE VELOCITY: 774 fps
MAXIMUM RANGE: 5,200 yards

9.5-inch Howitzer Mk1

ADOPTION DATE: 1904
CALIBER: 9.5-inch
WEIGHT: 19,152 pounds
BREECH: interrupted screw
BARREL LENGTH: 76 inches

ELEVATION: 63°
TRAVERSAL: 19°
PROJECTILE WEIGHT: 280 pounds
MUZZLE VELOCITY: 925 fps
MAXIMUM RANGE: 7,650 pounds

9.2-inch Howitzer Mk1

ADOPTION DATE: 1914
CALIBER: 9.2-inch
WEIGHT: 29,961 pounds
BREECH: interrupted screw
BARREL LENGTH: 119.6 inches

ELEVATION: 55°
TRAVERSAL: 60°
PROJECTILE WEIGHT: 290 pounds
MUZZLE VELOCITY: 1,184 fps
MAXIMUM RANGE: 10,061 yards

6-inch, 26-cwt Howitzer Mk1

ADOPTION DATE: 1915
CALIBER: 6-inch
WEIGHT: 6,797 pounds
BREECH: interrupted screw
BARREL LENGTH: 78 inches

ELEVATION: 45°
TRAVERSAL: 8°
PROJECTILE WEIGHT: 100 pounds
MUZZLE VELOCITY: 411 fps
MAXIMUM RANGE: 9,499 yards

GREAT BRITAIN: 8-INCH HOWITZER MK1
(Courtesy Art-Tech)

8-inch Howitzer Mk1

ADOPTION DATE: 1915
CALIBER: 8-inch
WEIGHT: 31,306 pounds
BREECH: interrupted screw
BARREL LENGTH: 112 inches

ELEVATION: 45°
TRAVERSAL: —
PROJECTILE WEIGHT: 200 pounds
MUZZLE VELOCITY: 1,299 fps
MAXIMUM RANGE: 10,500 yards

15-inch Howitzer Mk1

ADOPTION DATE: 1915
CALIBER: 15-inch
WEIGHT: —
BREECH: interrupted screw
BARREL LENGTH: 150 inches

ELEVATION: 45°
TRAVERSAL: 25°
PROJECTILE WEIGHT: 1,400 pounds
MUZZLE VELOCITY: 1,116 fps
MAXIMUM RANGE: 10,794 yards

GREAT BRITAIN: 9.2-INCH HOWITZER MK2
(Courtesy Art-Tech)

9.2-inch Howitzer Mk2

ADOPTION DATE: 1916
CALIBER: 9.2-inch
WEIGHT: 36,288 pounds
BREECH: interrupted screw
BARREL LENGTH: 156.4 inches

ELEVATION: 50°
TRAVERSAL: 60°
PROJECTILE WEIGHT: 290 pounds
MUZZLE VELOCITY: 1,339 fps
MAXIMUM RANGE: 13,944 yards

8-inch Howitzer Mk7

ADOPTION DATE: 1917
CALIBER: 8-inch
WEIGHT: 19,820 pounds
BREECH: interrupted screw
BARREL LENGTH: 136 inches

ELEVATION: 45°
TRAVERSAL: 8°
PROJECTILE WEIGHT: 200 pounds
MUZZLE VELOCITY: 1,558 fps
MAXIMUM RANGE: 12,303 yards

12-inch Howitzer Mk1

ADOPTION DATE: 1917
CALIBER: 12-inch
WEIGHT: 83,996 pounds
BREECH: interrupted screw
BARREL LENGTH: 204 inches

ELEVATION: 65°
TRAVERSAL: 60°
PROJECTILE WEIGHT: 750 pounds
MUZZLE VELOCITY: 1,466 fps
MAXIMUM RANGE: 14,348 yards

CZECHOSLOVAKIA

150mm Gun vz15/16
ADOPTION DATE: 1919
CALIBER: 150mm
WEIGHT: 36,332 pounds
BREECH: —
BARREL LENGTH: 236 inches

ELEVATION: 45°
TRAVERSAL: —
PROJECTILE WEIGHT: 120 pounds
MUZZLE VELOCITY: 2,296 fps
MAXIMUM RANGE: 21,982 yards

149mm Howitzer vz14/16
ADOPTION DATE: 1919
CALIBER: 149mm
WEIGHT: 6,460 pounds
BREECH: —
BARREL LENGTH: 81.2 inches

ELEVATION: —
TRAVERSAL: —
PROJECTILE WEIGHT: 92.5 pounds
MUZZLE VELOCITY: 1,148 fps
MAXIMUM RANGE: 9,460 yards

150mm Field Howitzer vz15
ADOPTION DATE: 1919
CALIBER: 150mm
WEIGHT: 8,378 pounds
BREECH: —
BARREL LENGTH: 236 inches

ELEVATION: 65°
TRAVERSAL: —
PROJECTILE WEIGHT: 92.5 pounds
MUZZLE VELOCITY: 1,640 fps
MAXIMUM RANGE: 12,992 yards

210mm Howitzer vz18
ADOPTION DATE: 1919
CALIBER: 210mm
WEIGHT: 19,934 pounds
BREECH: —
BARREL LENGTH: 85 inches

ELEVATION: 70°
TRAVERSAL: 360°
PROJECTILE WEIGHT: 298 pounds
MUZZLE VELOCITY: 1,247 fps
MAXIMUM RANGE: 11,046 yards

FRANCE

120mm Short Gun Mle 90
ADOPTION DATE: 1890
CALIBER: 120mm
WEIGHT: 3,252 pounds
BREECH: interrupted screw
BARREL LENGTH: 65.8 inches

ELEVATION: 44°
TRAVERSAL: 10°
PROJECTILE WEIGHT: 40 pounds
MUZZLE VELOCITY: 951 fps
MAXIMUM RANGE: 6,343 yards

139mm Gun Mle 10

ADOPTION DATE: 1912
CALIBER: 139mm
WEIGHT: 24,251 pounds
BREECH: interrupted screw
BARREL LENGTH: 313.5 inches

ELEVATION: 30°
TRAVERSAL: 6°
PROJECTILE WEIGHT: 67 pounds
MUZZLE VELOCITY: 2,707 fps
MAXIMUM RANGE: 19,029 yards

155mm Gun Mle 77/14

ADOPTION DATE: 1914
CALIBER: 155mm
WEIGHT: 13,250 pounds
BREECH: interrupted screw
BARREL LENGTH: 164.7 inches

ELEVATION: 42°
TRAVERSAL: 5°
PROJECTILE WEIGHT: 95 pounds
MUZZLE VELOCITY: 1,837 fps
MAXIMUM RANGE: 12,467 yards

145mm Gun Mle 16

ADOPTION DATE: 1916
CALIBER: 145mm
WEIGHT: 27,558 pounds
BREECH: interrupted screw
BARREL LENGTH: 285 inches

ELEVATION: 38°
TRAVERSAL: 6°
PROJECTILE WEIGHT: 74 pounds
MUZZLE VELOCITY: 2,625 fps
MAXIMUM RANGE: 20,231 yards

155mm Gun Mle 17LS

ADOPTION DATE: 1917
CALIBER: 155mm
WEIGHT: 19,731 pounds
BREECH: interrupted screw
BARREL LENGTH: 195.2 inches

ELEVATION: 40°
TRAVERSAL: 5°
PROJECTILE WEIGHT: 95 pounds
MUZZLE VELOCITY: 2,133 fps
MAXIMUM RANGE: 17,498 yards

155mm Gun Mle 17 GPF

ADOPTION DATE: 1917
CALIBER: 155mm
WEIGHT: 23,700 pounds
BREECH: interrupted screw
BARREL LENGTH: 231.8 inches

ELEVATION: 35°
TRAVERSAL: 60°
PROJECTILE WEIGHT: 95 pounds
MUZZLE VELOCITY: 2,411 fps
MAXIMUM RANGE: 17,717 yards

220mm Gun Mle 17

ADOPTION DATE: 1917
CALIBER: 220mm
WEIGHT: 55,116 pounds
BREECH: interrupted screw
BARREL LENGTH: 240.8 inches

ELEVATION: 37°
TRAVERSAL: 21°
PROJECTILE WEIGHT: 228 pounds
MUZZLE VELOCITY: 2,510 fps
MAXIMUM RANGE: 24,934 yards

155mm Gun Mle 18

ADOPTION DATE: 1918
CALIBER: 155mm
WEIGHT: 11,089 pounds
BREECH: interrupted screw
BARREL LENGTH: 164.7 inches

ELEVATION: 44°
TRAVERSAL: 6°
PROJECTILE WEIGHT: 95 pounds
MUZZLE VELOCITY: 1,837 fps
MAXIMUM RANGE: 13,123 yards

270mm Howitzer Mle 85

ADOPTION DATE: 1885
CALIBER: 270mm
WEIGHT: 36,376 pounds
BREECH: interrupted screw
BARREL LENGTH: 101.76 inches

ELEVATION: 70°
TRAVERSAL: 30°
PROJECTILE WEIGHT: 335 pounds
MUZZLE VELOCITY: 1,070 fps
MAXIMUM RANGE: 8,749 yards

FRANCE: 220MM HOWITZER MLE 01
(Courtesy Art-Tech)

220mm Howitzer Mle 01

ADOPTION DATE: 1903
CALIBER: 220mm
WEIGHT: 19,739 pounds
BREECH: interrupted screw
BARREL LENGTH: 77.4 inches

ELEVATION: 40°
TRAVERSAL: 40°
PROJECTILE WEIGHT: 220 pounds
MUZZLE VELOCITY: —
MAXIMUM RANGE: 7,655 yards

155mm Howitzer Rimailho Mle 04

ADOPTION DATE: 1905
CALIBER: 155mm
WEIGHT: 7,055 pounds
BREECH: interrupted screw
BARREL LENGTH: 91.5 inches

ELEVATION: 41°
TRAVERSAL: 5°
PROJECTILE WEIGHT: 89 pounds
MUZZLE VELOCITY: 1,050 fps
MAXIMUM RANGE: 6,562 yards

120mm Howitzer Mle 15TR

ADOPTION DATE: 1915
CALIBER: 120mm
WEIGHT: 3,252 pounds
BREECH: interrupted screw
BARREL LENGTH: 65.8 inches

ELEVATION: 44°
TRAVERSAL: 10°
PROJECTILE WEIGHT: 40 pounds
MUZZLE VELOCITY: 951 fps
MAXIMUM RANGE: 6,343 yards

220m Howitzer Mle 16

ADOPTION DATE: 1915
CALIBER: 220mm
WEIGHT: 17,196 pounds
BREECH: interrupted screw
BARREL LENGTH: 88.58 inches

ELEVATION: 65°
TRAVERSAL: 6°
PROJECTILE WEIGHT: 220
MUZZLE VELOCITY: 1,362 fps
MAXIMUM RANGE: 12,030 yards

155mm Howitzer Mle 17

ADOPTION DATE: 1917
CALIBER: 155mm
WEIGHT: 7,275 pounds
BREECH: interrupted screw
BARREL LENGTH: 91.5 inches

ELEVATION: 43°
TRAVERSAL: 6°
PROJECTILE WEIGHT: 96 pounds
MUZZLE VELOCITY: 1,476 fps
MAXIMUM RANGE: 12,577 yards

279mm Mortar Schneider

ADOPTION DATE: 1917
CALIBER: 279mm
WEIGHT: 3,638 pounds
BREECH: interrupted screw
BARREL LENGTH: 104.5 inches

ELEVATION: 60°
TRAVERSAL: 20°
PROJECTILE WEIGHT: 452 pounds
MUZZLE VELOCITY: —
MAXIMUM RANGE: 11,924 yards

GERMANY

150mm sFH02

ADOPTION DATE: 1902
CALIBER: 150mm
WEIGHT: 4,826 pounds
BREECH: horizontal sliding block
BARREL LENGTH: 64.9 inches

ELEVATION: 65°
TRAVERSAL: —
PROJECTILE WEIGHT: 87 pounds
MUZZLE VELOCITY: 906 fps
MAXIMUM RANGE: —

420mm "Gamma" H

ADOPTION DATE: 1911
CALIBER: 420mm
WEIGHT: 175 tons
BREECH: horizontal sliding block
BARREL LENGTH: 201.6 inches

ELEVATION: 75°
TRAVERSAL: 46°
PROJECTILE WEIGHT: 2,535 pounds
MUZZLE VELOCITY: 1,483 fps
MAXIMUM RANGE: 8.8 miles

GERMANY: 420MM L/14 "BIG BERTHA"
(Courtesy Art-Tech)

420mm L/14 "Big Bertha"

ADOPTION DATE: 1914
CALIBER: 420mm
WEIGHT: 41.3 tons
BREECH: horizontal sliding block
BARREL LENGTH: 231 inches

ELEVATION: 70°
TRAVERSAL: 360°
PROJECTILE WEIGHT: 1,719 pounds
MUZZLE VELOCITY: 2,676.5 fps
MAXIMUM RANGE: 10,253 yards

150mm sFH113

ADOPTION DATE: 1917
CALIBER: 150mm
WEIGHT: 4,960 pounds
BREECH: horizontal sliding block
BARREL LENGTH: 82.6 inches

ELEVATION: 45°
TRAVERSAL: 9°
PROJECTILE WEIGHT: 92.5 pounds
MUZZLE VELOCITY: 1,250 fps
MAXIMUM RANGE: 9,405 yards

150mm K16

ADOPTION DATE: 1917
CALIBER: 150mm
WEIGHT: 23,964 pounds
BREECH: horizontal sliding block
BARREL LENGTH: —

ELEVATION: 43°
TRAVERSAL: 8°
PROJECTILE WEIGHT: 113 pounds
MUZZLE VELOCITY: 2,484 fps
MAXIMUM RANGE: 24,060 yards

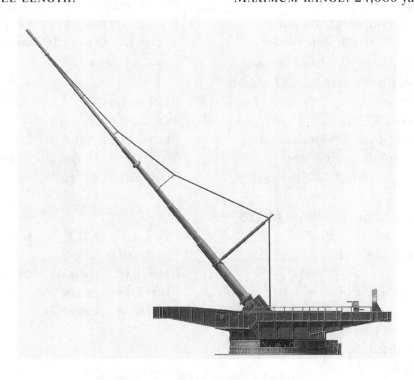

GERMANY:210MM PARIS GUN
(Courtesy Art-Tech)

210mm Paris Gun

ADOPTION DATE: 1918
CALIBER: 210mm
WEIGHT: 1,653,470 pounds
BREECH: horizontal sliding block
BARREL LENGTH: 2,550 inches

ELEVATION: 35°
TRAVERSAL: 360°
PROJECTILE WEIGHT: 264 pounds
MUZZLE VELOCITY: 5,085 fps
MAXIMUM RANGE: 82 miles

ITALY

155mm Canoneda 155/25

ADOPTION DATE: 1908
CALIBER: 155mm
WEIGHT: 15,829 pounds
BREECH: interrupted screw
BARREL LENGTH: 152.5 inches

ELEVATION: 28°
TRAVERSAL: —
PROJECTILE WEIGHT: 95 pounds
MUZZLE VELOCITY: 1,640 fps
MAXIMUM RANGE: 12,467 yards

149mm Canone da 149/35

ADOPTION DATE: 1910
CALIBER: 149mm
WEIGHT: 18,078 pounds
BREECH: interrupted screw
BARREL LENGTH: 206.5 inches

ELEVATION: 33°
TRAVERSAL: —
PROJECTILE WEIGHT: 101 pounds
MUZZLE VELOCITY: 2,297 fps
MAXIMUM RANGE: 10,608 yards

152.4mm Canone da 152/37 Mo.15

ADOPTION DATE: 1915
CALIBER: 152.4mm
WEIGHT: 26,213 pounds
BREECH: interrupted screw
BARREL LENGTH: 222 inches

ELEVATION: 45°
TRAVERSAL: 6°
PROJECTILE WEIGHT: 120 pounds
MUZZLE VELOCITY: 2,297 fps
MAXIMUM RANGE: 26,794 yards

149mm Canone da 149/40 Mo.35

ADOPTION DATE: 1935
CALIBER: 149mm
WEIGHT: 25,309 pounds
BREECH: interrupted screw
BARREL LENGTH: 236 inches

ELEVATION: 45°
TRAVERSAL: 60°
PROJECTILE WEIGHT: 112 pounds
MUZZLE VELOCITY: 2,625 fps
MAXIMUM RANGE: 24,060 yards

149mm Obice da 149/12

ADOPTION DATE: —
CALIBER: 149mm
WEIGHT: 5,269 pounds
BREECH: horizontal sliding block
BARREL LENGTH: 70.8 inches

ELEVATION: 65°
TRAVERSAL: 5°
PROJECTILE WEIGHT: 90 pounds
MUZZLE VELOCITY: 984 fps
MAXIMUM RANGE: 7,218 yards

210mm Mortaio da 210/8

ADOPTION DATE: —
CALIBER: 210mm
WEIGHT: 24,108 pounds
BREECH: —
BARREL LENGTH: 65.6 inches

ELEVATION: 70°
TRAVERSAL: 360°
PROJECTILE WEIGHT: 222 pounds
MUZZLE VELOCITY: 1,214 fps
MAXIMUM RANGE: 8,449 yards

149mm Obice da 149/13 M14/15

ADOPTION DATE: 1915
CALIBER: 149mm
WEIGHT: 6,162 pounds
BREECH: horizontal sliding block
BARREL LENGTH: 76.7 inches

ELEVATION: 70°
TRAVERSAL: 6°
PROJECTILE WEIGHT: 93 pounds
MUZZLE VELOCITY: 1,132 fps
MAXIMUM RANGE: 9,569 yards

305mm Obice da 305/17DS

ADOPTION DATE: 1915
CALIBER: 305mm
WEIGHT: 75,596 pounds
BREECH: interrupted screw
BARREL LENGTH: 204 inches

ELEVATION: 65°
TRAVERSAL: —
PROJECTILE WEIGHT: 772 pounds
MUZZLE VELOCITY: 1,788 fps
MAXIMUM RANGE: 19,193 yards

260mm Mortaio da 260/9 Mo.16

ADOPTION DATE: 1916
CALIBER: 260mm
WEIGHT: 26,081 pounds
BREECH: interrupted screw
BARREL LENGTH: 91.8 inches

ELEVATION: 65°
TRAVERSAL: 30°
PROJECTILE WEIGHT: 483 pounds
MUZZLE VELOCITY: 984 fps
MAXIMUM RANGE: 9,952 yards

305mm Mortaio da 305/8 Mo.11/16

ADOPTION DATE: 1916
CALIBER: 305mm
WEIGHT: 46,032 pounds
BREECH: interrupted screw
BARREL LENGTH: 96 inches

ELEVATION: 73°
TRAVERSAL: 120°
PROJECTILE WEIGHT: 838 pounds
MUZZLE VELOCITY: 1,312 fps
MAXIMUM RANGE: 12,030 yards

210mm Obice da 210/22 Mo.35

ADOPTION DATE: 1934
CALIBER: 210mm
WEIGHT: 34,833 pounds
BREECH: interrupted screw
BARREL LENGTH: 210 inches

ELEVATION: 70°
TRAVERSAL: 30°
PROJECTILE WEIGHT: 225 pounds
MUZZLE VELOCITY: 1,870 fps
MAXIMUM RANGE: 17,500 yards

JAPAN

120mm Field Howitzer Meiji 38

ADOPTION DATE: 1905
CALIBER: 120mm
WEIGHT: 2,767 pounds
BREECH: quick-firing
BARREL LENGTH: 56.4 inches

ELEVATION: 43°
TRAVERSAL: 64°
PROJECTILE WEIGHT: 44 pounds
MUZZLE VELOCITY: 902 fps
MAXIMUM RANGE: 6,300 yards

105mm Howitzer Meiji 38

ADOPTION DATE: 1905
CALIBER: 105mm
WEIGHT: 4,597 pounds
BREECH: quick-firing
BARREL LENGTH: 70.8 inches

ELEVATION: 43°
TRAVERSAL: 3°
PROJECTILE WEIGHT: 79 pounds
MUZZLE VELOCITY: 902 fps
MAXIMUM RANGE: 6,452 yards

240mm Howitzer Meiji 45

ADOPTION DATE: 1912
CALIBER: 240mm
WEIGHT: —
BREECH: —
BARREL LENGTH: —

ELEVATION: —
TRAVERSAL: —
PROJECTILE WEIGHT: 399 pounds
MUZZLE VELOCITY: 1,197 fps
MAXIMUM RANGE: 11,303 yards

150mm Howitzer Taisho 4

ADOPTION DATE: 1915
CALIBER: 150mm
WEIGHT: 6,173 pounds
BREECH: vertical sliding block
BARREL LENGTH: 129.8 inches

ELEVATION: 63°
TRAVERSAL: 6°
PROJECTILE WEIGHT: 92 pounds
MUZZLE VELOCITY: 1,345 fps
MAXIMUM RANGE: 10,444 yards

Coastal Artillery
UNITED STATES

2.24-inch RF Gun M1900

ADOPTION DATE: 1900
CALIBER: 2.24-inch
WEIGHT: —
BREECH: rapid fire
BARREL LENGTH: 112 inches

ELEVATION: 12°
TRAVERSAL: 360°
PROJECTILE WEIGHT: 6 pounds
MUZZLE VELOCITY: 2,398 fps
MAXIMUM RANGE: 6,213 yards

3-inch Gun M1902

ADOPTION DATE: 1902
CALIBER: 3-inch
WEIGHT: —
BREECH: —
BARREL LENGTH: 150 inches

ELEVATION: 15°
TRAVERSAL: 360°
PROJECTILE WEIGHT: 15 pounds
MUZZLE VELOCITY: 2,598 fps
MAXIMUM RANGE: 8,671 yards

3-inch Gun M1903

ADOPTION DATE: 1903
CALIBER: 3-inch
WEIGHT: 9,311 pounds
BREECH: —
BARREL LENGTH: 165 inches

ELEVATION: 16°
TRAVERSAL: 360°
PROJECTILE WEIGHT: 15 pounds
MUZZLE VELOCITY: 2,798 fps
MAXIMUM RANGE: 11,282 yards

4-inch Driggs-Schroeder

ADOPTION DATE: 1900
CALIBER: 4-inch
WEIGHT: —
BREECH: quick-firing
BARREL LENGTH: 160 inches

ELEVATION: 15°
TRAVERSAL: 360°
PROJECTILE WEIGHT: 33 pounds
MUZZLE VELOCITY: 2,296 fps
MAXIMUM RANGE: 8,829 yards

4.72-inch Armstrong

ADOPTION DATE: 1895
CALIBER: 4.72-inch
WEIGHT: —
BREECH: quick-firing
BARREL LENGTH: 228.5 inches

ELEVATION: 20°
TRAVERSAL: 360°
PROJECTILE WEIGHT: 45 pounds
MUZZLE VELOCITY: 2,598 fps
MAXIMUM RANGE: 11,172 yards

5-inch Gun M1900

ADOPTION DATE: 1900
CALIBER: 5-inch
WEIGHT: —
BREECH: quick-firing
BARREL LENGTH: 250 inches

ELEVATION: 15°
TRAVERSAL: 360°
PROJECTILE WEIGHT: 59 pounds
MUZZLE VELOCITY: 2,598 fps
MAXIMUM RANGE: 11,750 yards

6-inch RF Armstrong

ADOPTION DATE: 1896
CALIBER: 6-inch
WEIGHT: —
BREECH: rapid fire
BARREL LENGTH: 240 inches

ELEVATION: 16°
TRAVERSAL: 360°
PROJECTILE WEIGHT: 106 pounds
MUZZLE VELOCITY: 2,148 fps
MAXIMUM RANGE: 10,164 yards

6-inch M1897

ADOPTION DATE: 1900
CALIBER: 6-inch
WEIGHT: —
BREECH: —
BARREL LENGTH: 270 inches

ELEVATION: 15°
TRAVERSAL: 170°
PROJECTILE WEIGHT: 90 pounds
MUZZLE VELOCITY: 2,598 fps
MAXIMUM RANGE: 11,772 yards

6-inch Gun M1900

ADOPTION DATE: 1903
CALIBER: 6-inch
WEIGHT: 45,681 pounds
BREECH: —
BARREL LENGTH: 300 inches

ELEVATION: —
TRAVERSAL: —
PROJECTILE WEIGHT: 90 pounds
MUZZLE VELOCITY: 2,749 fps
MAXIMUM RANGE: 16,459 yards

6-inch Gun M1903

ADOPTION DATE: 1905
CALIBER: 6-inch
WEIGHT: —
BREECH: —
BARREL LENGTH: 300 inches

ELEVATION: 15°
TRAVERSAL: 170°
PROJECTILE WEIGHT: 90 pounds
MUZZLE VELOCITY: 2,749 fps
MAXIMUM RANGE: 16,895 yards

6-inch Gun M1905

ADOPTION DATE: 1908
CALIBER: 6-inch
WEIGHT: 159,395 pounds
BREECH: —
BARREL LENGTH: 300 inches

ELEVATION: 47°
TRAVERSAL: 360°
PROJECTILE WEIGHT: 105 pounds
MUZZLE VELOCITY: 2,798 fps
MAXIMUM RANGE: 274,135 yards

6-inch Gun M1908

ADOPTION DATE: 1910
CALIBER: 6-inch
WEIGHT: 42,355 pounds
BREECH: —
BARREL LENGTH: 270 inches

ELEVATION: 15°
TRAVERSAL: 120°
PROJECTILE WEIGHT: 90 pounds
MUZZLE VELOCITY: 1,548 fps
MAXIMUM RANGE: 14,742 yards

8-inch Gun M1888

ADOPTION DATE: 1896
CALIBER: 8-inch
WEIGHT: —
BREECH: —
BARREL LENGTH: 256 inches

ELEVATION: 18°
TRAVERSAL: 360°
PROJECTILE WEIGHT: 324 pounds
MUZZLE VELOCITY: 2,198 fps
MAXIMUM RANGE: 16,241 yards

10-inch Gun M1888M1

ADOPTION DATE: 1891
CALIBER: 10-inch
WEIGHT: 144,954 pounds
BREECH: —
BARREL LENGTH: 340 inches

ELEVATION: 15°
TRAVERSAL: 320°
PROJECTILE WEIGHT: 1,050 pounds
MUZZLE VELOCITY: 2,247 fps
MAXIMUM RANGE: 16,241 yards

10-inch Gun M1900

ADOPTION DATE: 1902
CALIBER: 10-inch
WEIGHT: 398,971 pounds
BREECH: —
BARREL LENGTH: 400 inches

ELEVATION: 12°
TRAVERSAL: 170°
PROJECTILE WEIGHT: 619 pounds
MUZZLE VELOCITY: 2,247 fps
MAXIMUM RANGE: 16,241 yards

12-inch Mortar M1890

ADOPTION DATE: 1892
CALIBER: 12-inch
WEIGHT: 157,385 pounds
BREECH: —
BARREL LENGTH: 120 inches

ELEVATION: 70°
TRAVERSAL: 360°
PROJECTILE WEIGHT: 1,050 pounds
MUZZLE VELOCITY: 1,696 fps
MAXIMUM RANGE: 11,979 yards

12-inch Mortar M1908

ADOPTION DATE: 1910
CALIBER: 12-inch
WEIGHT: 144,556 pounds
BREECH: —
BARREL LENGTH: 120 inches

ELEVATION: 70°
TRAVERSAL: 360°
PROJECTILE WEIGHT: 1,050 pounds
MUZZLE VELOCITY: 1,000 fps
MAXIMUM RANGE: 9,156 yards

12-inch Mortar M1912

ADOPTION DATE: 1913
CALIBER: 12-inch
WEIGHT: 165,706 pounds
BREECH: —
BARREL LENGTH: 180 inches

ELEVATION: 65°
TRAVERSAL: 360°
PROJECTILE WEIGHT: 700.5 pounds
MUZZLE VELOCITY: 1,804 fps
MAXIMUM RANGE: 19,255 yards

12-inch Gun M1888

ADOPTION DATE: 1895
CALIBER: 12-inch
WEIGHT: 229,564 pounds
BREECH: —
BARREL LENGTH: 408 inches

ELEVATION: 15°
TRAVERSAL: 360°
PROJECTILE WEIGHT: 977 pounds
MUZZLE VELOCITY: 2,234 fps
MAXIMUM RANGE: 18,339 yards

12-inch Gun M1895

ADOPTION DATE: 1898
CALIBER: 12-inch
WEIGHT: 407,701 pounds
BREECH: —
BARREL LENGTH: 420 inches

ELEVATION: 35°
TRAVERSAL: 360°
PROJECTILE WEIGHT: 977 pounds
MUZZLE VELOCITY: 2,257 fps
MAXIMUM RANGE: 30,002 yards

12-inch Gun M1900

ADOPTION DATE: 1902
CALIBER: 12-inch
WEIGHT: 675,045 pounds
BREECH: —
BARREL LENGTH: 480 inches

ELEVATION: 10°
TRAVERSAL: 360°
PROJECTILE WEIGHT: 1,072 pounds
MUZZLE VELOCITY: 2,247 fps
MAXIMUM RANGE: 17,277 yards

14-inch M1907M1

ADOPTION DATE: 1908
CALIBER: 14-inch
WEIGHT: 637,563 pounds
BREECH: —
BARREL LENGTH: 476 inches

ELEVATION: 20°
TRAVERSAL: 360°
PROJECTILE WEIGHT: 1,662 pounds
MUZZLE VELOCITY: 2,348 fps
MAXIMUM RANGE: 22,727 yards

14-inch M1909 in Turret Mount

ADOPTION DATE: 1913
CALIBER: 14-inch
WEIGHT: 2,321,687 pounds (two guns and mounting)
BREECH: —
BARREL LENGTH: 560 inches

ELEVATION: 15°
TRAVERSAL: 360°
PROJECTILE WEIGHT: 1,209 pounds
MUZZLE VELOCITY: 2,368 fps
MAXIMUM RANGE: 22,705 yards

14-inch M1910

ADOPTION DATE: 1913
CALIBER: 14-inch
WEIGHT: 683,675 pounds
BREECH: —
BARREL LENGTH: 560 inches

ELEVATION: 20°
TRAVERSAL: 170°
PROJECTILE WEIGHT: 1,662 pounds
MUZZLE VELOCITY: 2,348 fps
MAXIMUM RANGE: 22,727 yards

16-inch Gun M1895

ADOPTION DATE: 1917
CALIBER: 16-inch
WEIGHT: 1,277,119 pounds
BREECH: —
BARREL LENGTH: 560 inches

ELEVATION: 20°
TRAVERSAL: 170°
PROJECTILE WEIGHT: 2,404 pounds
MUZZLE VELOCITY: 2,247 fps
MAXIMUM RANGE: 27,277 yards

GREAT BRITAIN

3-pdr Hotchkiss Mk1

ADOPTION DATE: 1885
CALIBER: 1.8-inch
WEIGHT: 2,469 pounds
BREECH: vertical sliding block
BARREL LENGTH: 74 inches

ELEVATION: 9°
TRAVERSAL: 360°
PROJECTILE WEIGHT: 3.3 pounds
MUZZLE VELOCITY: 1,824 fps
MAXIMUM RANGE: 7,491 yards

6-pdr Hotchkiss Mk1

ADOPTION DATE: 1885
CALIBER: 2.2-inch
WEIGHT: 3,350 pounds
BREECH: vertical sliding block
BARREL LENGTH: 88 inches

ELEVATION: 20°
TRAVERSAL: 360°
PROJECTILE WEIGHT: 6 pounds
MUZZLE VELOCITY: 590 fps
MAXIMUM RANGE: 7,502 yards

6-pdr Nordenfelt Mk1

ADOPTION DATE: 1885
CALIBER: 2.2-inch
WEIGHT: —
BREECH: vertical sliding block
BARREL LENGTH: 92.4 inches

ELEVATION: 20°
TRAVERSAL: 360°
PROJECTILE WEIGHT: 6 pounds
MUZZLE VELOCITY: 1,772 fps
MAXIMUM RANGE: 7,300 yards

4.7-inch Mk2

ADOPTION DATE: 1888
CALIBER: 4.7-inch
WEIGHT: —
BREECH: quick-firing
BARREL LENGTH: 188 inches

ELEVATION: 20°
TRAVERSAL: 360°
PROJECTILE WEIGHT: 45 pounds
MUZZLE VELOCITY: 2,123 fps
MAXIMUM RANGE: 12,992 yards

10-inch Mk3

ADOPTION DATE: 1888
CALIBER: 10-inch
WEIGHT: 291,208 pounds
BREECH: interrupted screw
BARREL LENGTH: 340 inches

ELEVATION: 15°
TRAVERSAL: 360°
PROJECTILE WEIGHT: 500 pounds
MUZZLE VELOCITY: 2,037 fps
MAXIMUM RANGE: 11,483 yards

3-pdr Nordenfelt Mk1

ADOPTION DATE: 1889
CALIBER: 1.8-inch
WEIGHT: —
BREECH: vertical sliding block
BARREL LENGTH: 81 inches

ELEVATION: 9°
TRAVERSAL: 360°
PROJECTILE WEIGHT: 3 pounds
MUZZLE VELOCITY: 2,465 fps
MAXIMUM RANGE: 7,491 yards

13.5-inch Mk3F

ADOPTION DATE: 1892
CALIBER: 13.5-inch
WEIGHT: —
BREECH: interrupted screw
BARREL LENGTH: 405 inches

ELEVATION: 15°
TRAVERSAL: 360°
PROJECTILE WEIGHT: 1,250 pounds
MUZZLE VELOCITY: 2,100 fps
MAXIMUM RANGE: —

12-pdr, 12-cwt Mk1

ADOPTION DATE: 1894
CALIBER: 3-inch
WEIGHT: 9,237 pounds
BREECH: quick-firing
BARREL LENGTH: 120 inches

ELEVATION: 20°
TRAVERSAL: 360°
PROJECTILE WEIGHT: 12.5 pounds
MUZZLE VELOCITY: 2,257 fps
MAXIMUM RANGE: 10,100 yards

6-inch Mk7

ADOPTION DATE: 1898
CALIBER: 6-inch
WEIGHT: 35,896 pounds
BREECH: interrupted screw
BARREL LENGTH: 270 inches

ELEVATION: —
TRAVERSAL: —
PROJECTILE WEIGHT: 100 pounds
MUZZLE VELOCITY: 760 fps
MAXIMUM RANGE: 12,598 yards

4.7-inch Mk5

ADOPTION DATE: 1900
CALIBER: 4.7-inch
WEIGHT: 19,434 pounds
BREECH: quick-firing
BARREL LENGTH: 211.5 inches

ELEVATION: 20°
TRAVERSAL: 360°
PROJECTILE WEIGHT: 45 pounds
MUZZLE VELOCITY: 2,349 fps
MAXIMUM RANGE: 16,500 yards

9.2-inch Mk10

ADOPTION DATE: 1900
CALIBER: 9.2-inch
WEIGHT: 279,987 pounds
BREECH: interrupted screw
BARREL LENGTH: —

ELEVATION: 35°
TRAVERSAL: 360°
PROJECTILE WEIGHT: 379 pounds
MUZZLE VELOCITY: 2,822 fps
MAXIMUM RANGE: 36,691 yards

7.5-inch Mk2

ADOPTION DATE: 1905
CALIBER: 7.5-inch
WEIGHT: 114,255 pounds
BREECH: interrupted screw
BARREL LENGTH: 375 inches

ELEVATION: 20°
TRAVERSAL: 360°
PROJECTILE WEIGHT: 200 pounds
MUZZLE VELOCITY: 2,800 fps
MAXIMUM RANGE: 21,708 yards

9.2-inch High Angle

ADOPTION DATE: 1905
CALIBER: 9.2-inch
WEIGHT: 153,221 pounds
BREECH: interrupted screw
BARREL LENGTH: 294.4 inches

ELEVATION: 45°
TRAVERSAL: 360°
PROJECTILE WEIGHT: 289 pounds
MUZZLE VELOCITY: 2,050 fps
MAXIMUM RANGE: 16,601 yards

4-inch Mk3

ADOPTION DATE: 1906
CALIBER: 4-inch
WEIGHT: 15,512 pounds
BREECH: quick-firing
BARREL LENGTH: 160 inches

ELEVATION: 20°
TRAVERSAL: 360°
PROJECTILE WEIGHT: 25 pounds
MUZZLE VELOCITY: 2,254 fps
MAXIMUM RANGE: 11,200 yards

4-inch Mk5

ADOPTION DATE: 1915
CALIBER: 4-inch
WEIGHT: 25,541 pounds
BREECH: semiautomatic horizontal
    sliding block
BARREL LENGTH: 180 inches

ELEVATION: 20°
TRAVERSAL: 360°
PROJECTILE WEIGHT: 31 pounds
MUZZLE VELOCITY: 2,641 fps
MAXIMUM RANGE: 14,797 yards

GERMANY

283mm SK L/40

ADOPTION DATE: 1901
CALIBER: 283mm
WEIGHT: —
BREECH: horizontal sliding block
BARREL LENGTH: 444 inches

ELEVATION: 45°
TRAVERSAL: 360°
PROJECTILE WEIGHT: 529 pounds
MUZZLE VELOCITY: 2,690 fps
MAXIMUM RANGE: 32,262 yards

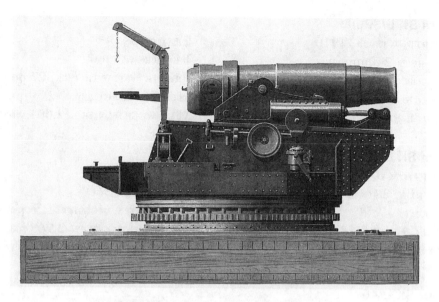

GERMANY: 283MM KÜSTEN HAUBITZE
(Courtesy Art-Tech)

283mm Küsten Haubitze

ADOPTION DATE: 1903
CALIBER: 283mm
WEIGHT: 81,571 pounds
BREECH: horizontal sliding block
BARREL LENGTH: 121 inches

ELEVATION: 70°
TRAVERSAL: 360°
PROJECTILE WEIGHT: 772 pounds
MUZZLE VELOCITY: 1,243 fps
MAXIMUM RANGE: 12,467 yards

283mm SK L/45

ADOPTION DATE: 1907
CALIBER: 283mm
WEIGHT: —
BREECH: horizontal sliding block
BARREL LENGTH: 49.5 inches

ELEVATION: 45°
TRAVERSAL: 360°
PROJECTILE WEIGHT: 626 pounds
MUZZLE VELOCITY: 2,871 fps
MAXIMUM RANGE: 39,479 yards

173mm SK L/40

ADOPTION DATE: 1908
CALIBER: 173mm
WEIGHT: —
BREECH: horizontal sliding block
BARREL LENGTH: 272 inches

ELEVATION: 45°
TRAVERSAL: 360°
PROJECTILE WEIGHT: 138 pounds
MUZZLE VELOCITY: 2,871 fps
MAXIMUM RANGE: 29,746 yards

240mm SK L/35

ADOPTION DATE: 1910
CALIBER: 240mm
WEIGHT: —
BREECH: horizontal sliding block
BARREL LENGTH: 330 inches

ELEVATION: 45°
TRAVERSAL: 360°
PROJECTILE WEIGHT: 327 pounds
MUZZLE VELOCITY: 2,215 fps
MAXIMUM RANGE: 22,091 yards

283mm SK L/50

ADOPTION DATE: 1910
CALIBER: 283mm
WEIGHT: —
BREECH: horizontal sliding block
BARREL LENGTH: 550 inches

ELEVATION: 45°
TRAVERSAL: 360°
PROJECTILE WEIGHT: 626 pounds
MUZZLE VELOCITY: 2,969 fps
MAXIMUM RANGE: 42,760 yards

149mm SK L/40

ADOPTION DATE: 1914
CALIBER: 149mm
WEIGHT: —
BREECH: horizontal sliding block
BARREL LENGTH: 236 inches

ELEVATION: 30°
TRAVERSAL: 360°
PROJECTILE WEIGHT: 100 pounds
MUZZLE VELOCITY: 2,641 fps
MAXIMUM RANGE: 21,872 yards

240mm SK L/40

ADOPTION DATE: 1914
CALIBER: 240mm
WEIGHT: —
BREECH: horizontal sliding block
BARREL LENGTH: 377.6 inches

ELEVATION: 45°
TRAVERSAL: 360°
PROJECTILE WEIGHT: 327 pounds
MUZZLE VELOCITY: 2,657 fps
MAXIMUM RANGE: 29,254 yards

356mm SK L52.5

ADOPTION DATE: 1914
CALIBER: 356mm
WEIGHT: —
BREECH: horizontal sliding block
BARREL LENGTH: 728 inches

ELEVATION: 52°
TRAVERSAL: 360°
PROJECTILE WEIGHT: 1,180 pounds
MUZZLE VELOCITY: —
MAXIMUM RANGE: 55,665 yards

JAPAN

149mm Gun Meiji 45

ADOPTION DATE: 1912
CALIBER: 149mm
WEIGHT: —
BREECH: quick-firing
BARREL LENGTH: 295 inches

ELEVATION: 45°
TRAVERSAL: 360°
PROJECTILE WEIGHT: 123 pounds
MUZZLE VELOCITY: 2,903 fps
MAXIMUM RANGE: 25,973 yards

127mm AA/CD Taisho 3

ADOPTION DATE: 1914
CALIBER: 127mm
WEIGHT: —
BREECH: quick-firing
BARREL LENGTH: 250 inches

ELEVATION: 77°
TRAVERSAL: 360°
PROJECTILE WEIGHT: 51 pounds
MUZZLE VELOCITY: 2,985 fps
MAXIMUM RANGE: 20,177 yards

105mm Gun Taisho 7

ADOPTION DATE: 1918
CALIBER: 105mm
WEIGHT: —
BREECH: semiautomatic horizontal
    sliding block
BARREL LENGTH: 184.5 inches

ELEVATION: 20°
TRAVERSAL: 360°
PROJECTILE WEIGHT: —
MUZZLE VELOCITY: 2,297 fps
MAXIMUM RANGE: 11,100 yards

305mm Howitzer Taisho 7 (Long)

ADOPTION DATE: —
CALIBER: 305mm
WEIGHT: 44,125 pounds
BREECH: interrupted screw
BARREL LENGTH: 288 inches

ELEVATION: 73°
TRAVERSAL: 360°
PROJECTILE WEIGHT: 1,098 pounds
MUZZLE VELOCITY: 1,608 fps
MAXIMUM RANGE: 16,678 yards

305mm Howitzer Taisho 7 (Short)

ADOPTION DATE: 1918
CALIBER: 305mm
WEIGHT: 32,849 pounds
BREECH: interrupted screw
BARREL LENGTH: 192 inches

ELEVATION: 73°
TRAVERSAL: 360°
PROJECTILE WEIGHT: 882 pounds
MUZZLE VELOCITY: 1,299 fps
MAXIMUM RANGE: 12,000 yards

Railway Artillery
UNITED STATES

8-inch Gun M1888M1

ADOPTION DATE: 1918
CALIBER: 8-inch
WEIGHT: 15,813 pounds
BREECH: —
BARREL LENGTH: 256 inches

ELEVATION: 42°
TRAVERSAL: 360°
PROJECTILE WEIGHT: 260.5 pounds
MUZZLE VELOCITY: 2,598 fps
MAXIMUM RANGE: 23,817 yards

10-inch Gun M1888M1

ADOPTION DATE: 1918
CALIBER: 10-inch
WEIGHT: 38,814 pounds
BREECH: —
BARREL LENGTH: 340 inches

ELEVATION: 54°
TRAVERSAL: 0°
PROJECTILE WEIGHT: 511 pounds
MUZZLE VELOCITY: 2,398 fps
MAXIMUM RANGE: 23,926 yards

12-inch Mortar M1890

ADOPTION DATE: 1918
CALIBER: 12-inch
WEIGHT: 17,724 pounds
BREECH: —
BARREL LENGTH: 120 inches

ELEVATION: 65°
TRAVERSAL: 360°
PROJECTILE WEIGHT: 700.5 pounds
MUZZLE VELOCITY: 1,499 fps
MAXIMUM RANGE: 30,896 yards

14-inch Gun M1919

ADOPTION DATE: 1919
CALIBER: 14-inch
WEIGHT: 575,000 pounds
BREECH: —
BARREL LENGTH: 560 inches

ELEVATION: 30°
TRAVERSAL: 10°
PROJECTILE WEIGHT: 1,400 pounds
MUZZLE VELOCITY: —
MAXIMUM RANGE: 42,487 yards

14-inch M1919M1

ADOPTION DATE: 1920
CALIBER: 14-inch
WEIGHT: 730,016 pounds
BREECH: —
BARREL LENGTH: 700 inches

ELEVATION: 50°
TRAVERSAL: 7°
PROJECTILE WEIGHT: 1,200 pounds
MUZZLE VELOCITY: —
MAXIMUM RANGE: 48,228 yards

14-inch M1920M1

ADOPTION DATE: 1920
CALIBER: 14-inch
WEIGHT: 730,016 pounds
BREECH: —
BARREL LENGTH: 700 inches

ELEVATION: 50°
TRAVERSAL: 7°
PROJECTILE WEIGHT: 1,000 pounds
MUZZLE VELOCITY: 2,999 fps
MAXIMUM RANGE: 48,228 yards

AUSTRIA

350mm Railroad M16

ADOPTION DATE: 1916
CALIBER: 350mm
WEIGHT: 451,947 pounds
BREECH: —
BARREL LENGTH: 616.5 inches

ELEVATION: 50°
TRAVERSAL: 360°
PROJECTILE WEIGHT: 1,543 pounds
MUZZLE VELOCITY: —
MAXIMUM RANGE: 32,808 yards

380mm Railroad "Lulo"

ADOPTION DATE: 1917
CALIBER: 380mm
WEIGHT: —
BREECH: —
BARREL LENGTH: 596 inches

ELEVATION: —
TRAVERSAL: —
PROJECTILE WEIGHT: 1,874 pounds
MUZZLE VELOCITY: 2,608 fps
MAXIMUM RANGE: 41,557 yards

GREAT BRITAIN

9.2-inch Gun Mk3

ADOPTION DATE: 1915
CALIBER: 9.2-inch
WEIGHT: 134,394 pounds
BREECH: interrupted screw
BARREL LENGTH: 275 inches

ELEVATION: 35°
TRAVERSAL: 20°
PROJECTILE WEIGHT: 379 pounds
MUZZLE VELOCITY: 2,100 fps
MAXIMUM RANGE:

12-inch Gun Mk9

ADOPTION DATE: 1915
CALIBER: 12-inch
WEIGHT: —
BREECH: interrupted screw
BARREL LENGTH: 480 inches

ELEVATION: 30°
TRAVERSAL: 2°
PROJECTILE WEIGHT: 849 pounds
MUZZLE VELOCITY: 2,500 fps
MAXIMUM RANGE: 32,700 yards

GREAT BRITAIN: 9.2-INCH GUN MK10
(Courtesy Art-Tech)

9.2-inch Gun Mk10

ADOPTION DATE: 1916
CALIBER: 9.2-inch
WEIGHT: 201,613 pounds
BREECH: interrupted screw
BARREL LENGTH: 414 inches

ELEVATION: 30°
TRAVERSAL: 360°
PROJECTILE WEIGHT: 379 pounds
MUZZLE VELOCITY: 2,697 fps
MAXIMUM RANGE: 21,000 yards

12-inch Howitzer Mk1

ADOPTION DATE: 1916
CALIBER: 12-inch
WEIGHT: 129,588 pounds
BREECH: interrupted screw
BARREL LENGTH: 144 inches

ELEVATION: 65°
TRAVERSAL: 40°
PROJECTILE WEIGHT: 750 pounds
MUZZLE VELOCITY: 1,175 fps
MAXIMUM RANGE: 11,133 yards

12-inch Howitzer Mk3

ADOPTION DATE: 1916
CALIBER: 12-inch
WEIGHT: 136,080 pounds
BREECH: interrupted screw
BARREL LENGTH: 204 inches

ELEVATION: 65°
TRAVERSAL: 40°
PROJECTILE WEIGHT: 750 pounds
MUZZLE VELOCITY: 1,470 fps
MAXIMUM RANGE: 15,000 yards

14-inch Gun Mk3 "Boche-Buster"

ADOPTION DATE: 1916
CALIBER: 14-inch
WEIGHT: 555,532 pounds
BREECH: interrupted screw
BARREL LENGTH: 630 inches

ELEVATION: 40°
TRAVERSAL: 4°
PROJECTILE WEIGHT: 1,653 pounds
MUZZLE VELOCITY: 2,448 fps
MAXIMUM RANGE: 21.6 miles

12-inch Gun MkII

ADOPTION DATE: 1918
CALIBER: 12-inch
WEIGHT: 1,091,400 pounds
BREECH: —
BARREL LENGTH: 600 inches

ELEVATION: 45°
TRAVERSAL: 2°
PROJECTILE WEIGHT: 849 pounds
MUZZLE VELOCITY: 2,749 fps
MAXIMUM RANGE: 37,800 yards

18-inch Howitzer Mk1

ADOPTION DATE: 1920
CALIBER: 18-inch
WEIGHT: 781,483 pounds
BREECH: interrupted screw
BARREL LENGTH: 630 inches

ELEVATION: 40°
TRAVERSAL: 4°
PROJECTILE WEIGHT: 2,500 pounds
MUZZLE VELOCITY: 1,900 fps
MAXIMUM RANGE: 22,720 yards

FRANCE

164.7mm Matériel de 164 Mle93/96

ADOPTION DATE: 1912
CALIBER: 164.7mm
WEIGHT: 125,663 pounds
BREECH: —
BARREL LENGTH: 164.7 inches

ELEVATION: 40°
TRAVERSAL: 360°
PROJECTILE WEIGHT: 110 pounds
MUZZLE VELOCITY: 2,723 fps
MAXIMUM RANGE: 21,000 yards

194.4mm Matériel de 194 Mle70/94

ADOPTION DATE: 1914
CALIBER: 194.4mm
WEIGHT: 143,300 pounds
BREECH: interrupted screw
BARREL LENGTH: 182.4 inches

ELEVATION: 40°
TRAVERSAL: 360°
PROJECTILE WEIGHT: 183 pounds
MUZZLE VELOCITY: 2,723 fps
MAXIMUM RANGE: 15,100 yards

240mm Canon de 240 Mle 84

ADOPTION DATE: 1915
CALIBER: 240mm
WEIGHT: 198,416 pounds
BREECH: interrupted screw
BARREL LENGTH: 197.4 inches

ELEVATION: 38°
TRAVERSAL: 360°
PROJECTILE WEIGHT: 350.5 pounds
MUZZLE VELOCITY: 1,886 fps
MAXIMUM RANGE: 19,030 yards

240mm Canon de 240 Mle 93/96

ADOPTION DATE: —
CALIBER: 240mm
WEIGHT: 310,852 pounds
BREECH: interrupted screw
BARREL LENGTH: 291.4 inches

ELEVATION: 35°
TRAVERSAL: 360°
PROJECTILE WEIGHT: 357 pounds
MUZZLE VELOCITY: 2,756 fps
MAXIMUM RANGE: 24,825 yards

305mm Matériel de 305 Mle 93/96

ADOPTION DATE: 1915
CALIBER: 305mm
WEIGHT: —
BREECH: interrupted screw
BARREL LENGTH: 360 inches

ELEVATION: 40°
TRAVERSAL: 0°
PROJECTILE WEIGHT: 767 pounds
MUZZLE VELOCITY: 2,608 fps
MAXIMUM RANGE: 30,000 yards

320mm Matériel de 320 Mle 74

ADOPTION DATE: 1915
CALIBER: 320mm
WEIGHT: 357,149 pounds
BREECH: interrupted screw
BARREL LENGTH: 377.7 inches

ELEVATION: 40°
TRAVERSAL: 0°
PROJECTILE WEIGHT: 855 pounds
MUZZLE VELOCITY: 2,200 fps
MAXIMUM RANGE: 27,000 yards

340mm Matériel de 340 Mle 12

ADOPTION DATE: 1915
CALIBER: 340mm
WEIGHT: —
BREECH: interrupted screw
BARREL LENGTH: 598.5 inches

ELEVATION: 37°
TRAVERSAL: 0°
PROJECTILE WEIGHT: 950 pounds
MUZZLE VELOCITY: 3,000 fps
MAXIMUM RANGE: 41,000 yards

370mm Canon de 370 Mle 75/79

ADOPTION DATE: 1915
CALIBER: 370mm
WEIGHT: 551,155 pounds
BREECH: interrupted screw
BARREL LENGTH: 319.2 inches

ELEVATION: 40°
TRAVERSAL: 0°
PROJECTILE WEIGHT: 1,563 pounds
MUZZLE VELOCITY: 1,969 fps
MAXIMUM RANGE: 26,247 yards

274mm Matériel de 274 Mle 87/93
ADOPTION DATE: 1916
CALIBER: 274mm
WEIGHT: 335,102 pounds
BREECH: interrupted screw
BARREL LENGTH: 485.1 inches

ELEVATION: 40°
TRAVERSAL: 0°
PROJECTILE WEIGHT: 522.5 pounds
MUZZLE VELOCITY: 2,487 fps
MAXIMUM RANGE: 28,900 yards

305mm Canon de 305 Mle 06
ADOPTION DATE: 1916
CALIBER: 305mm
WEIGHT: 392,423 pounds
BREECH: interrupted screw
BARREL LENGTH: 456 inches

ELEVATION: 40°
TRAVERSAL: 0°
PROJECTILE WEIGHT: 855 pounds
MUZZLE VELOCITY: 2,211 fps
MAXIMUM RANGE: 30,730 yards

305mm Matériel de 305 Mle 06/10
ADOPTION DATE: 1916
CALIBER: 305mm
WEIGHT: 458,561 pounds
BREECH: interrupted screw
BARREL LENGTH: 540 inches

ELEVATION: 38°
TRAVERSAL: 0°
PROJECTILE WEIGHT: 760 pounds
MUZZLE VELOCITY: 2,818 fps
MAXIMUM RANGE: 33,683 yards

285mm Canon de 285 Mle 17
ADOPTION DATE: 1917
CALIBER: 285mm
WEIGHT: 335,102 pounds
BREECH: —
BARREL LENGTH: 425.6 inches

ELEVATION: 40°
TRAVERSAL: 0°
PROJECTILE WEIGHT: 595 pounds
MUZZLE VELOCITY: 2,428 fps
MAXIMUM RANGE: 29,965 yards

320mm Canon de 320 Mle 17
ADOPTION DATE: 1917
CALIBER: 320mm
WEIGHT: 392,423 pounds
BREECH: interrupted screw
BARREL LENGTH: 440.65 inches

ELEVATION: 40°
TRAVERSAL: —
PROJECTILE WEIGHT: 864 pounds
MUZZLE VELOCITY: 2,264 fps
MAXIMUM RANGE: 30,840 yards

340mm Canon de 340 Mle 84
ADOPTION DATE: 1917
CALIBER: 340mm
WEIGHT: 412,264 pounds
BREECH: interrupted screw
BARREL LENGTH: 374.64 inches

ELEVATION: 40°
TRAVERSAL: 10°
PROJECTILE WEIGHT: 996.5 pounds
MUZZLE VELOCITY: 1,900 fps
MAXIMUM RANGE: 20,000 yards

340mm Canon de 340 Mle 93

ADOPTION DATE: 1917
CALIBER: 340mm
WEIGHT: 403,446 pounds
BREECH: interrupted screw
BARREL LENGTH: 468.3 inches
ELEVATION: 40°

TRAVERSAL: 10°
PROJECTILE WEIGHT: 1,018.5 pounds
MUZZLE VELOCITY: 2,428 fps
MAXIMUM RANGE: 29,400 yards

370mm Matériel de 370 Mle 15

ADOPTION DATE: 1917
CALIBER: 370mm
WEIGHT: 286,601 pounds
BREECH: interrupted screw
BARREL LENGTH: 362.5 inches

ELEVATION: 65°
TRAVERSAL: 12°
PROJECTILE WEIGHT: 1,138 pounds
MUZZLE VELOCITY: 1,755 fps
MAXIMUM RANGE: 15,967 yards

400mm Matériel de 400 Mle 15/16

ADOPTION DATE: 1917
CALIBER: 400mm
WEIGHT: 308,647 pounds
BREECH: interrupted screw
BARREL LENGTH: 393.5 inches

ELEVATION: 65°
TRAVERSAL: 12°
PROJECTILE WEIGHT: 1,413 pounds
MUZZLE VELOCITY: 1,739 fps
MAXIMUM RANGE: 17,498 yards

520mm Obusier de 520

ADOPTION DATE: 1918
CALIBER: 520mm
WEIGHT: 573,202 pounds
BREECH: interrupted screw
BARREL LENGTH: 389 inches

ELEVATION: 60°
TRAVERSAL: 0°
PROJECTILE WEIGHT: 3,645 pounds
MUZZLE VELOCITY: 1,476 fps
MAXIMUM RANGE: 15,967 yards

GERMANY

170mm K (E) Samuel

ADOPTION DATE: 1916
CALIBER: 173mm
WEIGHT: 132,227 pounds
BREECH: horizontal sliding block
BARREL LENGTH: 272 inches

ELEVATION: 47°
TRAVERSAL: 12°
PROJECTILE WEIGHT: 138 pounds
MUZZLE VELOCITY: 2,674 fps
MAXIMUM RANGE: 26,270 yards

210mm SKL/40 Peter Adalbert

ADOPTION DATE: 1916
CALIBER: 209mm
WEIGHT: —
BREECH: horizontal sliding block
BARREL LENGTH: 328 inches

ELEVATION: 43°
TRAVERSAL: 0°
PROJECTILE WEIGHT: 253.5 pounds
MUZZLE VELOCITY: 2,559 fps
MAXIMUM RANGE: 27,975 yards

380mm SK L/45 "Max"

ADOPTION DATE: 1916
CALIBER: 381mm
WEIGHT: 595,248 pounds
BREECH: horizontal sliding block
BARREL LENGTH: 675 inches

ELEVATION: 55°
TRAVERSAL: 2°
PROJECTILE WEIGHT: 882 pounds
MUZZLE VELOCITY: —
MAXIMUM RANGE: 51,950 yards

350mm K (E)

ADOPTION DATE: 1917
CALIBER: 350mm
WEIGHT: 451,947 pounds
BREECH: horizontal sliding block
BARREL LENGTH: 616.5 inches

ELEVATION: 50°
TRAVERSAL: 360°
PROJECTILE WEIGHT: 1,543 pounds
MUZZLE VELOCITY: —
MAXIMUM RANGE: 32,808 yards

CHAPTER SEVEN SPECIFICATIONS:

1921–1945

Field Artillery
UNITED STATES

75mm Gun Model 1920 MII
ADOPTION DATE: 1920
CALIBER: 75mm
WEIGHT: —
BREECH: —
BARREL LENGTH: —

ELEVATION: —
TRAVERSAL: —
PROJECTILE WEIGHT: —
MUZZLE VELOCITY: —
MAXIMUM RANGE: 15,100 yards

75mm M1897A2 on Carriage M2A2
ADOPTION DATE: 1934
CALIBER: 75mm
WEIGHT: 3,472 pounds
BREECH: Nordenfelt screw
BARREL LENGTH: 120 inches

ELEVATION: 46°
TRAVERSAL: 85°
PROJECTILE WEIGHT: 15 pounds
MUZZLE VELOCITY: 2,182 fps
MAXIMUM RANGE: 14,977 yards

75mm Howitzer M1 on Carriage M3A1
ADOPTION DATE: 1940
CALIBER: 75mm
WEIGHT: 1,885 pounds
BREECH: Nordenfelt screw
BARREL LENGTH: 57 inches

ELEVATION: 49°
TRAVERSAL: 55°
PROJECTILE WEIGHT: 15 pounds
MUZZLE VELOCITY: 1,247 fps
MAXIMUM RANGE: 9,625 yards

Note: — indicates the information is unavailable.

UNITED STATES: 105MM HOWITZER M101 (M2A1)
(Courtesy Art-Tech)

105mm Howitzer M101 (M2A1)

ADOPTION DATE: 1940
CALIBER: 105mm
WEIGHT: 4,475 pounds
BREECH: horizontal sliding block
BARREL LENGTH: 91 inches

ELEVATION: 66°
TRAVERSAL: 46°
PROJECTILE WEIGHT: 33 pounds
MUZZLE VELOCITY: 1,550 fps
MAXIMUM RANGE: 12,250 yards

105mm Howitzer M3A1

ADOPTION DATE: 1942
CALIBER: 105mm
WEIGHT: 2,500 pounds
BREECH: horizontal sliding block
BARREL LENGTH: 74 inches

ELEVATION: 49°
TRAVERSAL: 55°
PROJECTILE WEIGHT: 33 pounds
MUZZLE VELOCITY: 1,017 fps
MAXIMUM RANGE: 8,295 yards

BELGIUM

120mm Gun M32

ADOPTION DATE: 1932
CALIBER: 120mm
WEIGHT: 12,015 pounds
BREECH: horizontal sliding block
BARREL LENGTH: 175 inches

ELEVATION: 40°
TRAVERSAL: 60°
PROJECTILE WEIGHT: 48 pounds
MUZZLE VELOCITY: 2,526 fps
MAXIMUM RANGE: 19,850 yards

GREAT BRITAIN

GREAT BRITAIN: 25-PDR MK2
(Courtesy Art-Tech)

3.4-inch 25-pdr Mk2

ADOPTION DATE: 1940
CALIBER: 3.4-inch
WEIGHT: 3,968 pounds
BREECH: vertical sliding block
BARREL LENGTH: 92 inches

ELEVATION: 40°
TRAVERSAL: 8°
PROJECTILE WEIGHT: 29 pounds
MUZZLE VELOCITY: 1,700 fps
MAXIMUM RANGE: 13,400 yards

3.4-inch 25-pdr Short Mk1

ADOPTION DATE: 1944
CALIBER: 3.4-inch
WEIGHT: 3,009 pounds
BREECH: vertical sliding block
BARREL LENGTH: —

ELEVATION: 40°
TRAVERSAL: 8°
PROJECTILE WEIGHT: 25 pounds
MUZZLE VELOCITY: 1,280 fps
MAXIMUM RANGE: 11,811 yards

3-inch Smith Gun

ADOPTION DATE: 1940
CALIBER: 3-inch
WEIGHT: 604 pounds
BREECH: —
BARREL LENGTH: 54 inches

ELEVATION: 40°
TRAVERSAL: 360°
PROJECTILE WEIGHT: 8 pounds
MUZZLE VELOCITY: 400 fps
MAXIMUM RANGE: 550 yards

CZECHOSLOVAKIA

75mm Field Gun vz35
ADOPTION DATE: 1934
CALIBER: 75mm
WEIGHT: 2,293 pounds
BREECH: horizontal sliding block
BARREL LENGTH: 63 inches

ELEVATION: 45°
TRAVERSAL: 50°
PROJECTILE WEIGHT: 14 pounds
MUZZLE VELOCITY: 1,575 fps
MAXIMUM RANGE: 11,155 yards

76.5mm Field Gun vz30
ADOPTION DATE: 1934
CALIBER: 76.5mm
WEIGHT: —
BREECH: horizontal sliding block
BARREL LENGTH: 120 inches

ELEVATION: 80°
TRAVERSAL: 8°
PROJECTILE WEIGHT: 18 pounds
MUZZLE VELOCITY: 1,970 fps
MAXIMUM RANGE: 14,755 yards

100mm Field Gun vz35
ADOPTION DATE: 1934
CALIBER: 100mm
WEIGHT: 2,300 pounds
BREECH: horizontal sliding block
BARREL LENGTH: 82.5 inches

ELEVATION: 45°
TRAVERSAL: 50°
PROJECTILE WEIGHT: 40 pounds
MUZZLE VELOCITY: 1,575 fps
MAXIMUM RANGE: 11,155 yards

76.5mm Field Gun vz30
ADOPTION DATE: 1934
CALIBER: 76.5mm
WEIGHT: 4,000 pounds
BREECH: horizontal sliding block
BARREL LENGTH: 120 inches

ELEVATION: 80°
TRAVERSAL: 8°
PROJECTILE WEIGHT: 17.6 pounds
MUZZLE VELOCITY: 1,969 fps
MAXIMUM RANGE: 14,764 yards

76.5mm Field Gun vz39

ADOPTION DATE: 1939
CALIBER: 76.5mm
WEIGHT: 3,142 pounds
BREECH: horizontal sliding block
BARREL LENGTH: 90 inches

ELEVATION: 45°
TRAVERSAL: 50°
PROJECTILE WEIGHT: 18 pounds
MUZZLE VELOCITY: 1,870 fps
MAXIMUM RANGE: 13,123 yards

100mm Field Howitzer vz14/19

ADOPTION DATE: 1923
CALIBER: 100mm
WEIGHT: 3,413 pounds
BREECH: horizontal sliding block
BARREL LENGTH: 94 inches

ELEVATION: 50°
TRAVERSAL: 6°
PROJECTILE WEIGHT: 35 pounds
MUZZLE VELOCITY: 1,296 fps
MAXIMUM RANGE: 10,717 yards

100mm Field Howitzer vz30/34

ADOPTION DATE: 1934
CALIBER: 100mm
WEIGHT: 3,893 pounds
BREECH: —
BARREL LENGTH: 98 inches

ELEVATION: 70°
TRAVERSAL: 8°
PROJECTILE WEIGHT: 35 pounds
MUZZLE VELOCITY: 1,411 fps
MAXIMUM RANGE: 13,342 yards

100mm Field Howitzer H3

ADOPTION DATE: 1939
CALIBER: 100mm
WEIGHT: 4,321 pounds
BREECH: —
BARREL LENGTH: 118 inches

ELEVATION: 70°
TRAVERSAL: 50°
PROJECTILE WEIGHT: 35 pounds
MUZZLE VELOCITY: 1,722 fps
MAXIMUM RANGE: 13,342 yards

FRANCE

75mm St. Chamond

ADOPTION DATE: 1923
CALIBER: 75mm
WEIGHT: —
BREECH: vertical sliding block
BARREL LENGTH: —

ELEVATION: 70°
TRAVERSAL: 40°
PROJECTILE WEIGHT: 6.6 pounds
MUZZLE VELOCITY: —
MAXIMUM RANGE: 1,969 yards

105mm Howitzer Mle 35

ADOPTION DATE: 1937
CALIBER: 105mm
WEIGHT: 3,587 pounds
BREECH: horizontal sliding block
BARREL LENGTH: 70 inches

ELEVATION: 70°
TRAVERSAL: 50°
PROJECTILE WEIGHT: 35 pounds
MUZZLE VELOCITY: 1,450 fps
MAXIMUM RANGE: 13,123 yards

105mm Gun Mle 36

ADOPTION DATE: 1937
CALIBER: 105mm
WEIGHT: 7,804 pounds
BREECH: horizontal sliding block
BARREL LENGTH: 157 inches

ELEVATION: 48°
TRAVERSAL: 50°
PROJECTILE WEIGHT: 35 pounds
MUZZLE VELOCITY: 2,379 fps
MAXIMUM RANGE: 17,500 yards

105mm Cannon Court Mle 35B

ADOPTION DATE: 1940
CALIBER: 105mm
WEIGHT: 3,587 pounds
BREECH: —
BARREL LENGTH: 69.29 inches

ELEVATION: 50°
TRAVERSAL: 58°
PROJECTILE WEIGHT: 34.6 pounds
MUZZLE VELOCITY: 1,450 fps
MAXIMUM RANGE: 11,264 yards

45mm Nordenfelt M1923

ADOPTION DATE: 1923
CALIBER: 45mm
WEIGHT: 436.5 pounds
BREECH: Nordenfelt screw
BARREL LENGTH: —

ELEVATION: 45°
TRAVERSAL: 7°
PROJECTILE WEIGHT: 4 pounds
MUZZLE VELOCITY: 1,476 fps
MAXIMUM RANGE: 6,015 yards

GERMANY

75mmm Field Gun FK15nA

ADOPTION DATE: 1933
CALIBER: 75mm
WEIGHT: —
BREECH: horizontal sliding block
BARREL LENGTH: 81 inches

ELEVATION: 44°
TRAVERSAL: 4°
PROJECTILE WEIGHT: 13 pounds
MUZZLE VELOCITY: 2,172 fps
MAXIMUM RANGE: 13,451 yards

75mm FK38

ADOPTION DATE: 1942
CALIBER: 75mm
WEIGHT: 3,009 pounds
BREECH: semiautomatic horizontal
  sliding block
BARREL LENGTH: 75 inches

ELEVATION: 45°
TRAVERSAL: 50°
PROJECTILE WEIGHT: 13 pounds
MUZZLE VELOCITY: 1,985 fps
MAXIMUM RANGE: 12,577 yards

75mm FK7M85

ADOPTION DATE: 1944
CALIBER: 75mm
WEIGHT: 3,009 pounds
BREECH: semiautomatic horizontal
  sliding block
BARREL LENGTH: 99 inches

ELEVATION: 45°
TRAVERSAL: 50°
PROJECTILE WEIGHT: 13 pounds
MUZZLE VELOCITY: —
MAXIMUM RANGE: 12,577 yards

75mm IG18

ADOPTION DATE: 1927
CALIBER: 75mm
WEIGHT: 882 pounds
BREECH: vertical sliding block
BARREL LENGTH: 33 inches

ELEVATION: 75°
TRAVERSAL: 12°
PROJECTILE WEIGHT: 13 pounds
MUZZLE VELOCITY: 2,264 fps
MAXIMUM RANGE: 3,700 yards

GERMANY: 150MM SIG33
(Courtesy Art-Tech)

150mm sIG33

ADOPTION DATE: 1933
CALIBER: 150mm
WEIGHT: 3,750 pounds
BREECH: horizontal sliding block
BARREL LENGTH: —

ELEVATION: 73°
TRAVERSAL: 23°
PROJECTILE WEIGHT: 84 pounds
MUZZLE VELOCITY: 787 fps
MAXIMUM RANGE: 5,140 yards

75mm IG L/13

ADOPTION DATE: 1936
CALIBER: 75mm
WEIGHT: 830 pounds
BREECH: horizontal sliding block
BARREL LENGTH: 39 inches

ELEVATION: 50°
TRAVERSAL: 43°
PROJECTILE WEIGHT: 14 pounds
MUZZLE VELOCITY: 738 fps
MAXIMUM RANGE: 4,200 yards

75mm IG37

ADOPTION DATE: 1944
CALIBER: 75mm
WEIGHT: 1,225 pounds
BREECH: semiautomatic vertical
   sliding block
BARREL LENGTH: 60 inches

ELEVATION: 40°
TRAVERSAL: 58°
PROJECTILE WEIGHT: 12 pounds
MUZZLE VELOCITY: 920 fps
MAXIMUM RANGE: 5,632 yards

75mm IG42

ADOPTION DATE: 1944
CALIBER: 75mm
WEIGHT: 1,300 pounds
BREECH: semiautomatic vertical
  sliding block
BARREL LENGTH: 60 inches

ELEVATION: 32°
TRAVERSAL: 60°
PROJECTILE WEIGHT: 12 pounds
MUZZLE VELOCITY: 920 fps
MAXIMUM RANGE: 5,030 yards

105mm 1eFH18

ADOPTION DATE: 1935
CALIBER: 105mm
WEIGHT: 4,376 pounds
BREECH: horizontal sliding block
BARREL LENGTH: 99 inches

ELEVATION: 40°
TRAVERSAL: 56°
PROJECTILE WEIGHT: 33 pounds
MUZZLE VELOCITY: 1,542 fps
MAXIMUM RANGE: 11,675 yards

105mm 1eFH18M

ADOPTION DATE: 1940
CALIBER: 105mm
WEIGHT: —
BREECH: horizontal sliding block
BARREL LENGTH: 99 inches

ELEVATION: 40°
TRAVERSAL: 56°
PROJECTILE WEIGHT: 31 pounds
MUZZLE VELOCITY: 1,772 fps
MAXIMUM RANGE: 13,479 yards

105mm 1eFH18/40

ADOPTION DATE: 1941
CALIBER: 105mm
WEIGHT: 4,310 pounds
BREECH: horizontal sliding block
BARREL LENGTH: 103 inches

ELEVATION: 40°
TRAVERSAL: 56°
PROJECTILE WEIGHT: 31 pounds
MUZZLE VELOCITY: 1,772 fps
MAXIMUM RANGE: 13,479 yards

105mm 1eFH42

ADOPTION DATE: 1942
CALIBER: 105mm
WEIGHT: 3,594 pounds
BREECH: horizontal sliding block
BARREL LENGTH: 103 inches

ELEVATION: 45°
TRAVERSAL: 70°
PROJECTILE WEIGHT: 33 pounds
MUZZLE VELOCITY: 1,952 fps
MAXIMUM RANGE: 14,217 yards

105mm 1eFH43 (Skoda)

ADOPTION DATE: 1944
CALIBER: 105mm
WEIGHT: 2,001 pounds
BREECH: horizontal sliding block
BARREL LENGTH: 95 inches

ELEVATION: 75°
TRAVERSAL: 360°
PROJECTILE WEIGHT: 33 pounds
MUZZLE VELOCITY: 2,001 fps
MAXIMUM RANGE: 16,404 yards

ITALY

75mm Obice da 75/18 Mo.35

ADOPTION DATE: 1935
CALIBER: 75mm
WEIGHT: 2,425 pounds
BREECH: horizontal sliding block
BARREL LENGTH: 54 inches

ELEVATION: 45°
TRAVERSAL: 50°
PROJECTILE WEIGHT: 14 pounds
MUZZLE VELOCITY: 1,427 fps
MAXIMUM RANGE: 10,280 yards

ITALY: 75/32 MO.37
(Courtesy Art-Tech)

75mm 75/32 Mo.37

ADOPTION DATE: 1937
CALIBER: 75mm
WEIGHT: 2,613 pounds
BREECH: horizontal sliding block
BARREL LENGTH: 96 inches

ELEVATION: 45°
TRAVERSAL: 50°
PROJECTILE WEIGHT: 14 pounds
MUZZLE VELOCITY: 1,970 fps
MAXIMUM RANGE: 13,670 yards

105mm 105/40 Mo.42
ADOPTION DATE: 1942
CALIBER: 105mm
WEIGHT: 8,510 pounds
BREECH: horizontal sliding block
BARREL LENGTH: 165 inches

ELEVATION: 45°
TRAVERSAL: 50°
PROJECTILE WEIGHT: 38.5 pounds
MUZZLE VELOCITY: 2,329 fps
MAXIMUM RANGE: 19,248 yards

JAPAN

37mm Infantry Gun Taisho 11
ADOPTION DATE: 1922
CALIBER: 37mm
WEIGHT: 207 pounds
BREECH: semiautomatic vertical
   sliding block
BARREL LENGTH: 36 inches

ELEVATION: 14°
TRAVERSAL: 33°
PROJECTILE WEIGHT: 1.3 pounds
MUZZLE VELOCITY: 1,476 fps
MAXIMUM RANGE: 5,468 yards

105mm Gun Taisho 14
ADOPTION DATE: 1925
CALIBER: 105mm
WEIGHT: 6,856 pounds
BREECH: quick-firing
BARREL LENGTH: 140 inches

ELEVATION: 43°
TRAVERSAL: 30°
PROJECTILE WEIGHT: 35 pounds
MUZZLE VELOCITY: 2,034 fps
MAXIMUM RANGE: 16,404 yards

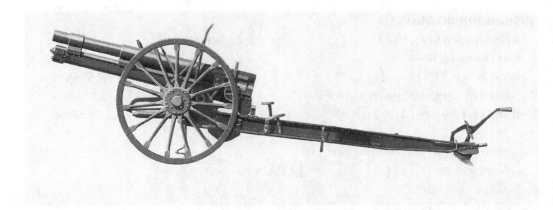

JAPAN: 75MM FIELD GUN
(Courtesy Art-Tech)

75mm Field Gun Model 90

ADOPTION DATE: 1930

CALIBER: 75mm

WEIGHT: 3,087 pounds

BREECH: horizontal sliding block

BARREL LENGTH: 132 inches

ELEVATION: 43°

TRAVERSAL: 43°

PROJECTILE WEIGHT: 14 pounds

MUZZLE VELOCITY: 2,300 fps

MAXIMUM RANGE: 16,350 yards

105mm Gun Model 92

ADOPTION DATE: 1932

CALIBER: 105mm

WEIGHT: 8,201 pounds

BREECH: quick-firing

BARREL LENGTH: 186 inches

ELEVATION: 45°

TRAVERSAL: 36°

PROJECTILE WEIGHT: 35 pounds

MUZZLE VELOCITY: 2,493 fps

MAXIMUM RANGE: 19,958 yards

75mm Field Gun Model 95

ADOPTION DATE: 1935

CALIBER: 75mm

WEIGHT: —

BREECH: horizontal sliding block

BARREL LENGTH: 93 inches

ELEVATION: 43°

TRAVERSAL: 50°

PROJECTILE WEIGHT: 14 pounds

MUZZLE VELOCITY: 2,436 fps

MAXIMUM RANGE: 12,000 yards

105mm Howitzer Model 91

ADOPTION DATE: 1931
CALIBER: 105mm
WEIGHT: 3,296 pounds
BREECH: quick-firing
BARREL LENGTH: 99 inches

ELEVATION: 45°
TRAVERSAL: 40°
PROJECTILE WEIGHT: 35 pounds
MUZZLE VELOCITY: 1,788 fps
MAXIMUM RANGE: 11,773 yards

70mm Infantry Howitzer M92

ADOPTION DATE: 1932
CALIBER: 70mm
WEIGHT: 467 pounds
BREECH: quick-firing
BARREL LENGTH: 25 inches

ELEVATION: 50°
TRAVERSAL: 45°
PROJECTILE WEIGHT: 8 pounds
MUZZLE VELOCITY: 656 fps
MAXIMUM RANGE: 3,062 yards

SOVIET UNION

76.2mm Regimental Gun M27

ADOPTION DATE: 1927
CALIBER: 76.2mm
WEIGHT: 1,927 pounds
BREECH: quick-firing
BARREL LENGTH: 45 inches

ELEVATION: 25°
TRAVERSAL: 6°
PROJECTILE WEIGHT: 14 pounds
MUZZLE VELOCITY: 2,346 fps
MAXIMUM RANGE: 14,873 yards

76.2mm M02/30

ADOPTION DATE: 1930
CALIBER: 76.2mm
WEIGHT: 2,976 pounds
BREECH: quick-firing
BARREL LENGTH: 120 inches

ELEVATION: 37°
TRAVERSAL: 5°
PROJECTILE WEIGHT: 14 pounds
MUZZLE VELOCITY: 2,231 fps
MAXIMUM RANGE: 14,217 yards

SOVIET UNION: 107MM GUN M10/30
(Courtesy Art-Tech)

107mm Gun M10/30

ADOPTION DATE: 1930
CALIBER: 107mm
WEIGHT: 5,247 pounds
BREECH: quick-firing
BARREL LENGTH: 160 inches

ELEVATION: 37°
TRAVERSAL: 6°
PROJECTILE WEIGHT: 38 pounds
MUZZLE VELOCITY: 2,198 fps
MAXIMUM RANGE: 17,880 yards

76.2mm Divisional Gun USV

ADOPTION DATE: 1939
CALIBER: 76.2mm
WEIGHT: 3,272 pounds
BREECH: vertical sliding block
BARREL LENGTH: 126 inches

ELEVATION: 45°
TRAVERSAL: 60°
PROJECTILE WEIGHT: 13.5 pounds
MUZZLE VELOCITY: 2,198 fps
MAXIMUM RANGE: 13,326 yards

107mm Gun M40

ADOPTION DATE: 1940
CALIBER: 107mm
WEIGHT: 8,719 pounds
BREECH: horizontal sliding block
BARREL LENGTH: 185 inches

ELEVATION: 44°
TRAVERSAL: 60°
PROJECTILE WEIGHT: 38 pounds
MUZZLE VELOCITY: 2,362 fps
MAXIMUM RANGE: 19,084 yards

76.2mm Gun M41

ADOPTION DATE: 1941
CALIBER: 76.2mm
WEIGHT: 2,425 pounds
BREECH: vertical sliding block
BARREL LENGTH: 129 inches

ELEVATION: 18°
TRAVERSAL: 54°
PROJECTILE WEIGHT: 13.5 pounds
MUZZLE VELOCITY: 2,231 fps
Maximum range: —

76.2mm Gun ZIS-3

ADOPTION DATE: 1942
CALIBER: 76.2mm
WEIGHT: 2,460 pounds
BREECH: semiautomatic vertical
  sliding block
BARREL LENGTH: 126 inches

ELEVATION: 37°
TRAVERSAL: 54°
PROJECTILE WEIGHT: 13.5 pounds
MUZZLE VELOCITY: 2,231 fps
MAXIMUM RANGE: 14,217 yards

85mm Divisional Gun D-44

ADOPTION DATE: 1944
CALIBER: 85mm
WEIGHT: 3,755 pounds
BREECH: semiautomatic vertical
  sliding block
BARREL LENGTH: 185 inches

ELEVATION: 35°
TRAVERSAL: 54°
PROJECTILE WEIGHT: 21 pounds
MUZZLE VELOCITY: 2,602 fps
MAXIMUM RANGE: 16,951 yards

85mm Divisional Gun D-48

ADOPTION DATE: 1945
CALIBER: 85mm
WEIGHT: 4,630 pounds
BREECH: semiautomatic vertical
  sliding block
BARREL LENGTH: 184 inches

ELEVATION: 40°
TRAVERSAL: 54°
PROJECTILE WEIGHT: 21 pounds
MUZZLE VELOCITY: 2,602 fps
MAXIMUM RANGE: 17,498 yards

122mm Howitzer M1938 (M-30)

ADOPTION DATE: 1938
CALIBER: 122mm
WEIGHT: 4,960 pounds
BREECH: quick-firing
BARREL LENGTH: 110 inches

ELEVATION: 63°
TRAVERSAL: 50°
PROJECTILE WEIGHT: 48 pounds
MUZZLE VELOCITY: 1,640 fps
MAXIMUM RANGE: 12,900 yards

SWEDEN

75mm Gun M02/33

ADOPTION DATE: 1934
CALIBER: 75mm
WEIGHT: 2,976 pounds
BREECH: horizontal sliding block
BARREL LENGTH: 88.5 inches

ELEVATION: 42°
TRAVERSAL: 50°
PROJECTILE WEIGHT: 14 pounds
MUZZLE VELOCITY: 1,772 fps
MAXIMUM RANGE: 12,030 yards

75mm Gun M40

ADOPTION DATE: 1940
CALIBER: 75mm
WEIGHT: 3,307 pounds
BREECH: horizontal sliding block
BARREL LENGTH: 118 inches

ELEVATION: 43°
TRAVERSAL: 50°
PROJECTILE WEIGHT: 14 pounds
MUZZLE VELOCITY: 2,296 fps
MAXIMUM RANGE: 15,311 yards

75mm Light Gun

ADOPTION DATE: 1935
CALIBER: 75mm
WEIGHT: 2,028 pounds
BREECH: semiautomatic horizontal
   sliding block
BARREL LENGTH: 68 inches

ELEVATION: 50°
TRAVERSAL: 6°
PROJECTILE WEIGHT: 14 pounds
MUZZLE VELOCITY: 1,640 fps
MAXIMUM RANGE: 11,159 yards

105mm Gun M28

ADOPTION DATE: 1927
CALIBER: 105mm
WEIGHT: 3,300 pounds
BREECH: quick-firing
BARREL LENGTH: 173 inches

ELEVATION: 45°
TRAVERSAL: 60°
PROJECTILE WEIGHT: 35 pounds
MUZZLE VELOCITY: 2,379 fps
MAXIMUM RANGE: 17,717 yards

105mm Gun L/42

ADOPTION DATE: 1934
CALIBER: 105mm
WEIGHT: 8,267 pounds
BREECH: horizontal sliding block
BARREL LENGTH: 173 inches

ELEVATION: 42°
TRAVERSAL: 60°
PROJECTILE WEIGHT: 34 pounds
MUZZLE VELOCITY: 2,575 fps
MAXIMUM RANGE: 18,920 yards

105mm Gun M37

ADOPTION DATE: 1937
CALIBER: 105mm
WEIGHT: 9,921 pounds
BREECH: horizontal sliding block
BARREL LENGTH: 206 inches

ELEVATION: 45°
TRAVERSAL: 60°
PROJECTILE WEIGHT: 34 pounds
MUZZLE VELOCITY: 2,625 fps
MAXIMUM RANGE: 17,826 yards

105mm Howitzer M40

ADOPTION DATE: 1940
CALIBER: 105mm
WEIGHT: 4,057 pounds
BREECH: horizontal sliding block
BARREL LENGTH: 91 inches

ELEVATION: 45°
TRAVERSAL: 50°
PROJECTILE WEIGHT: 34 pounds
MUZZLE VELOCITY: 1,509 fps
MAXIMUM RANGE: 10,936 yards

SWITZERLAND

75mm Gun M03/22

ADOPTION DATE: 1923
CALIBER: 75mm
WEIGHT: 2,416 pounds
BREECH: horizontal sliding block
BARREL LENGTH: 88.5 inches

ELEVATION: 25°
TRAVERSAL: 8°
PROJECTILE WEIGHT: 14 pounds
MUZZLE VELOCITY: 1,591 fps
MAXIMUM RANGE: 10,936 yards

105mm Gun M35

ADOPTION DATE: 1935
CALIBER: 105mm
WEIGHT: 9,359 pounds
BREECH: horizontal sliding block
BARREL LENGTH: —

ELEVATION: 45°
TRAVERSAL: 60°
PROJECTILE WEIGHT: 33 pounds
MUZZLE VELOCITY: 2,625 fps
MAXIMUM RANGE: 19,138 yards

Mountain Artillery
UNITED STATES

UNITED STATES: 75MM PACK HOWITZER M1
(Courtesy Art-Tech)

75mm Pack Howitzer M1

ADOPTION DATE: 1927
CALIBER: 75mm
WEIGHT: 1,268 pounds
BREECH: horizontal sliding block
BARREL LENGTH: 57 inches

ELEVATION: 45°
TRAVERSAL: 5°
PROJECTILE WEIGHT: 15 pounds
MUZZLE VELOCITY: 1,247 fps
MAXIMUM RANGE: 9,186 yards

CZECHOSLOVAKIA

100mm Mountain Howitzer vz16/19

ADOPTION DATE: 1920
CALIBER: 100mm
WEIGHT: 2,976 pounds
BREECH: horizontal sliding block
BARREL LENGTH: 94 inches

ELEVATION: 70°
TRAVERSAL: 5°
PROJECTILE WEIGHT: 35 pounds
MUZZLE VELOCITY: 1,296 fps
MAXIMUM RANGE: 10,500 yards

FRANCE

75mm Schneider
ADOPTION DATE: 1932
CALIBER: 75mm
WEIGHT: 882 pounds
BREECH: quick-firing
BARREL LENGTH: —

ELEVATION: —
TRAVERSAL: —
PROJECTILE WEIGHT: 14 pounds
MUZZLE VELOCITY: 722 fps
MAXIMUM RANGE: 4,484 yards

GERMANY

75mm Geb K15
ADOPTION DATE: 1925
CALIBER: 75mm
WEIGHT: 1,389 pounds
BREECH: horizontal sliding block
BARREL LENGTH: 45 inches

ELEVATION: 50°
TRAVERSAL: 14°
PROJECTILE WEIGHT: 12 pounds
MUZZLE VELOCITY: 1,266 fps
MAXIMUM RANGE: 7,245 yards

75mm Geb G36
ADOPTION DATE: 1938
CALIBER: 75mm
WEIGHT: 1,654 pounds
BREECH: horizontal sliding block
BARREL LENGTH: 57 inches

ELEVATION: 70°
TRAVERSAL: 40°
PROJECTILE WEIGHT: 12.5 pounds
MUZZLE VELOCITY: 1,558 fps
MAXIMUM RANGE: 10,000 yards

105mm Geb H40
ADOPTION DATE: 1942
CALIBER: 105mm
WEIGHT: 3,527 pounds
BREECH: horizontal sliding block
BARREL LENGTH: 132 inches

ELEVATION: 71°
TRAVERSAL: 51°
PROJECTILE WEIGHT: 32 pounds
MUZZLE VELOCITY: 1,854 fps
MAXIMUM RANGE: 18,307 yards

ITALY

75mm Canone da 75/13 Skoda

ADOPTION DATE: 1922
CALIBER: 75mm
WEIGHT: —
BREECH: horizontal sliding block
BARREL LENGTH: 39 inches

ELEVATION: —
TRAVERSAL: —
PROJECTILE WEIGHT: —
MUZZLE VELOCITY: —
MAXIMUM RANGE: —

75mm Obice da 75/18 Mo.34

ADOPTION DATE: 1935
CALIBER: 75mm
WEIGHT: 1,764 pounds
BREECH: horizontal sliding block
BARREL LENGTH: 54 inches

ELEVATION: 65°
TRAVERSAL: 48°
PROJECTILE WEIGHT: 14 pounds
MUZZLE VELOCITY: 1,427 fps
MAXIMUM RANGE: 9,400 yards

JAPAN

75mm Model 94

ADOPTION DATE: 1934
CALIBER: 75mm
WEIGHT: 1,180 pounds
BREECH: horizontal sliding block
BARREL LENGTH: 63 inches

ELEVATION: 45°
TRAVERSAL: 45°
PROJECTILE WEIGHT: 14 pounds
MUZZLE VELOCITY: 1,263 fps
MAXIMUM RANGE: 9,077 yards

SOVIET UNION

76.2mm Gun M38

ADOPTION DATE: 1938
CALIBER: 76.2mm
WEIGHT: 1,731 pounds
BREECH: —
BARREL LENGTH: 69 inches

ELEVATION: 70°
TRAVERSAL: 10°
PROJECTILE WEIGHT: 13 pounds
MUZZLE VELOCITY: 1,624 fps
MAXIMUM RANGE: 11,046 yards

SWEDEN

90mm Howitzer Bofors

ADOPTION DATE: 1935
CALIBER: 90mm
WEIGHT: 1,742 pounds
BREECH: semiautomatic horizontal
  sliding block
BARREL LENGTH: 60 inches

ELEVATION: 50°
TRAVERSAL: 6°
PROJECTILE WEIGHT: 20 pounds
MUZZLE VELOCITY: 1,148 fps
MAXIMUM RANGE: 8,366 yards

SWITZERLAND

75mm Gun M33

ADOPTION DATE: 1933
CALIBER: 75mm
WEIGHT: 1,741 pounds
BREECH: horizontal sliding block
BARREL LENGTH: 65 inches

ELEVATION: 50°
TRAVERSAL: 6°
PROJECTILE WEIGHT: 14 pounds
MUZZLE VELOCITY: 1,640 fps
MAXIMUM RANGE: 11,483 yards

Antitank Artillery
UNITED STATES

37mm Gun M3

ADOPTION DATE: 1938
CALIBER: 37mm
WEIGHT: 913 pounds
BREECH: vertical sliding block
BARREL LENGTH: 78 inches

ELEVATION: 15°
TRAVERSAL: 60°
PROJECTILE WEIGHT: 1.5 pounds
MUZZLE VELOCITY: 2,897 fps
MAXIMUM RANGE: 12,850 yards

57mm Gun M1

ADOPTION DATE: 1941
CALIBER: 57mm
WEIGHT: 2,809 pounds
BREECH: semiautomatic vertical
  sliding block
BARREL LENGTH: 112 inches

ELEVATION: 15°
TRAVERSAL: 90°
PROJECTILE WEIGHT: 6 pounds
MUZZLE VELOCITY: 2,798 fps
MAXIMUM RANGE: 12,670 yards

3-inch M5

ADOPTION DATE: 1941
CALIBER: 3-inch
WEIGHT: 4,877 pounds
BREECH: horizontal sliding block
BARREL LENGTH: 150 inches

ELEVATION: 30°
TRAVERSAL: 45°
PROJECTILE WEIGHT: 13 pounds
MUZZLE VELOCITY: 2,799 fps
MAXIMUM RANGE: 15,311 yards

90mm T8 Antitank Gun

ADOPTION DATE: 1944
CALIBER: 90mm
WEIGHT: 6,799 pounds
BREECH: semiautomatic horizontal
    sliding block
BARREL LENGTH: 184 inches

ELEVATION: 20°
TRAVERSAL: 60°
PROJECTILE WEIGHT: 24 pounds
MUZZLE VELOCITY: 2,798 fps
MAXIMUM RANGE: 21,435 yards

BELGIUM

47mm FRC

ADOPTION DATE: 1932
CALIBER: 47mm
WEIGHT: 1,252 pounds
BREECH: horizontal sliding block
BARREL LENGTH: 55.5 inches

ELEVATION: 20°
TRAVERSAL: 40°
PROJECTILE WEIGHT: 3.3 pounds
MUZZLE VELOCITY: 2,215 fps
MAXIMUM RANGE: 5,687 yards

GREAT BRITAIN

40mm 2-pdr Mk9

ADOPTION DATE: 1936
CALIBER: 40mm
WEIGHT: 1,755 pounds
BREECH: semiautomatic vertical
    sliding block
BARREL LENGTH: 78.5 inches

ELEVATION: 15°
TRAVERSAL: 360°
PROJECTILE WEIGHT: —
MUZZLE VELOCITY: 2,648 fps
MAXIMUM RANGE: 6,452 yards

57mm 6-pdr, 7-cwt Mk2

ADOPTION DATE: 1941
CALIBER: 57mm
WEIGHT: 2,520 pounds
BREECH: semiautomatic vertical
sliding block
BARREL LENGTH: 96 inches

ELEVATION: 15°
TRAVERSAL: 90°
PROJECTILE WEIGHT: 6 pounds
MUZZLE VELOCITY: 2690 fps
MAXIMUM RANGE: 16,503 yards

3-inch 17-pdr Mk1

ADOPTION DATE: 1942
CALIBER: 3-inch
WEIGHT: 4,623 pounds
BREECH: semiautomatic vertical
sliding block
BARREL LENGTH: 165 inches

ELEVATION: 16.5°
TRAVERSAL: 60°
PROJECTILE WEIGHT: 17 pounds
MUZZLE VELOCITY: 2,900 fps
MAXIMUM RANGE: 10,000 yards

CZECHOSLOVAKIA

40mm vz30

ADOPTION DATE: 1930
CALIBER: 40mm
WEIGHT: —
BREECH: horizontal sliding block
BARREL LENGTH: 111.5 inches

ELEVATION: —
TRAVERSAL: —
PROJECTILE WEIGHT: 2.3 pounds
MUZZLE VELOCITY: 3,117 fps
MAXIMUM RANGE: 9,996 yards

37mm vz34

ADOPTION DATE: 1934
CALIBER: 37mm
WEIGHT: 606 pounds
BREECH: —
BARREL LENGTH: 56.5 inches

ELEVATION: 30°
TRAVERSAL: 50°
PROJECTILE WEIGHT: 2 pounds
MUZZLE VELOCITY: 2,215 fps
MAXIMUM RANGE: 5,468 yards

37mm vz37

ADOPTION DATE: 1937
CALIBER: 37mm
WEIGHT: 816 pounds
BREECH: —
BARREL LENGTH: 70 inches

ELEVATION: 26°
TRAVERSAL: 50°
PROJECTILE WEIGHT: 2 pounds
MUZZLE VELOCITY: 2,461 fps
MAXIMUM RANGE: 5,468 yards

47mm vz39

ADOPTION DATE: 1938
CALIBER: 47mm
WEIGHT: 1,257 pounds
BREECH: —
BARREL LENGTH: 81 inches

ELEVATION: 26°
TRAVERSAL: 50°
PROJECTILE WEIGHT: 3.7 pounds
MUZZLE VELOCITY: 2,543 fps
MAXIMUM RANGE: 6,343 yards

FRANCE

25mm Hotchkiss Mle 34

ADOPTION DATE: 1934
CALIBER: 25mm
WEIGHT: 1,058 pounds
BREECH: semiautomatic vertical
    sliding block
BARREL LENGTH: 88 inches

ELEVATION: 15°
TRAVERSAL: 60°
PROJECTILE WEIGHT: 0.7 pound
MUZZLE VELOCITY: 3,012 fps
MAXIMUM RANGE: 1,914 yards

GERMANY

37mm PaK36

ADOPTION DATE: 1936
CALIBER: 37mm
WEIGHT: 952 pounds
BREECH: horizontal sliding block
BARREL LENGTH: 61 inches

ELEVATION: 25°
TRAVERSAL: 60°
PROJECTILE WEIGHT: 1.5 pounds
MUZZLE VELOCITY: 2,500 fps
MAXIMUM RANGE: 4,402 yards

GERMANY: 50MM PAK38
(Courtesy Art-Tech)

50mm PaK38

ADOPTION DATE: 1940
CALIBER: 50mm
WEIGHT: 2,174 pounds
BREECH: semiautomatic horizontal
    sliding block
BARREL LENGTH: 110 inches

ELEVATION: 27°
TRAVERSAL: 65°
PROJECTILE WEIGHT: 4.8 pounds
MUZZLE VELOCITY: 2,700 fps
MAXIMUM RANGE: 2,898 yards

42mm LePaK41 Taper-bore

ADOPTION DATE: 1941
CALIBER: 42/30mm
WEIGHT: 992 pounds
BREECH: semiautomatic horizontal
    sliding block
BARREL LENGTH: 82.5 inches

ELEVATION: 32°
TRAVERSAL: 60°
PROJECTILE WEIGHT: 0.7 pound
MUZZLE VELOCITY: 4,150 fps
MAXIMUM RANGE: 1,094 yards

75mm PaK41 Squeezebore

ADOPTION DATE: 1942
CALIBER: 75/55mm
WEIGHT: 2,990 pounds
BREECH: semiautomatic horizontal
    sliding block
BARREL LENGTH: 120 inches

ELEVATION: 17°
TRAVERSAL: 60°
PROJECTILE WEIGHT: 16.5 pounds
MUZZLE VELOCITY: 3,691 fps
MAXIMUM RANGE: 4,593 yards

28mm Schweres Panzerbuchse 41

ADOPTION DATE: 1942
CALIBER: 28mm-20mm
WEIGHT: 496 pounds
BREECH: —
BARREL LENGTH: 67 inches

ELEVATION: 45°
TRAVERSAL: 90°
PROJECTILE WEIGHT: .28 pounds
MUZZLE VELOCITY: 4,590 fps
MAXIMUM RANGE: 2,187 yards

75mm PaK40

ADOPTION DATE: 1941
CALIBER: 75mm
WEIGHT: 3,420 pounds
BREECH: horizontal sliding block
BARREL LENGTH: 126 inches

ELEVATION: 65°
TRAVERSAL: 22°
PROJECTILE WEIGHT: 33 pounds
MUZZLE VELOCITY: 1,870 fps
MAXIMUM RANGE: 8,400 yards

75mm PaK97/38

ADOPTION DATE: 1941
CALIBER: 75mm
WEIGHT: 2,624 pounds
BREECH: Nordenfelt screw
BARREL LENGTH: 99 inches

ELEVATION: 25°
TRAVERSAL: 60°
PROJECTILE WEIGHT: 10 pounds
MUZZLE VELOCITY: 2,078 fps
MAXIMUM RANGE: 2,078 yards

76.2mm PaK36(r)

ADOPTION DATE: 1942
CALIBER: 76.2mm
WEIGHT: 3,814 pounds
BREECH: semiautomatic vertical
sliding block
BARREL LENGTH: 114 inches

ELEVATION: 25°
TRAVERSAL: 60°
PROJECTILE WEIGHT: 16.5 pounds
MUZZLE VELOCITY: 2,428 fps
MAXIMUM RANGE: 9,843 yards

88mm PaK43 Panzer
Abwehr Kanone

ADOPTION DATE: 1943
CALIBER: 88mm
WEIGHT: 8,157 pounds
BREECH: semiautomatic vertical
sliding block
BARREL LENGTH: 235 inches

ELEVATION: 40°
TRAVERSAL: 360°
PROJECTILE WEIGHT: 23 pounds
MUZZLE VELOCITY: 3,707 fps
MAXIMUM RANGE: 11 miles

88mm PaK43/41

ADOPTION DATE: 1943
CALIBER: 88mm
WEIGHT: —
BREECH: semiautomatic horizontal
    sliding block
BARREL LENGTH: 235 inches

ELEVATION: 38°
TRAVERSAL: 56°
PROJECTILE WEIGHT: 23 pounds
MUZZLE VELOCITY: 3,281 fps
MAXIMUM RANGE: 19,138 yards

81mm Panzer Abwher Werfer 600

ADOPTION DATE: 1943
CALIBER: 81mm
WEIGHT: 1,323 pounds
BREECH: vertical sliding block
BARREL LENGTH: 111 inches

ELEVATION: 32°
TRAVERSAL: 55°
PROJECTILE WEIGHT: 6 pounds
MUZZLE VELOCITY: 1,706 fps
MAXIMUM RANGE: 6,780 yards

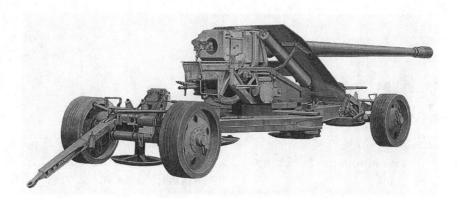

GERMANY: 128MM PAK44
(Courtesy Art-Tech)

128mm PaK44

ADOPTION DATE: 1945
CALIBER: 128mm
WEIGHT: 22,400 pounds
BREECH: semiautomatic horizontal
    sliding block
BARREL LENGTH: 252.5 inches

ELEVATION: 45°
TRAVERSAL: 360°
PROJECTILE WEIGHT: 62 pounds
MUZZLE VELOCITY: 3,281 fps
MAXIMUM RANGE: 26,684 yards

ITALY

47mm Canon da 45/30 Mo.35

ADOPTION DATE: 1935
CALIBER: 47mm
WEIGHT: 584 pounds
BREECH: horizontal sliding block
BARREL LENGTH: 66.5 inches

ELEVATION: 58°
TRAVERSAL: 60°
PROJECTILE WEIGHT: 3.3 pounds
MUZZLE VELOCITY: 2,067 fps
MAXIMUM RANGE: 8,968 yards

47mm Canon da 47/32 Mo.39

ADOPTION DATE: 1939
CALIBER: 47mm
WEIGHT: 611 pounds
BREECH: horizontal sliding block
BARREL LENGTH: 66.5 inches

ELEVATION: 56°
TRAVERSAL: 60°
PROJECTILE WEIGHT: 3.3 pounds
MUZZLE VELOCITY: 2,067 fps
MAXIMUM RANGE: 7,655 yards

JAPAN

37mm Model 94

ADOPTION DATE: 1934
CALIBER: 37mm
WEIGHT: 816 pounds
BREECH: semiautomatic horizontal
    sliding block
BARREL LENGTH: 65 inches

ELEVATION: 27°
TRAVERSAL: 60°
PROJECTILE WEIGHT: 1.5 pounds
MUZZLE VELOCITY: 2,297 fps
MAXIMUM RANGE: 5,031 yards

37mm Model Ra-97

ADOPTION DATE: 1937
CALIBER: 37mm
WEIGHT: 992 pounds
BREECH: semiautomatic horizontal
    sliding block
BARREL LENGTH: 61 inches

ELEVATION: 16°
TRAVERSAL: 90°
PROJECTILE WEIGHT: 2 pounds
MUZZLE VELOCITY: 2,625 fps
MAXIMUM RANGE: 4,374 yards

47mm Model 01

ADOPTION DATE: 1941
CALIBER: 47mm
WEIGHT: 1,665 pounds
BREECH: semiautomatic horizontal
    sliding block
BARREL LENGTH: 120 inches

ELEVATION: 19°
TRAVERSAL: 60°
PROJECTILE WEIGHT: 2.3 pounds
MUZZLE VELOCITY: 2,723 fps
MAXIMUM RANGE: 8,394 yards

SOVIET UNION

45mm M1932

ADOPTION DATE: 1932
CALIBER: 45mm
WEIGHT: 1,124 pounds
BREECH: vertical sliding block
BARREL LENGTH: 81 inches

ELEVATION: 25°
TRAVERSAL: 60°
PROJECTILE WEIGHT: 4.6 pounds
MUZZLE VELOCITY: 2,494 fps
MAXIMUM RANGE: 9,733 yards

45mm M1937

ADOPTION DATE: 1937
CALIBER: 45mm
WEIGHT: 1,120 pounds
BREECH: vertical sliding block
BARREL LENGTH: 64 inches

ELEVATION: 25°
TRAVERSAL: 60°
PROJECTILE WEIGHT: 5.5 pounds
MUZZLE VELOCITY: 2,510 fps
MAXIMUM RANGE: 9,733 yards

45mm M42

ADOPTION DATE: 1942
CALIBER: 45mm
WEIGHT: 1,257 pounds
BREECH: semiautomatic vertical slid-
    ing block
BARREL LENGTH: 117 inches

ELEVATION: 25°
TRAVERSAL: 60°
PROJECTILE WEIGHT: 4.6 pounds
MUZZLE VELOCITY: 2,690 fps
MAXIMUM RANGE: 9,733 yards

57mm ZIS-2

ADOPTION DATE: 1943
CALIBER: 57mm
WEIGHT: 2,535 pounds
BREECH: semiautomatic vertical slid-
    ing block
BARREL LENGTH: 163.5 inches

ELEVATION: 25°
TRAVERSAL: 56°
PROJECTILE WEIGHT: 8.4 pounds
MUZZLE VELOCITY: 3,248 fps
MAXIMUM RANGE: 9,186 yards

100mm Field Gun M1944 (BS-3)

ADOPTION DATE: 1944
CALIBER: 100mm
WEIGHT: 7,617 pounds
BREECH: semiautomatic vertical
    sliding block
BARREL LENGTH: 239 inches

ELEVATION: 45°
TRAVERSAL: 58°
PROJECTILE WEIGHT: 35 pounds
MUZZLE VELOCITY: 2,953 fps
MAXIMUM RANGE: 22,966 yards

85mm Antitank Gun D-48

ADOPTION DATE: 1955
CALIBER: 85mm
WEIGHT: —
BREECH: semiautomatic vertical
    sliding block
BARREL LENGTH: 255.5 inches

ELEVATION: 35°
TRAVERSAL: 54°
PROJECTILE WEIGHT: 21 pounds
MUZZLE VELOCITY: 3,281 fps
MAXIMUM RANGE: 20,746 yards

Antiaircraft Artillery
UNITED STATES

105mm AA M3

ADOPTION DATE: 1927
CALIBER: 105mm
WEIGHT: 33,537 pounds
BREECH: semiautomatic vertical
    sliding block
BARREL LENGTH: 248 inches

ELEVATION: 80°
TRAVERSAL: 360°
PROJECTILE WEIGHT: 33 pounds
MUZZLE VELOCITY: 2,798 fps
MAXIMUM CEILING: 42,000 feet

3-inch M3 Antiaircraft Gun

ADOPTION DATE: 1928
CALIBER: 3-inch
WEIGHT: 12,203 pounds
BREECH: semiautomatic vertical
    sliding block
BARREL LENGTH: 150 inches

ELEVATION: 80°
TRAVERSAL: 360°
PROJECTILE WEIGHT: 12.7 pounds
MUZZLE VELOCITY: 2,800 fps
MAXIMUM CEILING: 31,000 feet

3-inch M4 Antiaircraft Gun

ADOPTION DATE: 1931
CALIBER: 3-inch
WEIGHT: 14,991 pounds
BREECH: semiautomatic vertical
  sliding block
BARREL LENGTH: 165 inches

ELEVATION: 85°
TRAVERSAL: 360°
PROJECTILE WEIGHT: —
MUZZLE VELOCITY: 2,800 fps
MAXIMUM CEILING: 29,035 feet

37mm M1 Antiaircraft Gun

ADOPTION DATE: 1938
CALIBER: 37mm
WEIGHT: 6,124 pounds
BREECH: semiautomatic vertical
  sliding block
BARREL LENGTH: 78 inches

ELEVATION: 90°
TRAVERSAL: 360°
PROJECTILE WEIGHT: 1.3 pounds
MUZZLE VELOCITY: 2,598 fps
MAXIMUM CEILING: 18,602 feet

UNITED STATES: 90MM M1 ANTIAIRCRAFT GUN
(Courtesy Art-Tech)

90mm M1 Antiaircraft Gun

ADOPTION DATE: 1940
CALIBER: 90mm
WEIGHT: 17,754 pounds
BREECH: semiautomatic vertical
  sliding block
BARREL LENGTH: 177 inches

ELEVATION: 80°
TRAVERSAL: 360°
PROJECTILE WEIGHT: 23 pounds
MUZZLE VELOCITY: 2,697 fps
MAXIMUM CEILING: 32,000 feet

120mm Gun M1

ADOPTION DATE: 1943
CALIBER: 120mm
WEIGHT: 48,800 pounds
BREECH: semiautomatic vertical
sliding block
BARREL LENGTH: 283 inches

ELEVATION: 80°
TRAVERSAL: 360°
PROJECTILE WEIGHT: 50 pounds
MUZZLE VELOCITY: —
MAXIMUM CEILING: 57,415 feet

GREAT BRITAIN

4.5-inch Mk2

ADOPTION DATE: 1936
CALIBER: 4.5-inch
WEIGHT: 33,038 pounds
BREECH: semiautomatic horizontal
sliding block
BARREL LENGTH: 202.5 inches

ELEVATION: 80°
TRAVERSAL: 360°
PROJECTILE WEIGHT: 54.4 pounds
MUZZLE VELOCITY: 2,393 fps
MAXIMUM CEILING: 42,585 feet

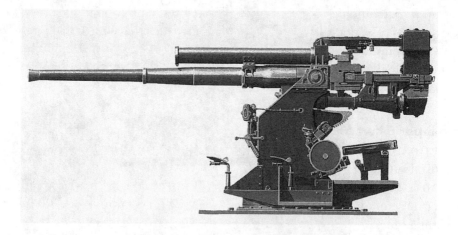

GREAT BRITAIN: 3.7-INCH MK1
(Courtesy Art-Tech)

3.7-inch Mk1

ADOPTION DATE: 1937
CALIBER: 3.7-inch
WEIGHT: 20,540 pounds
BREECH: semiautomatic horizontal
sliding block
BARREL LENGTH: 185 inches

ELEVATION: 80°
TRAVERSAL: 360°
PROJECTILE WEIGHT: 28 pounds
MUZZLE VELOCITY: 3,468 fps
MAXIMUM CEILING: 59,300 feet

40mm 2-pdr Mk8 Twin

ADOPTION DATE: 1939
CALIBER: 40mm
WEIGHT: 16,689 pounds
BREECH: automatic vertical sliding
    block
BARREL LENGTH: 67 inches

ELEVATION: 80°
TRAVERSAL: 360°
PROJECTILE WEIGHT: 2 pounds
MUZZLE VELOCITY: 2,274 fps
MAXIMUM CEILING: 7,200 feet

3.7-inch Mk6

ADOPTION DATE: 1942
CALIBER: 3.7-inch
WEIGHT: 38,360 pounds
BREECH: semiautomatic horizontal
    sliding block
BARREL LENGTH: 240.5 inches

ELEVATION: 80°
TRAVERSAL: 360°
PROJECTILE WEIGHT: 28 pounds
MUZZLE VELOCITY: 3,468 fps
MAXIMUM CEILING: 59,301 feet

5.25-inch Mk2

ADOPTION DATE: 1942
CALIBER: 5.25-inch
WEIGHT: 67,871 pounds
BREECH: semiautomatic horizontal
    sliding block
BARREL LENGTH: 262.5 inches

ELEVATION: 70°
TRAVERSAL: 360°
PROJECTILE WEIGHT: 80 pounds
MUZZLE VELOCITY: 2,800 fps
MAXIMUM CEILING: 55,610 feet

40mm 6-pdr 6-cwt Mk1

ADOPTION DATE: 1944
CALIBER: 40mm
WEIGHT: 24,639 pounds
BREECH: semiautomatic vertical
    sliding block
BARREL LENGTH: 88 inches

ELEVATION: 85°
TRAVERSAL: 360°
PROJECTILE WEIGHT: 6 pounds
MUZZLE VELOCITY: 2,700 fps
MAXIMUM CEILING: —

CZECHOSLOVAKIA

83.5mm Kan PL vz22

ADOPTION DATE: 1925
CALIBER: 83.5mm
WEIGHT: 18,188 pounds
BREECH: semiautomatic horizontal
    sliding block
BARREL LENGTH: 180 inches

ELEVATION: 85°
TRAVERSAL: 360°
PROJECTILE WEIGHT: 22 pounds
MUZZLE VELOCITY: 2,625 fps
MAXIMUM CEILING: 36,098 feet

76.2mm Kan PP Let vz28

ADOPTION DATE: 1928
CALIBER: 76.2mm
WEIGHT: 12,028 pounds
BREECH: —
BARREL LENGTH: 162 inches

ELEVATION: 85°
TRAVERSAL: 360°
PROJECTILE WEIGHT: 17.6 pounds
MUZZLE VELOCITY: 2,625 fps
MAXIMUM CEILING: 37,400 feet

75mm Kan PP Let vz32

ADOPTION DATE: 1932
CALIBER: 75mm
WEIGHT: 5,611 pounds
BREECH: semiautomatic vertical
    sliding block
BARREL LENGTH: 150 inches

ELEVATION: 85°
TRAVERSAL: 360°
PROJECTILE WEIGHT: 14 pounds
MUZZLE VELOCITY: 2,690 fps
MAXIMUM CEILING: 32,000 feet

37mm vz37

ADOPTION DATE: 1938
CALIBER: 37mm
WEIGHT: —
BREECH: semiautomatic vertical
    sliding block
BARREL LENGTH: —

ELEVATION: 85°
TRAVERSAL: 360°
PROJECTILE WEIGHT: 3.3 pounds
MUZZLE VELOCITY: 2,625 fps
MAXIMUM CEILING: 23,294 feet

GERMANY

75mm FlaK38

ADOPTION DATE: 1928
CALIBER: 75mm
WEIGHT: 7,000 pounds
BREECH: horizontal sliding block
BARREL LENGTH: 180 inches

ELEVATION: 85°
TRAVERSAL: 360°
PROJECTILE WEIGHT: 14 pounds
MUZZLE VELOCITY: 2,779 fps
MAXIMUM CEILING: 37,730 feet

88mm FlaK18 and 36

ADOPTION DATE: 1931, 1937
CALIBER: 88mm
WEIGHT: 10,990 pounds
BREECH: semiautomatic horizontal
    sliding block
BARREL LENGTH: 183 inches

ELEVATION: 85°
TRAVERSAL: 360°
PROJECTILE WEIGHT: 21 pounds
MUZZLE VELOCITY: 2,690 fps
MAXIMUM CEILING: 26,247 feet

37mm Flak18, 36, and 37

ADOPTION DATE: 1937
CALIBER: 37mm
WEIGHT: 3,850 pounds
BREECH: automatic
BARREL LENGTH: 123 inches

ELEVATION: 85°
TRAVERSAL: 360°
PROJECTILE WEIGHT: 1.5 pounds
MUZZLE VELOCITY: 2,690 fps
MAXIMUM CEILING: 15,750 feet

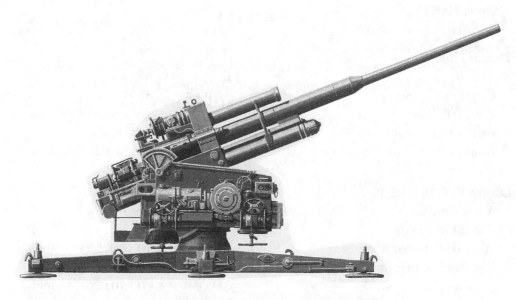

GERMANY: 105MM FLAK38 AND 39
(Courtesy Art-Tech)

105mm Flak38 and 39
ADOPTION DATE: 1938, 1939
CALIBER: 105mm
WEIGHT: 22,540 pounds
BREECH: semiautomatic horizontal
  sliding block
BARREL LENGTH: 219 inches

ELEVATION: 85°
TRAVERSAL: 360°
PROJECTILE WEIGHT: 33 pounds
MUZZLE VELOCITY: 2,890 fps
MAXIMUM CEILING: 37,400 feet

50mm FlaK41
ADOPTION DATE: 1941
CALIBER: 50mm
WEIGHT: 6,834 pounds
BREECH: automatic vertical sliding
  block
BARREL LENGTH: 133 inches

ELEVATION: 90°
TRAVERSAL: 360°
PROJECTILE WEIGHT: 4.8 pounds
MUZZLE VELOCITY: 2,756 fps
MAXIMUM CEILING: 59,528 feet

88mm FlaK41
ADOPTION DATE: 1943
CALIBER: 88mm
WEIGHT: 17,196 pounds
BREECH: semiautomatic horizontal
  sliding block
BARREL LENGTH: 249 inches

ELEVATION: 90°
TRAVERSAL: 360°
PROJECTILE WEIGHT: 21 pounds
MUZZLE VELOCITY: 3,280 fps
MAXIMUM CEILING: 36,213 feet

128mm FlaK40

ADOPTION DATE: 1942
CALIBER: 128mm
WEIGHT: 59,525 pounds
BREECH: semiautomatic horizontal
  sliding block
BARREL LENGTH: 292 inches

ELEVATION: 88°
TRAVERSAL: 360°
PROJECTILE WEIGHT: 57 pounds
MUZZLE VELOCITY: 2,887 fps
MAXIMUM CEILING: 48,556 feet

ITALY

37mm Breda 37/54

ADOPTION DATE: 1925
CALIBER: 37mm
WEIGHT: —
BREECH: vertical sliding block
BARREL LENGTH: 78 inches

ELEVATION: 90°
TRAVERSAL: 360°
PROJECTILE WEIGHT: 1.7 pounds
MUZZLE VELOCITY: 3,625 fps
MAXIMUM CEILING: 13,780 feet

75mm 75/46 Mo.35 Ansaldo

ADOPTION DATE: 1935
CALIBER: 75mm
WEIGHT: 7,385 pounds
BREECH: semiautomatic horizontal
  sliding block
BARREL LENGTH: 138 inches

ELEVATION: 90°
TRAVERSAL: 360°
PROJECTILE WEIGHT: 14 pounds
MUZZLE VELOCITY: 2,346 fps
MAXIMUM CEILING: 30,500 feet

75mm 75/49 Skoda

ADOPTION DATE: 1935
CALIBER: 75mm
WEIGHT: 6,283 pounds
BREECH: vertical sliding block
BARREL LENGTH: 147 inches

ELEVATION: 85°
TRAVERSAL: 360°
PROJECTILE WEIGHT: 14 pounds
MUZZLE VELOCITY: 2.690 fps
MAXIMUM CEILING: 30,000 feet

75mm 75/50 Ansaldo

ADOPTION DATE: 1938
CALIBER: 75mm
WEIGHT: 11,464 pounds
BREECH: semiautomatic horizontal
  sliding block
BARREL LENGTH: 150 inches

ELEVATION: 90°
TRAVERSAL: 360°
PROJECTILE WEIGHT: 14 pounds
MUZZLE VELOCITY: 3.200 fps
MAXIMUM CEILING: 27,559 feet

90mm 90/53 Ansaldo

ADOPTION DATE: 1938
CALIBER: 90mm
WEIGHT: 11,420 pounds
BREECH: —
BARREL LENGTH: —

ELEVATION: 85°
TRAVERSAL: 360°
PROJECTILE WEIGHT: 22 pounds
MUZZLE VELOCITY: 2.756 fps
MAXIMUM CEILING: 39,370 feet

102mm 102/35

ADOPTION DATE: 1938
CALIBER: 102mm
WEIGHT: —
BREECH: —
BARREL LENGTH: 140 inches

ELEVATION: 70°
TRAVERSAL: 360°
PROJECTILE WEIGHT: 29 pounds
MUZZLE VELOCITY: 2.477 fps
MAXIMUM CEILING: 31,168 feet

JAPAN

80mm Taisho 10

ADOPTION DATE: 1921
CALIBER: 80mm
WEIGHT: 5.291 pounds
BREECH: vertical sliding block
BARREL LENGTH: 125.5 inches

ELEVATION: 75°
TRAVERSAL: 360°
PROJECTILE WEIGHT: 13.5 pounds
MUZZLE VELOCITY: 2.231 fps
MAXIMUM CEILING: 25,263 feet

105mm Taisho 14

ADOPTION DATE: 1925
CALIBER: 105mm
WEIGHT: 9,877 pounds
BREECH: semiautomatic horizontal
  sliding block
BARREL LENGTH: 165 inches

ELEVATION: 85°
TRAVERSAL: 360°
PROJECTILE WEIGHT: 35 pounds
MUZZLE VELOCITY: 2,296 fps
MAXIMUM CEILING: 35,925 feet

75mm Model 88

ADOPTION DATE: 1928
CALIBER: 75mm
WEIGHT: 5,379 pounds
BREECH: semiautomatic horizontal
  sliding block
BARREL LENGTH: 132 inches

ELEVATION: 85°
TRAVERSAL: 360°
PROJECTILE WEIGHT: 14 pounds
MUZZLE VELOCITY: 2,362 fps
MAXIMUM CEILING: 29,000 feet

40mm Model 91

ADOPTION DATE: 1931
CALIBER: 40mm
WEIGHT: 1,962 pounds
BREECH: automatic
BARREL LENGTH: 61 inches

ELEVATION: 85°
TRAVERSAL: 360°
PROJECTILE WEIGHT: 1.7 pounds
MUZZLE VELOCITY: 2,000 fps
MAXIMUM CEILING: 12,560 feet

80m Model 99

ADOPTION DATE: 1939
CALIBER: 80mm
WEIGHT: 14,495 pounds
BREECH: semiautomatic vertical
   sliding block
BARREL LENGTH: 141 inches

ELEVATION: 80°
TRAVERSAL: 360°
PROJECTILE WEIGHT: 20 pounds
MUZZLE VELOCITY: 2,625 fps
MAXIMUM CEILING: 32,000 feet

120mm Type 3

ADOPTION DATE: 1943
CALIBER: 120mm
WEIGHT: 48,502 pounds
BREECH: horizontal sliding block
BARREL LENGTH: 307 inches

ELEVATION: 90°
TRAVERSAL: 360°
PROJECTILE WEIGHT: 57 pounds
MUZZLE VELOCITY: 2,805 fps
MAXIMUM CEILING: 48,000 feet

75mm Type 4

ADOPTION DATE: 1944
CALIBER: 75mm
WEIGHT: 7,496 pounds
BREECH: semiautomatic horizontal
   sliding block
BARREL LENGTH: 168 inches

ELEVATION: 85°
TRAVERSAL: 360°
PROJECTILE WEIGHT: 14 pounds
MUZZLE VELOCITY: 2,822 fps
MAXIMUM CEILING: 32,972 feet

150mm Prototype

ADOPTION DATE: 1944
CALIBER: 150mm
WEIGHT: 120,813 pounds
BREECH: horizontal sliding block
BARREL LENGTH: 354 inches

ELEVATION: 85°
TRAVERSAL: 360°
PROJECTILE WEIGHT: 98 pounds
MUZZLE VELOCITY: 3,051 fps
MAXIMUM CEILING: 62,336 feet

SOVIET UNION

76.2mm M31

ADOPTION DATE: 1931
CALIBER: 76.2mm
WEIGHT: 6,063 pounds
BREECH: vertical sliding block
BARREL LENGTH: 165 inches

ELEVATION: 82°
TRAVERSAL: 360°
PROJECTILE WEIGHT: 14 pounds
MUZZLE VELOCITY: 2,674 fps
MAXIMUM CEILING: 31,168 feet

76.2mm M38

ADOPTION DATE: 1938
CALIBER: 76.2mm
WEIGHT: 9,480 pounds
BREECH: semiautomatic vertical
    sliding block
BARREL LENGTH: 165 inches

ELEVATION: 82°
TRAVERSAL: 360°
PROJECTILE WEIGHT: 14 pounds
MUZZLE VELOCITY: 2,674 fps
MAXIMUM CEILING: 31,168 feet

37mm Gun M39

ADOPTION DATE: 1939
CALIBER: 37mm
WEIGHT: 4,409 pounds
BREECH: vertical sliding block
BARREL LENGTH: 53.5 inches

ELEVATION: 85°
TRAVERSAL: 360°
PROJECTILE WEIGHT: 1.5 pounds
MUZZLE VELOCITY: 3,150 fps
MAXIMUM CEILING: 19,685 feet

85mm M39

ADOPTION DATE: 1939
CALIBER: 85mm
WEIGHT: 9,480 pounds
BREECH: semiautomatic vertical
    sliding block
BARREL LENGTH: 184 inches

ELEVATION: 82°
TRAVERSAL: 360°
PROJECTILE WEIGHT: 20 pounds
MUZZLE VELOCITY: 2,625 fps
MAXIMUM CEILING: 27,165 feet

SOVIET UNION: 85MM M44

(Courtesy Art-Tech)

85mm M44

ADOPTION DATE: 1944
CALIBER: 85mm
WEIGHT: 10,781 pounds
BREECH: semiautomatic vertical
   sliding block
BARREL LENGTH: —

ELEVATION: —
TRAVERSAL: —
PROJECTILE WEIGHT: 20 pounds
MUZZLE VELOCITY: 2,953 fps
MAXIMUM CEILING: 33,465 feet

SWEDEN

SWEDEN: 40MM L/60 (M33)
(Courtesy Art-Tech)

40mm L/60 Bofors (M33)

ADOPTION DATE: 1933
CALIBER: 40mm
WEIGHT: 3,814 pounds
BREECH: automatic vertical sliding
block
BARREL LENGTH: 94 inches

ELEVATION: 90°
TRAVERSAL: 360°
PROJECTILE WEIGHT: 2 pounds
MUZZLE VELOCITY: 2,953 fps
MAXIMUM CEILING: 7,200 feet

75mm L/52 Bofors

ADOPTION DATE: 1936
CALIBER: 75mm
WEIGHT: 8,819 pounds
BREECH: semiautomatic horizontal
sliding block
BARREL LENGTH: 153 inches

ELEVATION: 85°
TRAVERSAL: 360°
PROJECTILE WEIGHT: 14 pounds
MUZZLE VELOCITY: 2,756 fps
MAXIMUM CEILING: 39,370 feet

80mm L/50 Bofors

ADOPTION DATE: 1936
CALIBER: 80mm
WEIGHT: 7,716 pounds
BREECH: semiautomatic horizontal
   sliding block
BARREL LENGTH: 157 inches

ELEVATION: 85°
TRAVERSAL: 360°
PROJECTILE WEIGHT: 17.5 pounds
MUZZLE VELOCITY: —
MAXIMUM CEILING: 49,213 feet

Heavy Artillery
UNITED STATES

UNITED STATES: 8-INCH HOWITZER M1 (M115)
(Courtesy Art-Tech)

8-inch Howitzer M1 (M115)

ADOPTION DATE: 1940
CALIBER: 8-inch
WEIGHT: 29,701 pounds
BREECH: interrupted screw
BARREL LENGTH: 200 inches

ELEVATION: 65°
TRAVERSAL: 60°
PROJECTILE WEIGHT: 95 pounds
MUZZLE VELOCITY: 2,245 fps
MAXIMUM RANGE: 19,794 yards

UNITED STATES: 155MM GUN M1 "LONG TOM"
(Courtesy Art-Tech)

155mm Gun M1 "Long Tom"
ADOPTION DATE: 1938
CALIBER: 155mm
WEIGHT: 28,000 pounds
BREECH: interrupted screw
BARREL LENGTH: 275 inches

ELEVATION: 63°
TRAVERSAL: 60°
PROJECTILE WEIGHT: 96 pounds
MUZZLE VELOCITY: 2,800 fps
MAXIMUM RANGE: 25,700 yards

4.5-inch Gun M1
ADOPTION DATE: 1941
CALIBER: 4.5-inch
WEIGHT: 12,070 pounds
BREECH: interrupted screw
BARREL LENGTH: 193.5 inches

ELEVATION: 65°
TRAVERSAL: 53°
PROJECTILE WEIGHT: 55 pounds
MUZZLE VELOCITY: 2,264 fps
MAXIMUM RANGE: 20,505 yards

8-inch Gun M1
ADOPTION DATE: 1943
CALIBER: 8-inch
WEIGHT: 69,302 pounds
BREECH: interrupted screw
BARREL LENGTH: 400 inches

ELEVATION: 50°
TRAVERSAL: 30°
PROJECTILE WEIGHT: 240 pounds
MUZZLE VELOCITY: 2,838 fps
MAXIMUM RANGE: 35,357 yards

155mm Howitzer M1 (M114)
ADOPTION DATE: 1941
CALIBER: 155mm
WEIGHT: 12,700 pounds
BREECH: interrupted screw
BARREL LENGTH: 149 inches

ELEVATION: 65°
TRAVERSAL: 50°
PROJECTILE WEIGHT: 95 pounds
MUZZLE VELOCITY: 2,089 fps
MAXIMUM RANGE: 15,966 yards

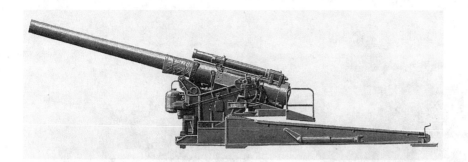

UNITED STATES: 240MM HOWITZER M1
(Courtesy Art-Tech)

240mm Howitzer M1

ADOPTION DATE: 1943
CALIBER: 240mm
WEIGHT: 64,706 pounds
BREECH: interrupted screw
BARREL LENGTH: 330 inches

ELEVATION: —
TRAVERSAL: —
PROJECTILE WEIGHT: 360 pounds
MUZZLE VELOCITY: 2,297 fps
MAXIMUM RANGE: 25,224 yards

BELGIUM

155mm Howitzer M24

ADOPTION DATE: 1924
CALIBER: 155mm
WEIGHT: 38,105 pounds
BREECH: interrupted screw
BARREL LENGTH: 180 inches

ELEVATION: 45°
TRAVERSAL: 8°
PROJECTILE WEIGHT: 95 pounds
MUZZLE VELOCITY: 2,182 fps
MAXIMUM RANGE: 18,591 yards

GREAT BRITAIN

4.5-inch Gun Mk2

ADOPTION DATE: 1939
CALIBER: 4.5-inch
WEIGHT: 12,086 pounds
BREECH: interrupted screw
BARREL LENGTH: 184.5 inches

ELEVATION: 45°
TRAVERSAL: 60°
PROJECTILE WEIGHT: 55 pounds
MUZZLE VELOCITY: 2,247 fps
MAXIMUM RANGE: 20,500 yards

GREAT BRITAIN: 5.5-INCH GUN MK3
(Courtesy Art-Tech)

5.5-inch Gun Mk3

ADOPTION DATE: 1941
CALIBER: 5.5-inch
WEIGHT: 13,647 pounds
BREECH: interrupted screw
BARREL LENGTH: 165 inches

ELEVATION: 45°
TRAVERSAL: 60°
PROJECTILE WEIGHT: 100 pounds
MUZZLE VELOCITY: 1,673 fps
MAXIMUM RANGE: 16,196 yards

7.2-inch Howitzer Mk1

ADOPTION DATE: 1941
CALIBER: 7.2-inch
WEIGHT: 22,758 pounds
BREECH: interrupted screw
BARREL LENGTH: 158.4 inches

ELEVATION: 45°
TRAVERSAL: 8°
PROJECTILE WEIGHT: 213 pounds
MUZZLE VELOCITY: 1,700 fps
MAXIMUM RANGE: 16,896 yards

7.2-inch Howitzer Mk6

ADOPTION DATE: 1943
CALIBER: 7.2-inch
WEIGHT: 32,562 pounds
BREECH: interrupted screw
BARREL LENGTH: 237.6 inches

ELEVATION: 63°
TRAVERSAL: 60°
PROJECTILE WEIGHT: 202 pounds
MUZZLE VELOCITY: 1,922 fps
MAXIMUM RANGE: 19,603 yards

CZECHOSLOVAKIA

149mm Howitzer vz25

ADOPTION DATE: 1925
CALIBER: 149mm
WEIGHT: 8,378 pounds
BREECH: —
BARREL LENGTH: 105 inches

ELEVATION: 70°
TRAVERSAL: 7°
PROJECTILE WEIGHT: 92.5 pounds
MUZZLE VELOCITY: 1,476 fps
MAXIMUM RANGE: 12,905 yards

149mm Howitzer vz37

ADOPTION DATE: 1937
CALIBER: 149mm
WEIGHT: 11,464 pounds
BREECH: interrupted screw
BARREL LENGTH: 140.5 inches

ELEVATION: 70°
TRAVERSAL: 45°
PROJECTILE WEIGHT: 92.5 pounds
MUZZLE VELOCITY: 1,903 fps
MAXIMUM RANGE: 16,514 yards

FRANCE

155mm Gun Mle 32

ADOPTION DATE: 1933
CALIBER: 155mm
WEIGHT: 36,156 pounds
BREECH: interrupted screw
BARREL LENGTH: 305 inches

ELEVATION: 45°
TRAVERSAL: 360°
PROJECTILE WEIGHT: 110 pounds
MUZZLE VELOCITY: 2,953 fps
MAXIMUM RANGE: 28,434 yards

155mm Howitzer Mle 29

ADOPTION DATE: 1930
CALIBER: 155mm
WEIGHT: 11,387 pounds
BREECH: interrupted screw
BARREL LENGTH: 134 inches

ELEVATION: 45°
TRAVERSAL: 40°
PROJECTILE WEIGHT: 85 pounds
MUZZLE VELOCITY: 2,083 fps
MAXIMUM RANGE: 16,404 yards

GERMANY

105mm sK18

ADOPTION DATE: 1934
CALIBER: 105mm
WEIGHT: 12,438 pounds
BREECH: horizontal sliding block
BARREL LENGTH: 206.5 inches

ELEVATION: 48°
TRAVERSAL: 64°
PROJECTILE WEIGHT: 33 pounds
MUZZLE VELOCITY: 2,740 fps
MAXIMUM RANGE: 20,861 yards

238mm KL/46

ADOPTION DATE: 1937
CALIBER: 238mm
WEIGHT: 99,649 pounds
BREECH: horizontal sliding block
BARREL LENGTH: 412.5 inches

ELEVATION: 45°
TRAVERSAL: 360°
PROJECTILE WEIGHT: 397 pounds
MUZZLE VELOCITY: 2,789 fps
MAXIMUM RANGE: 35,000 yards

150mm K18

ADOPTION DATE: 1938
CALIBER: 150mm
WEIGHT: —
BREECH: horizontal sliding block
BARREL LENGTH: 254 inches

ELEVATION: 45°
TRAVERSAL: 10°
PROJECTILE WEIGHT: 95 pounds
MUZZLE VELOCITY: 2,920 fps
MAXIMUM RANGE: 26,794 yards

240mm K3

ADOPTION DATE: 1938
CALIBER: 240mm
WEIGHT: 120,959 pounds
BREECH: horizontal sliding block
BARREL LENGTH: 491 inches

ELEVATION: 56°
TRAVERSAL: 360°
PROJECTILE WEIGHT: 334 pounds
MUZZLE VELOCITY: 3,182 fps
MAXIMUM RANGE: 19,138 yards

149mm K39

ADOPTION DATE: 1940
CALIBER: 149mm
WEIGHT: 26,896 pounds
BREECH: horizontal sliding block
BARREL LENGTH: 98.5 inches

ELEVATION: 46°
TRAVERSAL: 60°
PROJECTILE WEIGHT: 95 pounds
MUZZLE VELOCITY: 2,838 fps
MAXIMUM RANGE: 27,000 yards

105mm sK18/40

ADOPTION DATE: 1941
CALIBER: 105mm
WEIGHT: 12,522 pounds
BREECH: horizontal sliding block
BARREL LENGTH: 190 inches

ELEVATION: 45°
TRAVERSAL: 56°
PROJECTILE WEIGHT: 33 pounds
MUZZLE VELOCITY: 2,805 fps
MAXIMUM RANGE: 22,800 yards

149mm SKC/28 in Mörserlaf

ADOPTION DATE: 1941
CALIBER: 149mm
WEIGHT: 37,192 pounds
BREECH: horizontal sliding block
BARREL LENGTH: 310.5 inches

ELEVATION: 50°
TRAVERSAL: 16°
PROJECTILE WEIGHT: 95 pounds
MUZZLE VELOCITY: 2,920 fps
MAXIMUM RANGE: 25,900 yards

GERMANY: 173MM K18 IN MÖRSERLAF
(Courtesy Art-Tech)

173mm K18 in Mörserlaf

ADOPTION DATE: 1941
CALIBER: 173mm
WEIGHT: 38,625 pounds
BREECH: horizontal sliding block
BARREL LENGTH: 320 inches

ELEVATION: 50°
TRAVERSAL: 16°
PROJECTILE WEIGHT: 138 pounds
MUZZLE VELOCITY: 3,035 fps
MAXIMUM RANGE: 25,520 yards

211mm K38

ADOPTION DATE: 1943
CALIBER: 211mm
WEIGHT: 55,777 pounds
BREECH: horizontal sliding block
BARREL LENGTH: 432 inches

ELEVATION: 50°
TRAVERSAL: 17°
PROJECTILE WEIGHT: 264.5 pounds
MUZZLE VELOCITY: 2,969 fps
MAXIMUM RANGE: 37,000 yards

210mm K39

ADOPTION DATE: 1943
CALIBER: 210mm
WEIGHT: 74,516 pounds
BREECH: interrupted screw
BARREL LENGTH: 289 inches

ELEVATION: 45°
TRAVERSAL: 360°
PROJECTILE WEIGHT: 297.5 pounds
MUZZLE VELOCITY: 2,625 fps
MAXIMUM RANGE: 32,800 yards

150mm sFH18

ADOPTION DATE: 1934
CALIBER: 150mm
WEIGHT: 12,152 pounds
BREECH: horizontal sliding block
BARREL LENGTH: 159 inches

ELEVATION: 45°
TRAVERSAL: 64°
PROJECTILE WEIGHT: 96 pounds
MUZZLE VELOCITY: 1,624 fps
MAXIMUM RANGE: 14,490 yards

150mm sFH36

ADOPTION DATE: 1938
CALIBER: 150mm
WEIGHT: 7,231 pounds
BREECH: horizontal sliding block
BARREL LENGTH: 94 inches

ELEVATION: 45°
TRAVERSAL: 56°
PROJECTILE WEIGHT: 96 pounds
MUZZLE VELOCITY: 1,591 fps
MAXIMUM RANGE: 13,451 yards

211mm Mörser 18

ADOPTION DATE: 1939
CALIBER: 211mm
WEIGHT: 36,817 pounds
BREECH: horizontal sliding block
BARREL LENGTH: 232 inches

ELEVATION: 70°
TRAVERSAL: 16°
PROJECTILE WEIGHT: 293 pounds
MUZZLE VELOCITY: 1,853 fps
MAXIMUM RANGE: 18,263 yards

356mm H M1

ADOPTION DATE: 1939
CALIBER: 356mm
WEIGHT: 165,347 pounds
BREECH: horizontal sliding block
BARREL LENGTH: 308 inches

ELEVATION: 75°
TRAVERSAL: 360°
PROJECTILE WEIGHT: 1,268 pounds
MUZZLE VELOCITY: 1,870 fps
MAXIMUM RANGE: 21,872 yards

538mm SP Mrs Karl

ADOPTION DATE: 1939
CALIBER: 538mm
WEIGHT: 271,168 pounds
BREECH: horizontal sliding block
BARREL LENGTH: 233 inches

ELEVATION: 70°
TRAVERSAL: 5°
PROJECTILE WEIGHT: 2,749 pounds
MUZZLE VELOCITY: 984 fps
MAXIMUM RANGE: 13,670 yards

598mm SP Mrs Karl

ADOPTION DATE: 1939
CALIBER: 598mm
WEIGHT: 271,168 pounds
BREECH: —
BARREL LENGTH: 165 inches

ELEVATION: 75°
TRAVERSAL: 4°
PROJECTILE WEIGHT: 3,475 pounds
MUZZLE VELOCITY: 935 fps
MAXIMUM RANGE: 7,300 yards

240mm H39

ADOPTION DATE: 1940
CALIBER: 240mm
WEIGHT: 59,525 pounds
BREECH: interrupted screw
BARREL LENGTH: 236 inches

ELEVATION: 70°
TRAVERSAL: 360°
PROJECTILE WEIGHT: 366 pounds
MUZZLE VELOCITY: 1,968 fps
MAXIMUM RANGE: 19,685 yards

150mm Hochdruckpumpe

ADOPTION DATE: 1943
CALIBER: 150mm
WEIGHT: —
BREECH: —
BARREL LENGTH: 492 feet

ELEVATION: —
TRAVERSAL: —
PROJECTILE WEIGHT: 308.5 pounds
MUZZLE VELOCITY: 4,921 fps
MAXIMUM RANGE: 18,045 yards

ITALY

149mm Canone da 149/40 Mo.35

ADOPTION DATE: 1935
CALIBER: 149mm
WEIGHT: 25,309 pounds
BREECH: interrupted screw
BARREL LENGTH: 234 inches

ELEVATION: 45°
TRAVERSAL: 60°
PROJECTILE WEIGHT: 112 pounds
MUZZLE VELOCITY: 2,625 fps
MAXIMUM RANGE: 24,060 yards

210mm Obice da 210/22 Mo.35 Howitzer

ADOPTION DATE: 1934
CALIBER: 210mm
WEIGHT: 34,833 pounds
BREECH: interrupted screw
BARREL LENGTH: 182 inches

ELEVATION: 70°
TRAVERSAL: 30°
PROJECTILE WEIGHT: 225 pounds
MUZZLE VELOCITY: 1,870 fps
MAXIMUM RANGE: 17,500 yards

JAPAN

150mm Gun Model 89

ADOPTION DATE: 1929
CALIBER: 150mm
WEIGHT: 22,928 pounds
BREECH: interrupted screw
BARREL LENGTH: —

ELEVATION: —
TRAVERSAL: —
PROJECTILE WEIGHT: 101 pounds
MUZZLE VELOCITY: 2,247 fps
MAXIMUM RANGE: 21,763 yards

150mm Howitzer Model 96

ADOPTION DATE: 1936
CALIBER: 150mm
WEIGHT: 9,116 pounds
BREECH: quick-firing
BARREL LENGTH: 130 inches

ELEVATION: 65°
TRAVERSAL: 30°
PROJECTILE WEIGHT: 69 pounds
MUZZLE VELOCITY: 2,641 fps
MAXIMUM RANGE: 12,959 yards

410mm Siege Howitzer

ADOPTION DATE: —
CALIBER: 410mm
WEIGHT: 179,192 pounds
BREECH: interrupted screw
BARREL LENGTH: 484 inches

ELEVATION: 45°
TRAVERSAL: 360°
PROJECTILE WEIGHT: 2,198 pounds
MUZZLE VELOCITY: 1,755 fps
MAXIMUM RANGE: 21,194 yards

SOVIET UNION

152mm Gun M10/30

ADOPTION DATE: 1930
CALIBER: 152mm
WEIGHT: 14,771 pounds
BREECH: interrupted screw
BARREL LENGTH: 167 inches

ELEVATION: 37°
TRAVERSAL: 5°
PROJECTILE WEIGHT: 96 pounds
MUZZLE VELOCITY: 2,133 fps
MAXIMUM RANGE: 18,700 yards

152mm Gun M10/34

ADOPTION DATE: 1934
CALIBER: 152mm
WEIGHT: 15,653 pounds
BREECH: vertical sliding block
BARREL LENGTH: 173 inches

ELEVATION: 45°
TRAVERSAL: 58°
PROJECTILE WEIGHT: 96 pounds
MUZZLE VELOCITY: 2,150 fps
MAXIMUM RANGE: 17,717 yards

152mm Gun BR-2

ADOPTION DATE: 1935
CALIBER: 152mm
WEIGHT: 40,455 pounds
BREECH: interrupted screw
BARREL LENGTH: 269 inches

ELEVATION: 60°
TRAVERSAL: 8°
PROJECTILE WEIGHT: 108 pounds
MUZZLE VELOCITY: 2,887 fps
MAXIMUM RANGE: 29,500 yards

152mm Gun-Howitzer ML-20

ADOPTION DATE: 1937
CALIBER: 152mm
WEIGHT: 15,719 pounds
BREECH: interrupted screw
BARREL LENGTH: 173 inches

ELEVATION: 65°
TRAVERSAL: 58°
PROJECTILE WEIGHT: 95.5 pounds
MUZZLE VELOCITY: 2,149 fps
MAXIMUM RANGE: 18,898 yards

122mm Corps Gun M31/37 (A-19)

ADOPTION DATE: 1938
CALIBER: 122mm
WEIGHT: 15,697 pounds
BREECH: quick-firing
BARREL LENGTH: 216 inches

ELEVATION: 65°
TRAVERSAL: 58°
PROJECTILE WEIGHT: 55 pounds
MUZZLE VELOCITY: 2,625 fps
MAXIMUM RANGE: 22,747 yards

122mm Howitzer M1938 (M-30)

ADOPTION DATE: 1939
CALIBER: 122mm
WEIGHT: 5,401 pounds
BREECH: hinged screw
BARREL LENGTH: 110 inches

ELEVATION: 63.5°
TRAVERSAL: 49°
PROJECTILE WEIGHT: 48 pounds
MUZZLE VELOCITY: 1,690 fps
MAXIMUM RANGE: —

210mm Gun M39/40

ADOPTION DATE: 1940
CALIBER: 210mm
WEIGHT: 95,196 pounds
BREECH: interrupted screw
BARREL LENGTH: 396.5 inches

ELEVATION: 50°
TRAVERSAL: 22°
PROJECTILE WEIGHT: 297 pounds
MUZZLE VELOCITY: 2,625 fps
MAXIMUM RANGE: 33,279 yards

203mm Howitzer L-25

ADOPTION DATE: 1931
CALIBER: 203mm
WEIGHT: 39,022 pounds
BREECH: interrupted screw
BARREL LENGTH: 200 inches

ELEVATION: 60°
TRAVERSAL: 8°
PROJECTILE WEIGHT: 217 pounds
MUZZLE VELOCITY: 1,988 fps
MAXIMUM RANGE: 19,685 yards

152mm Howitzer M-10

ADOPTION DATE: 1938
CALIBER: 152mm
WEIGHT: 9,182 pounds
BREECH: quick-firing
BARREL LENGTH: 149.5 inches

ELEVATION: 65°
TRAVERSAL: 50°
PROJECTILE WEIGHT: 88 pounds
MUZZLE VELOCITY: 1,667 fps
MAXIMUM RANGE: 13,561 yards

305mm Howitzer BR-18

ADOPTION DATE: 1940
CALIBER: 305mm
WEIGHT: 136,929 pounds
BREECH: interrupted screw
BARREL LENGTH: 264 inches

ELEVATION: 77°
TRAVERSAL: 360°
PROJECTILE WEIGHT: 727.5 pounds
MUZZLE VELOCITY: 1,739 fps
MAXIMUM RANGE: 17,935 yards

152mm Howitzer D-1

ADOPTION DATE: 1943
CALIBER: 152mm
WEIGHT: 7,937 pounds
BREECH: —
BARREL LENGTH: 137.5 inches

ELEVATION: 63°
TRAVERSAL: 35°
PROJECTILE WEIGHT: 88 pounds
MUZZLE VELOCITY: 1,673 fps
MAXIMUM RANGE: 13,561 yards

Coastal Artillery
UNITED STATES

16-inch Gun M1919 MII

ADOPTION DATE: 1923
CALIBER: 16-inch
WEIGHT: 1,248,040 pounds
BREECH: interrupted screw
BARREL LENGTH: 800 inches

ELEVATION: 30°
TRAVERSAL: 360°
PROJECTILE WEIGHT: 2,339 pounds
MUZZLE VELOCITY: 2,249 fps
MAXIMUM RANGE: 41,601 yards

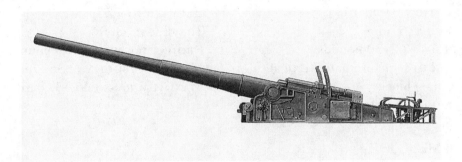

UNITED STATES: 16-INCH GUN M1919
(Courtesy Art-Tech)

16-inch Gun M1919

ADOPTION DATE: —
CALIBER: 16-inch
WEIGHT: 1,085,000 pounds
BREECH: interrupted screw
BARREL LENGTH: 800 inches

ELEVATION: 65°
TRAVERSAL: 360°
PROJECTILE WEIGHT: 2,240 pounds
MUZZLE VELOCITY: 2,697 fps
MAXIMUM RANGE: 50,000 yards

16-inch Howitzer M1920

ADOPTION DATE: 1927
CALIBER: 16-inch
WEIGHT: 900,015 pounds
BREECH: interrupted screw
BARREL LENGTH: 400 inches

ELEVATION: 65°
TRAVERSAL: 360°
PROJECTILE WEIGHT: 2,099 pounds
MUZZLE VELOCITY: 1,949 fps
MAXIMUM RANGE: 73,491 yards

GREAT BRITAIN

15-inch Mk1

ADOPTION DATE: 1936
CALIBER: 15-inch
WEIGHT: 834,974 pounds
BREECH: interrupted screw
BARREL LENGTH: 630 inches

ELEVATION: 45°
TRAVERSAL: 48°
PROJECTILE WEIGHT: 1,940 pounds
MUZZLE VELOCITY: 2.680 fps
MAXIMUM RANGE: 42,000 yards

6-pdr 10-cwt Mk1 Twin

ADOPTION DATE: 1937
CALIBER: 57mm
WEIGHT: 22,130 pounds
BREECH: semiautomatic vertical
    sliding block
BARREL LENGTH: 105 inches

ELEVATION: 7.5°
TRAVERSAL: 360°
PROJECTILE WEIGHT: 6 pounds
MUZZLE VELOCITY: 2,362 fps
MAXIMUM RANGE: 5,151 yards

6-inch Mk24

ADOPTION DATE: 1939
CALIBER: 6-inch
WEIGHT: —
BREECH: interrupted screw
BARREL LENGTH: 270 inches

ELEVATION: 45°
TRAVERSAL: 360°
PROJECTILE WEIGHT: 100 pounds
MUZZLE VELOCITY: 2,857 fps
MAXIMUM RANGE: 21,708 yards

8-inch Mk8

ADOPTION DATE: 1942
CALIBER: 8-inch
WEIGHT: —
BREECH: interrupted screw
BARREL LENGTH: 400 inches

ELEVATION: 70°
TRAVERSAL: 170°
PROJECTILE WEIGHT: 256 pounds
MUZZLE VELOCITY: 2,723 fps
MAXIMUM RANGE: 29,200 yards

GERMANY

305mm SK L/50

ADOPTION DATE: 1932
CALIBER: 305mm
WEIGHT: 390,218 pounds
BREECH: horizontal sliding block
BARREL LENGTH: 600 inches

ELEVATION: 45°
TRAVERSAL: 360°
PROJECTILE WEIGHT: 551 pounds
MUZZLE VELOCITY: 3,675 fps
MAXIMUM RANGE: 55,774 yards

37mm SK C/30

ADOPTION DATE: 1934
CALIBER: 37mm
WEIGHT: —
BREECH: semiautomatic vertical
   sliding block
BARREL LENGTH: 116 inches

ELEVATION: 80°
TRAVERSAL: 260°
PROJECTILE WEIGHT: 1.5 pounds
MUZZLE VELOCITY: 3,281 fps
MAXIMUM RANGE: 7,201 yards

105mm SK C/32

ADOPTION DATE: 1934
CALIBER: 105mm
WEIGHT: 33,579 pounds
BREECH: vertical sliding block
BARREL LENGTH: 162 inches

ELEVATION: 79°
TRAVERSAL: 360°
PROJECTILE WEIGHT: 33 pounds
MUZZLE VELOCITY: 2,575 fps
MAXIMUM RANGE: 16,678 yards

150mm Ubts & Tbts K L/45

ADOPTION DATE: 1934
CALIBER: 150mm
WEIGHT: —
BREECH: horizontal sliding block
BARREL LENGTH: 265.5 inches

ELEVATION: 45°
TRAVERSAL: 360°
PROJECTILE WEIGHT: 100 pounds
MUZZLE VELOCITY: 2,231 fps
MAXIMUM RANGE: 17,498 yards

203mm SK C/340

ADOPTION DATE: 1934
CALIBER: 203mm
WEIGHT: —
BREECH: horizontal sliding block
BARREL LENGTH: 455 inches

ELEVATION: 30°
TRAVERSAL: 360°
PROJECTILE WEIGHT: 269 pounds
MUZZLE VELOCITY: 3,035 fps
MAXIMUM RANGE: 40,464 yards

88mm SK C/35

ADOPTION DATE: 1935
CALIBER: 88mm
WEIGHT: —
BREECH: semiautomatic vertical
   sliding block
BARREL LENGTH: 145 inches

ELEVATION: 30°
TRAVERSAL: 360°
PROJECTILE WEIGHT: —
MUZZLE VELOCITY: 2,297 fps
MAXIMUM RANGE: 13,506 yards

149mm SK C/28

ADOPTION DATE: 1936
CALIBER: 149mm
WEIGHT: —
BREECH: semiautomatic vertical
  sliding block
BARREL LENGTH: 305 inches

ELEVATION: 35°
TRAVERSAL: 360°
PROJECTILE WEIGHT: 100 pounds
MUZZLE VELOCITY: 2,575 fps
MAXIMUM RANGE: 25,700 yards

149mm TbtsK C/36

ADOPTION DATE: 1937
CALIBER: 149mm
WEIGHT: —
BREECH: horizontal sliding block
BARREL LENGTH: 264 inches

ELEVATION: 40°
TRAVERSAL: 120°
PROJECTILE WEIGHT: 100 pounds
MUZZLE VELOCITY: 2,740 fps
MAXIMUM RANGE: 21,353 yards

105mm SK L/60

ADOPTION DATE: 1938
CALIBER: 105mm
WEIGHT: 25,904 pounds
BREECH: semiautomatic vertical
  sliding block
BARREL LENGTH: 248 inches

ELEVATION: 80°
TRAVERSAL: 360°
PROJECTILE WEIGHT: 33 pounds
MUZZLE VELOCITY: 2,953 fps
MAXIMUM RANGE: 19,138 yards

406mm SK C/34

ADOPTION DATE: 1939
CALIBER: 406mm
WEIGHT: —
BREECH: horizontal sliding block
BARREL LENGTH: 719 inches

ELEVATION: 60°
TRAVERSAL: 360°
PROJECTILE WEIGHT: 2,271 pounds
MUZZLE VELOCITY: 2,000 fps
MAXIMUM RANGE: 61,242 yards

406mm K (E) Adolf

ADOPTION DATE: 1940
CALIBER: 406mm
WEIGHT: 712,093 pounds
BREECH: horizontal sliding block
BARREL LENGTH: 767 inches

ELEVATION: 45 °
TRAVERSAL: 0°
PROJECTILE WEIGHT: 2,271 pounds
MUZZLE VELOCITY: 2,000 fps
MAXIMUM RANGE: 35 miles

Railroad Artillery
UNITED STATES

8-inch Gun Mk VI Model 3A2

ADOPTION DATE: 1940
CALIBER: 8-inch
WEIGHT: 230,000 pounds
BREECH: interrupted screw
BARREL LENGTH: 360 inches

ELEVATION: 45°
TRAVERSAL: 360°
PROJECTILE WEIGHT: 260 pounds
MUZZLE VELOCITY: 2,750 fps
MAXIMUM RANGE: 35,296 yards

GERMANY

238mm K (E) Theodor Bruno

ADOPTION DATE: 1936
CALIBER: 238mm
WEIGHT: 207,234 pounds
BREECH: horizontal sliding block
BARREL LENGTH: 304 inches

ELEVATION: 45°
TRAVERSAL: 1°
PROJECTILE WEIGHT: 327 pounds
MUZZLE VELOCITY: 2,215 fps
MAXIMUM RANGE: 12.5 miles

283mm K (E) Lange Bruno

ADOPTION DATE: 1937
CALIBER: 283mm
WEIGHT: 242,000 pounds
BREECH: horizontal sliding block
BARREL LENGTH: 440 inches

ELEVATION: 45°
TRAVERSAL: 1°
PROJECTILE WEIGHT: 626 pounds
MUZZLE VELOCITY: 2,871 fps
MAXIMUM RANGE: 22.4 miles

283mm K (E) Kurze Bruno

ADOPTION DATE: 1937
CALIBER: 283mm
WEIGHT: 252,000 pounds
BREECH: horizontal sliding block
BARREL LENGTH: 418 inches

ELEVATION: 45°
TRAVERSAL: 1°
PROJECTILE WEIGHT: 529 pounds
MUZZLE VELOCITY: 2,690 fps
MAXIMUM RANGE: 32,262 yards

283mm K (E) Schwerer Bruno

ADOPTION DATE: 1937
CALIBER: 283mm
WEIGHT: 260,145 pounds
BREECH: horizontal sliding block
BARREL LENGTH: 446 inches

ELEVATION: 45°
TRAVERSAL: 1°
PROJECTILE WEIGHT: 626 pounds
MUZZLE VELOCITY: 2,821 fps
MAXIMUM RANGE: 22 miles

283mm K (E) Neue Bruno

ADOPTION DATE: 1940
CALIBER: 283mm
WEIGHT: 294,000 pounds
BREECH: horizontal sliding block
BARREL LENGTH: 601.5 inches

ELEVATION: 50°
TRAVERSAL: 1°
PROJECTILE WEIGHT: 584 pounds
MUZZLE VELOCITY: 3,264 fps
MAXIMUM RANGE: 23 miles

149mm K in Eisenbahnlafette

ADOPTION DATE: 1937
CALIBER: 149mm
WEIGHT: 165,347 pounds
BREECH: vertical sliding block
BARREL LENGTH: 217 inches

ELEVATION: 45°
TRAVERSAL: 360°
PROJECTILE WEIGHT: 95 pounds
MUZZLE VELOCITY: 2,641 fps
MAXIMUM RANGE: 24,606 yards

173mcm K (E)

ADOPTION DATE: 1938
CALIBER: 173mm
WEIGHT: 176,370 pounds
BREECH: horizontal sliding block
BARREL LENGTH: 191 inches

ELEVATION: 45°
TRAVERSAL: 360°
PROJECTILE WEIGHT: 138 pounds
MUZZLE VELOCITY: 2,871 fps
MAXIMUM RANGE: 29,746 yards

211mm K12 (E)

ADOPTION DATE: 1939
CALIBER: 211mm
WEIGHT: 196,000 pounds
BREECH: horizontal sliding block
BARREL LENGTH: 1,260 inches

ELEVATION: 55°
TRAVERSAL: 0°
PROJECTILE WEIGHT: 237 pounds
MUZZLE VELOCITY: 4,921 fps
MAXIMUM RANGE: 93 miles

283mm K5 (E)

ADOPTION DATE: 1940
CALIBER: 283mm
WEIGHT: 480,607 pounds
BREECH: horizontal sliding block
BARREL LENGTH: 802 inches

ELEVATION: 50°
TRAVERSAL: 1°
PROJECTILE WEIGHT: 561 pounds
MUZZLE VELOCITY: 3,700 fps
MAXIMUM RANGE: 39 miles

380mm K (E) Siegfried

ADOPTION DATE: 1938
CALIBER: 380mm
WEIGHT: 648,159 pounds
BREECH: horizontal sliding block
BARREL LENGTH: 703 inches

ELEVATION: 45°
TRAVERSAL: 360°
PROJECTILE WEIGHT: 1,091 pounds
MUZZLE VELOCITY: 3,445 fps
MAXIMUM RANGE: 26 miles

203mm K (E)

ADOPTION DATE: 1941
CALIBER: 203mm
WEIGHT: 189,818 pounds
BREECH: horizontal sliding block
BARREL LENGTH: 455 inches

ELEVATION: 45°
TRAVERSAL: 0°
PROJECTILE WEIGHT: 269 pounds
MUZZLE VELOCITY: 3,035 fps
MAXIMUM RANGE: 40,464 yards

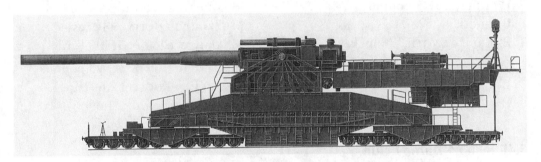

GERMANY: 80CM K (E) GUSTAV ("DORA GERAT")
(Courtesy Art-Tech)

800mm K (E) Gustav ("Dora Gerat")

ADOPTION DATE: 1941
CALIBER: 800mm
WEIGHT: 2,658,000 pounds
BREECH: horizontal sliding block
BARREL LENGTH: 1,134 inches
ELEVATION: 65°

TRAVERSAL: 0°
PROJECTILE WEIGHT: 14,000 pounds
MUZZLE VELOCITY: 2,690 fps
MAXIMUM RANGE: 24 miles

Recoilless Artillery
UNITED STATES

57mm RCL Rifle M18

ADOPTION DATE: 1945
CALIBER: 57mm
WEIGHT: 44 pounds
BREECH: —
BARREL LENGTH: 60.5 inches

ELEVATION: 65°
TRAVERSAL: 360°
PROJECTILE WEIGHT: 2.5 pounds
MUZZLE VELOCITY: 1,197 fps
MAXIMUM RANGE: 4,921 yards

75mm RCL Rifle M20

ADOPTION DATE: 1945
CALIBER: 75mm
WEIGHT: 167.5 pounds
BREECH: —
BARREL LENGTH: 78 inches

ELEVATION: 65°
TRAVERSAL: 360°
PROJECTILE WEIGHT: 14 pounds
MUZZLE VELOCITY: 984 fps
MAXIMUM RANGE: 7,300 yards

GREAT BRITAIN

3.45-inch P1 Burney Gun

ADOPTION DATE: 1944
CALIBER: 3.45-inch
WEIGHT: —
BREECH: —
BARREL LENGTH: 45 inches

ELEVATION: —
TRAVERSAL: —
PROJECTILE WEIGHT: 3.7 pounds
MUZZLE VELOCITY: 909 fps
MAXIMUM RANGE: 547 yards

3.7-inch Mk1

ADOPTION DATE: 1944
CALIBER: 3.7-inch
WEIGHT: 375 pounds
BREECH: —
BARREL LENGTH: 81 inches

ELEVATION: 10°
TRAVERSAL: 20°
PROJECTILE WEIGHT: 22.5 pounds
MUZZLE VELOCITY: 1,000 fps
MAXIMUM RANGE: 1,996 yards

7.2-inch P1

ADOPTION DATE: 1944
CALIBER: 7.2-inch
WEIGHT: 3,582.5 pounds
BREECH: interrupted screw
BARREL LENGTH: 130 inches

ELEVATION: 15°
TRAVERSAL: 30°
PROJECTILE WEIGHT: 120 pounds
MUZZLE VELOCITY: 902 fps
MAXIMUM RANGE: 3,401 yards

95mm Mk1

ADOPTION DATE: 1945
CALIBER: 95mm
WEIGHT: 2,350 pounds
BREECH: —
BARREL LENGTH: 101 inches

ELEVATION: 35°
TRAVERSAL: 60°
PROJECTILE WEIGHT: 25 pounds
MUZZLE VELOCITY: 1,598 fps
MAXIMUM RANGE: 10,800 yards

GERMANY

75mm LG40

ADOPTION DATE: 1941
CALIBER: 75mm
WEIGHT: 320 pounds
BREECH: horizontal sliding block
BARREL LENGTH: 52 inches

ELEVATION: 42°
TRAVERSAL: 360°
PROJECTILE WEIGHT: 1.8 pounds
MUZZLE VELOCITY: 1,148 fps
MAXIMUM RANGE: 7,436 yards

105mm LG40

ADOPTION DATE: 1941
CALIBER: 105mm
WEIGHT: 855 pounds
BREECH: special
BARREL LENGTH: 53.5 inches

ELEVATION: 41°
TRAVERSAL: 80°
PROJECTILE WEIGHT: 32.6 pounds
MUZZLE VELOCITY: 1,099 fps
MAXIMUM RANGE: 8,694 yards

105mm LG42

ADOPTION DATE: 1941
CALIBER: 105mm
WEIGHT: 1,190.5 pounds
BREECH: horizontal sliding block
BARREL LENGTH: 53.5 inches

ELEVATION: 42°
TRAVERSAL: 360°
PROJECTILE WEIGHT: 32.6 pounds
MUZZLE VELOCITY: 2,739 fps
MAXIMUM RANGE: 8,694 yards

75mm RFK43

ADOPTION DATE: 1944
CALIBER: 75mm
WEIGHT: 95 pounds
BREECH: special
BARREL LENGTH: 26 inches

ELEVATION: 45°
TRAVERSAL: 360°
PROJECTILE WEIGHT: 9 pounds
MUZZLE VELOCITY: 558 fps
MAXIMUM RANGE: 2,187 yards

Self-propelled Artillery
UNITED STATES

75mm Gun Motor Carriage M3

ADOPTION DATE: 1940
CALIBER: 75mm
WEIGHT: 20,000 pounds
BREECH: Nordenfelt screw
BARREL LENGTH: —

ELEVATION: 29°
TRAVERSAL: 40°
PROJECTILE WEIGHT: 15 pounds
MUZZLE VELOCITY: 2,000 fps
MAXIMUM RANGE: 1,933 yards

UNITED STATES: 105MM HOWITZER MOTOR CARRIAGE M7
(Courtesy Art-Tech)

105mm Howitzer Motor Carriage M7

ADOPTION DATE: 1941
CALIBER: 105mm
WEIGHT: 8,050 pounds
BREECH: horizontal sliding block
BARREL LENGTH: —

ELEVATION: 30°
TRAVERSAL: 15°
PROJECTILE WEIGHT: 33 pounds
MUZZLE VELOCITY: 1,017 fps
MAXIMUM RANGE: 11,600 yards

UNITED STATES: 155MM GUN MOTOR CARRIAGE M12
(Courtesy Art-Tech)

155mm Gun Motor Carriage M12

ADOPTION DATE: 1941
CALIBER: 155mm
WEIGHT: 58,974 pounds
BREECH: interrupted screw
BARREL LENGTH: —

ELEVATION: 30°
TRAVERSAL: 28°
PROJECTILE WEIGHT: 96 pounds
MUZZLE VELOCITY: 2,800 fps
MAXIMUM RANGE: 21,982 yards

37mm Gun Motor Carriage M6

ADOPTION DATE: 1942
CALIBER: 37mm
WEIGHT: 7,352 pounds
BREECH: —
BARREL LENGTH: —

ELEVATION: 15°
TRAVERSAL: 360°
PROJECTILE WEIGHT: 1.9 pounds
MUZZLE VELOCITY: 2,900 fps
MAXIMUM RANGE: 1,094 yards

75mm Howitzer Motor Carriage M8

ADOPTION DATE: 1942
CALIBER: 75mm
WEIGHT: 34,613 pounds
BREECH: Nordenfelt screw
BARREL LENGTH: —

ELEVATION: 40°
TRAVERSAL: 360°
PROJECTILE WEIGHT: 15 pounds
MUZZLE VELOCITY: 1,250 fps
MAXIMUM RANGE: 9,613 yards

3-inch Gun Motor Carriage M10

ADOPTION DATE: 1942
CALIBER: 3-inch
WEIGHT: 65,995 pounds
BREECH: —
BARREL LENGTH: —

ELEVATION: 19°
TRAVERSAL: 360°
PROJECTILE WEIGHT: 15 pounds
MUZZLE VELOCITY: 2,592 fps
MAXIMUM RANGE: 15,967 yards

57mm Gun Motor Carriage T48

ADOPTION DATE: 1942
CALIBER: 57mm
WEIGHT: 19,000 pounds
BREECH: —
BARREL LENGTH: —

ELEVATION: 15°
TRAVERSAL: 55°
PROJECTILE WEIGHT: 6 pounds
MUZZLE VELOCITY: 2,800 fps
MAXIMUM RANGE: 2,625 yards

76mm Gun Motor Carriage M18 "Hellcat"

ADOPTION DATE: 1944
CALIBER: 76.2mm
WEIGHT: 37,556 pounds
BREECH: —
BARREL LENGTH: —

ELEVATION: 20°
TRAVERSAL: 360°
PROJECTILE WEIGHT: 15 pounds
MUZZLE VELOCITY: 2,625 fps
MAXIMUM RANGE: 3,281 yards

Twin 40mm Gun Motor Carriage M19

ADOPTION DATE: 1944
CALIBER: 40mm
WEIGHT: 38,471 pounds
BREECH: —
BARREL LENGTH: —

ELEVATION: 85°
TRAVERSAL: 360°
PROJECTILE WEIGHT: —
MUZZLE VELOCITY: 2,870 fps
MAXIMUM RANGE: 9,475 yards

UNITED STATES: 90MM GUN MOTOR CARRIAGE M36
(Courtesy Art-Tech)

90mm Gun Motor Carriage M36 "Jackson"

ADOPTION DATE: 1944
CALIBER: 90mm
WEIGHT: 61,994 pounds
BREECH: horizontal sliding block
BARREL LENGTH: —

ELEVATION: 20°
TRAVERSAL: 360°
PROJECTILE WEIGHT: 24 pounds
MUZZLE VELOCITY: 2,798 fps
MAXIMUM RANGE: 17,060 yards

105mm Howitzer Motor Carriage M37

ADOPTION DATE: 1945
CALIBER: 105mm
WEIGHT: 46,000 pounds
BREECH: horizontal sliding block
BARREL LENGTH: —

ELEVATION: 43°
TRAVERSAL: 45°
PROJECTILE WEIGHT: 33 pounds
MUZZLE VELOCITY: —
MAXIMUM RANGE: 12,000 yards

155mm Gun Motor Carriage M40

ADOPTION DATE: 1945
CALIBER: 155mm
WEIGHT: —
BREECH: interrupted screw
BARREL LENGTH: —

ELEVATION: 55°
TRAVERSAL: 36°
PROJECTILE WEIGHT: 95 pounds
MUZZLE VELOCITY: —
MAXIMUM RANGE: 25,722 yards

155mm Howitzer Motor Carriage M41

ADOPTION DATE: 1945
CALIBER: 155mm
WEIGHT: 40,995 pounds
BREECH: interrupted screw
BARREL LENGTH: —

ELEVATION: 45°
TRAVERSAL: 37.5°
PROJECTILE WEIGHT: 95 pounds
MUZZLE VELOCITY: 2,089 fps
MAXIMUM RANGE: 16,360 yards

8-inch Howitzer Motor Carriage M43

ADOPTION DATE: 1945
CALIBER: 8-inch
WEIGHT: 83,026 pounds
BREECH: interrupted screw
BARREL LENGTH: —

ELEVATION: 52°
TRAVERSAL: 34°
PROJECTILE WEIGHT: 200 pounds
MUZZLE VELOCITY: 2,245 fps
MAXIMUM RANGE: 18,515 yards

240mm Howitzer Motor Carriage T92 and 8-inch Gun Motor Carriage T93

ADOPTION DATE: 1945
CALIBER: 240mm (Howitzer) 8-inch
   (Gun)
WEIGHT: 137,500 pounds (Howitzer)
   131,400 pounds (Gun)
BREECH: interrupted screw
BARREL LENGTH: —

ELEVATION: 50°
TRAVERSAL: 22°
PROJECTILE WEIGHT: 360 pounds
   (Howitzer)
MUZZLE VELOCITY: —
MAXIMUM RANGE: 25,262 yards
   (Howitzer)

GREAT BRITAIN

Birch Gun
ADOPTION DATE: 1925
CALIBER: 84mm
WEIGHT: 27,900 pounds
BREECH: —
BARREL LENGTH: —

ELEVATION: 37.5°
TRAVERSAL: 360°
PROJECTILE WEIGHT: 18 pounds
MUZZLE VELOCITY: —
MAXIMUM RANGE: 10,500 yards

Bishop
ADOPTION DATE: 1942
CALIBER: 87mm
WEIGHT: 38,471 pounds
BREECH: vertical sliding block
BARREL LENGTH: —

ELEVATION: 15°
TRAVERSAL: 8°
PROJECTILE WEIGHT: 25 pounds
MUZZLE VELOCITY: —
MAXIMUM RANGE: 6,398 yards

Priest
ADOPTION DATE: 1941
CALIBER: 105mm
WEIGHT: —
BREECH: horizontal sliding block
BARREL LENGTH: 91 inches

ELEVATION: —
TRAVERSAL: —
PROJECTILE WEIGHT: 33 pounds
MUZZLE VELOCITY: —
MAXIMUM RANGE: —

Deacon
ADOPTION DATE: 1942
CALIBER: 57mm
WEIGHT: 26,896 pounds
BREECH: —
BARREL LENGTH: —

ELEVATION: 15°
TRAVERSAL: 360°
PROJECTILE WEIGHT: —
MUZZLE VELOCITY: —
MAXIMUM RANGE: 1,094 yards

Sexton
ADOPTION DATE: 1943
CALIBER: 87mm
WEIGHT: 10,800 pounds
BREECH: vertical sliding block
BARREL LENGTH: —

ELEVATION: 40°
TRAVERSAL: 50°
PROJECTILE WEIGHT: 25 pounds
MUZZLE VELOCITY: —
MAXIMUM RANGE: 13,402 yards

Achilles

ADOPTION DATE: 1944

CALIBER: 76mm

WEIGHT: 65,213 pounds

BREECH: —

BARREL LENGTH: —

ELEVATION: 20°

TRAVERSAL: 360°

PROJECTILE WEIGHT: —

MUZZLE VELOCITY: —

MAXIMUM RANGE: 2,187 yards

GREAT BRITAIN: ARCHER
(Courtesy Art-Tech)

Archer

ADOPTION DATE: 1944

CALIBER: 75mm

WEIGHT: 36,509 pounds

BREECH: —

BARREL LENGTH: —

ELEVATION: 70°

TRAVERSAL: 360°

PROJECTILE WEIGHT: 17 pounds

MUZZLE VELOCITY: —

MAXIMUM RANGE: 18,591 yards

GERMANY

150mm sIG auf Pzkwl

ADOPTION DATE: 1940

CALIBER: 150mm

WEIGHT: 18,739 pounds

BREECH: horizontal sliding block

Barrel length: —

ELEVATION: 75°

TRAVERSAL: 25°

PROJECTILE WEIGHT: 84 pounds

MUZZLE VELOCITY: 787 fps

MAXIMUM RANGE: 5,140 yards

GERMANY: KARL 040
(Courtesy Art-Tech)

Karl 040

ADOPTION DATE: 1940

CALIBER: 600mm

WEIGHT: 244,000 pounds

BREECH: —

BARREL LENGTH: —

ELEVATION: 70°

TRAVERSAL: 8°

PROJECTILE WEIGHT: 3,472 pounds

MUZZLE VELOCITY: —

MAXIMUM RANGE: 7,300 yards

Sturmgeschütz 40

ADOPTION DATE: 1940
CALIBER: 75mm
WEIGHT: 48,502 pounds
BREECH: horizontal sliding block
BARREL LENGTH: —

ELEVATION: 20°
TRAVERSAL: 24°
PROJECTILE WEIGHT: 13 pounds
MUZZLE VELOCITY: —
MAXIMUM RANGE: 5,468 yards

150mm sIG auf PzKwII

ADOPTION DATE: 1941
CALIBER: 150mm
WEIGHT: 24,692 pounds
BREECH: horizontal sliding block
BARREL LENGTH: —

ELEVATION: 50°
TRAVERSAL: 20°
PROJECTILE WEIGHT: 84 pounds
MUZZLE VELOCITY: —
MAXIMUM RANGE: 5,140 yards

Wespe

ADOPTION DATE: —
CALIBER: 105mm
WEIGHT: 25,794 pounds
BREECH: horizontal sliding block
BARREL LENGTH: —

ELEVATION: 45°
TRAVERSAL: 34°
PROJECTILE WEIGHT: 33 pounds
MUZZLE VELOCITY: 1,542 fps
MAXIMUM RANGE: 11,674 yards

150mm sIG auf PzKw 38(t)

ADOPTION DATE: 1943
CALIBER: 150mm
WEIGHT: 25,355 pounds
BREECH: horizontal sliding block
BARREL LENGTH: —

ELEVATION: 72°
TRAVERSAL: 10°
PROJECTILE WEIGHT: 95 pounds
MUZZLE VELOCITY: —
MAXIMUM RANGE: 5,140 yards

Sturmpanzer IV "Brummbär"

ADOPTION DATE: 1943
CALIBER: 150mm
WEIGHT: 62,170 pounds
BREECH: horizontal sliding block
BARREL LENGTH: —

ELEVATION: 30°
TRAVERSAL: 10°
PROJECTILE WEIGHT: 95 pounds
MUZZLE VELOCITY: —
MAXIMUM RANGE: 4 miles

150mm Schweres Infantriegeschütz 33 (Sf) auf PzKpfw 38(t) Ausf. H, Grille

ADOPTION DATE: 1943
CALIBER: 150mm
WEIGHT: 25,353 pounds
BREECH: horizontal sliding block
BARREL LENGTH: —

ELEVATION: 72°
TRAVERSAL: 5°
PROJECTILE WEIGHT: 95 pounds
MUZZLE VELOCITY: —
MAXIMUM RANGE: 5,140 yards

150mm Schwere Panzerhaubitze auf Fahrgestell Panzerkampfwagen III/IV (SdKfz 165) Hummel

ADOPTION DATE: 1943
CALIBER: 150mm
WEIGHT: 51,809 pounds
BREECH: horizontal sliding block
BARREL LENGTH: —

ELEVATION: 42°
TRAVERSAL: 15°
PROJECTILE WEIGHT: 95 pounds
MUZZLE VELOCITY: —
MAXIMUM RANGE: 7.8 miles

88mm PaK43/1 (L/71) auf Fahrgestell Panzerkampfwagen III/IV (Sf) "Nashorn" (Hornisse)

ADOPTION DATE: 1943
CALIBER: 88mm
WEIGHT: 52,801 pounds
BREECH: horizontal sliding block
BARREL LENGTH: —

ELEVATION: 20°
TRAVERSAL: 15°
PROJECTILE WEIGHT: 23 pounds
MUZZLE VELOCITY: —
MAXIMUM RANGE: 3,280 yards

Sturmgeschütz m/8.8cm Pak43/2 Sd Kfz 184 "Elefant"

ADOPTION DATE: 1943
CALIBER: 88mm
WEIGHT: 143,300 pounds
BREECH: horizontal sliding block
BARREL LENGTH: —

ELEVATION: 14°
TRAVERSAL: 14°
PROJECTILE WEIGHT: 23 pounds
MUZZLE VELOCITY: —
MAXIMUM RANGE: —

Jagdpanzer 38(t) Hetzer Sd. Kfz. 138/2

ADOPTION DATE: 1944
CALIBER: 75mm
WEIGHT: 31,400 pounds
BREECH: horizontal sliding block
BARREL LENGTH: —

ELEVATION: 12°
TRAVERSAL: 5° left 11° right
PROJECTILE WEIGHT: 13 pounds
MUZZLE VELOCITY: —
MAXIMUM RANGE: 2,187 yards

Sturmgeschütz IV

ADOPTION DATE: 1944
CALIBER: 75mm
WEIGHT: 56,880 pounds
BREECH: horizontal sliding block
BARREL LENGTH: —

ELEVATION: 15°
TRAVERSAL: 12°
PROJECTILE WEIGHT: 13 pounds
MUZZLE VELOCITY: —
MAXIMUM RANGE: 8,393 yards

GERMANY: JAGDPANTHER
(Courtesy Art-Tech)

Jagdpanther

ADOPTION DATE: 1944
CALIBER: 88mm
WEIGHT: 100,310 pounds
BREECH: horizontal sliding block
BARREL LENGTH: —

ELEVATION: 14°
TRAVERSAL: 26°
PROJECTILE WEIGHT: 23 pounds
MUZZLE VELOCITY: —
MAXIMUM RANGE: 3,281 yards

Jagdpanzer VI/Jagdtiger (SdKfz 186)

ADOPTION DATE: 1944
CALIBER: 128mm
WEIGHT: 158,071 pounds
BREECH: horizontal sliding block
BARREL LENGTH: —

ELEVATION: 15°
TRAVERSAL: 20°
PROJECTILE WEIGHT: 62 pounds
MUZZLE VELOCITY: —
MAXIMUM RANGE: 4,374 yards

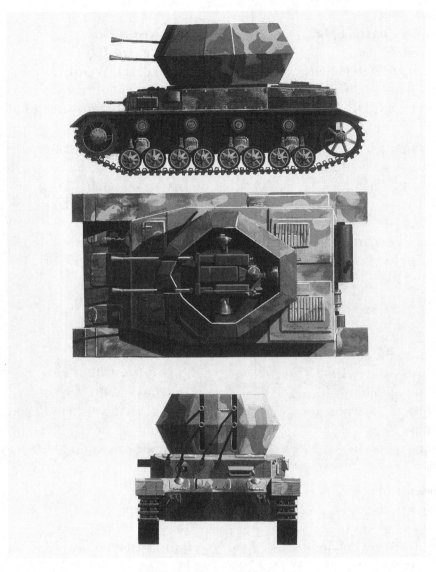

GERMANY: WIRBELWIND
(Courtesy Art-Tech)

Wirbelwind

ADOPTION DATE: 1944

CALIBER: 20mm

WEIGHT: 48,502 pounds

BREECH: —

BARREL LENGTH: —

ELEVATION: 90°

TRAVERSAL: 360°

PROJECTILE WEIGHT: —

MUZZLE VELOCITY: —

MAXIMUM CEILING: 10,500 feet

Ostwind

ADOPTION DATE: 1944
CALIBER: 37mm
WEIGHT: 55,226 pounds
BREECH: —
BARREL LENGTH: —

ELEVATION: 90°
TRAVERSAL: 360°
PROJECTILE WEIGHT: —
MUZZLE VELOCITY: —
MAXIMUM CEILING: 13,123 feet

Möbelwagen

ADOPTION DATE: 1944
CALIBER: 37mm
WEIGHT: —
BREECH: —
BARREL LENGTH: —

ELEVATION: —
TRAVERSAL: 360°
PROJECTILE WEIGHT: —
MUZZLE VELOCITY: —
MAXIMUM RANGE: —

ITALY

Semovente 90/53

ADOPTION DATE: 1942
CALIBER: 90mm
WEIGHT: 37,479 pounds
BREECH: —
BARREL LENGTH: —

ELEVATION: 24°
TRAVERSAL: 90°
PROJECTILE WEIGHT: 22 pounds
MUZZLE VELOCITY: 2,760 fps
MAXIMUM RANGE: 20,779 yards

Semovente 149

ADOPTION DATE: —
CALIBER: 149mm
WEIGHT: 39,683 pounds
BREECH: —
BARREL LENGTH: —

ELEVATION: 45°
TRAVERSAL: 60°
PROJECTILE WEIGHT: 110 pounds
MUZZLE VELOCITY: 2,625 fps
MAXIMUM RANGE: 14.8 miles

SOVIET UNION

SU76
ADOPTION DATE: 1943
CALIBER: 76.2mm
WEIGHT: 24,692 pounds
BREECH: —
BARREL LENGTH: —

ELEVATION: —
TRAVERSAL: —
PROJECTILE WEIGHT: —
MUZZLE VELOCITY: —
MAXIMUM RANGE: —

SU85
ADOPTION DATE: 1943
CALIBER: 85mm
WEIGHT: 25,257 pounds
BREECH: —
BARREL LENGTH: —

ELEVATION: 20°
TRAVERSAL: 20°
PROJECTILE WEIGHT: —
MUZZLE VELOCITY: —
MAXIMUM RANGE: —

SU122
ADOPTION DATE: 1943
CALIBER: 122mm
WEIGHT: 90,830 pounds
BREECH: —
BARREL LENGTH: —

ELEVATION: —
TRAVERSAL: —
PROJECTILE WEIGHT: —
MUZZLE VELOCITY: —
MAXIMUM RANGE: —

SU152
ADOPTION DATE: 1943
CALIBER: 152.4mm
WEIGHT: 92,153 pounds
BREECH: —
BARREL LENGTH: —

ELEVATION: 18°
TRAVERSAL: 12°
PROJECTILE WEIGHT: —
MUZZLE VELOCITY: —
MAXIMUM RANGE: —

SU100
ADOPTION DATE: 1944
CALIBER: 100mm
WEIGHT: 69,666 pounds
BREECH: —
BARREL LENGTH: —

ELEVATION: 20°
TRAVERSAL: 20°
PROJECTILE WEIGHT: —
MUZZLE VELOCITY: —
MAXIMUM RANGE: 3,281 yards

CHAPTER EIGHT SPECIFICATIONS: POST–WORLD WAR II AND LATE-TWENTIETH-CENTURY DEVELOPMENTS

Towed Artillery
UNITED STATES

105mm Howitzer M102

ADOPTION DATE: 1965
CALIBER: 105mm
WEIGHT: 3,298 pounds
BREECH: vertical sliding block
BARREL LENGTH: 124 inches

ELEVATION: 76°
TRAVERSAL: 360°
PROJECTILE WEIGHT: 33 pounds
MUZZLE VELOCITY: 1,621 fps
MAXIMUM RANGE: 12,577 yards

75mm Pack Howitzer M116

ADOPTION DATE: 1955
CALIBER: 75mm
WEIGHT: 1,440 pounds
BREECH: horizontal sliding block
BARREL LENGTH: 57 inches

ELEVATION: 45°
TRAVERSAL: 6°
PROJECTILE WEIGHT: 15 pounds
MUZZLE VELOCITY: 1,260 fps
MAXIMUM RANGE: 9,055 yards

155mm Howitzer M198

ADOPTION DATE: 1978
CALIBER: 155mm
WEIGHT: 15,792 pounds
BREECH: interrupted screw
BARREL LENGTH: 240 inches

ELEVATION: 72°
TRAVERSAL: 45°
PROJECTILE WEIGHT: 95 pounds
MUZZLE VELOCITY: 2,245 fps
MAXIMUM RANGE: 19,794 yards

AUSTRIA

Noricum GH N-45 155mm Gun-Howitzer

ADOPTION DATE: —
CALIBER: 155mm
WEIGHT: 22,201 pounds
BREECH: semiautomatic
BARREL LENGTH: 277 inches

ELEVATION: 72°
TRAVERSAL: 70°
PROJECTILE WEIGHT: —
MUZZLE VELOCITY: —
MAXIMUM RANGE: 43,307 yards

GREAT BRITAIN

105mm Pack L10A1

ADOPTION DATE: 1956
CALIBER: 105mm
WEIGHT: 2,807 pounds
BREECH: semiautomatic vertical
  sliding block
BARREL LENGTH: 83 inches

ELEVATION: 65°
TRAVERSAL: 56°
PROJECTILE WEIGHT: 33 pounds
MUZZLE VELOCITY: 1,378 fps
MAXIMUM RANGE: 11,000 yards

Note: — indicates the information is unavailable.

GREAT BRITAIN: 105MM LIGHT GUN L118
(Courtesy Art-Tech)

105mm Light Gun L118

ADOPTION DATE: 1981
CALIBER: 105mm
WEIGHT: 4,008 pounds
BREECH: semiautomatic vertical
sliding block
BARREL LENGTH: 124 inches

ELEVATION: 70°
TRAVERSAL: 11°
PROJECTILE WEIGHT: 35.5 pounds
MUZZLE VELOCITY: 2,024 fps
MAXIMUM RANGE: 16,480 yards

155mm Ultralightweight Field Howitzer (UFH)

ADOPTION DATE: 1997
CALIBER: 155mm
WEIGHT: 7,000 pounds
BREECH: interrupted screw
BARREL LENGTH: 240 inches

ELEVATION: 70°
TRAVERSAL: 45°
PROJECTILE WEIGHT: —
MUZZLE VELOCITY: 2,713 fps
MAXIMUM RANGE: 29,528 yards

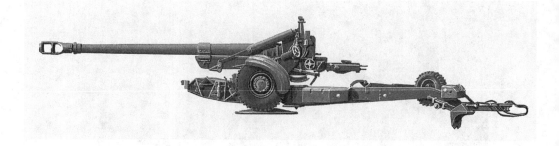

GREAT BRITAIN: 155MM HOWITZER FH70
(Courtesy Art-Tech)

155mm Howitzer FH70

ADOPTION DATE: 1978
CALIBER: 155mm
WEIGHT: 20,503 pounds
BREECH: semiautomatic vertical
    sliding block
BARREL LENGTH: 232 inches

ELEVATION: 70°
TRAVERSAL: 56°
PROJECTILE WEIGHT: 96 pounds
MUZZLE VELOCITY: 2,887 fps
MAXIMUM RANGE: 26,247 yards

PEOPLE'S REPUBLIC OF CHINA

NORINCO 203mm Howitzer

ADOPTION DATE: early 1990s
CALIBER: 203mm
WEIGHT: —
BREECH: vertical sliding block
BARREL LENGTH: 364 inches

ELEVATION: —
TRAVERSAL: —
PROJECTILE WEIGHT: 101.1 pounds
MUZZLE VELOCITY: 3,061 fps
MAXIMUM RANGE: 54,680 yards
    (ERFB-BB)

NORINCO 155mm Gun-Howitzer Type WA 021

ADOPTION DATE: 1991
CALIBER: 155mm
WEIGHT: 20,944 pounds
BREECH: —
BARREL LENGTH: 277 inches

ELEVATION: 72°
TRAVERSAL: 70°
PROJECTILE WEIGHT: —
MUZZLE VELOCITY: —
MAXIMUM RANGE: 42,650 yards

NORINCO 155mm GUN XP52

ADOPTION DATE: 1993
CALIBER: 155mm
WEIGHT: 21,385 pounds
BREECH: —
BARREL LENGTH: 348 inches

ELEVATION: 45°
TRAVERSAL: 50°
PROJECTILE WEIGHT: —
MUZZLE VELOCITY: —
MAXIMUM RANGE: —

NORINCO 155mm Gun-Howitzer Type GM-45

ADOPTION DATE: —
CALIBER: 155mm
WEIGHT: 17,968 pounds
BREECH: —
BARREL LENGTH: —

ELEVATION: 55°
TRAVERSAL: 50°
PROJECTILE WEIGHT: —
MUZZLE VELOCITY: —
MAXIMUM RANGE: —

NORINCO 152mm Gun Type 83

ADOPTION DATE: —
CALIBER: 152mm
WEIGHT: 21,385 pounds
BREECH: —
BARREL LENGTH: 269 inches

ELEVATION: 45°
TRAVERSAL: 50°
PROJECTILE WEIGHT: 106 pounds
MUZZLE VELOCITY: 3,133 fps
MAXIMUM RANGE: 41,557 yards
    (ERFB-BB)

NORINCO 152mm Gun-Howitzer Type 66

ADOPTION DATE: —
CALIBER: 152mm
WEIGHT: 12,610 pounds
BREECH: semiautomatic vertical
    sliding block
BARREL LENGTH: 204.5 inches

ELEVATION: 45°
TRAVERSAL: 58°
PROJECTILE WEIGHT: 96 pounds
MUZZLE VELOCITY: 2,132 fps
MAXIMUM RANGE: 13,375 yards

NORINCO 130mm Field Gun
Type 59-1
ADOPTION DATE: —
CALIBER: 130mm
WEIGHT: 13,889 pounds
BREECH: semiautomatic vertical sliding block
BARREL LENGTH: —

ELEVATION: 45°
TRAVERSAL: 58°
PROJECTILE WEIGHT: 73.5 pounds
MUZZLE VELOCITY: 3,051 fps
MAXIMUM RANGE: 30,063 yards

NORINCO 122mm Howitzer
Type 59-1
ADOPTION DATE: —
CALIBER: 122mm
WEIGHT: 7,055 pounds
BREECH: —
BARREL LENGTH: —

ELEVATION: 70°
TRAVERSAL: 360°
PROJECTILE WEIGHT: 48 pounds
MUZZLE VELOCITY: 2,264 fps
MAXIMUM RANGE: 16,732 yards

NORINCO 122mm Howitzer
Type 54-1
ADOPTION DATE: —
CALIBER: 122mm
WEIGHT: 5,512 pounds
BREECH: hinged screw
BARREL LENGTH: 110 inches

ELEVATION: 60.5°
TRAVERSAL: 49°
PROJECTILE WEIGHT: 48 pounds
MUZZLE VELOCITY: 1,690 fps
MAXIMUM RANGE: 12,905 yards

NORINCO 100mm Field Gun
ADOPTION DATE: —
CALIBER: 100mm
WEIGHT: 7,606 pounds
BREECH: semiautomatic vertical sliding block
BARREL LENGTH: 362.6 inches

ELEVATION: 45°
TRAVERSAL: 50°
PROJECTILE WEIGHT: 59.5 pounds
MUZZLE VELOCITY: 2,936 fps
MAXIMUM RANGE: 21,872 yards

NORINCO 100mm Antitank Gun
Type 86
ADOPTION DATE: —
CALIBER: 100mm
WEIGHT: 8,069 pounds
BREECH: vertical sliding block
BARREL LENGTH: —

ELEVATION: 38°
TRAVERSAL: 50°
PROJECTILE WEIGHT: —
MUZZLE VELOCITY: —
MAXIMUM RANGE: 14,932 yards

NORINCO 85mm Field Gun Type 56

ADOPTION DATE: 1960s
CALIBER: 85mm
WEIGHT: 3,858 pounds
BREECH: semiautomatic vertical
   sliding block
BARREL LENGTH: 185 inches

ELEVATION: 35°
TRAVERSAL: 54°
PROJECTILE WEIGHT: —
MUZZLE VELOCITY: —
MAXIMUM RANGE: 17,115 yards

NORINCO 152mm Type 54 Howitzer

ADOPTION DATE: —
CALIBER: 152mm
WEIGHT: 7,937 pounds
BREECH: —
BARREL LENGTH: —

ELEVATION: —
TRAVERSAL: —
PROJECTILE WEIGHT: —
MUZZLE VELOCITY: —
MAXIMUM RANGE: 13,560 yards

NORINCO 122mm Type 83 Howitzer

ADOPTION DATE: 1984
CALIBER: 122mm
WEIGHT: 5,882 pounds
BREECH: —
BARREL LENGTH: —

ELEVATION: 65°
TRAVERSAL: 65°
PROJECTILE WEIGHT: —
MUZZLE VELOCITY: 2,027 fps
MAXIMUM RANGE: 19,685 yards

NORINCO 122mm Type 60 Field Gun

ADOPTION DATE: —
CALIBER: 122mm
WEIGHT: 12,125 pounds
BREECH: —
BARREL LENGTH: —

ELEVATION: —
TRAVERSAL: —
PROJECTILE WEIGHT: —
MUZZLE VELOCITY: —
MAXIMUM RANGE: 26,247 yards

CZECHOSLOVAKIA

85mm Field Gun vz52

ADOPTION DATE: 1953
CALIBER: 85mm
WEIGHT: 4,619 pounds
BREECH: semiautomatic vertical
   sliding block
BARREL LENGTH: 199.6 inches

ELEVATION: 38°
TRAVERSAL: 60°
PROJECTILE WEIGHT: 20.5 pounds
MUZZLE VELOCITY: 2,641 fps
MAXIMUM RANGE: 16,160 yards

100mm Field Gun vz53

ADOPTION DATE: 1954
CALIBER: 100mm
WEIGHT: 9,281 pounds
BREECH: horizontal sliding block
BARREL LENGTH: 265 inches

ELEVATION: 42°
TRAVERSAL: 60°
PROJECTILE WEIGHT: 35 pounds
MUZZLE VELOCITY: —
MAXIMUM RANGE: 21,000 yards

FINLAND

Tampella 122mm M-60 Field Gun

ADOPTION DATE: 1964
CALIBER: 122mm
WEIGHT: 18,739 pounds
BREECH: horizontal sliding block
BARREL LENGTH: 254.5 inches

ELEVATION: 50°
TRAVERSAL: 90°
PROJECTILE WEIGHT: 55 pounds
MUZZLE VELOCITY: 3,117 fps
MAXIMUM RANGE: 27,340 yards

Tampella 155mm Gun-Howitzer M-74

ADOPTION DATE: —
CALIBER: 155mm
WEIGHT: 20,944 pounds
BREECH: horizontal sliding block
BARREL LENGTH: 236 inches

ELEVATION: 52°
TRAVERSAL: 90°
PROJECTILE WEIGHT: —
MUZZLE VELOCITY: —
MAXIMUM RANGE: 26,247 yards

VAMMAS 155mm M-83 Howitzer

ADOPTION DATE: 1991
CALIBER: 155mm
WEIGHT: 20,955 pounds
BREECH: semiautomatic horizontal
   sliding block
BARREL LENGTH: 236 inches

ELEVATION: —
TRAVERSAL: —
PROJECTILE WEIGHT: —
MUZZLE VELOCITY: —
MAXIMUM RANGE: 43,307 yards
   (long version)

VAMMAS 155mm 155GH52 APU

ADOPTION DATE: 1991
CALIBER: 155mm
WEIGHT: 29,762 pounds
BREECH: semiautomatic horizontal
   sliding block
BARREL LENGTH: 317 inches

ELEVATION: 70°
TRAVERSAL: 70°
PROJECTILE WEIGHT: —
MUZZLE VELOCITY: 3,084 fps
MAXIMUM RANGE: 29,527 yards

FRANCE

155mm Howitzer Model 50

ADOPTION DATE: —
CALIBER: 155mm
WEIGHT: 17,857 pounds
BREECH: interrupted screw
BARREL LENGTH: 174 inches

ELEVATION: 60°
TRAVERSAL: 80°
PROJECTILE WEIGHT: 96 pounds
MUZZLE VELOCITY: 2,132 fps
MAXIMUM RANGE: 19,412 yards

Giat Industries 155mm Howitzer M114F

ADOPTION DATE: 1987
CALIBER: 155mm
WEIGHT: 16,094 pounds
BREECH: horizontal sliding block
BARREL LENGTH: 244 inches

ELEVATION: 63°
TRAVERSAL: 49°
PROJECTILE WEIGHT: —
MUZZLE VELOCITY: —
MAXIMUM RANGE: 20,231 yards

Giat Industries 155mm Towed Gun TR

ADOPTION DATE: 1989
CALIBER: 155mm
WEIGHT: 23,700 pounds
BREECH: semiautomatic horizontal
  sliding block
BARREL LENGTH: 244 inches

ELEVATION: 66°
TRAVERSAL: 65°
PROJECTILE WEIGHT: —
MUZZLE VELOCITY: —
MAXIMUM RANGE: 35,000 yards

Giat Industries 105mm LG1 MKII Light Gun

ADOPTION DATE: 1990
CALIBER: 105mm
WEIGHT: 3,351 pounds
BREECH: semiautomatic vertical
  sliding block
BARREL LENGTH: 124 inches

ELEVATION: 70°
TRAVERSAL: 36°
PROJECTILE WEIGHT: —
MUZZLE VELOCITY: —
MAXIMUM RANGE: 20,000 yards

INDIA

Indian Ordnance Factories 105mm Light Field Gun

ADOPTION DATE: early 1990s
CALIBER: 105mm
WEIGHT: 5,247 pounds
BREECH: vertical sliding block
BARREL LENGTH: 153 inches

ELEVATION: 73°
TRAVERSAL: 360°
PROJECTILE WEIGHT: —
MUZZLE VELOCITY: —
MAXIMUM RANGE: 18,810 yards

ISRAEL

Soltam 155mm M68 Gun-Howitzer

ADOPTION DATE: 1970
CALIBER: 155mm
WEIGHT: 18,739 pounds
BREECH: semiautomatic horizontal sliding block
BARREL LENGTH: 183 inches

ELEVATION: 52°
TRAVERSAL: 90°
PROJECTILE WEIGHT: 97 pounds
MUZZLE VELOCITY: 2,380 fps
MAXIMUM RANGE: 22,966 yards

Soltam 155mm M71 Gun-Howitzer

ADOPTION DATE: 1975
CALIBER: 155mm
WEIGHT: 19,842 pounds
BREECH: horizontal sliding block
BARREL LENGTH: 238 inches

ELEVATION: 52°
TRAVERSAL: 84°
PROJECTILE WEIGHT: —
MUZZLE VELOCITY: 2,510 fps
MAXIMUM RANGE: 25,153 yards

Soltam 155mm Model 839P

ADOPTION DATE: 1983
CALIBER: 155mm
WEIGHT: 23,920 pounds
BREECH: horizontal sliding block
BARREL LENGTH: 238 inches

ELEVATION: 70°
TRAVERSAL: 78°
PROJECTILE WEIGHT: 97 pounds
MUZZLE VELOCITY: —
MAXIMUM RANGE: 33,900 yards

Soltam 155mm Model 845P

ADOPTION DATE: 1984
CALIBER: 155mm
WEIGHT: 25,794 pounds
BREECH: horizontal sliding block
BARREL LENGTH: 275 inches

ELEVATION: 70°
TRAVERSAL: 78°
PROJECTILE WEIGHT: 97 pounds
MUZZLE VELOCITY: —
MAXIMUM RANGE: 42,650 yards

Soltam 155mm M-46 Field Gun Upgrade

ADOPTION DATE: —
CALIBER: 155mm
WEIGHT: 19,511 pounds
BREECH: semiautomatic horizontal
  sliding block
BARREL LENGTH: 303 inches

ELEVATION: 45°
TRAVERSAL: 50°
PROJECTILE WEIGHT: —
MUZZLE VELOCITY: —
MAXIMUM RANGE: 42,650 yards
  (high-performance)

Soltam 155mm M114S Howitzer Upgrade

ADOPTION DATE: —
CALIBER: 155mm
WEIGHT: 13,007 pounds
BREECH: —
BARREL LENGTH: 201 inches

ELEVATION: 65°
TRAVERSAL: 49°
PROJECTILE WEIGHT: —
MUZZLE VELOCITY: —
MAXIMUM RANGE: 19,794 yards

ITALY

Oto Melara 105mm Model 56 Pack Howitzer

ADOPTION DATE: 1957
CALIBER: 105mm
WEIGHT: 2,844 pounds
BREECH: semiautomatic vertical
  sliding block
BARREL LENGTH: 58 inches

ELEVATION: 65°
TRAVERSAL: 36°
PROJECTILE WEIGHT: 33 pounds
MUZZLE VELOCITY: 1,365 fps
MAXIMUM RANGE: 11,565 yards

SOUTH KOREA

105mm KH178 Light Howitzer

ADOPTION DATE: 1984
CALIBER: 105mm
WEIGHT: 5,842 pounds
BREECH: horizontal sliding block
BARREL LENGTH: 176 inches

ELEVATION: 65°
TRAVERSAL: 45.5°
PROJECTILE WEIGHT: —
MUZZLE VELOCITY: 2,172 fps
MAXIMUM RANGE: 16,076 yards

155mm KH179 Howitzer

ADOPTION DATE: 1983
CALIBER: 155mm
WEIGHT: 15,190 pounds
BREECH: interrupted screw
BARREL LENGTH: 279.5 inches

ELEVATION: 68°
TRAVERSAL: 48.7°
PROJECTILE WEIGHT: —
MUZZLE VELOCITY: 2,710 fps
MAXIMUM RANGE: 24,060 yards

SOUTH AFRICA

Denel 155mm G5
Gun-Howitzer

ADOPTION DATE: 1983
CALIBER: 155mm
WEIGHT: 30,314 pounds
BREECH: semiautomatic interrupted
  screw
BARREL LENGTH: 275 inches

ELEVATION: 75°
TRAVERSAL: 82°
PROJECTILE WEIGHT: —
MUZZLE VELOCITY: —
MAXIMUM RANGE: 32,808 yards

SOVIET UNION/RUSSIA

122mm Field Gun M-46 (M1954)

ADOPTION DATE: 1954
CALIBER: 122mm
WEIGHT: —
BREECH: —
BARREL LENGTH: —

ELEVATION: —
TRAVERSAL: —
PROJECTILE WEIGHT: 74 pounds
MUZZLE VELOCITY: —
MAXIMUM RANGE: 29,690 yards

76mm Gun M69

ADOPTION DATE: 1969
CALIBER: 76.2mm
WEIGHT: 1,720 pounds
BREECH: horizontal sliding block
BARREL LENGTH: —

ELEVATION: 65°
TRAVERSAL: 50°
PROJECTILE WEIGHT: 14 pounds
MUZZLE VELOCITY: —
MAXIMUM RANGE: 12,030 yards

57mm CH-26

ADOPTION DATE: 1955
CALIBER: 57mm
WEIGHT: 4,630 pounds
BREECH: semiautomatic vertical
    sliding block
BARREL LENGTH: 163.5 inches

ELEVATION: 35°
TRAVERSAL: 54°
PROJECTILE WEIGHT: 6.8 pounds
MUZZLE VELOCITY: 3,281 fps
MAXIMUM RANGE: 9,186 yards

100mm T-12

ADOPTION DATE: 1955
CALIBER: 100mm
WEIGHT: 5,953 pounds
BREECH: semiautomatic vertical
    sliding block
BARREL LENGTH: 212 inches

ELEVATION: 40°
TRAVERSAL: 55°
PROJECTILE WEIGHT: 34.6 pounds
MUZZLE VELOCITY: 2,953 fps
MAXIMUM RANGE: 22,966 yards

57mm M50

ADOPTION DATE: 1950
CALIBER: 57mm
WEIGHT: 8,818.5 pounds
BREECH: —
BARREL LENGTH: 163.5 inches

ELEVATION: 90°
TRAVERSAL: 360°
PROJECTILE WEIGHT: 6 pounds
MUZZLE VELOCITY: 3,200 fps
MAXIMUM CEILING: 13,123 feet

130mm Gun M46

ADOPTION DATE: 1954
CALIBER: 130mm
WEIGHT: 18,629 pounds
BREECH: horizontal sliding block
BARREL LENGTH: 281 inches

ELEVATION: 45°
TRAVERSAL: 50°
PROJECTILE WEIGHT: 74 pounds
MUZZLE VELOCITY: 3,051 fps
MAXIMUM RANGE: 29,528 yards

122mm Field Gun M1955 (D-74)

ADOPTION DATE: 1955
CALIBER: 122mm
WEIGHT: 11,023 pounds
BREECH: vertical sliding block
BARREL LENGTH: 216 inches

ELEVATION: —
TRAVERSAL: —
PROJECTILE WEIGHT: 56 pounds
MUZZLE VELOCITY: 2,625 fps
MAXIMUM RANGE: 22,966 yards

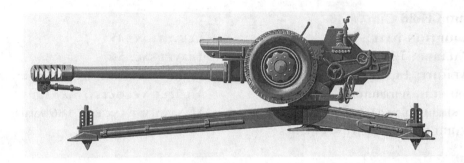

SOVIET UNION/RUSSIA: 122MM HOWITZER D-30
(Courtesy Art-Tech)

122mm Howitzer D-30

ADOPTION DATE: early 1960s
CALIBER: 122mm
WEIGHT: 6,944 pounds
BREECH: semiautomatic vertical
    sliding block
BARREL LENGTH: 192 inches

ELEVATION: 70°
TRAVERSAL: 360°
PROJECTILE WEIGHT: 48 pounds
MUZZLE VELOCITY: 2,264 fps
MAXIMUM RANGE: 16,732 yards

152mm Gun-Howitzer D-20

ADOPTION DATE: 1955
CALIBER: 152mm
WEIGHT: 13,007 pounds
BREECH: vertical sliding block
BARREL LENGTH: 221 inches

ELEVATION: 63°
TRAVERSAL: 60°
PROJECTILE WEIGHT: 96 pounds
MUZZLE VELOCITY: 2,198 fps
MAXIMUM RANGE: 19,040 yards

180mm Gun S-23

ADOPTION DATE: 1955
CALIBER: 180mm
WEIGHT: 47,289 pounds
BREECH: interrupted screw
BARREL LENGTH: 319 inches

ELEVATION: 50°
TRAVERSAL: 44°
PROJECTILE WEIGHT: 194 pounds
MUZZLE VELOCITY: 2,592 fps
MAXIMUM RANGE: 33,246 yards

240mm Mortar M-240

ADOPTION DATE: 1953
CALIBER: 240mm
WEIGHT: 9,149 pounds
BREECH: —
BARREL LENGTH: 210 inches

ELEVATION: 65°
TRAVERSAL: 18°
PROJECTILE WEIGHT: 288 pounds
MUZZLE VELOCITY: —
MAXIMUM RANGE: 10,608 yards

130mm Field Gun M-46

ADOPTION DATE: 1954
CALIBER: 130mm
WEIGHT: 16,976 pounds
BREECH: horizontal sliding block
BARREL LENGTH: 299 inches

ELEVATION: 45°
TRAVERSAL: 50°
PROJECTILE WEIGHT: 74 pounds
MUZZLE VELOCITY: 3,051 fps
MAXIMUM RANGE: 29,690 yards

180mm Gun S-23

ADOPTION DATE: 1955
CALIBER: 180mm
WEIGHT: 47,289 pounds
BREECH: interrupted screw
BARREL LENGTH: 346 inches

ELEVATION: 50°
TRAVERSAL: 44°
PROJECTILE WEIGHT: 194 pounds
MUZZLE VELOCITY: 2,592 fps
MAXIMUM RANGE: 33,246 yards

152mm Gun 2A36 (M1976)

ADOPTION DATE: 1981
CALIBER: 152mm
WEIGHT: 21,517 pounds
BREECH: semiautomatic horizontal
   sliding block
BARREL LENGTH: 323 inches

ELEVATION: 57°
TRAVERSAL: 25°
PROJECTILE WEIGHT: 101 pounds
MUZZLE VELOCITY: 2,625 fps
MAXIMUM RANGE: 43,745 yards

152mm Howitzer 2A65 (M1987)

ADOPTION DATE: —
CALIBER: 152mm
WEIGHT: 15,432 pounds
BREECH: semiautomatic
BARREL LENGTH: —

ELEVATION: 70°
TRAVERSAL: 27°
PROJECTILE WEIGHT: 96 pounds
MUZZLE VELOCITY: 2,657 fps
MAXIMUM RANGE: 27,012 yards

125mm 2A45M Antitank Gun

ADOPTION DATE: 1955
CALIBER: 125mm
WEIGHT: 14,495 pounds
BREECH: semiautomatic vertical
    sliding block
BARREL LENGTH: —

ELEVATION: 25°
TRAVERSAL: 360°
PROJECTILE WEIGHT: 15.5 pounds
    (AP)
MUZZLE VELOCITY: 5,577 fps
MAXIMUM RANGE: 2,296 yards (AP)

120mm 2B16 (NONA-K)
Combination Gun

ADOPTION DATE: 1986
CALIBER: 120mm
WEIGHT: 2,645.5 pounds
BREECH: vertical sliding block
BARREL LENGTH: —

ELEVATION: 60°
TRAVERSAL: 80°
PROJECTILE WEIGHT: —
MUZZLE VELOCITY: —
MAXIMUM RANGE: 9,514 yards

100mm Antitank Gun T-12 and MT-12

ADOPTION DATE: 1955
CALIBER: 100mm
WEIGHT: 6,063 pounds
BREECH: semiautomatic vertical
    sliding block
BARREL LENGTH: 248 inches

ELEVATION: 20°
TRAVERSAL: 27°
PROJECTILE WEIGHT: 50.7 pounds
MUZZLE VELOCITY: 3,199 fps
MAXIMUM RANGE: 3,199 yards

152mm 2A61 Howitzer

ADOPTION DATE: early 1990s
CALIBER: 152mm
WEIGHT: 9,590 pounds
BREECH: —
BARREL LENGTH: —

ELEVATION: 70°
TRAVERSAL: 360°
PROJECTILE WEIGHT: —
MUZZLE VELOCITY: —
MAXIMUM RANGE: 16,404 yards

85mm Auxiliary-Propelled Field Gun
SD-44

ADOPTION DATE: —
CALIBER: 85mm
WEIGHT: 4,960 pounds
BREECH: semiautomatic vertical
    sliding block
BARREL LENGTH: 185 inches

ELEVATION: 35°
TRAVERSAL: 54°
PROJECTILE WEIGHT: 8 pounds
    (HE)
MUZZLE VELOCITY: 2,598 fps
MAXIMUM RANGE: 17,115 yards

82mm Vasilyek Automatic Mortar (2B9)

ADOPTION DATE: early 1970s
CALIBER: 82mm
WEIGHT: 1,422 pounds
BREECH: semiautomatic
BARREL LENGTH: —

ELEVATION: 85°
TRAVERSAL: 60°
PROJECTILE WEIGHT: 7 pounds
MUZZLE VELOCITY: 886 fps
MAXIMUM RANGE: 4,670 yards

76mm Mountain Gun GP (M1966)

ADOPTION DATE: 1966
CALIBER: 76mm
WEIGHT: 1,720 pounds
BREECH: horizontal sliding block
BARREL LENGTH: —

ELEVATION: 65°
TRAVERSAL: 50°
PROJECTILE WEIGHT: —
MUZZLE VELOCITY: 1,969 fps
MAXIMUM RANGE: 12,576 yards

SPAIN

105mm M/26 Field Howitzer

ADOPTION DATE: early 1950s
CALIBER: 105mm
WEIGHT: —
BREECH: horizontal sliding block
BARREL LENGTH: 132 inches

ELEVATION: 45°
TRAVERSAL: 50°
PROJECTILE WEIGHT: —
MUZZLE VELOCITY: —
MAXIMUM RANGE: 12,522 yards

Santa Barbara 155mm SB 155/39 Towed Howitzer

ADOPTION DATE: 1994
CALIBER: 155mm
WEIGHT: —
BREECH: semiautomatic vertical
  sliding block
BARREL LENGTH: 238 inches

ELEVATION: 70°
TRAVERSAL: 60°
PROJECTILE WEIGHT: 96 pounds
MUZZLE VELOCITY: —
MAXIMUM RANGE: 26,247 yards

SWEDEN

105mm Howitzer Bofors 4140
ADOPTION DATE: 1955
CALIBER: 105mm
WEIGHT: 6,173 pounds
BREECH: semiautomatic vertical
sliding block
BARREL LENGTH: 132 inches

ELEVATION: 60°
TRAVERSAL: 360°
PROJECTILE WEIGHT: 34 pounds
MUZZLE VELOCITY: 2,100 fps
MAXIMUM RANGE: 17,060 yards

155mm Bofors Field Howitzer Field 77A
ADOPTION DATE: 1973
CALIBER: 155mm
WEIGHT: 25,353 pounds
BREECH: semiautomatic vertical
sliding block
BARREL LENGTH: 232 inches

ELEVATION: 50°
TRAVERSAL: 50°
PROJECTILE WEIGHT: 94 pounds
MUZZLE VELOCITY: 2,539 fps
MAXIMUM RANGE: 24,060 yards

155mm Bofors Field Howitzer Field 77B
ADOPTION DATE: 1986
CALIBER: 155mm
WEIGHT: 26,235 pounds
BREECH: interrupted screw
BARREL LENGTH: 238 inches

ELEVATION: 70°
TRAVERSAL: 60°
PROJECTILE WEIGHT: 94 pounds
MUZZLE VELOCITY: 2,713 fps
MAXIMUM RANGE: 26,247 yards

SWITZERLAND

105mm Field Howitzer M46
ADOPTION DATE: 1943
CALIBER: 105mm
WEIGHT: 4,057 pounds
BREECH: horizontal sliding block
BARREL LENGTH: 91 inches

ELEVATION: 67°
TRAVERSAL: 72°
PROJECTILE WEIGHT: 33 pounds
MUZZLE VELOCITY: 1,608 fps
MAXIMUM RANGE: 10,936 yards

90mm M50
ADOPTION DATE: 1950
CALIBER: 90mm
WEIGHT: 1,226 pounds
BREECH: semiautomatic vertical sliding block
BARREL LENGTH: 113 inches

ELEVATION: 32°
TRAVERSAL: 66°
PROJECTILE WEIGHT: 4 pounds
MUZZLE VELOCITY: 1,969 fps
MAXIMUM RANGE: 3,281 yards

90mm M57
ADOPTION DATE: 1957
CALIBER: 90mm
WEIGHT: 1,257 pounds
BREECH: semiautomatic vertical sliding block
BARREL LENGTH: 117 inches

ELEVATION: 23°
TRAVERSAL: 70°
PROJECTILE WEIGHT: 6 pounds
MUZZLE VELOCITY: 1,969 fps
MAXIMUM RANGE: 3,281 yards

(FORMER) YUGOSLAVIA

76mm Mountain Gun M48
ADOPTION DATE: 1948
CALIBER: 76mm
WEIGHT: 1,554 pounds
BREECH: —
BARREL LENGTH: 46 inches

ELEVATION: 45°
TRAVERSAL: 50°
PROJECTILE WEIGHT: 13.5 pounds
MUZZLE VELOCITY: 1,306 fps
MAXIMUM RANGE: 9,569 yards

155mm Converted Gun M46/84
ADOPTION DATE: —
CALIBER: 155mm
WEIGHT: 16,931 pounds
BREECH: horizontal sliding block
BARREL LENGTH: 275 inches

ELEVATION: 45°
TRAVERSAL: 50°
PROJECTILE WEIGHT: —
MUZZLE VELOCITY: —
MAXIMUM RANGE: 42,650 yards

152mm Gun-Howitzer M84, M84B1, and M84B2
ADOPTION DATE: —
CALIBER: 152mm
WEIGHT: 15,609 pounds
BREECH: semiautomatic vertical sliding block
BARREL LENGTH: 238 inches

ELEVATION: 63°
TRAVERSAL: 50°
PROJECTILE WEIGHT: —
MUZZLE VELOCITY: 2,658 fps
MAXIMUM RANGE: 29,528 yards
  (M84B1, M84B2)

105mm Howitzer M56

ADOPTION DATE: —
CALIBER: 105mm
WEIGHT: 4,542 pounds
BREECH: horizontal sliding block
BARREL LENGTH: 137 inches

ELEVATION: 68°
TRAVERSAL: 52°
PROJECTILE WEIGHT: —
MUZZLE VELOCITY: —
MAXIMUM RANGE: 14,217 yards

100mm M87 Antitank Gun TOPAZ

ADOPTION DATE: —
CALIBER: 100mm
WEIGHT: —
BREECH: —
BARREL LENGTH: 248 inches

ELEVATION: 18°
TRAVERSAL: 360°
PROJECTILE WEIGHT: —
MUZZLE VELOCITY: 3,199 fps
MAXIMUM RANGE: 1,312 yards

Self-Propelled Artillery
UNITED STATES

105mm Howitzer Motor Carriage M52

ADOPTION DATE: 1951
CALIBER: 105mm
WEIGHT: 53,021 pounds
BREECH: —
BARREL LENGTH: —

ELEVATION: 65°
TRAVERSAL: 120°
PROJECTILE WEIGHT: —
MUZZLE VELOCITY: —
MAXIMUM RANGE: 12,325 yards

155mm Gun Motor Carriage M53

ADOPTION DATE: 1951
CALIBER: 155mm
WEIGHT: 90,011 pounds
BREECH: —
BARREL LENGTH: —

ELEVATION: 65°
TRAVERSAL: 60°
PROJECTILE WEIGHT: —
MUZZLE VELOCITY: —
MAXIMUM RANGE: 25,400 yards

203mm Howitzer Motor Carriage M55

ADOPTION DATE: 1951
CALIBER: 203mm
WEIGHT: 98,000 pounds
BREECH: —
BARREL LENGTH: —

ELEVATION: 65°
TRAVERSAL: 60°
PROJECTILE WEIGHT: —
MUZZLE VELOCITY: —
MAXIMUM RANGE: 18,373 yards

40mm Self-Propelled Gun M42A1 "Duster"

ADOPTION DATE: 1951
CALIBER: 40mm
WEIGHT: 49,494 pounds
BREECH: —
BARREL LENGTH: —

ELEVATION: 85°
TRAVERSAL: 360°
PROJECTILE WEIGHT: —
MUZZLE VELOCITY: —
MAXIMUM RANGE: 5,468 yards

155mm Howitzer Motor Carriage M44

ADOPTION DATE: 1952
CALIBER: 155mm
WEIGHT: 64,000 pounds
BREECH: —
BARREL LENGTH: —

ELEVATION: 65°
TRAVERSAL: 60°
PROJECTILE WEIGHT: —
MUZZLE VELOCITY: —
MAXIMUM RANGE: 15,967 yards

90mm Gun Motor Carriage M56 "Scorpion"

ADOPTION DATE: 1953
CALIBER: 90mm
WEIGHT: 15,510 pounds
BREECH: —
BARREL LENGTH: —

ELEVATION: 15°
TRAVERSAL: 60°
PROJECTILE WEIGHT: —
MUZZLE VELOCITY: —
MAXIMUM RANGE: 2,734 yards

UNITED STATES: GUN MOTOR CARRIAGE M107
(Courtesy Art-Tech)

175mm SP Gun M107

ADOPTION DATE: 1963
CALIBER: 175mm
WEIGHT: 62,100 pounds
BREECH: interrupted screw
BARREL LENGTH: 413 inches

ELEVATION: 65°
TRAVERSAL: 30°
PROJECTILE WEIGHT: 147 pounds
MUZZLE VELOCITY: 3,028 fps
MAXIMUM RANGE: 35,761 yards

105mm Self-Propelled Howitzer M108

ADOPTION DATE: 1961
CALIBER: 105mm
WEIGHT: 49,500 pounds
BREECH: —
BARREL LENGTH: —

ELEVATION: 74°
TRAVERSAL: 360°
PROJECTILE WEIGHT: 33 pounds
MUZZLE VELOCITY: 1,550 fps
MAXIMUM RANGE: 12,577 yards

UNITED STATES: HOWITZER MOTOR CARRIAGE M109

(Courtesy Art-Tech)

155mm Self-Propelled Howitzer M109

ADOPTION DATE: 1962
CALIBER: 155mm
WEIGHT: 52,460 pounds
BREECH: —
BARREL LENGTH: —

ELEVATION: 75°
TRAVERSAL: 360°
PROJECTILE WEIGHT: 95 pounds
MUZZLE VELOCITY: 1,840 fps
MAXIMUM RANGE: 15,967 yards

155mm Self-Propelled Howitzer M109A2

ADOPTION DATE: 1978
CALIBER: 155mm
WEIGHT: 55,005 pounds
BREECH: —
BARREL LENGTH: —

ELEVATION: 75°
TRAVERSAL: 360°
PROJECTILE WEIGHT: —
MUZZLE VELOCITY: —
MAXIMUM RANGE: 19,795 yards

155mm M109A6 Paladin Self-Propelled Howitzer

ADOPTION DATE: 1992
CALIBER: 155mm
WEIGHT: 63,600 pounds
BREECH: —
BARREL LENGTH: 238 inches

ELEVATION: 75°
TRAVERSAL: 360°
PROJECTILE WEIGHT: —
MUZZLE VELOCITY: —
MAXIMUM RANGE: —

UNITED STATES: HOWITZER MOTOR CARRIAGE M110A2
(Courtesy Art-Tech)

8-Inch Self-Propelled Howitzer M110

ADOPTION DATE: 1962
CALIBER: 8-inch
WEIGHT: 58,422 pounds
BREECH: interrupted screw
BARREL LENGTH: —

ELEVATION: 65°
TRAVERSAL: 60°
PROJECTILE WEIGHT: 204 pounds
MUZZLE VELOCITY: 1,926 fps
MAXIMUM RANGE: 18,373 yards

GREAT BRITAIN

105mm Vickers Defence Systems L13 "Abbott" Self-Propelled Gun

ADOPTION DATE: 1964
CALIBER: 105mm
WEIGHT: 36,500 pounds
BREECH: semiautomatic vertical sliding block
BARREL LENGTH: 153 inches

ELEVATION: 70°
TRAVERSAL: 360°
PROJECTILE WEIGHT: 35.3 pounds
MUZZLE VELOCITY: 2,313 fps
MAXIMUM RANGE: 18,920 yards

PEOPLES' REPUBLIC OF CHINA

NORINCO 122mm Self-Propelled Howitzer Type 54-1

ADOPTION DATE: —
CALIBER: 122mm
WEIGHT: 33,731 pounds
BREECH: —
BARREL LENGTH: —

ELEVATION: 63°
TRAVERSAL: 45°
PROJECTILE WEIGHT: 48 pounds
MUZZLE VELOCITY: 1,690 fps
MAXIMUM RANGE: 12,905 yards

NORINCO 122mm Self-Propelled Howitzer Type 85

ADOPTION DATE: —
CALIBER: 122mm
WEIGHT: 36,375 pounds
BREECH: —
BARREL LENGTH: —
ELEVATION: 70°

TRAVERSAL: 45°
PROJECTILE WEIGHT: 48 pounds
MUZZLE VELOCITY: —
MAXIMUM RANGE: 22,966 yards
  (ERFB)

NORINCO Type 83 152mm Self-Propelled Gun-Howitzer and 130mm Self-Propelled Gun

ADOPTION DATE: 1984
CALIBER: 152mm
WEIGHT: 66,139 pounds
BREECH: —
BARREL LENGTH: —

ELEVATION: 65°
TRAVERSAL: 360°
PROJECTILE WEIGHT: —
MUZZLE VELOCITY: 2,149 fps
MAXIMUM RANGE: 18,843 yards

NORINCO 155mm 45 Caliber Self-Propelled Gun

ADOPTION DATE: 1988
CALIBER: 155mm
WEIGHT: 70,548 pounds
BREECH: semiautomatic horizontal
  sliding block
BARREL LENGTH: 277.5 inches

ELEVATION: 72°
TRAVERSAL: 360°
PROJECTILE WEIGHT: —
MUZZLE VELOCITY: 2,963 fps
MAXIMUM RANGE: 42,651 yards

CZECHOSLOVAKIA (CZECH REPUBLIC)

CZECHOSLOVAKIA (CZECH REPUBLIC): 152MM ZTS SELF-PROPELLED GUN-HOWITZER DANA (VZ.77)
(Courtesy Art-Tech)

152mm ZTS Self-Propelled Gun-Howitzer DANA (vz.77)

ADOPTION DATE: 1981
CALIBER: 152mm
WEIGHT: 64,485 pounds
BREECH: semiautomatic horizontal sliding block
BARREL LENGTH: 220 inches

ELEVATION: 70°
TRAVERSAL: 225°
PROJECTILE WEIGHT: 96 pounds
MUZZLE VELOCITY: 2,274 fps
MAXIMUM RANGE: 20,450 yards

120mm ZTS PRAM-S Self-Propelled Mortar System

ADOPTION DATE: 1992
CALIBER: 120mm
WEIGHT: 37,412 pounds
BREECH: —
BARREL LENGTH: 316 inches

ELEVATION: 80°
TRAVERSAL: 30°
PROJECTILE WEIGHT: —
MUZZLE VELOCITY: —
MAXIMUM RANGE: 8,788 yards

FRANCE

105mm Howitzer Modèle 50 sur affût Automoteur

ADOPTION DATE: 1952
CALIBER: 105mm
WEIGHT: 36,376 pounds
BREECH: —
BARREL LENGTH: —

ELEVATION: 66°
TRAVERSAL: 40°
PROJECTILE WEIGHT: —
MUZZLE VELOCITY: —
MAXIMUM RANGE: 16,404 yards

155mm Giat Industries Self-Propelled Gun F3 (Cn-155-F3-Am)

ADOPTION DATE: early 1950s
CALIBER: 155mm
WEIGHT: 38,360 pounds
BREECH: interrupted screw
BARREL LENGTH: 201 inches

ELEVATION: 67°
TRAVERSAL: 50°
PROJECTILE WEIGHT: 96 pounds
MUZZLE VELOCITY: 2,379 fps
MAXIMUM RANGE: 21,927 yards

30mm AMX-13 DCA

ADOPTION DATE: 1964
CALIBER: 30mm
WEIGHT: 37,919 pounds
BREECH: —
BARREL LENGTH: —

ELEVATION: 85°
TRAVERSAL: 360°
PROJECTILE WEIGHT: —
MUZZLE VELOCITY: —
MAXIMUM CEILING: 11,483 feet

155mm SP Gun GCT (155 AUF1 T)

ADOPTION DATE: 1979
CALIBER: 155mm
WEIGHT: 92,594 pounds
BREECH: vertical sliding block
BARREL LENGTH: 244 inches

ELEVATION: 66°
TRAVERSAL: 360°
PROJECTILE WEIGHT: 95 pounds
MUZZLE VELOCITY: 2,658 fps
MAXIMUM RANGE: 25,514 yards

Giat Industries/Hägglunds Vehicle CV 90105 TML Tank Destroyer

ADOPTION DATE: 1994
CALIBER: 105mm
WEIGHT: 52,911 pounds
BREECH: —
BARREL LENGTH: —

ELEVATION: 20°
TRAVERSAL: 360°
PROJECTILE WEIGHT: —
MUZZLE VELOCITY: —
MAXIMUM RANGE: —

155mm Giat Industries CAESAR Self-Propelled Gun

ADOPTION DATE: 1994
CALIBER: 155mm
WEIGHT: —
BREECH: —
BARREL LENGTH: 317 inches

ELEVATION: 66°
TRAVERSAL: 30°
PROJECTILE WEIGHT: —
MUZZLE VELOCITY: —
MAXIMUM RANGE: 46,000 yards

GERMANY

90mm Thyssen Hhenschel Jagdpanzer Kanon (JPZ 4-5)

ADOPTION DATE: 1965

CALIBER: 90mm

WEIGHT: 60,621 pounds

BREECH: —

BARREL LENGTH: —

ELEVATION: 15°

TRAVERSAL: 15°

PROJECTILE WEIGHT: —

MUZZLE VELOCITY: —

MAXIMUM RANGE: 2,187 yards

GERMANY: GEPARD
(Courtesy Art-Tech)

Gepard

ADOPTION DATE: 1973

CALIBER: 35mm

WEIGHT: 104,279 pounds

BREECH: —

BARREL LENGTH: 124 inches

ELEVATION: 85°

TRAVERSAL: 360°

PROJECTILE WEIGHT: —

MUZZLE VELOCITY: —

MAXIMUM CEILING: 11,483 feet

155mm Wegmann/MaK Panzerhaubitze 2000 (PzH2000) Self-Propelled Howitzer

ADOPTION DATE: 1986
CALIBER: 155mm
WEIGHT: 121,254 pounds
BREECH: —
BARREL LENGTH: 317 inches
ELEVATION: 65°

TRAVERSAL: 360°
PROJECTILE WEIGHT: —
MUZZLE VELOCITY: —
MAXIMUM RANGE: 43,745 yards
  (extended-range)

155mm Rheinmetall M109A36

ADOPTION DATE: mid-1990s
CALIBER: 155mm
WEIGHT: —
BREECH: —
BARREL LENGTH: 238 inches
ELEVATION: —

TRAVERSAL: —
PROJECTILE WEIGHT: —
MUZZLE VELOCITY: 2,247 fps
MAXIMUM RANGE: 32,808 yards
  (extended-range)

ISRAEL

155mm Self-Propelled Howitzer M50

ADOPTION DATE: 1958
CALIBER: 155mm
WEIGHT: 68,343 pounds
BREECH: —
BARREL LENGTH: —

ELEVATION: 69°
TRAVERSAL: 40°
PROJECTILE WEIGHT: 95 pounds
MUZZLE VELOCITY: 2,132 fps
MAXIMUM RANGE: 19,248 yards

ISRAEL: 155MM SOLTAM SELF-PROPELLED GUN-HOWITZER L33
(Courtesy Art-Tech)

155mm Soltam Self-Propelled Gun-Howitzer L33

ADOPTION DATE: 1973
CALIBER: 155mm
WEIGHT: 91,492 pounds
BREECH: horizontal sliding block
BARREL LENGTH: 201 inches

ELEVATION: 52°
TRAVERSAL: 60°
PROJECTILE WEIGHT: 95 pounds
MUZZLE VELOCITY: 2,378 fps
MAXIMUM RANGE: 21,872 yards

155mm Soltam Rascal Light Self-Propelled Howitzer

ADOPTION DATE: 1994
CALIBER: 155mm
WEIGHT: 19,500 pounds
BREECH: —
BARREL LENGTH: 238 inches

ELEVATION: 60°
TRAVERSAL: 120°
PROJECTILE WEIGHT: 95 pounds
MUZZLE VELOCITY: —
MAXIMUM RANGE: 27,340 yards

ITALY

76mm OTO-Melara 76

ADOPTION DATE: 1984
CALIBER: 76mm
WEIGHT: 110,231 pounds
BREECH: —
BARREL LENGTH: —

ELEVATION: 60°
TRAVERSAL: 360°
PROJECTILE WEIGHT: —
MUZZLE VELOCITY: —
MAXIMUM CEILING: 19,686 feet

JAPAN

106mm Type 60 Self-Propelled Recoilless Gun

ADOPTION DATE: 1960
CALIBER: 106mm
WEIGHT: 17,637 pounds
BREECH: —
BARREL LENGTH: 131 inches

ELEVATION: 15°
TRAVERSAL: 60°
PROJECTILE WEIGHT: —
MUZZLE VELOCITY: —
MAXIMUM RANGE: 1,203 yards

SOVIET UNION/RUSSIA

SOVIET UNION/RUSSIA: ZSU-57-2
(Courtesy Art-Tech)

ZSU-57-2

ADOPTION DATE: 1954
CALIBER: 57mm
WEIGHT: 61,950 pounds
BREECH: —
BARREL LENGTH: —

ELEVATION: 85°
TRAVERSAL: 360°
PROJECTILE WEIGHT: —
MUZZLE VELOCITY: —
MAXIMUM CEILING: 13,123 feet

ASU57

ADOPTION DATE: 1957
CALIBER: 57mm
WEIGHT: 16,314 pounds
BREECH: —
BARREL LENGTH: —

ELEVATION: 12°
TRAVERSAL: 16°
PROJECTILE WEIGHT: —
MUZZLE VELOCITY: —
MAXIMUM RANGE: 1,094 yards

ASU85

ADOPTION DATE: 1961
CALIBER: 85mm
WEIGHT: 30,865 pounds
BREECH: —
BARREL LENGTH: —

ELEVATION: 15°
TRAVERSAL: 12°
PROJECTILE WEIGHT: —
MUZZLE VELOCITY: —
MAXIMUM RANGE: 3,281 yards

152mm Self-Propelled Gun-Howitzer M-1973 (SO-152) Akatsiya

ADOPTION DATE: 1971
CALIBER: 152mm
WEIGHT: 60,627 pounds
BREECH: —
BARREL LENGTH: —

ELEVATION: 60°
TRAVERSAL: 360°
PROJECTILE WEIGHT: 96 pounds
MUZZLE VELOCITY: —
MAXIMUM RANGE: 20,232 yards

SOVIET UNION/RUSSIA:
122MM SELF-PROPELLED HOWITZER M1974 (SO-122 GVOZDIKA)
(Courtesy Art-Tech)

122mm Self-Propelled Howitzer M1974 (SO-122, Gvozdika)

ADOPTION DATE: 1971
CALIBER: 122mm
WEIGHT: 34,172 pounds
BREECH: —
BARREL LENGTH: —

ELEVATION: 70°
TRAVERSAL: 360°
PROJECTILE WEIGHT: 48 pounds
MUZZLE VELOCITY: 2,264 fps
MAXIMUM RANGE: 16,732 yards

240mm Self-Propelled Mortar M-1975 (SM-240) Tyul'pan

ADOPTION DATE: 1975
CALIBER: 240mm
WEIGHT: 60,627 pounds
BREECH: —
BARREL LENGTH: —

ELEVATION: 80°
TRAVERSAL: 10°
PROJECTILE WEIGHT: 286.5 pounds
MUZZLE VELOCITY: —
MAXIMUM RANGE: 10,553 yards (HE)

203mm Self-Propelled Gun M-1975 (SO-203) Pion

ADOPTION DATE: 1975
CALIBER: 203mm
WEIGHT: 102,515 pounds
BREECH: interrupted screw
BARREL LENGTH: 449 inches

ELEVATION: 60°
TRAVERSAL: 30°
PROJECTILE WEIGHT: 242.5 pounds
MUZZLE VELOCITY: 3,150 fps
MAXIMUM RANGE: 41,010 yards (HE)

152mm Self-Propelled Gun (2S5) Giatsint

ADOPTION DATE: 1976
CALIBER: 152mm
WEIGHT: 62,170 pounds
BREECH: —
BARREL LENGTH: —

ELEVATION: 57°
TRAVERSAL: 30°
PROJECTILE WEIGHT: 101 pounds
MUZZLE VELOCITY: —
MAXIMUM RANGE: 31,059 yards (HE)

120mm SO-120 Self-Propelled Howitzer/Mortar (2S9) Anona

ADOPTION DATE: 1981
CALIBER: 120mm
WEIGHT: 19,180 pounds
BREECH: —
BARREL LENGTH: —

ELEVATION: 80°
TRAVERSAL: 70°
PROJECTILE WEIGHT: —
MUZZLE VELOCITY: 1,204 fps
MAXIMUM RANGE: 9,684 yards

152mm Self-Propelled Artillery System 2S19

ADOPTION DATE: 1989
CALIBER: 152mm
WEIGHT: —
BREECH: —
BARREL LENGTH: —

ELEVATION: 68°
TRAVERSAL: 360°
PROJECTILE WEIGHT: —
MUZZLE VELOCITY: —
MAXIMUM RANGE: 31,605 yards

120mm 2S23 self-Propelled Gun-Mortar System

ADOPTION DATE: 1990
CALIBER: 120mm
WEIGHT: 19,180 pounds
BREECH: —
BARREL LENGTH: —
ELEVATION: 80°

TRAVERSAL: 35°
PROJECTILE WEIGHT: 41.5 pounds
MUZZLE VELOCITY: 1,204 fps
MAXIMUM RANGE: 14,217 yards
    (HE-RAP)

Recoilless Artillery
UNITED STATES

90mm RCL Rifle M67
ADOPTION DATE: 1955
CALIBER: 90mm
WEIGHT: 77 pounds
BREECH: —
BARREL LENGTH: 53 inches

ELEVATION: 65°
TRAVERSAL: 360°
PROJECTILE WEIGHT: 6.8 pounds
MUZZLE VELOCITY: 705 fps
MAXIMUM RANGE: 820 yards

120mm RCL M28 Davy Crockett
ADOPTION DATE: 1958
CALIBER: 120mm
WEIGHT: 103.5 pounds
BREECH: —
BARREL LENGTH: 56.5 inches

ELEVATION: 45°
TRAVERSAL: 360°
PROJECTILE WEIGHT: —
MUZZLE VELOCITY: 459 fps
MAXIMUM RANGE: 2,187 yards

155mm RCL M29 Davy Crockett
ADOPTION DATE: 1958
CALIBER: 155mm
WEIGHT: 311 pounds
BREECH: —
BARREL LENGTH: 97.5 inches

ELEVATION: 45°
TRAVERSAL: 360°
PROJECTILE WEIGHT: —
MUZZLE VELOCITY: 656 fps
MAXIMUM RANGE: 4,375 yards

106mm RCL Rifle M40A1
ADOPTION DATE: 1965
CALIBER: 106mm
WEIGHT: 483 pounds
BREECH: —
BARREL LENGTH: 133 inches

ELEVATION: 65°
TRAVERSAL: 360°
PROJECTILE WEIGHT: 17 pounds
MUZZLE VELOCITY: 1,634 fps
MAXIMUM RANGE: 7,518 yards

GREAT BRITAIN

120 BAT L1
ADOPTION DATE: 1952
CALIBER: 120mm
WEIGHT: 2,205 pounds
BREECH: vertical sliding block
BARREL LENGTH: 156 inches

ELEVATION: 24°
TRAVERSAL: 40°
PROJECTILE WEIGHT: 28 pounds
MUZZLE VELOCITY: 1,516 fps
MAXIMUM RANGE: 1,094 yards

GLOSSARY

Air burst: The detonation of a timed shell over a target to rain shrapnel down on enemy troops.

Antiaircraft artillery: Artillery for use against aircraft and mounted on carriages to allow a high degree of elevation and 360° traversal.

Antitank artillery: High-velocity artillery firing armor-piercing projectiles used against tanks and other armored vehicles.

Assault gun: A form of self-propelled artillery intended to accompany advancing infantry.

Automatic: A breech system that mechanically loads the piece and ejects the spent casings to achieve rapid fire.

Barbette: A mounting used in fortifications to allow artillery to fire over the parapet rather than through an embrasure.

Barrage: A heavy blanket of artillery fire typically intended to disrupt enemy troops in preparation of an assault.

Battery: A grouping of usually four or six artillery pieces.

Bell mouth: A flared cannon muzzle resembling a bell.

Bolt: A solid elongated projectile.

Box trail: A single, solid carriage trail.

Breech: The rear section of the cannon barrel.

Built-up gun: A gun tube reinforced by the addition of external metal sleeves.

Caisson: A large two-wheeled cart used to carry two or more ammunition chests.

Caliber: The diameter of the cannon's bore designated either by inches, millimeters, centimeters, or the weight of the projectile.

Canister: An antipersonnel projectile consisting of a metal can filled with iron or lead round shot.

Capsquare: The curved metal component of the carriage that passes over and secures a trunnion.

Carronade: A short-barreled, high-caliber naval cannon of the late eighteenth and early nineteenth centuries.

Cascabel: The rounded knob on the breech of a muzzle-loaded cannon. Naval cascabels often had a lateral hole to accommodate a securing rope.

Case shot: A projectile filled with a bursting charge and round iron or lead shot.

Ceiling: The maximum range of antiaircraft artillery, typically expressed in feet.

Chamber: The rear portion of the cannon's bore that accommodates the propellant and projectile.

Counter-battery fire: The practice of directing fire against opposing artillery.

Cradle: The component attached to the carriage that supports the barrel and recoil mechanism.

Cruciform carriage: A carriage with X-shaped supports that provides extra stability. Cruciform carriages often provide 360° traversal and are commonly used with antiaircraft artillery.

Direct fire: A method of firing at a relatively flat trajectory at a target that is within the gun crew's line of sight.

Disappearing carriage: A type of carriage that depresses beneath the edge of the defensive parapet to allow reloading in relative safety; most often used with late nineteenth and early twentieth century seacoast guns.

Elevation: The degree to which the cannon's barrel can be raised or lowered to achieve the desired range.

Embrasure: An opening through a fortification's wall to accommodate a cannon's muzzle.

Extractor: A typically claw-like component that removes the spent shell casing from the breech after firing.

Firing lanyard: A cord attached at one end to the primer and pulled by the gunner to fire the piece.

Fume extractor: A gas-filled cylindrical chamber fitted around a barrel that pulls spent propellant fumes forward out of the bore rather than allowing them to vent rearward from the breech. Particularly necessary with tanks and self-propelled artillery when the breech is within an enclosed space such as a turret.

Fuse setter: A mechanical or electronic device used to automatically fix the detonation time of a shell's fuse.

Gun: An artillery piece with a flat trajectory.

Handspike: A wood pole inserted into mounts located on the trail of a muzzle-loaded cannon and used to traverse the piece.

Howitzer: A cannon capable of achieving a high trajectory.

Indirect fire: The practice of firing at a relatively high trajectory at targets beyond the line of sight.

Limber: The two-wheeled cart for carrying ammunition chests.

Mortar: A squat cannon capable of firing a relatively large explosive shell at a high trajectory.

Muzzle brake: An attachment to the end of the gun tube's muzzle that deflects a portion of the gas backwards to reduce recoil.

Muzzle velocity: The speed at which the projectile leaves the muzzle of the piece, usually expressed in feet-per-second (fps) or meters-per-second (mps).

Obturation: The closure of a cannon's breech to prevent the escape of gasses and energy upon firing.

Outriggers: Projections mounted to a cannon's mounting to provide added stability.

Pack howitzer: A lightweight howitzer often designed to be easily disassembled to facilitate transportation over difficult terrain.

Pedestal mount: A fixed support often used with naval or coast artillery.

Pintle: A metal pin attached to the rear of a limber or towing vehicle to which a piece's trail can be attached for towing. Also, the heavy metal pin on the front of a barbette carriage that allows it to traverse.

Primer: The flammable material or mechanical or electrical device that ignites the cannon's main powder charge.

Recoil: The rearward motion of the piece initiated by its discharge.

Recuperator: The component of the recoil mechanism that returns the barrel to its original position after firing, usually incorporating springs or compressed air or gas.

Rifling: Spiraling grooves cut within the bore of the piece that impart a spin to its projectile thus improving its range and accuracy.

Salvo: The multiple discharge of several pieces.

Semiautomatic breech: A breech mechanism that diverts a portion of the energy of the piece's discharge to mechanically open the breech, eject the spent cartridge casing, insert a fresh round, and then close the breech.

Shell: A hollow projectile filled with a bursting charge.

Shrapnel: A type of projectile designed to burst into numerous fragments.

Sliding Block: A type of breech mechanism utilizing a heavy metal block that slides either vertically or horizontally to seal the breech.

Spade: Shovel-like projections on a piece's trail or on the chassis of a self-propelled weapon that, when lowered, absorb recoil and increase stability for firing.

Spiking: The practice of hammering a metal rod or spike into the vent of a muzzle-loaded piece's vent to prevent its use by an enemy if captured.

Split trail carriage: A mounting incorporating two hinged trails that can be closed for transport and opened to provide stability in preparation to firing.

Tank destroyer: A self-propelled piece specifically designed as an antitank weapon.

Tompion: A plug inserted into the muzzle of a cannon to prevent the entry of moisture or debris.

Trail: The rearward projection of an artillery carriage.

Trajectory: The arc of a projectile's flight.

Traversal: The side-to-side movement of the piece's barrel expressed in degrees.

Traversing gear: A mechanical device to aid in the left-to-right movement of a cannon's barrel.

Truck carriage: An early four-wheeled naval carriage.

Trunnion: The projections to either side of the barrel by which it is mounted to its carriage.

Turret: An enclosed protective housing for a gun that is typically capable of 360° traversal.

Vent: The small hole drilled near the rear of a muzzle-loaded cannon's barrel to allow the insertion of a primer.

Windage: The space between the inside of the bore and the actual projectile.

BIBLIOGRAPHY

Bailey, J. B. A. 1989. *Field Artillery and Firepower*. Oxford: Military Press.

Batchelor, John, and Ian Hogg. 1972. *Artillery*. New York: Charles Scribner's Sons.

Chartrand, Rene. 2003. *Napoleon's Guns 1792–1815*. Vol. 2: *Heavy and Siege Artillery*. Oxford: Osprey Publishing.

Comparato, Frank E. 1965. *Age of Great Guns, Cannon Kings and Cannoneers Who Forged the Firepower of Artillery*. Harrisburg, PA: Stackpole Company.

Connolly, Peter. 1981. *Greece and Rome at War*. Englewood Cliffs, NJ: Prentice-Hall.

Contamine, Phillipe. 1985. *War in the Middle Ages*. Trans. by Michael Jones. New York: Basil Blackwell.

Cullen, Tony, and Christopher F. Foss, eds. 1996. *Jane's Armour and Artillery Upgrades 1995–1996*. Coulsdon, Surrey: Jane's Information Group.

Daniel, Larry J., and Riley W. Gunter. 1977. *Confederate Cannon Foundries*. Union City, TN: Pioneer Press.

De Camp, L. Sprague. 1963. *The Ancient Engineers*. New York: Doubleday and Company.

DeVries, Kelly (volume editor). 2002. "The Forgotten Battle of Bevershoutsveld, 3 May, 1382: Technological Innovation and Military Significance." Chapter VIII in *Guns and Men in Medieval Europe, 1200–1500: Studies in Military History and Technology*. Aldershot, Hampshire: Ashgate Publishing.

DeVries, Kelly (volume edtior). 2002. "The Use of Gunpowder Weaponry by and against Joan of Arc during the Hundred Years War." Chapter IX in *Guns and Men in Medieval Europe, 1200–1500: Studies in Military History and Technology*. Aldershot, Hampshire: Ashgate Publishing.

DeVries, Kelly (volume edtior). 2002. "Gunpowder Weapons at the Siege of Constantinople, 1453." Chapter X in *Guns and Men in Medieval Europe, 1200–1500: Studies in Military History and Technology*. Aldershot, Hampshire: Ashgate Publishing.

DeVries, Kelly (volume edtior). 2002. "Gunpowder and Early Gunpowder Weapons." Chapter XI in *Guns and Men in Medieval Europe, 1200–1500: Studies in Military History and Technology*. Aldershot, Hampshire: Ashgate Publishing.

DeVries, Kelly (volume edtior). 2002. "The Technology of Gunpowder Weaponry in Western Europe during the Hundred Years War." Chapter XII in *Guns and Men in Medieval Europe, 1200–1500: Studies in Military History and Technology*. Aldershot, Hampshire: Ashgate Publishing.

DeVries, Kelly (volume edtior). 2002. "The Impact of Gunpowder Weaponry on Siege Warfare in the Hundred Years War." Chapter XIII in *Guns and Men in Medieval Europe, 1200–1500: Studies in Military History and Technology*. Aldershot, Hampshire: Ashgate Publishing.

DeVries, Kelly (volume edtior). 2002. "The Effectiveness of Fifteenth-Century Shipboard Artillery." Chapter XIV in *Guns and Men in Medieval Europe, 1200–1500: Studies in Military History and Technology*. Aldershot, Hampshire: Ashgate Publishing.

Dupuy, R. Ernest, and Trevor N. Dupuy. 1993. *The Harper Encyclopedia of Military History from 3500 B.C. to the Present*. New York: Harper Collins Publishers.

Foss, Christopher F., ed. 1995. *Jane's Armour and Artillery 1994–1995, 15th ed*. Coulsdon, Surrey: Jane's Information Group.

Gudmundsson, Bruce I. 1993. *On Artillery*. Westport, CT: Praeger Publishers.

Guilmartin, John Francis, Jr. 1974. *Gunpowder and Galleys: Changing Technology and Mediterranean Warfare at Sea in the Sixteenth Century*. Cambridge: Cambridge University Press.

Hall, Bert S. 1997. *Weapons and Warfare in Renaissance Europe: Gunpowder, Technology, and Tactics*. Baltimore: Johns Hopkins Press.

Henry, Chris. 2003. *British Napoleonic Artillery 1793–1815*. Vol. 2: *Siege and Coastal Artillery*. Oxford: Osprey Publishing.

Henry, Chris. 2004. *Napoleonic Naval Armaments 1792–1815*. Oxford: Osprey Publishing.

Hogg, Ian V. 1974. *A History of Artillery*. London: Hamlyn Publishing Group.

Hogg, Ian V. 1986. *The Weapons that Changed the World*. New York: Arbor House Publishing Company.

Hogg, Ian V. 1988. *An Illustrated History of Artillery*. Secaucus: Chartwell Books.

Josephus. 1987. *The Works of Josephus, Complete and Unabridged*. Trans. by William Whiston. Peabody, MA: Hendrickson Publishers.

Kagay, Donald J., and L. J. Andrew Villalon. 2003. *Crusaders, Condottieri, and Cannon: Medieval Warfare in Societies around the Mediterranean*. Leiden, Boston: Brill.

Keegan, John. 1993. *A History of Warfare*. New York: Alfred A. Knopf.

Kiley, Kevin F. 2004. *Artillery of the Napoleonic Wars 1792–1815*. London: Greenhill Books.

Koch, H. W. 1981. *History of Warfare*. New York: Gallery Books.

Konstam, Angus. 2003. *Lepanto 1571: The Greatest Naval Battle of the Renaissance*. Oxford: Osprey Publishing.

Manucy, Albert. 2001. *Artillery through the Ages*. Honolulu: University Press of the Pacific.

Marsden, E. W. 1969. *Greek and Roman Artillery, Historical Development*. Oxford: Oxford at the Clarendon Press.

Marsden, E. W. 1971. *Greek and Roman Artillery: Technical Treatises*. Oxford: Oxford at the Clarendon Press.

Mercer, General Cavalie. 1995. *Journal of the Waterloo Campaign, Kept throughout the Campaign of 1815*. New York: Da Capo Press.

Nicolle, David. 2002. *Medieval Siege Weapons*. Vol. 1. Oxford: Osprey Publishing.

Norris, John. 2003. *Early Gunpowder Artillery, c. 1300–1600*. Ramsbury: Crowood Press.

Olmstead, Edwin, Wayne E. Stark, and Spencer C. Tucker. 1997. *The Big Guns: Civil War Siege, Seacoast and Naval Cannon*. Bloomfield, Ontario: Museum Restoration Service.

Parker, Geoffrey. 1996. *The Military Revolution: Military Innovation and the Rise of the West*. Cambridge: Cambridge University Press.

Partington, J. R. 1960. *A History of Greek Fire and Gunpowder*. New York: Barnes and Noble.

Peterson, Harold L. 1969. *Round Shot and Rammers*. New York: Bonanza Books.

Solka, Michael. 2004. *German Armies 1870–71*. Vol. 1. Oxford: Osprey Publishing.

Trawin, Len. 1997. *Early British Quick Firing Artillery (Field and Horse)*. Hemel Hempstead: Nexus Special Interests.

Tucker, Spencer C. 1989. *Arming the Fleet*. Annapolis: Naval Institute Press.

Warry, John. 1980. *Warfare in the Classical World*. London: Salamander Books.

Wise, Terence. 1976. *Medieval Warfare*. New York: Hastings House Publishers.

INDEX

ABOUT THE AUTHOR

JEFF KINARD is a military historian who lives in High Point, North Carolina with his wife, Kelly, and son, Luka. His earlier books include *The Battle of the Crater, Lafayette of the South: Prince Camille de Polignac and the American Civil War,* and *Pistols: An Illustrated History of Their Impact.*